PERESTROIKA AND SOVIET
NATIONAL SECURITY

Michael MccGwire

PERESTROIKA AND SOVIET NATIONAL SECURITY

THE BROOKINGS INSTITUTION
Washington, D.C.

Copyright © 1991 by
THE BROOKINGS INSTITUTION
1775 Massachusetts Avenue, N.W., Washington, D.C. 20036

Library of Congress Cataloging-in-Publication data

MccGwire, Michael.
 Perestroika and Soviet national security / Michael K. MccGwire.
  p.   cm.
 Includes bibliographical references and index.
 ISBN 0-8157-5554-6 (alk. paper) — ISBN 0-8157-5553-8
(pbk. : alk. paper)
  1. Soviet Union—National security. 2. Perestroĭka. 3. Soviet
Union—Foreign relations—1985– I. Title.
UA770.M3993   1991
355′.033047—dc20   90-46529
                                                                  CIP

9 8 7 6 5 4 3 2 1

Ⅱ THE BROOKINGS INSTITUTION

The Brookings Institution is an independent organization devoted to nonpartisan research, education, and publication in economics, government, foreign policy, and the social sciences generally. Its principal purposes are to aid in the development of sound public policies and to promote public understanding of issues of national importance.

The Institution was founded on December 8, 1927, to merge the activities of the Institute for Government Research, founded in 1916, the Institute of Economics, founded in 1922, and the Robert Brookings Graduate School of Economics and Government, founded in 1924.

The Board of Trustees is responsible for the general administration of the Institution, while the immediate direction of the policies, program, and staff is vested in the President, assisted by an advisory committee of the officers and staff. The by-laws of the Institution state: "It is the function of the Trustees to make possible the conduct of scientific research, and publication, under the most favorable conditions, and to safeguard the independence of the research staff in the pursuit of their studies and in the publication of the results of such studies. It is not a part of their function to determine, control, or influence the conduct of particular investigations or the conclusions reached."

The President bears final responsibility for the decision to publish a manuscript as a Brookings book. In reaching his judgment on the competence, accuracy, and objectivity of each study, the President is advised by the director of the appropriate research program and weighs the views of a panel of expert outside readers who report to him in confidence on the quality of the work. Publication of a work signifies that it is deemed a competent treatment worthy of public consideration but does not imply endorsement of conclusions or recommendations.

The Institution maintains its position of neutrality on issues of public policy in order to safeguard the intellectual freedom of the staff. Hence interpretations or conclusions in Brookings publications should be understood to be solely those of the authors and should not be attributed to the Institution, to its trustees, officers, or other staff members, or to the organizations that support its research.

Foreword

THE INTERPRETATION of Soviet policy has long been a matter of intense concern among the Western countries. For many it has been a source of unsettling mystery, for some a threat of ominous clarity, for most an occasion for defining their strongest convictions and political values. Understandably, we have tended to see the Soviet Union in terms of the way we understand and justify our own history.

In recent years, however, standard Western conceptions of the Soviet Union have had to be re-evaluated. What once appeared to be immutable axioms of central economic control and of authoritarian political rule have yielded to market principles and consensual politics that at least in aspiration clearly resemble our own standards. The military confrontation that has defined a major period of history is rapidly dissolving under the impetus of a dramatic shift in Soviet policy initiated by Mikhail Gorbachev in 1987. The implications are now reverberating throughout the world.

In this book Michael MccGwire presents the logic and the historical genesis of this change in Soviet policy. He identifies a driving assumption, which, when altered, transformed the entire character of this policy. Specifically, the long-standing Soviet commitment to prepare for the contingency of world war has been replaced by a commitment to prevent such a war by reversing the preparations to fight it. The new Soviet policy, MccGwire argues, proceeds on the assumption that war will in fact be avoided and that Soviet state security is to be accomplished by means of international cooperation.

MccGwire traces the origins of this policy shift, documenting its lengthy gestation prior to the rise of Gorbachev as its leading champion. He develops his account by reconstructing Soviet logic using the advantages of hindsight. He makes little reference to American or other Western perspectives and instead strives to understand the Soviet Union in its own terms. Those terms are inferred from a variety of sources— policy statements, implementing actions, and their practical effects. Both the exercise of logical reconstruction and the subordination of American perspectives are controversial but central features of the book. They are designed to stimulate thinking and improve understanding of a remarkable series of events.

When he wrote this book, MccGwire was a senior fellow in the Brookings Foreign Policy Studies program. The author's debt to fellow analysts is evident in his footnotes, but he wishes to express his particular appreciation to Karen Dawisha, Margot Light, and Elizabeth Valkenier, whose expertise and comments were especially valuable, and to Raymond L. Garthoff, an unfailing touchstone and generous fund of knowledge. John D. Steinbruner was important to shaping the central argument and justifying the analytical approach. Vaughan Altemus, Richard K. Betts, Thomas Bjorkman, Franklyn Griffiths, Selig Harrison, Dale Herspring, Ed A. Hewett, John Hines, Christopher Jones, Jacob Kipp, John McDonnell, Gur Ofer, Bruce Parrott, and Cynthia Roberts each contributed to the study in different ways. So did fellow members of the Writings Analysis Group and the Washington Forum on Soviet Affairs, who dissected early versions of the underlying analysis.

Andrew Portocarrero provided outstanding research support and was responsible for coordinating preparations for publication. He had part-time assistance from Robin Wornall and Kyle Ray; Mark Thibault provided research support during the exploratory analysis. Thomas Somuah typed the early drafts of the manuscript, and Annette D. Leak the final version. Alice M. Carroll edited the manuscript, Vernon L. Kelly and Michael Levin verified it, and Fred L. Kepler prepared the index.

Brookings gratefully acknowledges the Carnegie Corporation of New York and the John D. and Catherine T. MacArthur Foundation for providing financial support for this project.

The views expressed are solely those of the author and should not be ascribed to the persons whose assistance is acknowledged above, to the sources of funding support, or to the trustees, officers, or other staff members of the Brookings Institution.

BRUCE K. MACLAURY
President

November 1990
Washington, D.C.

Contents

Abbreviations of Frequently Cited Sources

PERESTROIKA AND SOVIET
NATIONAL SECURITY

CHAPTER 1

Introduction

BY THE SUMMER OF 1988 most Western observers had been persuaded that Mikhail Gorbachev was indeed embarked on a process of revolutionary change. The Nineteenth All-Union Party Conference, the first to be held since 1941, had displayed on television a range of vigorous controversy that had not been seen since the debates of the 1920s.

However, few of those observers foresaw that within six months Gorbachev would announce a unilateral force cut of 500,000 men. And even fewer expected that in 1989 Moscow would actively encourage the replacement of communist regimes throughout Europe.

It was true that some Soviet intellectuals had advocated unilateral force reductions, but the few Western analysts who chose to bet on that outcome did so on the basis of Gorbachev being unpredictable. Almost no one foresaw the peaceful dissolution of the Eastern European "empire." And none of those analysts had a logical explanation for these and other closely related developments.

Yet there was such an explanation. It lay in the fundamental change in Soviet military doctrine that was clearly signaled in the Warsaw Pact statement in May 1987, and then spelled out in detail by the chief of the Soviet General Staff in December that year. Once the implications of that change had been grasped, the feasibility of unilateral force cuts became clear, as did the fact that Eastern Europe was no longer needed as a defensive glacis or a springboard for an offensive westward.

This was not, of course, the only reason for those radical developments, which were driven by the complex of impulses that underlay the whole perestroika process which forms the subject of this book. However, for fundamental change to occur, the removal of obstacles is at least as important as the presence of impulses to change. And while

1

the pressures for change will build up over a prolonged period, the removal of obstacles, whether by force majeur or deliberate choice, will usually determine the timing of the change.

The process of reformulating military doctrine that was initiated in January 1987 removed what had been an absolute obstacle to change.

Impulses and Obstacles to Change

The political impulse for economic perestroika and what the Soviets term "the new political thinking about international relations" went back to Yuri Andropov's interregnum as general secretary in 1982–84, while the intellectual roots lay in the 1970s and even earlier. An absolute obstacle to adopting these ideas in the form they took under Gorbachev was a leadership comprising men who had experienced the fateful years of 1920 to 1960. Besides the cost in material resources and human suffering, those years seemed to prove the rightness of Marx's diagnosis of capitalist imperialism and confirm the Marxist-Leninist prognosis of history.

But even when that generation was dead or gone, there remained another absolute obstacle to restructuring the Soviet political economy. This was the doctrinal assumption that fundamental differences between socialism and capitalism made world war inherently possible, even though unintended. That assumption generated the core military requirement to be able to fight such a war—a war the Soviets absolutely wanted to avoid but could not afford to lose. They could not afford to lose because U.S. statements and Western military capabilities made it clear that in such a war the capitalist objective would be to overthrow the Soviet state and destroy the socialist system.

The requirement to cover the worst-case contingency of world war was not peculiar to the Soviets, for it was the same requirement that had determined the size and shape of Western forces since World War II. However, because of the Soviet Union's geostrategic and geopolitical situation, and because of disparities between the two economic systems, the economic burden of covering that contingency had been quite disproportionate. Unless the Soviets could shed a significant part of that defense burden and shift resources to the civilian economy, then economic perestroika must surely fail.

There were other asymmetries. If the Soviets were not ultimately to lose a world war, they would need to deny the United States a bridgehead in Europe. This meant that the armies of the Warsaw Treaty Organization (the Warsaw Pact) must defeat the armies of the North Atlantic Treaty Organization (NATO) in Europe and evict U.S. forces from the Continent, which required an offensive posture and operational surprise. In order to improve their chances of averting the resort to nuclear weapons in Europe, thereby reducing the danger of escalation to strategic strikes on the Soviet Union, the Soviets restructured their forces in the 1970s to provide conventional superiority over NATO. In doing so they alarmed the West, raised tension, and increased the danger of the very war they sought to avoid.

Added to the heightened danger of world war and the ever-growing burden of defense were the political costs of the need for ground force superiority over NATO. Besides souring relations with the NATO nations and supporting the charge of aggressive intentions, this superiority prevented any meaningful negotiations on the mutual reduction of forces in Europe. It also justified the United States dragging its feet in negotiating reductions in strategic nuclear weapons. They were needed to deter the aggressive urge that was implicit in the Soviet military posture.

While the impulses for change were strong and growing, the obstacle to change seemed immovable. After all, world war was conceivable and therefore possible. How, then, could the Soviets justify jettisoning that commonsense assumption (which they shared with the West) and rule instead that world war was not possible? There was no middle ground. World war was either possible or not possible; it could not be both.

The answer lay in the distinction between a factual statement that world war was conceivable and a planning assumption that world war could and would be prevented by political means. In other words, the obstacle to change could be removed by instructing the military establishment to cease planning for world war and instead to develop plans for a range of lesser contingencies involving conflict on the Soviet periphery. World war would be averted by political means.

This would require a revolution in Soviet military thought. For some forty years, from 1948 through 1986, military requirements had been driven by the open-ended and increasingly demanding objective of "not losing" a world war. In the future, requirements would be shaped by an inherently limited objective such as protecting the territorial integrity of the Soviet Union.

This was not, however, just a politically astute way of escaping the costs of the old assumption. Gorbachev had made it clear that he believed that ceasing to prepare for world war would, of itself, act to lessen the danger of world war. This reflected his belief that national security must rely primarily on political means and that the age-old adage "if you want peace, prepare for war" did not hold good in the nuclear age. The sharp improvement in the climate of international relations since he began to act on those beliefs in 1987 suggests they had substance.

By the end of 1989 the assumption of "no world war" had yet to be articulated publicly, but there were persuasive ideological and pragmatic reasons for this reticence. The assumption had, however, been made all but explicit in a wide range of authoritative doctrinal statements from 1987 on, and it had been evinced by the unilateral force reductions announced at the end of 1988, by the readiness to negotiate asymmetric cuts in conventional forces, and by the acceptance of peaceful revolution in Eastern Europe in 1989.

The assumption that war would be prevented by political means affected the five services differently, with the strategic nuclear forces becoming the subject of political rather than military calculations, and the ground forces requiring complete restructuring. If "no world war," the capability to launch a blitzkrieg into Western Europe was not a strategic imperative and there was no longer a requirement for superiority in conventional ground forces. Unilateral cuts to remove the offensive overhang were therefore in order. Similarly, Eastern Europe was no longer needed as an offensive springboard, and there was no requirement for a defensive glacis.

The new assumption did not mean that "defense of the homeland" could or would be neglected, but there was vast scope for argument over what forces would be needed and how much would be "enough." The room for disagreement was increased by the fact that the future threat environment would depend on negotiations with the West and China, and their outcome remained uncertain.

The military, meanwhile, had to deal with the world as it still was, with massive forces arrayed on either side. The General Staff had to plan for an extended strategic withdrawal from the existing configuration of forces that were structured and postured for the contingency of world war to some new defensive posture that had yet to be decided.

Outline of the Argument

The crucial catalyst for change was Gorbachev's acceptance in mid-1986 that democracy was essential if real change was to come about, if perestroika was not to fail. To wrench the Soviet economy from extensive to intensive development and to speed up technological innovation required more than efficient economic mechanisms and tauter labor discipline. It demanded that the energies of the people be engaged directly, through a process of democratization. This conclusion had momentous consequences.

Democratization implied domestic destabilization, making a peaceful international environment absolutely essential. Economic perestroika would need assistance from the capitalist world. Both these requirements meant that good relations with the United States became an imperative, rather than a policy option. But good relations were not to be had for the asking, and the two main obstacles were the size and shape of the Soviet armed forces and the Marxist-Leninist theory of international relations. The former was by far the more important. Few Americans attach much importance to theory, but the West had consistently used the size, posture, and disposition of the Soviet armed forces as a prime indicator of Soviet motivations.

During the last three months of 1986 economic perestroika, political democratization, changes in military doctrine, and the new thinking about international relations became truly interdependent. This symbiotic relationship yielded a coherent set of policy objectives that drove developments in the direction that has surprised so many in the West.

This is not to claim that Gorbachev and his supporters foresaw the exact timing of those developments, the depressing slowness of economic restructuring, or the unnerving speed with which events moved in Eastern Europe. But at the Central Committee plenum in January 1987, when Gorbachev pushed through democratization and the need for a new military doctrine, he did understand that he had set the ship of state on a completely new course, and what the implications were. As he said: "There was a particular situation before the January plenum, and after it events went in a completely different direction."[1] And he did have a timetable that was tied to the start of the Thirteenth Five-Year Plan in 1991.

1. *Pravda,* July 15, 1987, in *FBIS*-87-135, p. R2.

Chapters 7–9 of this book explain the course of events in the wake of the January plenum, while chapter 6 fills in what happened from the time that Andropov made Gorbachev his de facto deputy for domestic affairs in 1983. These chapters are the core of the book and describe truly momentous developments, including the introduction of democracy, the reversal of military policy, the redirection of foreign policy, the withdrawal from Afghanistan, and the redefinition of Soviet national security.

However, to perceive the present correctly, the trajectory of past developments must be understood. Western analysts have had difficulty in predicting events because they could not see how the Soviets could have got to where they are today from where they were thought to have been yesterday. In fact they were somewhere else.

The record is reexamined in chapters 2–4. Chapter 2 explains how Soviet military requirements evolved from the immediate postwar period, when the threat was seen as a resurgent Germany in fifteen to twenty years time, to the increasingly demanding objective of not losing a world war. Chapter 3 discusses strategic weapons and arms control, an area of considerable misunderstanding. And chapter 4 describes the evolution of Soviet foreign policy from 1971, a time of seeming U.S.-Soviet understanding that actually concealed fundamental misunderstanding and conflicts of interest which came to dominate East-West relations by the end of the decade.

Chapter 5 pieces together the important policy reappraisal in 1983–84 that rejected many of the assumptions underlying Brezhnev's 1971 peace program and returned Soviet policy toward the United States to a more intransigent course. Gorbachev introduced greater flexibility and a different style of diplomatic discourse when he took office in March 1985, but the main direction of Soviet foreign policy did not change until two years later in the spring of 1987. The conclusions of the 1983–84 reappraisal were almost the opposite of those that would be reached by Gorbachev and his supporters at the end of 1986, but evidence of the reappraisal was obscured by the shooting down of the Korean airliner, the generational change in leadership, and the histrionics of the negotiations on intermediate-range nuclear forces. To further confuse matters, the reappraisal legitimized certain terms and concepts that were exploited by Gorbachev in 1987–88 to achieve very different ends, giving a false impression of continuity.

The last chapter looks to the future, but it also considers whether the changes in the Soviet Union were helped or hindered by the confrontational policies of the Reagan administration. And it discusses the very fundamental difference between Gorbachev's new political thinking about international relations, based on the "new realities" of the nuclear age, and the established Western approach, noting that the divergence of opinion is not between the Soviet Union and the United States but between two well-established bodies of Western political thought, and that the new political thinking is supported by a growing number of world elites and by several Western political parties.

The Focus on Security

To understand Soviet foreign policy one must be sensitive to Soviet national security concerns and to the military requirements that flow from them.[2] In *Military Objectives in Soviet Foreign Policy,* I showed how the requirement to cover the contingency of world war seriously distorted Soviet foreign policy behavior and grossly overburdened the domestic economy during the forty years 1947–86.[3] Even now, when the meaning of national security and the way it is best ensured have undergone a metamorphosis, it remains central to interpreting and predicting Soviet foreign policy behavior and the Soviet response to domestic developments that threaten the integrity of the Union. And this despite the manifold impulses and diverse effects of the perestroika process.

The focus on national security in this study is doubly important because of the emphasis the West has always placed on Soviet military behavior as evidence of the motivations underlying Soviet foreign policy. The prevalence of worst-case analysis, the emphasis on military capabilities, and Western neglect of Soviet interests and intentions produced an oversimplified and distorted image of Soviet aspirations and concerns, and how the Soviets viewed the world. In particular, the West chose to ignore the reality of the military threat that has faced the Soviet Union.

2. "It is hard to overstate the importance of the military factor in Soviet history." Thane Gustafson, "Conclusions: Towards a Crisis in Civil-Military Relations?" in Timothy J. Colton and Thane Gustafson, eds., *Soldiers and the Soviet State* (Princeton University Press, 1990), p. 334.

3. Michael MccGwire, *Military Objectives in Soviet Foreign Policy* (Brookings, 1987).

The emerging threat of war was a driving force behind the rapid industrialization of the 1930s, which in turn justified the collectivization of agriculture. The arms race that got under way in the late 1940s skewed the Soviets' plans for rebuilding their war-shattered economy, a race where they came from far behind in every area except field artillery, tanks, and the mathematics of rocketry. The defense industry has comprised a distinct sector of the Soviet economy, with a priority claim on high-quality manufactured goods, materials, skilled manpower, managerial talent, and the rest. The technological arms race steadily increased this disparity in the economy, while secrecy and the structure of Soviet industry prevented the diffusion of defense-related technology to other sectors.

The West chose to interpret this heavy burden of defense-related investment as compensation for the socioeconomic inadequacies of Soviet communism, as an attempt to coerce adherence to socialism, since persuasion must fail. It chose to ignore that the price of defeat in World War I was the punitive Treaty of Brest-Litovsk, which was designed to turn Eastern Europe and the westernmost parts of Russia into a German preserve through a system of satellite states and economic exploitation; that the civil war that followed the October Revolution drew in foreign powers including Great Britain, France, Japan, and the United States, who sought to overthrow the new Soviet state; that in 1941 invading Axis forces advanced six hundred miles into Soviet territory in four months on their whole front and were only checked after twelve months, by when their southern armies had advanced a thousand miles into the Soviet Union; or that in 1959 the U.S. Strategic Air Command had 1,750 bombers capable of nuclear strikes on the Soviet Union, which lacked an effective means of attacking the United States.

There are, of course, many reasons besides avoiding defeat in war for possessing armed forces, and the Soviets are the first to assert that it was not until they had matched the American strategic nuclear capability that the United States was prepared to deal with them seriously. However, the West has all but ignored the Soviet Union's legitimate security concerns and had chosen to interpret its military capabilities as an expression of foreign policy ambitions, even to the extent of claiming that Soviet communism sought military domination of the world.[4] That

4. This view was widely held in the first Reagan administration, and it seems to have been believed that the Soviets had embarked on the necessary military buildup in the wake of the Cuban missile crisis. See, for example, statements by Secretary of Defense Caspar Weinberger

is why the West has had difficulty in seeing how the Soviets could have gotten to where they are today from where they were yesterday.

The Analytical Approach

The emphasis in this book is on providing the context for developments since Gorbachev took office and explaining how and why those changes came about. Rather than describing Soviet military and foreign policy behavior, it focuses on the reasons that prompted that behavior, paying particular attention to the deep assumptions and hidden objectives that underlie policy but often remain silent.

Describing Soviet policy in terms of its underlying assumptions and objectives has many advantages. By its very nature, policy implies the existence of some kind of objective, explicit or implicit, and in a mono-organizational society like the Soviet Union, objectives lie at the center of the policy process. This is particularly true of military affairs where the systematic approach reflects the combined influence of the General Staff and the Marxist belief in the existence of basic regularities in all aspects of human endeavor, including war.

Assumptions and objectives are specified in Soviet military doctrine, which is a continually evolving system of officially accepted views on basic questions about war, much of which is highly classified. There are also silent (but vital) assumptions reflecting universally accepted beliefs that are taken as self-evident. Given a sufficient body of evidence over time (and there is more than enough in the Soviet case), higher-order assumptions and objectives can usually be inferred.

Two types of assumption have been central to Soviet military behavior in the postwar period. One concerned the likelihood of world war. Whether it was assumed to be inevitable (as it was before 1957) or merely possible, the Soviet Union had to be ready to fight such a war. This assumption (or contingency) determined the overall size and structure of the Soviet armed forces through 1988.

The other key assumption was about the nature of a world war. Until 1987, when it was decided to plan on the assumption that such a war could and would be prevented, the likely nature of a world war lay at the

in "Face the Nation," CBS television, March 13, 1983; interview with *USA Today,* August 11, 1983; Fred Hiatt, "Pentagon Sees Space Buildup by Soviets," *Washington Post,* April 11, 1984.

core of Soviet military doctrine. The crucial question was whether or not it would inevitably escalate to massive nuclear strikes on the Soviet Union. The assumption on this score determined the way that world war would be fought, the range of possible objectives, and the peacetime force posture required to cover the contingency of world war.

The validity of the inferred assumptions and higher-order objectives can be tested by using a combination of inductive and deductive analysis to reconstruct a hierarchy of strategic objectives that reaches from the apex of "not losing" a war down to the detailed missions and tasks of the individual services. The evidence ranges from the concrete details of force structure, operational concepts, and weapons programs to doctrinal statements and professional debates. The result is a complex hypothesis that can be tested in part and in whole. It also serves as an analytical matrix that both orders and reinterprets the existing mass of evidence and directs one to new evidence. This methodology is outlined in appendix A.

Major changes in policy usually stem from changes in the underlying assumptions and objectives, which is why their identification is so important. Such changes are, however, rarely made explicit, particularly if they have major implications for military requirements. Sometimes change can be inferred from subtle adjustments in the wording of key statements in the wake of a decision. In other cases anomalies in established patterns of weapons production or operational behavior may be the first indicators of a change higher up the hierarchy and much further back in time.

A change in either of the key assumptions will not necessarily generate change in the hierarchy of objectives. When the Soviets decided in 1956 that war between the two social systems was no longer fatalistically inevitable, the decision had no effect on military requirements, since such a war remained a possibility and the contingency had still to be covered.

However, when it was ruled in late 1966 that it was no longer inevitable that world war would be nuclear and involve massive strikes on the Soviet Union, the new decision required that the strategic hierarchy be completely restructured, starting with the two primary objectives and moving on down. This decision had major repercussions in terms of Soviet strategy, concepts of operation, and military requirements.[5]

5. MccGwire, *Military Objectives*, chap. 3.

Similarly, at the beginning of 1987, when the Soviets moved from assuming that world war was possible to assuming that world war was not possible (because it would be averted by political means), this change in assumptions had momentous effects, and the Soviets are still debating and working out the full implications, only this time they are doing it partly in public.

Doctrinal rulings of this kind involved clear-cut decisions. World war was either possible or not possible; nuclear escalation was either inevitable or not inevitable; it could not be both. This way of thinking is foreign to Western analysts, who are uncomfortable with the idea of far-reaching changes in policy being generated by seemingly subtle shifts in underlying assumptions. This is partly because Western defense and foreign policy changed little in their essentials for more than forty years. The central assumptions of a Soviet urge to aggression and the use of nuclear weapons were enshrined and perpetuated in the doctrine of nuclear deterrence, and any changes in Western policy that did occur were usually the result of incremental decisions or political compromises.

This experiential viewpoint was buttressed by the way that evidence of change in the Soviet Union, until recently, emerged progressively and belatedly, and by the emphasis in Western analyses on describing the flow of events (the *what* of policy) rather than identifying the underlying objectives (the *why* of policy). Explaining changes of policy in terms of clear-cut decisions is therefore said to be "all too tidy." But this reflects confusion between what brings about a decision, often an untidy process, and the decision itself. There is also confusion between the multiple factors that lead to a decision and the rationalization that is used to justify the decision, which then takes on a life of its own.[6]

The tidiness complaint reflects the untidy political process that the United States enjoys, which is, however, *sui generis*. Besides the fragmentation of political authority, few countries are rich, secure, and powerful enough to indulge the U.S. luxury of continually deferring or fudging key political decisions, least of all the Soviet Union. Analytical methods that work for U.S. policy will not necessarily work for the Union of Soviet Socialist Republics (USSR) or vice versa. Tidiness is

6. This is a widespread phenomenon. While the U.S. "strategic triad" rationalized institutional interests, the concept became a powerful determinant of resource allocation in its own right. Similarly, the doctrine of nuclear deterrence, which in the early 1950s rationalized the U.S. air force's strategic aspirations and the NATO allies' unwillingness to pay the costs of conventional defense against the Soviet threat, became an autonomous concept that was used to justify an improbable array of policies, military deployments, and weapons programs.

therefore not an issue. Proof of a pudding lies in the eating, and validation of a methodology lies in its explanatory power and whether it can identify change and predict the consequences. Meanwhile, there is a dearth of alternative explanations of Soviet defense and foreign policy that have the scope of this study and draw on a comparable range of evidence.[7]

In *Military Objectives* I developed a fully articulated but "tidy" hypothesis that provided a comprehensive explanation for Soviet military behavior from 1945 through 1985; it included weapons programs, arms control, and involvement in the third world. This clear-cut hypothesis allowed me to recognize in the spring of 1987 that Soviet behavior was not conforming to that explanation, and by that fall to identify the underlying cause—namely, a change in assumptions about the likelihood of world war.[8] I was then able to predict what would henceforth be possible on the basis of purely military considerations (unilateral force cuts in Europe, for example), assuming that political considerations favored such a course of action.

Some caveats are in order. An explanation tied to a series of discreet policy decisions will undoubtedly produce a more orderly and coherent picture than the inevitably untidy outcome of the actual policy process. But imposing order on the evidence in this way allows one to grasp the process of change, while not distorting reality. It simplifies much less than the accepted practice of describing policy in terms of successive general secretaries.

Meanwhile the relative coherence of the narrative does not imply a deterministic view of Soviet military developments. In describing the outcomes of the policy process, I do not suggest that they were inevitable or necessarily the optimum decisions. Similarly, in describing the strategic rationale underlying successive changes in policy, I am not arguing that this was the only or always the most important reason for adopting the policies in questions. As long as they are not mutually exclusive, there is no limit to the number of impulses that can be added to the causal heap.

7. Appendix A details the varied kinds of information and different analytical techniques that yield this unusually broad range of evidence. It also argues the importance of an externally derived frame of reference for analyzing these different kinds of information, with particular reference to textual material, which is inherently ambiguous. For a critique of contrary explanations based on partial analyses and worst-case assumptions, see MccGwire, *Military Objectives,* pp. 353–73.

8. Michael MccGwire, "Rethinking War: The Soviets and European Security," *Brookings Review,* vol. 6 (Spring 1988), pp. 3–10, identified the change in assumptions, but I did not date the decision correctly until the summer of 1988.

These methodological questions are relevant but they should not be allowed to obscure the purpose of the study. It is to clarify the nature of developments in Soviet foreign policy and in the Soviet approach to national security at the turn of the 1990s. At that level of analysis the focus is on the policy that prevailed and on the reasoning that justified its adoption, and little attention is paid to bureaucratic politics or the jostling for power in the Kremlin. Political disagreement and conflict are background conditions, but the focus of the study is on the emergence of new policy and not on the substance of the political debate or its participants.[9]

The analytical approach can be seen as applying a historical perspective to contemporary events, explaining developments in terms of primary determinants, underlying assumptions, broad impulses, and major obstacles to change. This approach imputes a purposefulness and coherency to the Soviet policy process that is undoubtedly much more clearly defined than the immediate participants would perceive. It has, however, proven to be an unusually successful way of understanding the flow of events, particularly when fast moving.

---

9. There is a school of thought that policy cannot be understood without analyzing the bureaucratic politics that underlay the decision. That may well be true of the United States but is only sometimes true of the Soviet Union, and then mainly in the domestic field. The importance of bureaucratic politics depends largely on the level of analysis. In this study, which focuses mainly on outcomes, it is only occasionally useful as an aid to understanding.

CHAPTER 2

Evolving Military Requirements, 1945–86

THE STATED mission of the Soviet armed forces has traditionally been to secure the defense of the homeland. The evolving structure of those forces since World War II provides evidence that Soviet military requirements have in practice been determined by the worst case of world war, a war the Soviets absolutely wanted to avoid but could not afford to lose.[1] If that contingency could be handled, so could any lesser conflict. If, however, the Soviet Union lost a world war, the Soviet state would be overthrown and the armed forces would have failed in their mission.

Underlying the evolution of Soviet military requirements have been a series of more or less major decisions prompted by changes in doctrine on the likely nature of world war, by reassessments of the threat, and by developments in military technology. Each decision generated changes, evidence of which emerged during the following ten to fifteen years, overlapping the evidence of earlier changes. The complex tangle of information on Soviet military requirements can best be presented by calendar decades, which roughly match the major shifts in Soviet strategy. The decades locate successive strategies in time, while suggesting the drawn-out process of restructuring forces and introducing new concepts of operation as strategies change.[2] The underlying decisions

1. This is a central thesis of Michael MccGwire, *Military Objectives in Soviet Foreign Policy* (Brookings, 1987).
2. This periodization was implied by Marshal Nikolay V. Ogarkov, who distinguished between the 1960s, on the one hand, and the 1970s and 1980s, on the other, in *Istorya uchit bditel'nosti* (*History Teaches Vigilance*) (Moscow: Voenizdat, 1985), p. 51.

14

for each decade between World War II and the 1980s were taken toward the end of the preceding decade and the new strategy was not ready to be fully implemented until the middle of the decade in question.

Except in the 1950s, the relative likelihood of world war and how it might come about were not critical conditions. Rather, it was the U.S. objective in such a war of destroying the Soviet system that provided the impetus for Soviet military requirements. It was in response to this perceived capitalist objective, inferred from Western statements over the years and from the logic of Marxism-Leninism, that the Soviets formulated their objectives. That logic emphasized the inherent possibility of war between the two social systems, war that would be precipitated by the imperialists. And since that assessment was reinforced by U.S. foreign policy behavior and the thrust of U.S. weapons programs, Soviet defense policy centered on preparing to fight and "not lose" such a war.

"Not losing" is a more meaningful and more accurate way of formulating the Soviet objective in world war than "winning" or "victory." "Winning," under the 1960s nuclear strategy, meant no more than the survival of the socialist system, while "losing" implied its extinction.[3] Similarly, the force structure developed to support the 1970s strategy did not provide for the kind of victory over the capitalist system that the Allies achieved over their opponents in World Wars I and II. The Soviets required victory in Western Europe, but thereafter there would be some kind of geostrategic standoff. The optimum outcome would then be a negotiated peace with the United States. In both the 1960s and the 1970s strategies, the essential objective was not to lose, because defeat implied the demise of the Soviet state.

Given that minimum objective, the structure of Soviet forces has been determined by the probable nature of a world war. Soviet assessments of the likelihood of such a war have influenced the scale of resources to be invested in fleshing out that structure and the urgency of such investment. How the Soviets planned, at various periods, to fight a world war, should it be unavoidable, has led to the changes in Soviet military requirements.

The assumption that world war would be precipitated in some way by the imperialists did not imply that the Soviets were willing to forgo the advantage of initiating or escalating armed conflict. On the contrary,

3. On the meaning of "victory," see Stephen Shenfield, *The Nuclear Predicament: Explorations in Soviet Ideology,* Chatham House Paper 37 (London: Routledge and Kegan Paul, 1987), pp. 12–13.

they have consistently emphasized the importance of the first blow, of striking before the opponent is ready, of deception and surprise. Yet these well-attested beliefs and the offensive posture of some of their forces did not imply that the Soviets saw armed conflict with the United States as being in their interest, or that they had aggressive designs on Western Europe.

To the extent there is any paradox here, it is explained by the distinction the Soviets make between military doctrine at the sociopolitical and military-technical levels. The sociopolitical level is dominant, thus allowing the Soviets to claim that their military doctrine has always been defensive. In the sense that they have actively sought to avoid war and have never advocated a policy of military conquest such as Hitler's or (more pertinent) the European colonial expansion, that is true. Until recently, however, their doctrine at the military-technical level, the level of applied strategy, has been predominantly offensive.

Soviet intellectuals now disingenuously blame this offensive doctrine on a lack of civilian involvement in military decisionmaking. At least the members of the Defense Council and probably many others in the political apparatus would have been aware of underlying concepts and understood the significance of Soviet war plans. Furthermore, given the geostrategic capabilities of the two opponents, some form of offensive preemption was essential if the Soviets were not ultimately to lose a world war.

For most of the postwar period the Soviets lagged behind the West in overall military capability. As fast as they caught up or developed a counter in one area of military technology, the United States would introduce a new weapon system that outflanked them. As a consequence, particularly where nuclear weapons were concerned, it was largely the West that dictated the nature of a war. In the 1950s it was the United States that enunciated the policy of devastating strikes on the Soviet Union known as massive retaliation; it was NATO (the North Atlantic Treaty Organization) that declared that it had integrated its arsenals and would use conventional or atomic weapons as appropriate. Soviet war planners had to accept these and other constraints, and (to borrow economics terms) they were strategy takers, unlike the Germans in World War II who were strategy setters.

The German offensives in 1940 and 1941 assumed that war was beneficial to Germany; to initiate conflict was to harvest its fruits. Soviet plans for the contingency of world war in the 1950s, 1960s, and 1970s saw war as disastrous for the Soviet Union; to initiate conflict could, however, mitigate its effects. If world war were inevitable, then to launch an offensive into Western Europe or to launch a nuclear attack on North America would be to choose a lesser evil. The final outcome would be somewhat better (or, more properly, less bad) than if the Soviet Union were to wait for the West to initiate conflict on its own terms.

This tough-minded reasoning took shape in the 1950s and was the Soviet counterpart to the process of "thinking the unthinkable" that was under way in the United States. The Soviets did not, however, follow the Americans down the convoluted byways of Western deterrence theory. The catastrophic results of losing a world war justified the massive cost of developing and maintaining a preemptive offensive capability, whose makeup had to change with each successive strategy. Never mind the obvious difficulty of identifying the circumstances that would make world war unavoidable. It was the military's responsibility to provide the Soviet Union with the means to exercise the preemptive option, should the political leadership so decide.

The distinction between the Soviet view of an offensive into Western Europe as a lesser of two evils and the German view of it as an intrinsically desirable move helps to explain the new Soviet readiness to forgo the capability for such an offensive. That readiness was signaled in the Warsaw Pact statement of May 1987.

The Postwar Strategies

In 1944–45 as World War II drew to a close, Marxist theory still held that war between the two social systems was inevitable. Stalin did not, however, see that as an immediate danger, and it was even hoped that the wartime relationship with the United States would in some fashion persist in peacetime. The primary threat was seen as the resurgence of a powerful Germany, perhaps supported by a restored Japan.

The Soviets' strategy in the 1940s was to meet this potential threat by exacting punitive reparations that would destroy Germany's war-making potential. They also sought to establish a protective barrier of Soviet-oriented buffer states and to build up their capability to counter a German military threat, should it ever reemerge. Stalin hoped to be able to achieve security for the Soviet Union within fifteen to twenty years.

This reassuring view of Germany as the main but future threat was replaced in 1947–48 by a much less sanguine assessment. A reevaluation of the evidence led to the conclusion that by 1953 the Soviet Union would face the very real threat of a premeditated attack by a capitalist coalition. Its objective would be to oust the communists from Eastern Europe, to destroy the Soviets' nascent nuclear capability, and to overthrow their system of government. It would be built around a radical new partnership between France and Germany, the recognized proponents of large ground forces, and led by the United States and Great Britain.[4]

The accumulating evidence suggested to the Soviets what they might face in the not too distant future even if President Harry S. Truman could resist domestic pressures for a preventive strike against Soviet atomic research and development facilities. Some pretext, of the kind the Germans had used for aggressive incursions in 1938–41, might be found to justify a capitalist intervention in the name of freedom. It might involve picking off a single country under Soviet control or be an intervention across the board. It could be limited to the Western European continental armies, with the Anglo-Saxon allies standing back to deter a Soviet reaction, or it might include the full panoply of Western military power from the start.

The Soviets had to plan for the worst case, which could include massive land offensives across the German plain and through the Balkans; major amphibious landings on the Baltic and Black Sea coasts, opening up fronts in the Soviet rear and mobilizing anti-Soviet partisans; and massive air attacks by conventional and atomic bombers throughout the Soviet Union.

The Soviets' strategy in the 1950s was mainly an extrapolation of their recent experience and can be described as improved World War II. On the plus side the de facto front line ran across the narrowest part of Europe and was five hundred miles to the west of the Soviet border. On the minus side, the Soviet Union's former allies would now be ranged against it, together with its erstwhile enemies, Italy and the more important elements of Germany. However, the Soviet rear was covered by China and North Korea, which removed the danger of a second land front. The minimum requirement was to be able to rebuff Western aggression. The larger requirement was to defeat the capitalist bloc, and

---

4. MccGwire, *Military Objectives*, pp. 13–22; Michael MccGwire, "The Genesis of Soviet Threat Perceptions" (Brookings, 1988).

that implied going over to the offensive. To achieve victory and a durable peace would require a major offensive into Western Europe and the accession to power of pro-Soviet or genuinely neutral governments throughout the area.

The offensive operations would have the dual purpose of defeating NATO forces and denying the United States a bridgehead. To the extent that the Soviets were concerned about the reliability of Eastern Europe, a factor that varied between peoples, offensive operations would make defections less likely. Offensive operations also offered some protection to Soviet front-line forces against nuclear attack, a factor that became increasingly important as the United States built up its arsenal. And as the nuclear threat to the Soviet homeland increased, the capability for a rapid offensive into Western Europe offered some deterrent to a premeditated attack by the U.S. Strategic Air Command.

The major new element of the threat was strategic bombardment, which had imposed such heavy costs on Germany and Japan, costs that would be multiplied as atomic and nuclear weapons became more readily available. The scope of the air threat had been spelled out by the retiring chief of staff of the U.S. Air Force. He had written in 1948 about destroying "a few hundred square miles of industrial area in a score of Russian cities." He had stressed the need for forward bases from which U.S. bombers could mount an air offensive against Russia's industrial heartland; eventually, intercontinental supersonic bombers and guided missiles carrying atomic warheads would make the bases unnecessary.[5]

The initial Soviet response to the threat of strategic air attack included the establishment in 1948 of a national air defense system. Then, as the U.S. Strategic Air Command developed a network of staging bases around the periphery of the Soviet Union, a Soviet doctrine of preemptive attacks against these bases emerged. To carry out these attacks, the Soviets had to rely on medium-range aircraft and (for most of the 1950s) on the use of conventional weapons, but the concept of preemption became operationally more attractive at the end of the decade, when Soviet medium- and intermediate-range ballistic missiles (MRBMs and IRBMs) armed with nuclear warheads began to enter service. Meanwhile the Soviets sought to break the U.S. strategic monopoly by developing

---

5. General Carl Spatz, "If We Should Have to Fight Again," *Life Magazine,* July 5, 1948, pp. 33–44, and "General Spatz on Atomic Warfare," ibid., August 16, 1948, pp. 90–104. The discussion was pitched in terms of responding to a Soviet attack, but the logic was equally valid for a war incited by the United States.

their own means of delivering nuclear weapons against North America, as described in chapter 3.

Until at least 1953, the Soviets took the threat of premeditated military aggression by the West very seriously, although NATO's failure to press ahead with the buildup of a Franco-German army meant that the threat remained only latent. The reassessment that followed Stalin's death downgraded the threat of territorial aggression and emphasized the danger of a disarming nuclear strike, but the immediacy of that threat steadily diminished. In 1956 it was ruled that a deliberate capitalist attack on the Soviet Union was no longer inevitable (because of Soviet strength) and later that year, Western inaction during the Hungarian crisis reinforced the more sanguine trend. By the end of the 1950s the Soviets had largely discounted the kind of cold-blooded premeditated U.S. attack that they had feared in the early 1950s.

This change in perceptions had been progressive, fostered by the increasing Soviet capability to rebuff an aggressor and a growing understanding of the distinction between U.S. urges and actions. Nikita Khrushchev's visit to America in 1959 was almost certainly a major factor in the final appreciation. The change did not mean that the Soviets thought that the U.S. urge to change the political complexion of Eastern Europe had evaporated. The danger of Western intervention to exploit a perceived opportunity to discomfort the Soviet Union would persist and remained a potential cause of war. But as the status quo in Europe gained de facto acceptance, so did that particular danger diminish. However, the Soviet Union had growing international commitments that broadened the scope of superpower competition and increased the likelihood of confrontation in other parts of the world. The antagonisms of the two social systems contained the seeds of global conflict.

War would be precipitated in some way by the aggressive behavior of imperialism. But whereas in the early 1950s the Soviets thought it would come like World War II as the result of a deliberate policy of aggression, carefully thought out and skillfully planned, by the end of the decade they thought more in terms of World War I, where war would come through a chain of circumstances.

This made little practical difference from the military viewpoint. It had to be assumed that if the capitalists concluded that war was likely, they would choose to initiate military action on their own terms. This assumption was reflected in Soviet military writings and exercises. It did not exclude the possibility that the Soviets might be able to beat the

West to the punch, and the advantages of successful preemption were stressed. But the emphasis on the importance of surprise is more likely to have reflected Soviet concern about the possibility of the Soviet Union being surprised by the West than the reverse.

The 1960s Strategy

During the latter part of the 1950s, the emerging implications of nuclear weapons and of missile delivery systems (the second revolution in military affairs) forced a basic reassessment of established military theory and concepts of operation. Much of the reassessment focused on how to integrate the new weapons into traditional ground force operations at the theater level and on what this meant for force structure and the balance between arms. But the Soviets were also rethinking the nature of a war involving the superpowers, a crucial factor in their deliberations being U.S. and NATO doctrine on the role of nuclear weapons in such a war.

The central conclusion was that a major conflict would inevitably develop into a full-scale intercontinental nuclear exchange. In the initial stages of such a conflict each power would carry out massive nuclear strikes on the other's territory to deprive its enemy of the military, political, and economic means of waging war. The war would be violent and swift moving. The use of nuclear weapons at the theater level was inevitable, and indeed necessary, and massive casualties would have to be accepted. Both the Soviet Union and the United States would be devastated and, although hostilities might drag on, the outcome of the war would be decided by the initial nuclear exchanges.

The doctrinal reassessment, which culminated in December 1959, led to a series of decisions that included the establishment of the strategic rocket forces as a separate branch of service. The reassessment was subsequently validated by the rapid buildup of U.S. strategic delivery systems (Minuteman and Polaris) initiated by the Kennedy administration on taking office in January 1961, and by the introduction of a completely new family of tactical nuclear systems throughout NATO in the 1962–64 period.

A world war of the kind described would represent the decisive clash between the capitalist and socialist systems. It would be a fight to the finish, where survival was all that would be expected of victory and defeat would be synonymous with extinction. In order not to lose such a war, the Soviets would have to *preserve the socialist system* and *destroy the capitalist system*. These were the primary military objectives.

The apparently limited objective of preserving the socialist system was the best available, given Soviet doctrine on the likely nature of a world war. It is a universal axiom of military planning that success in war depends in part on choosing an objective that is achievable in the given circumstances. It is a recipe for disaster to choose a more ambitious objective that is unachievable. By doctrinal definition, the Soviet Union would be devastated and suffer massive casualties in a world war, and in such circumstances the survival of the socialist system was the optimal outcome.

The destruction of the capitalist system required a nuclear attack on North America. If the weapons could strike home before the United States launched its own strike, such an attack would also help to preserve the socialist system by diminishing the weight of the nuclear attack on the USSR. The importance of getting in the first blow meant that, in theory at least, a Soviet decision that war was inescapable would lead automatically to the decision to strike at North America and at the nuclear bases on the continental and maritime periphery of the Soviet Union. Terminologically, this would be closer to a preventive attack than to preemption.

The difficulty of deciding that war was inescapable and the political constraints on launching such strikes were obvious, but an offensive damage-limiting strategy was the least of all evils. The Soviets' limited intercontinental capability during the early 1960s did not undermine such a strategy. If an exchange was inevitable, the USSR would be slightly less worse off if it could get in the first blow, even if only a modest strike.

In the late 1950s, the evidence suggests that Soviet production of intercontinental ballistic missiles (ICBMs) was programmed to yield a force of about 1,200 ICBMs by 1970. This force would have had the capacity to devastate North America, while targets on the European periphery were to be struck by MRBMs and IRBMs and medium-range bombers. These missile programs were disrupted and augmented by the need to respond to the surge in deployment of Minuteman missiles in the first half of the 1960s. But the underlying principle did not change and the Soviets were set on achieving strategic nuclear superiority.[6]

6. Soviet ICBM programs belie the idea that the Soviet Union ever seriously entertained the idea of minimum deterrence as an operational policy. To the extent that the Soviet Union

They were also seeking to develop an antiballistic missile (ABM) system that would help protect the center of government in Moscow. The Soviets could not, therefore, entertain arms control proposals that would constrain their attempt to attain these objectives.

The requirement to destroy those elements of the capitalist system located on the Eurasian continent had to be balanced against the need for an alternative socioeconomic base to help rebuild the socialist economies in the Soviet Union and Eastern Europe. Military operations in Western Europe had therefore to be designed so as to defeat NATO forces and overthrow the existing governments while attempting to preserve the productive resources of the various economies. The United States would be in no position to mount a transoceanic assault, so the Soviets would not need to establish military control beyond that needed for economic exploitation. The people of the Warsaw Pact would have first call on resources, and concern for the people of NATO would be directly related to their capacity to produce such resources and their willingness to join the socialist camp.

The importance of Western Europe as an alternative socioeconomic base focused Soviet attention on the West's sea-based nuclear delivery capability, which increased sharply in the early 1960s with the deployment of the Polaris system and the entry into service of the aircraft carriers ordered in the wake of the Korean War. These nuclear delivery systems could be withheld from the initial exchange and, unless matched by a comparable Soviet capability, would be able to dictate the outcome of the war. The Soviets responded with the Yankee nuclear-powered ballistic-missile submarine (SSBN) program that was probably planned to yield a matching force of 70 submarines carrying 1,260 missiles for delivery in 1968–77.[7]

But the U.S. sea-based systems could also be used to deny the Soviets the use of Western Europe as an alternative socioeconomic base. The Soviets would be unable to defend Western Europe against attacks from sea and the only possible response was to counter the sea-based systems directly. As one element of their response, the Soviets deployed naval forces to those sea areas from which nuclear strikes could be launched against the Soviet Union and Europe. The Soviets reasoned that if they

achieved a measure of "assured response" in the late 1960s, it was by deploying large numbers of ICBMs. Even if Khrushchev toyed with the notion in 1959, the surge in U.S. ICBM production in 1961 would have made it impractical.

7. MccGwire, *Military Objectives,* pp. 410–15.

maintained forces within weapons range of U.S. nuclear strike platforms, the United States would have to choose between using its systems at the onset of war or losing them and would no longer have the option of withholding them from the initial exchange.

The Soviet navy's shift to forward deployment began in 1963, but it soon became clear that without access to facilities ashore the navy could not sustain the necessary level and tempo of operations. The mission of countering the strike carrier and Polaris had to be discharged at the very onset of war (after which the Soviet forces were expendable), and this introduced a new requirement for overseas bases in peacetime. Access to Egyptian facilities was secured in the wake of the 1967 Arab-Israeli War and to Somalian facilities in 1968–69.

There remained the question of China. By 1957 the rift with China was wide enough for it to be seen as a rival rather than an ally. Thus in the event of a world war it would probably be necessary for the Soviets to strike China with enough nuclear weapons to ensure that it would not by default take over the leadership of the socialist system. It would make sense to spare Manchuria, so that it would remain available for use as an alternative socioeconomic base.

The 1970s Strategy

Toward the end of 1966 the Soviets concluded that a world war would not necessarily be nuclear and that, even if it were, it would not necessarily include massive strikes on the USSR. This change in doctrine was probably engendered by the strategic reassessment that would have been necessitated by France's withdrawal from NATO in July 1966, a reassessment that brought several developments into focus.[8] The United States' advocacy of flexible response in Europe and the adoption of "assured destruction" as the criterion for sizing its strategic forces suggested a deep reluctance to resort to strategic nuclear weapons except in response to a direct attack on the United States. This implied that there was a real possibility that the Soviet ICBMs that were beginning to enter service in large numbers would be able to deter the United States

8. The circumstantial, empirical, and textual evidence for the July 1966 dating, in ibid., pp. 385–405, excludes the "natural" decision point of the Twenty-third Party Congress held in March 1966, which leaves the French withdrawal as the most likely precipitating cause.

Table 2-1. *Soviet Doctrine on the Nature of World War*

Aspect	The 1960s	The 1970s
	Nature of world war	
Military	Inevitably nuclear, including nuclear strikes on the USSR	May not be nuclear. Strikes on the USSR are not inevitable
Political	A fight to the finish between two social systems	A critical campaign in the ongoing struggle between the two systems
	Primary military objectives	
Own survival	Preserve the socialist system	Avoid the nuclear devastation of the USSR
Enemy's defeat	Destroy the capitalist system	Gravely weaken the capitalist system

Source: Michael MccGwire, *Military Objectives in Soviet Foreign Policy* (Brookings, 1987), p. 45.

from launching a nuclear attack on the USSR, even if U.S. forces faced defeat in Europe.

Meanwhile, the NATO doctrine of flexible response offered the Soviets a new strategic opportunity. If, during this initial conventional phase of a war in Europe, they could neutralize NATO's theater nuclear forces, that would remove the first rung of escalation. If the Soviets could knock NATO out of the war using nonnuclear forces, the question of intercontinental escalation might become moot.

The new doctrine on the likely nature of world war meant that it became logically possible (and hence necessary) for the Soviets to adopt the wartime objective of avoiding the nuclear devastation of the Soviet Union (see table 2-1). As a corollary, they had to forgo the objective of destroying the capitalist system since this could only be achieved by launching a nuclear attack on the United States, which would result in retaliatory strikes on the USSR.

Nuclear attack on North America had also been intended to reduce the weight of attack on the Soviet Union, but by 1966 it was clear that the number and diversity of U.S. nuclear systems meant that the practical benefits of a preemptive strike would, in that respect, be marginal. Forgoing such an attack would, however, mean that the U.S. military-industrial base would remain intact, and it therefore became essential to deny the United States a bridgehead in Europe from which to mount an offensive against the USSR at a subsequent stage of the war.

Another corollary of sparing North America was that the Soviets had to think in terms of a two-phase war. A first phase of initially intense operations, leading to the defeat of NATO forces in Europe, would be followed (if possible) by some kind of armistice and peace agreement. If peace were not possible, the war would move into a second phase involving a protracted global struggle, whose course and duration would be hard to predict. A major objective would be to prevent the return of capitalist forces to the Eurasian continent.[9]

In phase one the main theater of war would be Europe, and the Western theater of military action (TVD) would be the main TVD in the European theater. Phase one can be visualized for planning purposes as including three stages.[10] The first stage (lasting twelve to twenty days) would cover the period of the offensive into Western Europe and the operations designed to knock NATO out of the war. The second stage (lasting twenty to thirty days) would cover the redeployment of forces and the completion of offensive operations on the secondary axes of advance, as well as the occupation of territories to the rear of the defeated enemy's main forces. The third stage (lasting another two to three months) would cover the establishment of an extended defensive perimeter, exploiting natural defensive barriers in order to economize force.

The southern boundary of the defense perimeter would probably run along the Sahara Desert and angle down to meet the Indian Ocean at the Horn of Africa. To the west, there could be some kind of "Atlantic wall" that would include Iceland and the British Isles. To the east, the defense perimeter would run north past the inhospitable shores of the Arabian Peninsula, up through Baluchistan to Afghanistan, and then along the Chinese border to the Pacific. Such an alignment would make maximum

9. The concept of a two-phase war is a logical deduction based on strategic analysis and German experience in World War II. Obviously, the Soviets do not spell out their war plans publicly, but Admiral Sergey S. Gorshkov's 1972 analysis of naval operations in World War II makes sense only in the context of a debate on the Soviet navy's role in the second phase of a world war. The change in the nature of Soviet military involvement in Somalia can also be explained in these terms. See ibid., pp. 106–07, 196–203, 468–70.

10. The concept of stages was spelled out by Major General V. Zemskov in "Characteristic Features of Modern Wars and Possible Methods of Conducting Them," *VM*, no. 7 (July 1969), in U.S. Foreign Broadcast Information Service, *Foreign Press Digest*, 0022/70, April 6, 1970, pp. 19–27 (see Abbreviations of Frequently Cited Sources). He describes the initial stage as "a short period of time during which the most immediate strategic goals of the war will be achieved in the theaters of military operation." Estimated lengths of the three stages are based on Western officials' statements over the years about the Soviet capability to reach the Channel, on the daily rates of advance used in Soviet planning, and on the opinion of Western specialists on Soviet theater operations.

use of the obstructive nature of oceans and deserts and would also encompass the bulk of petroleum resources lying outside the western hemisphere.

Among the strategic requirements there remained the problem, in the event of war, of how to defeat NATO in Europe without precipitating a nuclear attack on the USSR. The Soviets would try to prevent the initial resort to nuclear weapons in the theater and, if that were not possible, to limit its extent. They would exploit the NATO concept of flexible response (which foresaw a conventional phase at the start of war in Europe) by launching preventive attacks against NATO's nuclear delivery systems, command, control, and communications (C^3) nodes, and higher command structure, at the same time mounting a massive blitzkrieg offensive striking deep to the rear, all of this using conventional means only. The ensuing disruption would, they hoped, paralyze NATO's decisionmaking processes and encourage the European members to accept defeat without resorting to the use of nuclear weapons. If, nevertheless, NATO did go nuclear, its capability would have been considerably diminished and the escalatory momentum lessened.

In 1967–68 the Soviets embarked on the process of restructuring their forces to carry out these conventional offensive operations, and the new capability was largely in place by the second half of the 1970s. In 1973–74 it was decreed that the Soviet Union would not initiate the use of nuclear weapons.[11] This policy was later supplemented by a political campaign to persuade NATO to adopt a policy of "no first use" of nuclear weapons in the theater and to persuade the United States that the resort to nuclear weapons in Europe would inevitably lead to strikes on North America.

The 1970s strategy was the *preferred* one (see table 2-2), but the Soviets had to be *prepared* for a much wider range of contingencies. At one extreme NATO might succeed in checking the Warsaw Pact offensive without resort to nuclear weapons, and the Soviets would be faced with the prospect of protracted conventional war. At the other extreme the Soviets might successfully implement their plans for a

---

11. Raymond L. Garthoff, *Deterrence and the Revolution in Soviet Military Doctrine* (Brookings, 1990), p. 83, cites an article in *VM,* no. 1 (January 1975), that refers to these secret instructions. By 1973–74, the General Staff had concluded that offensive military operations would not be helped by the use of nuclear weapons and that in certain types of terrain they would be hindered.

Table 2-2. *A Comparison of the 1960s and 1970s Strategic Hierarchies*

The 1960s hierarchy	The 1970s hierarchy
Objectives	
Preserve the socialist system	Avoid the nuclear devastation of the USSR
Protect the physical structure of government and secure its capacity for effective operation throughout the Soviet state	Hamper NATO's resort to nuclear weapons
Guarantee the survival of a proportion of the nation's industrial base and working population	Deter nuclear strikes on the USSR
Secure an alternative economic base to contribute to the rebuilding of a socialist society in the USSR	Insure against the fixed-silo deterrent being rendered impotent
Destroy the capitalist system	Gravely weaken the capitalist system
Destroy enemy forces in being	Establish physical control of Europe
Destroy the system's war-making potential	Deny the United States access to the western parts of Eurasia
Destroy the system's structure of governmental and social control	Establish hegemony over Japan and South Korea
Type of war	
Short, all-out nuclear war, including intercontinental nuclear exchange	Two-phase war; no intercontinental exchange
	One: Short, high-intensity offensive operations in Europe, preferably nonnuclear
	Two: Long-drawn-out, primarily defensive operations; course unpredictable

Source: MccGwire, *Military Objectives*, p. 47.

blitzkrieg offensive but fail to deter the U.S. president from launching a nuclear attack on the USSR when faced by the defeat of U.S. forces in Europe. In that case, the Soviets had to be prepared to revert to the 1960s strategy for global nuclear war; the terms would be considerably more unfavorable than if the Soviets had themselves initiated the use of nuclear weapons.

The restructuring of Soviet theater forces also required a significant increase in the capability of individual formations and units. The Soviets were therefore in no position to negotiate constructively at the talks on mutual and balanced force reductions (MBFR) in Europe.[12] However, the opposite consideration applied to strategic nuclear forces, because Soviet requirements in this area changed radically with the change in objectives and the new strategy and operational concepts that flowed from those objectives.

The primary mission of the Soviet ICBM force was no longer to destroy the capitalist system by devastating North America, but to deter the United States from striking at the Soviet Union in the course of a war, particularly when faced by the imminent defeat of U.S. forces in Europe. In calculating what would be needed to deter a U.S. nuclear strike, the Soviets could reasonably have argued that if the president were not deterred by the threatened destruction of the five or ten largest U.S. cities, he would not be deterred by threats to fifty or even five hundred. In other words, deterrence would work at a fairly low level or not at all.

If deterrence failed, the smaller the U.S. strategic arsenal, the less devastating the result of a nuclear attack on the USSR. Soviet interests would therefore be best served by parity at as low a level as possible. Parity was necessary to thwart the avowed U.S. policy of negotiating from a position of strength in peacetime, and also to cover the possibility that wartime deterrence would fail, in which case the Soviets wanted to be on an even footing with the United States. Rough numerical parity was already in sight, but to reduce the level of the strategic arsenals would require agreement with the United States. This military rationale clinched the argument of those Soviet leaders who advocated arms control negotiations as a means of promoting détente. Agreement on limiting the buildup of strategic weapons as a first step to reducing the size of the nuclear arsenals became an end in itself.

An important aspect of this new requirement for wartime deterrence was credibility. As a way of minimizing pressure on the United States to escalate, the 1970s strategy required the Soviets to eschew intercontinental preemption and adopt a policy of launch on warning.[13] In conse-

12. Having been unresponsive to NATO proposals in 1968 and 1970, the Soviets finally agreed to negotiations in 1972 (which got under way in 1973) in order to reap specific political benefits. They did not, however, begin to negotiate seriously until January 1976, and that response was elicited by the specific nature of a NATO proposal involving an offer to withdraw nuclear strike weapons in exchange for a reduction in Soviet tanks. MccGwire, *Military Objectives,* p. 245.

13. This is confirmed in Bruce A. Blair, *The Logic of Accidental Nuclear War* (Brookings, forthcoming).

quence, a Soviet retaliatory strike was likely to comprise only a fraction of the original ICBM force. This meant that it would be much more important to halt the development of a U.S. ABM system than to deploy a marginally effective Soviet one.[14] The Soviets therefore pressed for the maximum limitations on ABM systems from the start of the SALT negotiations in November 1969. They were even willing to consider a complete ban, which would have required them to dismantle the existing ABM sites around Moscow.

The West seems to have assumed that this reversal of policy on ABM meant that the Soviets now subscribed to the Western version of deterrence theory, and Westerners remained unaware of the underlying change in Soviet wartime strategy. Reticence about their new interest in reducing offensive nuclear forces, however, was costly for the Soviets, reinforcing the perception that they had to be dragged to the negotiating table and justifying U.S. development of new weapon systems. In theory, the new systems were to be used as bargaining chips; in practice they augmented the U.S. arsenal and put new obstacles in the path of limiting nuclear inventories.

Under the 1970s strategy the fixed-silo ICBM force would be the primary wartime deterrent of the Soviets, but they had to insure against the possibility that American technological ingenuity would find some way of rendering it impotent. A force of mobile ICBMs would have met the requirement, but that was not an option. Problems with solid-fuel propulsion meant that the SS-13 missile, which had been intended to provide a survivable strategic reserve, would have to be emplaced in silos. The insurance force thus had to be deployed at sea, as the adaptation of the projected SSBN and associated missile programs to produce the Delta class SSBN indicate.

The changes in design specifications were necessary because the operational requirements for the Delta-Typhoon insurance force in the 1970s strategy were significantly more demanding than those for the Yankee matching force in the 1960s strategy. The Yankees' mission of matching the U.S. sea-based capability would have only become operative after an intercontinental nuclear exchange, when the SSBN force would probably have constituted the major element of the remain-

14. Difficulties experienced in developing an effective Soviet ABM system would obviously have influenced the debate. However, it would have been out of character for the Soviets to desist in their efforts to deploy some form of ballistic missile defense, however inadequate, while they persisted in trying to develop a better system; something other than technical difficulties must explain this uncharacteristic change in policy on ABMs.

ing Soviet nuclear war-fighting capability. By then the West's antisubmarine warfare (ASW) capability would have been seriously degraded and the Yankees could have anticipated little difficulty in deploying to within striking range of their targets.

By contrast the Deltas' insurance mission would become operative before a nuclear exchange, an exchange that the Soviets hoped to deter. From the onset of war, the insurance force would have to withstand determined Western efforts to degrade its capability, which meant it would have to be deployed in protected waters close to home and its missiles would have to be capable of striking directly at North America from those waters. These SSBNs would need to be protected by ships and submarines armed with both conventional and nuclear ordnance and capable of sustained combat operations. This implied a major change in design specifications for general-purpose naval forces and required scaling up the size of all types of major combatant. Initially, the Soviets intended to use the Arctic Ocean as the primary deployment area for SSBNs, turning it into an enclosed sea by blocking the Bering and Canadian straits and establishing command of the Norwegian Sea.[15]

Another naval consequence of the 1970s strategy was to relax the requirement to pose a permanent counter in peacetime to U.S. sea-based strike systems, because it was no longer planned to attack them with nuclear weapons at the onset of war. Indeed, such attacks would be prohibited since they would provide grounds for nuclear escalation by NATO. The 1970s strategy also changed the nature of the Soviets' war-related requirements in the third world, which lost their former urgency. Whereas naval support facilities had previously been required in peacetime, the new concept called for an extended defense perimeter and possibly a need to supply the Far East by sea, both of which would only become operative in phase two of a world war.

The 1970s strategy had major implications for war plans in the Far East. Avoiding a two-front war continued to be a primary objective but it became necessary to deter China from seeking to profit from war in Europe. This had to be achieved with conventional forces, lest resort to nuclear weapons in the Far East encourage their use by NATO. This is likely to have been the main consideration underlying the buildup of Soviet forces facing China from twenty divisions in 1965 to forty-five in 1973. If the 1960s strategy had remained operative, the threat of Chinese

---

15. MccGwire, *Military Objectives,* pp. 146–53.

attack would have been covered by the existing capability for preventive nuclear strikes.

The Soviets' objective in dealing with China in phase two of a world war would have been to achieve a reasonably stable political situation that could be sustained at not too great a cost in military resources and that would deny China to the United States as a potential ally in the ongoing global struggle between the two social systems. The concentration of forces on the Manchurian sector of the border with China suggests that the Soviets might have planned to separate Manchuria from the rest of China, believing that they would gain significant long-term benefits if Manchuria were in friendly and malleable hands, while its loss would seriously weaken China.

Regardless of whether the USSR found itself at war with China in phase one, Soviet military planners had to cover the possibility that at some stage in phase two the United States might arrange to use China as an avenue for assault on the Russian heartland, following the path of the Mongol hordes. By advancing through western China, U.S. forces would outflank eastern and central Siberia, gaining access to the Kirghiz steppes and the West Siberian Plain. The Soviets had therefore to think in terms of a secondary defense perimeter following the north-south line of the Yenisey River and had to ensure that key strategic assets, such as ballistic-missile early-warning radars, were located to the west of that line.

The Early 1980s

Although the 1980s would turn out to be a period of change, the early impression was one of continuity. The new family of more capable general-purpose naval combatants began to enter service in the early 1980s, flight testing of the fifth generation of ballistic missiles began in 1982–83, and in the ground-air forces, which had achieved a capability for a conventional blitzkrieg, emphasis shifted to improving their sustainability in case the offensive into Western Europe should bog down.[16] As the Soviet military entered the 1980s its focus was on fleshing out the

16. Beginning in 1981, a preoccupation with protracted conventional war surfaced in Soviet military writing; see James McConnell "Shifts in Soviet Views on the Proper Focus of Military Development," *World Politics,* vol. 37 (April 1985), pp. 330–36.

new force structure and making adjustments in its original operational concept in order to improve its ability to implement the 1970s strategy.

Other developments, however, helped to prepare the ground for the fundamental change in Soviet defense policy that would be introduced by the new leadership in the second half of the decade.

Modifying the 1970s Strategy

The 1970s strategy probably became fully operational in 1976. Coincidentally, Marshal Grechko died in April that year, to be followed as minister of defense by Dmitriy F. Ustinov, and Marshal Ogarkov was made chief of the General Staff in January 1977. A series of developments that can be dated to about 1976–77 suggest a major review at that time of the decisions taken in 1967–68 and of their practical outcomes.[17]

By 1978 a high command for the Far Eastern TVD had been established, reflecting the concept that, in a world war, the Soviets would hold in the east, while war in the European theater (the main theater) would be run out of Moscow by the Stavka, as in World War II. In the European theater, the Soviets appear to have streamlined their command structure to provide a better balance between coordination and delegation. It was probably at this time that they decided to resuscitate the World War II concept of the mobile (now operational maneuver) group, as a response to developments in NATO operational doctrine.

The requirements for a long-range bomber and a new kind of IRBM are likely to have been formulated in this period, though possibly somewhat earlier. The long-range bomber had no place in the 1960s strategy because ICBMs had been selected as the means of intercontinental nuclear delivery, and air bases were expected to be destroyed in the initial exchange. The 1970s strategy meant that air bases would remain available, and the concept of a two-phase war generated a variety of general-purpose roles for the long-range bomber. Its heavy payload and reusability offered considerable advantages over missiles armed with conventional warheads. Its likely targets would include Western invasion forces as well as threatening troop formations and military bases that might be established outside the extended defense perimeter.

The most far-reaching modification in the 1970s strategy was the plan to use the Arctic Ocean as a secure deployment zone for the SSBN

---

17. A fine-grained analysis of this decision period has yet to be undertaken.

insurance force. The plan as conceived in 1967–68 had involved closing off the Arctic by establishing command of the Norwegian Sea, which required control of key islands in the area and much of the surrounding coastline. Even if deferred to the second stage of phase one, this plan would have involved major ground-air operations, and in phase two it would have been necessary to occupy large parts of Norway, whose geography favored resistance movements.

The military costs of the plan were extremely high, as were the costs in new naval building programs. The chances of excluding U.S. nuclear attack submarines (SSNs) from the Arctic were low and the new class of SSN that would enter service in the second half of the 1970s had been designed specifically to operate against Soviet SSBNs. In 1975 the Soviets appear to have decided to downgrade the importance of the Arctic as a deployment area for SSBNs and to give priority to making the Sea of Okhotsk secure by improving the military and physical defense of the Kurile island chain and by reinforcing the Pacific Fleet. Relaxing the requirement to establish command of the Norwegian Sea did not, however, imply conceding command to NATO, and that area probably reverted to its former status as an outer defense zone for the Northern Fleet.[18]

This significantly reduced requirement allowed the cancelation, curtailment, or amendment of naval programs that had been designed to support the concept of closing off the Arctic Ocean; those programs included the Typhoon SSBN and the Oscar nuclear-powered guided-missile submarine (SSGN).[19] It also put an end to argument about the navy's role in phase two of a world war and reversed the increase in political clout that the navy had acquired during the first half of the 1970s.[20] A significant part of the navy's more ambitious requirements was related to phase two of the 1970s strategy. Only if Soviet ground-air operations in the Western TVD were successful in the first stage of phase

18. MccGwire, *Military Objectives,* pp. 100–02, 146–53, 174–75. There was a warming of Soviet-Japanese relations in the first half of the 1970s, including indications of some flexibility on the question of the "northern territories." However, early in 1976 Soviet intransigence returned, when Brezhnev stated in his report to the Twenty-fifth Party Congress on February 24, 1976, that Japan's claim to the four southernmost islands of the Kurile chain was "unfounded and unlawful." Tsuyoshi Hasegawa, *Japan-Soviet Relations under Gorbachev,* Occasional Paper 5 (Tokyo: Research Institute for Peace and Security, May 1987), p. 11.

19. MccGwire, *Military Objectives,* pp. 110–12, 438–47.

20. Ibid., pp. 464–76.

one would there be a phase two of the kind envisaged by the navy. Its requirements had, therefore, to yield priority.

The decision to curtail naval programs was made possible, in part, by evidence that the United States was reducing the size of its navy to about 475 ships, centered on twelve carrier battle groups (CBGs). In 1981 the Reagan administration reversed that policy and sought appropriations for fifteen CBGs, while U.S. naval spokesmen talked of attacking Soviet naval bases in the Arctic and the Pacific. Thus the Soviets in 1982–83 remitted the cuts in those naval programs building anticarrier classes, the Kirov and Slava (and perhaps the Oscar) programs.[21]

A New Threat of Regional War

A series of events between 1979 and 1982 made major Soviet-U.S. conflict in the region north of the Persian Gulf area a real possibility.[22] No matter how likely the Soviets thought such conflict, they were forced to address the issue in concrete terms. Throughout the 1970s the General Staff had been occupied with day-to-day problems of implementing and modifying the 1970s strategy, while objective circumstances since the 1950s had made the possibility of major conflict with the United States outside of Europe extremely remote. Such contingencies had been discussed in the theoretical literature, but before 1979 the Soviets had probably made their plans on the assumption that major conflict with the United States implied war in Europe and hence world war.

21. This can be inferred from the pattern of deliveries. The second Kirov class battle cruiser was launched in May 1981, its place on the slip being taken by a 32,000-ton command-communication ship. It was followed on the slip by a third and fourth Kirov in May 1983 and April 1986, respectively. Similarly, the third Slava-class missile cruiser was laid down in 1979 and launched in 1983, and a fourth one was not laid down until 1986. There a comparable break between the second Oscar-class SSGN and the third, after which the building rate may have picked up.

22. By late 1978, the overthrow of the shah of Iran was a strong possibility, bringing with it the possibility of U.S. intervention to keep him in power. The Soviets probably saw the possibility as remote, but it was bolstered in early 1979 by the U.S. supply of airborne warning and control system (AWACS) aircraft to Saudi Arabia and arms to North Yemen. The possibility of military intervention increased sharply at the end of the year. The U.S. embassy in Tehran was taken hostage on November 4, 1979, the Soviets invaded Afghanistan at Christmas, Carter declared the Persian Gulf a region of vital U.S. interest, and a rapid-deployment joint task force was officially constituted on March 1, 1980, following the signing of basing agreements. The likelihood of inadvertent conflict increased thereafter with the outbreak of the Iran-Iraq war in September 1980, the Israeli attack on the Iraqi nuclear reactor in June 1981, the Israeli invasion of Lebanon in June 1982, and the steadily increasing involvement of the United States in the war in Lebanon.

Events in 1979–82 challenged this assumption, forcing Moscow to decide whether major conflict with the United States in the Persian Gulf region would necessarily escalate to world war. If escalation was inevitable, then the existing contingency plans would still apply, and the existing posture was satisfactory; once U.S. forces had been committed to the Gulf, the Soviets would launch an offensive against NATO. If, however, the Soviets concluded that escalation was not inevitable, their primary objective would be to contain the war, and that would preclude an offensive into Europe. Instead of advancing into Europe, the Soviets would need to "hold" on their western front, while engaging U.S. forces to the south.

It can be inferred that the Soviets concluded that such a regional conflict would not inevitably escalate to world war and that they would have to hold in the west. This conclusion was implicit in the shift toward mending fences with China that was signaled by Leonid Brezhnev in Tashkent in March 1982.[23] It was more explicit in the establishment in 1984 of high commands for the Western, Southwestern, and Southern TVDs.[24] The Soviets wanted to be able (if necessary) to hold in the east and in the west, fight to the south, and possibly also fight in the southwest. They had also to cover the possibility that the conflict would not be contained and be ready to revert to their contingency plans for world war, involving an offensive into Western Europe. Such a complex strategy would be extremely difficult to manage successfully from Moscow and required that operational command be delegated to the TVD level.

While hardly surprising, the decision to hold in the west would have

23. MTS, March 24, 1982, in *FBIS*-82-058, p. R1. Work on normalizing relations began in October 1982, according to Kazuko Mori, "Sino-Soviet Relations: From Confrontation to Cooperation," *Japan Review of International Affairs*, vol. 2 (Spring-Summer 1988), p. 57. Raymond L. Garthoff (personal communication) has noted that the fairly steady stream of informative surveys of Chinese military developments and criticisms of Chinese policies that had appeared in *VM* since the latter 1960s ceased abruptly in early 1982. The first step toward improving relations with China had, however, been signaled in Brezhnev's speech to the Twenty-sixth Party Congress in February 1981.

24. The concept of regional war would explain: what had changed between 1978, when the Far Eastern High Command was established, and the establishment in 1984 of the three TVD high commands; the alignment of the boundary between the Southern and Southwestern TVDs, which does not make sense for a world war contingency, but is ideal for the contingency of regional war; and the absence of a high command in the Northwestern TVD. The reorganization in the early 1980s of medium-range strike aircraft into six air armies, which facilitated their redeployment between TVDs, supports this analysis. The merging of territorial and field air defense and its subordination to the existing structure of military districts is compatible with this conclusion but is more likely to have reflected the new and diversified threat from long-range cruise missiles flying different courses at subsonic speed.

placed in question a tenet of Soviet military thought that had its roots in tsarist days. Since before World War I, a prerequisite for success in major war was the capability to mount a continental-scale offensive to the west. This enduring requirement underlay Russian strategy in World War I, was central to Marshal Tukhachevsky's strategic plans in the 1930s, and had been triumphantly validated by the experience of World War II. In the postwar period, the ground offensive to the west remained a central concept in the successive reformulations of strategy.

The new requirement to hold in the west also raised the question whether forces facing NATO must necessarily be postured offensively. The military viewpoint would favor the existing posture, since it covered the worst-case contingency of escalation to world war and at the same time pinned down U.S. forces that might otherwise be redeployed to the Persian Gulf. The political viewpoint would emphasize the heavy political and military costs of an offensive posture, costs that were only too evident in the 1979–82 period. Since the military-technical factors favored the status quo, there was no operational urgency to resolve this question, but it is likely to have been placed on the agenda.

Other developments in 1979–82 favored a shift in emphasis toward defensive operations. In the European theater emphasis moved from restructuring Soviet forces facing NATO to increasing their sustainability, reflecting the possibility that NATO might check the blitzkrieg offensive and that the Soviets might be forced onto the defensive. The Western response in 1978–79 to the Soviet buildup of conventional forces facing NATO included various concepts of active defense, such as striking at Soviet second- and third-echelon forces and interdiction attacks on the deep rear. Thus a new emphasis on defensive operations cannot be tied to the emergence of a concrete possibility of regional war and the new requirement to hold in the west.[25] But the key point is that

25. By the early 1980s, a number of studies on defensive operations were under way, under the auspices of the General Staff. A series of high-level military conferences exploring the role of defensive operations in combat culminated in a conference held in 1981, on the fortieth anniversary of the German invasion; see Stephen M. Meyer, "The Sources and Prospects of Gorbachev's New Political Thinking on Security," *International Security*, vol. 13 (Fall 1988), pp. 153, 155. There was also an increase in the number of articles on defensive operations, although discussion could sometimes be referring to NATO's strategy of active defense as well as to Soviet requirements. Besides those in *VIZh*, the first appearing in October 1979, Raymond Garthoff (personal communication) has noted nine articles that appeared in *VM* between August 1979 and July 1984. They were identified by Army General D. T. Yazov, writing in February 1987, and the main cluster of five articles appeared in 1982–83. Meyer notes that in 1983 *Voennyy vestnik* (*Military Herald*) began devoting a special issue to defensive operations in war. The increased emphasis on defense was evident in the

the concept of holding in the west effectively downgraded a requirement that for over seventy years had been seen as a strategic imperative, thereby withdrawing a linchpin from the established framework of geostrategic assumptions.

Nuclear War

The destructive power of nuclear weapons inevitably raises the question of whether it is realistic to think of actually fighting a nuclear war. Besides the categorical alternatives of yes or no, there are qualified answers that take account of specific scenarios and there are also reasons for evading the question, such as the demands of troop morale or the credibility of deterrence.

Questions about nuclear war have persistently raised their heads in Soviet theoretical writings since the mid-1950s, but the debates have been of little practical relevance in military terms.[26] The West had actively espoused nuclear weapons, which meant that the Soviets had the choice of preparing to fight a nuclear war or not fighting at all, and the latter was not an option. The Soviet preference was, however, clearly signaled when the theoretical possibility emerged in the second half of the 1960s of preventing NATO's resort to nuclear weapons in the event of war. The Soviets responded by embarking on the extremely costly process of restructuring their forces to make that possibility a real one, if still relatively slim. By 1974 it had been formally decreed that the Soviet Union would not initiate the use of nuclear weapons.[27]

It is unlikely that the Soviets assessed the chance of preventing

---

1983 edition of *Combined Arms Exercises and Manoeuvers,* an updated version of *Tactical Exercises and Manoeuvers* (1977), written by the same author, Colonel General M. A. Gareev (see William Burgess, "Soviets Size up AirLand Battle," *Army,* July 1986, p. 40). M. A. Gareev reaffirmed this viewpoint in *M. V. Frunze: Voennyy teoretik (M. V. Frunze: Military Theorist)* (Moscow: Voenizdat, 1985), p. 230, using the experience of World War II to stress that defensive operations could not be seen as "an intermediate task" before moving over the offensive but required particular deployment of troops and weapons, a different kind of command and control, and logistic and engineering support prepared in advance. However, the book, which went for typesetting in August 1984, probably reflects the conclusions of the 1983–84 review.

26. See Mary C. FitzGerald, *Changing Soviet Doctrine on Nuclear War* (Halifax, Nova Scotia: Dalhousie University, Center for Foreign Policy Studies, 1988), pp. 42–48, who builds on the work of James McConnell. I have the impression that open discussion of these problems in official circles has, at times, been much more explicit and realistic in the Soviet Union than in the West, where officials glossed over the implications of nuclear deterrence doctrine, leaving antinuclear writers and activists to highlight the problems.

27. See note 11 above.

NATO's resort to nuclear weapons as more than even and probably much less. Soviet forces had therefore to be prepared to wage nuclear war, at least in the European theater, and troop morale remained a critical factor. It was therefore a major step when Brezhnev, in his report to the Twenty-sixth Party Congress in 1981, formally declared that "to count on victory in nuclear war [is] dangerous madness." The underlying ambiguity of this declaration was removed by Yuri Andropov's statement at the Central Committee plenum in June 1983 that "a military clash would be disastrous to mankind." This invited the question "why, then, prepare to fight it?"

The military did not address this question, but growing doubts were expressed in the early 1980s that a world war could be kept limited. One author advocated, in effect, a return to the 1960s strategy of nuclear preemption as the lesser evil in a war that would inevitably escalate to a global exchange.[28] More significant, writing in the wake of the Twenty-sixth Party Congress, the chief of the General Staff Marshal Nikolay V. Ogarkov asserted that a world war would use "the entire arsenal of means for armed struggle" and that such a war would be the "decisive clash between two opposing social systems," while the use of modern weapons would mean that "the future of all mankind would be at stake."[29] Reference to "the decisive clash" was a return to the language of the 1960s and to the assumption that escalation to massive strikes on the Soviet Union could not be avoided.

Euromissiles

Whether or not escalation to global nuclear war could be avoided, the Soviet military position in Europe was seriously damaged by the U.S. deployment of nuclear-armed Pershing II IRBMs and ground-launched cruise missiles (GLCMs) that began at the end of 1983, nominally in response to the Soviet deployment of the SS-20 missile. The most serious threat came from the Pershing II. It could be assumed that, if or when NATO resorted to nuclear weapons, these missiles would be used against Soviet command centers and communicating nodes, depriving the Sovi-

28. N. N. Azovtsev, *V. I. Lenin i sovetskaya voennaya nauka* (*V. I. Lenin and Soviet Military Science*) (Moscow: Izdatel'stvo Nauka, 1981), pp. 299–301. In a section new to this edition, Azovtsev invokes the Twenty-second and Twenty-third Party Congresses (1961 and 1966) when discussing the contemporary development of the armed services and military science.

29. N. Ogarkov, "Guarding Peaceful Labor," *Kommunist*, no. 10 (July 1981), p. 85.

ets of effective operational control at this crucial juncture. Meanwhile, the terrain-hugging GLCM, which for years to come would be virtually unstoppable, threatened their logistic infrastructure to a depth of twelve hundred miles or more.

The planned deployment of Euromissiles would more than double the number of quick-reaction intermediate-range nuclear systems that were under direct U.S. control in Europe, from just under five hundred to well over one thousand. In the longer term it opened the possibility of a premeditated disarming strike on the Soviet Union, with Pershing II being used for a decapitating attack on the national command authority, preparing the way for a successful counterforce strike by MX and D-5 intercontinental missiles.[30]

U.S. Application of Emerging Technologies

Once clear of Vietnam, the U.S. military establishment had been able to refocus its vast energy and technological ingenuity on the problem of war in Europe. Its short-term preoccupation was to reequip the U.S. armed forces and match the buildup in Soviet conventional capability that had taken place in the 1970s. The longer-term approach was to develop new operational concepts that would exploit emerging technologies in surveillance and target-acquisition techniques and in precision-guided munitions. The immediate objective was to be able to strike at Soviet second-echelon forces, as well as those already committed to battle. If successful, such strikes could disrupt a Soviet offensive into Western Europe.

These innovative Western initiatives called for major Soviet investment in new forms of countermeasures and the development of comparable capabilities. But the challenge did not stop there. These emerging technologies also meant that conventional weapons were approaching the effectiveness of nuclear weapons in reach and lethality, and this would have serious implications for activities in the Soviet deep rear in the initial stage of a war. And in the future lay the prospect of "even

---

30. MccGwire, *Military Objectives,* pp. 258–61. Soviet sensitivity to the deployment of Euromissiles was first evidenced in October 1979, when Brezhnev offered to reduce the overall number of intermediate-range missiles emplaced in the western USSR. By then the Soviets had recognized that the SS-20 and Euromissile deployments were inextricably linked and they demonstrated their concern over this threat throughout the initial negotiations in 1981–83 on intermediate-range nuclear forces and in their acceptance of the final INF treaty in 1987. Ibid., pp. 508–14, 549–57.

more destructive and previously unknown types of weapon based on new physical principles."[31]

The outlook was depressing. As the Soviets completed the process of restructuring their forces in Europe in accord with their 1970s strategy, they were faced by a completely new kind of Western capability. And as long as Soviet contingency plans called for defeating NATO and evicting U.S. forces from Europe there was no way of breaking this action-reaction cycle. It was virtually inevitable that in one way or another NATO would counter Soviet attempts to acquire the margin of military superiority needed for a successful offensive into Western Europe.

Besides the seeming inevitability of an unending arms race in Europe, emerging technology meant that the Soviet rear could no longer be seen as a partial sanctuary. This, combined with the capacity of future weapons systems to pinpoint and destroy moving targets, meant that conventional war, like nuclear war before it, was rapidly becoming "too difficult" to wage in any meaningful way.[32]

The 1983–84 Review

The Soviets in 1983–84 faced up to the fact that in covering the worst case of world war, they had made more likely a contingency that had become increasingly remote and in the process had incurred massive economic, political, and even military costs. By justifying the deployment of Pershing II, they had jeopardized the success of their European offensive, which was a prerequisite for evicting U.S. forces from the Continent and not losing such a war.

The obvious way to escape this vicious circle was to forgo the requirement to be able to fight such a war, but in 1983–84 that was not a practical option. Instead, the Soviets focused on the primary cause of Western concern, the Soviet offensive posture facing NATO. They reasoned that if they adopted a defensive posture and reduced their capability for surprise attack, this would relax tension, release the pressure for increasing Western military strength, and increase the influence of "peace-loving forces" in the West.

31. Interview with Marshal N. V. Ogarkov, "The Defense of Socialism: The Experience of History and Today," *KZ*, May 9, 1984, p. 2.

32. In his impromptu comments following a formal presentation at the Royal United Services Institution in London on October 19, 1988, General Makhmut A. Gareev noted that "neither nuclear war nor conventional war can . . . serve any sensible political objective."

Whereas the existing strategy meant they were poised to launch a blitzkrieg offensive and preemptive conventional strikes at the very onset of a conflict in Europe, in future they planned to remain on the defensive for twenty to thirty days to allow time to negotiate termination of the conflict.[33] If the attempt at negotiation was unsuccessful, Soviet forces would move over to the offensive and execute the 1970s strategy.

A defensive posture would make it harder to defeat NATO in Europe and evict U.S. forces from the Continent. But this reversal of long-established strategic concepts is likely to have been made easier by the fact that in 1979–82 the General Staff had been forced to focus on the requirement to hold in the west, in the event of conflict in the area north of the Persian Gulf. The new strategy did, however, require that doctrine be amended at the military-technical level. The objective of averting world war had always had precedence at the military-political level of doctrine, but it would now be given precedence at the level of applied strategy as well.[34] Averting world war now took precedence over not losing it, thereby legitimizing a defensive posture.

The adoption of a defensive doctrine, along with specific proposals for mutual cuts in forces and for reducing the threat of surprise attack, was announced in a Warsaw Pact statement, the Budapest Appeal of June 1986.[35] It is, however, important to note the very limited scope of the initiatives that were adopted in the first half of 1984. The contingency of world war continued to be the focus of Soviet security concerns and would continue to drive military requirements. The latter would actually increase as a result of forgoing the advantage of strategic surprise. The defensive doctrine would only apply for twenty to thirty days, after which the Soviets would revert to their established concepts of operation with some modified version of the 1970s offensive strategy. And the

33. In his talks with U.S. Defense Secretary Frank Carlucci and during his visit to Washington in July 1988, Akhromeev made it known that the defensive stage of a war in Europe would last about twenty to thirty days, after which the Soviets would move to a counteroffensive. Ambassador Paul Nitze, "East-West Relations," WORLDNET (U.S. Information Agency television), December 12, 1988.

34. *VES*, 1986 ed., p. 712. A twelve-word statement to this effect, tacked on the end of an eighteen-hundred word entry for "military strategy," is the only substantive amendment to the entry in the 1983 edition of *VES*. In the entry for "military doctrine" in the 1986 edition (p. 240) "averting world war" is added to "securing the defense of the socialist Fatherland" as the primary direction-focus of military doctrine. The 1983 edition was released for printing in January 1983 and the 1986 edition was sent for typesetting on August 6, 1985.

35. *Pravda*, June 12, 1986, p. 1. The statement followed the annual meeting in Budapest of the Political Consultative Committee, comprising the foreign and defense ministers of the member states.

proposals to cut both sides' forces in Europe by equal numbers had no real substance, given the Soviets' offensive overhang and NATO's long-established position at the MBFR negotiations.

Planning for the Worst Case

Western observers have difficulty accepting the idea that concern about world war is the explanation for Soviet military behavior since World War II. It is hard to recapture the rancorous tone of international discourse in the immediate postwar years, or the outspoken hostility in Western leadership circles to the Soviet Union, driven mostly by fear of communist encroachment. How ever much Western behavior may have been justified by Soviet behavior, that has no bearing on Soviet perceptions of threat. In the 1948–53 period, East and West mirrored and fulfilled each other's threat perceptions. There was ample evidence to fuel the apprehensions of both sides. The pattern of military confrontation was thus established.

In effect, both sides prepared for the possibility of world war and they had the common objective of not losing such a war. But in order not to lose, the Soviets had to defeat NATO in Europe and evict U.S. forces from the Continent, which required an offensive posture and a measure of military superiority. All NATO had to do was retain a bridgehead in Europe and its requirements were therefore inherently defensive. The United States could even afford to lose in Europe and still would not have lost the war. Soviet requirements were inherently offensive, while NATO's requirements were primarily defensive.

The belief that NATO was founded on held that war could only come as the result of an aggressive action by the Soviets that the allies had failed to deter. The Soviet urge to aggression was codified in the Western doctrine of deterrence, and the Soviet capability for aggression not only remained in place but increased significantly in the 1970s. Although it became steadily more difficult to conceive how Soviet interests could be served by invading Western Europe, the West became adept at redefining the temptation that NATO was designed to deter.

Underlying the Western doctrine of deterrence is the implicit assumption that deterrence will not fail and therefore the likelihood of world war is negligible. The force structure, posture, and infrastructure of NATO all demonstrate that it does not take the possibility of world war (as distinct from the need to deter aggression) fully seriously and the West has found it hard to accept that the Soviets should see things differently. But Yuri Andropov was speaking his mind when he accused the Reagan administration of having a flippant attitude toward the issue of war and peace,[36] and a senior Soviet adviser summed the situation up when he commented that "the danger of war [in U.S. policy] lies in the fact that politics are carried on as if there were no danger of war."[37]

This concern about world war is vital to understanding Soviet defense and foreign policy and how it has changed. From the inception of the Soviet state in 1917 until the mid-1950s, the Soviets lived either with war or with the expectation that it would come to their territory. Defense of the homeland depended on the ability to repel, or at least to absorb an attack and then to go on to win the subsequent war, a capability that might also deter an aggressor in the first place. And although the threat of premeditated aggression was perceived to wane after the first half of the 1950s, accidental war remained an inherent possibility in the structure of international relations and in the historical evolution from capitalism to socialism.

Deterrence is only relevant to situations where an opponent is tempted to take the action being deterred. By definition, therefore, accidental war could not be deterred. Given the prevailing circumstances and the experiences of individual Soviet leaders since the early 1930s, a mixture of political prudence, Marxist ideology, and military habit was sufficient to ensure that the possibility of world war remained at the center of Soviet security concerns.

36. "Answers of Yuri V. Andropov to the Questions of a *Pravda* Correspondent," *Pravda,* March 27, 1983, p. 1.
37. Comment by Georgiy Arbatov, cited in Charles Kiselyak, "Round the Prickly Pear: SALT and Survival," *Orbis,* vol. 22 (Winter 1979), p. 833.

CHAPTER 3

Strategic Weapons and Arms Control

FAR-REACHING changes in the nature of Soviet requirements for general-purpose forces would take place in 1987–88, but the crucial change for strategic nuclear forces had already been decided by the end of the 1960s. In response to the new doctrine on the likely nature of a world war and to the consequential change in wartime objectives, the requirement for nuclear superiority was dropped and replaced by the objective of parity at as low a level as possible.

It so happened that this new objective, adopted in the late 1960s for reasons of strategic advantage, was fully compatible with Soviet thinking about international relations and the danger of world war that emerged in 1985. Mikhail Gorbachev added an important new political rationale and introduced a new approach to arms control negotiations, but in terms of force size and structure, the policy objective remained the same.

Except in bare numbers of missiles, it would have been hard to achieve parity, let alone reduce the size of the existing arsenals, in 1968–69. The United States was eager to halt the buildup of Soviet ballistic missiles and reduce the Soviet inventory of heavy intercontinental ballistic missiles (ICBMs). But it also wanted to preserve the overall strategic superiority that the United States had enjoyed since World War II. It would seek to achieve this through technological developments and by avoiding limitations in those areas where it held a unilateral advantage.

The arms race would therefore continue and, except for throw-weight, advantage in the race would lie with the United States. For example, by introducing multiple independently targeted reentry vehicles (MIRVs), the United States increased the number of its warheads from about 1,900 to 6,850 between 1970 and 1975, the period of most intense negotiations on arms limitations; Soviet warheads increased from about 1,700 to 2,700.[1] Similarly, development of the conceptually new strategic-range cruise missile was authorized at this period. The United States would not relinquish superiority without a struggle.

The Soviets had to halt and reverse this arms race and do so without conceding effective superiority to their opponent. The only way they could do this was by orchestrating their own strategic weapons programs, while pursuing negotiations with the United States, and here the Soviets were constrained by the need for secrecy. Besides weakening their negotiating position, a sudden display of enthusiasm for arms control would alert the West to the shift in Soviet strategic concepts. This would expose their vulnerability as they restructured their general-purpose forces to implement the 1970s strategy, and they would forfeit operational surprise in the event of world war.

Soviet secrecy is one reason why the West did not recognize the fundamental shift in strategic weapons policy for what it was. Information about the deployment of Soviet missiles and about the strategic arms limitations talks (SALT) came from U.S. statements and leaks, which, quite properly, were aimed at enhancing the U.S. image and increasing the United States' negotiating leverage. But the more important reason is that the deployment of Soviet ICBMs was described but never analyzed, and it was easy to present the process as a relentless buildup; as Defense Secretary Harold Brown put it, "We build, they build; we stop, they build."

This aphorism overlooked the fact that the Soviets were always coming from behind. In 1959, when the Soviets still lacked an effective means of delivering nuclear weapons on North America, the U.S. Strategic Air Command had 1,750 bombers and was beginning to deploy ICBMs.[2] Ten years later, when the Soviets adopted the 1970s strategy, their ICBM force still lagged behind the U.S. force in numbers, accuracy, reliability, and response time. Their missiles were larger, but that was

1. John M. Collins, *U.S.-Soviet Military Balance: Concepts and Capabilities 1960–1980* (McGraw-Hill, 1980), pp. 444, 448.
2. The Soviets had no ICBMs in 1959. About 110 turboprop Bear and 85 jet Bison bombers were delivered in 1957–60. The SS-N-4 surface-launched 350-mile-range ballistic missile and nuclear-armed torpedoes were deployed aboard diesel submarines, and nuclear-powered submarines were about to enter service. Robert P. Berman, *Soviet Air Power in Transition* (Brookings, 1978), p. 25.

because the United States had chosen miniaturization and small payloads as the most advantageous policy.

Another point that is overlooked is that the urgency of the situation, the Soviets' technological backwardness, and the organization of their weapons procurement led them to deploy and then replace successive generations of missiles until their systems approached the capability of U.S. systems. This wasteful process created a false impression of developmental dynamism.

Strategic Weapons Policy

In 1945, the immediate requirement facing the Soviets had been to break the U.S. strategic monopoly by developing their own means of delivering atomic weapons against North America. By the early 1950s four submarine, two bomber, and two ballistic-missile programs were under way. The United States had by then embarked on establishing a network of forward bases within bomber range of the Soviet Union, which generated an additional requirement for strategic strikes that would be met by medium-range bombers and missiles. However, in 1957–58 the Soviets decided that the land-based ballistic missile was the most expedient means of strategic delivery, and the other programs were either canceled or the launch platforms reassigned to other tasks.[3]

By 1988 the Soviets had deployed five generations of strategic missiles and a sixth was under development. They had embarked on development of at least fifteen intercontinental-range systems, of which eleven had been deployed and ten had entered service. They had also deployed five regional- or intermediate-range systems, of which three had entered service.

As a result of shifts in Soviet strategy, changes in U.S. capabilities, technological problems, or the constraints of arms control, few of these programs ran to plan. Soviet procurement of weapons is a centrally planned process that ideally would move in a regular, unbroken pattern, with successive generations of weapons following each other into service. Production problems and changes in requirements leading to the cancelation or amendment of plans create faults or folds in the

3. Michael MccGwire, *Military Objectives in Soviet Foreign Policy* (Brookings, 1987), pp. 94–96.

process like those that appear in rock formations. Like the geologist who extracts a series of cores to infer the history of a rock formation, the military analyst with an understanding of the larger picture can infer what the structure of the Soviet weapons programs was before external forces brought about change. The Soviet practice of continuous procurement, the five-year planning process, the emphasis on series production, the way the Soviets allocate production facilities, and the fact that they are usually working within clearly defined constraints, all make it possible to reconstruct the history of Soviet missile programs. This is done in appendix B, and that evidence is central to the analysis in this chapter.

The 1960s Strategy

The strategic rocket forces (SRF) were established in 1959 as a fifth branch of service[4] and contributed directly to both of the primary wartime missions under the 1960s strategy. By devastating North America and Western states on the Eurasian periphery, they were to provide the means of destroying the capitalist system. And by preemptively attacking Western facilities for launching nuclear strikes on the Soviet Union, they were to help preserve the socialist system.

The 1960s strategy was a war-fighting strategy based on the use of nuclear weapons and it required nuclear superiority. That was a corollary of strategic preemption, since it would be necessary to destroy all the enemy's strategic delivery systems and have other weapons with which to attack administrative, economic, and conventional military targets. Furthermore, in a fight to the finish between two social systems, the side that started with an advantage in nuclear delivery systems was likely to have some left when the other's had run out.

Superiority did not have to be strictly numerical and the characteristics of their ICBM programs in the 1960s suggest that in the 1950s the Soviets had planned to achieve their objective through area devastation, using large warheads to destroy all facilities, political, military, and economic, in a given area. But whatever the means of achieving it, the doctrinal requirement for superiority was never in doubt, and the Soviets regularly

4. The Soviets classify ballistic missiles with a range of 2,000 kilometers or more as strategic. Although the range of the SS-4 was only 1,750 kilometers, it was classified as a strategic system in 1959.

insisted that they needed nothing less than qualitative superiority over their true enemies.

Regional Systems

The regional-range missiles of the SRF covered a preplanned set of targets on the continental periphery of the Soviet Union, priority being given to those that would be the source of strikes on the USSR or contribute to such strikes—bomber staging airfields were particularly important.[5] When the requirement was formulated in the second half of the 1950s, it was probably planned to deploy about 1,200 missiles in 1959–65, half of them being the first-generation 1,000-mile SS-4 and the other half being the second-generation 2,200-mile SS-5. It was apparently planned to begin replacing these two systems in 1966 with the third-generation SS-14 and SS-15 mobile missiles. But the SS-5 program was cut short at about 100 missiles, probably to release production facilities to meet the unexpected increase in the requirement for ICBMs.[6] And the SS-14 and SS-15 never entered service, seemingly because of problems with their solid-fuel propulsion;[7] the SS-4 and SS-5 therefore had to soldier on.

Intercontinental Systems

The main requirement of the SRF was for an ICBM force that could destroy military, economic, and political targets in North America. A strategic reserve that could survive the initial U.S. strikes on the USSR was needed also.

North America's industrial capacity and administrative facilities were mainly clustered in large conurbations. Many of the more important military installations were located in these more densely populated areas, and most of the remainder were located nearby. Given the shortage of fissile material for warheads and the constraints on mass-producing

5. Robert P. Berman and John C. Baker, *Soviet Strategic Forces: Requirements and Responses* (Brookings, 1982), p. 135, estimated the number of targets in the early 1960s was 1,145–1,410; in the latter 1950s there would have been additional Strategic Air Command (SAC) bases on the list.

6. About 730 of these regional-range missiles were deployed in 1959–66, of which more than 600 were SS-4s.

7. There is also likely to have been a shortage of production capacity because of the demands imposed by the unforeseen SS-11 program. See app. B.

intercontinental-range missiles, the most cost-effective way of destroying these different kinds of soft targets was to use large warheads that would devastate large areas.

The evidence suggests that it was originally planned to deploy a force of 960 ICBMs in 1961–70 (480 second-generation 5-megaton SS-7s and SS-8s, followed by 480 third-generation 20-megaton SS-9s and SS-10s) that would have the nominal capacity to devastate most of the populated areas of the United States.[8] A fourth generation of ICBMs with 50–100-megaton warheads were planned for deployment beginning in 1970, probably replacing the relatively primitive second-generation systems.[9] In addition to these first-strike weapons, it was planned to deploy a strategic reserve of 480 mobile 600-kiloton ICBMs in 1966–75, comprising 240 third-generation SS-13s, followed by 240 fourth-generation SS-16s.[10]

This plan was thrown off track in the first half of 1961 by the U.S. decision to deploy a large but unspecified number of Minuteman ICBMs at a rate of 240–300 a year.[11] These would be emplaced in silos in the American Midwest, creating a qualitatively new set of targets that would escape the planned area devastation.[12] The initial (and typical) Soviet response to this new requirement was to match the Minuteman deployment with a hastily contrived program to deploy 240 1-megaton SS-11s a year, starting in 1966.[13] The poor accuracy of the system was less important than the fact that the whole Minuteman force would be put directly at risk.

The later and more measured response was to target the Minuteman

8. See MccGwire, *Military Objectives*, pp. 480–83, particularly note 7. The SS-7 and SS-9 used storable liquid propellant and were designed by Yangel. The SS-8 and SS-10 used nonstorable liquid propellant and were designed by Korolev, who had also designed the first-generation SS-6, which was never operational.

9. Ibid., particularly note 6. The Proton space booster, which was first tested in 1965, was probably originally intended as the military system to carry these very large warheads.

10. Problems with solid-fuel propulsion badly delayed the SS-13 program and the 60 missiles that were deployed had to be emplaced in fixed silos.

11. In 1961 Minuteman production had been programmed at 360 missiles a year and there was talk of doubling it. The U.S. Joint Chiefs of Staff favored a force of 1,600 Minuteman missiles (SAC was lobbying for 10,000) and during 1961–63 the "approved" size of the force fluctuated between 800 and 1,300, before settling down at 1,000.

12. In 1961 SAC had over 1,500 bombers and 63 ICBMs; the Soviets' planned area devastation would have covered its airfields and missile sites. By the end of 1964 the U.S. ICBM force was up to 931, of which 698 were Minutemen in silos. This was sufficient reason for the Soviets in 1962 to adopt the expedient of targeting the United States with SS-4 and SS-5 medium- and intermediate-range missiles emplaced in Cuba.

13. The SS-11 ICBM was an adaption of a variable-range ballistic missile being developed in Chelomey's design bureau for use against U.S. carrier battle groups preparing to launch nuclear strikes against Russia. Berman and Baker, *Soviet Strategic Forces*, p. 55.

control centers (there was one for every ten launchers) with the 20-megaton SS-9, whose deployment was probably advanced by one year. The SS-10, fueled by nonstorable liquid, was canceled, but the planned production run of the SS-9 was extended to ten years (as was the production run of the SS-11) to allow time to develop fourth-generation systems designed to meet the altered requirements. At a combined deployment rate of 288 a year (48 SS-9s and 240 SS-11s), this would yield a force of almost 3,000 third-generation first-strike ICBMs by the end of 1975, beside which there would be the solid-fuel ICBMs in the strategic reserve.

However, by 1967 it was certain that the U.S. Minuteman force would not exceed 1,000 missiles. The Soviets responded by reassigning four-fifths of the SS-11 production facilities to building a so-called variable-range version of that missile for use against regional targets in adjacent land and sea areas; this left 48 SS-11s a year for the intercontinental role.[14] The reallocation of production facilities would have resulted in an SS-11 deployment of 960 ICBMs and 1,200 variable-range ballistic missiles (VRBMs) by the end of the ten years' production run in 1975. The force of 1,200 VRBMs, which would approximate the number of regional-range systems that had originally been planned, was probably intended to replace the SS-4 and SS-5 force, following the failure of the SS-14 and SS-15.

The 1970s Strategy

The 1960s strategy had been a nuclear-war-fighting strategy. The 1970s strategy was a nuclear-war-avoidance one. The new objective was to avert or at least limit the use of nuclear weapons in the event of war, and the role of the SRF's intercontinental systems was to deter the United States from striking at the Soviet Union in the course of a war, particularly if faced by the defeat of NATO in Europe.

The 1970s strategy did not require nuclear superiority. The shift from a strategy of intercontinental preemption to one of launching on warning of a U.S. attack meant that a large proportion of the original target set would cease to have military significance, since the birds would already

14. See table B-1. The partial hiatus in deployments in 1968–69 indicates the decision had been made by 1967.

have flown. After the Twenty-fifth Party Congress in February and March 1976, reference to the doctrinal requirement to maintain "qualitative superiority over the armies of our true enemies" all but disappeared from Soviet public pronouncements.[15] In his speech at Tula in January 1977, Leonid Brezhnev formally denied it was Soviet policy to seek such superiority "with the aim of delivering a first strike," the statement being limited by implication to intercontinental nuclear systems.

The new objective of Soviet strategic weapons policy was parity with the United States at as low a level as possible. Wartime deterrence would either work at a fairly low level or not at all. If it failed, a smaller U.S. arsenal would mean less devastation of the USSR. Parity would ensure an even footing in such circumstances. But parity was also needed to negotiate reductions in the two sides' nuclear arsenals. Experience had shown that the United States would not accept constraints on its military capability in areas where it held a perceived advantage.

The Soviets recognized that the process of checking the U.S. buildup would be incremental, with the arms race continuing in uncontrolled areas. In 1968–69 they therefore adopted a two-track policy of negotiating arms limitations and reductions where possible, while continuing to modernize their forces and developing strategic nuclear-delivery vehicles (SNDVs) to match the new types of weapons being developed by the United States. Arms control would, however, have priority and the process itself became important as the only means of reducing the U.S. arsenal. It was also seen as an important contribution to détente.

Intercontinental Ballistic Missiles

The base line for initial parity was provided by the size of the U.S. force in 1968–69: 1,000 modern ICBMs. The Soviets had adopted this ceiling by the end of 1969 and the ceiling was still 1,000 ICBMs in their 1983 proposals at the strategic arms reduction talks (START). This fundamental Soviet decision was obscured during SALT I (1969–72) by the 360 SS-11 VRBMs that had to be counted as ICBMs, and by the presence of 209 second-generation systems. The Soviets did, however,

---

15. William V. Gardner, *Soviet Threat Perceptions of NATO's Eurostrategic Missiles* (Paris: Atlantic Institute for International Affairs, 1983), p. 72. Raymond L. Garthoff considers that there were no authoritative Soviet statements advocating superiority as a goal after the Twenty-fourth Party Congress in 1971 (*Détente and Confrontation: American-Soviet Relations from Nixon to Reagan* [Brookings, 1985], p. 54).

Table 3-1. *Effect of SALT I Limits on Plans for Missile Deployment*

Type of missile	Intercontinental ballistic missiles		Variable-range ballistic missiles	
	Planned	Actual	Planned	Actual
SS-9	480	288	. . .	. . .
SS-11	960	670	1,200	360
SS-13	240	60	. . .	. . .
Total	1,680	1,018	1,200	360

Source: Appendix B.

signal that they were halting the buildup of their ICBM force by abandoning the construction of 78 silos in the spring of 1970. This was observed by the United States but not publicized.[16]

The result of SALT I was a significantly smaller force of third-generation systems than had been originally planned, of which 1,018 would be targeted on North America (table 3-1). Particularly significant was the abandonment of construction of 18 of 24 new silos for the SS-9 heavy missile that so concerned the United States. The 6 silos that were completed topped out the SS-9 force at 288, or six years' deployment.[17] The abandoned 18 silos were hard evidence of at least a seventh year's deployment, supporting the circumstantial evidence of a ten-year program.

The United States continued to press for an arbitrary ceiling of 250 heavy missiles, despite the Soviets' already having curtailed their deployment by 40 percent. In 1971, the Soviets responded to this obduracy by starting construction of 4 additional silos at 5 of the 48 SS-9 sites. The implied threat was to complete the 480 SS-9 silos, as originally planned. The message got through, but the final number of heavy missiles was now 308, rather than the 288 the Soviets had tacitly accepted.

Numerical parity would turn out to be a moving target as the United States changed the units of account. SALT I was only concerned with the number of missiles, bombers being excluded; SALT II (1973–79) would impose limits on the number of missiles with MIRVs and would include bombers but exclude land- and sea-based cruise missiles; and START (1982–83) would seek to concentrate on the number of warheads and throw-weight. But in 1969 the immediate problem was to achieve

16. See app. B.
17. This force could adequately target the 100 Minuteman launch control centers. Berman and Baker, *Soviet Strategic Forces*, p. 138.

qualitative parity, while shaping an ICBM force that would meet the requirements of the 1970s strategy.

Soviet targeting requirements were much the same as for the 1960s strategy, but there was a new emphasis on survivability. The 1960s strategy had been predicated on launching first, whereas the 1970s strategy forbade preemption. The best that could be hoped for was to launch on warning of an attack, and the Soviets had to be prepared to ride out a nuclear strike. In 1968–69, the development of fourth-generation systems was already far advanced, so they and the third-generation missiles would have to rely on hardening the launch silos. The fifth generation of missiles could be designed to use mobility to improve their chances of survival.

The fourth generation of ICBMs, whose general specifications for the 1960s strategy would have been formulated in about 1963–64, had been designed to replace the three relatively crude types of missile that made up the family of adapted third-generation systems. It was planned that the heavy SS-9 would be succeeded by the even heavier SS-18. The 600-kiloton SS-16 would continue the endeavor, unsuccessful in the SS-13, to provide a mobile, land-based missile that would serve as a strategic reserve. And the SS-17 and SS-19, similar missiles developed by competing design bureaus, would meet the new requirement for an accurate missile with a medium payload for use against dispersed and hardened targets such as missile silos, a task that was beyond the SS-11.

The 1970s strategy did not invalidate this force mix. Only part of the ICBM force was likely to survive a U.S. first strike, and the credibility of the land-based deterrent was enhanced by the increased capacity of each heavy missile to inflict punishment. Meanwhile the impending availability of MIRVs introduced a new flexibility to targeting. It was, however, decided not to deploy the SS-16, for reasons discussed in appendix B. Instead, the SS-16 propulsion system would be adapted to produce the SS-20 intermediate-range ballistic missile (IRBM), which would not be limited by SALT.

The fourth generation of ICBMs was programmed for deployment at 144 a year between 1975 and 1984. The conversion of existing silos to launch these missiles got under way in the first half of the 1970s and about 920 silos were under construction or completed when SALT II was signed in June 1979. A central feature of the SALT II agreement was a ceiling of 820 MIRVed ICBMs. All three of the new Soviet systems had been tested in the MIRVed mode and therefore came within this

Table 3-2. *Effect of SALT II Limits on Plans*
for Missile Deployment

Type of missile	Intercontinental ballistic missiles		Variable-range ballistic missiles	
	Planned	Actual	Planned	Actual
SS-11	0	340	0	180
SS-13	0	60	...	...
SS-18	308	308	...	...
SS-17	} 730	150	...	...
SS-19		180	360	180
Total	1,038	1,038	360	360

Source: Appendix B.

ceiling. To abide by the treaty, the Soviets had to abort the conversion of about 100 silos.

Complying with SALT II meant forgoing the replacement of nearly 40 percent of the Soviet intercontinental force and half of the 360 regionally targeted VRBMs (table 3-2).[18] The Soviets were, however, able to deploy 638 MIRVed ICBMs targeted on North America, balancing the U.S. force of 550 MIRVed Minuteman III missiles.

By 1970, the Soviets would have realized that the SALT process would penalize them for using VRBMs to cover targets on the Eurasian periphery. A fifth generation of ICBMs would therefore be needed if they were to meet the requirements of the 1970s strategy and the rather different objective of achieving numerical and qualitative parity with the United States. Parity would continue as the prerequisite for negotiating mutual force reductions.

Looking forward to that fifth generation, the Soviets would need to optimize about two-thirds of the 1,000 ICBMs for retaliation against a planned set of targets, mainly in the United States. This implied MIRVed systems, and it was decided to continue with light and heavy variants. The other third would serve as a war-fighting strategic reserve, implying a small, single-warhead, fully mobile system. They would also need a fifth-generation IRBM to replace the VRBMs that covered targets on the Eurasian periphery.

The Soviets already had respectable fourth-generation MIRVed systems and there was no real need to replace the heavy SS-18, since it

18. The SS-19 replaced the 180 SS-11 VRBMs in southwest Russia.

could not be made truly mobile. Nevertheless, the development of the heavy SS-26 was put in hand, with flight testing and deployment to be decided in the light of future circumstances. There were stronger reasons for replacing the light SS-17 and SS-19 with a fifth-generation SS-24, since that could be made rail-mobile, thus improving its survivability. The decision on moving to series production of the SS-24 may have been tied to the United States' decision to build the MX missile.

There was no alternative to a fifth-generation system for the strategic reserve. The Soviets demonstrated that a new reserve missile was their first priority by initially insisting that the one new missile to be permitted under the terms of SALT II should have a single warhead.[19] The SS-25 would be the lineal successor to the SS-16 missile and its unsuccessful predecessor the SS-13.

The fifth-generation systems would not be ready for deployment until the mid-1980s, but the Soviets would have had those systems in mind as they negotiated with the United States in the 1970s. Hence the importance that the Soviets attached to the joint statement of principles for negotiating arms limitations that was issued at the 1974 Vladivostok summit and their flat rejection of the 1977 Carter proposals which ignored those principles.

The intended structure of that intercontinental force can be inferred from the numbers agreed at SALT I and II, the projected and actual weapons programs, and the internal arithmetic of the Soviet proposals at START in 1983 (table 3-3). The Soviets would match the United States' 1,000 Minuteman ICBMs exactly. They would also deploy 950 submarine-launched ballistic missiles (SLBMs) of which at least 576 would be MIRVed (400 aboard Typhoons and at least 176 aboard Delta IIIs), to match the Poseidon force, while the single-warhead SLBMs (aboard Delta Is and IIs) would balance the remaining sea-based systems, both aircraft and missile.[20] The numbers of ICBMs and SLBMs were not, however, sacrosanct. If the United States signaled an intention to reduce either, the Soviets would adjust their plans accordingly—as they did at the 1983 talks when they reduced the number of SLBMs to 680.

19. Such a rule would have blocked deployment of the United States' MX missile. The Soviets built the SS-25 to conform to the parameters of the SS-13 and claimed that it did not count as new. The United States disputed this claim.

20. In 1969 there would have been doubts as to exactly when the SS-N-18 system would be ready for fitting aboard the Delta SSBN. As ultimately deployed, the original Delta force (I, II, and III) carried 280 single-warhead and 224 MIRVed SLBMs.

Table 3-3. *Soviet Force Structure Implicit in START Position in November 1983*

Delivery system	Single	MIRV	Total
Intercontinental ballistic missiles	320	680	1,000
SS-11, SS-13	0	...	...
SS-17, SS-19 (SS-24)	...	372	...
SS-18 (SS-26)	...	308	...
SS-25	320	...	...
Sea-launched ballistic missiles	280	400	680
Delta I	64	...	...
Delta II	216	...	...
Delta III	...	224	...
Delta IV/Typhoon	...	176	...
Bombers	...	120	120
Totals			
SALT II, 1979	930	1,320	2,250
START, 1983	600	1,200	1,800
Reduction	330	120	450

Source: Appendix B.

Regional Ballistic Missiles

The decision to forgo production of the SS-16 ICBM and to use its components to build the SS-20 IRBM would have been taken by 1972 and possibly earlier.[21] The operational reasons for doing so were persuasive. It was important to replace the aging SS-4s and SS-5s facing NATO with a more accurate and survivable system. And the SALT counting rules meant that the Soviet intercontinental capability would be diminished if the SS-11 VRBMs were not replaced by IRBMs.

The plan apparently was to deploy 486 of the fourth-generation SS-20s, a number that may have been determined by the original plan to deploy the SS-16s at the established rate of 48 a year for ten years. The SS-20, however, would be deployed in about seven years at an average rate of about 75 launchers a year, starting in 1977 (see appendix B).

The construction of missile bases for the SS-20 launcher began in 1975 and by 1978 emplacements were being started at a rate of nine bases (to house 81 launchers) a year. However, the SS-20 deployment had become

21. Flight-testing of the SS-20 began in 1974 (Andrew C. Goldberg, "Moscow's INF Experience," in Michael Mandelbaum, ed., *The Other Side of the Table: The Soviet Approach to Arms Control* [New York: Council on Foreign Relations Press, 1990], p. 100).

the center of intense controversy in NATO and in October 1979 Brezhnev offered to reduce the overall number of IRBMs facing Western Europe.[22] The production of SS-20s appears to have been halted at this time, although it was not publicized until March 1982, when Brezhnev announced a moratorium on SS-20 deployments in the western part of Russia.[23] This break in production meant that only 378 SS-20s were deployed in 42 bases during the 1977–83 period, 243 of them within range of Western Europe.

Production of the SS-20 was resumed following the Soviet Union's withdrawal from the negotiations on intermediate-range nuclear forces (INF) in November 1983. By April 1985 another 4 missile bases had been built with 36 SS-20s deployed, and work was proceeding on 8 more bases. This would bring the force up to its originally planned strength of 486 SS-20s deployed in 54 bases.[24]

A logical consequence of adopting the 1970s strategy was a redefinition of nuclear target sets. Under the 1960s strategy, missile range had been the critical factor, with the distinction between intercontinental and regional (or continental) target sets. The 1970s strategy made it necessary to distinguish between different levels of conflict that would be separate in time: theater nuclear war, limited to the Eurasian continent and surrounding seas, and global nuclear war, which would include massive strikes on the Soviet Union and North America. The global war set would include fixed political and economic targets on the Eurasian continent and could be preplanned. The theater war set would mainly comprise military targets whose location and even existence could not be forecast in peacetime.

Even under the 1960s strategy there had been a requirement to attack movable military targets, and in late 1972 the Soviets had claimed that the SRF had the capability to destroy "troops and naval groupings in the land and maritime" theaters of military action (TVDs).[25] Some of the SS-11 VRBMs had that role, while others covered targets in the

22. Brezhnev spoke as chairman of the Defense Council. See "Further Reportage on Brezhnev Visit to GDR," Moscow TASS, October 1979, in *FBIS*-79-196, p. F4 (see Abbreviations of Frequently Cited Sources).

23. In 1978 and 1979 work had started on emplacements for 81 launchers, but new starts fell off in 1980 and tapered to a halt in 1982. Similarly, the actual deployment of SS-20 missile launchers built up to a plateau in 1980 and 1981 and then fell away over the next three years. These patterns were typical of a sudden decision to halt production, while completing those systems that were already in the production pipeline.

24. "New Soviet Missile Sites Reported," *New York Times,* April 23, 1985, p. A4.

25. A. A. Grechko, "A Socialist, Multinational Army," *KZ,* December 12, 1972.

regional set that had been left uncovered by the truncated SS-5 program. This became clear when the SS-19 VRBMs replaced the SS-11s in the western USSR, whereas the SS-20 IRBMs replaced the SS-4s and SS-5s in the western USSR and part of the SS-11 force in the Far East.[26]

But the 1970s targets for theater war generated a new requirement for a missile with a very flexible targeting capability. It would have to be able to survive attempts to destroy it during the conventional phase of a war and would therefore need to be relatively invulnerable. The fifth-generation missile that seems to have been intended to meet this requirement did not begin testing until 1985, suggesting that the need to redefine target sets may not have come into focus until 1976–77.[27]

The redefinition of target sets curtailed but did not invalidate the SS-20's role. Besides the preplanned political, military, and economic global-war targets in the European theater, there was a comparable set of targets in China and some in Japan. It is possible that in the European theater this core group of targets numbered about 135—that was the number of SS-4s and SS-5s that were emplaced in silos in the 1963–66 period, and near the minimum number of SS-20s the Soviets seemed willing to accept at the INF negotiations in October and November 1983.

Negotiating Arms Reductions

The many changes between the planned and actual deployments of missiles illustrate how disruptive negotiations and agreements on arms control were for Soviet strategic weapons programs. Meanwhile, the effect on U.S. plans was minimal; the SALT limits did not really bite until 1985, when the U.S. navy had to dismantle a twenty-year-old 16-tube Poseidon submarine to bring a 24-tube Trident on line.

Though public perception was the very reverse, the SALT negotiations must be seen as one of the great successes of U.S. public diplomacy since World War II. The widespread impression was of the United States as the initiator, continually pressing for negotiations and agreement, while the Soviet Union had to be dragged to the negotiating table. The Soviets did tend to respond to U.S. proposals rather than initiating their own. And they continued to play their cards close to their chest, never

26. MccGwire, *Military Objectives,* pp. 249–57, 502–15.
27. Testing of a new generation of medium-range missile was first reported in April 1985. Michael J. Bonafield, *Washington Times,* April 10, 1985, p. 1.

changing the propagandistic and inflexible style of negotiation. But that was only half the story.

Over the years, Soviet arms control proposals, negotiations, and agreements have served many purposes—political, economic, and military. However, at the heart of serious negotiations have lain two somewhat contradictory objectives: to reduce the danger of war and, should war prove unavoidable, to improve the USSR's military prospects. Between 1922 and 1967, serious negotiations to limit arms had not been in the Soviet interest. The Soviet Union was in a position of overall military inferiority and there was no reason to suppose that its likely opponents would embark on significant force reductions or accept unilateral constraints, allowing the Soviets to catch up. If there had been any doubts on this score, they would have been removed by the negotiations on banning atomic weapons in 1945–46, which the Soviets did take seriously.

Nor could it be shown that arms control agreements served to lower tension and reduce the danger of war. Rather, those treaties that were signed before the SALT negotiations came about as the result of a previous lessening of tension, rather than the other way around. Soviet arms control proposals before 1967 were therefore largely propagandistic, designed to halt or sidetrack military developments that were unfavorable to Soviet interests, such as the rearming of Germany in the 1950s.[28] The exception were those few areas where agreement would limit the future threat, as in the Nuclear Non-Proliferation Treaty, or fence off areas from future competition, such as the treaties on Antarctica, outer space, and the sea bed.

In the late 1960s the cost-benefit calculus for strategic nuclear weapons was reversed. Negotiations on limiting intercontinental systems had become a key factor in the move toward détente, thereby reducing the danger of world war. And the new wartime strategy meant that there was now an inverse relation between Soviet prospects in such a war and the size of the U.S. strategic arsenal. Negotiations were the only way of reducing the size of the U.S. nuclear arsenal, and thereby reducing the devastation of the USSR should war escalate to intercontinental strikes.

The calculus did not, however, change for general-purpose forces. Rather, the 1970s strategy produced additional reasons for resisting limits on those forces, particularly in Europe. The new strategy required

28. The Soviet campaign to prevent the deployment of neutron weapons in the 1970s and the introduction of new Euromissiles in the 1980s are other examples.

the Soviets to provide their forces with the capability for massive blitzkrieg operations and for deep disarming strikes against NATO's in-theater nuclear capability, relying in both cases on conventional means only. The Soviets were therefore unresponsive in 1968–70 when NATO proposed discussing what came to be referred to as mutual and balanced force reductions (MBFR) in the central region of Europe.

The talks did ultimately get under way in 1973. By then the restructuring of Soviet forces was well in hand and the political dividends of agreeing to negotiate were more clearly defined, but the Soviets did not negotiate seriously until January 1976. And then, having spent five years refusing to discuss MBFR and the next three stonewalling in the negotiations, the Soviets responded to a NATO proposal within a month.

In December 1975 NATO had offered to withdraw 90 nuclear delivery systems, together with 1,000 warheads, if the Soviets would withdraw a Soviet tank corps, reduce tank strength by 1,700, and agree in principle to bringing Warsaw Pact and ground force manpower into balance at reduced levels.[29]

The Soviets could not, of course, agree to the reduction of 250,000 men that was called for by Western calculations of the balance, nor could they agree to a sizable reduction in their tank force, which was essential for offensive operations. On the other hand, U.S. withdrawal of 54 F-4 Phantom aircraft and 36 Pershing I missiles would directly support the Soviet objective of eliminating NATO nuclear delivery systems during the conventional phase of a war. The Soviets therefore responded promptly by proposing to match and extend the NATO offer with cuts in their own nuclear capability.[30]

That, of course, was unacceptable to NATO. The abortive exchange illustrated the impossibility of negotiating mutual force reductions when the two sides had diametrically opposed operational requirements. The Soviets were clearly aware of this, but negotiations on MBFR was the price they had to pay for Western agreement to participate in the Conference on Security and Cooperation in Europe, which they valued

29. This limited and conditional NATO offer was intended to break the deadlock at Vienna and was seen by the West as a way of trading nuclear systems for Soviet tanks. See Lothar Ruehl, *MBFR: Lessons and Problems,* Adelphi Paper 176 (London: International Institute for Strategic Studies, 1982), pp. 9, 15.

30. The Soviets offered to trade 54 Su-7 (Fitter) aircraft and 54 SS-1cs (Scud B) missiles, and an unspecified number of surface-to-air (SAM-2) missiles to be matched by U.S. Nike-Hercules SAM systems. In all three cases, the Soviet systems were significantly less capable than the U.S. ones. Ibid., p. 19.

as legitimizing the postwar political settlement of Europe. Fruitful negotiations were, however, out of the question as long as Soviet military requirements were driven by the objective of not losing a world war.

Intercontinental-Range Systems

A five-week preliminary session of SALT in November and December 1969 appears to have convinced the Soviets that the United States was serious about negotiating limits on strategic weapons. The Soviets responded in the spring of 1970 by curtailing the deployment of third-generation ICBMs. This involved abandoning 78 launch silos that were in an early stage of construction, although they got no credit for this unilateral concession. The remaining silos were completed and the match between the 1,000 modern Minutemen and the 1,018 (later 1,038) Soviet third-generation systems targeted on North America was obscured by the final total of 1,607 missiles that counted as Soviet ICBMs. This number included 360 SS-11s targeted on the Soviet periphery and 209 of the already obsolescent second-generation systems.

Although this match was pointed out informally,[31] the Soviets gave no indication of the extent to which the SALT I standstill agreement had curtailed their deployment plans. For ICBMs and VRBMs the cut approached 50 percent (about 1,500 missiles) and for submarine-launched ballistic missiles (SLBMs) it was roughly 25 percent (over 300),[32] but the arguments for not publicizing this information would have been persuasive. In the short term, cuts of that order implied a radical shift in strategy, something the Soviets did not wish to advertise, nor did they want to divulge their targeting philosophy. In the longer term they had to balance the conflicting objectives of halting and reversing the arms race while ensuring that they were not left at a military disadvantage. Within the detailed provisions of any treaty they had to maximize their future relative capability, bearing in mind the intended characteristics of the fifth-generation systems that they would not begin

31. Raymond L. Garthoff told me that in November 1971, N. S. Kishilov claimed in a private conversation with him that "the number of Soviet ICBM silos is approximately the same as the number of U.S. ICBM silos," although Kishilov never explained (and may not have known) the rationale for this assertion.

32. The ten-year program of 35 16-tube Yankee Is followed by 35 20-tube Yankee IIs would have yielded 1,260 SLBMs, which would have roughly matched the number of Western sea-based missile and aircraft systems that could be held back from the initial exchange. MccGwire, *Military Objectives*, p. 411.

to test until the early 1980s. The need to conceal both the shift in wartime strategy and their negotiating objectives at SALT would have outweighed the uncertain benefits that might have accrued from publicizing the cuts in Soviet weapons programs.

Because the VRBMs were counted as ICBMs, the Soviets initially resisted U.S. pressure to negotiate a reduction in the limits agreed at SALT I. However, it became clear that such reductions were essential if agreement on a broader treaty was to be reached, and by the fall of 1974 considerable progress had been made in developing a formal treaty whose lineaments were very similar to those of the SALT II Treaty, which was finally signed in June 1979. The main disagreements were resolved in principle at the Vladivostok summit in November 1974, when the United States withdrew its demands for cuts in heavy missiles and the Soviet Union withdrew its demands concerning forward-based nuclear delivery systems. The summit also established principles and guidelines for the continuing negotiations.

To reach this agreement, the Soviets made concessions that were much greater than the United States realized. Complying with its terms meant limiting the number of fourth-generation missiles to less than 60 percent of the number already programmed, and that meant forgoing the replacement of nearly 40 percent of the Soviet intercontinental force and half of the regionally targeted VRBMs (table 3-2). It was no wonder that the Soviet military objected strenuously to these new concessions, or that "Brezhnev had to spill political blood to get the Vladivostok accords."[33]

Soviet rejection of the proposals advanced by President Jimmy Carter shortly after he took office in 1977 must be viewed in the light of these accords and of the fact that negotiations had slowly ground to a halt as U.S. attention turned to the presidential election. Virtually ignoring the Vladivostok guidelines, the Carter administration proposed a 25 percent cut in the aggregate ceilings that had already been agreed, a unilateral 50 percent cut in Soviet heavy missiles, and a cap of 550 on MIRVed ICBMs,[34] which the Soviets had recently begun to deploy. The Carter proposals left U.S. force structure and plans unaffected while requiring the Soviets to immediately curtail the deployment of fourth-generation

33. Georgy Kornienko, Andrey Gromyko's senior deputy, quoted by Paul Warnke, director of the U.S. Arms Control and Disarmament Agency. See Garthoff, *Détente and Confrontation*, p. 465.
34. This was the exact number of Minuteman III, the U.S. MIRVed ICBM.

missiles and to make major cuts in their forces already in the field. No compensating concessions were offered and, to add insult to injury, the proposal was leaked in Washington before it was presented to the Soviets.

Soviet rejection of the Carter proposals does not, therefore, undermine the conclusion that under the 1970s strategy the Soviet objective was to negotiate parity at as low a level as possible. It does illustrate the U.S. approach to arms control.

Americans have always been deeply ambivalent about arms control. From the earliest arguments concerning the use of the atomic bomb in 1945, the American body politic has been afflicted by deep divisions and contrary impulses about the desirability of arms control rather than military superiority.[35] Parity does not sit well with the American people. From the time of the Baruch Plan, arms control negotiations have been used, in practice if not in theory, as a way of capping and, if possible, reducing Soviet inventories in areas where the Soviets were catching up or moving ahead. Although Richard Nixon, in effect, accepted the idea of parity in 1969, he had campaigned for the presidency on the promise to restore clear-cut military superiority. Throughout the 1970s there was tenacious resistance to the idea of sufficiency, parity, or equivalence, and in the first half of the 1980s the Reagan administration explicitly sought to regain some measure of superiority.

Even with administrations that were mainly predisposed to seek agreement with the Soviets on arms control, divisions in the body politic constrained the possibilities for wide-ranging negotiations. Nixon and Kissinger saw SALT "as simply one key piece on the political chess board," and were not primarily concerned to limit the arms race.[36] In general, Americans were not persuaded that arms racing led to war. For many, qualitative arms racing was a way of preserving U.S. superiority by exploiting the United States' technological advantage; for others, only certain kinds of arms racing were destabilizing and hence undesirable.[37] By the early 1980s, with a U.S. administration that actively distrusted arms control, the clear purpose of negotiations was to placate

---

35. See the Council on Foreign Relations book by Michael Krepon, *Strategic Stalemate: Nuclear Weapons and Arms Control in American Politics* (St. Martin's Press, 1984), particularly pp. 1–2, 108–20.

36. Garthoff, *Détente and Confrontation*, p. 149.

37. This explains the fourfold increase in U.S. warheads between 1970 and 1975 and the U.S. insistence on introducing long-range cruise missiles as a completely new category of strategic nuclear delivery vehicle. The Soviets matched both of these technological innovations.

domestic and allied opinion and to discomfort the Soviets, rather than to reach agreement on reducing the level of armaments.

In one sense, then, it could be said that the United States lacked a consistent policy on arms control, and it became a truism that the most difficult negotiations took place in Washington, not in Geneva. But that is only true if arms control is seen as a way of limiting and reducing the size of the nuclear arsenals. If, however, its purpose was to preserve American superiority, U.S. policy was both consistent and remarkably successful.

The theoretical objective of U.S. arms control strategy, based on a concept of crisis stability, was to enhance that stability. But the criteria for pursuing the objective were changeable and they were applied selectively. Stability was apparently unaffected when the United States deployed MIRVed missiles, but it became an issue when the Soviet Union followed suit. The United States, while extolling the virtues of SSBNs as invulnerable second-strike systems for its own forces, not only refused to negotiate constraints on antisubmarine operations that would have reinforced that invulnerability but actively developed the means of attacking Soviet SSBNs. And the U.S. position on the destabilizing effects of mobile ICBMs changed in measure with projected U.S. programs.

In U.S. arms control theory, lower force levels were not a necessary adjunct of crisis stability, and the Soviets had to pursue their objective within the negotiating parameters established by the United States. Hence the perception that they would only respond and not initiate proposals. But besides providing the nominal theory that was meant to shape negotiations, the United States also dictated the scope of the negotiations and chose the units of account. Furthermore, it successively redefined both of these parameters as necessary to favor its evolving interests.

Thus at SALT I, when the United States had already started deploying MIRVed missiles but the Soviets lacked that capability, it was only missile launchers that were counted; at SALT II, when the Soviets were about to replace their third-generation missiles with fourth-generation MIRVed systems, the key units became delivery vehicles carrying multiple warheads; and at START in 1982–83, after the Soviets had deployed a somewhat truncated fourth-generation ICBM force, the United States insisted on throw-weight and reentry vehicles as the units of account. Similarly, SALT I excluded bombers, of which the United

States had a virtual monopoly; SALT II included bombers but effectively excluded land- and sea-launched cruise missiles from the account, while the limits on air-launched cruise missiles allowed the United States to add 3,360 of these ALCMs to its strategic inventory;[38] and none of the negotiations took account of the British and French nuclear arsenals or the U.S. forward-based systems, all of which were, or could be, targeted on the Soviet Union.[39]

Soviet acceptance of these unfavorable terms, albeit under protest, demonstrates the importance the Soviets attached to the arms control process. It did them little good, however, since their resistance to the successive changes was publicized as a reluctance to negotiate, and this was used to justify new U.S. weapons programs to be used as so-called bargaining chips. The impression persisted, despite the knowledge of officials such as Alexander Haig, secretary of state in the first Reagan administration, of Soviet eagerness to enter into arms control talks.[40]

In practical terms, domestic ambivalence about arms control strengthened the American hand, while the Soviets were handicapped by their obsessive concern for secrecy and by their intransigent style of negotiation. In fact, the two sides' tactical objectives were similar. Both were skillful in pursuing relative advantage—capping the other side's capabilities and fencing off dangerous new developments whenever possible, while seeking to protect their own programs and the possibilities for future development. But the Americans cultivated an impression of greater flexibility in negotiations and the United States succeeded in focusing public attention on ICBMs. The impression was created that the Soviet emphasis on that means of delivery was particularly threatening and somehow unfair. Unilateral concessions were therefore in order.

The Soviets did, indeed, offer further unilateral concessions. In November 1983 their revised proposals at the strategic arms reduction talks represented significant reductions in the SALT II limits and would

38. This would have involved trading in gravity bombs and short-range and stand-off weapons.

39. Forward-based forces had been included in the U.S. strike plan since at least 1961. After SALT I Henry Kissinger publicly acknowledged the fact, implying that about 330 units were targeted on the Soviet Union. Raymond L. Garthoff, *Perspectives on the Strategic Balance* (Brookings, 1983), pp. 20–21; John Prados, *The Soviet Estimate* (Dial Press, 1982), p. 121.

40. Haig later noted: "The Soviets were eager to enter into arms control talks with the United States. Dobrynin raised the subject in his first talk with me [in January 1981] and never failed to mention it in subsequent encounters. The Soviets were willing to talk on almost any basis." Alexander M. Haig, Jr., *Caveat: Realism, Reagan and Foreign Policy* (Macmillan, 1984), p. 228.

have required them to reduce their MIRVed ICBM force by a further 138 missiles (see table 3-3).[41] The proposal was also accommodating in that it offered aggregate totals similar to those proposed by President Carter in 1977. The new ceiling on MIRVed missiles provided for the 100 MX missiles that were in Carter's fiscal 1982 budget and it would have allowed construction of the 18 Trident SSBNs that were implicit in the SALT II limits.[42]

The Reagan administration was not, however, interested in negotiating. The United States' START proposals were subsequently described by Haig as a "non-negotiable package" and a "two-faced proposal." The proposals ignored the agreed-on guidelines for negotiations and required the Soviets to reduce their number of existing warheads by 60 percent and dismantle almost 70 percent of their modern MIRVed missiles. American plans would meanwhile remain unaffected.[43]

For the Soviet Union, these developments would not have been completely unexpected since the arms control process and the move toward détente had been steadily unraveling. For domestic political reasons the treaties on a Nuclear Threshold Test Ban (signed by Nixon in 1974) and Peaceful Nuclear Explosions (signed by Ford in 1976) were never submitted to the U.S. Senate for ratification. The word *détente* was banned from Republican statements during the 1976 presidential campaign. And while the SALT II negotiations made erratic progress toward the treaty that was signed in 1979, the negotiations on ancillary arms control issues initiated by the Carter administration in 1977 had virtually ground to a halt because of U.S. lack of interest. The negotiations on a comprehensive test ban were symptomatic of the larger problem. The Soviet Union had made significant concessions in late 1977, but the United States responded by continually adjusting its position, limiting the scope of the proposed agreement, and hardening its terms, until it broke off the talks in 1980.[44]

41. National Academy of Sciences, *Nuclear Arms Control: Background and Issues* (Washington, D.C.: National Academy Press, 1985), p. 67.

42. The proposed ceiling on MIRVed ICBMs was 680; 100 MXs added to the 550 Minuteman IIIs equal 650. Only 2 ICBMs would have had to be sacrificed to deploy 18 Trident SSBNs carrying 24 MIRVed missiles each.

43. Roy Gutman, *Newsday*, August 12, 1984. See also Haig, *Caveat*, p. 223; National Academy of Sciences, *Nuclear Arms Control*, pp. 74–75.

44. Garthoff, *Détente and Confrontation*, pp. 756–58. The United States declined to resume negotiations on the demilitarization of the Indian Ocean in the fall of 1978 and the talks on limiting the transfer of conventional arms collapsed in December 1978 after an apparent reversal of U.S. policy.

Given the slow progress of negotiations after the 1974 Vladivostok summit, there must have been considerable doubt within the Soviet Union as to whether SALT II would ever be signed, let alone ratified. This would explain the Soviet decision to continue converting silos to launch the fourth-generation systems even though the conversions that went beyond the limits generally agreed at Vladivostok in 1974 would have to be aborted once the treaty was signed.

Given the deteriorating international situation and the growing influence of "aggressive circles" in the United States, there would have been those in the Soviet Union who argued that ten years of arms control had imposed severe cuts in the Soviet Union's potential capability, while allowing the United States to steadily increase the size and diversity of its nuclear arsenal. Despite unilateral Soviet concessions, the negotiations had been singularly unsuccessful in halting the arms race, let alone effecting reductions.

It is a measure of the Soviets' commitment to the underlying strategic rationale that they persisted in their efforts despite these massive discouragements.

Intermediate-Range Nuclear Forces

The long-range objective of Soviet arms control policy has been to reduce the weight of attack on the Russian homeland in the event of world war. Such attacks could be delivered by U.S. intercontinental systems, U.S. forward-based systems, and the British and French nuclear arsenals. In the strategic arms limitation talks the Soviets had consistently pushed for the inclusion of U.S. intermediate-range systems that were based on the periphery of the Soviet Union, and the United States had as consistently refused to include them.

It therefore seems likely that intermediate-range systems did not come into focus as a separate negotiating category until 1976–77, when a number of developments came together, although not in such a way as to lead to clear-cut policy prescriptions. The 1970s strategy for world war probably came into full effect in 1976, at about the same time that a review of the decisions taken in 1967–68 and their practical outcomes apparently took place. In April 1976 Dmitriy Ustinov became minister of defense and in January 1977 Nikolay Ogarkov (who had served as the second-ranking member of the SALT delegation) was appointed chief of the General Staff.

By January 1976 the Soviets had realized that it might be possible to reduce NATO's theater strike capability by peacetime negotiations rather than wartime conventional strikes. By 1974 the leadership had decreed that the Soviet Union would not initiate the use of nuclear weapons in the European theater, both because of the dangers of escalation to strikes on the USSR and because the military had concluded that, on balance, the use of nuclear weapons was not in their operational interests. In other words, the Soviets would welcome a nonnuclear Europe. The December 1975 proposal by NATO at the MBFR talks to withdraw ninety so-called long-range theater nuclear delivery systems opened Soviet eyes to the potential of nuclear arms control as a way of improving their military prospects.

It was not, however, obvious how this potential could be actualized. For NATO, nuclear weapons were a way of compensating for the Warsaw Pact's conventional superiority, to be used if a Warsaw Pact offensive could not be checked by conventional means. The Soviets would need theater nuclear systems to respond in kind and also to discourage NATO's resort to nuclear weapons in the first place. So much was clear. What was not clear was whether the United States could be persuaded to negotiate mutual reductions in such systems.

It is in this light that the deployment of SS-20 IRBMs in 1977 must be viewed. The rightness of the decision to produce this fourth-generation missile (taken by 1972) would have been confirmed by the realization that the new limits on MIRVed ICBMs would preclude the replacement of about half of the SS-11 VRBM force.[45] The military rationale would still have been compelling in 1976–77, despite the redefinition of target sets that is likely to have taken place, since developing an appropriate response to that new requirement would take eight to ten years. Meanwhile, because of its vulnerability, the SS-4 and SS-5 force was more a hindrance than a help to the 1970s strategy and there were strong operational reasons for replacing it with a more responsive, accurate, and survivable system.

In 1976–77, it could have been argued that the SS-20 might encourage NATO to negotiate mutual reductions in theater systems. And these modern missiles could be seen as an American-style bargaining chip. In any case, it is unlikely that the Soviets expected this belated replacement of obsolescent systems to cause much of a stir in NATO; it was

45. The general parameters of these limits were proposed by Henry Kissinger in Moscow in October 1974 and generally agreed on (ibid., pp. 443–44).

comparable to the periodic upgrading of NATO's quick-reaction strike aircraft that went largely unremarked and was fully in accord with both the spirit and the letter of the SALT agreements.

But Soviet expectations were proven wrong. Proponents of U.S. ground-launched cruise missiles (GLCMs) and Pershing II intermediate-range missiles seized this opportunity to argue for deployment of these systems in Western Europe. Nominally, they would be a matching response to the SS-20s, but in practice they would introduce a qualitatively new capability, which the Soviets claimed would circumvent SALT II by posing a dangerous new threat to Soviet territory. Though NATO as a whole was dubious about this initiative, in December 1979 it adopted a two-track policy allowing the United States to negotiate the withdrawal of the SS-20 while preparing to deploy Euromissiles in the event that negotiations were unsuccessful.

The Soviets had been pressing for negotiations on INF since May 1978. In October 1979, speaking as chairman of the Defense Council and hoping to head off the deployment of Euromissiles, Brezhnev offered to reduce the overall number of IRBMs facing NATO. Production of the SS-20 appears to have been halted as this stage, but the United States was not interested in negotiations. Following the Soviet invasion of Afghanistan at Christmas 1979, the United States broke off most of its dealings with the Soviet Union, and the Reagan administration that took office in January 1981 was concerned to make America strong rather than to reach agreement on arms control. It was not until November 1981 that the realities of alliance politics caused the United States to initiate talks.

It did so with the so-called zero-zero option, a proposal designed to be nonnegotiable.[46] The United States offered to forgo the deployment of Euromissiles in return for the Soviet Union completely dismantling all SS-4, SS-5, and SS-20 systems. Secretary of State Haig commented subsequently that the proposal raised the suspicion that the United States "was disingenuously engaging in arms control negotiations simply as a cover . . . to build up its nuclear arsenal." He considered it "absurd to expect the Soviets to dismantle an existing force of 1,100 warheads . . .

---

46. Richard Allen, the president's national security adviser, had publicly derided a less sweeping version of the zero option for being nonnegotiable. Richard Burt, Haig's principal arms control deputy, described the purpose of the INF negotiations to be the "maximum political advantage. It is not arms control we are engaged in, it's alliance management." Strobe Talbott, "Behind Closed Doors," *Time,* December 5, 1983, p. 19.

in exchange for a promise from the United States not to deploy a missile force [it] had not yet begun to build.''[47]

This time it was Western expectations that were proven wrong. By December 1982 (following Yuri Andropov's appointment as general secretary) the Soviets had formally proposed a ceiling of 162 SS-20s,[48] and their proposals in October–November 1983 suggested that the lowest they could go lay between 120 and 140 launchers.[49] The "walk-in-the-woods" formula arrived at unofficially in July 1982 raises the possibility that the Soviets were prepared to contemplate going even lower, but it seems more likely that this was a probe designed to find out what it would cost to prevent the deployment of the Pershing II.[50] These numbers must be compared with the 600 IRBMs within range of Western Europe during most of the 1960s and 1970s and the 423 in place at the end of 1983, including 243 SS-20s.

The scale of the concessions indicates how seriously the Soviets took the threat of Euromissiles, particularly the Pershing II. But it also raises the question of why, if they were prepared to go that far, they were not prepared to go further.

The answer is likely to have reflected what the Soviets saw as their prompt targeting requirements in a world war. The new Euromissiles were only a part of NATO's nuclear delivery capability. Soviet negotiators had to look to a future where all of the fifth-generation ICBMs would be targeted on North America and there would be no VRBMs for use against targets on the Eurasian periphery. The fifth-generation IRBMs would therefore have to cover the newly designated theater-war set.

---

47. Haig, *Caveat*, p. 229. The absurdity was compounded in March 1983 when the United States proposed (as a concession) limiting the deployment of GLCMs and Pershing IIs in NATO Europe to between 50 and 450 warheads, if the Soviets would reduce the number of warheads on IRBMs in all parts of the Soviet Union to the same level.

48. This matched the combined inventory of British and French missiles.

49. Andropov proposed "about 140" on October 26, 1983; the exact number was probably 144, since SS-20s were deployed in multiples of nine. The number of SS-20 warheads (432) would equal the number of British and French warheads as calculated by the Soviets. An informal proposal in November would have had the effect of bringing this number down to 129 or (according to the Arms Control Association) even lower. A ceiling of 135 would have allowed 15 missile bases. MccGwire, *Military Objectives,* pp. 250, 508–09.

50. The package, which was negotiated informally by Ambassadors Paul Nitze (who was responsible for the initiative) and Yuli Kvitsinsky, would have imposed a common ceiling of 75 missile launchers in the European theater, where 1 GLCM launcher (carrying 4 single-warhead missiles) would equal 1 SS-20 (carrying 3 warheads); the Pershing II would have been banned. Medium-range aircraft on both sides would be limited to 150, and the British and French systems would not count. Both governments disavowed the initiative. John Cartwright and Julian Critchley, *Nuclear Weapons in Europe* (Brussels: North Atlantic Assembly, 1984), p. 27.

Meanwhile in 1982–83, when the Soviets saw the danger of world war as having reached a level unmatched since the height of the cold war, immediate military requirements would have been at the front of their minds.[51] The similarity between the ceiling of 120–140 SS-20s and the 135 SS-4s and SS-5s that were emplaced in silos in the mid-1960s may have been more than coincidental.[52]

The Soviets sought to compensate for their unfavorable negotiating position through public diplomacy, most notably by encouraging NATO electorates to bring pressure, directly or through their own governments, on the Reagan administration to forgo, or at least delay, the deployment of Euromissiles. Hoping to influence antiwar groups and advocates of arms control negotiations, the Soviets threatened that if NATO went ahead with the deployment while negotiations were still in progress, they would break off START as well as the INF talks. And this they duly did in November 1983, when the first Pershing IIs arrived in Germany.

In Western eyes, this was a mistake, but that judgment was hasty. Perhaps the Soviets should not have given the ultimatum in the first place, but future credibility required that it be followed through. And what was to be gained by continuing the unproductive and increasingly rancorous negotiations? The Soviets had failed to prevent the deployment of the Euromissiles and it was now best to revert to the original plan, complete the deployment of the SS-20s, analyze what went wrong on the political front, and let the dust settle before returning to try to negotiate the removal of the Pershing IIs in 1985.

While the Soviet withdrawal left the field to the United States, who could be said to have "won," it was the long term that mattered. True, the Soviets had lost the short-term propaganda battle as the Western media rallied in support of the alliance. But breakdown in negotiations had long-term political consequences for evolving attitudes among European electorates and their doubts about the confrontational style of alliance leadership provided by the Reagan administration.

Strategic Defense Systems

The 1970s strategy placed a premium on the credibility of the wartime deterrent and hence on the certainty that Soviet ballistic missiles, once

51. McGwire, *Military Objectives,* pp. 300–09. This assessment was confirmed by the revelations of a defector, Oleg A. Gordievskiy, in 1986 (ibid., p. 363).

52. Why did the Soviets harden only 135 of some 650 SS-4s and SS-5s deployed in the western USSR? The 1960s strategy was predicated on Soviet preemption, but the Soviets

launched, would strike home on their U.S. targets. Never inclined to underestimate the American capacity for implementing futuristic technological concepts, the Soviets gave first priority in arms control negotiations to limiting the development and deployment of U.S. antiballistic missile systems, and they achieved this objective with the signing of the ABM Treaty in 1972.

Another corollary of the 1970s strategy, the need to eschew the option of striking first, meant that the best the Soviets could hope for was to launch their ICBMs on warning of attack. The longer the warning, the more likely the hope would be fulfilled, and this put a premium on effective means of early warning. Ballistic-missile early-warning systems (BMEWSs) had always received the highest priority, but their vital importance was no longer limited to the onset of war and its initial stages. Under the 1970s strategy, early warning would be a critical factor for the whole course of the conflict.

Assuming that the Soviets succeeded in defeating NATO in Europe and evicting U.S. forces from the Continent during the first phase of a world war, a worst-case contingency in the second phase would be for the United States to mount an invasion of the Soviet Union through Xinjiang in northwest China. Such a land offensive would outflank eastern Siberia and the Central Siberian Plateau; the Soviet General Staff had to think in terms of being forced to give up these sparsely populated areas and concentrate on securing the industrially important West Siberian Plain. Terrain and other factors suggest that this fall-back defense perimeter would run roughly north-south, to the east of the line of the Yenisey River.

Military prudence would argue that all major facilities should be located to the west of that line, except for those specifically directed toward the Asian-Pacific region. And that is, indeed, the general pattern.[53] Location to the west of this defense perimeter was particularly important for the early-warning radars.

This new constraint on the location of early-warning radars emerged at about the same time as the requirement to deploy additional BMEWSs to cover a new arc of threat that was opened by the U.S. Trident SSBN

---

had to be prepared for a first blow by NATO, in which case many of the military targets in their preemptive set would lose their importance. But the destruction of a hard core of political and military targets would remain critical to the outcome of a war in Europe; key strategic targets of this type change very slowly.

53. U.S. Department of Defense, *Soviet Military Power, 1986,* 5th ed. (U.S. Government Printing Office, 1986), pp. 23, 100, 101.

program. The Polaris and Poseidon systems had lacked the range to strike at the central Soviet Union from the Pacific. Both the projected Trident missile systems would be able to do so and would even be able to reach Moscow from those waters. Highlighting this new arc of threat, the U.S. navy announced that a new base for Trident nuclear-powered ballistic-missile submarines (SSBNs) would be built on the West Coast of the United States.

To cover the threat, the Soviets set about building two new early-warning radars. The one at Pechora, looking out across the Arctic toward the north and northeastern parts of the North Pacific, would also cover the Minuteman ICBM fields. The other at Abalakova, near Krasnoyarsk, would cover the north and central parts of the North Pacific.[54] That radar lies inside the Yenisey defense perimeter and is located about 470 miles from the southern periphery of the Soviet Union, looking northeast across about 4,000 miles of Soviet territory.

The Krasnoyarsk radar is therefore in breach of the technical provisions of the ABM Treaty, which requires that early-warning radars be deployed on the periphery of national territory and oriented outward. The Soviets may not have realized this future conflict at the time they signed the treaty, but whenever it was that they appreciated the problem, the strategic rationale for the Krasnoyarsk location was compelling.[55] They could not, however, have argued their case without disclosing the fundamental shift in strategy. Given their hopes of détente and the constructive functioning of the Standing Consultative Commission at Geneva, they may have reckoned on being able to negotiate their way around the treaty provisions when the time came to actually build the radar. It is unlikely that they foresaw the deterioration in Soviet-American relations or the disruptive approach to arms control adopted by the Reagan administration.

Eventually, the location of the Krasnoyarsk radar provided an important lever for those in the United States who disparaged existing arms control agreements and who argued against continued adherence to the ABM Treaty and for the adoption of a space-based ballistic-missile defense (BMD) system.

The strategic defense initiative (SDI) announced by President Reagan

54. The Trident threat from the Indian Ocean is covered by a radar near Astrakhan that looks south. Ibid., pp. 43–45.

55. The strategic rationale provides a more plausible explanation for trying to finesse the letter of the ABM Treaty than does bureaucratic incompetence, the problems of permafrost, or an attempt to break out of a treaty that the Soviets saw as serving a vital interest.

in March 1983 adversely affected Soviet interests in several ways. In the most general sense it could be seen as an attempt to recapture the territorial invulnerability that the United States had enjoyed until the 1960s, an attempt admitted by the U.S. secretary of defense.[56] The SDI was another piece of evidence that the United States was seeking to restore the military preponderance it had enjoyed for twenty-five years after World War II, including a first-strike nuclear capability.[57] Indeed, its leaders were open in their belief that by building American military power the United States could once more operate from a position of strength and would be able to constrain Soviet foreign policy behavior.

Whether or not the United States was successful in establishing a space-based BMD system, a serious attempt to do so would move the arms race into a new arena. The Soviet Union would have to follow suit, increasing the defense burden immeasurably. Since the United States could be expected to develop the relevant technology much more rapidly than the Soviet Union, the Soviets would also need to develop offensive means of neutralizing or outflanking the U.S. capability. As the race took hold and each side's weapons programs fulfilled the other side's prophecies of aggressiveness, tension would rise and the danger of war would increase.

If SDI went ahead, the adverse effect on the Soviet objective of avoiding world war would be immediate and would become increasingly dangerous as the new round of the arms race gathered momentum. For example, could the Soviet Union allow the United States to assemble its space-based weapon systems without interference or would it decide that deployment had to be physically prevented?

The adverse effect on the Soviet objective of not losing a world war was longer term, but it was also more concrete. The stated objective of the SDI was to develop a BMD system that would be "a thoroughly reliable defense against incoming Soviet missiles."[58] The existing Soviet

---

56. In congressional testimony on February 1, 1984, Defense Secretary Caspar Weinberger noted, "If we can get a system which is effective and which we know can render their weapons impotent, we would be back in a situation we were in, for example, when we were the only nation with nuclear weapons and we did not threaten others with it." *Department of Defense Authorization for Appropriations for Fiscal Year 1985: Part I: U.S. Military Posture,* Hearings before the Senate Committee on Armed Services, 98 Cong. 2 sess. (GPO, 1984), pt. 1, p. 89.

57. For example, a U.S. Air Force booklet, which outlined basic doctrine, included the requirement to gain and maintain superiority in space. This requirement had been established in 1982, at the latest. Fred Hiatt, *Washington Post,* January 15, 1985.

58. *Military Posture,* Hearings, pt. 1, p. 55.

deterrent would be rendered impotent and the United States would have the option of striking at the USSR at any time it chose, without fear of retaliation. Even if the U.S. system of defense against ballistic missiles were only partially effective, it would become more likely that the United States would attempt a disarming nuclear attack on the Soviet Union if faced by an impending defeat of its forces in NATO.

The crucial significance of the United States' BMD systems to Soviet wartime strategy had been implicit in the priority given by the Soviet Union to negotiating the 1972 ABM Treaty. The treaty was of unlimited duration, but a signatory could withdraw if it decided "that extraordinary events relating to the Treaty jeopardized its supreme interests."[59] The SDI set the United States on a path that was intended to breach the treaty's provisions.[60] Neither an "extraordinary event" nor jeopardy to U.S. "supreme interests," but rather a change of mood in the country and a change of fashion in strategic thought were responsible for the breach.

The defense aspect of the strategic defense initiative was, however, only one part of the implicit threat. Weapons designed for use in space could be adapted for use from space. Similarly, the underlying research programs would generate new ways of exploiting the potential of space, such as the kinetic energy of orbiting bodies. The move into space would lead to a completely new species of offensive weapons that could be directed at Soviet assets inside the Soviet Union, and against which the Soviets would have to contrive new defenses.

Retrospect

For the Soviets, looking back fifteen years from 1985, the record in respect to policies for strategic weapons and arms control was discouraging. The ABM Treaty, which had seemed an irreversible gain, was in growing jeopardy as the United States sought to develop the means of deploying strike weapons in space, weapons that would pose an offensive threat to Soviet territory while negating the Soviet Union's wartime deterrent.

59. United States Arms Control and Disarmament Agency, *Arms Control and Disarmament Agreements* (GPO, 1982), p. 142.
60. This was before the attempt to reinterpret the meaning of the treaty's provisions, and the official U.S. interpretation was that the treaty specifically prohibited the development and testing of components for space-based BMD systems.

Negotiations on intercontinental weapons had caused the Soviets to make major cuts in current deployments and future production plans while leaving U.S. plans untouched. Rather than weakening the United States' drive to preserve its military superiority, negotiations had provided the U.S. military establishment with a novel rationale for developing new means of delivering strategic nuclear weapons, such as the long-range cruise missile.

The situation regarding regional-range missiles was even worse. In carrying out what had been seen as the routine replacement of obsolescent systems, the Soviets had managed to justify the U.S. deployment of two new categories of weapon that jeopardized the success of Soviet war plans in Europe and posed a new threat to the Soviet homeland.

There had been no progress on negotiating a comprehensive test ban, notwithstanding significant concessions by the Soviet Union, and talks had been broken off by the United States in 1980. Despite hard evidence of U.S. ambivalence about limiting nuclear weapons and the expressed lack of interest of the Reagan administration, it was the Soviet Union that acquired the public image of a reluctant negotiator while the United States was thought to be eager for arms control—it was, but only in the sense of cutting back the Soviet inventory of ICBMs at no cost to itself.

The Soviets would have also had to ask themselves why it was that the Western electorates' resistance to Euromissiles was never quite sufficient to prevent their deployment. One factor would have been evident. The conventional superiority and offensive posture of Warsaw Pact forces facing NATO belied the claim that the Soviets had a defensive doctrine and posed no threat to Western Europe.

The fifteen-year record was one of almost complete failure. Not only had the Soviets been unable to achieve their immediate negotiating objectives, but in respect to the underlying objectives of arms control, they were worse off than when they started. In Soviet eyes (and in the eyes of many Europeans and some Americans) the danger of world war had increased sharply since 1978. At the same time, the Soviet Union's chances of not losing such a war had been reduced in the short term by the deployment of Euromissiles, particularly Pershing II, and in the longer term its chances would be seriously jeopardized by the deployment of a space-based BMD system.

However, the fact that the Soviets had been unsuccessful in achieving their objectives did not mean that the objectives were invalid or, for that matter, unachievable. The military logic of a nonnuclear Europe and of parity in strategic weapons at as low a level as possible remained valid. And if less was better, then it could be argued that zero was best. To these military-technical reasons for negotiating the reduction and if possible the elimination of the two sides' nuclear arsenals, in 1985 Gorbachev added the political-military argument that the only certain way of averting the catastrophe of nuclear war was to get rid of nuclear weapons.

Meanwhile, any military reason to conceal the Soviet interest in arms reductions had dissolved. By 1980, Soviet ground-air forces facing NATO had been mainly restructured, and Western analysts had demonstrated their awareness of the 1970s strategy. And by 1985 the Soviets had largely achieved the strategic force structure they had projected in 1970, with the fourth-generation systems in place and the fifth-generation ICBMs ready to begin deployment. The military-technical constraints on openness were lifted, and in 1985 Gorbachev added the political-military argument that in the nuclear age national security had to be secured mainly by political rather than military means.

With Gorbachev's appointment, public advocacy of nuclear arms control became an important element of Soviet national security policy. Gorbachev also insisted on a new style of negotiation, focusing on the objective of achieving reductions, rather than "winning" the negotiations. Despite these important changes in style and the new political-military arguments in favor of arms control, the negotiating objectives remained the same. The underlying consistency of Soviet strategic weapons policy can be seen in the evolving Soviet negotiating positions, shown in table 3-4. The ceilings on units of account move steadily downward, while the Soviets maximize their capability in areas where no constraints limit them. Such numerical discontinuities as do exist stem from U.S.-dictated changes in the units of account and not from changes in Soviet policy.

Table 3-4. *Specific or Implied Limits on Arms Accepted or Proposed by the Soviet Union, 1972–87*[a]

Delivery system	SALT I, 1972	SALT II, 1979	START, 1983	START, 1987
Strategic nuclear delivery vehicles	...	2,250	1,800	1,600
MIRVed SNDVs	...	1,320	1,200	...
Warheads[b]	...	9,550	[12,580]	6,000
Ballistic missiles	2,348[c]	2,130	[1,680]	...
MIRVed BMs	Excluded	1,200	1,080	...
Warheads[b]	2,348	9,430	[10,180]	4,900
Intercontinental ballistic missiles	1,038[c,d]	1,038[c]	[1,000]	...
MIRVed ICBMs	...	820	680	...
Warheads[b]	1,038	6,418	[7,100]	3,300
Heavy ICBMs	308	308	308	154
Warheads[b]	308	3,080	3,080	1,540
Sea-launched ballistic missiles	950	732	[680]	...
MIRVed SLBMs	...	380	400	...
Warheads[b]	950	3,012	3,080	Limits
Bombers	Excluded	120	120	...
ALCM bombers[e]	...	120	120	...
Warheads	...	3,360	2,400	1,100
ALCMs	...	...	...	900
Sea-launched cruise missiles	...	Excluded	Excluded	Limits

Sources: Michael MccGwire, *Military Objectives in Soviet Foreign Policy* (Brookings, 1987), pp. 516–18; *Arms Control Reporter 1987* (Brookline, Mass.: Institute for Defense and Disarmament Studies), pp. 607.A.3–7, 611.A.6–7, 611.B.418, 611.B.430.

a. Limits specified in the agreement or in the Soviet proposal are in italics; limits inferred from Soviet force structure at the time of the proposal are in brackets.

b. Numbers reflect actual or impending deployments and are not theoretical maximums.

c. Excludes the obsolescent second-generation systems that were phased out and replaced by SLBMs in the 1970s.

d. Excludes the 360 VRBMs targeted on the Soviet periphery.

e. Air-launched cruise missile bombers.

CHAPTER 4

International Relations, 1970–83

INTERNATIONAL developments in the 1970s and the first half of the 1980s set the scene for the far-reaching changes that took place after 1987. The Soviet world view during this period continued to be determined largely by the Marxist-Leninist theory of international relations. It can be inferred that foreign policy was generally shaped by the hierarchy of objectives shown in figure 4-1.

Since the 1920s, two enduring and interdependent factors have been central to Soviet analyses of international relations.[1] One is the international correlation of forces, whose trend is manifest in the outcome of the ongoing competition for world influence. The other is the danger of war, which stems from capitalism's innately aggressive tendencies and is latent in arms racing.

The Competition for World Influence

For the Soviets, the competition for world influence has been conducted under the rubric of "peaceful coexistence." The concept goes back to Lenin's day and, while it has evolved over the years, the goal of shifting the inevitable conflict between the socialist and capitalist systems

---

1. The theoretical aspects of this chapter are based on Margot Light, *The Soviet Theory of International Relations* (St. Martin's Press, 1988); Allen Lynch, *The Soviet Study of International Relations* (Cambridge University Press, 1987); Michael J. Deane, *The Soviet Concept of the "Correlation of Forces,"* Project 4383, SSC-TN-4383-1, DARPA Contract MDA903-75-C-0347 (Palo Alto, Calif.: Stanford Research Institute, May 1976).

Figure 4-1. *The Hierarchy of Foreign Policy Objectives, 1970–86*

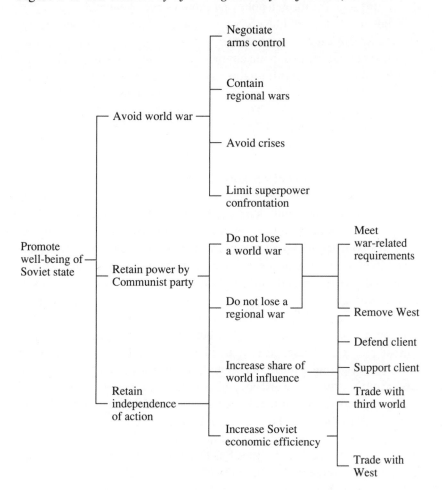

Source: This is an extension of the hierarchy of objectives developed in Michael MccGwire, *Military Objectives in Soviet Foreign Policy* (Brookings, 1987), pp. 37–42; it includes suggestions made by Roderick Pitty.

away from military confrontation to the economic and ideological spheres has always been integral to the Soviet definition. Initially a tactic, peaceful coexistence was extended to a long-term strategy and subsequently became an abiding principle of Soviet foreign policy, enshrined in the new 1977 Soviet Constitution. The possibility of achieving peaceful coexistence has depended on being able to constrain the aggressive behavior and ambitions of the capitalist states, since (by definition) socialist foreign policy has always been peaceful.[2]

While excluding military confrontation, peaceful coexistence remained a manifestation of the international class struggle and therefore assumed continuing economic competition and ideological conflict. The concept allowed support for national liberation movements, a duty that came under the rubric of "proletarian internationalism," the other pillar of Soviet foreign policy. The Soviets came to think of peaceful coexistence as the principle, while détente was the process, although there is a significant distinction between the two concepts. When the correlation of forces favored capitalism, peaceful coexistence was used as a strategy to defeat capitalist aggression. When the correlation of forces favored socialism, détente became the "natural" relationship between the two systems and could therefore be imposed on a reluctant West.[3]

Like peaceful coexistence, the concept of a correlation of forces goes back to Lenin and its scope has evolved over the years. In essence, it is a multifactor analysis of the relative power of the two social systems, evaluated across a broad range of indexes. Some of these are more or less quantifiable (for example, economic and military capabilities), others are not (social, political, and ideological factors, for instance), and the indexes include intangible qualities like the general crisis of capitalism, the struggle for national liberation, the mobilization of mass anti-imperialist movements, and the stratification of the Western leadership's attitude toward cooperation with the socialist community.[4]

Soviet theorists insist that the correlation of forces is quite different from Western theories of a balance of power, which they see as a static concept, mainly concerned with military power. They argue that the correlation of forces reflects the objective nature of Marxist analysis and is a dynamic concept since it addresses a historical process—namely, the inevitable shift in relative power from capitalism to socialism.

The long-term trend is therefore preordained, and the policy problem is of two kinds—to decide the current trend in the rate of change from capitalism to socialism, and to assess the correlation in a particular set of circumstances, in order to select the appropriate Soviet policies.[5]

---

2. Light, *Soviet Theory,* pp. 29, 31, 54.

3. Ibid., pp. 54–57. I am indebted to Karen Dawisha for pointing out this important distinction between peaceful coexistence and détente.

4. Deane, *Soviet Concept,* pp. 20–24, 33.

5. Light, *Soviet Theory,* p. 250.

While the displacement of capitalism by socialism is seen as a long-term process, there have been three major shifts in the correlation of forces in favor of socialism. The first was in 1917 when the first socialist state emerged from the Russian revolution. The second was in 1945, which saw the defeat of fascist Germany and the emergence on the world scene of a much stronger Soviet Union. It also saw the addition of several "democratic" states to the socialist camp and the beginning of the European withdrawal from empire and the emergence of national liberation movements.

The third major shift was in 1969–70. By 1961 the correlation was already seen to be in the socialists' favor (or so Nikita S. Khrushchev claimed at the Twenty-second Party Congress in October that year), but in 1969–70 the United States implicitly acknowledged that the Soviets had achieved a form of strategic nuclear parity, by entering into negotiations on limiting strategic arms. The Soviets saw this parity as having been critical in persuading the United States to accept the principle of peaceful coexistence, as embodied in the process of détente.[6]

The Brezhnev Peace Program

The third shift was widely acknowledged in retrospect, but at the time Leonid I. Brezhnev had to overcome significant opposition to his policy of securing improved relations with the United States,[7] which was announced at the Twenty-fourth Party Congress in March 1971. That congress, at which Brezhnev declared that peaceful coexistence was the basis of Soviet-American relations and announced what came to be called the peace program, set the direction of Soviet foreign policy for the next twelve years.

The new direction was confirmed by the Central Committee plenum in April 1973, which resolved that peaceful coexistence was now the general rule for relations between states with different social systems and stressed the importance of making détente irreversible. Current

6. Deane, *Soviet Concept,* sets out these periods. Light (who links the correlation of forces to stages in the crisis of capitalism) points to the importance of parity being recognized by others in 1969–70 (*Soviet Theory,* p. 291, note 10). In the Soviet view, "by the start of the 1970s, this change had essentially assumed an irreversible nature. The turning point in the change in the correlation of forces between the two systems was the elimination of imperialism's superiority in the military sphere" (V. V. Zagladin, *Mirovoe kommunisticheskoe dvizhenie* [*The World Communist Movement*] [Moscow: Politizdat, 1982], p. 19).

7. Raymond L. Garthoff, *Détente and Confrontation: American-Soviet Relations from Nixon to Reagan* (Brookings, 1985), p. 42.

developments gave reason for optimism. Besides progress in the strategic arms limitation talks (SALT) and the flowering of détente, West Germany's new Ostpolitik had resulted in a de facto peace settlement in Europe. This was embodied in treaties with the USSR and Poland in August and December 1970 and with East Germany in December 1972, while the Quadripartite Agreement on Berlin was signed in September 1971. West Germany had also finally signed the Nuclear Non-Proliferation Treaty in 1969 (and ratified it in 1973). Meanwhile this whole process had served to open the stopcock of West German trade with the Soviet Union, following Soviet trade agreements with France (1965), Italy (1966), and Great Britain (1970). Like détente with the United States, however, trade with the West was a controversial policy among Soviet leaders.[8]

Long-term trends were also propitious. Contradictions within the capitalist system were growing. The United States had lost its position of absolute economic superiority over its allies, and Western Europe and Japan were steadily closing the gap. The dollar crisis in 1971 had caused the Bretton Woods international monetary agreement to collapse and with it the postwar economic order. The emergence of the less developed countries and the nonaligned states as pressure groups in the international community was undermining the global preponderance that the capitalist West had enjoyed since World War II. And the lesson of Vietnam that liberation movements could succeed against strong imperialist opposition augured well for the relatively few territories still in colonial hands.

Reinforcing the latter trend was the doctrine announced by President Richard M. Nixon at Guam in 1969, indicating that the United States intended to rely on regional proxies to halt the progress of socialism and suggesting that in future it would be reluctant to intervene with ground forces overseas. Meanwhile the U.S. involvement in Vietnam had been a source of disunity in the West and, although the last U.S. combat units were withdrawn in August 1972, the war and its aftermath were continuing to rend the U.S. political fabric. This could be seen as further evidence of the growing crisis of capitalism.[9]

There were of course minuses, the most serious being the resumption of Sino-American relations after a twenty-year rift, against which the

8. Ibid., p. 354; Robin Edmonds, *Soviet Foreign Policy: The Brezhnev Years* (Oxford University Press, 1983), pp. 86, 88–90, 101.
    9. Lynch, *Soviet Study,* pp. 98–101; Deane, *Soviet Concept,* p. 36.

Indo-Soviet Treaty of 1971 did not weigh heavily. China was not only actively hostile toward the Soviet Union, it was increasingly unpredictable. Another minus was Eastern Europe, where the invasion of Czechoslovakia in 1968 and the fall of the Polish government at the end of 1970 (following food riots) indicated the underlying fragility of the political system. And then there was the Soviet economy.

It had long been clear that Khrushchev's ambitious projections of overtaking and then outpacing the capitalist economies had been hopelessly optimistic, and that the gap between the Soviet Union and the industrialized West was steadily getting larger. Meanwhile, the annual growth rate, while still a healthy 5 percent, was falling steadily. However, it was still hoped that could be remedied by adjusting the economic machinery, and Brezhnev mistakenly believed that the arms control process would halt the arms race and allow the Soviets to reallocate resources from defense. In other words, the scale of the economic problem and its structural nature had yet to be appreciated.

Nevertheless, developments in the 1970–73 period justified the Soviets' conclusion that the change in the correlation of forces was accelerating, and it was not unreasonable for them to carry this sanguine assessment through to the Twenty-fifth Party Congress in February 1976. After all, there had been a "historically significant turn" in Soviet-U.S. relations, involving a transition from cold war to genuine peaceful coexistence, including the development of "mutually advantageous cooperation in many spheres."[10]

At the Moscow summit in May 1972, besides the Antiballistic Missile (ABM) Treaty and the SALT interim agreement, eight other agreements had been signed, including the Basic Principles of U.S.-Soviet Relations, which represented a charter for détente. In June 1973, following an unprecedented visit to Bonn, Brezhnev had visited Washington for the return summit, when ten new agreements were signed including one on the Prevention of Nuclear War, something to which the Soviets attached particular importance. And the Conference on Security and Cooperation in Europe had convened in early July, achieving another long-term Soviet goal.[11]

Nor did events in the remainder of 1973 through 1975 seem to justify a different assessment. While President Nixon and Secretary of State

10. G. Arbatov, "Soviet-American Relations at a New Stage," *Pravda*, July 22, 1973, commenting on developments during the fourteen months following the 1972 summit.
11. Garthoff, *Détente and Confrontation*, pp. 290, 334–45.

Henry Kissinger had ignored Soviet warnings about the danger of an Arab-Israeli war,[12] when it did break out in October 1973 the superpowers had managed to contain it, albeit rather clumsily. The fourfold increase in oil prices that was triggered by the war caused economic disruption in the West but favored the Soviet Union, a net oil exporter. The Arab-Israeli war had also caused rifts in the NATO alliance, with most European members refusing to allow the use of U.S. bases on their territory in the airborne resupply of Israeli forces. As unrelated developments, the right-wing regime in Lisbon was overthrown in April 1974, to be replaced by a government that granted independence to Portugal's colonies and continued moving to the left in 1975. In Cyprus, a right-wing coup prompted a Turkish invasion and the partition of the island, which led to the replacement of the right-wing junta in Athens by a moderate government, intensified Turko-Greek enmity, and weakened NATO.[13] And by May 1975, the North Vietnamese had taken over South Vietnam, the United States having reneged on its implicit promise of support.[14]

Soviet commentators saw these developments as merely the latest cycle in the "general crisis of capitalism," a historic period sparked by the international situation following World War I, that would see the worldwide replacement of capitalism by socialism. There was general agreement that the 1973–75 crisis was the worst since World War I and its geographic breadth unique. At the party congress in 1976 Brezhnev compared the current economic crisis in the West to the beginning of the 1930s and, noting the intensification of the ideological and social crisis in bourgeois society (this was after the Watergate investigation and Nixon's resignation), concluded that "capitalism is a society devoid of a future."[15]

In general, then, the favorable trend could be expected to persist, although the emerging opposition in America to the very concept of détente meant a continual struggle would be needed to make it irreversible. The problem was seen to lie in a failure of realism among

---

12. Ibid., p. 331.
13. Ibid., pp. 401–05, 485.
14. Adam B. Ulam, *Dangerous Relations: The Soviet Union in World Politics, 1970–1982* (Oxford University Press, 1983), pp. 127–28.
15. Deane, *Soviet Concept*, pp. 29–33; Ulam, *Dangerous Relations*, pp. 146–47. For an exposition of why this misplaced optimism could be justified in terms of Marxist-Leninist theory, see R. Judson Mitchell, "A New Brezhnev Doctrine," *World Politics*, vol. 30 (April 1978), pp. 388–90.

Western opponents of détente, and an inability within "aggressive circles" to appreciate the objective factor that had "compelled" the United States to accept peaceful coexistence as the basis of relations between the two social systems. Soviet pronouncements at the party congress were therefore generally upbeat.

But the Soviet analysts had got it wrong, and the tide had already turned.

Soviet Misperceptions

One mistake had been to underestimate the strength of the capitalist economies and their inherent resilience. This was compounded by a failure to recognize the underlying weakness of the Soviet economy and the structural problems that afflicted it and its work force. Another mistake had been to overestimate the relevance and attractiveness of the Soviet model to nations in the third world. A third mistake had been to ignore the likely Western reaction to the restructuring of Soviet forces to implement the 1970s strategy for the contingency of world war, a restructuring that involved a major buildup of conventional forces facing NATO and in the Far East. But the most serious mistake had been to misjudge the U.S. political scene, to misunderstand the reasons that led the Nixon administration to seek arms control and détente, and to misread the changing mood of the American people in the wake of Vietnam.

There was a fundamental disjunction in the two sides' understanding of détente. Besides its role in reducing the danger of world war, the Soviets saw détente as a means of managing the peaceful transition of the United States into a world marked by political parity rather than by American predominance.[16] American leaders saw détente and arms control as elements in a much larger global game; they valued them as means to an end and were not convinced of their intrinsic worth. This would become embarrassingly clear to the Soviets when Nixon and Kissinger published their memoirs.[17]

Kissinger's emphasis on managing Soviet power, disciplining Soviet

16. Garthoff, *Détente and Confrontation*, p. 38.
17. Henry Trofimenko refers to the memoirs of Nixon, published in 1978, and Kissinger's, published in 1979 and 1982, in "The Third World and the U.S.-Soviet Competition: A Soviet View," *Foreign Affairs*, vol. 59 (Summer 1981), pp. 1024–25. Those memoirs and Brzezinski's, published in 1983, would have given the Soviets insights to U.S. thinking that would have been important inputs in the 1983–84 Soviet review of policy.

behavior, and restraining Soviet actions indicated that primacy remained an American goal, and he assumed that Washington could dictate the terms on which détente proceeded.[18] Kissinger put it bluntly when discussing the role of détente in the outcome of the 1973 Arab-Israeli war: U.S. policy was "to reduce and where possible to eliminate Soviet influence in the Middle East . . . under the cover of détente." As he explained, "détente . . . was partly necessity; partly a tranquilizer for Moscow as we sought to draw the Middle East into closer relations with us at Soviet expense; partly the moral imperative of the nuclear age."[19]

Nixon and Kissinger were not really interested in the theoretical concept of peaceful coexistence or in the Soviets' more extensive understanding of what détente implied. They paid little attention to repeated Soviet assertions that the ideological struggle would continue and that it would include national wars of liberation. For their different reasons, Nixon and Kissinger encouraged the public impression that as a result of their personal relationships and diplomatic skills, the Soviet Union was now willing to accept U.S. global predominance, no longer believed in the historical progression from capitalism to socialism, and would cease supporting the opponents of U.S. protégés and clients.

The bulk of the American people, bruised by the experience of withdrawing from Vietnam, were ready to believe this, and perceptions of the threat posed by the Soviet Union fell steadily. Disillusionment was inevitable and the turning point came in October 1973, when the Arab-Israeli war served as cause and catalyst for a reversal of U.S. public opinion.

Both the final outcome of the war and Israel's near defeat in the initial stages persuaded its influential political lobby in the United States that Israel had been ill served by détente and that a high level of perceived Soviet threat was in Israel's best interests.[20] There were many others who accepted the U.S. administration's version of events and believed that the Soviet Union had breached the recent agreements on superpower

18. Mike Bowker and Phil Williams, *Superpower Détente: A Reappraisal* (London: Sage Publications, 1988), pp. 58–59.

19. Henry A. Kissinger, *Years of Upheaval* (Little, Brown, 1982), p. 594, cited in Garthoff, *Détente and Confrontation,* p. 393.

20. For the rationale see Garthoff, *Détente and Confrontation,* pp. 405–08. Besides the danger to Israeli interests of a Soviet-American condominium, a high level of Soviet threat would ensure that Israel would be seen by the American people as an ally and an asset in the struggle against communist expansion, rather than as a burden and part of the problem in the Middle East.

behavior in crises, and therefore could not be trusted.[21] But besides those who responded to the event itself, there was a wide range of political actors who, for different reasons, had never accepted the move toward détente and were waiting for the opportunity to reverse existing policies.

The latter group included those who rejected the concept of parity and believed that the United States' interests (and those of the free world) required superiority over the Soviet Union, and those who saw the USSR as essentially evil, bent on expansion and with no concern for world order. The powerful political voice of these and other activists, joined in the 1976 presidential campaign, was responsible for having the word *détente* banned from Republican pronouncements. Their varied interests were given an institutional voice in the mid-1970s by the establishment of organizations such as the Heritage Foundation and the Committee on the Present Danger. The latter was particularly important because of its influential and nominally bipartisan composition and its clear-cut agenda, which denigrated arms control negotiations, called for an across-the-board buildup of U.S. military strength, unabashedly supported Israel as a bastion against Soviet expansion, and raised the specter of a "window of vulnerability" to a surprise Soviet missile attack.

The reversal of U.S. attitudes was accelerated in 1975 by the outcome of the struggle for power in Angola following the granting of independence, an outcome that was widely seen in the United States as demonstrating the consequences of the post-Vietnam reluctance to intervene against Soviet expansionism. Never mind that the Soviets had been providing support to the Popular Movement for the Liberation of Angola (MPLA) since 1964, and that the colonial power Portugal was an ally of the United States. There was a tacit assumption that once European colonial rule collapsed, it should by right be replaced by U.S. economic and political influence and that the Soviet Union should keep out.[22]

The political impact of the Angolan war was compounded by the involvement of Cuba, itself a painful issue for many Americans. In May and June 1975 there were 230 Cuban military advisers to the MPLA, but

---

21. For the contrary view that the Soviets had adhered to the agreements, see ibid., pp. 385–93.

22. This description of U.S. assumptions reflects the Soviet viewpoint (Ulam, *Dangerous Relations*, p. 135), but it is none the less valid for that.

in response to incursions by South African forces, several hundred more advisers and some 700 combat troops soon became involved. The South Africans escalated their involvement in late October and the Cubans responded with a large-scale infusion of troops, initially using their own ships and aircraft; by the end of January 1976 the Cuban expeditionary force numbered 10,000–12,000.[23]

The New American Mood

By 1977 the new anti-Soviet trend in U.S. opinion was firmly established and the realignment of superpower clients in the Horn of Africa was seen as confirmation of communist expansionism. Following the overthrow of Emperor Haile Selassie in 1974, Ethiopia had moved steadily away from its close relationship with the United States to a new relationship with the Soviet Union that was finally publicized in May 1977. Somalia, a Soviet client since the 1960s, was meanwhile chafing under Soviet restraints on its irredentist claims to the Ogaden, the large southern province of Ethiopia that was an area ethnically Somali.[24]

Soviet-Cuban attempts at resolving the conflict by establishing a Marxist regional federation failed, and by May 1977 at least three thousand Somalia-supported guerrillas were operating in the Ogaden. Encouraged by U.S. statements that implied a readiness to supply arms if Somalia switched patrons, regular troops were committed in mid-June and by the end of July the Somalis had "liberated" much of the Ogaden.[25]

Because the Organization of African Unity had declared for Ethiopia and against aggression, the United States backed away from the possibility of supplying arms, but Somalia was fully committed. By the end of September the Somalis had driven the Ethiopians out of 90 percent of the Ogaden and it looked as if Ethiopia might disintegrate because the Eritrean secessionist movement and other provincial rebellions were also achieving successes against the overstretched Ethiopian forces. However, the Somali invasion bogged down and the Ethiopians managed to stabilize the Ogaden front.

Starting in November, Ethiopia received a massive infusion of Cuban advisers and Soviet arms, and in January 1978, directly supported by

23. Bowker and Williams, *Superpower Détente*, pp. 122–25; Garthoff, *Détente and Confrontation*, pp. 502–19, 533–37, 1112.
24. Garthoff, *Détente and Confrontation*, pp. 630–53.
25. Ibid., pp. 633–37.

some fifteen thousand Cuban combat troops, Ethiopian forces launched a counteroffensive in the Ogaden. The operation was planned and conducted by a Soviet military staff led by a senior Soviet general, and Ethiopia had substantial superiority. Its forces were soon successful, but the Ethiopians halted their offensive at the border and did not invade Somali territory.[26]

While it was hard to portray the Soviet involvement as breaking the norms of international behavior (although President Jimmy Carter's national security adviser sought to do so),[27] and it cost the Soviets their bases in Somalia, on balance the Soviets were seen to have "won." More important, the impression of U.S. vacillation and impotence, due partly to divided counsel, compared unfavorably with the seemingly directed style of Soviet policy.

President Carter's stance toward the Soviet Union toughened after the Ogaden war and the balance within his administration shifted toward Zbigniew Brzezinski's hardline policies. Groups such as the Committee on the Present Danger became increasingly influential in the U.S. political debate and unfolding events could be taken as confirming their argument that the problem lay in U.S. military weakness and the post-Vietnam lack of political will.

The revolution in Iran that broke surface in late 1978 led to the collapse of that pro-American bastion of power and the taking hostage of the U.S. embassy in Tehran in November 1979. While the revolution could not be ascribed directly to the Soviets, many of their own statements implied their own belief that it offered them opportunities for future advances. In the West, it resurrected the myth of a Russian "drive for warm water ports" in the area.[28] The overthrow of the Daoud government in Kabul in April 1978 and its replacement by a doctrinaire Marxist regime led ultimately to the Soviet invasion of Afghanistan in December 1979. That

26. Ibid., pp. 630–53.
27. Zbigniew Brzezinski, *Power and Principle: Memoirs of the National Security Advisor, 1977–1981* (Farrar, Straus and Giroux, 1983), p. 181.
28. Russia's western border with Iran was established in 1828 and the eastern one in 1881. In 1939–40 the Soviets rebuffed German attempts to direct their interests away from the Balkans toward the Persian Gulf. The reputed "drive for warm water ports" was a British distortion during the imperial competition with Russia in the nineteenth century. From the ninth through the eighteenth centuries the Russians and their forebears had striven repeatedly to gain access to the Black Sea. They also had faced the problem of securing free passage for the products of the steppes through the Black Sea exits, which were controlled by the Ottoman Empire. See Michael MccGwire, *Miliary Objectives in Soviet Foreign Policy* (Brookings, 1987), p. 186. For the negotiations with Germany, see Garthoff, *Détente and Confrontation,* p. 941, note 152.

was seen as confirming the Soviets' interest in the Indian Ocean and their drive for world domination, a drive that could only be encouraged by American weakness and inaction.

The invasion of Afghanistan focused and provided an outlet for American frustration with the course of world events. It evoked a strong political response from the Carter administration that combined punitive sanctions, a freeze on Soviet-American relations, closer links with China, and the rebuilding of a position of military strength in Southwest Asia.[29] Reflecting deeply felt domestic discontent more than calculations of national interest, these initiatives formalized U.S. disillusionment with a policy of détente and marked the end of progress on strategic arms control. The United States' policy toward the Soviet Union became increasingly confrontational.

The Soviet leadership has been criticized for not being more sensitive to U.S. concern about communist expansionism. But broader forces were moving U.S. opinion in a confrontational direction, and the Soviets provided a scapegoat. Underlying everything was the diminished global status of the United States. By the mid-1970s, the United States no longer had the substantial advantage in economic and military strength that it had enjoyed for the first twenty-five years after World War II. But instead of viewing this change as part of a desirable process brought about in large part by its own enlightened policies, the United States saw its new role as a sign of failure. That view was strengthened by a deep resentment about the Vietnam War among a silent and bemused majority who remembered the good intentions with which their nation had embarked on the enterprise. Despite intentions, the effort went sour, partly because of the political failure on the home front and partly because of the carping of U.S. allies, but mainly because the United States had not been tough enough.

The oil shocks of 1973–74 showed clearly that the United States no longer enjoyed energy independence and could actually be held ransom by barely developed Arab countries. Next, the Japanese began to encroach on markets (such as automobiles) that the United States viewed as part of its own natural preserve and as the just rewards of its technological preeminence. The New International Economic Order, demands for technology transfer, and the endless Law of the Sea negotiations, all added to the sense of unfairness. The final insult was

29. Garthoff, *Détente and Confrontation,* p. 958.

the Iranian hostage crisis, which the United States could do little about but chose to wallow in. With the U.S. economic downturn at the end of the 1970s and the insecurity of rising unemployment, it is not surprising that Americans returned to the motto, "Don't tread on me."

The Soviets did misjudge the American mood and U.S. readiness to accept the changing correlation of forces, but they had little control over unfolding international events in the 1970s. In Angola and the Horn of Africa the Soviets had to weigh the potentially high costs of inaction. They were sensitive to the charge that their narrow interest in détente took precedence over support for the struggle for national liberation. When Egypt, six weeks after the 1972 Moscow summit, requested the Soviet Union to withdraw its forces, the Soviets probably welcomed the request as an opportunity to extricate themselves from direct involvement in an inherently unstable area but also recognized their eviction as a blow to their image in the third world.[30]

In the complex struggle for power in Angola in 1975 there was the added complication of Chinese involvement, and the Soviet Union's inaction would have been detrimental to its role as leader of the world socialist movement. Even though it was Cuba that led the decision to respond to South Africa's involvement by introducing combat troops, the Soviet Union could not afford to give in to U.S. diplomatic pressure, when power was within the MPLA's grasp. African opinion was overwhelmingly in favor of Soviet-Cuban support for the MPLA against South African–backed forces.[31]

Similarly in 1977 in the Horn of Africa, numerous players were seeking to change a complex flow of events. Some of those players, including Saudi Arabia and Iran, were willing to accept the dismemberment of Ethiopia (until recently a U.S. protégé), if that was what was needed to persuade Somalia to switch sides.[32] This meant that the Soviet Union had three choices: to support Somalia's irredentist claims; to help Ethiopia repel the Somali invasion; or to do nothing and lose a point d'appui that would be strategically important in the event of world war.[33]

The Soviet invasion of Afghanistan came into a quite separate category

---

30. Ibid., p. 315. MccGwire, *Military Objectives,* pp. 197–99, explains why the Soviets, while retaining access to naval support bases, were ready to withdraw the twenty thousand troops that had been deployed in 1970 to provide air defense against deep interdiction by the Israelis.
31. Garthoff, *Détente and Confrontation,* p. 688.
32. Ibid., pp. 632–33.
33. MccGwire, *Military Objectives,* pp. 192–210.

of events. The West chose to classify it as a particularly ominous example of Soviet expansion in the third world, because it was the first time the Soviet Union had deployed ground forces beyond the borders of the bloc. However, the Soviets saw Afghanistan as part of their national security zone, and their intervention was directly comparable to those in Hungary in 1956 and Czechoslovakia in 1968 and was not some new departure.[34]

It did not reflect an urge to extend Soviet frontiers. Although the USSR's borders with Afghanistan and Iran cut through a single ethnic area that makes the Soviet Union particularly sensitive to Muslim irredentism, that does not imply a strategic imperative to turn those countries into communist satellites. The Soviets have had the military capability to invade Afghanistan at any time since the mid-1950s. There was nothing to prevent them from doing so in 1958 in response to the formation of the Central Treaty Organization,[35] or in the mid-1960s after the United States had committed sizable forces to Vietnam and before détente became the Soviet goal.

The record of the last one hundred years suggests that Russian interests had been reasonably well served by Afghanistan as a more or less independent buffer to the south, whereas the procommunist coup in Kabul in 1978 was followed by a slide toward anarchy. This led to Soviet military intervention and a major setback in the competition for world influence. The political costs were significant, not only among the thirty-eight Muslim states, but in the third world at large. A United Nations resolution condemning the Soviet intervention was supported by an unprecedented 104 votes.

The Unfavorable Trend in the Correlation of Forces

The Carter administration chose to characterize the invasion of Afghanistan as a major tilt in the East-West geostrategic balance in favor of the Soviet Union, whereas it was just the opposite. But that mistaken assessment conformed with U.S. assertions about unchecked Soviet advances in the third world. In fact, the overall picture was very different.

---

34. For the reasons underlying the Soviet decision to invade Afghanistan, see Garthoff, *Détente and Confrontation,* pp. 915–37, 1074–75.

35. The treaty linked Turkey, Iran, and Pakistan with the United States and Britain in an anti-Soviet alliance; it could be seen as breaching the Soviet-Iranian treaty of 1924.

While it had been possible in 1976 to argue that broader developments meant the trend in the correlation of forces was still favorable for the Soviets, in concrete terms they had barely broken even during the first half of the decade.

The Egyptian request that Soviet troops withdraw in 1972 was followed by the loss of naval support facilities in 1975 and the abrogation of the Treaty of Friendship in 1976, as Anwar al-Sadat moved across to the U.S. camp. Kissinger's diplomatic maneuvering was successful in squeezing the Soviet Union out of the Middle East negotiations; meanwhile the buildup of Iran to serve as the U.S. proconsul in the region was moving ahead. A rift had developed with Sudan after a failed communist coup in 1971; in Chile, Salvador Allende was overthrown and killed in 1973. And while developments in Angola, Mozambique, and Vietnam could be counted as favoring the Soviet Union, they had to be weighed against the more far-reaching implications of the U.S. rapprochement with China and the renewal of Sino-Japanese diplomatic relations.

In the second half of the decade the balance was clearly unfavorable. Soviet influence in Vietnam increased the distrust of other states in the area. In the Horn, the Soviets had to choose between Ethiopia and Somalia, losing their investment in Somalia and acquiring large political problems in Ethiopia. Although South Yemen had come their way, they now had to face a new American influence in Egypt, Sudan, Somalia, and Kenya. Angola became enmeshed in a drawn-out civil war, tying down significant Cuban forces; Zimbabwe gained its independence and turned a cold shoulder to Moscow; by the end of the decade Mozambique had begun to ease its way to accommodation with South Africa; and in 1979 there was a rash of antileftist coups in Africa. In Southwest Asia, Saudi Arabia and Iran were becoming increasingly effective as U.S. political proxies; there was a progressive loss of Soviet influence in Iraq; Syria demanded Soviet arms but gave little in return; and after the fall of the shah, the Soviet Union was reviled by the Iranian revolutionaries almost as much as was the United States.[36]

Much of this could be explained as the vagaries of unfolding events, but there were more serious developments at the structural level of international relations that could not be discounted so easily. In 1978 the

36. Garthoff, *Détente and Confrontation,* pp. 666–89, 1079–82.

United States moved from Kissinger and Cyrus R. Vance's policy of triangular diplomacy, whereby it kept its relations with China and the Soviet Union roughly in balance, to the Brzezinski policy of an informal alliance with China against the Soviet Union. The new stance was formalized in December 1978 by the announcement of Deng Xiaoping's forthcoming visit to Washington and of the impending establishment of diplomatic relations; this would be followed by technological assistance, the supply of arms and equipment by Western Europe, and agreement to establish U.S. intelligence facilities on Chinese territory. That same year China and Japan signed a peace treaty containing an antihegemonic clause directed at the Soviet Union. These realignments paralleled the shift toward a more confrontational approach in U.S. policy, reflecting a steady swing in public opinion and the accretion of power by Brzezinski, whose anti-Soviet views came to dominate the Carter administration.[37]

Another structural problem was the failure of the United States to respond to détente in the way the Soviets had assumed it would. Rather than recognizing the change in objective circumstances and acknowledging the trend in the correlation of forces that existed at the beginning of the 1970s, the United States had become increasingly assertive in resisting this historical process. It ignored Soviet injunctions that the status quo must be seen as a flow of progressive change and Soviet explanations that peaceful coexistence assumed the continuation of the ideological struggle between the two social systems. Instead, the Nixon administration created the impression that the Soviets had agreed to a policy of socialist inaction in the third world, while the United States was entitled to defend the status quo of capitalist neocolonialism in the name of freedom.[38]

Reviewing this increasingly unfavorable situation in his report to the Twenty-sixth Party Congress in February 1981, Brezhnev characterized the world situation as an intense struggle between two trends: one toward curbing the arms race and strengthening peace and détente and the other toward undermining détente, boosting the arms race, and suppressing the struggle for national liberation. In response to this situation the party congress reaffirmed the peace program proclaimed at the congresses in 1971 and 1976, the arms race was identified as the greatest threat, and

37. Ibid., pp. 690–716.
38. For an elaboration of this view, see Trofimenko, "Third World and U.S.-Soviet Competition," pp. 1025–26.

the defense and consolidation of peace was defined as the party's most important task.[39] This echoed the line agreed at the special plenum held eight months earlier, when it was ruled that détente was the natural result of the prevailing correlation of forces in the world, and that continued negotiations should be able to avert a return to the cold war.[40]

This Pollyannaish conclusion was possible because it was judged that the five years since the Twenty-fifth Party Congress had seen "further aggravation of the general crisis of capitalism," which was currently going through its third economic recession in ten years. Inflation had reached unprecedented levels and was increasing, unemployment in developed capitalist countries had doubled in ten years, totaling some 19 million people by 1980, and the number of people involved in strikes had increased by one-third. Meanwhile, the struggle among capitalist countries for markets and sources of raw materials was increasing.[41]

These problems were used to explain the acerbic style of Western policies. And while the new U.S. administration was overtly bellicose, Moscow hoped that President Reagan would come to look at things more realistically. There were, meanwhile, forces in the United States that supported arms control and détente, and these appeared to be growing apace with those that opposed détente. Furthermore, détente was still alive in Europe where "peaceful cooperation among countries of the two systems" was generally developing quite well, and Soviet trade with West Germany had almost doubled during the five years.

These were slim grounds for persisting with the existing policies, but the Soviet leadership had a lot invested in them. It had not been easy for Brezhnev and his supporters to persuade their political colleagues and the military to accept the peace program in 1970, with its pillars of détente and arms control, strategic parity, and trade with the West and, at least initially, the policy had seemed highly successful. Besides, the Soviets had become increasingly convinced that the peace program was not only in the interest of the Soviet Union and the world socialist movement, but also essential if world war was to be avoided. The

---

39. "Brezhnev's report to the Twenty-sixth Party Congress," MDS, February 23, 1981, in *FBIS*-81-036, supp. 1, pp. 5, 16, 19, 20 (see Abbreviations of Frequently Cited Sources).

40. The plenum considered the appropriate Soviet response to the shelving of the SALT II Treaty and the sharp shift in U.S. policy following Afghanistan, and to the unrelated NATO decision in December 1979 to deploy theater nuclear weapons capable of striking targets well within the Soviet Union (*Kommunist*, no. 10 [July 1980], pp. 8–10).

41. "Brezhnev's report," pp. 14–17.

problem was not with Soviet policy but with aggressive imperialist forces that were unwilling "to consider the realities of the contemporary world."[42]

The Danger of War

Harsh experience and Marxist theory ensured that war and its avoidance loomed large in Soviet considerations. The October Revolution was spawned by three years of world war and followed by three years of civil war where the forces of counterrevolution included Russia's erstwhile allies. Little more then twenty years later the country was first ravaged by the Axis invasion, which penetrated one thousand miles into Soviet territory, and then devastated as the enemy was driven back to final defeat at the cost of well over twenty million Soviet lives.

This experience could be seen as confirming Lenin's claim that the very nature of monopoly capitalism inevitably led to war. Imperialist wars could be of three kinds: with another imperial power in a competition for markets and resources, with a socialist state in an attempt to crush the proletarian revolution, or with an indigenous people seeking national liberation from colonial status.[43] The first two were of immediate concern to the Soviet Union. There was some argument as to whether war was more likely as a by-product of conflict between imperialist states or as a direct attack on socialism (World War II could be categorized as either or both), but there was little disagreement that war between the two systems was fatalistically inevitable. Nor was this doctrine unrealistic, given the situation in the 1930s and again in 1948–53.

The belief that war was inevitable did not imply that the Soviets saw it as being in their interest.[44] From its earliest days, a constant refrain of the Soviet state was that peace was needed to allow the building of socialism, unlike capitalism, which thrived on arms racing. Josef V. Stalin used the threat of war to support the forced industrialization of the Soviet economy in the 1930s, and in 1939 took the opportunity to

42. *Kommunist*, no. 10 (July 1980), p. 8.
43. Light, *Soviet Theory*, pp. 212–13.
44. Malcolm Mackintosh, an assitant secretary in the British Cabinet and a special adviser to the government on Soviet military affairs for more than twenty years, asserts that "the Russian people are not and never have been a militaristic nation devoted to the solution of their problems or the achievement of their goals by war" ("The Russian Attitude to Defence and Disarmament," *International Affairs*, vol. 61 [Summer 1985], p. 393).

improve the USSR's geostrategic position vis-à-vis Germany,[45] but meanwhile did his utmost to avoid being drawn into the conflict.

Nor could war be justified by the argument that it created the kind of domestic turmoil that, in some cases, could enable a socialist revolution. The Soviets have consistently refuted the idea that war by itself causes revolution or that revolution can be exported, a lesson they first learned from Poland in 1920. A revolution can only occur when the necessary material requisites have matured within society. There remains, however, the problem that the Soviet Union has a theoretical obligation to support the just wars of oppressed people, whether colonial wars of national liberation or civil wars between the proletariat and the bourgeoisie. The potential cost of this obligation was one reason for the doctrinal ruling that revolution could come about by peaceful means.[46]

At the Twentieth Party Congress in 1956, Khrushchev announced that war was no longer fatalistically inevitable. A move in this direction had already been taken by Stalin in 1952 when he strongly implied that although wars between imperialist states were still inevitable, wars between socialism and capitalism were avoidable because the capitalists knew that it would mean their demise.[47] Khrushchev went further and, blurring the distinction between the different kinds of war, implied that all wars had ceased to be fatalistically inevitable because socialism and its supporters had the moral and material means to prevent aggression. He reaffirmed that "war is not fatally inevitable" at the twenty-first and twenty-second party congresses (in 1959 and 1961), but it became increasingly clear that what was avoidable was war between socialism and capitalism—that is, world war. In 1959 Khrushchev also asserted that it would be possible to eliminate world war from the life of society before the complete triumph of socialism, and words to that effect were included in the 1961 party program. Both formulations were endorsed by Brezhnev after he came to power.[48]

---

45. If the Soviets had not moved into Poland when the Germans invaded in September 1939, the German army would have ended up on the USSR's borders and some 150 miles closer to Moscow. If the Germans had held the Baltic states and Finnish Karelia, Leningrad would surely have fallen.

46. Light, *Soviet Theory,* pp. 222, 228.

47. Stalin's stress on wars among imperialists rebutted the ideas of the economist Yevgeniy Varga, who argued that the capitalists' wartime experience of state intervention in the economy meant that the Marxist prognosis was no longer valid. Although discredited, Varga's ideas continued to influence Soviet analysis and underlay perestroika and the new political thinking on international relations. Lynch, *Soviet Study,* pp. 20–25.

48. Light, *Soviet Theory,* pp. 216–18, 278.

While war between the two social systems was no longer inevitable, it remained possible. The Soviets therefore continued to prepare for the worst case of world war, which in the 1960s was assumed to involve the inevitable use of nuclear weapons and the devastation of the Soviet homeland. Nobody pretended that world war could be in the interest of socialism, even though it meant the demise of capitalism, but for reasons of troop morale and deterring capitalist adventurism, it had to be publicly insisted that such a war, if unavoidable, was worth fighting and could be won.

Soviet statements seemed to Westerners to imply a belief that the Clausewitzian dictum of war being an extension of policy applied to global nuclear war. The misinterpretation of Soviet beliefs arose from the fact that the Russian *politika* translates both as *politics* and as *policy*. Hence its use both in the operational concept of "war as an instrument of policy" and in the analytical description of "war as a continuation of politics." Soviet theorists and spokesmen emphatically denied that nuclear war was a practical instrument of policy. Soviet theorists persisted, however, in seeing the phenomenon of war, even nuclear war, as being the outgrowth of the political system (analyzed in class terms) and considered that the essence of any war could not be understood without studying its political roots.[49]

Economic Reality

Underlying the theoretical debate on whether world war was inevitable and whether it was realistic to think in terms of eliminating such a war as a social phenomenon was the reality of the crippling defense burden. Long- and short-term assessments of the threat facing the Soviet Union were central to decisions on how to allocate scarce resources between the military and civilian sectors of the economy. For example, in the reassessment following Stalin's death, downgrading the threat of invasion allowed major reductions in troop strength and the reallocation of resources to the civilian economy; the cuts in naval building programs were the most notable.[50]

49. See Robert L. Arnett, "Soviet Attitudes towards Nuclear War: Do They Really Think They Can Win?" *Journal of Strategic Studies,* vol. 2 (September 1979), pp. 172–91.

50. It is now accepted that during 1955–56, Soviet forces were reduced by about 1.8 million men. I estimate that the 1953–54 and 1957–58 decisions resulted in the planned annual construction of naval tonnage being cut by about 60 percent (Michael MccGwire, "Soviet Naval Procurement," in *The Soviet Union in Europe and the Near East: Her Capabilities and Intentions* [London: Royal United Services Institution, 1970], pp. 74–87).

The nature of a world war determined the structure of the forces required to fight it. The likelihood of such a war and its imminence determined the level of resources allocated to fleshing out that structure. Nuclear weapons introduced a new factor, and the belief that nuclear war was unthinkable offered the tempting idea that it could be averted through the possession of a minimum nuclear capability. But deterrence was only relevant when the urge existed to take the action being deterred. A minimum nuclear capability would deter a premeditated attack but could not prevent inadvertent war or nuclear escalation through an unforeseeable chain of events. Nuclear war therefore remained possible and the armed forces had to be prepared to fight such a war.

Beyond the possibility of global nuclear war, there remained the question of whether the use of nuclear weapons, particularly nuclear-armed missiles, would reduce the requirement for conventional forces. This was a controversial subject, with Khrushchev and his supporters seeing the "nuclear-missile revolution" as a way of cutting back on conventional forces and shifting resources into the domestic sector of the economy. In 1958–59 Soviet forces were cut by 300,000, and a further reduction of 1.2 million was announced in January 1960, to be completed within two years.

This reduction was halted in mid-1961, prompted nominally by the call-up of U.S. forces during the Berlin crisis. In practice it marked closure of the main debate, which had extended to include the appropriate Soviet response to the military buildup initiated by the Kennedy administration on taking office in January 1961. It was ruled that while strategic nuclear strikes would be decisive, a war could only be won through the combined operations of all arms. In other words, the advent of nuclear missiles offered few prospects for reducing the investment in defense, at least as far as ground forces were concerned.[51]

None of this had anything to do with the likelihood of world war, and it is probable that Khrushchev's frequent references to the noninevitability of such a war and to the possibility of eliminating world war as a social phenomenon were directed mainly at the military establishment's resistance to his unilateral cuts in conventional forces and the redirection of resources to the civilian economy. The lack of positive initiatives is

51. John McDonnell, "Khrushchev and the Soviet Military-Industrial Complex: Soviet Defense Policy, 1959–1961" (Halifax, Nova Scotia: Dalhousie University, Center for Foreign Policy Studies, 1979), pp. 73–82; Thomas W. Wolfe, *Soviet Power and Europe, 1945–70* (Johns Hopkins Press, 1970), p. 196.

not, however, surprising, since the only means of reducing the danger of world war available to the Soviet Union was to accept U.S. global domination and renounce its right to independent action in the international arena. This would have left the Soviet Union open to nuclear blackmail of the kind spelled out in U.S. deterrence (and compellence) theory and demonstrated against North Korea in 1953, China in 1955, and China and the Soviet Union in 1958[52] and implied by U.S. military moves during the Cuban missile crisis.[53] Throughout the 1960s the Soviets were still strategy takers, and it was the United States and its massive nuclear arsenal that dictated the nature of a future world war.

This situation changed toward the end of the 1960s. The reformulation of Soviet military doctrine about the inevitability of a world war being nuclear and involving massive strikes on Russia reversed the cost-benefit calculus of strategic arms control from negative to positive. Soviet willingness to negotiate limits on strategic weapons made it possible for the United States to move toward a détente in relations with the Soviet Union, and détente was the essential prerequisite for East-West trade and the transfer of technology.

Averting World War

Soviet-American détente was also a critical step toward the goal of eliminating the possibility of world war, without having to await the final victory of socialism. It allowed Brezhnev to launch his peace program in 1971, with its emphasis on the need to avert war, on the dangers of the arms race, and on the positive benefits of the negotiating process. It was the military logic of the Soviets' 1970s strategy for world war that allowed Brezhnev to renounce the requirement for strategic superiority at Tula in 1977 (shortly before Jimmy Carter's inauguration as president),[54] and to make a unilateral declaration of no first use of nuclear

52. Richard K. Betts, *Nuclear Blackmail and Nuclear Balance* (Brookings, 1987), pp. 42–44, 59, 71–72, 119. During the U.S. landings in Lebanon in the summer of 1958, the Strategic Air Command was put on alert with more than 1,100 aircraft positioned for takeoff against the Soviet Union (ibid., pp. 66–67).

53. For a survey of these moves and how they might have been construed by the Soviets see Raymond L. Garthoff, *Reflections on the Cuban Missile Crisis* (Brookings, 1987), pp. 58–62, 68–69. For a Soviet exposition of how the United States used crises and the threat of nuclear escalation as blackmail, see Anatoliy A. Gromyko, "The Caribbean Crisis," *Voprosy istorii (Questions of History)*, no. 8 (1971), pp. 121–29.

54. Strategic superiority had been a requirement of the 1960s strategy. At Tula, Brezhnev formally denied that it was Soviet policy to seek superiority "with the aim of delivering a first strike." This made explicit what had been implicit in Soviet strategic missile programs since 1970. "Leonid Brezhnev's Speech in Tula," January 18, 1977, in *FBIS*-77-12, p. R9.

weapons in June 1982.[55] These initiatives were seen as contributing to the objective of averting world war, although both could also be justified on military grounds.

Just as there was a disjunction between the way the Soviets and the Americans viewed the value and purpose of détente, so was there a disjunction between the way the two sides viewed the danger of world war and the threat to mankind that was inherent in the nuclear arsenals of the two sides. This persistent fundamental divergence was well illustrated in the negotiations leading up to the agreement on the Prevention of Nuclear War that was first proposed by the Soviet Union in April 1972 and finally signed at the June 1973 summit in Washington.

At the core of the original Soviet proposal was agreement by the superpowers not to use nuclear weapons against each other's homeland. The United States could not even contemplate such an agreement, because NATO strategy was based on the concept of nuclear deterrence. Henry Kissinger characterized the proposal as "a colossal piece of effrontery," but entered into negotiations nevertheless as a way of "setting additional bait" to discourage the Soviets from siding with Hanoi as the United States extricated itself from Vietnam. In the course of more than a year's defensive maneuvering, the U.S. side managed to transform the original proposal renouncing the use of nuclear weapons aginst each other into "a somewhat banal statement that our objective was peace." Kissinger described the final agreement as no more than "a bland set of principles that had been systematically stripped of all implications harmful to [U.S.] interests" and congratulated himself on having "skillfully pulled the teeth of a dangerous Soviet maneuver to lure us into renouncing the use of nuclear weapons."[56]

The disjunction in views stemmed from the differing perceptions of the nature of the danger faced by the two societies. For the West, the primary threat was Soviet aggression, which was held at bay by threatening that it would inevitably lead to world war. Identified in the 1948–53 period, the threat of Soviet aggression was codified in Western

55. *Pravda*, June 16, 1982, reporting Brezhnev's speech to the United Nations Second Special Session on Disarmament. In December 1970 the Soviets had taken informal soundings at SALT on a no-first-use agreement but were warned off by U.S. negotiators. A public proposal for a mutual agreement was made by the Warsaw Pact following their annual meeting in November 1976. MccGwire, *Military Objectives*, pp. 54–55.

56. Henry A. Kissinger, *Years of Upheaval*, pp. 274–75, 284, and *White House Years* (Little, Brown, 1979), p. 1152. His description of these negotiations shows Kissinger at his most cynical and self-satisfied.

deterrence doctrine, which also fostered the belief that there would be no world war as long as the credibility of deterrence was not weakened. Nuclear superiority for the United States served the double purpose of preventing Soviet aggression by strengthening deterrence, thereby making world war impossible, while improving the U.S. capability to wage such a war.

In the 1948–53 period the Soviets had likewise feared a premeditated attack, but by the end of the 1950s the likelihood of such an attack had been largely discounted. The greatest danger was seen to be inadvertent world war, precipitated in some way by the imperialists. Such a war might be averted but it could not be deterred, given the absence of intent.

As a way of averting war, the Soviet Union attached considerable importance to establishing principles that would provide the two sides with an agreed code of conduct.[57] The United States did not share that view but humored the Soviets, and an agreement on the Basic Principles of U.S.-Soviet Relations was signed at the Moscow summit in May 1972. The Soviets saw their proposal on the Prevention of Nuclear War as another way of helping to avert world war. Admittedly, such an agreement would also support the objectives of the 1970 strategy, since it offered a means, other than the threat of retaliation, of avoiding the nuclear devastation of the Soviet Union in the event of world war. But the proposal had the prior purpose of averting such a war.

The two sides' viewpoints and their interests were fundamentally incompatible. The U.S. side took the likelihood of deliberate Soviet aggression seriously but discounted the possibiity of nuclear war. The Soviets took the likelihood of inadvertent nuclear war seriously but discounted the possibility of a deliberate U.S. attack on the Soviet Union.

The U.S. side believed that anything that lessened Soviet concern about world war would weaken nuclear deterrence, "on which the free world's defense after all depended."[58] While neither side wanted nuclear war, Western policy had come to be based on the political readiness to escalate to such a war.

The Soviets were meanwhile beginning to take the first tentative intellectual steps in the other direction. In his speech to the Polish

---

57. Garthoff describes the importance the Soviets attached to the Basic Principles (*Détente and Confrontation*, pp. 290–98). Brezhnev told Nixon he considered the Basic Principles even more important than the SALT agreements.

58. Kissinger, *Years of Upheaval*, pp. 274, 278.

parliament in July 1974, Brezhnev referred to the centuries-old formula "if you want peace, prepare for war," and went on to note that "in our nuclear age this formula conceals particular danger."[59]

Limiting the Use of Nuclear Weapons

The replacement of the 1960s strategy for world war by the 1970s version, and the prospect of moving from being strategy takers to strategy setters, explains a seeming paradox in the trend of Soviet military theoretical writing about the winnability of nuclear world war. At the very time that great political efforts were being made to make nuclear war less likely, military statements about winning such a war became more optimistic.[60] But because a nuclear war may in theory be winnable, it does not follow that nuclear war is a useful instrument of policy, even in theory.[61] Soviet theory stresses that the initiation of war can only be justified if victory is virtually certain and the benefits will outweigh the costs. Neither of these criteria applies to nuclear war and the Soviets have been consistent in their view that it would be an unmitigated disaster, as would any kind of world war.[62]

The change in the nature of the war that Soviet theory was addressing explains the paradox. The 1960s strategy assumed the nuclear devastation of Russia and that while "the whole system of capitalism would find its grave in such a war," the struggle for socialism would be immeasurably set back. Under the 1970s strategy, while there was a high probability that NATO would resort to nuclear weapons in Europe, the Soviets planned to spare North America and meanwhile to deter the United States from striking at the Soviet Union (see tables 2-1 and 2-2).[63]

---

59. *Pravda*, July 22, 1974, noted by Thomas Bjorknon and Thomas Zamostny in "Soviet Politics and Strategy towards the West: Three Cases," *World Politics*, no. 2 (January 1984), p. 202.

60. Light, *Soviet Theory*, p. 219, quoting A. S. Milovidov, ed., *Philosophical Heritage of V. I. Lenin and Problems of Contemporary War* (Moscow: Voenizdat, 1972), U.S. Air Force translation (U.S. Government Printing Office, 1977), pp. 17, 128. Light dates this quotation 1977, when the translation was published, rather than 1971, when the original book was typeset.

61. Stephen Shenfield, *The Nuclear Predicament: Explorations in Soviet Ideology*, Chatham House Paper 37 (London: Routledge and Kegan Paul, 1987), pp. 9–15.

62. See Peter H. Vigor, *The Soviet View of War, Peace, and Neutrality* (London: Routledge and Kegan Paul, 1975), pp. 127, 133, 159.

63. Milovidov, *Philosophical Heritage*, p. 127, refers to restraining influences on the use of imperialist nuclear weapons, "including the nuclear weapons in the possession of the USSR."

In 1970–71 the Soviets' optimism that they would be able to impose their strategy on NATO would have been at its height. The United States was still mired in Vietnam, politically and militarily, and the Soviets could not foresee the very different situation that could pertain in the second half of the 1970s, when their new strategy was to become fully operational. The contingency was still a world war in which nuclear weapons would be used, but it was quite different from what the Soviets had prepared for under the 1960s strategy, and there were grounds for hope that such a war would not "signify the irrevocable doom of mankind."[64]

Whatever hopes may have existed in the 1970s, the tenor of their statements at the beginning of the 1980s suggested that the Soviets were by then far less sanguine about avoiding intercontinental escalation.[65] At this time, however, the Soviets were responding to NATO's December 1979 decision to go ahead with the deployment of Euromissiles and the leaking in July 1980 of U.S. Presidential Directive (PD) 59.

In Soviet eyes, the Euromissiles provided the United States with the means to fight a nuclear war against Russia that would be limited to the European continent, while avoiding or at least minimizing nuclear destruction in the United States.[66] This conclusion was reinforced by PD 59, which set forth the basis of a "countervailing strategy" and reinforced the concept of "escalation dominance." The idea was to increase the U.S. capacity for proportional response and provide for multiple nuclear options that would allow controlled escalation.

Soviet commentators were emphatic that a war of that kind could not be kept limited but would inevitably escalate to include North America. At the Twenty-sixth Party Congress in February 1981 Brezhnev referred to PD 59 as intended "to make people believe that nuclear war can be

64. A. A. Shirman, "Social Activity of the Masses and the Defense of Socialism," in ibid., p. 128. It is relevant that Shirman writes of "the existence of sophisticated hardware making possible the annihilation of hundreds of millions of persons" but does not write about the use of this hardware. He also warns against ruling out the future possibility of antimissile defenses. This is all part of an argument against "nuclear fatalism" and is concerned to persuade military readers that if world war were unavoidable it would still be worth fighting and could be won. He does not contradict the new line that had been established by the beginning of the 1970s, aspects of which were articulated by Brezhnev at Tula in January 1977, when he denied that the Soviet Union sought strategic superiority.

65. See Mary C. FitzGerald, *Changing Soviet Doctrine on Nuclear War* (Halifax, Nova Scotia: Dalhousie University, Center for Foreign Policy Studies, 1988), pp. 33–42.

66. These points are based on the analyses by William V. Gardner, *Soviet Threat Perceptions of NATO's Eurostrategic Missiles* (Paris: Atlantic Institute for International Affairs, 1983), pp. 11–44, and Raymond L. Garthoff, "The Soviet SS-20 Decision," *Survival*, vol. 25 (May–June 1983), pp. 110–14.

kept limited" and dismissed the possibility that the United States could "remain untouched by the flames of war."[67] The assertion that a U.S. resort to nuclear weapons in Europe would inevitably escalate to a worldwide holocaust was repeated and echoed in numerous Soviet statements and articles.[68]

It seems likely that the primary purpose of this orchestrated outburst was to influence the domestic debate in the NATO nations on the wisdom of deploying Euromissiles, and also to discourage the United States from going farther down the road it had mapped out in PD 59.[69] The statements were certainly propagandistic because they implied that the Soviet Union would initiate strikes on North America. But any attack on the continental United States would precipitate a nuclear attack on the Soviet Union and ensure its devastation, and the primary objective of the 1970s strategy was to avoid the devastation of the USSR.

The Soviets' 1970s strategy was in fact predicated on being able to deter escalation from theater nuclear war. It was also hoped to prevent the resort to nuclear weapons in the theater, as much for reasons of operational advantage as the danger of escalation. Presidential Directive 59 made NATO's resort to nuclear weapons in Europe virtually inevitable and implied that limited nuclear strikes against targets in the Soviet Union were also likely.

In the late 1960s through the mid-1970s, the Soviets thought they had extricated themselves from the fatal trap of an inevitable nuclear exchange, should world war be unavoidable. They saw themselves as strategy setters, able to impose their conventional strategy on NATO and deter nuclear strikes on the USSR. But by the end of the decade this optimism was being undermined by developments in U.S. military doctrine and technological capability, while no alternative Soviet policy was in sight. Although Brezhnev noted in his report to the party congress in 1981 that "to count on victory in a nuclear war [is] dangerous madness," this denoted official acceptance that "victory" in a nuclear war was meaningless.[70] It begged the question of exactly what was meant

---

67. "Brezhnev's report," p. 15.

68. For a selection of references, see FitzGerald, *Changing Soviet Doctrine,* pp. 62–70.

69. The official justification for PD 59 was that the Soviets believed they could fight and win a nuclear war, were preparing to do so, and could only be deterred from initiating such a war by a comparable U.S. capability. This assessment was partly the result of combining the evidence of Soviet missile programs in the 1970s with doctrinal writings that were only relevant to the outdated 1960s strategy.

70. "Brezhnev's report," p. 16.

by nuclear war and whether, in the event of world war, escalation to massive nuclear strikes on the USSR could be avoided.

Despite these doubts, the peace program that had first been proclaimed in 1971 and then reaffirmed in 1976 was reaffirmed yet again in 1981, as was the importance of strengthening and deepening détente. And in November 1982, at his first plenum after being elected general secretary, Yuri Andropov reaffirmed the foreign policy line established by his predecessor, emphasized that détente would persist into the future and was not some passing phenomenon, and once again stressed the danger of the arms race.[71]

Meanwhile, the 1981 party congress had identified the arms race as the primary threat to peace, and curbing it had acquired a special significance and urgency. Rapid and profound changes were taking place in military technology, which would make it extremely difficult (if not impossible) to negotiate limits on such weapons. A new stage in the arms race would disrupt international stability and greatly intensify the danger of war.[72]

Washington's Political-Military Offensive

Although the Soviet leadership continued to hew to the foreign policy line established in 1971 and to assert that détente was still alive, it did acknowledge that Soviet-American relations had deteriorated and that East-West tension had risen along with the danger of war. Reviewing the international situation in the wake of Afghanistan, the June 1980 plenum noted that in the 1970s there had been an obvious abatement of the cold war, but "of late . . . aggressive imperial forces" were opposing the trend and the United States was seeking to change the existing military balance. The Central Committee was, however, confident that a slide toward a new cold war could be prevented.

At the party congress in 1981 the situation was described as an "intensive struggle of two trends in world politics," the U.S. line being to undermine détente and boost the arms race. In October 1982, speaking to the military leadership, Brezhnev noted that "two lines clash," the U.S. line being for deepening tension and arms racing. In June 1983, Andrey Gromyko spoke of "the confrontation of two lines"

71. *Kommunist,* no. 17 (November 1982), pp. 19–21.
72. "Brezhnev's report," pp. 5, 16, 18.

and at this same plenum Andropov described U.S. policy as being "extremely dangerous to mankind." And the plenum decree noted that "a sharp exacerbation of the struggle between the two social systems, two diametrically opposite world outlooks, a struggle unprecedented in the postwar period" was taking place.[73]

Until that forthright decree, the semantic adjustments to successive Soviet reviews of the international situation had been a pale reflection of deteriorating relations. The American mood had changed in the 1970s, anti-Soviet fervor had built up in the second half of the decade, President Carter's stance had hardened in the wake of the Ogaden war in 1977–78, and U.S. policy had changed direction after the Soviet invasion of Afghanistan.

A series of incidents during the last two years of the Carter administration, accompanied by rises in the U.S. defense budget of 3 percent and then 21.6 percent, fed Russian fears that the United States was determined to isolate the Soviet Union and was set on a path to regain clear-cut military superiority. First, Carter approved the MX missile program, one week before he signed the SALT II agreement in June 1979. Then the United States reacted to the rediscovery of a Soviet brigade that had been in Cuba since 1962 with what the Soviets saw as a trumped-up furor designed to prevent ratification of SALT II by the Senate. In October the United States announced that Secretary of Defense Harold Brown would visit China in January 1980, opening up the possibility of Sino-American cooperation in the military field. Early in 1980 the United States responded to the Soviet entry into Afghanistan in what Moscow perceived as an exaggerated way. And in July PD 59 was deliberately leaked to the press.

To the Soviet Union, its invasion of Afghanistan was a police action necessary to reestablish control within its national security zone. The Soviets viewed it as similar to their actions in Hungary and Czechoslovakia, which had been accepted, though with loud protests, by the West. Certainly the United States had never hesitated to use force in its national security zone. Yet the Carter administration had responded to the Soviet action in Afghanistan as if it was unprecedented. The Soviets suspected the United States of using Afghanistan as an excuse to take punitive measures against the Soviet Union and to justify the use of U.S. military

73. "Meeting of military leaders in the Kremlin," *Pravda,* October 28, 1982, p. 1; A. A. Gromyko, *Pravda,* June 17, 1983, pp. 2–3; *Kommunist,* no. 9 (June 1983), pp. 5, 40.

power in Southwest Asia, which Brzezinski had defined as an arc of crisis.

In many ways, PD 59 provided the logical framework that gave coherence to much of the other evidence. It set forth a "countervailing strategy" based on a U.S. war-fighting capability which, it was claimed, would enhance nuclear deterrence. Considering the massive capabilities already available to the United States, the Soviets would have dismissed the deterrence explanation and focused on the aspects of PD 59 describing the U.S. capability for war fighting.

Within that framework the weapons programs authorized during the Carter administration took on an ominous cast. The new Minuteman warhead, the intercontinental MX missile, the D-5 missile to be carried by the new Trident II submarine were all destined to possess a counterforce capability, while the Pershing II, with its short time of flight and thirty-meter accuracy, could be used for "decapitation" strikes against the Soviet leadership. Around the Soviet Union the United States intended to deploy thousands of cruise missiles that would be able to destroy hard targets.

The origins of the presidential directive were equally worrying. The directive was presented as a refinement and elaboration of the 1974 Schlesinger doctrine. In other words, the reevaluation had been under way for at least six years, thus casting doubts on the nature of U.S. objectives at the strategic arms limitation talks. Ostensiby, the SALT process aimed at reducing weapons inventories on both sides. But in SALT I a cap had been placed on the Soviet missile buildup, at no cost to U.S. programs. In SALT II the number of Soviet ICBMs had been reduced, while the United States had increased its capability of striking at the USSR with systems that were not constrained by the agreements.

From Bad to Worse

Jimmy Carter was followed by President Ronald Reagan, who strongly distrusted arms control and had campaigned on the promise to restore American military superiority in order to negotiate from a position of strength. Reagan's first administration was characterized by an unmitigated and vituperative hostility toward the Soviet Union. Three interlocking themes ran through its rhetoric.[74]

74. Alexander Dallin and Gail W. Lapidus, "Reagan and the Russians: United States Policy toward the Soviet Union and Eastern Europe," in Kenneth A. Oye, Robert J. Lieber, and Donald Rothchild, eds., *Eagle Defiant: United States Foreign Policy in the 1980s*

One was the assumption that Soviet communism was a political aberration and an evil that was not only destined to fail but should be made to fail. Another was the idea that an important function of the U.S. arms buildup was to force an arms race on Russia that would break its economy. Third was the concept of a "crusade for freedom." This crusade, Reagan told the British Parliament in June 1982, was to assist all people living under Marxist-Leninist regimes, including those in the Soviet Union.[75]

In other words, the Reagan administration denied the legitimacy of the Soviet state and was set on undermining it, one way or another. The American people were bombarded with the idea of a "relentless Soviet expansion" that would have to be checked with military force if necessary.[76] The Soviets had an "increasing proclivity to support change . . . by rule of force, by bloodshed, terrorism, so-called wars of liberation."[77]

There was also a distinct change in tone as senior officials talked about the likelihood of war. The idea of an inevitable conflict with the Soviet Union emerged for the first time since the 1950s,[78] prompting a surge in peace and antinuclear movements throughout the West. In May 1982 the gist of American military policy for 1984–85 contained in the U.S.

(Little, Brown, 1983), pp. 191–236, provide a good impression of how outside observers, including foreign policy analysts in Moscow, would have perceived Ronald Reagan's policies. In describing the ideological makeup of the U.S. administration, Dallin and Lapidus distinguish between three main perspectives on the Soviet Union. Essentialists saw the Soviet Union as inherently evil, bent on expansion and with no concern for world order. Mechanists saw the USSR primarily as a geopolitical threat that must be met with countervailing force. And interactionists recognized the U.S. role in Soviet policy and viewed the world in multipolar terms. In the Reagan administration, essentialists were represented in unprecedented force.

75. "Address to Members of Parliament," June 8, 1982, *Weekly Compilation of Presidential Documents*, vol. 18 (June 14, 1982), p. 768. In 1981 Richard Pipes, the senior Soviet specialist on the National Security Council staff, had asserted, "Soviet leaders would have to choose between peacefully changing their Communist system . . . or going to war." This statement was repudiated by the administration ("U.S. Repudiates a Hard-Line Aide," *New York Times*, March 19, 1981).

76. George C. Wilson, "Weinberger, in His First Message, Says Mission Is to Rearm America," *Washington Post*, January 23, 1981.

77. Secretary Alexander M. Haig, interviewed for the *Wall Street Journal*, reported in *Department of State Bulletin*, vol. 81, no. 2054 (GPO, 1981), p. 25.

78. In October 1981 Major General Robert L. Schweitzer, the military assistant to the national security adviser, was reassigned after making unauthorized comments that there was "a drift toward war," that the Soviets were "on the move" and "were going to strike" ("Security Adviser Ousted for Talk Hinting at War," *New York Times*, October 21, 1981). Although Schweitzer's statements were extreme, the assumption was widespread in military circles that strategic parity would prompt the Soviets into military adventures that would lead to conflict. See, for example, Fred Hiatt, "Limited War Held 'Almost Inevitable,'" *Washington Post*, June 22, 1984.

Defense Guidance was leaked to the press.[79] Among other things, the document reaffirmed the PD 59 policy of being able to prevail in a protracted nuclear war and established a decapitation strategy aimed at Soviet political and military command, control, and communications systems. It called for development of space-based weapons and research on other new weaponry and for development of special forces for use in Eastern Europe. Maximum economic pressure would be put on the Soviet Union through trade policies and denial of advanced technology, and new weapons would be introduced with the idea of making Soviet inventories obsolete.

A year later, after a period in which the war in Lebanon and mid-term congressional elections had preoccupied Americans, a series of developments reaffirmed the stark thrust of Reagan's policies. In late March of 1983 the president announced that the United States would develop a space-based system for defense against ballistic missiles. The strategic defense initiative (SDI) was further evidence that the United States was not interested in arms control but was seeking military superiority. One of the more influential U.S. groups advocating the move into space was explicit that its objective was "to implement a basic change in U.S. grand strategy and make a technological end-run on the Soviets."[80]

Two weeks before Reagan unveiled the SDI in his "Star Wars" speech, he had described the Soviet leadership as "the focus of evil in the modern world" and the Soviet bloc as "an evil empire" and he had also implied that the Soviet Union was comparable to Nazi Germany.[81] In June Secretary of State Shultz was reported as saying that changing the internal system of the Soviet Union was a U.S. objective, seeming to confirm the reported existence of a presidential directive to that effect. In August, the U.S. administration greeted with skepticism and disinterest a revised draft treaty on weapons in space submitted by the Soviet Union to the United Nations.[82]

79. Richard Halloran, *New York Times,* May 30, 1982.
80. Daniel O. Graham, *The High Frontier: A New National Strategy* (Washington, D.C.: High Frontier, 1982), p. ix.
81. "National Association of Evangelicals," Remarks at the Annual Convention, March 8, 1983, *Weekly Compilation of Presidential Documents,* vol. 19 (March 14, 1983), p. 369.
82. Dan Oberdorfer, "Shultz Outlines Policy of Opposing Soviets," *Washington Post,* June 16, 1983; *United States–Soviet Relations,* Hearings before the Senate Committee on Foreign Relations, 98 Cong. 1 sess. (GPO, 1983), pt. 1, p. 5. The substance of the presidential directive was somewhat more moderate than reports implied, but the Soviet Union was not to know that. The Soviet draft space treaty included proposals for the control of antisatellite

With the shooting down of a Korean airliner by a Soviet aircraft shortly after the airliner flew over Soviet Sakhalin at the beginning of September 1983, relations worsened. The Soviets were unpersuaded that the aircraft's wanderings were accidental and were convinced that they had been set up by the United States. Three weeks later, Vice President George Bush, in a tough policy address in Vienna, offered political and economic support to countries such as Hungary and Romania (which he had just visited) if they distanced themselves from the Soviet Union. He also rejected any acceptance of the status quo in Eastern Europe.[83]

Bush also insulted historical Russia, and denied its European roots. He noted that it had missed out on the three great events of European history: the Renaissance, the Reformation, and the Enlightenment. And he spoke of "brutal murder" when he referred to the Korean airliner incident. He was echoing Reagan, who had spoken of a "terrorist act," an "inexcusable act of brutality," and an "act of barbarism" that was "inexplicable to civilized people everywhere."[84] It could be inferred that the White House considered the Russians essentially uncivilized, and the rhetoric implied that the focus of all evil was as much Russia as its Marxist-Leninist form of government.

Enough Is Enough

In the arms control negotiations on intermediate nuclear forces and strategic arms reductions, the United States' approach offered little hope that the Reagan administration's verbal assaults were just rhetoric. On the contrary, deeply entrenched beliefs seemed to be structuring objectives, shaping policy, and animating action. The administration had been able to gain congressional support for a large and sustained

weapons, which took account of the critical comments by notable American scientists on the 1981 Soviet draft treaty (Richard L. Garwin, Kurt Gottfried, and Donald L. Hafner, "Antisatellite Weapons," *Scientific American,* vol. 250 [June 1984], p. 53).

83. George Bush explicitly rejected the acceptance of the status quo in Europe, which the Soviets saw as the key element in the 1974 Helsinki accords. Citing Hungary and Romania, Bush said that the United States would improve "political, economic and cultural relations" with Eastern European countries that asserted greater independence from Moscow. "Bush: U.S. Will Aid Maverick Soviet Bloc States," *Washington Post,* September 22, 1983.

84. See "Soviet Attack on Korean Civilian Airliner," Remarks to Reporters, September 2, 1983, *Weekly Compilation of Presidential Documents,* vol. 19 (September 12, 1983), pp. 1193, 1197, 1199–1200.

defense buildup at the cost of domestic programs. Clearly, the people supported Reagan's moves to restore American strength and adopt a more assertive foreign policy.

The outward response of the Politburo to the Reagan administration's political offensive was one of patience. By the end of September 1983 the Soviet leaders had endured thirty-two months of "the most aggressive anti-Soviet and anti-Communist rhetoric in 25 years, backed by record [U.S.] defense budgets, an uncompromising stance in nuclear arms control negotiations, and the highly visible commitment of American power to the Middle East and Central America."[85] The U.S. secretary of state was amazed that they had "stayed very, very moderate, very, very responsible."[86] However, the Soviets had already embarked on a review of their foreign and defense policy that would carry through into 1984.

85. Coit D. Blacker, "The United States and the Soviet Union," *Current History,* vol. 83 (October 1984), p. 310.
86. Roy Gutman, *Newsday,* August 12, 1984.

CHAPTER 5

The 1983–84 Reappraisal

DESPITE the steady deterioration in East-West relations and in the Soviet Union's world standing, the aging Soviet leadership was clearly reluctant to jettison the tenets underlying the 1971 peace program. In recommending that Yuri Andropov be elected general secretary in November 1982, Konstantin Chernenko expressed the Politburo's confidence that he would continue Leonid Brezhnev's style of leadership and that he had a "predilection for collective work." And on taking office Andropov found it politic to reaffirm the twelve-year-old foreign policy line.

Ronald Reagan's speech in March 1983 announcing the strategic defense initiative (SDI) appears to have provided the grounds for questioning that line. In his report to the party congress in 1981 Brezhnev had stressed the emerging danger of a qualitatively new stage of the arms race and the importance of strategic parity in ensuring peace. The SDI was a clear bid to restore U.S. strategic superiority. It required the emplacement of strike weapons in space and that the ABM Treaty be abrogated. It directly challenged key assumptions underlying the 1971 peace program.[1]

Following the Star Wars speech there was a radical shift in the tone of Soviet internal propaganda and, for the first time since Stalin's death, the threat of war rather than the likelihood of avoiding war became Moscow's dominant theme.[2] Andropov dropped the conciliatory tone he had adopted on taking office and by April was accusing the United

---

1. The significance of Reagan's Star Wars speech as a catalyst in Soviet foreign policy is implied by the emphasis that Gorbachev placed from the start of his leadership on the dangers of a qualitatively new stage in the arms race and the need to prevent an arms race in space.

2. Vladimir E. Shlapentokh, "Moscow's War Propaganda and Soviet Public Opinion," *Problems of Communism*, vol. 33 (September–October 1984), pp. 89, 91–92.

States of seeking military superiority, including the capability for a disarming strike, and of having a flippant attitude toward the issue of peace and war.[3]

At the plenum in June Foreign Minister Andrey A. Gromyko spoke of "the confrontation of two lines," hardening the position he had taken in an article written before Reagan's speech. Andropov noted that an "unprecedented sharpening of the struggle" between the two social systems had taken place. He went on to say that the "threat of nuclear war overhanging mankind causes one to reappraise the principal goals of the activities of the entire communist movement."[4] Thereafter no senior Soviet official spoke out in detail on relations with Washington until September 28,[5] when Andropov made a formal declaration in his capacity as general secretary of the Communist party and chairman of the Presidium of the Supreme Soviet of the USSR.[6]

In the West, the full significance of the declaration was missed because the shooting down of the Korean airliner at the beginning of September still dominated the news, and this was Andropov's first major statement since the incident. Although he made some reference to the matter, it was not the reason for the declaration, which reflected a new evaluation that had been gestating for some time.[7] The declaration had an "electrifying and sobering effect" on the Soviet people, and its content and style of presentation implied a major break with the foreign policy line that had endured for twelve years.[8]

It is likely that President Reagan's strategic defense initiative had

3. "Replies by Yuri V. Andropov to Questions from a Correspondent of Pravda," *Pravda,* March 27, 1983, p. 1; "Replies by Yuri V. Andropov to the Journal *Spiegel,*" *Pravda,* April 25, 1983, pp. 1–2.

4. *Pravda,* June 17, 1983, pp. 2–3; A. A. Gromyko, "V. I. Lenin and the Foreign Policy of the Soviet State," *Kommunist,* no. 6 (April 1983), pp. 11–32; "Speech of the General Secretary of the CC [of the] CPSU Comrade Yuri V. Andropov," *Kommunist,* no. 9 (June 1983), p. 13.

5. Coit D. Blacker, "The United States and the Soviet Union," *Current History,* vol. 83 (October 1984), p. 313.

6. The mode of presentation was unprecedented in recent years, perhaps because Andropov was too sick to appear in public. The statement was read on television and radio on September 28 and published in a front-page article headlined "DECLARATION . . . of Yuri V. Andropov" in *Pravda,* September 29, 1983.

7. Personal communication from Raymond L. Garthoff, of Brookings, who was in Moscow at the time the declaration was published; a member of the Central Committee conveyed this information to him.

8. Personal communication from Garthoff. A regional party chief told Garthoff that after a local party meeting convened to discuss the declaration, several women asked if it meant their sons would have to go to war.

tilted the balance in favor of those in Moscow who had been arguing that the established foreign policy line was no longer serving the interests of the world socialist movement. By June the need for a special foreign policy review had probably been accepted. None had been carried out since the review in the first half of 1980 in response to the redirection of U.S. policy following the Soviets' entry into Afghanistan, and that review had reaffirmed the correctness of the established line.

The review in the summer of 1983, it can be inferred, concluded that the existing line was no longer tenable and that it would be necessary to "reappraise the basic purport of the activities of the entire communist movement," as Andropov had predicted in June. The September declaration was, therefore, a decision-in-principle. Normally such decisions lead to a series of policy prescriptions and implementing decisions, the more important of which emerge from futher analysis and debate.[9]

The essence of Andropov's declaration was that the United States had launched a crusade against socialism and was bent on military domination, that there was no possibility that the U.S. administration would change its ways, and that the Soviet Union would respond as necessary to any attempt to disrupt the existing military balance.

Six weeks later Minister of Defense Dmitriy F. Ustinov gave a structured analysis of U.S. objectives to a special gathering of generals, admirals, and other officers.[10] His presentation echoed less formal assessments by Marshal Aleksey A. Yepishev, Marshal Nikolay V. Ogarkov, and himself during the summer. All concluded that the United States, with the rest of the capitalist bloc trailing along more or less willingly, had embarked on a crusade against communism and was determined to eliminate socialism as a sociopolitical system.[11]

According to the marshals, it was this objective that drove the economic, political, ideological, and military policies of the United States. These policies pursued three main lines of attack: (1) a sustained attempt to achieve military superiority, including the capability for a

9. "Speech of the General Secretary of the CC," p. 13. If the process of coming to such a decision is pictured as a wave form, the rear slope represents the period when perceptions of the need for change are building to a decision-in-principle at the crest, and the front slope represents the following series of implementing decisions. See app. A.

10. "For High Combat Readiness," *KZ*, November 12, 1983, p. 3 (see Abbreviations of Frequently Cited Sources).

11. A. A. Yepishev, "A Historic Milestone in the Peoples' Destinies," *KZ*, May 9, 1983, pp. 1–2; "At the Level of the Party's Demands," *KZ*, June 22, 1983, p. 2; "Reliable Defense for Peace," *Izvestiya*, September 23, 1983, in *FBIS*-83-186, pp. AA1–6.

disarming first strike, and a determination to break the military balance between East and West; (2) a general militarization of the international arena, drawing more nations into the U.S. military orbit and encouraging them to build up their forces, while steadily increasing the scale, scope, and global diversity of U.S. military exercises; and (3) a massive "psychological" attack against the socialist community aimed at preparing the people of the capitalist bloc for the possibility of military action against socialist states and at subverting the peoples of the socialist bloc.

Policy pronouncements, budgetary decisions, and the operational behavior of the United States, all provided concrete evidence of these three lines of attack. And to those who argued that this assessment ignored the complexities of the American political system and the ability of Congress and public opinion to hold the executive branch in check, it could be pointed out that one of the striking characteristics of the Reagan administration had been its ability to get its way. This reflected the fact that the American people were basically anti-Soviet, and that they therefore approved of a confrontational policy as long as it did not actually lead to war.

The U.S. policies posed a serious threat to the Soviet Union's three first-order national objectives.[12] First, the retention of power by the Communist party was being threatened by the massive psychological attack. Second, Soviet independence of international action was being undermined by the U.S. attempt to reestablish military superiority and by the prospective U.S. capability for a disarming strike, accompanied by a more active geopolitical policy. And third, the avoidance of world war had been made more difficult by the shift from détente to confrontation; by the steadily increasing scale, scope, and diversity of U.S. military exercises and operational deployments; and by the general militarization of the international arena, drawing in ever more countries to the U.S. military orbit and encouraging them to build up their military strength.[13]

Issues in Debate

The review carried out during the summer of 1983 put in doubt the appropriateness of policies pursued by the Soviet Union in the 1970s.

12. MccGwire, *Military Objectives,* pp. 37–39.
13. These are Ustinov's descriptions of U.S. policy in "For High Combat Readiness."

Over the next six to nine months, a fundamental "reappraisal of the basic purport of the activities of the whole communist movement" was undertaken.

A number of operational questions that were important at the time turned out to have no long-term significance. They concerned the imminence of world war in 1983–84 and whether or not it was in the Soviet interest to continue negotiating with the United States.[14] The more fundamental questions involved Marxist-Leninist theory and came under the general headings of the correlation of forces and the danger of world war. Those aspects of the reappraisal can only be postulated because they were overtaken by Gorbachev's new political thinking. But Soviet criticism of past approaches to foreign policy that began to be articulated in 1987 provides evidence of issues that were evaded and decisions not made in 1983–84.

All of the questions addressed were more or less interdependent and the underlying issues were entangled. The reappraisal would have been permeated by the Soviet establishment's resentment toward the United States and anger at the way the Soviet Union was being treated by the Reagan administration. Reagan's rhetoric disparaged the USSR's national culture as well as its social system and depicted the Soviet Union as both threatening to take over the world and bound for the ash heap of history.

But the Soviets also had substantive reasons to be angry. Détente, a relationship that had been the cornerstone of Soviet foreign and domestic policy for fifteen years and represented a major political investment, had been ruptured. At the same time, Reagan's policies had increased the danger of war in the short term; and in the longer term the strategic defense initiative would open a Pandora's box with unforeseeable consequences. Meanwhile, these and other negative developments threatened the economic well-being of the Soviet Union and its people.

The Imminence of War

The Soviets distinguish between the military threat and the danger of war. In 1983 few Soviets would have disagreed with the proposition that

14. On various military-technical debates such as the proper balance between nuclear and conventional forces, the threat from emerging technologies, and the need for revolutionary rather than evolutionary change that are not germane to this analysis, see Mary C. FitzGerald, *Changing Soviet Doctrine on Nuclear War* (Halifax, Nova Scotia: Dalhousie University, Center for Foreign Policy Studies, 1989); Rose E. Gottemoeller, *Conflict and Consensus in the Soviet Armed Forces,* R3759AF (Santa Monica, Calif.: Rand Corp., October 1989); Dale

the military threat to the USSR had increased over the previous five years and had to be responded to. The more contentious question was the extent to which the danger of war had increased. If war was imminent, the Soviet Union should move its economy to a war footing and adopt an intransigent international demeanor, both to deter and to avoid conceding anything to the enemy. On the other hand, if the likelihood of war had increased, but it was still not imminent, then precipitous action would achieve the worst of all worlds. Of itself, moving to a war footing would increase the danger of war and might prompt competitive mobilization. It would certainly damage the domestic economy while denying the military the future fruit of ripening research and development. It would force the USSR to forgo the potential gains of negotiations.

Marshal Ogarkov, chief of the General Staff, had been pressing the more alarmist view for some time. In 1981, following a pessimistic review of U.S. policies, he wrote of the need for an improved war mobilization capability and concluded by stressing the seriousness of the international situation and the danger of war.[15] And although the official depiction of the danger of war became sharply more pessimistic at the end of March 1983, Ogarkov continued to be more outspoken on this score than his political masters.[16]

The argument was one of degree and about competing claims on resources. There is little doubt that the Soviet political leadership considered that war had become significantly more likely and had taken certain precautionary measures. In 1981, the KGB (the Committee on State Security) had been required to divert additional assets into monitoring warning indicators of possible Western attack.[17] The length of political warning time appears to have been reduced between 1981 and 1984, and after the deployment of Euromissiles in December 1983 some, if not all, Soviet armed forces were placed on a higher level of day-to-day readiness.[18]

In April 1984 General Secretary Konstantin Chernenko found it necessary to reassure the Soviet people that the danger of war was not serious enough to justify extending the five-day work week, implying

R. Herspring, "Nikolay Ogarkov and the Scientific-Technical Revolution in Soviet Military Affairs," *Comparative Strategy,* vol. 6, no. 1 (1987).

15. N. Ogarkov, "Guarding Peaceful Labor," *Kommunist,* no. 10 (July 1981), pp. 80–91.

16. Dale R. Herspring, *The Soviet High Command, 1967–1989: Personalities and Politics* (Princeton University Press, 1990), chap. 6.

17. Murrey Marder, *Washington Post,* August 8, 1986, p. A1.

18. See p. 391 (text related to fn. 24).

that other influential leaders felt that more far-reaching measures were required, including a six-day week.[19] But by July it appears that the issue had been resolved, and in early September Ogarkov was relieved of his position as first deputy minister of defense and chief of the General Staff.

Press statements at the time of Ogarkov's removal, and his assignment as the commander-in-chief of the newly formed Western theater of military action (TVD), clarified certain aspects of the debate. Although it would be necessary to divert additional resources to strengthening the country's security, the broad social programs that had been outlined by the 1981 party congress would not be curtailed.[20] The military was put firmly in its place regarding the allocation of resources. Its operational concerns, however, were addressed directly by setting up in peacetime the high commands that would be needed in the event of war. The alarmists had lost on the matter of economic mobilization for war, but they had won on the question of operational readiness for war.

The guns or butter argument was of course nothing new. It went back to the earliest days of the Soviet state, and its salience steadily increased following the 1956 doctrinal revision that war with the capitalist bloc was no longer fatalistically inevitable. Nor had the Soviet military received everything it asked for, as demonstrated repeatedly over the years.[21] However, the security of the Soviet Union still ranked high as a national priority that was accepted by the people at large. Given the general perception that both the threat and the danger of war had increased, in 1983–84 there would have been considerable support throughout the political establishment for improving the Soviet Union's preparedness for war. There remained the questions of the best way of achieving this state and what resources should be shifted to the defense sector at the expense of the domestic economy. Those arguments would have been merged with the broader debate over improving the efficiency of the Soviet economy.

Doubts about Dialogue

Since 1980, if not earlier, a growing body of opinion has supported the argument that détente and diplomacy were dead and that Soviet

19. *Pravda,* April 30, 1984, pp. 1–2.
20. "For Soviet Man," *Pravda,* September 5, 1984, p. 1; "For the Good of the People," *KZ,* September 6, 1984, p. 1.
21. See, for example, MccGwire, *Military Objectives,* apps. B, D.

interests would be best served by a "unilaterist" approach.[22] After September 1983 adherents of the "diplomatist" side of the debate were forced to abandon many of their original positions as hopelessly optimistic. The parameters of the debate moved sharply toward obduracy, with the constituents on the two sides remaining roughly the same. In the overlapping arguments about dialogue and the imminence of war, opinion then divided between "tough negotiators" and "intransigent alarmists."

The intransigent alarmists included those who argued that the conciliatory posture adopted during the previous three years (and duly noted by Alexander Haig, the U.S. secretary of state)[23] had worked against the Soviet Union's interest and emboldened the United States. There were also those who believed that more should be done to prepare for war, such as shifting additional resources and assembly lines from civil to military production, increasing the number of shifts worked, and improving the readiness of army divisions.

It seems that neither the negotiators nor the alarmists considered a conciliatory approach appropriate in the short term. The Soviets' response to the deployment of Euromissiles was to withdraw from the negotiations on intermediate-range nuclear forces (INF) and to make offsetting deployments on their own. They also reduced Soviet-American contacts and business to a trickle.[24]

In June 1984, doubts in the U.S. Congress about the arms control implications of testing the U.S. antisatellite (ASAT) system provided a crucial opening for those in Moscow who favored negotiation. The United States' ASAT program was important because of the inherent relationship of such programs to space-based defense systems and the opportunity it offered the United States for evading the provisions of the Antiballistic Missile (ABM) Treaty. Halting the development of the U.S. antisatellite system was therefore a high priority Soviet objective, both in its own right and as a means of checking the momentum behind the strategic defense initiative.[25] On June 29 the Soviets proposed that the

22. Dan L. Strode and Rebecca V. Strode, "Diplomacy and Defense in Soviet National Security Policy," *International Security,* vol. 8 (Fall 1983), pp. 91–116.

23. Roy Gutman, *Newsday,* August 12, 1984.

24. Personal communication from Garthoff. He was told by knowledgeable Soviet officials that the decision to withdraw from the negotiations, and to take offsetting deployments and publicize them, was finally taken in November 1983.

25. The Soviets' own antisatellite program, which had been under way since 1967, was much more primitive and had virtually no potential for ballistic-missile defense.

two sides should meet to discuss how to prevent the militarization of space by banning the testing or deployment of antisatellite and other weapons. The process of reestablishing a dialogue had begun;[26] ultimately it would lead to the nuclear and space talks (NST) that got under way in March 1985.[27]

The intransigent alarmists could still argue that the United States was not prepared to negotiate in good faith and that any discussions would be manipulated to Soviet disadvantage in world opinion. This contention was reinforced by President Reagan's speech to the Irish Parliament, also in June 1984, in which he recalled the appeal he made for "a crusade for freedom" when he had addressed the British Parliament two years previously. Further support for the alarmists' point of view was provided by the Republican platform adopted in August 1984, which stressed the need for U.S. military superiority. And in September, a Central Intelligence Agency memorandum was leaked that concluded that the Soviet empire had "entered its terminal phase."[28]

The intransigent alarmists could not, however, deny the vital importance of derailing the strategic defense initiative, an objective that justified incurring significant diplomatic costs, and by July their case had been lost. The alarmists' political leverage had derived mainly from the thrust and urgency of their arguments about the danger of war, rather than from high-level support in the Politburo. The main strength of this viewpoint lay in its support by the military, who had a legitimate concern about the core issues and contributed their professional authority.

The Correlation of Forces: Soviet-U.S. Relations

Soviet policy toward the United States was shaped to some extent by prevailing views of the nature of the U.S. policy process and its

26. On June 11 Konstantin Chernenko reaffirmed the Soviet Union's continued adherence to the unilateral moratorium on ASAT testing declared by Andropov ten months earlier. This move elicited a vote in the U.S. House of Representatives to block ASAT testing for a year. Paul B. Stares, *The Militarization of Space: U.S. Policy, 1945–84* (Cornell University Press, 1985), pp. 233–34.

27. See Franklyn Griffiths, "The Soviet Experience of Arms Control," *International Journal* (Canada), vol. 44 (Spring 1989), pp. 341–54.

28. "CIA Says Soviets in Terminal Phase," *Washington Times*, September 21, 1984. In August, on the fortieth anniversary of the Warsaw uprising, Reagan had declared that the United States would not accept "the permanent subjection of the people of Eastern Europe" and rejected "any interpretation of the Yalta agreement that suggests American consent for the division of Europe into spheres of influence."

underlying power structure. These views reflected four competing images of the nature of capitalism and its capacity to adapt to changing circumstances. The dominance of one or other of these images can explain which of the four main tendencies in Soviet foreign policy prevailed at any particular period.[29]

At one extreme was the view that prevailed in the Stalin era, which advocates frontal opposition to U.S. policies, high levels of defense preparedness, a readiness to repress counterrevolutionary activities within the socialist camp, and a policy that does not differentiate between members of the capitalist camp. Because the dictatorship of the proletariat is impossible without the economic collapse of capitalism, this view advocates an active policy to deny capitalism access to markets and raw materials in the third world.

At the other extreme is a view that was relatively underrepresented and largely academic throughout the Brezhnev era. Building on ideas advanced by Evgeniy S. Varga in the postwar years, this view notes that capitalism has not evolved exactly as Marx predicted. It envisages a substantially modified form of U.S. imperialism, where aggressiveness is not an inevitable corollary, and a form of capitalism where the state acts as regulator and arbiter of differences within the ruling class and between capital and labor. In this view the principal goal of Soviet foreign policy should be to ensure general peace and avoid nuclear war, in order to allow the internal reform and democratization of Soviet socialism.

In between these extremes lay the two tendencies that have shaped Soviet foreign policy since Stalin's death. They differ in how they see imperialism and the relationship between the two social systems, but the two views have coexisted. The harder "expansionist" line, however, has tended to prevail. Its view is that it is not imperialism that has changed but the conditions of its existence, which constrain imperialist behavior. This implied that Soviet policy should reinforce those constraints by matching the U.S. military capability, by using détente

---

29. Franklyn Griffiths successfully links the relative salience of these images in the Soviet literature with the dominant tendency in Soviet foreign policy since 1922 ("The Sources of American Conduct: Soviet Perspectives and Their Policy Implications," *International Security*, vol. 9 [Fall 1984], pp. 3–50). Analyzing the attitudes of Soviet elites in 1973, Dina Rome Spechler identifies three images of U.S.-Soviet relations which are roughly similar to three of Griffiths's four main tendencies ("The USSR and Third World Conflicts: Domestic Debates and Soviet Policy in the Middle East, 1967–73," *World Politics*, vol. 38 [April 1986], pp. 447–50).

to accentuate divisions between and within Western countries, by encouraging revolutionary change in the third world, and by generally working to contain and isolate the United States. The focus is not on Soviet-American bilateral relations as such, but on accelerating the favorable trend in the correlation of forces.

The softer, "reformative" line sees change in imperialist policies as reflecting a new realism that needs to be reinforced by Soviet policies that encourage American moderation and the stabilization of political and military relations. The emphasis was on avoiding nuclear war and moving the competition into economic and ideological channels. Soviet diplomacy is not only concerned to structure the external environment of U.S. policymaking, but also to modify American public opinion.

This spectrum of views would have been represented in the internal debate that accompanied the reappraisal of the world communist movement's policies, with the largely discredited Stalinist view gaining new currency (see figure 5-1). The debate would have been influenced by the more immediate preoccupation with the imminence of world war and the advisability of negotiating with the United States. The less ideological, cooperative viewpoint would have been largely ignored in the angry and resentful mood of 1983–84.

The scope for debate was almost endless, but the Soviets would have had to address three interrelated questions: why had détente failed; was détente in the Soviet interest; and what relationship with the United States should the Soviets seek in the future? And in considering why the optimistic projection made in 1971–73 had failed so miserably, the Soviets would have had to consider, explicitly or not, whether the reasons lay in mistaken Soviet policies, in unalterable U.S. policies, in a misreading of the world scene, or in some combination of the three.

Why Did Détente Fail?

In the 1970s it was regularly asserted that détente had been made possible by the increasingly favorable trend in the correlation of forces, which had compelled the capitalists to finally accept the concept of strategic parity and peaceful coexistence. Did the failure of détente mean that the assessment of the situation in 1969–70 had been too optimistic, resulting in a premature turn to détente, and that it was only necessary to wait for a further improvement in the correlation of forces for sustained détente to be possible? Or was the long-term trend in the correlation of

Figure 5-1. *The Dominant Ideological View Shaping Foreign Policy, 1971–89*

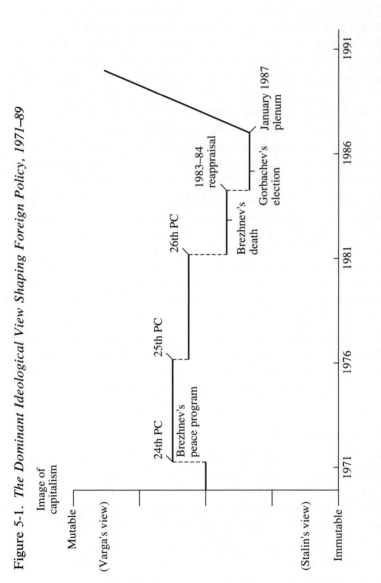

Source: This impressionistic curve, showing successive changes in the dominant image of capitalism and hence in Soviet policy toward the United States, draws on the concepts analysis of Franklyn Griffiths, "The Sources of American Conduct," *International Security*, vol. 9 (Fall 1984), pp. 3–50.

forces not as favorable as had been assumed? Had the crisis of capitalism been exaggerated so that the Soviets could not just sit and wait for capitalism to fail but must take more vigorous action to improve the strength of the communist system?

Alternatively, had the calculation of the correlation of forces been correct but the Reagan administration so blinded by anticommunism that it was unable to draw "realistic" conclusions from the objective situation? Or perhaps the problem lay in the Leninist concept of peaceful coexistence, which was limited to the military sphere and specifically excluded the ideological struggle, where the principle of irreconcilability still pertained.[30]

It seems likely that the reappraisal in 1983–84 would have placed the main blame for the failure of détente on the abiding anti-Sovietism of certain sectors of American opinion, on the innate imperialism of U.S. capitalism, and on a failure of realism in Washington, perhaps coupled with the conclusion that the correlation of forces had not in fact been favorable enough to compel the United States to accept détente.

The Soviets were probably not ready to admit that they had overestimated the speed with which the influence of socialism would spread and had underestimated the ability of capitalism to adapt to new conditions.[31] Clearly, the leadership was not prepared to jettison the original concept of peaceful coexistence, with its emphasis on the ideological struggle. However, the reformulation of established international relations theory that got under way in 1987, including criticism of peaceful coexistence as then defined, suggests that the concept was challenged in 1983–84.[32]

In this respect it is noteworthy that in his September 1983 declaration Andropov had asserted that "the transfer of ideological conflict to the sphere of relations between states has never benefited the one who resorted to it in external affairs."[33] While this was nominally directed at the Reagan administration's ideological onslaught, it applied equally to the Soviet concept of peaceful coexistence.

30. A. S. Milovidov and V. G. Kozlov, eds., *The Philosophical Heritage of V. I. Lenin and Problems of Contemporary War* (Moscow: Voenizdat, 1972), U.S. Air Force translation (U.S. Government Printing Office, 1977), p. 217.

31. This began to be admitted publicly in 1987. See, for example, E. G. Plimak, *Voprosy filosofii (Questions of Philosophy)*, no. 6 (June 1987), p. 87; Aleksandr Bovin, *Izvestiya,* July 11, 1987, in *FBIS*-87-137, pp. R17–22.

32. See, for example, Ye. Primakov, *Pravda,* July 9, 1987, in *FBIS*-87-134, pp. CC5–10; he describes the traditional interpretation of peaceful coexistence as "clearly inadequate and inaccurate."

33. *Pravda,* September 29, 1983.

Is Détente in the Interest of World Communism?

Even assuming that détente could be reestablished, was that necessarily in the interest of the Soviet Union and world communism? There had always been a contradiction between the concepts of peaceful coexistence and the international class struggle, and peaceful coexistence could not help but delay the world revolution. While peace provided the most favorable conditions for building socialism, it also provided the conditions under which capitalism could consolidate itself, and it could be argued (as did the Chinese communists in the 1950s) that peaceful coexistence implied selling out to capitalism. The counterargument was that it was history that would destroy capitalism; meanwhile peaceful coexistence allowed socialism to outpace capitalism.[34]

The peaceful coexistence of the two social systems was a sine qua non in a nuclear world, but that did not necessarily imply Soviet-American détente. By definition, détente imposed constraints on Soviet behavior that in the past had incurred costs in terms of opportunities forgone, while the restraint itself went unrewarded. Soviet restraint in the Greek civil war in the latter 1940s had not prevented the Soviets from being portrayed as the instigators, justifying the Truman Doctrine, containment, and the move to cold war. Soviet restraint in the western hemisphere in the 1970s had not prevented the Soviets from being blamed for the various upheavals in Central and South America.

It could be argued that the 1970s détente had brought problems at home and few benefits abroad. At the height of détente Salvador Allende was brought down in Chile, the United States achieved rapprochement with China, and the Soviets were squeezed out of the Middle East. It was not a period of net gain in Soviet world influence, and the gains made were not a by-product of détente. In the strategic field the importance of détente had been used to justify asymmetrical concessions in the strategic arms limitations talks (SALT). Despite Soviet concessions, the U.S. Senate had been reluctant to ratify SALT II, and meanwhile the Americans had sought to preserve their strategic superiority, first with multiple independently targeted reentry vehicles (MIRVs), then cruise missiles, and most recently the idea of space-based strike systems.

The memoirs of Richard M. Nixon and Henry Kissinger made it clear

---

34. Margot Light, *The Soviet Theory of International Relations* (St. Martin's Press, 1988), pp. 39–40, 49.

that they had seen détente as a way of tranquilizing Soviet opposition, while furthering U.S. interests around the world. The Reagan administration had demonstrated that the United States mistook moderate and conciliatory behavior as weakness. If the United States was emphasizing the role of military force in its global policy, then the Soviet Union should be prepared to respond in kind.

The U.S.-Soviet Relationship

Did the conflictual thrust of U.S. policy in the 1978–83 period represent a rightist deviation from the trend toward a more cooperative relationship? Or was it on trend, with the cooperative thrust of the 1969–75 period being a leftist deviation from a consistently conflictual relationship between the two social systems? Answers to these questions would have been strongly influenced by conclusions concerning the central tendency of the relationship between the superpowers.

A strong argument could be made that American policy toward the Soviet Union in 1978–83 conformed to the general thrust of U.S. policy over the forty years since World War II, whereas the years of relatively sustained détente in 1969–73, and the few brief periods before that, were atypical. The argument was even more persuasive if U.S. policy was surveyed over the sixty-six years since the Russian revolution and the formation of the Soviet state. For most of that period, the United States had demonstrated sustained hostility toward communism and the Soviet Union, and the collaborative relationship during World War II was a relatively brief exception to that norm.

There were, therefore, strong grounds for arguing that Reagan's policies were substantially the same as U.S. policies in the 1920s and the 1940s, that capitalist attitudes were immutable, and that the United States, the bastion of imperalism, was simply not prepared to accept the legitimacy of the socialist system or its leader, the Soviet Union.

Indeed, events in the 1970s bore a distinct resemblance to the move from collaboration to confrontation in 1945–47, although the 1970s process was more drawn out. By March 1946 the Anglo-Saxon powers had concluded that Russian behavior was such as to preclude the possibility of normal relations. They started girding themselves for a sustained struggle with the Soviet Union and world communism, although this was not formally announced until the Truman declaration of March 1947. It was not, however, until July 1947, after Foreign Minister

V. M. Molotov had withdrawn from the meeting called to discuss the European Recovery Program (the Marshall Plan), that the Soviets finally acknowledged the rupture with the West. It was formally announced at the organizing conference of the Cominform in September 1947.[35]

Similarly, in more recent times, the United States had concluded by 1978–79 that the détente relationship was no longer tenable, although the breach did not finally come until the Reagan administration. The Soviets, meanwhile, kept asserting that détente was irreversible. They blamed the deterioration in the superpower relationship on "certain influential forces" in the United States, rather than acknowledging it to be administration policy. It was not until the plenum in June 1983 that the Soviets formally admitted the split.

There were other similarities between the circumstances of September 1947 and September 1983. Andrey Zhdanov's statement and Andropov's declaration both announced the defeat of the cooperative tendencies in the West and the victory of those who sought confrontation with the Soviet Union, and both marked the end of a period of East-West collaboration or détente. Both Soviet statements depicted the world as having been split into two camps, with the capitalists embarked on a sustained offensive intended to destroy the socialist system.

What did this imply for the Soviet-American relationship in the second half of the 1980s? On the evidence of the past forty years it could be argued that the policy of détente adopted in 1971 had reflected a subjective yearning for a collaborative relationship with the other superpower, a relationship that was ruled out by objective factors. This did not mean that the Soviet Union could ignore the United States, which was by far the single most important actor in the international system. But the collaborative relationship that Brezhnev had envisaged in the agreements signed in 1972 and 1973 was wishful thinking.

There were, of course, several areas where the Soviet Union had no alternative to dealing closely with the United States—for example, on Middle East matters and especially on strategic arms control. There

---

35. Previously, the official Soviet line had been that there were two tendencies in Great Britain and the United States, one of which was prepared to continue with the decisionmaking system based on tripartite compromise and agreement that developed during the war, while the other sought world domination for the Anglo-Saxon powers (William Taubman, *Stalin's American Policy: From Entente to Détente to Cold War* [Norton, 1982], pp. 120–21). John C. Campbell, *The United States in World Affairs, 1945–47* (Harper, 1947), p. 480, characterized the Truman Doctrine as giving "the impression that the policy of attempting to cooperate with the Soviet Union had been given up, and that an eventual war between the 'two alternative ways of life' was inevitable."

were, however, other areas where it was realistic to think of developing long-term collaborative relationships with non-American members of the capitalist camp. Political détente in Europe had shown itself to have an existence independent of the United States, while domestic controversies over the deployment of Euromissiles had exposed new evidence of the relative strengths and alignments of latent political forces both within the countries of the Western bloc and among them.

Policy Implications

The relatively conciliatory style of Soviet policy that emerged in September 1984 said nothing about the strategic thrust of the reappraisal's conclusions. Having decided that war was not imminent, the Soviets were able to consider what style of diplomacy would best further their interests.[36] Derailing the strategic defense initiative and preserving the ABM Treaty was an immediate objective. That could only be done by influencing the debate in Congress and by enlisting the support of Western public opinion to halt the proposed move into space. Diplomatic initiatives, style, and concessions would be shaped to those immediate ends.

Two benchmarks in the strategic thrust of Soviet policy that emerged from the 1983–84 reappraisal stand out: the remark in Andropov's September 1983 declaration that "if anyone had any illusions about the possibility of an evolution for the better in the policy of the present American administration, recent events have dispelled them" and Gromyko's reference in his speech at the United Nations one year later to the "period of détente" as something in the past.[37]

To the extent the Soviets acknowledged that the failure of their foreign policy in the previous ten years stemmed from its very nature rather than from a misreading of the correlation of forces and of U.S. domestic trends, the correction would have been toward the Stalinist tendency of the spectrum (figure 5-1). There is no evidence that Soviet foreign policy shifted in the direction of the less ideological, cooperative tendency;

36. Gromyko is alleged to have said to his colleagues in the Ministry of Foreign Affairs in the early 1970s that one of the greatest weaknesses in U.S. foreign policy was that Americans did not comprehend the Soviets' final goals and that they mistook tactics for strategy. Arkady N. Shevchenko, *Breaking with Moscow* (Knopf, 1985), p. 279.

37. *Pravda,* September 29, 1983, p. 1; *TASS,* September 27, 1984, in *FBIS*-84-190, p. CC1.

certainly the criticisms of past policy that began to be leveled in 1987 imply that this tendency did not get a hearing in 1983–84. On the other hand, the harsh line toward West Germany that emerged in the summer of 1984, reacting to the growing rapprochement with East Germany and punishing the electorate's failure to thwart the deployment of Pershing II, was a clear break with the policy adopted in the 1970s and a return to the bullying style of the 1950s.

In the wake of Zhdanov's two-camps doctrine of 1947, Soviet policy had become assertively confrontational, the process of installing pro-Soviet regimes in the states of Eastern Europe had been hastened, and the constraints on the communist parties of Western Europe had been lifted. In other words, in response to Harry S. Truman's declaration of a crusade against communism and the depiction of the world as an unconstrained struggle between free people and those who sought to subjugate them, the Soviets had moved over to the political offensive.

Forty years later the Soviets may well have reached similar conclusions about the appropriate response to what they saw as Reagan's crusade against communism and his depiction of the world as divided between the forces of good and evil. In the 1940s the means available to the Soviets were restricted and somewhat crude, and their experience of international relations was limited. As a result, their offensive largely backfired. Forty years later the Soviets had gained considerable diplomatic experience, and the earlier failure would have been a reason for caution, but not necessarily for rejecting such a policy.

On balance, therefore, it seems likely that the line that emerged from the reappraisal would have ruled that Soviet policy must not be predicated on good relations (détente) with the United States, since the central tendency in American policy was toward accomplishing the downfall of Soviet communism and promoting U.S. global interests through the use of force. This conclusion did not call for cold war confrontation at the tactical level of policy, but it did mean that good relations with the United States were a means to an end, such as strategic arms control, and were not an end in themselves. Negotiations would be businesslike. Other interests would not be sacrificed for the sake of good relations.[38]

38. This conclusion runs counter to U.S. assessments in 1984–85, which assumed that good relations with Washington were the first priority of Soviet foreign policy. That assumption reflected the fact that the Soviets most frequently in contact with Americans came from the less ideological, cooperative tendency in foreign policy and that the Soviets wanted constructive negotiations on strategic arms control, which depended on U.S. goodwill.

The Correlation of Forces: Soviet Policy in the Third World

In appraising the results of their policies in the third world the Soviets had to consider two very different aspects. One concerned the question of supporting national liberation movements and "defending the gains of socialism" by thwarting U.S. attempts to overthrow fledgling progressive regimes by direct or indirect force. The other concerned the costs and benefits of Soviet involvement in the third world, and the fit between Marxist-Leninist theory on how less developed countries would move to socialism and what had been happening in practice. In discussing these results it is necessary to distinguish between Soviet military involvement and the application of Marxist-Leninist theory in the third world.

Military Involvement in the Third World

Soviet military involvement in the third world had been of two distinct kinds. One derived from the requirement to establish the political, physical, and operational infrastructure needed to support Soviet strategy in the event of world war. The other reflected the competition for world influence, a catchall category that extended beyond the struggle between the two social systems to include Sino-Soviet rivalry in the third world and the Soviets' need for access to certain raw materials.[39]

The 1960s strategy for world war required forward-deployed naval forces to attack U.S. sea-based nuclear delivery systems at the very onset of war. Establishing the necessary infrastructure therefore had high priority and the Soviets were willing to accept significant political and economic costs to gain peacetime access to the necessary facilities ashore. However, the 1970s strategy dropped that naval mission and with it the priority requirement for peacetime support facilities. While a naval base structure would be needed at a later stage of a world war, this did not justify incurring large political and economic costs in peacetime.

It happened at times that the war-related requirement conflicted with the objective of increasing Soviet influence, as in Somalia in 1968, when

39. The Soviet Union in 1980 imported 60 percent of the bauxite and alumina it consumed, 50 percent of the barium, 47 percent of the fluorine, 43 percent of the cobalt, and 10 percent of the tin and antimony. See V. V. Strishkov, "The Mineral Industry of the U.S.S.R. in 1980" (U.S. Department of the Interior, Bureau of Mines, Branch of Foreign Data, 1981), tables 7, 8.

the geostrategic requirement took priority.[40] But even when the political and strategic factors coincided, acquiring base rights usually consumed influence rather than increasing or preserving it—in the postcolonial era, it is the host country rather than its tenant who gains leverage in the concession of base rights.

THE ROLE OF THE MILITARY INSTRUMENT. The military instrument can be used to persuade, to support, or to coerce a target state. The Soviet objective was to acquire influence in the third world. It was therefore not surprising that through 1984 the Soviet Union had not used actual or latent military force to coerce a state that lay outside its national security zone (there was a minor exception involving the release of Soviet fishing trawlers seized by Ghana in 1972). The use of coercive force inside the Soviet national security zone had little bearing on the role of the military instrument in areas of the third world that were not adjacent to the Soviet Union's borders. Afghanistan, although a third world country in terms of its political and economic development, was part of the Soviet national security zone.

Outside that zone, the Soviets had consistently exercised restraint, even when base rights were at stake and they had significant forces on the ground and control of air terminals in the host country. Similarly, when the Soviets did apply supportive military force, either directly or through proxies, it was to protect their client, and not to punish their client's enemy, since it would be counterproductive to generate unnecessary hostility. The provision of air defense was the most typical form of supportive intervention, although in response to the Somali invasion of Ethiopia, the Soviets and Cubans gave direct support to the defense of Ethiopia. Soviet naval forces, besides serving as an earnest of Soviet commitment, were used primarily as a deterrent and shield against attacks by third parties on the external lines of supply (for example, against Israel in 1973, South Africa in 1975, and Somalia in 1978), or on the country itself (against Israel on behalf of Egypt in 1967 and of Syria in 1973).[41]

The Soviets had primarily used the military instrument in the third world to build influence through persuasion. Mostly, they trained person-

---

40. By becoming heavily committed to Somalia, the Soviet Union found itself on the opposite side from Kenya and Ethiopia. This involvement also provoked adverse reactions among the many French-speaking states that identified with Franco-Ethiopian interests in northeast Africa.

41. MccGwire, *Military Objectives*, pp. 221–22.

nel, both in the USSR and in the home country, and supplied arms. However, the Soviets also tried to increase the client's ability to defend itself against external intervention, thus raising the costs to the West of using military force to rectify unfavorable political developments.[42]

Fear that armed confrontation with U.S. forces would escalate to global nuclear war was a major constraint on the use of Soviet forces to promote the interests of world communism in the third world.[43] Adoption of the 1970s strategy, however, provided grounds for arguing against this constraint and in favor of an increased role for Soviet military force in the third world. If the 1970s concept of operations was predicated on deterring the United States from striking at the Soviet Union in the course of a world war, even when faced by the defeat of U.S. forces in Europe, then surely the Soviets could deter escalation of a local conflict to global nuclear war.

By 1969 the consensus on the dangers of escalation from local war began to break and a debate ensued, which in mid-1974 was set aside rather than resolved.[44] The pre-1967 doctrine stressing the dangers of escalation remained largely intact and the policy of avoiding superpower confrontation continued with minor adaptation, as did the general reluctance to commit Russian forces outside the Soviet national security zone. This outcome of the debate was no doubt influenced by the U.S. refusal to renounce the use of nuclear weapons outside of a NATO–Warsaw Pact conflict as part of the agreement on the Prevention of Nuclear War, and by the alerting of U.S. strategic nuclear forces during the Arab-Israeli war in October 1973.

Practical policy was as much the product of external events in the 1969–73 period as of theoretical considerations about escalation. The

42. The supply of arms has had two other objectives. As far back as the mid-1950s the Soviets sought to complicate the West's strategic situation by introducing threats in distant sea areas that would draw Western capability away from the Soviet Union. In the 1970s Soviet arms supply became increasingly important as a source of hard currency. Ibid., pp. 222–23.

43. Mark N. Katz, *The Third World in Soviet Military Thought* (Johns Hopkins University Press, 1982), pp. 18–21, 38–39.

44. Colonel G. Malinovskiy, "Local Wars in the Zone of National Liberation Movements," *VIZh,* no. 5 (May 1974), p. 97, quoted by Katz, *Third World,* p. 68, tied the new point of view directly to a statement made at a party conference in June 1969; Malinovskiy clearly defined the two points of view discussed in mid-1974. Publication of Malinovskiy's article coincided with publication of an article by Minister of Defense Andrey A. Grechko accepting an extended international role for the armed forces, which together with an earlier one by Admiral Sergey G. Gorshkov, commander-in-chief of the navy, indicated that some kind of compromise had been reached on the overseas role of the armed forces, if not on all the implications. See MccGwire, *Military Objectives,* pp. 216–19.

modified policy enabled the Soviet Union to affect the outcome of overseas conflict with direct support on the battlefield, while its political commitment remained strictly limited. The Soviets could restrict their involvement to providing advisers, weapons, and strategic logistic support. The combat role would be delegated to the Soviet-equipped forces of "revolutionary" states such as North Korea, Vietnam, and Cuba. The first example of this policy was provided by the Arab-Israeli war in October 1973.

This relatively relaxed policy of "win some, lose some" made good sense since the Soviets were confident that history was going their way. In 1969–74 the Soviet debate on the role of force was colored by optimism, almost euphoria, about the accelerating trend in the correlation of forces, and a sharp drop in the U.S. resort to military force in the third world was expected. This meant that proponents of the military instrument could be countered with the argument that the use of force was unnecessary as well as dangerous.

In 1983–84 none of the arguments justifying such a relaxed policy remained valid and the question of necessity would have been at the nub of the controversy. The Reagan administration seemed unwilling to tolerate the emergence of Marxist or socialist regimes and was prepared to use coercive military force to support perceived U.S. interests, including the overthrow of governments deemed unfriendly. And in June 1984 a new justification was added to the standard one of defending freedom. Washington threatened appropriate action against states that, in the administration's opinion, supported terrorism; three of the four names on the initial list were protégés of the Soviet Union.[45] Could the Soviets afford to stand idle while the United States set about punishing or overthrowing a socialist or pro-Soviet regime?

THE DANGER OF ESCALATION. In the early 1970s Soviet military thought was still largely conditioned by the ideas and attitudes that underlay the 1960s strategy, including the belief in inevitable escalation. The active political use of Soviet naval forces already deployed in distant sea areas only began in 1967–68 and built up slowly. In 1973 the Soviets had little experience of how the United States would react to armed confrontations in the third world, although the readiness with which the United States brought its strategic nuclear forces on alert during the Arab-Israeli war was not reassuring.

45. "Shultz Urges 'Active' Drive on Terrorism," *New York Times*, June 25, 1984, p. A3.

By 1983–84 the Soviets had new evidence on which to base their assessments of the danger of escalation. In his 1979 address in Brussels on "NATO and the Next Thirty Years," Henry Kissinger had ridiculed the idea that the United States would be willing to invite immolation by launching a strategic strike on Russia in defense of NATO. The deployment of Pershing II missiles and ground-launched cruise missiles (GLCMs) appeared to support his contention, since the military utility of these missiles was hard to discern unless the United States had decided that it no longer intended to honor its commitment to intercontinental escalation.[46] Such a decision would explain why the United States was willing to jeopardize the cohesion of the NATO alliance, as well as the domestic support for members' national defense policies, by insisting on the deployment.

The Kissinger address was only part of a growing body of evidence that the U.S. declaratory policy of deliberate escalation had been "a Grand Illusion or Great Lie."[47] Robert McNamara, secretary of defense under John F. Kennedy and Lyndon B. Johnson, had averred that he had "recommended [to both presidents], without qualification, that they never initiate, under any circumstances, the use of nuclear weapons," and he believed that his recommendation had been accepted. Samuel Huntington, a member of Jimmy Carter's National Security Council, had written of the "virtual certainty . . . that no American President [would] authorize the use of nuclear weapons in response to a conventional attack on Europe."[48]

If this was how U.S. officials felt about nuclear escalation in defense of Europe, where the United States had some 325,000 men on the ground and close cultural links, they would be even more reluctant to risk escalation in support of less tangible interests in the third world. Nor was there any evidence of U.S. domestic support for such a policy. The response to the perceived increase in the danger of war with the Soviet Union in 1981–83 had been the emergence of the ground zero and nuclear freeze movements in the United States and the declaration by some American communities that they were nuclear-free zones. Although the electorate generally approved of the U.S. administration's readiness to

46. Richard K. Betts, "Compound Deterrence vs. No-First-Use: What's Wrong Is What's Right," *Orbis*, vol. 28 (Winter 1985), p. 704.

47. Ibid., p. 702.

48. Robert S. McNamara, "The Military Role of Nuclear Weapons: Perceptions and Misperceptions," *Foreign Affairs*, vol. 62 (Fall 1983), p. 79; Samuel P. Huntington, "Correspondence," *International Security*, vol. 9 (Summer 1984), p. 212.

resort to force in the third world, this support had limited staying power and little tolerance for significant costs in men or major military units.

If there was little danger of escalation to global nuclear conflict, what then was the role of Soviet military force, latent or applied, as an instrument of policy in the third world? In 1983–84 it could be argued that renewed anticommunist militancy in the United States meant that the Soviet Union had to choose between two evils. Inaction could result in a serious setback to the Soviet Union's position in the third world and in the competition for world influence and could prejudice its ability to meet its war-related requirements. Action would risk military conflict with the United States, but that could almost certainly be contained, particularly if the confrontation took place in areas remote from the vital interests of either side.

TOWARD A MORE ASSERTIVE POLICY. Some proponents could have argued that the Soviet Union should therefore adopt a more assertive policy in the third world. It should be more active in supporting liberation movements and in providing help to consolidate the power of socialist regimes and protecting them from internal and external threats. It should also adopt a more active policy in Latin America where previously, in general, it had been sensitive to U.S. special interests. There could even be political advantage in provoking the United States to coercive intervention in Central and South America.

However, others could have argued that the real choice lay in different instruments of policy. It was not necessary for the Soviet Union to counter U.S. military intervention, since the United States' use of force to support its clients or to overthrow progressive regimes would inevitably estrange third world opinion. This outcome was being currently demonstrated in the Lebanon, where Arab respect for the United States plummeted in the period between October 1983, when a U.S. battleship was used to shell villages above Beirut, and February 1984, when the last marines were withdrawn from Beirut.[49] It was therefore far more important to concentrate on ensuring the economic development of the Soviet Union so that it could serve as a showcase for socialism and provide the necessary economic support to its protégés.

The question of Soviet involvement in the third world was part of the wider appraisal of the correlation of forces and the future direction of

---

49. Yahya Sadowski, "In the Wake of the Achille Lauro: Deterioration of the Egyptian-American Axis," University of California at Berkeley, 1987, p. 45.

Soviet-American relations. Arguments for a passive policy in the third world would not have had much of a hearing in 1983–84. In the 1969–74 debate Evgeniy M. Primakov and Vitaliy V. Zhurkin had argued against military intervention, primarily because of the danger of escalation to nuclear war.[50] They appear to have subscribed to the softer, "reformist" tendency in Soviet foreign policy and may even have favored the more cooperative, less ideological view. (In 1987 they were prominent exponents of Mikhail Gorbachev's new political thinking about international relations, arguing publicly against the zero-sum approach to third world problems that had pertained in the past.)[51]

In 1983–84, the stand that Primakov and Zhurkin had taken in 1969–74 could be turned against them.[52] The danger of escalation had been grossly exaggerated, and the withdrawal of U.S. marines from Lebanon less than four months after their barracks had been blown up in November 1983 suggested that the United States did not have the stomach for a real fight, confirming the lesson of Vietnam. Meanwhile, it would be argued that such success as the Soviets had achieved in the third world was the result of direct military involvement, with Angola and the Ogaden war as the best examples. And although the relationship with Egypt subsequently soured, the massive infusion of Soviet air defense forces in 1970 had saved Egypt from Israel's increasingly disruptive air attacks. Similarly, the restoration and improvement of Syria's air defense capacity in 1982–83, including the deployment of modern Soviet-manned SA-5 surface-to-air missile (SAM) systems, had stabilized a dangerous situation.[53] On the other hand, the Soviet unwillingness to commit

50. V. V. Zhurkin and Ye. M. Primakov, *Mezhdunarodnye konflikty* (*International Conflicts*) (Moscow: Izdatel'stvo Mezhdunarodnye Otnosheniya, 1972). Zhurkin was deputy director of the Institute for the Study of the United States and Canada and a leading commentator on American foreign policy. Primakov specialized in Middle East affairs at the Institute of World Economy and International Relations (IMEiMO) and went on to become head of the Institute of Oriental Studies.

51. Primakov took over as director of IMEiMO when Gorbachev moved Aleksandr Yakovlev to the Central Committee Secretariat in June 1985. Zhurkin became director of the European Studies Institute when it was constituted in 1987.

52. The cooperative view had been done enormous damage by the overthrow of the Chilean president in September 1973. The election of Salvador Allende on a Marxist-Leninist program had been cited as a prime example of the way in which détente served to restrain imperialist forces and opened up new opportunities for third world states to escape capitalist neocolonialism. The U.S.-backed military coup proved that view to be wrong and it could no longer be argued that Soviet restraint in the third world would be reciprocated. Spechler, "The USSR and Third World Conflicts," p. 459.

53. This was the first time the long-range SAM system had been deployed outside the Warsaw Pact area.

substantial resources to support the ruling Mozambique Liberation Front against the Pretoria-backed guerrillas had resulted in Maputo steadily slipping into the South African orbit.[54]

A seemingly authoritative exposition of the interventionist case was made by Major General Dolgopolov in the January 1984 issue of *Foreign Military Review*.[55] He cited the June 1983 plenum on the serious deterioration in the international political-military situation that had resulted from the attempt by the United States and its allies to reverse progressive change, and it identified the U.S. crusade against communism as being directed against all those who disagreed with U.S. expansionist imperialist policies. He ended with a call to watch vigilantly the machinations of the enemies of peace and socialist progress and to be in constant readiness to repulse them.

His article reviewed the use of force by the United States and its allies and asserted that in the postwar period "local wars have been one of the main instruments of the armed struggle of imperialist forces against the revolutionary and national-liberation movement, and one of the useable instruments of policy against the USSR and other countries of the socialist community." In the important closing paragraphs the article claimed that achieving strategic parity had not only allowed the socialist community to prevent a new world war, but also "to limit and in some cases to extinguish local conflicts." It went on to say that the Soviet Union consistently supported the struggle of those threatened by imperialist aggression, "rendering the necessary assistance, including military." A sentence later the article quoted General Secretary Andropov as saying that the Soviets were "resolutely and unchangeably on the side of those . . . who [were] compelled to repulse the aggressor's assault or [were] subjected to the threat of aggression." The final paragraph implied that if Western intervention were not resisted "the illusion [would be] created in imperialist circles of everything being permissible in the way of using force."[56]

Positive indications that the interventionist line had prevailed began

54. Francis Fukuyama, "Gorbachev and the Third World," *Foreign Affairs,* vol. 64 (Spring 1986), p. 723. Moscow increased its military and economic assistance to Mozambique incrementally during the early 1980s but did not arrange a military intervention to turn the tide in favor of FRELIMO. Maputo first turned to the West for help and eventually to a cease-fire agreement with South Africa in 1984.

55. E. Dolgopolov, "Local Wars in the Military Policy of Imperialism," *Zarubezhnoe voennoe obozrenie* (*Foreign Military Review*), January 1984, pp. 7–14.

56. Ibid., pp. 9, 13, 14.

to emerge in 1984, coinciding with a major Soviet diplomatic offensive in the Middle East. On January 8, in Havana for the twenty-fifth anniversary of the Cuban Revolution, Politburo member Petr Demichev made a particularly sharp attack on U.S. gunboat diplomacy and direct military intervention; and in March, the annual Soviet naval deployment to the Caribbean included a Moskva class antisubmarine helicopter cruiser.[57] In May 1984 the Soviets broke with precedent and agreed to provide North Korea with modern MiG-23 fighter aircraft, ending a decade-long hiatus in significant military assistance to that country.[58] In November that same year they supported the Vietnam dry-season offensive against the Cambodian resistance.

In 1984–85 the Soviets started providing support to the New People's Army in the Philippines. They had already concluded a $2 billion military and economic aid agreement with Angola by 1983 and in 1985 they directed a major offensive against UNITA rebel forces, with Soviet officers participating in the fighting down to the battalion level.[59] Meanwhile the Soviets continued to pay Vietnam and Cuba very large subsidies, and aid to Nicaragua, which had mounted steadily, probably included a commitment of $200 million made to President Ortega when he visited Moscow in April 1985.[60] In January 1986, when violent factional fighting led to a collapse of South Yemen's Marxist government, the Soviets intervened in support of the rebels, using Soviet ships to supply them with ammunition and Soviet and Cuban officers to direct their artillery fire.[61]

In December 1985 the Soviets supplied Libya with SA-5 surface-to-air missile systems just as a U.S.-Libyan crisis was breaking. And during the first stage of the U.S.-Libyan confrontation (from January 7 to

57. Moscow TASS International Service, January 8, 1984, in *FBIS*-84-05, p. K2. Demichev was minister of culture. The Soviet squadron included the newly built large antisubmarine ship *Udaloy* and the *Leningrad*, at 17,500 tons almost twice as big as the largest ship deployed to the Caribbean since deployments started in 1969.

58. Fukuyama, "Gorbachev," p. 725; Stephen Larrabee and Allen Lynch, "Gorbachev: The Road to Reykjavik," *Foreign Policy*, no. 65 (Winter 1986–87), p. 22. The Soviets also supplied SA-3 surface-to-air missile systems. They gained naval access to North Korean ports and overflight rights for aircraft enroute to the South China Sea.

59. Fukuyama, "Gorbachev," pp. 724–25; Francis Fukuyama, "Patterns of Soviet Third World Policy," *Problems of Communism*, vol. 36 (September–October 1987), p. 12.

60. In the years 1980–88, Soviet bloc military aid came to $2.7 billion. In 1982–88, bloc economic aid came to $2.8 billion; economic aid in 1980–81 can only be speculated. "Aid to Nicaragua," *New York Review of Books*, September 28, 1989, p. 77.

61. Neil McFarlane, "The USSR and the Third World: Continuity and Change under Gorbachev," in Paul Lerner, ed., *The Soviet Union 1988: Essays from the Harriman Institute Forum* (Crane Russak, 1989), p. 43.

February 14, 1986) the Soviets moored the flagship of their Mediterranean squadron in Tripoli and deployed other naval units to provide early warning and intelligence.

THE INTERPOSITION OF NAVAL FORCES. The military intervention in Libya was the first time the Soviets had interposed their ships between U.S. forces and a Soviet client in this blatant way.[62] It is unlikely to have been an impromptu response, because the crisis had been waiting to happen. From the earliest days of the first Reagan administration, Libya had been designated as a public enemy and the White House did not conceal its objective of overthrowing Muammar Muhammed Qaddafi as a lesson to other "terrorist states," notably the Soviet protégés Syria and North Korea.[63] Economic sanctions were imposed in 1981 and these were accompanied by a program of military intimidation that relied mainly on U.S. naval power.[64] This failed to topple Qaddafi and in the fall of 1985 the Reagan administration proposed to Egypt that the two countries should mount an invasion of Libya. Once Egypt had launched its assault, the United States would contribute 90,000 troops and air cover.[65] This impractical proposal, which was the subject of joint planning by U.S. and Egyptian military commanders, ultimately was deflected by President Hosni Mubarak.

Meanwhile, in the spring of 1984, following the U.S. setback in Lebanon, the Soviet Union had launched a major diplomatic offensive to regain a position in the Middle East. This involved greatly expanded assistance to Soviet protégés in the area (Libya, Syria, Iraq) and also determined efforts to establish relations with traditionally pro-American states, including Egypt.[66] The Soviets returned their ambassador to Cairo in July 1984 and the next month started to supply funds for a rural electrification project. For fear of worrying Washington, the Egyptians remained cautious until Mubarak's visit to Washington in March 1985, where he had hoped for an increase in economic aid but got lectured

---

62. The deployment of Soviet naval units to the Bay of Bengal during the Indo-Pakistan war in 1971 is not comparable. It was a diplomatic show of support for India, but the Soviets were not in position to interpose themselves in harm's way.

63. Seymour M. Hersh, "Target Qaddafi," *New York Times Magazine,* February 22, 1987, p. 2.

64. In August 1981, U.S. carrier aircraft shot down two Libyan fighters over the Gulf of Sidra. There were three aerial encounters in 1983, although no weapons were fired.

65. Bob Woodward, *Washington Post,* April 2, 1986.

66. Sadowski, "In the Wake of the Achille Lauro," pp. 45–46. Besides opening links with Saudi Arabia, the Soviets agreed to supply air defense systems to Jordan and used Kuwait to float a series of loans.

instead. Thereafter the relationship with the Soviet Union became warmer.

Relations between the United States and Egypt took a sharp turn for the worse in October 1985 when U.S. naval aircraft intercepted an Egyptian passenger aircraft in international airspace and forced it to land on a military airfield in Sicily. American officers took away the four Palestinian guerrillas who had hijacked the cruise ship *Achille Lauro* a week earlier. This high-handed action angered most Egyptians, including Mubarak.[67]

It was in these circumstances that the Soviets had to decide what position to take in the impending showdown between the United States and Libya. There were strong arguments in favor of standing clear. Washington had been largely successful in labeling Qaddafi a terrorist and he had many enemies among the Arab nations; the Eastern Mediterranean was already an area of tension, where the superpowers' vital interests overlapped; and the United States had overwhelming military superiority in the area and had demonstrated its readiness (even eagerness) to resort to force in disregard of world opinion.

The arguments in favor of Soviet involvement were much weaker. In addition to the general ones, involvement offered the possibility of exploiting Arab disenchantment with Washington's high-handed behavior while improving Moscow's standing in the Middle East. A more specific argument was that the Soviet Union was already committed to providing Libya with the SA-5 long-range SAM system and until the system had been set up and was operational, the Soviets were beholden to providing deterrent cover against U.S. preventive strikes.

This could explain the interposition of Soviet warships during the first stage of the U.S.-Libyan confrontation and their withdrawal before the second, violent stage from March 23 to April 15, 1986. It seems more likely, however, that the use of a Soviet naval presence reflected decisions that emerged from the 1983–84 reappraisal. Similarly, noninvolvement during the second stage of the confrontation reflected a

---

67. Ibid., pp. 1–8, 19–22, 48–49. Forcing down the passenger aircraft was, for the majority of Egyptians, "aerial piracy." It insulted Egypt and demolished months of careful diplomacy regarding the Jordanian–Palestinian Liberation Organization peace campaign, thereby crippling Egypt's foreign policy. Mubarak had arranged with PLO leader Yassir Arafat that the hijackers (who were from a dissident group) should be prosecuted by a special tribunal of the PLO in Tunis. When informed of this arrangement, the Americans, while skeptical, appeared to acquiesce but then acted unilaterally. Mubarak felt belittled and betrayed by this high-handed behavior.

change in Soviet policy. The Twenty-seventh Party Congress took place in the intervening period[68] and it saw major changes in the composition of the Central Committee, its Secretariat, and the Politburo, as Gorbachev consolidated his position. These included the removal of eighty-one-year-old Boris Ponomarev, candidate member of the Politburo and long-time head of the International Department (this change is discussed in chapter 6).

A decision in 1984 that the Soviets should be prepared to use countervailing force to thwart U.S. attempts to overthrow progressive regimes in the third world would have focused attention on the naval instrument. Given the United States' reliance on its navy to project force in distant parts of the globe, the long-term uncertainty of being able to rely on Cuba and others as Soviet proxies, and well-founded arguments against committing Soviet ground forces in direct support of third world regimes, Soviet naval forces were both the obvious and the only practical means of implementing such a policy.

In principle, this would involve extending the existing policy of using naval forces to deter attacks by third parties on Soviet protégés. In practice the new requirement was of a completely different order. Traditionally, the Soviet Union (like tsarist Russia) had placed little emphasis on the navy's peacetime role, and the use of naval forces in distant sea areas had been a by-product of the war-related requirement. Unlike the Western maritime powers, the Soviets had never built naval forces with the peacetime role primarily in mind. In the future, however, the peacetime role would be a consideration in deciding the navy's structure.

British experience in the 1982 Falklands War (which the Soviets had analyzed systematically)[69] argued that it was realistic to think in terms of deploying nuclear-powered attack submarines to deter, or if necessary prevent, U.S. naval intervention.[70] The Soviet submarine force was capable of performing such a role, but it would require surface support

68. From February 25 to March 5.
69. Jacob W. Kipp, "Naval Art and the Prism of Contemporaneity: Soviet Naval Officers and the Lessons of the Falklands Conflict," *Stratech Studies,* SS83-2 (Texas A & M University System, Center for Strategic Technology, 1983).
70. The British had successfully used four attack submarines (three of them nuclear powered) to impose a blockade against Argentine naval intervention in the Falklands conflict, which included sinking the cruiser *Belgrano*. Before that, it had been generally assumed that submarines had no role in local wars. N. P. V'yunenko and others, *Voenno-morskoy flot: rol', perspektivy razvitiya, ispol'zovanie (The Navy: Its Role, Prospects for Development, and Employment)* (Moscow: Voenizdat, 1988), p. 207.

to counter U.S. antisubmarine forces, and the surface forces would require sea-based air cover. This was an inversion of the debate in 1972–73 when the Soviet navy had argued that it needed additional resources if it was to fulfill its wartime missions under the new 1970s strategy and had used the peacetime role of such forces to support its case. Now, for the first time, the peacetime role would influence naval requirements by providing the additional justifications needed to authorize the construction of an American-style conventional takeoff and landing (CTOL) aircraft carrier.

THE NAVAL EVIDENCE. Objective circumstances in 1983–84 would have favored the Soviet Union's developing a policy of countervailing force. The interposition of Soviet naval forces in January 1986, despite obvious dangers and disadvantages, supports the argument that the Soviets set out to develop the capability for naval interposition. And in November 1988, what is likely to emerge as a fully capable CTOL carrier was laid down at a yard in Nikolayev.[71]

There are grounds for concluding that a CTOL carrier was authorized in 1974 but then canceled after the 1976–77 decision to forgo the attempt to close off the Arctic Ocean. Instead, the navy would have to make do with what Admiral Sergey G. Gorshkov, commander-in-chief, referred to disparagingly at the time as a "universal ship," combining the capabilities of the Kiev and Kirov classes in the single 60,000-ton Tbilisi-class hull.[72] However, in 1982–83, responding to the surge in U.S. naval appropriations and the confrontational style of U.S. foreign policy and naval operations, the Soviets restored programs for building countercarrier surface forces that had been cut in 1976–77 (Slava, Kirov). And it appears that in 1984 they decided to modify the design of the Tbilisi and its successor to allow a limited CTOL capability and to authorize the construction of a somewhat larger carrier that would have the full capability.[73]

71. Simon Elliot and Barbara Starr, *Jane's Defense Weekly*, March 25, 1989, p. 495.
72. MccGwire, *Military Objectives*, pp. 419–26, 441–42, 467–68.
73. Such a carrier is now building at Nikolayev and will follow two Tbilisi classes. The 67,000-ton Tbilisi was laid down in Janaury 1983 and launched in December 1985. It has a ski jump but no catapults. The Su-27 Flanker and MiG-29 Fulcrum fighters, both of which have a relatively short takeoff using after-burners, can take off and land from this ship. Riga is the same size as Tbilisi but may be fitted with a catapult. It was laid down in December 1985 and launched in November 1988. A third ship of 75,000 tons (almost 20 percent larger) was laid down in December 1988 and, according to the Soviets, will have a full CTOL capability. *Jane's Fighting Ships 1990–91*, p. 598; *Aviation Week and Space Technology*, February 12, 1990, p. 28. These dates are compatible with a design decision by mid-1984.

Further evidence of a new policy is provided in *The Navy: Its Role, Prospects for Development, and Employment,* which would have reflected the conclusions of the 1983–84 reappraisal, including the lipservice paid to a defensive doctrine.[74] The book was written by three well-known senior officers under the editorship of Admiral Gorshkov. It is not directly comparable to Gorshkov's 1970s book *Seapower of the State.*[75] Nevertheless it is relevant that Gorshkov's 404-page book had a 15-page section on local wars, whereas the 253-page *The Navy* had a 24-page section on local wars. In *The Navy* the section on local wars (that is, peacetime employment) constitutes one-third of the chapter on "Problems of Naval Employment," the last in the book. The other two-thirds of the chapter covers the three world-war missions of repelling an aerospace attack, suppressing the enemy's military-economic potential, and destroying the enemy's armed forces.

Gorshkov wrote the 3,500-word introduction to *The Navy.* About half of the introduction is devoted to castigating the confrontational policies of the Reagan administration and the role of the U.S. navy as "a policeman's truncheon, an instrument of military clashes, and the principal striking force in local wars and military conflicts unleashed by the United States in the postwar years, or alternatively as an instrument of state terrorism, now elevated by the American administration to the rank of state policy." Similarly, the section of the text on local wars discusses the threat that new wars will be unleashed by imperialist navies. It quotes foreign military specialists to the effect that the navy is the most suitable of all branches of service "for waging local wars at the present time and in the near future."[76] About 40 percent of the section is devoted to that kind of statement and the remainder to the lessons to be drawn from the Falklands War.

Earlier books of course had to make do with the examples of Vietnam and Korea. Nevertheless, the concentration in *The Navy* on local conflicts that have involved Western naval forces is striking. It is particularly significant that the book lacks the pointed criticism of senior

74. V'yunenko and others, *The Navy.* The book was sent for typesetting in June 1987, and I have been told that it had its origins in 1984. It can be seen as part of the debate that has been in progress since 1972–73 and a further step in the process of reasserting the navy's contribution to the assessment of military requirements. See Michael MccGwire, "Gorshkov's Navy—Part II," *U.S. Naval Institute Proceedings,* vol. 115 (September 1989), pp. 42–47.

75. S. G. Gorshkov, *Morskaya moshch' gosudarstva (Seapower of the State)* (Moscow: Voenizdat, 1976).

76. V'yunenko and others, *The Navy,* p. 6.

Soviet military leaders who did not understand seapower that was such a feature of both the 1976 and the 1979 edition of *Seapower of the State*. Gorshkov's tirade in his introduction to *The Navy* is against U.S.naval imperialism and not against the army-dominated Soviet military leadership.[77] The book is about what navies can do, and that includes their important peacetime role in local wars.[78]

OVERVIEW. Hard evidence of debate and decisions in the 1983–84 period on the role of a Soviet military presence in the third world is scarce. This is only to be expected given its classified nature.[79] Moreover, within twelve months Mikhail Gorbachev had assumed power and embarked on the process of reorienting the Soviet approach to international relations. There can be little doubt, however, that the third world would have been an important issue in any review of Soviet foreign and defense policy, given the bellicose rhetoric of the Reagan administration, its active support of counterrevolutionary forces in Nicaragua, Angola, and Afghanistan, the threats of action against Libya, the sudden invasion of Grenada in October 1983, the direct involvement of U.S. forces in Lebanon in 1982–84, and the withdrawal of U.S. marines under pressure in 1984.

The Soviet military presence in the third world was not a new issue, and earlier debate on the question had been set aside in 1974 rather than resolved. Since then, circumstances had changed fundamentally, and the changes favored a more assertive policy. A decision to that effect is supported by what evidence there is. The more tenuous evidence of a decision on naval interposition (the logical corollary of the more general conclusion) reinforces the assessment that in 1983–84 the Soviets decided on a more assertive policy in the third world.

The Third World in Theory and Practice

By 1983–84 a major reappraisal of Soviet theory and practice in the third world had already taken place.[80] Prompted by the overthrow of the

77. MccGwire, *Military Objectives*, pp. 471–72.

78. In a 1985 book, *History Teaches Vigilance* (Moscow: Voenizdat), Marshal Nikolay V. Ogarkov offers unexpected support for the assessment that in 1984 the Soviets set out to develop the capability for naval interposition; he implies that some such capability would be available to the Soviets in the future. See note 121 below.

79. Evidence of the debate on this issue that began in 1969 did not surface publicly until 1972 (MccGwire, *Military Objectives*, pp. 216–19). See also Katz, *Third World*, pp. 138–39, 151.

80. Elizabeth Kridl Valkenier, "Revolutionary Change in the Third World: Recent Soviet Assessments," *World Politics*, vol. 38 (April 1986), p. 426, and Jerry F. Hough, *The Struggle*

shah of Iran and by the political developments in Afghanistan that led to the Soviet takeover in December 1979, there had been a veritable revolution in the way that academic institutions addressed the problems of the developing world and in Soviet policies toward its members.

In his report to the 1981 party congress, Brezhnev observed that the new party program should (among other things) reflect the political changes that had taken place in the third world. In the wake of the congress the relevant institutes were instructed to research the role of the socialist system in the world market and the relations of socialist states with developing and industrially developed countries.[81] Andropov's comment at the June 1983 plenum that Soviet protégés in the third world must rely primarily on their own efforts was echoed in the new party program that was approved by the party congress in February 1986.[82] It is therefore likely that to the extent the 1983–84 policy review addressed Soviet relations with the countries of the third world, it would have confirmed the conclusions that had emerged from the earlier reappraisal.

The evolution of Soviet thinking about the third world had an importance that transcended the subject matter, because many of the problems addressed there had been those facing the Soviet political economy and those involving relations with the capitalist world and the rest of the socialist community. Soviet involvement with developing countries was based on basic Marxist-Leninst theories of economic, social, and political development, as well as theories of interstate relations and proletarian internationalism. But because the third world was never at the center of Soviet political concerns, development of theory about the developing countries was much freer and tolerance for disagreement much greater than in other areas. Because the growing number and diversity of examples made it hard to ignore experience when it contradicted theory,[83] a spirit of pragmatism and willingness to revise theory grew up, much of which had wider application.

---

for the Third World: Soviet Debates and American Options (Brookings, 1986), p. 92, cite authoritative works by Soviet academicians published in 1982 and 1983.

81. After the 1976 party congress, the institutes had been instructed to carry out research on the world socialist system, the developing countries, and contemporary capitalism, and to make an intensified analysis of advances in the economics of the developing countries under the influence of the world socialist system. Elizabeth Kridl Valkenier, *The Soviet Union and the Third World: An Economic Bind* (Praeger, 1983), p. 66.

82. "Speech of the General Secretary of the CC [of the] CPSU Comrade Yu. V. Andropov," *Kommunist,* no. 9 (June 1983), p. 15; *Kommunist,* no. 4 (March 1986), in *JPRS*-86-011, p. 163.

83. Light, *Soviet Theory,* pp. 137–38.

THEORY PREVAILS, 1945–74. Two objectives had underlain the traditional Marxist-Leninst approach to the third world. One was to set the exploited colonial people free and lead their oppressed masses along the road to socialism. The other was to weaken the capitalist powers by denying them access to overseas markets and raw material. The world communist movement would meanwhile be strengthened by acquiring the support of the newly independent states.

Since imperialism was a by-product of capitalism, the Soviets assumed a natural affinity between the socialist system and the colonial people's urge to independence. But once independence was achieved, the international alignment of the new state was likely to reflect the political orientation of the regime that took power. This raised two theoretical questions concerning the role of the national bourgeoisie and the focus of support by the world communist movement in the pre-independence state. Was the national bourgeoisie essential to shaking off the colonial yoke, or could independence be achieved by a mass-based communist-led movement? And if representatives of the national bourgeoisie did assume power on independence, would they soon be replaced by representatives of the workers and peasants, who would align themselves with the socialist system, or would the bourgeois leaders consolidate their position and align themselves with Western capitalism?[84]

Questions related to the ongoing struggle between socialism and capitalism in the developing world and of how newly independent countries could best be led to socialism persisted through the 1945–74 period. The Soviet Union had always given political support of varying kind and degree to the anticolonial movement[85] and, until the second half of the 1970s, it supported the economic claims of the newly independent nations on the developed Western world. However, in the mid-1950s, the developing countries began to assume their own role as an important economic component in the economic competition between socialism and capitalism.[86]

84. Ibid., pp. 116–34.
85. Soviet policy since 1917 can be divided into ten periods, alternating between the "right wing" strategy of encouraging local communist parties to ally themselves with other anti-imperialist groups such as bourgeois nationalists and national liberation movements, and the "left-wing" strategy of insisting that the local party focus on maintaining internal orthodoxy and discipline. Fukuyama, "Patterns of Soviet Third World Policy," pp. 2–4.
86. Valkenier, *The Soviet Union and the Third World*, pp. 1–22. The discussion in this section relies on Valkenier's analysis of Soviet economic policies, supplemented by Light's analysis of theory in *Soviet Theory*.

During the first seven years after World War II, the Soviets had been fully occupied in rebuilding their shattered economy, but by the end of 1952 they foresaw overproduction in machinery and equipment, which could be exchanged for raw materials from developing countries, such as rubber, nonferrous metals, cotton, jute, and foodstuffs. By mid-1952, they were actively courting the developing countries, both bilaterally and in the United Nations, and by the end of 1955 had negotiated trade agreements with countries in the Middle East, South and Southeast Asia, and Latin America.

By 1955, however, the Khrushchev leadership had come to recognize the potential role of a combination of trade and aid in establishing friendly relations with the develping countries. Trade-aid was used increasingly as a political weapon in the competition for world influence, drawing radical anti-Western regimes into close association and driving a wedge between moderate regimes and the West. In the short term, Soviet trade-aid was seen as a catalyst of economic liberation from the old colonial ties. In the longer term it was seen as a way of establishing a new world economic system based on the principles of "real equality and mutual aid" rather than the existing capitalist system of "oppression and exploitation of the weak by the strong."

By 1964, credits were being extended to thirty countries. The aid-trade offensive was successful in breaking the capitalist monopoly of influence in the third world and further improving the Soviet Union's anticolonial credentials. From the viewpoint of the developing countries, it increased their self-confidence, while prompting the West to give more aid at better terms, and forcing Western enterprises to accept less control and lower returns on their investments and to be more sensitive to the developing countries' sovereignty.

However, the priority given to political factors and to the competition with capitalism, along with Khrushchev's haphazard approach to economic factors, had disadvantages for both sides and were among the reasons leading to his ouster in 1964. Under Brezhnev, the pursuit of advantage became an important criterion for economic relations with the developing countries, the ideological rationale being that a strong Soviet economy was needed to properly support the revolutionary struggle. Aid to the developing countries was seen as an alternative to domestic investment, allowing the Soviet Union to import certain goods and materials more cheaply than it could produce them. This aid was justified in terms of the "socialist international division of labor," which applied to Eastern Europe as well as the developing world, and was based on the theory of two separate and competing world markets.

Political competition for the allegiance and the resources of developing countries therefore continued to be a major consideration. However, the emphasis on economic rationality allowed relations to be extended beyond the narrow circle of radically oriented states and meant that when such radicalism became self-destructive, the Soviets would refuse to shore up the economy of such states. As a consequence, by the 1970s it could be said that the Soviet Union had established stable and mutually advantageous trading relations with a number of countries and it seemed that it was set on a path to supply the less developed countries "with the products of its heavy industry in return for raw material and other goods that were either in short supply or too expensive to produce at home." However, while the increase in trade was significant in absolute terms, the Soviet Union was unable to increase its market share, and by 1975 the developing countries still conducted only 6 percent of their trade with the socialist bloc.[87]

The collapse of the Portuguese empire in 1974 revived hopes that the coming to power of Marxist regimes in newly independent countries would tilt the world balance of forces in favor of the socialist system. However, economic developments in the Soviet Union and in the third world invalidated the concept of a socialist global trading system. Meanwhile Soviet and third world economic interests, having been congruent for some twenty years, began to diverge.[88]

In the same way that Soviet views evolved concerning the role of the third world in the intersystem competition, so too did Soviet ideas on how best to set individual countries on the road to socialism. Initially, it was assumed that the key requirement was to rid the newly independent country of all vestiges of colonial rule and break the imperial powers' exploitative relationship. The focus would be on nationalizing foreign assets, central planning, and industrialization, and it was assumed that the combination of economic liberation, state capitalism, and aid from the Soviet Union would ensure rapid growth. The size of the state sector was seen as the key to increased production and import substitution and to the political strength of the new nationalist regime.

By the time of Khrushchev's ouster in 1964 it had become increasingly clear that this oversimplified approach was not working. The coups that

87. Valkenier, *The Soviet Union and the Third World*, p. 22.
88. Ibid., pp. 22–26.

overthrew several radical third world leaders in the second half of the 1960s were invariably justified by the chaotic economic conditions that prevailed. The economic disarray, combined with debt repayment problems, encouraged a less ideological and more pragmatic Soviet approach to the economic problems of the individual countries. The contribution of foreign investment, private business, and colonial trading patterns was reassessed, the inherent limitations on the effectiveness of the state sector in developing countries was acknowledged and more attention was paid to the role of the private sector, and the emphasis on industrialization at the expense of agriculture was moderated.[89]

This backtracking did not mean that the Soviets had relinquished the goal of leading their protégés to socialism, nor did the experience refute established theory. They had hoped to be able to repeat the experience of the 1920s when they had been able to skip the intermediate stage of capitalism by using massive infusions of aid to bring the feudal societies of the Caucasus, Central Asia, and Outer Mongolia through to socialism.[90] That had not, however, worked in the third world. Moreover, it had proved hard to apply traditional class analysis theory to countries where tribe, caste, race, and religion were often far more important than class and where there was often no proletariat or bourgeoisie. Nevertheless, many of the newly independent states, although not socialist (as were Cuba and North Vietnam), had opted for a "noncapitalist" path of development.

Originally, it had been expected that most ex-colonies would choose the noncapitalist path of development, and it was also expected that the transition to socialism would be relatively short. This optimism persisted for much of the Khrushchev era, with Cuba a shining example of successful change. By the end of the 1960s, however, the term "socialist orientation" was being used to describe these states and soon replaced "noncapitalist development." Although these states may have rejected capitalism and established organic links with the socialist system, they nevertheless remained dependent on the capitalist-dominated world economy.[91]

Meanwhile, Soviet theorists had gotten around the lack of a properly defined class structure in such states, and the fact that national liberation

89. Ibid., pp. 74–80.
90. Light, *Soviet Theory*, p. 131.
91. Ibid., pp. 127–28.

movements were usually led by military officers or members of the bourgeoisie, by describing their leaders as "revolutionary democrats," who were drawn from an "intermediate stratum" of society. This stratum comprised a broad cross-section, including the petty bourgeoisie, civilian and military intelligentsia, civil servants, traders, and artisans; the most radical elements in this stratum combined to form the revolutionary democrats. These theoretical formulations described the reality of the political situation, which did not fit the Western Marxist model, and it allowed the Soviets to incorporate military regimes in their class analysis.[92]

It turned out that Cuba's rapid move to socialism was an exception to the norm. Internal coups that ousted the charismatic leaders of several revolutionary democracies in the second half of the 1960s raised the question of how to prevent such reversals and how to ensure continuous progress toward a socialist state. The response, which became evident in the first half of the 1970s, was to emphasize support for self-proclaimed Marxist-Leninist regimes that were based on loosely organized mass parties and to help them form a disciplined political instrument—a formal Marxist-Leninist vanguard party, with an effective internal security system.[93]

THE EROSION OF THEORY, 1975–84. Until 1975 it was not too difficult to put a good face on the way things were turning out in the third world and to rationalize these developments in terms of Marxist-Leninist theory. Thereafter, it became increasingly hard to do so.

One reason was that in the first half of the 1970s the focus of Soviet analysis of developing countries had shifted. The key concern was no longer the competition for political allegiance and economic cooperation but each country's domestic potential, its position in the world economy, and the economic burden it would impose on the Soviet Union. It had become increasingly clear that the salient feature of the developing countries was not their similarity but the diversity of their circumstances, and this diversity did not fit well with established theory.[94] It had also become embarrassingly clear that most of the self-professed Marxist-Leninist states, of which there were almost twenty by the end of the 1970s, tended to be economically backward and most were beset with

92. Ibid., pp. 121–24.
93. Fukuyama, "Patterns of Soviet Third World Policy," pp. 4–5.
94. Valkenier, *The Soviet Union and the Third World*, p. 52.

political problems at home and wielded limited influence abroad. All depended on large amounts of Soviet aid.[95] Were these mainly impoverished radical states contributing to the cause of world socialism, or were they holding it back?

An even more important reason for the shift in focus was the steady erosion of the economic complementarity between the third world and the socialist bloc that had seemed to exist in the 1950s and 1960s. Some of the developing countries had outgrown the type of assistance and level of technology available from the Soviet Union. Others had regressed and were increasingly dependent on aid rather than trade, at a time that the Soviet economy was itself slowing down. Many of these poorer countries were badly hit by the sharp rise in oil prices following the Arab-Isreali war in 1973. Meanwhile those that had benefited from trade in oil could afford to increase their imports from the West and no longer needed long-term barter agreements trading oil for Soviet manufactured goods. Starting in 1975, Soviet trade with the developing countries turned down and the socialist proportion of aid to those developing countries fell sharply. By the end of the 1970s it was clear that, whether theoretically attractive or not, the idea of a separate socialist trading system within the world market could not be realized.[96]

Ultimately, the Soviets faced the fact that third world ideology and interests were increasingly diverging from those of the Soviet Union. In 1974, when the grievances and demands of developing countries were articulated in the Declaration of the New International Economic Order (NIEO), the Soviets had assumed that there was a natural affinity between the third world demand for a reordering of global economic relations and the objectives of world communism. However, by the fourth session of the United Nations Conference on Trade and Development (UNCTAD IV) in 1976, it was clear that the developing countries held the capitalist and socialist countries equally responsible for the plight of developing countries while third world "dependency theory" explained international economic exploitation in terms of the dichotomy between the rich industrial centers and the poor periphery supplying primary products, rather than Marxian class conflict.[97]

These divergencies prompted further rethinking on the Soviet side, leading to more explicit recognition that the developing countries were

95. Fukuyama, "Gorbachev," pp. 717–20.
96. Valkenier, *The Soviet Union and the Third World*, pp. 22–24.
97. Ibid., pp. 112–16.

becoming ever more closely bound to capitalism's main industrial centers, and that it would be difficult for the socialist bloc to increase its involvement in the third world. The Soviets therefore moved away from the idea of competing trading systems to that of a restructured global trading system, which would offer equitable participation by all groups, even before the defects of capitalism had been eliminated. Although these and other points were advanced at UNCTAD V in 1979, this did not imply a break with the NIEO. The Soviets continued to stress the affinity between the objectives of socialism and the third world in respect to the global economy, while emphasizing the responsibility of the industrialized West for the developing countries' problems and insisting on the benefits of adhering to Soviet priorities.[98]

These adjustments in the Soviet view of the global economy were part of a more general reassessment of theory, which extended to criticisms of the unilinear Marxist version of historical development by a minority of scholars.[99] In the 1970s the latter were in conflict with mainstream opinion in academic and political quarters, but the situation was reversed after 1979, because events in both Iran and Afghanistan had disproved the Marxist prognosis. The Soviets came to acknowledge that backwardness was not simply the product of imperialism, and new attention was directed to local traditions and culture. This focus allowed the Soviets to replace the simplistic notion of class with a recognition of the multistructural nature of the third world countries, the latter meaning that neither the experience of Western Europe nor that of the USSR was directly applicable to the developing countries. Events in the third world were, in fact, shaped by complex and distinctive interactions among the relevant economic, social, and cultural factors. These analyses led to increasing doubt that developing countries would evolve in ways that would bring them closer to the Soviet bloc.[100]

At this same period the inherent conflict between the objectives of the NIEO and the interests of the Soviet bloc became apparent, as did the adverse implications for Soviet trade with the West of the prevailing theory of two separate trading systems in one global market. At a preparatory meeting for UNCTAD VI in 1981, a Soviet statement omitted any reference to common interests with the third world and objected to manipulating trade for political purposes, which was said to

---

98. Ibid., pp. 115–17.
99. Valkenier, "Revolutionary Change," p. 426.
100. Light, *Soviet Theory,* p. 135; Valkenier, "Revolutionary Change," pp. 419–28.

conflict with the objective trends in the development of world economic activity.[101] By 1983 doubts were being expressed openly by Soviet specialists about whether Soviet and third world interests were, in fact, congruent and in 1984 an authoritative article asserted that the nonaligned nations had established an equidistant position between capitalism and socialism at the New Delhi summit in 1983. This was because the developing countries remained part of the capitalist world market and could not afford a principled anti-imperialist stand, nor (by implication) could the Soviet Union afford to support them in such a stand.[102]

Acknowledgment that the best interests of developing countries were as likely as not to be in conflict with those of the Soviet bloc and recognition of the manifold causes of economic backwardness encouraged a more objective approach to those Marxist-Leninist regimes that avowedly supported the socialist system. Increasingly, the vanguard parties came under criticism for elitism, misuse and abuse of power, and proliferating bureaucracies, and for trying to impose socialism before the necessary socioeconomic preconditions were in place.[103] As Andropov remarked rather sourly in 1983, "it is one thing to proclaim socialism as one's goal and quite another thing to build it."[104]

THEORY IN FLUX. In the evolution of Soviet policy toward the third world, Elizabeth Valkenier identifies three schools of thought.[105] The original, ideological school, besides pursuing the Marxist objective of helping oppressed colonial people, saw benefit in manipulating third world resentment in the competition with capitalism. Coexisting with this school were the skeptical realists. They assumed prominence during the middle Brezhnev years, arguing that developing countries were unbeholden actors in international relations and the world economy, and that the Soviet Union should base its policy toward the third world on cost-benefit considerations. A third, globalist viewpoint began to gain ascendancy after the reappraisal that followed the revolutions in Iran and Afghanistan. Besides accepting the reality of a single, capitalist-dominated global economy in which all nations must perforce participate,

101. Valkenier, *The Soviet Union and the Third World,* p. 116. However, the objection was probably aimed primarily at the U.S. use of trade restrictions to the disadvantage of the Soviet Union.
102. Valkenier, "Revolutionary Change," p. 431, citing an article by Karen Brutents, *MEiMO,* no. 5 (May 1984), pp. 26–41.
103. Light, *Soviet Theory,* p. 128; Valkenier, "Revolutionary Change," pp. 419–21.
104. June 1983 Plenum, *Kommunist,* no. 9 (June 1983), p. 15.
105. Valkenier, *The Soviet Union and the Third World,* pp. 148–49.

that school acknowledged that in the north-south divide the Soviet bloc was a part of the developed world and argued that the growing alienation of the underdeveloped third world was a long-term threat to peace.

By 1983–84 traditional Marxist-Leninist theory regarding the third world was in disarray, while Soviet policies were already moving toward greater emphasis on what was affordable, rather than theoretically desirable. The skeptical realists still held sway, but their view of developing countries in general and the self-proclaimed Marxist-Leninist states in particular was even more jaundiced than in the 1970s, and they had come to accept global interdependance as an economic reality.[106] Meanwhile, the lively debate on theory had implications for other aspects of Soviet foreign policy, and even more for Soviet domestic policy. While the failure of the Soviet model in producing growth in the third world could be explained by the multistructural nature of the societies involved and their extreme backwardness, much of the economic criticism reflected on the model per se, rather than its applicability in the third world.

By this time a majority of Soviet specialists on third world economies had become outspokenly contemptuous of the Soviet model as a means of promoting growth. That implies that the coming generation of leaders was already contemplating reform of the Soviet economy, in Jerry Hough's view.[107] Whether or not that was so (it is belied by the thrust of the Andropov-Gorbachev approach to the economy through mid-1986), the acknowledged failure of theories derived from traditional Marxist-Leninist analysis must have raised questions about the validity of that analysis in other spheres of international relations.

Policy Implications

By 1984, Soviet economic, political, and ideological interests in the third world were diverging sharply. On the one hand, ideological considerations favored providing political and economic support to all third world nations that chose a noncapitalist or socialist orientation, particularly those states with Marxist-Leninist vanguard parties. On the other hand, the costs involved and the reality of the capitalist global economy favored developing mutually beneficial trading relations with

---

106. Valkenier, "Revolutionary Change," p. 422–24.
107. Hough, *Sruggle for the Third World,* pp. 268–69.

the most appropriate third world nations, whatever their political alignment. Many of the self-professed Marxist-Leninist regimes had done
little beyond avowing their ideological allegiance and were, at best,
decades away from socialism. They not only imposed an economic
burden the Soviet Union could ill afford but undermined the credibility
of the world socialist system.

The ideological arguments were, however, reinforced by theoretical
concern about the adverse trend in the correlation of forces and by more
traditional considerations of realpolitik and superpower competition.
The Reagan administration had clearly articulated (and demonstrated)
its intention to reverse the gains of socialism, and the Soviet Union's
standing as a superpower and as leader of the world communist movement would be irreparably damaged if it withdrew from the struggle and
sacrificed its internationalist commitments and obligations for the sake
of its domestic well-being.

A strong Soviet economy was recognized as essential to the long-
term success of the communist world revolution. In 1984, however, the
Soviet leadership still believed that such an economy could be achieved
by shaking off the stagnation of the late Brezhnev years and following
through on fairly simple reforms, some of them proposed in the 1960s.
The reforms would include speeding up the shift from extensive to
intensive development; improving the planning of production, the allocation of resources, and the distribution of goods; eliminating waste; and
increasing the efficiency of managers and the discipline of the work
force.[108]

These conflicting considerations suggest that in reappraising policy
toward the third world in 1983–84 the Soviets would have adopted a
general rule that relations with third world nations would be based on
the principle of mutual benefit, but the Soviet Union would continue to
support existing clients and protégés, and would not withdraw from the
struggle against imperialism. Where possible, aid would be used as a
lever to shape the economic and political behavior of recipients and, in
the case of the newer Marxist-Leninist regimes, to moderate their
doctrinaire approach to the complex social, cultural, and economic
problems that faced them.

The resurgence of U.S. imperialist tendencies and readiness to resort
to force was a disturbing trend that would have to be countered.

108. The reforms are discussed in chap. 6.

This implied continued or increasing military support for regimes and movements whose downfall was being sought by the United States; it would include (if appropriate) the interposition of Soviet forces. It also implied continued support for states such as Libya and Syria where the primary link was their enmity toward the United States or its protégés.

The Danger of World War

In 1983–84 there was disagreement within the Soviet leadership about the imminence of war, but there was general agreement that world war had become significantly more likely and that the danger was, if anything, increasing. Ten years earlier world war had been thought to be becoming increasingly unthinkable. Blame for the change could be laid mainly at the American door, but in seeking to explain this adverse development the Soviets could not ignore the correlation between the restructuring of their forces facing NATO and the rise in East-West tension, culminating in the confrontation over the deployment of Euromissiles.

The Soviets were caught in a vicious circle. A first-order national objective was to avoid war but, should it be inescapable, the objective then became not to lose. By doctrinal definition (and by intelligence assessment), the capitalist objective in such a war would be to overthrow the Soviet system, but the Soviets could not respond by seeking to destroy the capitalist system. That would require a nuclear attack on North America, which would provoke retaliatory strikes resulting in the nuclear devastation of the USSR. The U.S. military-industrial base therefore had to be spared. This central element of the 1970s strategy implied that NATO must be defeated in Europe and that American forces must be evicted from the Continent to deny the United States a bridgehead from which to mount a land offensive against the USSR. To defeat NATO without NATO's resorting to nuclear weapons, Soviet forces had to be structured for conventional offensive operations and be provided with the necessary superiority.

The Soviets had restructured their forces in the 1970s to meet this new requirement. But in doing so they had caused the West to reaffirm its reliance on nuclear weapons, justified U.S. investment in new weapons systems that exploited emerging technologies, and prompted the U.S. concept of "limited nuclear options," which increased the probability that war would escalate to an intercontinental exchange.

Meanwhile, the Soviets' threatening military posture facing Europe reinforced the belief that the communist system sought military world domination and encouraged the United States to bolster its military superiority, this time through weapons in space. East-West tension steadily increased.

In other words, in preparing for the theoretical contingency of a war that was becoming increasingly less likely, the Soviets had reversed that favorable trend and actually made world war more likely. And despite the restructuring of Soviet forces, the chances in such a war of avoiding escalation to a nuclear exchange were slim. Nor could the Soviets be certain that their offensive in Europe would be successful, even if NATO did not resort to nuclear weapons. If the blitzkrieg failed, they would face a protracted conventional war against the industrial might of the United States and its allies.

Averting World War

Marxist-Leninist theory equated capitalist imperialism with war and socialism with peace. Only when socialism prevailed throughout the world could perfect peace occur, because only then would class antagonisms disappear and, with them, conflict and war. Until then, or at least until socialism became the predominant social system, the possibility of war could not be ruled out.

While accepting the possibility of war, the Soviets always gave high priority to averting it, adopting three approaches to that end. One was to mobilize world opinion in favor of peace. Another was to ensure that Soviet military strength was sufficient to deter military conflict between the two blocs and to prevent counterrevolutionary attacks on socialist states or national liberation movements. And the third was to pursue policies that enhanced peace, such as negotiating arms control and disarmament agreements and establishing collective security regimes.[109] Meanwhile, if war came nevertheless, it was essential not to lose, because defeat implied the overthrow of the Soviet state and the disintegration of the socialist system.

In 1983–84 it was clear that the measures taken in the 1970s to avoid defeat in world war had in practice made such a war more likely. Since

---

109. Light, *Soviet Theory*, pp. 238–42. The Soviets attempted to form a collective-security system against Germany in the 1930s, and they regard the Helsinki Agreement of 1975 as an acceptable initial outcome of similar efforts in the postwar period.

avoiding world war was a first-order national objective and prior to the objective of not losing such a war, the logical step was to cease preparing for it, ruling that such a war could and would be averted by political means. However, in the circumstances of 1983–84, when there was heated argument about the imminence of world war, such a course of action was hardly conceivable, let alone a practical option. Furthermore, besides the instinctive resistance to such a step, which was not limited to the military establishment, there were ideological objections.

Theoretically, the transition from a world of capitalism to one of socialism, and thereby from latent war to secure peace, was a continuous process that divided into stages, each having a different level of war danger. Achievement of rough strategic parity in the early 1970s and the move to détente marked the fourth stage, when the capitalists recognized that the outcome of the struggle could not be decided by military means. The next stage required that socialism become the predominant system, which would allow the possibility of neutralizing the threat of world war, but global peace would not be absolutely assured until a further stage, when socialism prevailed throughout the world.[110] Clearly, socialism was far from being the predominant system. On what grounds, then, could the Soviets justify ceasing to prepare for a war that they could not afford to lose?

However logical, ceasing to prepare for world war was not a live option in 1983–84.[111] At that time attention was focused on whether it was even realistic to think in terms of working to achieve enduring peace, however distant, a question that was part of the wider debate about the imminence of war, the feasibility of détente, and the future of Soviet-American relations.

That this was a central issue is evident in the writings of Marshal Nikolay V. Ogarkov, chief of the General Staff from 1977 to 1984. He undoubtedly was out of tune with key conclusions of the 1983–84 reappraisal (his abrupt reassignment away from Moscow in September 1984 to command the Western TVD is widely believed to have been in

---

110. Stephen Shenfield, *The Nuclear Predicament: Explorations in Soviet Ideology,* Chatham House Paper 37 (London: Routlege and Kegan Paul, 1987), p. 27.

111. In commenting on past mistakes in Soviet military and foreign policy, V. Zagladin noted a "conceptual inconsistency. While rejecting nuclear war and waging a struggle to avert it, we nonetheless proceeded from the possibility of winning it. . . . When we brought our concept into line with reality and logic, our whole policy started to be organized differently." Press conference at the 19th Party Conference, MTS, June 25, 1988, in *FBIS-88-123*, p. 2.

part disciplinary).[112] He is likely to have been against the plan to adopt a defensive doctrine that would sacrifice the crucial advantage of an offensive posture to the uncertain possibility of being able to develop political constraints on the outbreak of war. And the concern about Soviet military readiness and the imminence of war that is reflected in his writings led him to resist the conclusion that it was realistic to think in terms of an enduring peace at this time.[113]

It is generally considered that the political leadership required Ogarkov to recant his well-publicized opinions in the November 1984 issue of *Kommunist of the Armed Forces*. It can therefore be assumed that his statements in that article on the possibility of eliminating war as a social phenomenon represented the party line and reflected the conclusions of the 1983–84 reappraisal.[114] The trick had been to distinguish clearly between world war and other forms of war, and to distinguish between the danger of world war and the possibility of neutralizing it. World war had always lain at the center of Soviet concerns, but now the focus on averting world war was made explicit. It was claimed that qualitatively new sociopolitical and military-technical preconditions and circumstances were "objectively already creating conditions and possibilities for eliminating world wars from the life of society."[115]

The possibility of eliminating world war before the complete victory of socialism had been asserted as far back as the 1961 party program. What was new was the idea that circumstances were *already* creating the necessary conditions. While the threat of war still remained, "already it could be neutralized."[116] This was the "conclusion" drawn by the Communist party about the "absence [*otsutsvie*] of the fatal inevitability

---

112. For an analysis of where Ogarkov stood on more general military issues see Gottemoeller, *Conflict or Consensus*; Herspring, *The Soviet High Command*, chap. 8.

113. This conclusion derives from a comparison of his article, "The Unfading Glory of Soviet Arms," *Kommunist vooruzhennykh sil* (*Kommunist of the Armed Forces*), no. 21 (November 1984), with his subsequent book, *History Teaches Vigilance* (Moscow: Voenizdat, 1985).

114. "The Unfading Glory," pp. 23–24, 26. In his book, which was rushed to publication as Chernenko neared his death in March 1985, Ogarkov incorporated relevant paragraphs of his November article in a chapter headed "War Can and Must Be Averted" but changed the wording to stress that the possibility of eliminating war should not be confused with the reality of doing so, and that meanwhile the danger of war may actually increase (*History Teaches Vigilance*, p. 90). The book, sent for typesetting on February 29, was released to the press on April 8, 1985.

115. Ogarkov, *History Teaches Vigilance*, p. 90. Similar statements appear on p. 85, and in Ogarkov, "The Unfading Glory," pp. 23–24, 26.

116. Ogarkov, "The Unfading Glory," p. 24.

of war." In reaching the conclusion, the party had been "guided by the theory of Marxism-Leninism, creatively developing and enriching" the theory "as it applies to the *present* situation."[117]

Evidence of Gorbachev's involvement in this debate is provided by *The Second World War,* a book with a prestigious editorial board that was specifically written to commemorate the fortieth anniversary of victory. It was released for printing on February 27, 1985, but a six-page addition was made at a later date, after Gorbachev had been elected general secretary. It was this addition that asserted that "achieving a durable peace [was] a fully realistic task [*zadacha*]."[118] That conclusion had been reached by the Communist party of the Soviet Union and other Marxist-Leninist parties on the basis of a "comprehensive analysis of the manifestations and basic tendencies of contemporary social development."[119] The addition also noted that "the Communist Party [was] working out a military doctrine, having a defensive orientation." It dropped the standard reference to the 1971 and 1976 peace programs and referred only to the 1981 party congress and the development of the program at subsequent plenums. And it reaffirmed that the main lesson of World War II was the necessity to struggle against the military threat (the threat of war) "before the guns began to speak."[120]

117. Ogarkov, *History Teaches Vigilance,* pp. 85, 90. Emphasis added.

118. S. L. Sokolov, ed., *Vtoraya mirovaya voyna: itogi i uroki* (*Second World War: Review and Lessons*) (Moscow: Voenizdat, 1985), p. 417. The book was sent for typesetting in August 1984 and before it was released for printing on February 27, 1985, the chronology at the back was extended to the end of 1984 and the names of the editorial board were updated to include the new ministers of defense and new chief of the General Staff. The last numbered chapter of the main text, "Preserving Peace and Averting Nuclear War—the Main Contemporary Problem," has the structure and substance of a concluding chapter. However, this is followed by a six-page addition, headed "Conclusion," which is printed in a different style from the main text. It contains a quotation from the special plenum that elected Gorbachev on March 11, 1985, twelve days after the book had gone to the printers, and refers to a meeting with the leaders of Warsaw Pact nations that was held in mid-March (see note 119).

119. Sokolov, *Second World War,* p. 417. A meeting of the Warsaw Pact Political Consultative Committee had been planned for mid-January 1985 but was postponed because of Chernenko's terminal illness. However, in his report to the April plenum, Gorbachev referred to an "exchange of opinion that we had in the middle of March with the leaders of parties and states of the Warsaw Pact members" (*Pravda,* April 24, 1985, in *FBIS-85-079,* p. R16).

120. Sokolov, *Second World War,* pp. 415–18. The addition of these six pages lends credence to the argument that it was Gorbachev who was mainly instrumental in effecting Ogarkov's sudden transfer in September 1984, at a time when Chernenko was on vacation and Grigoriy G. Romanov, Ogarkov's main protagonist in the Politburo, was out of the country. Apart from Ogarkov's outspoken disregard for the party line, a more important reason for his reassignment away from Moscow is likely to have been the impending death of Ustinov. There was probably a significant group that favored Ogarkov as the next minister

What were the "preconditions and circumstances" that were said to be already creating conditions that would eliminate the danger of world war? The military-technical factor was the socialist community's capacity to guarantee the destruction of an aggressor, but that capacity had existed for some time. The sociopolitical factors working to that end included the deepening crisis of capitalism, the increasing role of socialism in international life, the steady development of the world socialist system, and the increased strength and activism of the non-aligned movements and of other peace-loving forces and movements. That, too, was a routine litany and the only new development was the surge of peace movements in the West, especially in Europe. They would be strengthened by a more skillful approach to arms control negotiations, and by the adoption of a defensive posture facing Europe.

By breaking out world war as the separate category that must absolutely be prevented, the Soviets sidestepped the difficulty that ideology still required them to actively support just wars, such as wars of national liberation. In 1984 they were not in a position to prevent local wars because they lacked the military-technical means "to guarantee the destruction of the aggressor," who (by definition) would be the Western imperialists. Ogarkov, however, did not see this as a permanent situation.

While noting that the conditions for eliminating world wars from the life of society were objectively already being created, Ogarkov also noted that "subsequently as advances are made, [the sociopolitical and military-technical preconditions and circumstances] will even create the conditions for eliminating local wars."[121] This is further evidence that

---

of defense. Such an appointment would have made it much harder, if not impossible, for Gorbachev to shift the emphasis from military to political means of ensuring national security. If it was indeed Gorbachev who killed whatever prospects Ogarkov had of becoming minister of defense, this would provide another reason why Gromyko threw his weight behind Gorbachev's candidacy for general secretary in March 1985. Not only did Gromyko and Ogarkov hold opposing views on the imminence of war and the need for dialogue, but in 1983 Ogarkov had gone out of his way to challenge Gromyko on the continuing desirability of détente. After the setback of the West German elections in March 1983, Gromyko had strongly defended détente as a policy, provided a lengthy list of agreements reached in the 1970s, and argued that Lenin's policy of differentiation among the various imperialist powers during the negotiations in the 1920s had produced positive results (*Kommunist*, no. 6 [April 1983], pp. 11–32). In a subsequent article Ogarkov noted that Lenin's disarmament proposals in the 1920s had come to nothing, and he chose to quote Lenin only on the need to avoid complacency ("Reliable Defense for Peace," *Izvestiya*, September 23, 1983, in *FBIS-83-186*, pp. AA1, 4).

121. Ogarkov, *History Teaches Vigilance*, p. 90.

by 1984 the Soviets had decided to develop the capability for naval interposition.

STRATEGIC STABILITY. Having agreed that it was realistic to think in terms of a durable peace, the Soviets had to decide on positive measures to achieve that objective. One answer was to challenge the West's concentration on crisis stability and crisis control, concepts that derived from the theory of nuclear deterrence and relied on the threat of unacceptable punishment to prevent escalation in a superpower confrontation over some issue that might or might not be crucial to both sides.

The Soviets considered the emphasis on crisis stability to be misplaced. Not without reason, they believed that U.S. leaders welcomed crises as a way of achieving gains or forcing concessions.[122] They also believed that the central problem was not how to ensure crisis stability, but how to prevent crises that were inherently unstable from arising. While sensitive to the danger of the unintentional use of nuclear weapons in a crisis, they saw this danger as less real than the danger of their threatened or actual use to shape the outcome of a crisis.[123] The primary requirement was not to be able to control crises, but to devise ways of averting them, and as an alternative to crisis stability, the Soviets advanced the notion of strategic stability. When the concept first emerged in mid-1984 it had very little substance and tended to be defined in terms of balance and the absence of military advantage.[124] However, this new concept was put to work by Gorbachev after 1987.

EXPANDING THE DEFENSE DEBATE. Another development that can be dated to the 1983–84 reappraisal was the decision to enlist the expertise of those in the social, natural, and technical sciences in analyses of Soviet security requirements. A new *nomenklatura* was established in the first half of 1984 that would concentrate on "a systems approach to

122. Discussing the nuclear alert he ordered during the Arab-Isreali war in October 1973, Henry A. Kissinger noted that the "Soviets subsided as soon as we showed our teeth. We were thus able to use the crisis to shape events and reverse alliances in the Middle East in defiance of the pressure of our allies, the preferences of the Soviets, and the rhetoric of Arab radicals" (*Years of Upheaval* [Little, Brown, 1982], p. 980). For Soviet discussion of the U.S. use of crises to make gains, see Anatoliy A. Gromyko, "The Caribbean Crisis," *Voprosy istorii,* no. 8 (1971), p. 125, as discussed in MccGwire, *Military Objectives,* p. 218.

123. MccGwire, *Military Objectives,* p. 275. For the occasions when the United States has threatened directly or by implication to use nuclear weapons, see Richard K. Betts, *Nuclear Blackmail and Nuclear Balance* (Brookings, 1987).

124. Soviet defense intellectuals began to use this term in discussions with their Western counterparts by May 1984. The 1986 edition of *VES* (sent for typesetting on August 6, 1985) had a new but uninformative entry for strategic stability on p. 703.

war and the army."[125] It appears that specialists in this area were primarily intended to address the problems introduced by Ronald Reagan's strategic defense initiative and to bring scientific methods to bear on the wider problems of strategic nuclear arms control. The gist of their work was probably reflected in the interests of the Committee of Soviet Scientists for Peace and against Nuclear War that was set up during this period and that focused on strategic issues.[126] However, Gorbachev was able to exploit the existence of this expanded *nomenklatura* in 1987, when, for the first time, defense intellectuals were brought into the debate on Soviet security requirements in Europe.[127]

A Defensive Doctrine—Of a Sort

Another way of dealing with the danger of world war was to address the source of East-West tension. If it was impractical to consider forgoing the military requirement to be able to fight a world war, tension would be reduced by the Soviets adopting a defensive posture facing NATO. This would allow them to continue covering the contingency of world war, while at least mitigating the political costs, if not actually achieving political benefits.

While there could be, and was, disagreement both among Western analysts and within the Soviet military establishment about whether the Warsaw Treaty Organization (WTO) had the kind of superiority that would ensure success in the event of war, there could be no argument that Soviet forces were offensively postured. More than anything, it was the Soviets' offensive posture and their inherent capability for surprise attack that had undercut the political campaign mounted by the peace movements in Western Europe to prevent the deployment of Pershing II missiles and GLCMs, a campaign that had gained surprisingly wide support among the electorates.

A defensive posture facing NATO would have to be justified in

125. M. A. Gareev, *M. V. Frunze: Voennyy teoretik* (*M. V. Frunze: Military Theorist*) (Moscow: Voenizdat, 1985), p. 422. First noted by Theodore Neeley III.

126. Stephen M. Meyer, "The Sources and Prospects of Gorbachev's New Political Thinking on Security," *International Security*, vol. 13 (Fall 1988), p. 130, note 14.

127. In May 1987 Soviet political-military analysts admitted that they had hardly addressed the issue. Robert Legvold, "The New Political Thinking and Gorbachev's Foreign Policy," *Japan-U.S. Joint Study on the Soviet Union*, Conference 2 (Tokyo: Research Institute for Peace and Security, May 1987), p. 25, citing an interview on May 12.

terms of military doctrine. At the political-military level Soviet military doctrine had, of course, always been explicitly defensive. The Soviets were prepared to use military force (albeit reluctantly because of the political costs) to "defend the gains of socialism," but they did not seek to spread communism by military conquest. However, at the military-technical level, at the level of applied strategy, doctrine had always been explicitly offensive, and it was this offensive doctrine that underlay Soviet strategy for world war.

That would have to change. The Soviets set out to develop a form of defensive doctrine at the military-technical level. As explained by Marshal Sergey F. Akhromeev, Ogarkov's successor as chief of the General Staff, this doctrine would have required the Warsaw Pact forces to remain on the defensive for twenty to thirty days, after which the Soviets would move to a counteroffensive and (it must be assumed) implement their contingency plans for world war.[128] This would of course make it harder to achieve the primary wartime objective of defeating NATO in Europe and evicting U.S. forces from the Continent.

The Soviets got around the doctrinal conflict between objectives by giving the objective of "averting world war" precedence at the military-technical as well as the political-military level of doctrine. It also acquired an instrumental character—henceforth, "the most important task of Soviet military strategy [would be] to solve the problem of averting war." And "averting world war" was added to "securing the defense of the socialist Fatherland" as the primary direction or focus of Soviet military doctrine.[129]

The practical implications of this reversal of priorities were significant. For example, while an offensive posture facing NATO improved the chance of a successful blitzkrieg in the event of war, it also increased Western concern, heightened tension, and made war more likely. Similarly, while precautionary mobilization might improve Soviet chances of not losing a war that seemed imminent, it would probably make that

128. Ambassador Paul Nitze, "East-West Relations," WORLDNET (U.S. Information Agency television), December 12, 1988.

129. *VES*, 1986 ed., p. 712. This 12-word statement tacked at the end of an 1,800-word entry for "military strategy" is the only substantive amendment to the entry in the 1983 edition of *VES* (which was released for printing in January 1983). In the entry for "military doctrine" in the 1986 edition of *VES*, "averting world war" is added to "securing the defense of the socialist Fatherland" as the primary direction or focus (p. 240). The 1986 edition was sent for typesetting August 6, 1985.

war inevitable.[130] In the future, therefore, it would be necessary to sacrifice a readiness to wage world war to the higher objective of averting it.

The new doctrine was reflected in the Warsaw Pact statement in June 1986 that came to be known as the Budapest Appeal. It proposed that each side reduce its forces by 100,000–150,000 troops within two years, with further reductions in the early 1990s that would bring the total up to 500,000, roughly equivalent to a 25 percent cut in troop strength. The need for on-site verification was acknowledged, and it would cover Europe from the Atlantic to the Urals. Reductions would be designed to preserve the existing military balance at lower force levels while reducing the danger of surprise attack and increasing confidence-building measures. The stated purpose was to lower military expenditures while enhancing military stability.[131]

Dating the Decisions

By the middle of 1984, the reappraisal signaled by Andropov's declaration in September 1983 appears to have been completed. One by-product of the implementing decisions, the new line on "strategic stability," had been decided by May 1984. According to Gareev, the new *nomenklatura* for defense analysis was established in the first half of 1984. Writing not later than August 1984, Gareev also noted that "in accord with the policy set out by the CPSU and the Soviet government, our military doctrine, including military strategy, has a strictly defensive nature";[132] the explicit reference to military strategy implied that the military-technical level of doctrine was included. The decision to resume the deployment of SS-20 missiles facing Europe was put into effect in June 1984.[133] Debate must have been closed off by August, at the very latest, in light of the ouster of Ogarkov from his post as chief of the General Staff at the beginning of September and his article in *Kommunist of the Armed Forces* in November.[134]

130. Gareev, *Frunze,* p. 242.
131. *Pravda,* June 12, 1986, in *FBIS*-86-114, pp. BB1–8. The statement followed a meeting in Budapest of the Political Consultative Committee comprising the heads of the member states and their communist parties, accompanied by their foreign and defense ministers.
132. Gareev, *Frunze,* pp. 422, 236. This book was sent for typesetting in late August 1984.
133. The date is inferred from Gorbachev's speech to French parliamentarians, TASS, October 3, 1985, in *FBIS*-85-193, p. G6.
134. Akhromeev's comment in 1988 that it took two years to develop the new defensive doctrine does not contradict this dating, even though the context of his remark implied that

In his analysis of Soviet doctrinal writings, Jacob Kipp likewise sees the first half of 1984 as a turning point. He notes that although strategic defense was being discussed in 1979 and was formally identified as a major topic for study in 1981, it was seen as "no more than a temporary measure, imposed by political or military conditions . . ." and the primacy of the offense was not questioned. But following the publication of an article by Akhromeev in February 1984, in which he used the Battle of Kursk to show the continuing relevance of "premeditated defense," the nature of the debate changed.[135]

The doctrinal adjustment that was decided by mid-1984 underlay the Budapest Appeal of June 1986 that proposed forgoing the capability for surprise attack. The limited change implied by the Warsaw Pact statement only required an adjustment in the relative priority given at the military-technical level of doctrine to averting world war as opposed to waging it.[136]

The Strategic Thrust of Foreign and Defense Policy in 1984

There is sufficient evidence, specific and circumstantial, to justify the conclusion that a reappraisal of Soviet defense and foreign policy took

---

the decision stemmed from the April plenum following Gorbachev's election as general secretary in March 1985 (Walter Pincus, *Washington Post*, July 13, 1988, p. A16). By April 1985 the doctrinal adjustment that was decided by mid-1984 was already being worked out (Sokolov, *Second World War*, p. 417). Akhromeev would have been referring to the subsequent and far more radical change in doctrine that was publicized in the Warsaw Pact statement of May 1987, which proposed forgoing the capability for offensive operations in general. In 1988 there was still a strong tendency for Soviet officials (but not Gorbachev) to link all new developments to Gorbachev's first plenum, and the May 1987 statement could be said to reflect the thrust of ideas on security put forward by Gorbachev in April 1985. The evidence indicates that the directive initiating this subsequent reworking of Soviet military doctrine was actually issued at the time of the plenum in January 1987 (see chap. 8), and its implications were not worked out (and then not fully) until December 1988. There was, in fact, a two-stage process, the first emerging from the reappraisal signaled by Andropov in 1983 and the second initiated by Gorbachev once he was firmly in the saddle, and the concept of a defensive doctrine implied quite different things in 1986 and 1987.

135. Jacob W. Kipp, "'A gde zhe ugroza?' An Historian's Reflections on Western Threat Perception and Soviet Military Doctrine in the Era of Change and Challenge" (June 1990), citing the article by Akhromeev in *VIZh*, no. 2 (February 1984), pp. 11–26.

136. The proposals in the 1987 statement were very different from those in 1986; the Soviet willingness to forgo "the capability for offensive operations in general" implied a fundamental change in planning assumptions. The 1987 statement was followed by a redefinition of the very substance of military doctrine, jettisoning a definition that had served the political-military establishment since the Soviet armed forces were first formed in the 1920s. Coming between the two Warsaw Pact statements was the January 1987 plenum. Gorbachev noted that "there was a particular situation before the January plenum, and after it events went in a completely different direction" (*Pravda*, July 15, 1987, in *FBIS*-87-135, p. R2).

place in 1983–84. It is unlikely to have been coincidental that a Communist party conference attended by the central committee secretaries of ruling communist parties responsible for international and ideological questions was held in Prague in July 1984. Previous conferences of this kind had been used to launch important foreign policy campaigns. The senior Soviet representative at the conference was Boris Ponomarev, candidate member of the Politburo and long-time head of the International Department.[137]

Whether there had been a formal reappraisal or instead a series of incremental decisions, the thrust of Soviet policy in mid-1984 was different from the policy that had prevailed through 1982, and its vector was generally in the opposite direction from the policies that Gorbachev began to introduce after January 1987. The prevailing circumstances were important. In 1983–84 the dominant mood among officials in Moscow was anger and resentment, directed mainly at the Reagan administration. On the basis of the latter's pronouncements and behavior they had good reason to conclude that the United States had embarked on a crusade against communism and was determined to regain military superiority and to eliminate socialism as a social system.

In terms of the four main tendencies in the Soviet view of what motivated U.S. policy, the harder "expansionist" line was already prevailing by the end of the 1970s. The events of the early 1980s would have reinforced this trend and given new credence to the doctrinaire Stalinist view that capitalism was incapable of changing its nature and that advocated frontal opposition to U.S. policies (see figure 5-1). However, the increased danger of accidental war resulting from the Reagan administration's confrontational policies would have been taken into account.

Given these circumstances, plus the experience of nearly seventy years since the October Revolution, it would have been reasonable to conclude that it was foolish for the Soviet Union to place the expectation of a cooperative relationship with the United States at the center of its foreign policy. This had been the opinion of those who opposed the move to détente in 1968–71, and it would have seemed that events had proven them correct.

This did not mean renouncing the objectives of Brezhnev's peace program in respect to strategic arms limitations and reductions, or to

---

137. *Pravda*, July 13, 1984, p. 4; John Van Oudenaren, *Soviet Policy towards Western Europe*, R-3310-AF (Santa Monica, Calif.: Rand Corp., February 1986), p. 68.

lessening the danger of war through superpower agreement on general principles. And of course the United States remained by far the most important player in the international arena and could not be ignored. But the proper relationship was that of the master mariner to an iceberg in the North Atlantic, or of the ringmaster to an unruly elephant at the circus. Good relations with the elephant were desirable, but the ringmaster would be foolish to count on its cooperation.

There were, of course, areas where the Soviets could not avoid a quasi-collaborative relationship with the United States, notably strategic arms control. But whereas in the 1970s the objective of détente had justified making significant concessions to reach agreement on arms limitations, negotiations would now reflect the narrower concerns of national security and reducing expenditure on defense. However, the overriding importance of derailing the strategic defense initiative and the potential role of the U.S. Congress in the U.S. debate meant that the Soviet negotiating position would be carefully attuned to how it would influence congressional perceptions.

Good relations with the United States would be a means to other ends and not an end in itself. Meanwhile the experience of the 1970s suggested that a more enduring cooperative relationship should be possible with the nations of Western Europe, allowing greater opportunities for beneficial trade and access to the latest technology. This objective would be furthered by the adoption of a defensive doctrine for Soviet forces facing NATO. By relaxing the offensive posture those forces had maintained for thirty-five years, the Soviets would strengthen the hand of Europeans who favored a collaborative economic relationship with the Soviet Union. The Conference on Disarmament in Europe (CDE) that convened in Stockholm in January 1984 to negotiate confidence and security-building measures and disarmament would work in the same direction.

Soviet policy toward the third world would have two strands. The reality of a single capitalist-dominated global economy having been accepted, economic relations could be diversified, giving priority to potential mutual benefit rather than political alignment. However, the political-ideological competition for world influence had sharpened significantly, increasing the importance of defending the gains of socialism against U.S. attempts to reverse them. This meant continuing to support Marxist-Leninist regimes and those that had adopted a socialist orientation, providing security assistance as necessary against internal subversion and external threats. In certain cases this assistance might extend beyond providing protection in the form of Soviet-manned air defense systems to interposing Soviet naval forces between a protégé and U.S. forces attempting military intervention.

This reorientation of Soviet foreign policy was reflected in Gromyko's comment in September 1984 that détente was something in the past and was in line with Andropov's remark a year earlier that there was no possibility that the U.S. administration would change its ways for the better. It also represented a compromise between two extreme approaches, one of which was actively pressed in 1983–84 and another that began to surface after Gorbachev took office.

In respect to the correlation of forces and relations with the United States, the hardline view was that decisionmaking in Washington was dominated by those with an abiding enmity toward the USSR and socialism. That being the case, negotiations on arms control and other matters were not in the Soviet interest, since the combination of American bad faith and the unpredictable American political system meant that the Soviet Union would always emerge worse off. The opposing viewpoint, which would not have had much of a hearing in the mood of 1983–84, was that it was assertive Soviet behavior, both in the third world and in respect to Soviet security requirements, that had provided U.S. aggressive circles with the opportunity to sabotage détente. There were, however, peaceloving forces in the United States whose influence would be strengthened by Soviet conciliatory behavior.

Both viewpoints took the danger of world war extremely seriously, but they differed in their prescriptions. The hardliners were convinced that national security could only be achieved by military means, and that the Soviet Union must be prepared for the worst case of world war, which despite nuclear weapons and emerging technologies could be fought and must not be lost. The others believed that the idea of waging world war in the nuclear age was nonsensical, that this was something that was increasingly recognized by world leaders, and that political rather than military means were increasingly important in ensuring national security.

There is no doubt that these opposing viewpoints existed in 1983–84, but the strategic thrust of the policy that emerged from the reappraisal was not middle-of-the-road. Given the beliefs and experience of the generation that still held power in Moscow, the conciliatory policies adopted by Gorbachev in 1987 were not a practical option in 1984. In the face of the confrontational rhetoric and behavior of the first Reagan administration, the real choice lay between a tougher but still moderate policy or responding in kind and reverting to the cold war of the 1948–53 period. Despite the extreme provocation, cooler heads prevailed in Moscow and the Soviets chose the more moderate road.

CHAPTER 6

Gorbachev Takes the Helm, 1984–86

THE PERESTROIKA PROCESS, often linked to the April 1985 plenum that followed Mikhail Gorbachev's election as general secretary in March, actually had its political origins in the Andropov period (1982–84). Its intellectual roots reached back much further. Initially it was seen as a matter of restructuring the Soviet political economy, but by the end of 1986 the need for radical change in all aspects of the Soviet polity, internal and external, military and civilian, was evident. The decision that democratization was unavoidable if perestroika was not to fail was the catalyst that led to domestic restructuring, new political thinking about international relations, and reconsideration of military doctrine about the possibility of world war.

Gorbachev may not initially have understood the fundamental nature of the problem facing the Soviet Union. Whether he took office with well-conceived goals and a strategy for achieving them, he certainly had such general objectives as making the Soviet economy globally competitive, restoring national self-respect and improving the well-being of the Soviet people, and ensuring the security of the homeland while reducing the danger of world war, as did most of his colleagues and, indeed, their predecessors. There seems no reason to disbelieve Gorbachev's statements to the effect that it took the new leadership some time to grasp the scale of the problem, that in April 1985 (and even much later) he did not foresee the direction in which events would lead, and that if that direction had then been suggested, he would probably have found the proposal unacceptable.[1]

1. Mikhail Gorbachev, *Perestroika: New Thinking for Our Country and the World* (Harper

Nevertheless, in his report to the important ideological conference in December 1984, Gorbachev pointed out that "profound transformations must be carried out in the economy and in the entire system of social relations." He spoke of the need to develop "socialist self-government by the people" and to enlist the "interests and energies of the masses" and said it was necessary to get rid of "obsolete approaches and methods" of socialist competition. He specifically advocated "glasnost" as a way of combating bureaucratic distortions. He castigated formalism and the bureaucratic approach as "the fierce enemy of lively thought and lively action." He noted that socialism's main influence on world development was exercised through successes in the socioeconomic sphere. And he stressed that in respect to world events and to the struggle between the two opposing systems, the party must be ready to make substantive and timely changes in theory and practice to bring them into line with reality.[2] Twenty months earlier he had used Lenin's writings to stress the importance of cost accounting and the intelligent use of commodity money relations and of material and moral incentives.[3]

Similarly, when Gorbachev addressed the British Parliament later that December he noted that the nuclear era dictated new political thinking about international relations and referred to Europe as "our common home."[4] In other words, at least three months before he was elected general secretary in March 1985, Gorbachev was speaking publicly in terms that would come to be associated with the perestroika process. And while he may not have had a clearly defined plan, he was certainly a radical (in the literal sense) and, if required to choose, was predisposed to the kind of decisions that were taken during the first two years of his tenure.

This may have reflected the influence of his undergraduate degree in law, which gave him unusual political insight and exposed him to the genesis of constitutional law, to the origins of ideas about the state, and to the history of political thought that had led ultimately to the ideas of Marx and Lenin.[5] But he seems also genuinely to have believed (with

and Row, 1987), p. 76. Addressing the Polish Sejm in July 1988, Gorbachev admitted that initially the new leadership had not understood "the necessity, or even [the] inevitability" of political reform and democratization (*Pravda*, July 12, 1988, p. 2).

2. *Pravda*, December 11, 1984, p. 2. His report was on the progress made on the ideological decisions taken at the plenum in June 1983.

3. Gorbachev, *Perestroika*, pp. 25–26.

4. "Gorbachev Speech before British Parliament," *Pravda*, December 19, 1984, p. 4.

5. Christian Schmidt-Häuer, *Gorbachev: The Path to Power* (Topsfield, Mass.: Salem House, 1986), p. 49.

Lenin) that "Marxism is not a dogma but a guide to action." Similarly, Leninism "is not a collection of congealed dogmas and ready panaceas, but is the theories and methods of a dialectic thinking and analysis for a revolutionary transformation of reality."[6] In any case, by the end of Gorbachev's first two years in office the Soviet Union had been set on a fundamentally new course in domestic and foreign policy, and battle lines for the internal political struggle were being hurriedly drawn up.

It was in November 1978 that Gorbachev had first achieved political prominence when he was summoned to Moscow to fill the post of Central Committee secretary in charge of agriculture that had been vacant since Fedor D. Kulakov's untimely death in July. For the previous eight years Gorbachev had been party first secretary of the predominantly agricultural Stavropol' region, a job that Kulakov had held in 1960–64.[7] Gorbachev had clearly been a successful first secretary, and he had come into close contact with Soviet party leaders such as Yuri Andropov, Aleksey Kosygin, and Mikhail Suslov when their chronic ailments brought them to the mineral spas in the area. In addition, Suslov had been first secretary of the Stavropol' region just before the war and still saw it as his territorial base. These personal contacts stood Gorbachev in good stead when he moved to Moscow, and he was elected a candidate member of the Politburo in November 1979. When he became a full member in October 1980, he was forty-nine years old, twenty-one years younger than the average member of that body.[8]

When Andropov succeeded Leonid Brezhnev in November 1982, he chose Gorbachev to take over responsibility for the economy and party personnel (cadre affairs). Andropov's health soon began to fail and Gorbachev emerged as his principal deputy, a role he continued to play after Andropov's death in February 1984. During Chernenko's even briefer tenure as general secretary, the responsibility for ideology, culture, and world communist affairs was added to Gorbachev's portfolio.[9] In other words, for more than two years before his election in March

6. Gorbachev, "Lenin Birthday Speech," *Pravda*, April 23, 1983, in *FBIS*-83-80, p. R3 (see Abbreviations of Frequently Cited Sources).

7. Schmidt-Häuer, *Path to Power*, pp. 58–59.

8. Donald Morrison, ed., *Mikhail S. Gorbachev: An Intimate Biography* (Time, Inc., 1988), pp. 100–05, 110–11; Alexander G. Rahr, *A Biographic Directory of 100 Leading Soviet Officials*, 4th ed. (Munich: Radio Liberty Research, January 1989), pp. 66–67.

9. Morrison, *Gorbachev*, pp. 113–17; Dimitri Simes, "Gorbachev: A New Foreign Policy?" *Foreign Affairs*, vol. 65, no. 3 (1987), p. 478; Archie Brown, "Gorbachev: New Man in the

1985, Gorbachev had had a large and growing measure of responsibility for the overall administration of Soviet internal affairs, with Andrey Gromyko having similar (but much less extensive) responsibility for foreign affairs. However, while Gorbachev had de facto day-to-day control, his de jure position and the continued predominance of the old guard in the Politburo meant that he was not in a position to institute fundamental changes in Soviet policy. And at no time was it certain that ultimately he would be chosen to lead the country.

Gorbachev seems not to have had a precisely formulated game plan when he took office, and the far-reaching goals that he subsequently pursued crystallized during his first two years as general secretary. He knew the general direction in which he must lead, cajole, prod, and drive his fellow citizens, but the sporting analogy is rugby, a far more fluid and unpredictable sport than American football, and one that lacks game plans and formalized plays. Gorbachev's style has been, when blocked, to kick ahead, not knowing which way the ball will bounce. Having leapfrogged the opposition, he has used political fleetness and dexterity to regain control of the ball and exploit the new openings.

Although Gorbachev did not have a game plan, it is clear that he had established well-defined time lines by when various things had to be achieved if economic perestroika was not to be imperiled. The end of this particular game was 1991, the beginning of the Thirteenth Five-Year Plan, by when the economy was to have been switched to the track of intensive development, which would allow dramatic improvements in the quantity and quality of national income. If 1991–95 was the target, the economy had to be up and running by 1990. This meant that 1989 was the start-up year and the end of 1988 an important deadline. By then the process of restructuring the obsolete economic mechanism, reallocating resources, and tapping the unused reserves of productive capacity would have to be largely complete.[10] It was that timetable that justified the audacious decision to democratize, because in mid-1986 it was already clear that the progress of economic perestroika was behind

---

Kremlin," *Problems of Communism,* May–June 1985, pp. 13–15; Rahr, *Biographic Directory,* p. 67.

10. In his campaigning for perestroika during his first eighteen months in office, Gorbachev placed great emphasis on these untapped reserves of industrial and labor capacity. Realization that these reserves could only be mobilized by enlisting the energies of the people (as he put it) would have been an important justification for democratization.

schedule. And although by 1990 economic reform had fallen two to three years behind schedule,[11] the original timetable could be seen in developments in domestic politics, ideological theory, and defense and foreign policy. The radical redirection of policy in the first six months of 1987 can be explained in part by the tyranny of time.

In seeking to escape the constraints of outdated ideology Gorbachev was skillful at gradually introducing doctrinally heretical ideas into the political discourse. But in conditions of glasnost it cannot be assumed that he agreed with every heretical concept when it was first voiced, even if he subsequently espoused it.[12] In some cases, he floated an idea himself; in others, the idea would surface in an academic journal, perhaps spontaneously, perhaps prompted by higher authority. It would appear that Gorbachev seized on ideas that would allow him to escape the straitjacket of ideological conformity and introduced them in whatever way was most appropriate in the prevailing political circumstances. Although the hallmark of his public pronouncements was forthrightness, Gorbachev showed himself to be a consummate politician, with a fine sense of what the market in ideas would bear.

In the perestroika process the emergence of new ideas did not lead in an orderly way to their adoption as policy. In the case of democratization it seems likely that Gorbachev was not convinced of the need for this politically dangerous policy until summer 1986. But in areas such as arms control and international relations, Gorbachev already had clearly defined ideas and had to wait for the politically opportune moment to turn them into policy. Yet even in those areas it is unlikely that his agenda was clear-cut, and many of the later ideas seem to have emerged from the process of learning by doing.

This outline of the perestroika process therefore concentrates on the formal political process and other concrete developments important to understanding developments in Soviet defense and foreign policy during Gorbachev's first two years. The genesis of domestic perestroika, and

11. To allow their use in 1991, new planning prices should have been introduced by the end of 1988, but they were not. At the plenum in February 1990 Gorbachev indicated that they would have to be introduced in 1991, come what may.

12. For a description of how Gorbachev introduced the concept of "socialist pluralism" into the mainstream of Soviet discourse (pluralism having been anathema hitherto), see Archie Brown, "The Soviet Leadership and the Struggle for Political Reform," in Paul Lerner, ed., *The Soviet Union—1988: Essays from the Harriman Institute Forum* (Crane Russak, 1989), p. 54.

Gorbachev's recognition of the democratic imperative, is described in chapter 7, although chronologically it should come here. The early course of perestroika is not, however, important to understanding the developments in Soviet defense and foreign policy during Gorbachev's first two years, which are discussed in this chapter. It is, however, essential to understanding the audacious decision in late 1986 to democratize, notwithstanding the obvious political risks.

There is absolutely no doubt that the formal adoption of democratization at the January 1987 plenum was a turning point in Soviet policy. As Gorbachev said later, "there was a particular situation before the January plenum and after it, events went in a completely different direction."[13]

New Political Thinking about International Relations

Gorbachev had referred to the need for "new political thinking about international relations" in his speech to the British Parliament in December 1984. The thrust of that thinking was latent in his report to the April 1985 plenum and was referred to specifically in his speech to the French Parliament in October and in his press conference following the Geneva summit in November. He fleshed out his ideas in an interview with *l'Humanité* in February 1986 and presented them formally in his report to the Twenty-seventh Party Congress at the end of that month.[14]

A notable feature of the new thinking was how little of it was actually new. What Gorbachev did was to take a number of interrelated proposals and concepts—many of which had already been featured in Brezhnev's report to the 1981 party congress,[15] while some went back even further—assemble them and other ideas into a coherent argument, add a

13. Gorbachev's own words to a group of senior officials of the Soviet press and creative unions in *Pravda*, July 15, 1987, in *FBIS*-87-135, p. R2.

14. See *Pravda*, December 19, 1984, p. 4, April 24, 1985, p. 1, October 4, 1985, p. 1; MTS, November 21, 1985, in *FBIS*-85-225, pp. 1–9. *Pravda*, February 8, 1986, p. 1, February 26, 1986, p. 1. His speech at the forum For a Nuclear Free World, For the Survival of Mankind (*Pravda*, February 17, 1987) gave a more extensive overview. Anatoliy Dobrynin, head of the Central Committee's International Department, provides an authoritative presentation of the new thinking in "For a Nuclear-Free World as We Approach the 21st Century," *Kommunist*, no. 9 (June 1986), while Alexander Bovin makes a wider-ranging argument (quoting Shakespeare) in "New Thinking—The Requirement of the Nuclear Age," *Kommunist*, no. 10 (July 1986). For other articles published either side of the party congress, see Charles Glickham, "New Directions for Soviet Foreign Policy," *RL* supp. 2/86 (September 6, 1986), notes 12, 20.

15. See MDS, February 23, 1981, in *FBIS*-81-36, supp. 01, pp. 18–21.

new note of urgency, and then promote the package as the way to think about international relations in the nuclear age.

However, few if any of the world's leaders were thinking in those terms, so the approach was in fact an important new departure. Gorbachev never claimed that the new political thinking he advocated was original and he noted that the underlying principles were embodied in the United Nations Charter. He subsequently stated that the new thinking "took into account and absorbed the conclusions and demands of the Non-Aligned Movement, of the public and scientific community of the movements of physicians, scientists and ecologists, and of various antiwar organizations."[16] He linked the approach to national security with that put forward by Olaf Palme when prime minister of Sweden and fleshed out by the report of the Palme Commission in 1982 (Georgiy A. Arbatov, head of the Institute of the United States and Canada and protégé of Andropov, was an active member of the commission, as was Cyrus Vance, President Carter's secretary of state). And a Soviet book entitled *New Thinking in the Nuclear Age* was already in circulation by 1984.[17]

The broader ideas that make up the new political thinking can be traced back to Soviet experience in the third world in the second half of the 1970s. Acceptance of the idea of a single world economy, and recognition that backwardness was a global problem and that underdevelopment threatened world civilization, had brought prominence to the globalists, who emphasized the existence of global problems that required global solutions, the interconnectedness of these problems, and

16. Written answer to question posed by *Washington Post–Newsweek* team, interview in Moscow May 18, 1988, *Washington Post,* May 22, 1988, p. A33.

17. Gorbachev, *Perestroika,* p. 207, citing Independent Commission on Disarmament and Security Issues (Palme Commission), *Common Security: A Blueprint for Survival* (Simon and Schuster, 1982), and Anotolii Gromyko and Vladimir Lomeiko, *Novye myshlenie v yadernyi vek* (*New Thinking in the Nuclear Age*) (Moscow: Mezhdunarodnye Otnoshenie, 1984). Also see Anotolii Gromyko and Vladimir Lomeiko, "Sleeping Mind Bears a Monster," *Novy mir* (*New World*), no. 10 (1984). Glickham, "New Directions," p. 9, considered that the last three chapters of *New Thinking* sounded like Gorbachev. Glickham noted an article by G. Shakhnazarov, "The Logic of Political Thinking in the Nuclear Era," *Voprosy filosofii* (*Questions of Philosophy*), no. 5 (May 1984), stating that "political ends do not exist that would justify the means liable to lead to nuclear war." Shakhnazarov was the long-time deputy head of a Central Committee department until 1986, when he became first deputy chief of the department for relations with other socialist countries (Archie Brown, "Soviet Political Developments and Prospects," *World Policy Journal,* vol. 4 [Winter 1986–87], p. 73). In 1988 Shakhnazarov was identified as an adviser (*pomoshchnik*) of Gorbachev; it was rumored in 1989 that he was head of the private cabinet (Michael Tatu, *SOVSET,* October 18, 1989).

the interdependence of the different actors in the international system.

In his report to the 1981 party congress, Brezhnev had noted the need for international cooperation to solve the problems facing all mankind such as illiteracy, disease, preservation of the environment, discovery of new sources of food and energy, and the peaceful exploration of outer space and the depths of the world ocean.[18] This litany was repeated (for example) by the Soviet spokesman at the meeting of the Council for Mutual Economic Assistance in Havana, Cuba, in October 1984.[19]

The emphasis on the interests of all mankind was not, of course, new. The legitimacy of the entire Soviet system and the ideological world view of its leaders has always depended on the validity of the identification of the world communist movement with the cause of mankind.[20] What was new was the implicit acknowledgment that the problems of the world did not all stem from capitalist imperialism and that the class struggle was irrelevant to many of the most pressing problems that faced mankind.

The new political thinking goes back many years and its roots spread very wide. The following summary of the new political thinking as it was originally articulated draws predominantly on speeches and statements by Gorbachev through the end of 1986 and makes considerable use of his own phraseology. He hammered away at the same points persistently, whether he was addressing the party congress, the Soviet people in casual encounter or on television, leaders of other nations, or assemblies of foreign elites.[21]

General Principles and Conclusions

The central new reality was that, for the first time since the emergence of civilization, mankind faced the very real possibility of extinction. The

18. MDS, February 23, 1981, in *FBIS*-81-36, supp. 01, p. 18. The paragraph in which these ideas appear starts with "Life demands," a catchphrase used continually by Gorbachev.

19. Speech by Nikolay Tikhonov, TASS, October 29, 1984, in *FBIS*-84-211, p. BB4.

20. Raymond L. Garthoff, *Détente and Confrontation: American-Soviet Relations from Nixon to Reagan* (Brookings, 1985), p. 680.

21. One of the first Western analyses of the new political thinking (and an invaluable source) was Glickham, "New Directions"; see also G. P. Armstrong, *Gorbachev's Foreign Policy*, D/StratA/Staff Note 8605 (Ottawa: Department of National Defense, June 1986); William F. Brazier and Joel S. Hellman, "Gorbachev's New World View," *Social Policy*, vol. 18 (Summer 1987), pp. 4–12; Robert Legvold, "The New Political Thinking on Soviet Foreign Policy," in *Japan-U.S. Joint Study on the Soviet Union, Conference 2* (Tokyo: Research Institute for Peace and Security, May 1987).

most immediate threat came from the existence of nuclear weapons, which had the inherent capacity to annihilate the human race. The more distant threat came from the onrush of technology and the growth in world population which, separately and together, laid the grounds for a global ecological catastrophe. Meanwhile, the growing contradictions between world poverty and wealth threatened to spark a global explosion.

"To be or not to be" was a question that now faced mankind rather than the individual, and the key issue was whether humanity was to survive or perish. This highlighted another fundamental reality of the contemporary world—its interrelatedness.

From these realities the Soviets drew the general conclusion that the present way of thinking about international relations was not only obsolete but extremely dangerous. They acknowledged that existing habits of thought go back hundreds and even thousands of years, and that it would be difficult to change these entrenched beliefs. They recognized that what they were advocating was profoundly revolutionary.

It would require moral courage to cast off comfortable patterns of thought, to break with traditional thinking about peace and war, and to adopt a new way of thinking about international relations that smacks of utopianism. There was, however, no alternative. Traditional views that were possibly correct thirty, twenty, even ten years ago were now hopelessly outdated, and time for corrective action was running out.

At the core of the new political thinking about international relations was an explicit recognition of the interdependence of peoples, states, and social systems. And since the need for security was the essence of international relations, it was necessary to think in terms of international security and forgo the search for national security.

New thinking about security was essential. A state that unilaterally sought to improve its own security would automatically reduce the security of others, meanwhile diminishing overall security by increasing the danger of war. In any case, the capability of modern weapons meant that physical security would no longer be ensured by military-technical means. Primary reliance had therefore to be placed on political means. National security could now only be achieved by cooperating with other states to provide mutual or universal security.

Security had to be defined in comprehensive terms, extending beyond political-military security to encompass its economic and cultural aspects. There could be no gain in security unless it was equal for all. This implied a shift in emphasis from competition to international cooperation. Peaceful coexistence had to become a universal principle of relations among states.

The concepts of mutual interdependence and universal security required a recognition that other countries had legitimate interests and that their viewpoints be respected. This implied that intervention by great powers in the internal affairs of other states was impermissible.

Specific Conclusions

Besides these general principles, the Soviets drew specific conclusions concerning the danger of nuclear war and the global problems of ecological disaster and mass impoverishment.

Although the global problems got less emphasis than the more immediate threat of nuclear annihilation, the direct relationship between the arms race and third world underdevelopment was stressed, and it was argued that the two realities were inextricably linked.[22] The main conclusion was that global problems could only be solved by mutual cooperation, both among the technologically advanced states and between them and the less-developed countries. There was, however, a more direct argument that developing countries must be allowed to choose their own path to development without external interference, since only they could judge their own best interests.

THE ARMS RACE. Soviet conclusions concerning the danger of nuclear war focused mainly on the arms race, the superpower relationship, and the substance of military doctrine. The danger of nuclear annihilation could be neutralized by averting war and eliminating nuclear weapons. The arms race worked against both these approaches, which was one reason why its dangers and iniquities dominated the exposition of new political thinking, both domestically and internationally. A second reason was the burden it imposed on the Soviet economy. Furthermore, the Soviets believed that in the United States an important body of opinion, including members of the Reagan administration, favored arms

22. Gorbachev refers to the nonbipolar and "globalist" aspects of the new thinking in most statements, including those that focus on the details of arms control. See his speech at the state dinner for India's prime minister (*KZ*, May 22, 1985, p. 1), the latter part of the Vladivostok speech (*Pravda*, July 29, 1986, p.1), his speech to the Indian Parliament (*Pravda*, November 27, 1986, p. 1), and the Delhi Declaration (*Pravda*, November 28, 1986, p. 1).

racing as a way of frustrating economic perestroika and bankrupting the Soviet Union.[23]

The Soviets asserted that the first imperative was to prevent an arms race in space and to terminate it on earth. Halting and then reversing the arms race was seen as a primary goal ("basic direction") of Soviet foreign policy. It was also seen as a prerequisite for a new world order and the main lever in the field of security.

The arms race was approaching a new frontier of technological complexity and numbers, which would affect man's ability to retain control. If not halted, the arms race would enter a qualitatively different stage involving weapons based on new physical principles, greater reliance on computers in decisionmaking, and the emplacement of strike weapons in space. The progression from terrestrial to space-based weapons was functionally equivalent to the progression from conventional to nuclear weapons in 1945. A situation was being approached where nuclear parity could no longer be relied on to prevent war.[24]

The danger of annihilation did not stem only from nuclear war. There were more than one hundred and fifty nuclear reactors in Europe and hundreds of chemical plants. The far-reaching fallout from the reactor explosion at Chernobyl could only hint at the catastrophic effects of a conventional war in Europe.

THE SUPERPOWER RELATIONSHIP. The major conclusion was that the imperative of peace took precedence over the competition between the two social systems, and the rivalry must not be allowed to lead to armed confrontation. Superpower involvement in regional conflicts carried the inherent risk of confrontation, and priority had to be given to resolving such conflicts rather than gaining relative advantage. The ultimate objective was a demilitarized world, a world without war. Competition between the two systems had to rely primarily on example and avoid military means.

23. Gorbachev refers to "people in the President's entourage" who resist agreement (*Pravda*, September 9, 1986). This U.S. viewpoint was implicit in the "competitive strategy" advocated by Defense Secretary Caspar Weinberger ("U.S. Defense Strategy," *Foreign Affairs*, vol. 64 [Spring 1986], pp. 694–96). It was explicit in the debate on the U.S. B-2 stealth bomber, where many supporters, including Senator Sam Nunn, "acknowledge that the airplanes' preeminent mission is economic: to compel the Soviet Union to spend an equivalent fortune on countermeasures" (Malcolm W. Browne, "Will the Stealth Bomber Work?" *New York Times Magazine*, July 17, 1988, p. 26).

24. See Gorbachev's view of the arms race in his statements on arms control (*Pravda*, January 16, 1986, p. 1) and on extending the Soviet moratorium on nuclear testing (*Pravda*, August 19, 1986, p. 1), and his interview with *Rude Pravo* (*Pravda*, September 9, 1986, p. 1).

A serious problem in the superpower relationship was that the leaders of the United States had yet to recognize the realities of the contemporary world and continued to strive for military superiority and to emphasize the role of force in U.S. foreign policy. However, this outdated approach reflected the narrow viewpoint of the U.S. military-industrial complex and militarist and right-wing groups, and there were other elements in American society that had a clearer appreciation of U.S. interests.

MILITARY DOCTRINE. A major conclusion was that military doctrine must pay as much attention to the problem of averting war as to ensuring the defense of the national homeland. To enhance mutual security, doctrine had to be inherently defensive. Mutual security could not be based on the offensive threat of nuclear retribution or retaliation, both because the threat induced tension and fueled the arms race, making war more likely, and because the concept of mutual deterrence was being undermined by technological developments.

It had to be explicitly acknowledged that a nuclear war could not be won and must never be fought, and it had to be recognized that an attempt by one superpower to achieve strategic superiority over the other was not only pointless, but extremely dangerous.

Policy Implications

The analysis led to the conclusion that it was essential to break with the past and to cast aside the customary approach to foreign policy. The injection of ideology into foreign policy had been counterproductive[25] and the new approach had to be based on realism, responsibility, and flexibility. A qualitatively higher level of flexibility was needed in all aspects of interstate relations, and realism required that foreign policy rely on pragmatic rather than ideological criteria. But most important was a sense of responsibility for the fate of mankind, a responsibility that bore especially heavily on the two superpowers, but must be shared by all the major powers, particularly the other nuclear states.

Peace was the dominant concern of Soviet foreign policy and the immediate goals were to prevent war, halt the arms race, settle existing conflicts, and start addressing global problems.[26] Preserving peace

25. Andropov noted that "transfer of the ideological conflict to the sphere of relations between states has never benefited the one who resorted to it in external affairs" (*Pravda,* September 28, 1983, p. 1).

26. Gorbachev listed these as the most important "common problems" requiring solution in his address to the British Parliament (*Pravda,* December 19, 1984, p. 4).

favored cooperation and the avoidance of confrontation, and a move from competition to interdependence. Similarly, global problems required global solutions and favored multilateral over bilateral approaches. This meant that the United Nations and other international institutions had to assume a prominent place in the conduct of Soviet foreign policy.

The move from competition to interdependence, the emphasis on flexibility and cooperation, and the acceptance of a multilateral approach were part of an explicit recognition that the Soviet leadership did not have all the answers and was willing to learn, that mistakes had been made in the past, and that the Soviet interpretation of communist ideology was not infallible. This reinforced the conclusion that individual states were the best judge of their own interests and that it was impermissible for major powers (including the Soviet Union) to intrude in the internal affairs of lesser brethren. Each state had to be allowed to choose its own path to development and the major powers must break their habit of using military force to resolve what they see as international problems.

The new approach to foreign policy should eschew confrontation and focus on dialogue and understanding. Implicit in the concept of mutual interdependence and universal security was rejection of the zero-sum approach to foreign policy, where one side gained at the expense of the other, and approval of an expanding-sum approach, where all parties stood to gain from cooperative negotiations.

Negotiations should involve a search for agreement and a willingness to make sensible compromises. The action-reaction cycle must be broken, particularly in regard to the arms race, where every new weapon had been matched by the other side, and where negotiations had been conducted on the basis of an eye for an eye, a tooth for a tooth.

The Danger of War

Gorbachev was not breaking new ground in 1985 when he stressed the threat of nuclear war and the danger of an arms race that was reaching a qualitatively new stage. Brezhnev had addressed the subject in his report to the 1981 party congress. Chernenko, in his message to the British prime minister in December 1984, had characterized the problem of how to parry the threat of nuclear war, of finding a means of halting the arms race, as one that pushed all others into the background, a problem where delay was inadmissible.[27] And the concluding chapter of the authoritative book published to mark the fortieth anniversary of the end of the Second World War had identified preserving peace and averting nuclear war as the main contemporary problem.[28]

Where Gorbachev differed from his predecessors was in the sense of urgency he brought to the problem and in his conviction that not only was it theoretically possible to neutralize the danger of nuclear war but thoroughly realistic to think in terms of turning that possibility into reality. As soon as he took office he got the leaders of the other Warsaw Pact nations to agree with him that "achieving a durable peace was a fully realistic task."[29] At the April 1985 plenum Gorbachev asserted his conviction that world war could be prevented[30] and early in November he was still insisting that it was realistic to think in these terms.[31]

A primary means of preventing nuclear war was to negotiate the reduction and ultimately the elimination of nuclear weapons. When the United States began to deploy Euromissiles in November 1983, the Soviets carried out their threat to walk out of the parallel negotiations on intermediate-range nuclear forces (INF) and the strategic arms reduction talks (START). They had made the threat in the hope of strengthening the hand of the European peace movements, and they had to carry it out if they wished to be believed in the future. It was not as if the negotiations were making any real progress. Rather, the Reagan administration had been using a series of "non-negotiable proposals to shift the blame for the erosion of East-West relations onto the Soviet Union as the U.S. military build-up continued."[32]

At the end of June 1984, when doubts were raised in the U.S. Congress about the wisdom of testing the U.S. antisatellite system, the Soviets had seized the opportunity to propose that the two sides meet to discuss how to prevent the militarization of space. The Reagan administration responded promptly by agreeing to some discussion of the issue, but

27. Quoted by Gorbachev in his speech to the British Parliament, *Pravda,* December 19, 1984, in *FBIS*-84-245, p. G3.

28. S. L. Sokolov, ed., *Vtoraya mirovaya voyna: itogi i uroki* (*Second World War: Review and Lessons*) (Moscow: Voenizdat, 1985).

29. Ibid., p. 417; that agreement was noted in the six-page "Conclusion" added after the book had been sent to the printers. See chap. 5, note 118.

30. *Kommunist,* no. 7 (May 1985), p. 16.

31. Speech at dinner for Mengistu Haile Mariam of Ethiopia, *Pravda,* November 3, 1985, p. 1.

32. Franklyn Griffiths, "The Soviet Experience of Arms Control," *International Journal* (Canada), vol. 44 (Spring 1989), p. 345.

only if the Soviets returned to the INF negotiations and START, a condition that it knew to be unacceptable. However, in the presidential election campaign Reagan gave increasing emphasis to nuclear arms control and, at the United Nations in late September, suggested that "umbrella talks" be considered. The idea was promptly followed up by Gromyko and in November 1984 the Soviets proposed privately that the two countries' foreign ministers should meet to establish a framework for a completely new set of negotiations on space and nuclear weapons.[33]

Soviet insistence that the talks be completely new was only incidentally a matter of face. The more important consideration was to start again from first principles and redress the adverse distortions established in the course of the earlier negotiations. Among the more blatant of these were the exclusion of U.S. forward-based systems from SALT and START, even though they could be and were targeted on the Soviet Union, and the refusal to take account of the British and French strategic capability in any of the negotiations, even those on INF in Europe. Similarly, the Soviets emphasized the comprehensive nature of the talks to make it harder for the United States to evade the issue of weapons in space, which would henceforth be on a par with intermediate and strategic nuclear forces.

Meeting in Geneva in January 1985, Gromyko and George Shultz, the U.S. secretary of state, agreed that the objective of the forthcoming nuclear and space talks would be "effective agreements aimed at preventing an arms race in space and terminating it on earth." Their joint statement declared that the negotiations should ultimately lead to "the complete elimination of nuclear arms everywhere."[34] Gorbachev attached considerable importance to that joint statement. To the question whether a world without weapons, without war, was really possible, he counterposed the question of whether it was conceivable that human civilization could be preserved by continuing the constantly accelerating arms race, fueling tension, and balancing on the steadily narrowing brink of war.[35]

Gorbachev's political objective of eliminating nuclear weapons fitted well with the long-standing Soviet military requirement for strategic

33. Ibid., pp. 346–49.
34. TASS, January 8, 1985, in *FBIS*-85-06, p. AA1. Gorbachev had proposed the complete elimination of nuclear weapons in his speech to the British Parliament in December 1984 (*Pravda,* December 19, 1984, p. 4).
35. "M. S. Gorbachev's Answers to Questions from the Newspaper l'Humanité," *Pravda,* February 8, 1986, in *FBIS*-86-27, p. CC9.

parity at as low a level as could be negotiated, with the established policy of no Soviet first use of nuclear weapons, and with the operational preference for a nonnuclear Europe. These desiderata were complicated by the on-going arms race in strategic and theater weapons, by military requirements in the event that wartime deterrence failed at either level, and by the need to ensure that the Soviet armed forces were not seriously disadvantaged in the process of effecting reductions. But while there were obvious practical difficulties in the final stages of eliminating nuclear weapons, at least Soviet military and political objectives were aligned in the same general direction.

This was not the case with the United States, where Reagan's personal aversion to nuclear weapons ran counter to the central doctrines of physical containment, strategic nuclear deterrence, and limited nuclear options,[36] and to the NATO concept of flexible response that was predicated on the first use of nuclear weapons in Europe. The U.S. military establishment continued to view arms control negotiations as a way of preserving the U.S. strategic advantage while diminishing the weight of a possible Soviet nuclear strike. Meanwhile the Reagan objectives of restoring U.S. military superiority (if it had ever lapsed) and developing space-based defenses implied new nuclear systems and would carry the arms race into space.

The only element of the joint statement of January 1985 that the Reagan administration could honestly support was "terminating the arms race on earth," and then only if the U.S. strategic advantage was perpetuated. However, electoral pressure in the United States and the other NATO nations required that lip service be paid to the agreed statement. And for its disparate reasons the Reagan administration welcomed the resumption of negotiations, not least because they provided the opportunity to repeat the propaganda success the United States had achieved at INF and START in 1982–83.

Negotiations got under way in March, by when it was clear that the U.S. defense budget provided for a surge of new spending on nuclear weapons and space research, which was justified as improving the U.S. bargaining position.[37] In April the U.S. Defense Department issued a reinterpretation of the 1972 ABM Treaty that would allow extensive testing of space weapons and (if adopted) would represent a de facto abrogation of the treaty as it had been universally understood for thirteen

36. Outlined in President Carter's Directive 59 (see chap. 4).
37. Bill Keller, *New York Times,* February 2, 1985, p. A1.

years.[38] Meanwhile, research on the strategic defense initiative (SDI) was moving ahead in the United States and subcontracts were being awarded to U.S. allies as a way of securing their political support.

At the negotiations in Geneva it had become clear that the United States had no intention of accepting any constraints on research, development, or the ultimate deployment of weapons in space, while in Washington support for the SDI had become a litmus test of loyalty to the Reagan administration. By May administration officials were raising doubts as to whether the United States would continue to abide by the provisions of SALT II. Grudging agreement to continue to honor the treaty was announced in June, but with no guarantee that this would extend beyond December 1985, when the treaty was to expire.

Gorbachev, undeterred by these developments, in speeches at home and abroad, to domestic audiences as well as to visiting foreigners, hammered away at the central importance of reversing the arms race and preventing it from spilling over into space.[39] Obviously, U.S. cooperation was critical to achieving this immediate objective and the longer-term objective of eliminating nuclear weapons. More important, the viability of Gorbachev's new political thinking about international relations depended on a measure of U.S. responsiveness. It was one thing for Gorbachev and his supporters to assert that the realities of the nuclear age meant that national security could only be achieved by cooperating with other states to achieve mutual security, and that guaranteeing national security was now primarily a political task rather than a military one. It was another for him to demonstrate it in practice to the satisfaction of a largely skeptical audience in Moscow. A lot would depend on how the United States responded to this new approach.

With the State Department pursuing one line and the Department of Defense quite another, it was hard to read the United States in 1985. And the president remained something of an enigma. Who was this man whose first administration had engineered the sharpest and most sustained rise in East-West tension since the late 1940s, who identified the Soviet Union as the source of all evil in the world, and who had

38. Ibid., April 21, 1985, p. A1. See also Raymond L. Garthoff, *Policy versus the Law: The Reinterpretation of the ABM Treaty* (Brookings, 1987), pp. 6–9.

39. Roderic Lyne noted that in his speeches to domestic audiences Gorbachev had "conducted what in the West would be called a single-issue campaign on the arms race" ("Making Waves: Mr. Gorbachev's Public Diplomacy, 1985–86," *International Affairs* [London], vol. 63 [Spring 1987], p. 219).

talked quite calmly of waging limited nuclear war in Europe?[40] At one time he claimed his ultimate goal to be the complete elimination of nuclear weapons, yet he made jokes in public about bombing Russia, and he asserted that even if agreement on eliminating nuclear weapons were reached, the United States would still want to develop a space-based defense system.[41] Did he believe his own rhetoric, or was he parroting the ideas of those around him? Was he in effective charge of the American foreign policy and defense process, or was he a puppet of the "aggressive circles" that had assumed such political prominence since he took office in 1981?[42]

Did Reagan really have a flippant attitude toward the issue of war and peace, as Andropov had claimed, or did he recognize the enormous responsibility the two superpowers had for the fate of the world?[43] To answer these questions and to persuade Reagan of the need for new political thinking, Gorbachev would have to meet the president, and he expressed his readiness to do so within a month of taking office.[44] Following Shevardnadze's appointment as foreign minister in early July, a date was set for November 19–20, 1985, in Geneva.

The Geneva summit was seen by the Soviet Union as a critical opportunity to reverse the deteriorating trend in East-West relations and the steady erosion of existing arms control agreements and, if possible, to take the steam out of the U.S. drive for military superiority. According to Gorbachev, one of the Soviet concerns was that the deterioration had gone too far for any agreement to be possible, even at a summit.

It was to help "pave the way for the Geneva meeting and create a

40. *New York Times,* October 18, 1981, p. A1; October 21, 1981, p. A1; October 22, 1981, p. A1. Reagan's unbriefed reply to a reporter's question indicated his unfamiliarity with the issues involved. At other times he had asserted that strategic cruise missiles could only be used defensively and that SLBMs could be recalled after launch. Strobe Talbott, *The Master of the Game: Paul Nitze and the Nuclear Peace* (Knopf, 1988), p. 5.

41. *New York Times,* January 10, 1985, p. B8; ibid., August 13, 1984, p. A16 (reporting that on August 11, during a voice-level test before a broadcast, Reagan had said that he had "just signed legislation which outlaws Russia. . . . The bombing begins in five minutes"); Bernard Weinraub, ibid., February 12, 1985, p. A1.

42. As Gorbachev put it a year later: "Where is the true face of the U.S. administration? . . . Either the President cannot cope with his entourage . . . or he himself wants things to be like this." "Vremya," MTS, October 22, 1986, in *FBIS-86-205,* p. AA6.

43. Gorbachev stressed this question of responsibility in the early part of his news conference following the Geneva talks (MTS, November 21, 1985, in *FBIS-85-225,* supp. 13, pp. 1–9) and it was a recurrent theme.

44. To use Gorbachev's own words: "The very complexity of the international situation convinced us that a direct conversation with the President . . . was essential because of the enormous role which both the Soviet Union and the United States play" (ibid., p. 1).

favorable climate for it"[45] that the Soviets decided to halt nuclear testing through the end of 1985 and to extend their unilateral moratorium on testing antisatellite weapons.[46] Gorbachev had already imposed a six-month halt in the deployment of SS-20 intercontinental-range ballistic missiles (IRBMs) in the European zone,[47] but he went even further in October by announcing that the total number facing Europe would be reduced to the 243 in place at the time negotiations were broken off in November 1983.

Similarly, at the April plenum Gorbachev had expressed a readiness to reduce strategic weapons by more than 25 percent. At the end of September 1985, however, the Soviets tabled a comprehensive proposal that included a 50 percent reduction in all types of strategic nuclear delivery vehicle (SNDV), with a subceiling of 6,000 "charges."[48] A 50 percent cut was a U.S. ideal that had been around since George Kennan first floated the idea in 1981, and the Soviets hoped that this talismanic figure would provide the key to derailing the SDI.[49]

From the Soviet viewpoint the main issue at Geneva was "war and peace, arms control. [That] was the crux of the . . . meeting." Gorbachev's primary purpose was to understand the "fundamental ideas behind the foreign policy of the [Reagan] administration" and discover, in particular, its "position on [the] cardinal issue . . . of war and peace." The Soviets put considerable effort into preparing for the summit and in the process concluded that the thing the two sides had in common was "an understanding of the fact that nuclear war is inadmissible, that it cannot be waged and it cannot have any victors."[50]

45. Ibid.

46. The unilateral moratorium began on August 6 (the anniversary of Hiroshima) and was twice extended. In the absence of any U.S. response it was finally ended in February 1987.

47. This was three weeks after he took office. ("Gorbachev Interview with the Editor of *Pravda*," *Pravda,* April 8, 1985, p. 1.) The initial deployment of SS-20s was in 1977, but a decision to curtail production appears to have been taken in 1979 as a concession to the INF negotiations (Michael MccGwire, *Military Objectives in Soviet Foreign Policy* [Brookings, 1987], p. 510; Gorbachev's speech to French parliamentarians October 3, 1985, *Pravda,* October 3, 1985, in *FBIS*-85-193, p. G3). Following the deployment of Euromissiles in November 1983, deployment of SS-20s was resumed in June 1984 (that date derives from Gorbachev's Paris speech and it fits well with the 1983–84 reappraisal; see chap. 5).

48. The Soviets defined SNDVs as delivery vehicles that could reach the territory of the other side, thus including U.S. forward-based systems. Nuclear charges included free-fall bombs and short-range attack missiles. The United States finally made a counterproposal on November 1 that among other things restricted the 50 percent cut to intercontinental and submarine-launched ballistic missiles (ICBMs and SLBMs).

49. Talbott, *The Master,* pp. 262–63.

50. Gorbachev postsummit press conference, MTS, November 21, 1985, in *FBIS*-85-225, supp. 13, pp. 2, 4.

Gorbachev was unable to persuade Reagan that in seeking to enhance U.S. security with a space-based defense system, the United States would diminish Soviet security and thereby increase the two countries' mutual insecurity. Nor would the U.S. side admit that the "star wars program [would] not only give an impulse to the arms race in all types of weapon, but [would] also put an end to all restraint in this race."[51] But while Gorbachev was not prepared to place any confidence in a U.S. promise to share the technology it developed for the SDI, he was convinced that Reagan believed that the SDI could only be seen as defensive.[52] And in his several hours of personal conversation with Reagan, he did discover that the president (if not his advisers) was in favor of a nonnuclear world and was absolutely sincere in his belief that "a nuclear war cannot be won and must not be fought."[53]

Never mind that U.S. support for the Geneva accords was subsequently belied by U.S. statements and behavior, in the following months Gorbachev would point to the significance of what had been achieved.[54] Besides the inadmissibility of nuclear war, the two leaders had agreed not to seek military superiority. They had reaffirmed the objectives of preventing an arms race in space and terminating it on earth that had already been agreed in January 1985. And they had accepted the principle of a 50 percent cut in intercontinental nuclear weapons, albeit with the caveat of "appropriately applied."[55]

Besides these statements of principle to which (as usual) the Soviets attached considerable importance, Gorbachev had established a personal rapport with the U.S. president. And while the run-up to the summit had shown that the "aggressive circles" in Washington still carried a lot of weight, in the final analysis the moderate view had prevailed.[56] The meeting would also have given Gorbachev some sense of the quasi-regal powers that a U.S. president has within his own administration, should he have the capacity and the will to wield them.

51. Ibid., p. 4.
52. Interview with *l'Humanité*, in *FBIS*-86-27, p. CC8.
53. Reagan had noted matter-of-factly, "Our ultimate goal, of course, is the complete elimination of nuclear weapons" (*New York Times*, January 10, 1985, p. B8).
54. See, for example, his interview with Indian journalists, MTS, November 23, 1986, in *FBIS*-86-226, pp. D1–10.
55. "Joint Soviet American Statement," Moscow TASS, November 21, 1985, in *FBIS*-85-225, supp. 13, pp. 2–4.
56. A letter from the secretary of defense to the president advising against committing the United States to continue adhering to the ABM and SALT II treaties was leaked in Washington as the president was on his way to Geneva. This was seen in both capitals as an attempt to sabotage the summit. *New York Times*, November 16, 1985, p. A1.

This whole process seems to have provided Gorbachev and Shevard-nadze with the confirmation they needed that the new political thinking about international relations was indeed the correct approach and that President Reagan offered an avenue for making progress in this direction. In December they took the first step in what would become a major reorganization of the upper echelons of the Ministry of Foreign Affairs, of which a minor but significant aspect was the establishment of a specialized arms control unit to be headed by Viktor Karpov, an experienced negotiator.[57] And then in January 1986, following a Politburo meeting, Gorbachev made an important statement drawing together earlier Soviet proposals and outlining a process that was intended to free "the world of nuclear weapons within the next 15 years, before the end of the century."[58]

Stressing that the task of freeing mankind from the threat of nuclear war must be fulfilled by the people of his own generation, Gorbachev proposed a three-stage process. The first stage, which would apply to the two superpowers and last five to eight years, would involve a halt to nuclear testing, the elimination of medium-range missiles in the European zone, and a 50 percent cut in intercontinental delivery vehicles, including a 6,000-warhead subceiling. However, if intercontinental arsenals were to be cut in this way, both sides would first have to renounce the development, testing, and deployment of space-based strike weapons. And if intermediate-range missiles were to be eliminated, Britain and France would have to agree to refrain from increasing their strategic forces.

The second stage, to begin by 1990 and last five to seven years, would bring the other nuclear powers into the process. Once the superpowers had completed the 50 percent cut in intercontinental systems, all nuclear powers would eliminate their tactical nuclear weapons. A ban would also be placed on the creation of new weapons of mass destruction based on new physical principles.

The third stage, to begin by 1995 and to be completed by 1999, would

57. As head of the Directorate for Problems of Arms Reduction and Disarmament, Karpov would have responsibility for all aspects of arms control negotiations, which had been fragmented until then. Subsequently, an arms control section was established in the International Department of the Central Committee, headed by Major General Viktor Starodubov (Glickham, "New Directions," p. 11). Karpov was promoted to deputy minister in November 1988, shortly before Gorbachev announced the unilateral cut of 500,000 troops.

58. *Pravda,* January 16, 1986, p. 1. The statement was also published in *Izvestiya,* TASS, MTS "Vremya," and MDS.

eliminate all remaining arms. Special procedures for the destruction of warheads and the dismantling, conversion, or destruction of delivery vehicles would be elaborated. Measures to verify the armaments subject to destruction or limitation would include on-site inspection and any other measures found necessary.

Practicing what he preached on the need for a new approach to arms negotiations, Gorbachev flouted the "logic" of the arms race (as he put it) by also announcing a three-month extension of the unilateral moratorium on nuclear testing, despite the failure of Washington to reciprocate. He stressed the vital necessity of preventing the arms race from spreading to space. He proposed the total elimination of chemical weapons and the industrial base that produced them, again to be strictly verified. He offered no major new initiatives in regard to the ongoing negotiations in Vienna and Stockholm on European security matters but expressed Soviet support for reducing conventional forces. And he rejected the idea that reductions in nuclear weapons should be held hostage to resolving regional disputes.

The U.S. response to Gorbachev's proposal four weeks later in a personal letter from Reagan seemed timed to arrive at the start of the Twenty-seventh Party Congress. In commenting on the reply, Gorbachev noted that while it agreed "in general with some of the Soviet attitudes and intentions on questions of disarmament and security . . . these positive pronouncements [were] lost in various kinds of reservations . . . making things conditional on each other and conditions which, in fact, block[ed] the solution of fundamental disarmament questions."[59] On the evidence available, this characterization was not unfair. Among other things, the letter said that many details of the Soviet plan could not be considered until conventional imbalances were addressed, treaties were complied with, and regional conflicts were resolved. It also indicated Reagan's desire to focus first on intermediate-range nuclear forces (INF).[60]

The Soviets faced a dilemma over INF. There was an obvious relationship between the SDI and the intercontinental offensive systems covered by START. But for the Soviets, the intermediate-range systems were also "strategic" since they could reach deep into Russian territory.

59. Gorbachev, "Report to 27th Party Congress," *Kommunist,* no. 4 (March 1986), in *JPRS*-86-011, p. 64.

60. Bernard Weinraub, *New York Times,* February 23, 1986, p. A1. Great Britain, meanwhile, rejected out of hand the idea that it should freeze its nuclear capability while the superpowers cut theirs by 50 percent.

The principle that the INF, START, and space issues must be resolved "in their interrelationship" had been conceded by the United States and included in the joint statement after the meeting in January 1985 between Shultz and Shevardnadze. Indeed, U.S. interest in some kind of package deal had been indicated at the meeting between Shultz and Ambassador Anatoliy Dobrynin in June 1985, and at the Geneva summit Reagan had presented Gorbachev with a proposed set of guidelines for the negotiations in all three areas.[61] However, for reasons of domestic and alliance politics, the United States now wanted to leave the START and the SDI on the back burner and press ahead with a separate agreement on INF.

In certain respects this would also serve Soviet interests since it would remove the threat of the Pershing II missile and be the first step toward a nonnuclear Europe. It would also reverse the adverse trend in the arms control process, which had run into the sand after a promising first six years (1969–75). There were, however, drawbacks. In military terms an agreement along the existing lines would have been a relatively small step toward a nonnuclear Europe. It would have required disproportionate Soviet concessions, since it was limited to missiles with a range greater than 1,000 kilometers, where the Soviets held a numerical advantage, and did not include nuclear-capable aircraft, where NATO had a strong edge.

The more serious drawback was that the *prospect* of an INF agreement was a political lever that might help persuade the United States to negotiate seriously on banning strike weapons from space. The 1981–83 experience could be read as demonstrating that European electorates attached great importance to INF and suggested that this could be translated into political pressure on Washington to abandon the SDI. On the other hand, congressional reluctance to fund the SDI was the key to halting its progress. It was possible that the Soviets' refusal to treat INF as a separate matter would rebound to their disadvantage by evoking "my country right or wrong" and rallying congressional support to the president.

It was not a clear-cut issue and this led to mixed signals from Moscow reflecting divergent opinions and changing positions in response to perceived shifts in the mood of Congress. However, the official Soviet

61. Talbott, *The Master*, pp. 264–66, 286.

line remained that the three elements were a single package, and agreement would be reached on all or none.

Essentially, formal negotiations on arms control went nowhere during the first nine months of 1986. While the State Department had wanted to respond positively to the January 15 proposal, that view did not prevail in Washington.[62] The U.S. administration was meanwhile pressing ahead with its efforts to make the SDI irreversible and insisting that its reinterpretation of the ABM Treaty was correct, although this was now being challenged in Congress. The continued observance of the SALT II Treaty was once more an issue in Washington, and at the end of May it was announced that production of bombers equipped with air-launched cruise missiles (ALCMs) would continue beyond the limit of 130 units, but that two old nuclear-powered ballistic-missile submarines (SSBNs) would be dismantled for budgetary reasons. It could be inferred from conflicting statements by senior U.S. officials that in the future the administration would suit itself as to what aspects of the treaty to observe and which to ignore.

At the same time, U.S. officials were pressing the Soviets to agree on a date for the next summit. At Geneva it had been agreed that there would be a full-scale summit in Washington in 1986 and a return one in Moscow in 1987, but Gorbachev refused to proceed in this matter unless there was substantial progress in arms control negotiations. He argued that those meetings should serve as the keystone of a major agreement on arms reductions and limitations, and no such agreement was in sight.

In late September, however, the Daniloff spy case provided the opportunity to maneuver the U.S. administration into agreeing to a mini summit in a neutral country where the two leaders would meet "one on one."[63] In Washington this was billed as the preliminary to a "regular" summit, but from the Soviet point of view its attraction was that it bypassed the unproductive negotiations at Geneva and provided direct

62. George Shultz is reported to have called the proposal "a very important breakthrough." Paul Nitze acknowledged the Soviet shift on British and French weapons. James McCartney, *Philadelphia Inquirer,* May 18, 1986, pp. 4–6.

63. Referring to the forthcoming meeting with Gorbachev in Reykjavik, Reagan said: "No . . . this is not a summit. This was a suggestion by him and that he and I, one on one, meet earlier and . . . in a neutral country" (*New York Times,* October 1, 1986, p. A8). Agreement on this mini summit was a key element in the negotiations to release Daniloff, the American accused of spying in Moscow. See also Larry Speakes, *Speaking Out* (Scribner, 1988), p. 140; Donald T. Regan, *For the Record* (Harcourt Brace Jovanovich, 1988), pp. 339–41.

access to Reagan. At the negotiations in Geneva, the U.S. side effectively refused to discuss banning weapons from space, while negotiations on existing offensive systems were bogged down in esoteric detail. To make matters worse, the Soviets faced a divided U.S. administration where one element seemed set on obstructing any agreement that did not involve grossly disproportionate concessions by the Soviet side.[64]

Reagan, and at least one of his advisers, believed in the goal of a nonnuclear world.[65] It was also known that there was an influential body of opinion in the United States, with adherents in the administration, that saw the possibility of a "grand compromise" where constraints on the SDI would be traded for major reductions in Soviet offensive forces.[66] It was hoped that if Reagan were presented an attractive package designed to achieve a nonnuclear world, he would be persuaded that space-based weapons were unnecessary. It was also hoped that by dealing one on one with Reagan, or two on two with Shevardnadze and Shultz joining in, Gorbachev would be able to "wrench arms control out of the hands of the bureaucrats"[67] and reach agreement in principle on the major arms control issues. This would provide the basis for an outline directive that would be given to the appropriate agencies in Moscow and Washington, which would develop three draft agreements that could be signed during a Washington summit.[68]

Gorbachev and his team arrived in Reykjavik, Iceland, well prepared. Following the precedent established by Reagan at Geneva where he presented Gorbachev with a set of proposed guidelines for the renewed negotiations in 1986,[69] the Soviets had prepared a set of "principles" for agreement by the Americans. These principles took at face value Reagan's stated objective of eliminating nuclear weapons completely and the jointly agreed objective of preventing an arms race in space and terminating it on earth. They incorporated the Soviet proposals made at the 1985 Geneva summit and in Gorbachev's January 15 statement. And they added important new concessions.

The Soviets were now willing to accept the lopsided U.S. definition

---

64. Talbott, *The Master,* pp. 289–303.

65. In March 1986 Paul Nitze had acknowledged that "the elimination of nuclear weapons is not an impossible goal, assuming cooperation between the two principal powers" (ibid., p. 214).

66. Ibid., p. 251.

67. Ibid., p. 315, quoting Gorbachev at the first session of the Reykjavik summit.

68. Gorbachev news conference following summit, MTS, October 12, 1986, in *FBIS*-86-198, p. DD29.

69. Talbott, *The Master,* p. 286.

of an SNDV, which excluded from consideration forward-based systems that were capable of striking at Soviet territory; they were willing to have the 50 percent cut in SNDVs apply to Soviet heavy missiles in particular as well as to each leg of the triad. In the INF negotiations, the Soviets would accept the 1981 zero-zero proposal to eliminate completely U.S. and Soviet medium-range missiles in Europe and to impose a freeze on shorter-range missiles.[70] They were also prepared to exclude British and French nuclear weapons from consideration and willing to negotiate on medium-range missiles in Asia.

The U.S. side was not well prepared for the Reykjavik meeting and seems to have put its effort into deciding which representatives of what factions should accompany the president rather than thinking through what lay behind the unexpected Soviet proposal for a mini summit.[71] Accepting the idea that he had come to Iceland for what was "essentially a private meeting" between himself and Gorbachev, Reagan did not expect any "substantive agreements"[72] and appears not even to have been prepared for substantive discussions.[73]

The Americans had been led to expect that intermediate-range systems would be the focal point of the meeting, and the concessions offered by the Soviets certainly made agreement in that area hard to avoid. But wishful thinking allowed the president's advisers to believe that when Gorbachev had written to Reagan of the need to provide an "impulse" to the stalled negotiations,[74] he had for some reason jettisoned the arms control objectives he had been proclaiming continually during the previous eighteen months. Of these the most important was preventing the arms race spreading to space, and in his letter proposing the mini summit Gorbachev had made specific proposals in that regard.[75]

70. According to Akhromeev, the Soviet military started work in 1986 on what such an INF agreement would imply in practical terms. (Interview on the television program "View," MTS, October 9, 1989, in *FBIS*-89-197, p. 102.)

71. *The Reykjavik Process: Preparation for and Conduct of the Iceland Summit and Its Implications for Arms Control Policy,* Committee Print, Report of the Defense Policy Panel to the House Armed Services Committee, 99 Cong. 2 sess. (GPO, January 1987).

72. David Hoffman, *Washington Post,* October 10, 1986, p. A1.

73. In a subsequent address to the Soviet people, Gorbachev noted "that the Americans came to Reykjavik completely empty handed. The impression was created that they had come there only to gather fruit into their basket with empty hands" (MTS, October 14, 1986, in *FBIS*-86-199, DD4). Talbott, *The Master,* p. 315, confirms this assessment.

74. Talbott, *The Master,* p. 315; Gorbachev, news conference, *FBIS*-86-198, p. DD28.

75. According to the president's chief of staff Donald Regan, Gorbachev proposed that any work on the SDI be confined to the laboratory and that the ABM Treaty be extended for an additional fifteen years, in return for which the Soviets would be willing to discuss significant reductions in strategic nuclear arms (*For the Record,* pp. 339–40). In other words, Gorbachev's

Certainly, Gorbachev was aware that the concessions he was offering would allow Reagan to claim a resounding victory on the INF negotiations, a victory that could serve the Republicans well in the mid-term congressional elections three weeks later. But this and the substantial concessions related to strategic systems were crafted to form a package so attractive that Reagan would be unable to refuse, even if acceptance meant forgoing his beloved SDI.

The fact that the U.S. side complained of being "ambushed" by the Soviets in Reykjavik spoke volumes of its inability to comprehend the nature of Soviet arms control objectives, let alone to believe them to be genuine. This incomprehension took the Americans on a fruitless search for some formula that would allow them to pocket the Soviet concessions while preserving the right to deploy space-based weapons. They thus accepted the proposal for a 50 percent cut in all three legs of the triad within five years and then proposed the elimination of all ballistic missiles within ten, which led on to Reagan accepting Gorbachev's amendment that *all kinds* of SNDV should be eliminated within those ten years.[76]

Nominally, the negotiations broke down over whether the ABM Treaty required that research on SDI be limited to the laboratory.[77] In actuality it was over whether or not strike weapons should be deployed in space. The Soviets, along with most of the Americans who had negotiated the ABM Treaty, considered that the treaty prohibited such developments, but the Reagan administration had unilaterally reinterpreted the treaty so as to allow the SDI to proceed. The Soviets

---

letter had clearly stated the agenda he expected to follow, but the U.S. administration was not paying attention.

76. At the final meeting of the two leaders, Gorbachev countered with a Soviet proposal to eliminate all SNDVs and short-range weapons as well, and Reagan replied "suits me fine" (Talbott, *The Master,* p. 325). President Reagan's agreement to eliminating *all* nuclear weapons (including ballistic missiles) is confirmed by Donald Regan (*For the Record,* p. 350) and Speakes (*Speaking Out,* p. 144). Shultz, who with Shevardnadze had sat in on this final meeting, stated that "the agreement that might have been, said [that] all offensive strategic arms and ballistic missiles would be eliminated" (*Department of State Bulletin,* vol. 86 [December 1986], p. 9, reporting Shultz's press conference following the break-up of the talks).

77. In July the U.S. side had offered to refrain from withdrawing from the treaty for seven and a half years, an empty concession since it would be at least seven and probably ten years before the SDI would be ready for initial test deployment. The Soviets had been seeking a firm U.S. commitment of fifteen to twenty years to the ABM Treaty, with protocols reaffirming and clarifying the original long-accepted interpretation. However, at Reykjavik they offered to accept ten years' strict observance during which research would be limited to the laboratory, obviating the possibility of early deployment of an operational system at the end of the period.

sought to have the original purpose of the treaty reaffirmed and the wording strengthened to remove any ambiguity on that score. The U.S. administration chose to characterize this as a "radical change," in that it would close a semantic loophole the administration was trying to exploit.[78]

The Soviets offered a raft of concessions to dissuade Reagan from extending the arms race into space, but he was not prepared to compromise on the strategic defense initiative. The U.S. side would agree to adhere to the ABM Treaty for another ten years, but only if research and development was not confined to the laboratory and if it was free to deploy a space-based system at the end of those ten years. And even that ten-year agreement was booby trapped.[79]

Despite the failure to achieve "the grand compromise," one that appealed to important elements in the Reagan administration,[80] Reykjavik could be seen as a major step toward achieving Gorbachev's broader objective. In January 1986, when he had announced a program to rid the world of nuclear weapons by the year 2000, it "was declared by many pillars of world politics to be an illusion and an unreasonable dream." Nine months later at Reykjavik, the leaders of the two superpowers had reached "agreement that such armaments . . . [could] and should be completely liquidated by 1996."[81]

Never mind that in the following days the U.S. administration claimed that Reagan had only meant to agree to the total elimination of ballistic missiles, and that cruise missiles and aircraft would only be cut by half; the genie was out of the bottle. With the whole world watching the outcome, the leaders of the two superpowers and their senior aides, including both foreign ministers and the Soviet chief of the General Staff, had agreed to eliminate all medium-range nuclear missiles from Europe and to cut 50 percent of all strategic nuclear delivery vehicles within five

---

78. *Department of State Bulletin,* vol. 86, p. 13.

79. The ten years were divided into one five-year period when SNDVs would be cut by 50 percent, and if the cuts had been properly implemented, a second five years during which the remaining ballistic missiles would be eliminated. The five-year break provided an opportunity for the United States to abrogate the treaty by claiming Soviet noncompliance. The second five years would remove all ballistic missiles, an area of perceived Soviet advantage, while the remaining cruise missiles and aircraft, an area of certain U.S. advantage, would be untouched. Thereafter, the Soviets would be unilaterally exposed to the threat of U.S. space-based weapons.

80. Talbott, *The Master,* pp. 251–53, 261–64.

81. "Vremya," MTS, October 22, 1986, in *FBIS*-86-205, pp. AA1, AA3.

years and eliminate the remaining SNDVs during the following five years. Comprehensive nuclear disarmament was being talked of as a practical possibility.[82]

Clearly, Gorbachev had achieved his oft-stated objective of "wrenching arms control from the arms of bureaucrats." It was regrettable that the U.S. administration had "come to the meeting unprepared . . . with their old baggage" and "not one new thought, not one fresh approach," and had responded to Gorbachev's sweeping proposals with a "load of old mothballed junk that was already stifling the Geneva talks, [such as] interim variants, numbers, levels, sub-limits and so on." It was also typical that in the wake of Reykjavik the Reagan administration sought to claim all the credit for what progress had been made, although it was the Soviets who made the concessions that had made progress possible. Nevertheless, the meeting had "raised the Soviet-U.S. dialogue to a new level, [bringing it] out of the plane of technical competition and numerical comparisons and on to new parameters and dimensions," from which height could "be seen new prospects for solving those problems that face us so acutely today."[83]

The meeting had been "a major event. A reappraisal [had taken] place. A qualitatively new situation [had] come about. Nobody [could] now act in the same way as he had acted before."[84] Even the U.S. administration, albeit for its own domestic political purposes, was now proclaiming that irreversible progress had been made at the summit. The interim ceilings of 1,600 SNDVs carrying no more than 6,000 nuclear charges became part of the accepted wisdom.[85]

Besides providing the sought-after "impulse" to negotiations, Reykjavik had clearly established in the eyes of the world's electorates (if not all their governments) that the Soviets were absolutely serious about nuclear disarmament, while "Reagan had thrown away the promise of a nuclear-free world by clinging to his version of a space-based defense—

82. Reykjavik "was not a failure; it was a breakthrough. That was not just another round of negotiations, but a moment of truth, when a momentous opportunity to embark on the path leading to a nuclear-weapon-free world was glimpsed" (Gorbachev addressing the forum "For a Nuclear-Free-World, For the Survival of Mankind," MTS, February 16, 1987, in *FBIS*-87-31, p. AA19).

83. Gorbachev television addresses on "Vremya," MTS, October 14, 1986, in *FBIS*-86-199, pp. DD4, DD10, and October 22, 1986, in *FBIS*-86-205, p. AA2.

84. Ibid.

85. "When to Hold 'Em—and to Fold 'Em," *Time,* October 27, 1986, p. 28.

even if there might be no missiles to defend against.''[86] And in seeking to persuade the American people that Gorbachev was responsible for the failure to agree by ''demanding a price he should have known Reagan would never pay,''[87] the administration's ''spin doctors'' identified the real root of the problem for the rest of the world.

While Reykjavik could be seen as a breakthrough in legitimizing ideas about ridding the world of nuclear weapons, it also highlighted ''how strong and influential the enemies of peace'' were in the United States. Even allowing that Reagan was personally wedded to the SDI, given that it was technologically impossible to implement his dream of a missile-tight shield, there must be other reasons why his administration would turn down such a cornucopia of concessions.

The unavoidable conclusion was that the United States was ''too dependent on the military industrial complex'' for which the arms race had become the ''means of making profits, the aim of [its] existence and the point of [its] activities.'' But there was more to it than that. ''The United States want[ed] to exhaust the Soviet Union economically through a race in the most up-to-date and expensive space weapons.'' Meanwhile the hawks in the Reagan administration seemed set on ''tak[ing] destructive, wrecking actions'' designed ''to poison the atmosphere'' whenever ''a ray of light appear[ed] in attitudes to the major questions of Soviet-U.S. relations [and] to the settlement of questions which involve the interests of the whole of mankind.''[88]

Reykjavik and its aftermath placed in sharp relief the conflicting elements within the Reagan administration and in the larger U.S. body politic. There was the coalition of those who were determined to preserve U.S. military superiority, who sought the downfall of the Soviet state, or who depended on a high level of threat and military expenditure for their well-being. And there were those who shared at least some of Gorbachev's urgent concern about the dangers that stemmed from large nuclear arsenals and the ongoing arms race. Reagan straddled both

86. This was the message being carried to the world by headlines announcing the failure of the summit. ''Forward Spin,'' *Time,* October 27, 1986, p. 24.

87. Ibid.

88. Gorbachev, ''Vremya,'' MTS, in *FBIS*-86-199, p. DD9, and *FBIS*-86-205, p. AA6. In August, Gorbachev had identified the probable interests of the ''right wing militarist group'' that represented the U.S. military-industrial complex as: preventing the profits from weapons' production from drying up; draining the Soviet Union economically and weakening it politically; and ultimately ensuring the United States a commanding position in the world, to fulfill ancient imperial ambitions, and to continue plundering the developing world (Gorbachev Statement, *Pravda,* August 19, 1986, in *FBIS*-86-160, p. AA4).

camps, having no difficulty with the fact that their ideas were largely mutually exclusive. He believed in a nonnuclear world but saw no contradiction in carrying the arms race into space and continuing to test nuclear weapons for use with space-based systems.

At Reykjavik, the combined influence of the American military-industrial complex and those who sought the downfall of the Soviet state was too strong for a "grand compromise" to emerge. In the wake of the summit, the challenge facing the Gorbachev leadership was to devise a course of action that would outflank these negative elements within the U.S. political structure and allow the superpowers to negotiate substantive agreements that would achieve the agreed objective of preventing an arms race in space and halting it on earth.

The Conduct of Foreign Affairs

Gorbachev believed that the situation created by the nuclear confrontation called for new approaches, methods, and forms of relations between different social systems, states, and regions. He came to power convinced that Soviet foreign policy had to make a "historic turn," and within four months he had taken the first major step in that direction.[89] At the July 1, 1985, Central Committee plenum Eduard Shevardnadze, then first secretary of the Georgian Republic, was elected a full member of the Politburo, the first to be chosen by Gorbachev from outside the Moscow apparatus. The next day Shevardnadze was appointed minister of foreign affairs. He replaced Gromyko who moved upstairs to the largely ceremonial post of president, while keeping his seat on the Politburo.

Gorbachev and Shevardnadze's acquaintance went back a long way, and it would seem that they were kindred spirits. When Gorbachev was first secretary of the Komsomol in the Stavropol' region in the late 1950s, Shevardnadze had the analogous post in neighboring Georgia, and in due course they both became first secretaries of their parties in their respective region and republic. While remaining as first secretary of Georgia, Shevardnadze was made a candidate member of the Politburo

89. Gorbachev referred to this turning point at the press conference following the Geneva summit (MTS, November 21, 1985, in *FBIS*-85-225, supp. 13, p. 5), and again in his speech to the 27th Party Congress (*Pravda*, February 26, 1986, p. 2). E. Primakov reasserted the historic nature of this turning point in *Pravda*, July 10, 1987, p. 4.

in 1978, the same year that Gorbachev moved to Moscow. As the Central Committee secretary responsible for agriculture, Gorbachev made repeated visits to see new management methods being tried out in Georgia and in 1984 he praised the Georgian party organization for persistently pursuing this issue.[90]

Shevardnadze, like Gorbachev (and Andropov), had a reputation for personal integrity and being tough on official corruption; he was an innovator in many different areas, and he had an almost legendary skill with people.[91] One can only assume that Gorbachev and Shevardnadze thought alike about international relations as well as how to run the Soviet political economy, and that they had developed great trust in each other's capabilities. Neither had any special experience in defense or foreign affairs, but for those who believed in the need for new thinking (and Shevardnadze was, if anything, more utopian than Gorbachev), this was a shared strength rather than a weakness.

Like the little boy who pointed out the emperor's nakedness, they saw the established approach to international relations as not only absurd, but highly dangerous and inherently unnecessary.[92] To fresh eyes, the nakedness of the underlying theories—socialism's class conflict and the correlation of forces, capitalism's military containment and nuclear deterrence—would have been exposed and the imperative need for a new approach to international relations would have become evident.

This is not to say that Gorbachev and Shevardnadze rejected the established objectives of Soviet foreign policy or that they disagreed with the thrust of the 1983–84 reappraisal and its main conclusions. Rather, they differed on relative priorities and the general approach to foreign affairs, and (most important) they favored a different style of diplomatic discourse. In large part it was a generational change, but it is too simple to assume that because Gromyko was kicked upstairs, he and Gorbachev must have differed fundamentally on the substance of foreign policy at this stage, particularly in respect to Soviet-American relations.

Certainly, Gorbachev gave a new urgency to halting the arms race, but the underlying tone of their public exchanges suggests that he and

90. Morrison, *Gorbachev,* p. 99.
91. Martin Walker, "Fresh Strategy to Defrost the Vodka," *Manchester Guardian Weekly,* November 5, 1989, p. 11.
92. A different form of "new awareness" can be seen in the West where senior officials and military officers, on being freed of the occupational preoccupations of government service and seeing the world through different lenses, sometimes adopt positions and advocate policies directly counter to those they sincerely supported when in office.

Gromyko held each other in high regard. After all, it was Gromyko who had moved away from military confrontation with China and embarked on the long path toward "normalizing relations." It was Gromyko who had publicly defended Soviet-American détente and the value of arms control negotiations well past their de facto demise during the first Reagan administration. It was Gromyko who had exploited the opportunity of Reagan's reference to a "bigger umbrella" in September 1984, who freed the arms control process from the constraints of the INF negotiations and SALT, and who reset them in the more promising framework of the nuclear and space talks (NST). It was Gromyko who had negotiated the joint statement on the objective of those talks, an objective that could have been written by Gorbachev himself. And it is unlikely to have been accidental that it was Gromyko's son and son-in-law who were the coauthors of the 1984 book *New Thinking in the Nuclear Age.*[93]

Gromyko's world view was less of a problem than the entrenched bureaucracy of the Ministry of Foreign Affairs (MFA). But Gromyko had been minister for twenty-eight years, the lines of patronage all ran in one direction, and if the style of Soviet foreign policy was to be refashioned, change must start at the top.

It was six months (and after the Geneva summit) before Gorbachev and Shevardnadze were ready to start radically rearranging the senior echelons of the MFA, and one of the first changes was to replace the deputy foreign minister for cadres with an experienced member of the Central Committee secretariat.[94] Within a year of Shevardnadze's appointment, only one hangover from the Brezhnev period and two from the Andropov period were still deputy foreign ministers. The other six deputies and both the first deputies were all new. Similarly, there had been a change of Soviet ambassador in over forty foreign capitals, including Washington, Beijing, Tokyo, London, Paris, and Bonn.[95]

In his report to the Twenty-seventh Party Congress at the end of February 1986, Gorbachev had expounded on the need for new political thinking, and by the second half of May he was ready to address a major in-house conference at the MFA. This was attended by the heads of

93. Gromyko and Lomeiko, *New Thinking.*
94. Valentin Nikiforov, who was appointed deputy foreign minister in December 1985, had previously been deputy head of the Organizational Party Work Department, which oversaw personnel policy (Elizabeth Teague, "Ambassadorial Merry-Go-Round," *RL* 132/86, [March 21, 1986], pp. 2–3).
95. Alexander Rahr, "Winds of Change Hit Foreign Ministery," *RL* 274/86 (July 16, 1986).

all Soviet diplomatic missions abroad and by the relevant Central Committee secretaries. Second-hand reports say that he outlined new foreign policy priorities and stressed the growing interdependence in the world; he required a new approach to negotiations, including those on arms control, where the emphasis was to be on flexibility; and he warned that corruption in the MFA would not be tolerated.[96]

But at this stage the "historic turn" in Soviet policy was more one of style than of substance. That would come in 1987. Meanwhile, the revamped foreign policy establishment continued to pursue the objectives that had emerged from the 1983–84 policy reappraisal.

Soviet-American Relations

There are no reasons for assuming that Gorbachev would have disputed the harsh indictment of U.S. policy leveled by Andropov in September 1983 nor was there reason for him to disagree with the Soviet assessment that the Reagan administration had embarked on a crusade against communism, that it was seeking to eliminate socialism as a sociopolitical system by one means or another, and that it was set on achieving military domination.

By the time that Gorbachev arrived in Moscow in 1978 the buildup of American anti-Sovietism had become palpable. He would have been aware of the adverse shift in U.S. policy in the second half of the Carter administration, the authorization of new U.S. nuclear weapons programs, and the leaking of Presidential Directive 59 with its nuclear-war-fighting strategy. As a member of the Politburo from 1980, he would have been fully cognizant of the details of the political-military offensive launched by the Reagan administration on taking office and of its rejection of détente and disparagement of arms control.

It would have been hard to interpret U.S. policy in 1980–85 as other than extremely hostile to the Soviet Union, and during Gorbachev's visits to Canada and Britain in 1983–84, Western observers were struck by his doctrinaire anti-Americanism.[97] After he took office, Gorbachev was quite explicit that he considered U.S. attitudes and policies as endangering the peace of the world and damaging Soviet interests. That these were sincerely held opinions rather than rhetoric is supported by

96. Rahr, "Winds of Change," p. 1; Glickham, "New Directions," p. 17.
97. Morrison, *Gorbachev*, pp. 126, 129.

the rapid progress of Aleksandr N. Yakovlev's career, once Gorbachev assumed power.

Yakovlev, who is more than six years older than Gorbachev and fought in World War II, had occupied rather important positions in the Central Committee propaganda apparatus under Khrushchev and Brezhnev. However, he fell out of favor in 1973 and was "exiled" to Ottawa as Soviet ambassador and was not brought back to Moscow by Andropov until after Gorbachev had visited Canada in the spring of 1983. Yakovlev, who was well known for harsh anti-American views that were confirmed rather than modified by his ten years as a U.S. watcher in Ottawa, returned to take up the newly vacant directorship of the influential Institute of World Economy and International Relations (IMEiMO).[98] Three months after Gorbachev became general secretary, Yakovlev rejoined the Central Committee secretariat as head of the Propaganda Department and soon came to be seen as one of Gorbachev's closest and most trusted advisers.[99]

Within nine months Yakovlev had been appointed secretary with overall responsibility for the media and culture; a year later he was a candidate member of the Politburo, and six months after that (June 1987) a full member, with overall responsibility for ideology. In that capacity he oversaw the work of Anatoliy Dobrynin, a career diplomat who, in March 1986, had been brought back from Washington to become a secretary of the Central Committee and head up the revamped International Department.

---

98. Rahr, *Biographic Directory*, pp. 226–27. For a taste of his views see Aleksandr Yakovlev, *On the Edge of the Abyss: From Truman to Reagan, the Doctrines and Realities of the Nuclear Age* (Moscow: Progress, 1985). In this book on U.S. grand strategy and military doctrine, Yakovlev portrays American society as prone to violence, governed by deceit, and fixed upon global hegemony and domination. The book links together three elements: a critique of American "political science" as a servant of the military-industrial complex and imperialism; the triumph of anti-Soviet hysteria in the late 1970s, with the rise of the radical right and neoconservatism; and various U.S. war plans of the 1940s and early 1950s and the linkage of these plans with various attempts at psychological warfare against the USSR. (Review by Jacob W. Kipp in *Journal of Soviet Military Studies*, vol. 1 [April 1988], pp. 147–48.) It has been suggested that Yakovlev's view of the United States was shaped in part by C. Wright Mills, *The Power Elite* (Oxford University Press, 1956), a book that was still a focus of interest in 1959 when Yakovlev was an exchange student at Columbia University in New York. Wright Mills was the first to publicize the existence of the American military-industrial complex, although he did not name it. He spoke instead of "military capitalism," and "a permanent-war economy" and "a political vacuum in which the corporate rich and high warlord, in their coinciding interest, rule" and he specified "the unity and the shape of the power elite in terms of the military ascendancy" (pp. 276–77).

99. Yakovlev was among the officials who accompanied Gorbachev to the Geneva summit in 1985.

Dobrynin had spent twenty-four years as ambassador to the United States and it was assumed by many that his new appointment signaled the rise of pro-American forces within the Soviet leadership. The assumption seemed to be confirmed when, within eight weeks, Yuliy M. Vorontsov was appointed as one of the two first deputy foreign ministers; he had served in Washington for ten years under Dobrynin and another six at the United Nations.[100] There is, however, no reason to conclude that Dobrynin's time in Washington made him pro-American and many reasons to assume the opposite. Doubtless, Dobrynin had cordial relations with many Americans and admired many aspects of the American nation. But liking the American people and their society is not synonymous with liking U.S. foreign policy.

Even to its friends, the United States is a difficult and unpredictable partner in foreign affairs. The division of powers between the legislative and the executive branches immeasurably complicates dealings with other nations and provides a unilateral escape clause to agreements freely entered into. The administration itself rarely speaks with one voice, and the fragmented system of government makes it hard to know which of the fiefdoms will prevail and whose view will become policy. There are also powerful forces outside government with the capacity to skew decisions to reflect their narrow sectional interests. This diffusion of power and authority allows subordinate political appointees within the different fiefdoms unparalleled influence over the nature and details of decisions on defense and foreign policy at the national level. Overlying everything is the populist tendency in U.S. foreign policy which focuses on making the American people "feel good" or "stand tall," rather than on the somewhat less nebulous (and more predictable) concept of national interest.

The populist tendency was particularly strong in the Reagan administration. Combined with it was a heavy bias toward the "essentialist" view of the Soviet Union as inherently evil and bent on military expansion.[101] The result was an actively hostile and deliberately confrontational policy toward the Soviet Union and clearly articulated U.S. objectives of restoring American military superiority and bringing about the collapse of the Soviet political system.

However sophisticated a diplomat, Dobrynin would have been hard

100. Vorontsov served as counselor in 1966–70 and then minister-counselor in 1970–77 (Rahr, "Winds of Change," p. 8).
101. See chap. 4, note 74.

pressed to have remained "pro-American" throughout this prolonged onslaught. He would have shared the feelings of those in Moscow who saw the years of effort they had invested in détente and the SALT process crumble because there had been a change of mood in the United States and a change of fashion in strategic thought.[102] More than most, Dobrynin would have been aware of the Reagan administration's double standards in the field of foreign policy and the skill with which it manipulated the facts and the media. And as a Soviet representative in Washington he would have had to endure the mixture of overt hostility and contempt that was fostered by the administration,[103] added to which Alexander Haig seemed to have gone out of his way to publicly humiliate Dobrynin in his early days as secretary of state.[104]

Dobrynin may have differed with Gromyko over matters of style and certain aspects of his approach to Soviet-American relations, but there was no reason why Dobrynin should have disagreed with the conclusions of the 1983–84 reappraisal, or with standard Soviet descriptions of what was driving U.S. foreign policy. The Soviets had seized on the term that President Dwight Eisenhower had coined when he warned against the U.S. military-industrial complex. There was no denying its pervasive influence throughout the U.S. political system, that it thrived on high threat perceptions, and that the complex's well-being was related to the prospects for profit and employment in a substantial proportion of U.S. congressional districts. Nor could it be denied that the military-industrial complex had grown to encompass a vast array of intellectual activity, which extended from universities and think tanks to myriad commercial consultancies, where the pressure was to tell the military and its political leadership what it wanted to hear.

And while the term "aggressive circles" might sound crass to Western ears, it became very clear during the first Reagan administration that there were indeed influential groups in the United States who saw the

102. Georgiy Arbatov, director of the Institute for the Study of the United States and Canada and generally assumed to be pro-American, made his disenchantment with U.S. policy in the early 1980s very clear in private conversations with Americans.

103. A junior member of the Soviet embassy in Washington in 1980–85 told me how thankful he was to be returning to Moscow and escaping the overt hostility directed toward his country, his family, and himself.

104. Haig acknowledges that Dobrynin "must have thought he had been deliberately humiliated" when, on his first visit with Haig, he was not allowed to enter the State Department via the basement garage he had used for years, and on proceeding to the main entrance, he was met by "a thicket of microphones and cameras" (Alexander M. Haig, Jr., *Caveat: Realism, Reagan and Foreign Policy* [Macmillan, 1984], pp. 101–02).

Soviet Union as an evil empire and as the sole cause of conflict in the world, and who envisaged U.S. foreign policy as a crusade to rectify this situation. There were also those who sought to restore U.S. military superiority, who sought the "high ground" of space and hoped to achieve a "strategic end run." There were others who focused on how to bring about the collapse of the Soviet economy by denying it access to the latest technology and hampering its efforts to trade with the West, while generating new kinds of military threat that would force the Soviet Union to invest in costly countermeasures. And there were those who saw the United States as the gendarme of the world with the inherent right if not a duty to "destabilize" regimes that did not conform to U.S.-determined norms of domestic and foreign behavior.

The Soviets have always been at pains to stress that the aggressive circles do not represent a majority in the United States or in the West.[105] But the crucial question was who had the greater influence over policy, and the experience of 1978–85 made it clear that it was not the "peace-loving forces" in the West. It is therefore likely that Dobrynin was brought back to Moscow not to counterbalance Yakovlev's overt anti-Americanism but rather to complement it with an intimate knowledge of the political process in Washington and the likely elements in U.S. decisionmaking on matters affecting the Soviet Union, particularly in crises.

Within the MFA, experience was biased in a different direction. All of Yuliy Vorontsov's service in America had been during the time of détente. His most recent appointments had been as ambassador to India (1977–83) and to France (1983–86). Anatoliy Kovalev, the other new first deputy foreign minister, had served in the German Democratic Republic in 1949–55, but since then had remained in Moscow. He had spent eight years in two of the European departments (heading one of them for six years), but since 1971 had been chief of the Foreign Policy Planning Administration.[106]

Vorontsov was responsible for global issues and disarmament, whereas his predecessor Georgiy Kornienko (who moved sideways to become Dobrynin's first deputy) had been responsible for the United

105. Georgiy Arbatov wrote of the struggle "between the mighty forces of the military-industrial complex, militarist forces, and extreme right wing politicians on the one hand, and on the other those sober-minded political and public circles which understand U.S. national interests . . . correctly." *Komsomol'skaya Pravda (Komsomol Truth)*, March 11, 1986, p. 3.

106. Rahr, "Winds of Change," p. 8.

States, plus the United Nations, the Middle East, and disarmament, all of which involved Soviet-U.S. interaction. Under the new arrangement, responsibility for the United States and the United Nations lay with a simple deputy minister, albeit one with significant expertise. Similarly, Kovalev was responsible for Western Europe and the Conference on Security and Cooperation in Europe (CSCE), whereas his predecessor Viktor Mal'tsev had been responsible for Eastern Europe, Southeast Asia, and China.

The result of these various appointments was to strengthen the capability of the Central Committee secretariat to support informed decisionmaking in hostile exchanges or crises involving the United States, and of the senior members of the MFA hierarchy to concentrate on longer-term policy in other parts of the world, particularly in Europe.

The same relative emphasis can be found in Gorbachev's report to the Twenty-seventh Party Congress at the end of February 1986, which preceded the major reshuffle at the MFA. Gorbachev used the classical concepts of tendencies and contradictions to organize his broad review of world trends, and he reaffirmed the Marxist-Leninist conclusion that history was not a "disorderly Brownian motion, but a law-governed onward process" in which "socialism [was] a realistic option open to all humanity." Socialism offered a new way of life "based on the principle of social justice, with neither oppressors nor oppressed, neither exploiter or exploited, where power belongs to the people."[107]

In discussing the most important group of contradictions, those between capitalism and socialism, Gorbachev put emphasis on the United States, whose ruling circles "refuse to assess the realities of the world . . . in sober terms." Addressing the growing contradictions within the capitalist world, he pointed to disagreements between its three main centers (the United States, Western Europe, and Japan) over exchange and interest rates and trading matters, and noted that for the first time "governments of some West European countries, the Social Democratic and Liberal parties, and the public at large have begun to openly discuss whether present U.S. policy coincides with Western Europe's notion about its own security."[108]

As Yakovlev had put it nine months earlier, "the distancing of Western Europe, Japan and other capitalist countries from U.S. strategic military plans in the near future is neither an excessively rash fantasy

107. Gorbachev, MTS, February 25, 1986, in *FBIS*-86-38, supp. 41, pp. O2–3.
108. Ibid., pp. O5–6.

nor a nebulous prospect,"[109] and this thought may have underlain Gorbachev's offer of bilateral negotiations with Britain and France on nuclear force reductions.[110] Similarly in the economic area, two months after taking office Gorbachev had raised the possibility of recognizing the Western European Economic Community as a political entity and establishing "mutually beneficial relations" between it and the Eastern European Council for Mutual Economic Assistance.[111]

An anti-American thrust had been very evident in Gorbachev's speech at the April 1985 plenum and this was sustained in his report to the party congress in 1986. In the section on the party's foreign policy strategy, it was the "right wing group which [had] come to power in the United States and its main fellow travellers in NATO [which had] turned sharply away from detente to a military policy of force. . . . The Washington administration [had] remained deaf to [Soviet] calls to halt the arms race." On the other hand, the party considered "one of the basic sectors of its foreign policy to be the European one."[112] Eight weeks later in East Berlin Gorbachev spoke of turning "away from confrontation and military rivalry to the path of peaceful coexistence by joint effort." Only in that sense could "our" continent be united. There was no suggestion that the United States had a place in this future shape of things, in "our common European house," and he had opened by affirming Soviet willingness to see the dismantling of the Warsaw Pact and NATO.[113]

This focus on the United States as an intractable problem was a salient feature of Shevardnadze's speech to the United Nations in late September 1986. It mainly comprised a polite but pointed and extensive attack on the failure of the United States to respond to the Soviet Union's arms control initiatives and on its continued insistence on emplacing strike weapons in space, policies that implied a disregard for the future of mankind. Shevardnadze also singled out the United States for its role in fomenting or prolonging internal conflict in countries led by left-leaning regimes.[114]

The relative emphasis in Gorbachev's and Shevardnadze's speeches,

---

109. Interview in *la Republica* (Rome), May 21, 1985, in *FBIS*-85-101, p. CC1.
110. On October 3, 1985, and January 15, 1986.
111. Gorbachev speech at dinner for Italian prime minister, MDS, May 29, 1985, in *FBIS*-85-104, p. G4. See F. Stephen Larrabee and Allen Lynch, "Gorbachev: The Road to Reykjavik," *Foreign Policy,* no. 65 (Winter 1986–87), pp. 8–9.
112. Gorbachev, MTS, in *FBIS*-86-38, supp. 41, pp. O28–29, O31.
113. MTS, April 21, 1986, in *FBIS*-86-77, pp. F1–5.
114. TASS, September 23, 1986, in *FBIS*-86-185, pp. CC1–10.

and in the pattern of appointments that emerged from the reshuffle of top MFA officials, conforms to the conclusion of the 1983–84 reappraisal. While the superpower relationship could never be less than central, in 1985–86 the United States was seen primarily as a problem, whereas the rest of the capitalist bloc was seen primarily as an opportunity. As Gorbachev noted in one of his first statements on foreign policy, "Relations between the U.S.S.R. and the United States are an exceptionally important factor." He did not say "good relations" and he went on to stress that "we do not look at the world solely through the prism of those relations."[115]

The United States was something unpredictable and often dangerous that required top-level attention on a day-to-day basis. Western Europe was seen as an area that needed to be cultivated and exploited over the long term, and good relations with the Western European nations were an end in themselves. Good relations with the United States were primarily the means to an end, that of averting world war, in part through negotiating the reduction and ultimately the elimination of nuclear weapons.

Relative priorities in the Soviet relationship with the United States were clearly demonstrated during 1986. The deterioration in Soviet-American relations and the increasing threat of war having been checked by the Geneva summit, the Soviets were not interested in another summit unless it had a real chance of achieving progress in halting the arms race on earth and preventing its spread into space. Nor were they prepared to sit quietly under provocation; they responded forcefully in March when two U.S. warships intruded into Soviet territorial waters in the Black Sea for the first time,[116] and they canceled a projected meeting between Shultz and Shevardnadze in response to the U.S. air attack on Libya in April.

The same hard-nosed policy could be seen in the diplomatic barging

115. *Pravda,* April 8, 1985, p. 1.
116. While U.S. ships deployed to the Black Sea on a regular basis, they had previously observed the twelve-mile territorial limit scrupulously, and this deliberate intrusion was a new departure. The Soviet protest threatened that future incursions would not go unpunished. In February 1988, when the same two ships entered territorial waters off Savastopol, the main naval base on the Black Sea, they were warned to leave. Receiving no reply, two Soviet frigates deliberately bumped the U.S. ships, causing slight damage but no injuries. The U.S. navy claimed its warships were conducting "routine operations" to exercise "the right of innocent passage." The operation, which had to be cleared by the White House, was hardly routine, while "the passage was not innocent under any credible interpretation of either customary or treaty-based laws of the sea." Rear Admiral Eugene J. Carroll, "Black Day on the Black Sea," *Arms Control Today,* vol. 18 (May 1988), pp. 14–17.

match that surfaced in 1985 and reached a crescendo at the end of August 1986 with the "Daniloff affair." Public concern in the United States about the espionage potential of Soviet diplomats had been rekindled in February 1985 by the publication of a book by Arkady Shevchenko, a senior member of the Soviet mission at the United Nations who had defected in 1978, and fuel was added with the exposure of the Walker brothers' naval spy ring in May. Among various responses, the administration rewrote U.S. counterintelligence plans, resulting in new restrictions on Soviet bloc citizens working in the United States and a presidential directive in March 1986 that the size of the Soviet UN mission was to be cut from 275 to 170 by April 1988.

The diplomatic climate continued to deteriorate and on August 23, 1986, Gennady Zakharov, a Soviet UN employee, was arrested for buying classified information. He had, indeed, been paying someone to collect technological information that was available through open sources, but the Federal Bureau of Investigation (FBI) had arranged for this intermediary to pass him some "secret" material, at which stage he was arrested. A week later the state security (KGB) service played the same trick on Daniloff, a U.S. correspondent in Moscow.[117] Washington cried foul and swore that a deal was out of the question, but by the end of September an exchange had been arranged, with Daniloff being freed on the 29th and Zakharov a day later.

Still denying there had been any trade, the Reagan administration was able to bury the issue with news of a mini summit at Reykjavik in ten days time, something that Gorbachev had proposed in a letter delivered by Shevardnadze on September 19th. This was hardball diplomacy of the kind Reagan's right wing aspired to, but they had been bested at their own game. Gorbachev's refusal to agree to a formal summit until there was progress on arms control still stood, but he might be able to break the logjam in negotiations by dealing directly with Reagan at Reykjavik. As for the U.S. administration, it had been maneuvered into accepting what it had hitherto condemned—an ill-prepared and unstructured meeting between the two leaders.

Meanwhile, the diplomatic posturing continued. On September 17th, twenty-five members of the Soviet mission to the United States were ordered to leave the United States by the end of the month. On October 21st, less than two weeks after the Reykjavik summit, the Soviets

---

117. Larry Speakes, then White House press secretary, has written that the two cases "were almost identical and were linked to each other" (*Speaking Out*, p. 140).

declared five American diplomats personae non gratae. Two days later the State Department expelled five Soviet diplomats and said that fifty more must leave by November 1st to bring representation in the two capitals into line. Two days after that the Soviets expelled another five U.S. diplomats and withdrew all two hundred and sixty Soviet service employees from the embassy. As the diplomats in Moscow did their own shopping, cooking, cleaning, and maintenance, Reagan's national security adviser remarked complacently: "We made our point. We are down to parity."

To close a rambunctious year, the Soviets rejected a U.S. proposal for an exchange of greetings at the New Year between the two leaders, because of U.S. reluctance to adhere to the informal agreements on arms reductions that had been reached at the Reykjavik summit. The New Year's exchange had been initiated the previous year in the wake of the Geneva summit, with each leader addressing the other's countrymen on national television channels for five minutes. Reagan did attempt to address the Soviet people on January 1, 1987, using the Voice of America, but the Soviets jammed the radio transmission.[118]

This diplomatic jousting, of no great interest in itself, highlights the style of Soviet discourse with the United States during the first two years of Gorbachev's regime. It contrasts sharply with the Soviet policy that began to emerge by the end of March 1987. This later policy held good relations with the United States to be an end in themselves and at times led to Soviet diplomatic behavior that verged on the ingratiating. But for most of Gorbachev's first two years, good relations with the United States continued to be a means to an end. And while the Soviets were willing to make concessions in areas such as arms control where this might bring about agreement on halting the arms race and preventing it from spreading into space, they were not prepared to ignore what they saw as U.S. provocations in the interest of good relations with Washington.

The Soviet National Security Zone

A nation's behavior in its national security zone is likely to be very different from its behavior toward the world at large. What constitutes

118. Bernard Weinraub, *New York Times*, December 31, 1986, p. 6. However, an edited version of Reagan's address was broadcast on a Radio Moscow news bulletin.

the national security zone varies with each country's capabilities, but this universal if somewhat fluid concept can be defined as the area surrounding a state's borders that it sees as critical to its well-being and security.

The salient feature of the hegemonic power's approach to developments in its national security zone is the general assumption that its ideological preferences and perceived security interests override the individual interests of other countries in the zone, an assumption that will have wide domestic political support. That is the approach that has been evident in U.S. policy over the years toward the states in its primary national security zone (the western hemisphere, north of the equator), and even more so in the case of the Soviet Union since World War II. The Soviets have not enjoyed the U.S. advantage of overwhelming predominance in a hemisphere that is remote from significant enemies.

Although the scope of a country's national security zone can change over time, it can be fairly clearly delineated at any one time. In 1985 the Soviet primary national security zone encompassed the members of the Warsaw Pact, plus Finland, Mongolia, and Afghanistan, and perhaps the northern part of Iran.

EASTERN EUROPE. From the late 1970s there had been an accelerating deterioration in political and economic conditions in most of Eastern Europe. In 1980-81 the situation in Poland had become critical, and Moscow had faced the question of whether it would have to intervene militarily, with all that implied in political costs within the Warsaw Treaty Organization (WTO) and in the world at large. These deteriorating conditions were matched by the Soviet Union's diminishing ability and willingness to bail out members whose misguided policies had resulted in economic distress.

This situation was no surprise to Gorbachev, since he had overall responsibility for relations with the Soviet bloc countries before his election as general secretary.[119] The obvious requirement was to turn Eastern Europe into an economic and political asset rather than a liability, and in April 1985 Gorbachev appears to have believed that Eastern Europe's problems were akin to those that bedeviled the Soviet Union. He assumed that the remedies he was applying to the Soviet domestic economy were equally applicable to Eastern Europe and that

119. Comment by Georgiy Shakhnazarov, Gorbachev's chief adviser on Eastern Europe, in an interview with the Soviet monthly *Gorizont*, no. 7, as reported in *RFE/RL* (U.S. Radio Free Europe–Radio Liberty) *Daily Report*, no. 216 (November 13, 1989), p. 5.

the main requirement was to improve the efficiency of the whole and its parts, streamline existing economic mechanisms, remove the slack from the system and make effective use of these untapped resources, invest more heavily in modern technology, and so on.

In other words there was nothing wrong with socialism per se, the problem lay in how it was applied both within the individual countries and within the structure of the Council for Mutual Economic Assistance (CMEA). And while Gorbachev recognized that the Eastern European economies were valuable seedbeds for innovative approaches, there were limits to what was acceptable. In mid-1985 he is said to have warned a closed meeting of high-level Eastern European economic planners against following China's example. "Many of you," he said, "see the solution to your problems in resorting to market mechanisms in place of direct planning. Some of you look to the market as a life saver for your economies. But comrades, you should not think about life savers, but about the ship. And the ship is socialism!"[120]

The CMEA had never succeeded in developing an economically coherent or politically feasible plan for promoting increased interaction, and while it was up to each member of the bloc to restructure its economy and bring it up to world standards, Gorbachev strongly believed that multilateral arrangements also needed improving.[121] A Comprehensive Program for Scientific and Technical Cooperation until the Year 2000 was agreed at the CMEA meeting in December 1985, and in October 1987 a Collective Concept for the Socialist International Division of Labor for the Period 1991–2005. The latter included an agreement that member states would plan and allocate production of key products according to the principle of comparative advantage.[122]

However, not all Eastern European countries were equally enthusiastic about the general thrust for reform, highlighting the contradiction that still lay at the heart of the perestroika process in 1985–86, both inside the Soviet Union and within the larger socialist community. This contradiction stemmed from the inherent conflicts between apparent

120. This is reported to have been said in a major policy speech to a closed meeting (Richard Nations, "Deng Xiaoping's Reforms Worry Kremlin's Bosses," *Far Eastern Economic Review,* August 14, 1986, p. 34).

121. "What is required are changes in the activity of the very headquarters of socialist integration—CEMA" (Gorbachev report to 27th Party Congress, MTS, February 25, 1986, in *FBIS-86-38,* supp. 41, p. O32).

122. Karen Dawisha, *Eastern Europe, Gorbachev and Reform: The Great Challenge* (Cambridge University Press, 1988), pp. 246, 249.

opposites like the diversity needed for progress and the conformity that ensured cohesion, or the interests of the larger system and those of its individual parts, whether people, parties, Union republics, or nation-states.

Recognition of the need for diversity was not something new and in his report to the party congress in 1981 Brezhnev had spoken of the "diverse, positive experience" accumulated by other members and the importance of learning from each other. Back in 1968, it had been authoritatively restated that "the peoples of socialist countries and the Communist Parties have and must have freedom to determine their countries' path of development." However, the statement went on to stress that their decisions must not damage socialism in their own country, the fundamental interests of other socialist countries, or the world communist movement.[123] This was in the wake of the Soviet invasion of Czechoslovakia, and the statement became known as the Brezhnev Doctrine, but it was not very different from what Gorbachev said almost twenty years later.

In his speech to the Tenth Polish Party Congress in June 1986 Gorbachev described socialism as "an international reality, as an alliance of states closely linked by political, economic, cultural, and defense interests." He then observed that "to threaten the socialist order, to try to undermine it from the outside, and tear one country or another from the socialist community means encroachment not only on the will of the people but also on the entire postwar order and, in the final analysis, on peace."[124] Although ostensibly directed at outside forces, this warning would apply equally to Eastern European initiatives that weakened the internal cohesion of the Warsaw Pact.

Gorbachev must surely have been aware that the implications of his warning ran counter to the new political thinking, which stressed that the viewpoint of other countries must be respected and their legitimate interests recognized, implying that intervention by great powers in the internal affairs of other states was impermissible. In his report to the Twenty-seventh Party Congress he called for "unconditional respect in international practice for the right of every people to choose the paths and forms of its development."[125] But this merely reflected the ambivalence that characterized Soviet policy toward the countries of Eastern

123. *Pravda,* September 15, 1968.
124. MTS, June 30, 1986, in *FBIS*-86-126, p. F3.
125. MTS, February 25, 1986, in *FBIS*-86-38, supp. 41, p. O34.

Europe during the first two years of perestroika. It also reflected the Soviet preoccupation at the time with the American policy of undermining "progressive regimes" in the third world, something the Soviets saw as quite different from their own "fraternal assistance" to ensure the retention of power by Soviet-approved regimes.

Soviet attitudes toward Eastern Europe in 1985–86 were complex, though understandable in the context of events since 1941.[126] Soviet forces entered Eastern Europe in the course of achieving final victory over the Axis armies, who fought as tenaciously in retreat as they had when advancing one thousand miles into Soviet territory. Germany did not capitulate until May 1945, after its armies went down to final defeat on native soil, and the Soviet advance through Eastern Europe was a prerequisite to that defeat.

Except in the most general terms it seems that Stalin did not have clear-cut plans for the countries that now comprise the Warsaw Pact. The basic requirement was to establish a buffer between the USSR and the resurgent Germany that could be expected to emerge in fifteen to twenty years, and this implied governments that were amicably disposed toward the Soviet Union, or at least not hostile. This would not be easy to achieve, since Romania and (to a much lesser extent) Hungary had fought against Russia in both world wars, and there was a centuries-old enmity with Poland, whose government had been actively hostile in the interwar years.

However, having been welcomed as liberators in Eastern Europe, the Soviets probably genuinely believed that governments that represented the mass of the people would be positively disposed toward the Soviet Union, a Marxist prediction that seemed to have been proved right in Albania and Yugoslavia, and again by the free elections held in Czechoslovakia in 1946. Nor was this assumption unjustified. The Communist parties of the Eastern European states were not alone in wanting the foreign policies of their countries to be based on an alliance with the USSR. Other political groups agreed that the Soviet Union was a surer safeguard against renewed German aggression than were the Anglo-Saxons or the French.[127]

The pattern that finally emerged in Eastern Europe was not preor-

---

126. For a broader historical context, skillfully portrayed, see Dawisha, *Eastern Europe,* pp. 7–19.

127. Peter Calvocoressi, *Survey of International Affairs, 1947–48* (London: Oxford University Press, 1952), p. 150.

dained, despite the ideological prejudice that the interests of the working class could only be properly represented by the world communist movement led from Moscow. Given the case of Finland and the differentiated Soviet approach to the other countries in 1945–47, it is likely that Stalin was prepared to live with a variety of left-leaning or resolutely neutral regimes. Communist control of the state apparatus was not seen as uniformly mandatory, although it may well have been the inevitable outcome in most countries.

This relatively relaxed approach changed abruptly in 1947–48, following the Truman declaration in March 1947, matched by Zhdanov's "two camps" doctrine in September. This led to a switch in Soviet threat assessments from "Germany in fifteen to twenty years" to the more immediate danger of a capitalist coalition led by the Anglo-Saxon powers that would be ready for war by 1953. Eastern Europe must now serve as a defensive glacis in both military and ideological terms, and the latter requirement evoked the worst kind of centrally enforced Stalinist orthodoxy.

During the next twenty years, Eastern Europe evolved from an ideological glacis to a cross between an ideological empire and an alliance and it became an important part of the metropolitan core of the growing socialist system and the expanding world communist movement. This was also the period when the Soviets still believed in the emergence of a socialist trading system that would progressively supplant the existing capitalist one. The economic aspects of the Eastern European alliance-empire therefore became steadily more important, in respect to both the material well-being of the Soviet Union and the strength of the larger socialist system.

Meanwhile, the importance of Eastern Europe as a military glacis increased steadily. Even though the Soviets had discounted the threat of a premeditated land offensive by the mid-1950s, the danger of war between the two social systems remained. The defensive role of Eastern Europe continued to be significant, but the area acquired a new importance as the springboard for offensive operations against Western Europe in the event of war. The 1970s wartime strategy increased the salience of that role, because the Soviets now needed to launch a conventional blitzkrieg at the onset of war, defeating NATO in Europe within three weeks and evicting U.S. forces from the Continent. The military significance of Eastern Europe (particularly East Germany, Czechoslovakia, and Poland) in Soviet contingency plans was further increased by the requirement that emerged from the 1983–84 reappraisal to remain on the defensive for the first twenty to thirty days of a major conflict.

During this same period, the Soviet military involvement in Eastern Europe had acquired political importance as an instrument of alliance cohesion. Starting in the first half of the 1960s the Soviets increasingly integrated the military forces of the Eastern European countries with their own. The conduct of joint exercises and officer training, the cross-posting between national forces, and the overlapping and interlocking of military staffs were all intended to serve a political as well as a military purpose, and this integrating process was important in promoting cohesion of the Warsaw Pact and enhancing the authority of the Communist party in member countries.

Despite this overlap, by 1985 the Soviet Union's military, ideological, and economic interests in Eastern Europe were badly out of balance.[128] Economically, the area was a net burden. East Germany, the most advanced of the CMEA countries, still lagged behind world standards and Hungary was no longer a seedbed for reformist ideas. Ideologically the leadership of the various countries was mostly moribund, while in Poland the legitimacy of the Communist party had been directly challenged. In all six countries, large sections of the populace were more or less openly hostile to the ruling elite and the government apparatus. In other words, a strong argument could be made on political, ideological, and economic grounds that the Soviet Union would be well rid of Eastern Europe, the loss of face notwithstanding.

The overriding objection to letting go of the CMEA countries, one that ruled out even contemplating such action in 1985–86, was the vital role of Eastern Europe in Soviet contingency plans. As long as the Soviet military was required to cover the possibility of world war, as long as its force posture and structure were determined by the objective of not losing such a war, the deployment of Soviet forces in Eastern Europe and the integration of national forces would continue to be a strategic imperative. A political prerequisite was that the six countries should remain part of the Soviet bloc (or socialist community, as Gorbachev called it), implying that the Communist party would remain in control of the respective governments, which would be careful not to diverge unduly from the centrally established line on key issues.

AFGHANISTAN. Within two months of the preemptive military coup

---

128. See, for example, F. Stephen Larrabee, *The Challenge to Soviet Interests in Eastern Europe,* R-3190-AF (Santa Monica, Calif.: Rand Corp., December 1984).

that overthrew the Daoud government in April 1978, a radical Marxist faction had gained ascendancy and begun to initiate a modernizing, secular, but not peculiarly communist revolution from above. This evoked growing Muslim-led resistance throughout most of Afghanistan, which escalated to a major insurgency in the city of Herat in March 1979. By the end of 1979, some forty thousand insurgents were operating inside Afghanistan, supported from bases in Pakistan.[129]

Moscow had signed a treaty of friendship with Afghanistan the previous December and in April 1979 it moved to assess and, if possible, to change the political-military situation in the country. This process included two visits by a large group of Soviet senior officers in April and again in August. The latter was led by Army General Ivan Pavlovsky, deputy defense minister and chief of the Soviet ground forces, and his sixty-three-man team included twelve other generals, who remained in Afghanistan for two months.[130]

As part of his instructions from Defense Minister Dmitriy F. Ustinov, General Pavlovsky had been told that it must be made clear that "in no circumstances" would the Soviet Union send troops into Afghanistan. During 1979 Moscow had refused no fewer than eighteen requests from Kabul for various kinds of direct but mainly limited assistance by Soviet forces, although an airborne battalion had been inserted at Bagram in July to secure the airfield.[131] Meanwhile, the situation in the countryside continued to deteriorate and, after an unsuccessful Soviet attempt to replace the Khalqi faction in September 1979, Hafizullah Amin emerged as the leader of the government in Kabul, a government that distrusted Moscow. Having failed in their efforts to bring about a change of course through forceful diplomacy, in December the Soviets resorted to military intervention.

The decision on what should be done about the deteriorating situation in Afghanistan in 1979 was not easy, in part because of the geostrategic context. Since the Ogaden war in 1977–78, Zbigniew Brzezinski's hard line had prevailed within the Carter administration, with its depiction of "an arc of crisis" in Southwest Asia and moves to implement the concept of a U.S. rapid deployment force. On January 1, 1979, U.S. diplomatic relations with China had been normalized (to be followed by a flood of

129. "The Introduction of Troops into Afghanistan: How the Decision Was Taken," *KZ*, November 18, 1989, p. 3.

130. Garthoff, *Détente and Confrontation,* pp. 901, 905.

131. "Introduction of Troops," *KZ,* p. 4.

U.S. official visits), and in April China had announced it would not renew the Sino-Soviet Treaty of Friendship that was due to expire in 1980. In August in a major speech in Beijing, the U.S. vice president had referred to the two nations' "parallel strategic interests," which he said the United States was "committed to . . . advanc[ing]." And an announcement on October 1 that the U.S. secretary of defense would visit China in January 1980 had been followed by a news leak indicating that the Carter administration intended to bolster China's military strength.[132] Meanwhile the Iranian revolution and the seizure of the U.S. embassy in Tehran had raised the possibility of a large-scale U.S. intervention in the Persian Gulf area.

It was against this deteriorating geopolitical background, with China enjoying direct (if tortuous) territorial access to Afghanistan, whose southern border was flanked by Pakistan, an ally of the United States, that the Soviets had to decide what to do about the growing insurgency and what to do about Amin, who would not take Soviet guidance and might be thinking of turning to the United States. In essence the Soviet leadership had to choose between withdrawing completely or moving in with greater strength. As with Hungary in 1956 and Czechoslovakia in 1968, the final decision reflected deep-seated attitudes regarding national security and political control.

It appears that the original plan involved the removal of Amin, his replacement by Babrak Karmal (whose more moderate Parcham faction had been ousted in June 1978), and the formation of a coalition. It was hoped that this would reconcile the various factions that had been involved in the 1978 coup and allow the Soviets to steer the government toward more moderate and constructive policies. The new leadership would request the assistance of additional Soviet forces who would be able to stabilize the military situation, allowing Kabul time to reverse the damage of the previous eighteen months and consolidate authority throughout the country.[133]

The political coup was botched but the Soviets went ahead as planned with the deployment of their forces in the final days of December. However, their sanguine expectations of stabilizing the military situation were not fulfilled, in part because the United States, Pakistan, and others moved to supply the insurgents with arms and other forms of support. As a consequence the Soviet Union found itself entangled in an unwinna-

132. Garthoff, *Détente and Confrontation*, pp. 748–50.
133. Ibid., pp. 925–36.

ble war against the Muslim guerrillas and committed to shoring up the fragmenting Afghan political economy. The insurgency grew enormously, as did the mass exodus of refugees to Pakistan and Iran.[134]

At an early stage, Moscow indicated its interest in a negotiated settlement of the internal conflict that would allow it to withdraw with good grace, and by January 1981 it had pushed Kabul into accepting the United Nations as an intermediary in negotiations with Pakistan, the overt supporter of the Afghan resistance movement. The first round of indirect negotiations began in June 1982 and those talks formalized agreement on the form, agenda, and broad elements of a comprehensive settlement, including the objective of a complete withdrawal of "foreign troops." To test Soviet intentions the UN negotiator prepared a rough draft of the settlement, including a clause stipulating that the withdrawal of forces would take place within a defined time (to be specified in the final agreement), and in October 1982 sent it to Gromyko, who did not respond.[135]

Although Andropov would have been involved in the original decision to deploy Soviet forces in Afghanistan, he may well have had doubts and it is possible that he argued against it in 1979.[136] In any case, on the occasion of Brezhnev's funeral in November 1982, Andropov gave the president of Pakistan the impression of a new flexibility in Soviet policy, and less than three weeks later Moscow had approved the UN rough draft.[137] The need to develop domestic support for a negotiated withdrawal would explain the new policy, which surfaced in February 1983, of the Soviet press admitting that there were casualties in Afghanistan and becoming increasingly explicit about the nature of the war.[138]

While skeptical of U.S. intentions, Andropov continued to respond

---

134. Ibid., pp. 895–915.

135. Selig S. Harrison, "Inside the Afghan Talks," *Foreign Policy*, no. 72 (Fall 1988), pp. 35–40.

136. Ibid., p. 35. By August 1979 a special Politburo subcommittee ("commission") had been formed comprising Brezhnev, Gromyko, Andropov (KGB), Ustinov (Defense), Kornienko (MFA), and Ogarkov (General Staff). Although the final decision to send Soviet troops in was taken in Brezhnev's office on December 12 without consulting the full Politburo, the general policy appears to have been decided by the time Pavlovsky returned from Afghanistan in November, based on Brezhnev's distrust of Amin ("Introduction of Troops," *KZ*, p. 4). According to Garthoff, the general decision was presented to the Central Committee plenum on November 27, and would have been cleared by the Politburo before that (*Détente and Confrontation*, p. 933).

137. Harrison, "Inside the Afghan Talks," p. 39.

138. Francis Fukuyama, *Soviet Civil-Military Relations and the Power Projection Mission*, R-3504-AF (Santa Monica, Calif.: Rand Corp., April 1987), p. 61.

positively during the first five months of 1983, although it could be argued that this was merely a diplomatic exercise to gain time for a military solution.[139] In any case, the movement toward agreement was suddenly checked in early June for reasons that remain obscure.[140] Meanwhile whatever its prospects, Andropov's constructive approach had been overtaken by the reappraisal of Soviet defense and foreign policy that began in mid-1983.

This reappraisal led to the conclusion that a Soviet response in kind was needed to counter the Reagan administration's attempt to reverse the course of history by engineering the downfall of progressive regimes. If such a response was required in the third world generally, it was even more important in the case of Afghanistan, which lay within the Soviet national security zone. It was, therefore, not surprising that for the remainder of Andropov's tenure and for the whole of Chernenko's, the Soviets mainly showed no interest in the UN-mediated negotiations and were intransigent over procedural issues.[141]

In 1979 Gorbachev would not have been in a position to influence the policy debate, but it is likely that subsequently he would have argued within the Politburo for a negotiated withdrawal, if only to slow diversion of scarce resources from the domestic economy.[142] In any case, at his first Central Committee plenum in April 1985, Gorbachev initiated a secret review of policy toward Afghanistan with a view to extricating the Soviet Union from an increasingly costly no-win situation.[143] Contemporary reports also suggested that the General Staff had been given twelve months in which to turn the tide. The reassignment of General Mikhail Zaitsev from commanding the Soviet Group of Forces in Germany to assuming charge of military operations in Afghanistan and

139. This was the general opinion in the State Department, which represented the "moderate" view within the Reagan administration. The hardliners saw Afghanistan as an opportunity to bleed the Soviet Union until it was willing to accept an anti-Soviet government in Kabul. Harrison develops a persuasive argument that Andropov was ready to accept a negotiated withdrawal on the proposed terms, which would have allowed the existing Afghan government to remain in power, but with a new leader ("Inside the Afghan Talks," pp. 40–47).

140. Ibid., pp. 45–47.

141. Ibid., pp. 46–50.

142. In a forthcoming book, Selig Harrison cites Soviet sources as saying that when Gorbachev's responsibilities were still limited to agriculture, he argued within the Politburo for a negotiated withdrawal on those grounds.

143. Gorbachev mentioned this fact in his report to the plenum in February 1988. *Kommunist*, no. 4 (March 1987), p. 27.

the heightened tempo of military activity during the remainder of 1985 lend credence to these reports.[144]

The Soviet military was, however, unable to significantly change the underlying situation. In his report to the Twenty-seventh Party Congress at the end of February 1986, Gorbachev referred to Afghanistan as a running sore and stated that the Soviet Union would like to withdraw Soviet forces as soon as possible. He went on to say that a timetable had been worked out with the Afghan side which would be implemented as soon as a political settlement had been achieved that would protect the Soviet Union's "vital national interest" in the future alignment of this bordering state.[145]

Following the April 1985 plenum, the Soviet approach to the UN-mediated negotiations had become more constructive. In June the Soviets had undercut Kabul's insistence that aid to the resistance must cease before a Soviet withdrawal began, and they quickly agreed to be a guarantor of the final settlement, while the United States dragged its feet. However, Kabul continued to obstruct progress and, in the wake of the 1986 party congress, Moscow arranged for Karmal to be replaced by Najibullah in time for the eighth round of negotiations that began early in May. Despite this change there continued to be problems with Kabul over the timetable for withdrawing "foreign forces," while the Soviets resisted Pakistan's demand for verification of the withdrawal and the cessation of aid.

In other words, Moscow was not yet ready to risk the overthrow of a socialist-oriented regime in Kabul and its replacement by a hostile government.

The World at Large

In his dealings with the world at large Gorbachev focused mainly on propagating the need for new political thinking about international relations and on accusing aggressive circles in the United States of being the malevolent force that sought to carry the arms race into space and that urged intervention in the third world. Gorbachev did launch a major political initiative concerning Asia and appears to have reversed or at least moderated the policy of interposing Soviet forces in the third world.

144. Harrison, "Inside the Afghan Talks," p. 50; Rosanne Klass, "Afghanistan: The Accords," *Foreign Affairs*, vol. 66 (Summer 1988), p. 930.
145. MTS, February 25, 1986, in *FBIS*-86-38, supp 41, p. O31.

In the main, however, he hammered away at the need for new thinking in the nuclear age, with particular emphasis on halting the arms race, a thesis he advanced in all his speeches abroad and to foreign elites and political leaders who came to Moscow.

His dealings with India provide an example of this approach. Prime Minister Rajiv Gandhi visited Moscow in the second half of May 1985, the first head of state to meet with the new leader since Chernenko's funeral. In his welcoming speech, Gorbachev stressed the long-standing and enduring friendship between the two nations. Among other things he noted the special importance of their common efforts to remove the threat of war and end the arms race, which would allow resources to be redeployed to help relieve poverty, hunger, disease, and illiteracy. And he pointed to the emergence of the third world and the Nonaligned Movement as one of the new realities of the present era.[146]

During his return visit to India at the end of November 1986 Gorbachev gave a more rounded exposition of his new political thinking, and the two leaders signed a Declaration of Principles for a Nuclear-Weapons-Free and Non-Violent World. Known as the Delhi Declaration, this blended the main strands of Gorbachev's argument with the precepts of the Pancha Sila and the more particular concerns of the third world to develop ten main points.

These stressed the supreme value of human life and the need for personal development; the indivisibility of international security, the need for peaceful coexistence, understanding, and trust, with nonviolence as the basis of community life; the need to redeploy resources from armaments to third world development; and the right of all states to political and economic independence. The ten principles had widespread appeal, focusing as they did on the danger of self-annihilation and the need for nuclear disarmament, the interrelatedness of the world and the need for combined efforts to solve global problems, and the importance of political and economic independence at the national level and the significance of the individual at the personal level.[147]

A natural corollary to the emphasis on global efforts to solve global problems and on the increasing interconnectedness of the international system was a greater emphasis on the potential role of the United Nations and other multinational organizations. Soviet policy toward the United Nations had formed during the first ten years of the organization's

146. *KZ,* May 22, 1985, p. 1.
147. *Pravda,* November 28, 1986, p. 1.

existence when it was seen (with considerable justification) as an instrument of Western policy. Coupled with the ideological belief that all the problems in the third world were the result of historical or contemporary exploitation by Western imperialist states, and with doctrinaire theories about competing economic systems, this meant that the Soviet Union had remained largely aloof from many of the operational activities of the UN Organization and its affiliates and had refused, for example, to contribute to the costs of peace-keeping operations.

Implicit in the new political thinking about international relations and the need for "a comprehensive system of international security" was a greater role for international institutions. At the Twenty-seventh Party Congress Gorbachev virtually listed the responsibilities of the UN family of organizations as he described the fundamental principles that would underlie such a comprehensive system. He called for the strengthening of existing forms and a search for new forms of cooperation, and for a "direct systematic dialogue" between the leaders of the world's nations, and particularly between the five permanent members of the Security Council when world peace was the issue.[148]

At its meeting in June 1986, the Warsaw Pact Political Consultative Committee declared in favor of "increasing the contributions of the United Nations and other international organizations" to the "cause of preserving peace . . . and to the solution of all global problems that mankind is faced with."[149] The socialist states supported the UN-sponsored Conference on the Relationship between Disarmament and Development, scheduled for July–August 1986 (the United States refused to participate), and one of the Soviet Union's more senior academicians was on the fourteen-member panel of "eminent personalities" that had the task of preparing a general statement of the problem to serve as a point of reference for the conference.[150]

The year was notable for the steady shift in Soviet policy toward the international institutions with which it was already involved and in the number of Soviet applications to join other ones, even if only as an

148. MTS, February 25, 1986, in *FBIS*-86-38, supp 41, p. O34.
149. *Pravda,* June 12, 1986. The PCC comprises the member states' party general secretaries, heads of state, and ministers of defense and foreign affairs.
150. France proposed the conference in 1984 and it finally convened in August and September 1987. More than 150 states participated, the United States being the only major power to absent itself. Oleg T. Bogomolov represented the Soviet Union on the fourteen-member panel, in his capacity as director of the Institute for the Study of the World Socialist Economy. *U.N. Chronicle,* vol. 23, no. 4, pp. 80–83; vol. 24, no. 7, pp. 23–25, 28.

observer. For example, after the Chernobyl reactor explosion in April, the Soviets turned to the International Atomic Energy Agency. In late summer 1986 they asked the General Agreement on Tariffs and Trade (GATT) for observer status at the round of talks due to begin in Uruguay that fall. They were turned down, but they were more successful in their lobbying to have limited representation at the November meeting of the Pacific Economic Cooperation Council and observer status at the April 1987 meeting of the Asian Development Bank. They took the process one stage further in July 1987 when they announced that they would join the Common Fund for Commodities and contribute their share ($29 million) to that UN-sponsored stabilization effort. In the fall they would pay $200 million in arrears to the United Nations for programs they had previously objected to.[151]

THE THIRD WORLD. Gorbachev continued the trend that had emerged in the early 1980s toward a more pragmatic appraisal of Soviet interests in the third world. The new Program of the Communist Party of the Soviet Union that was adopted at the 1986 party congress advocated good relations with countries that followed the capitalist path of development. In the Arab world this resulted in the abandonment of the unsuccessful efforts to forge a radical bloc and an effort instead to seek relationships with conservative and moderate regimes as well.[152] In his report to the party congress Gorbachev stressed that the most important contribution the Soviet Union could make to the world communist movement was a strong socialist economy. He offered little more than sympathy to members of the movement outside the Soviet bloc, emphasizing that they needed to rethink the established approaches to problems that faced them.

However, he did note the "acute and dynamic confrontation between progress and reaction" and reaffirmed Soviet support of "the forces of national and social liberation."[153] At the April 1985 plenum he had used much the same words, asserting that "solidarity with . . . countries and

151. Ed A. Hewett, "The Foreign Economic Factor in Perestroika," in Paul Lerner, ed., *The Soviet Union—1988,* pp. 133–34.
152. Galia Golan, "Gorbachev's Middle East Strategy," *Foreign Affairs,* vol. 66 (Fall 1987), pp. 48–49. For example, in July 1985 the Soviets established diplomatic relations with Oman. During the 1970s the Soviets had provided military assistance to the Marxist Popular Front for the Liberation of Oman and had continued to castigate the sultan and express support for the PFLO even after the front was defeated in 1975. Mark N. Katz, *Gorbachev's Military Policy in the Third World,* Washington Paper 140 (Praeger, 1989), pp. 36–37.
153. MTS, February 25, 1986, in *FBIS*-86-38, supp. 41, p. O33.

people fighting for their freedom and independence and against the onslaught of reaction" was "a matter of principle," that line being "as clear as it ever was."[154] In other words, the new economic pragmatism did not mean that the Soviet Union would desert those of its political protégés in the third world who were threatened by U.S. imperialism or other forms of aggression. For example, in June 1985 Vietnam received assurances that Soviet aid would more than double during 1986–90.[155]

ASIA AND THE PACIFIC. The Soviet Union's policy toward the Asian-Pacific region is dominated by the presence of China with whom it shares forty-five hundred miles of frontier and whose population of over one billion people continues to grow. For thirty years the two socialist countries were formally linked by a Treaty of Friendship, Alliance and Mutual Assistance (1950–80) that served them both well for the first five or six years. Thereafter, the military demands each posed on the other became increasingly unacceptable, leading to a Soviet-initiated split in 1959. This accelerated the ideological schism that had emerged in 1956 and saw its full flowering in the 1960s.[156]

In June 1969, following an escalating series of armed clashes on the Sino-Soviet border along the Ussuri and Amur rivers, Brezhnev advanced the idea of collective regional security in Asia. The clear purpose was to strengthen the Soviet position vis-à-vis an unpredictable China, where the Cultural Revolution had been under way since 1966. This was not, however, to be achieved by agreement on collective military action but through closer economic cooperation with nonsocialist states in the region.

While specifically respecting the existing rights of third parties (including U.S. military agreements), Brezhnev's proposal was intended both to contain China and to advance Soviet interests in an area where the British had already announced their withdrawal (from east of Suez) and the Americans were clearly set on extricating themselves (from the morass of Vietnam).[157] The idea failed, however, to evoke significant

154. *Kommunist,* no. 7, p. 17.
155. Bohdan Nahaylo, "Sino-Soviet Relations: Progress and Stagnation," *RL* 335/85 (October 4, 1985), p. 3.
156. Kazuko Mori, "Sino-Soviet Relations: From Confrontation to Cooperation," *Japan Review of International Affairs,* Spring–Summer 1988, pp. 43–54.
157. Kuniko Miyauchi, "Soviet Policy toward Asia under Gorbachev," Paper presented at the International Round Table Discussion, National Institute for Defense Studies, Tokyo, December 11–12, 1986, pp. 1–2.

interest in other countries in the region, and the unexpected rapprochement between the United States and China, which began in 1969 and
became public in 1971, ensured the demise of Brezhnev's proposal.

By the end of the 1970s China was once more near the center of Soviet
concerns, although this time because of developments in U.S. policy.
The U.S. shift from triangular diplomacy to Brzezinski's policy of an
informal alliance with China had been put into action at the beginning of
1979 by the establishment of diplomatic relations between Beijing and
Washington. During his visit to Washington at the end of January that
year, it appeared that Deng Xiaoping had been given the nod for the
Chinese invasion of Vietnam, a Soviet protégé, that was launched in
mid-February 1979.[158] The U.S. vice president's statement on the
"parallel strategic interests" of China and America and the U.S. secretary of defense's visit in January 1980 followed, and plans were made to
bolster China's military strength.

Moscow was faced with the prospect of a de facto military alliance
between China, South Korea, and Japan, with an increasingly belligerent
United States at its head. In his report to the Twenty-sixth Party
Congress in February 1981 Brezhnev moved to counter these adverse
developments by proposing the adoption of confidence-building measures in the Far East and by opening the door to improving relations
with China. The concept of confidence-building measures drew explicitly
on the experience of their use in Europe and, unlike the 1969 proposal
for collective security, these measures would include China as well as
Japan, the United States, and other interested countries.[159]

In respect to bilateral relations with China, while deploring that
Beijing's foreign policy came "close to imperialist policies," Brezhnev
went on to stress the Soviet Union's desire to normalize relations and
its respect and friendship for the Chinese people. These sentiments were
amplified in two articles that advocated promoting Sino-Soviet détente
and negotiating steps to pave the way for a bilateral agreement that
would be acceptable to both countries.[160] China responded in June by

158. This punitive invasion was in response to the Vietnamese invasion of Cambodia in
late December, the expulsion of ethnic Chinese from Vietnam, and the general deterioration
in Sino-Vietnamese relations in 1978. Garthoff, *Détente and Confrontation,* pp. 718–23.

159. "Brezhnev's report to the Twenty-sixth Party Congress," MDS, February 23, 1981,
in *FBIS*-81-036, supp. 1, pp. 20, 9. This important shift in Soviet policy in 1981 from collective
security to confidence-building measures was identified by Miyauchi, "Soviet Policy."

160. O. Borisov, "Several Aspects of China's Policies," *Kommunist,* no. 6 (April 1981),
and I. Aleksandrov, "Toward Soviet-Chinese Relations," *Pravda,* May 20, 1982 (cited in
Miyauchi, "Soviet Policy," notes 3, 4).

proposing renewed border talks. This action, coming three days after the visit by the U.S. secretary of state, was as much a gesture of independence from the United States as one of reconciliation with the USSR.[161]

With the perceived danger of major conflict with the United States steadily increasing, Brezhnev pushed the door ajar in his speech at Tashkent in March 1982. He referred to China as a socialist country for the first time in years and expressed a willingness to discuss the possibility of confidence-building measures in the border areas.[162] And in August, the Soviet statement following a Soviet-Mongolian summit noted that both countries were prepared to negotiate "with any interested country in the region" on ways to "radically improve the present situation" that would lead to mutual reductions in armed forces.[163]

The March statement on confidence-building measures and the August reference to "minimizing joint efforts for their national security" addressed obliquely one of the "three obstacles" to normalizing relations with China, and at the Twelfth Chinese Communist Party Congress in September, Chairman Hu Yaobang affirmed that an improvement in Sino-Soviet relations was possible, provided the Soviet Union took practical steps to remove the threat to China's security. In October 1982, talks were initiated between China and the Soviet Union at the deputy foreign minister level, and they became a regular biannual event.[164]

The prospects were reasonably auspicious at this time because the causes of the initial rift had mainly disappeared or been moderated. Ideological differences had been largely resolved by a major shift in China's position accompanied by changes in the international situation, while the Cultural Revolution, with its anti-Soviet revisionism, was admitted to have been a mistake. Most important, Beijing was coming to recognize that war was no longer inevitable and that ensuring peace

161. Garthoff, *Détente and Confrontation*, p. 1047.
162. TASS, March 24, 1982, in *FBIS*-82-57, p. R3.
163. TASS, August 20, 1982, in *FBIS*-82-163, p. C2. The words used were "so that the people can concentrate on the solution of the problems of socio-economic development and minimize their individual and collective efforts to ensure their security." The Mongolian version of the statement stopped short at "socio-economic development," saying nothing about minimizing the investment in security (TASS, August 30, 1982, in *FBIS*-82-169, p. C1). Meanwhile Mongolia (in May) and Vietnam, Cambodia, and Laos (in June) had proposed nonaggression treaties with China.
164. Eleven sessions had been held by the end of 1987. The "threat to China's security" was synonymous with the "three obstacles"—the Soviet invasion of Afghanistan, the Soviet-supported Vietnamese invasion of Cambodia, and Soviet force levels on the Sino-Soviet border (Mori, "Sino-Soviet Relations," pp. 57, 42).

through arms control and other means was the central problem.[165]
The process of normalizing Sino-Soviet relations therefore continued
steadily, if slowly. In June 1984 the Vietnamese withdrew more forces
from Cambodia (previous withdrawals having taken place in July 1982
and May 1983), and in August the general secretary of the Mongolian
Communist party, Y. Tsedenbal, was replaced. In December 1984 First
Deputy Premier Ivan V. Arkhipov, the highest-ranking Soviet official to
visit China in fifteen years, went to Beijing to negotiate agreements on
economic, scientific, and technical cooperation.[166]

In May 1985, when Gorbachev proposed in his speech welcoming the
Indian prime minister "a common, comprehensive approach to the
problems of security in Asia," he was not, therefore, breaking new
ground, although his ideas were somewhat more extensive. He noted
that both China and the Soviet Union had pledged not to make the first
use of nuclear weapons and, as had Brezhnev in 1981, he drew explicitly
on the experience in Europe (where "the concept of détente had come
into existence")—in this case on the Helsinki Agreement—to propose
a comparable "all-Asian forum."[167]

Gorbachev had meanwhile given renewed impetus to improving Sino-
Soviet relations. He met with Vice-President Li Pen on the occasion of
Chernenko's funeral and called for better bilateral relations in his report
to the April 1985 plenum, and in July the two countries signed their first
five-year trade agreement. Their foreign ministers met in New York in
September, political questions were added to the agenda for the seventh
session of the biannual talks in October 1985, and the ninth session of
the talks agreed to reopening discussion of border questions.[168]

The Soviet Union's "great neighbor, socialist China," received
special mention in Gorbachev's report to the party congress in February
1986, but the idea of an "all-Asian forum" was not pursued. This
omission was remedied in an official statement in April, which stressed
that the Soviet Union was one of the largest Asian and Pacific Ocean
powers and deplored the U.S. policy of forming selective alignments

165. Ibid., pp. 53–57.

166. Miyauchi, "Soviet Policy," p. 13; Nahaylo "Sino-Soviet Relations," p. 4.

167. *KZ*, May 22, 1985, pp. 1, 3. Gorbachev's proposal was elaborated by M. Isaev, "Asia: Peace and Security," *Mezhdunarodnaya zhizn'*, May 1985, and by V. Ovchinnikov, "Set About It Together," *Pravda*, June 22, 1985, and "Asia: Security But Not Confrontation," *Pravda*, September 26, 1985 (cited by Miyauchi, "Soviet Policy," p. 7, note 9).

168. Mori, "Sino-Soviet Relations," p. 58; Stephen M. Young, "Gorbachev's Asian Policy: Balancing the New and the Old," *Asian Survey*, vol. 28 (March 1988), pp. 322–23; Nahaylo, "Sino-Soviet Relations," p. 4.

rather than establishing "large-scale cooperation . . . between all countries of the Asia-Pacific region, irrespective . . . of their social systems."[169] It proposed working toward an "all-Asian forum" that would address this need for peaceful cooperation and also toward a separate meeting of the Pacific Ocean countries to consider matters of political and economic security.

In the 1970s, the Soviet Union had criticized proposals for Pacific cooperation on the grounds that this might lead to a new anti-Soviet military bloc. It was therefore significant that seven of the nine proposals in the April 1986 statement were similar to those in the May 1980 report of the Pacific Basin Cooperation Study Group commissioned by Japanese Prime Minister Masayoshi Ohira, who had strongly favored the concept.[170] The Soviet statement noted the "paramount attention" that was being given to Siberia and the Soviet Far East and the intention to seek sustained "trade-and-economic, technological, scientific and cultural cooperation with all interested countries" in that part of the world. Many of these large-scale and necessarily multinational projects could be best handled within the framework of existing UN machinery.

The significance of this formal policy statement was obscured by the explosion of the nuclear reactor at Chernobyl, and the new thrust in Soviet policy was not generally appreciated until Gorbachev's speech at Vladivostok on July 28. His speech was notable for the scope of its proposals and for the concessions it offered China. Although Gorbachev acknowledged that the United States was "a great Pacific Ocean power," his discussion of the Asian-Pacific area was permeated with criticism of U.S. militarism and imperialism. Once again Gorbachev drew on the precedent of Europe and the Helsinki Agreement, and he proposed a similar conference in Hiroshima to check the militarization of the Pacific, which had begun "to gather dangerous speed," and suggested more specific measures designed to reduce tension and build confidence.[171]

Noting that Soviet and Chinese priorities were similar—accelerating socioeconomic development—Gorbachev proposed joint development of the Amur basin, a rail link between Xinjiang and Kazakhstan, and the training of Chinese cosmonauts (China was also opposed to the U.S. strategic defense initiative). He officially accepted China's position on

169. "Soviet Government—Statement," TASS, April 23, 1986, in *FBIS*-86-78, pp. CC1–3.
170. Hiroshi Kimura, "Gorbachev's 'New Thinking' and Asia," in *Japan-U.S. Joint Study on the Soviet Union, Conference 2* (Tokyo: Research Institute for Peace and Security, May 1987), pp. 23–24.
171. MTS, July 28, 1986, in *FBIS*-86-145, pp. R11–19.

the rivers that formed part of the disputed border. He avoided the issue of Cambodia but spoke of withdrawing a large number of forces from Mongolia, and he formally announced that the "Soviet leadership" had decided to withdraw six regiments from Afghanistan by the end of 1986.[172]

The Vladivostok speech reflected very clearly the new political thinking about international relations, with its emphasis on cooperative rather than confrontational policies, on political and economic rather than military solutions, and on the need for comprehensive agreements on limiting and reducing armaments and for confidence-building measures. It was also a prime example of the strong anti-Americanism that colored Gorbachev's thinking throughout this period, reflecting his frustration with the U.S. refusal to acknowledge the new realities of the nuclear era and with the success of U.S. "aggressive circles" in perpetuating and extending the arms race, first by militarizing the world and then by moving on to space.

COUNTERING IMPERIALIST AGGRESSION. In almost every area of international relations, the objectives being pursued by the Soviet leadership in 1984–86 were the same as those identified or reaffirmed in the 1983–84 reappraisal. The major difference in policy reflected a change in scope, emphasis, and, most important, style. Even the "new political thinking" represented a skillful repackaging of well-established ideas, some Soviet, others Western, and its newness consisted of their being adopted by the leadership of a major power. However, among those ideas was the clear recognition that in the nuclear age national security must rely primarily on political and not military means and that military confrontation between the superpowers must be avoided. It was these principles that underlay the one significant reversal of Soviet policy during this period.

One of the questions that the 1983–84 reappraisal had had to address was how the Soviet Union should respond to the increasingly confrontational style of U.S. military behavior in the third world. The Reagan administration was clearly embarked on an attempt to check the course of history by using covert or overt force to bring about the downfall of "progressive" regimes, and several Soviet protégés had been labeled "terrorist" to justify U.S. military intervention. In the past the Soviet Union had adopted a fairly relaxed policy of "win some, lose some" in

172. Ibid.

the third world, but the new circumstances heightened the need for countervailing force to check this resurgence of capitalist imperialism.

The long-established approach was to provide advisers, training, arms, and equipment to increase the capability of target countries to resist internal subversion and external aggression. But by mid-1984 the Soviets had apparently decided to go beyond the more assertive use of advisers and supply of arms to developing the capability to interpose Soviet forces between a protégé and the threatening external forces. This was not a completely new departure, in that Soviet air-defense forces had been deployed to Egypt in 1970–73 to protect against Israeli deep strikes, and again to Syria in 1983–84. But it was now proposed that the countervailing force should comprise Soviet naval units that would be interposed between U.S. seaborne intervention forces and their target.

Although the Soviet Union still lacked a proper capability for this kind of operation, the policy of interposing naval forces was tried out during the first stage of the Libyan crisis in early 1986, when the Soviets moored the flagship of their Mediterranean squadron in Tripoli and deployed other ships in support. While the operational role of these forces was to provide early warning and intelligence to the SA-5 air-defense system with which the Soviets had provided the Libyans in late 1985, with the flagship acting as a communications link both with the ships deployed in the Eastern Mediterranean and with Moscow, the deployment had strong political symbolism. This was the first time that the Soviet Union had interposed its forces in this way between U.S. forces and a Soviet client, and there can be no doubt that the Soviets understood what was at stake, since the Reagan administration had been spoiling for a fight with Libya since 1981.

The Soviets withdrew their naval forces when the crisis went off the boil in mid-February. Nor did they redeploy them during the well-advertised second stage, which saw U.S. carrier strikes against Libyan naval forces and radar installations (March 24–25) and culminated in an air attack on Tripoli and Benghazi (April 15), following the terrorist bombing of a West German discotheque. In between these two series of events, the long-planned Twenty-seventh Party Congress convened in Moscow (from February 25 to March 6).

The party congress was an important occasion for Gorbachev to consolidate his authority as general secretary, which is reflected in part by the composition of the Central Committee, which is nominally elected at the five-yearly party congresses.[173] It is the Central Committee that elects the members of the Politburo, and among the changes announced at the final session of the congress was the retirement of eighty-one-year-old Boris Ponomarev.

Ponomarev was a candidate member of the Politburo and had been head of the Central Committee's International Department since 1955. One of the department's responsibilities was relations with liberation movements and with nonruling communist and other left-wing parties in the third world. Ponomarev had the reputation of being an unimaginative, inflexible Stalinist who believed adamantly in the world communist revolution, and he would have undoubtedly been a strong protagonist of an assertive Soviet policy designed to rebuff imperialist aggression and defend the gains of socialism.[174]

It is therefore unlikely to have been coincidental that the new policy regarding the interposition of Soviet naval forces in a third world crisis should have been revoked in the wake of a party congress that saw the retirement of Ponomarev, the announcement of the need for new political thinking, and the assertion as one of four principles underlying international security that "the confrontation between capitalism and socialism can take place only, and exclusively, in the field of peaceful coexistence and peaceful rivalry." All this was within the context of the more general statement by Gorbachev that "the situation of nuclear confrontation calls for new approaches, methods, and forms of relations between different social systems."[175]

Although it did not involve a comparable reversal of policy, similar considerations were reflected in what Gorbachev said at the congress about the future thrust of policy regarding the Soviet military involvement in Afghanistan. In essence, the policy would seek to neutralize the externally armed insurgency by political negotiation rather than countervailing force.[176]

---

173. In practice, a large proportion of seats was tied to the job rather than the individual. The 1986 congress provided the opportunity to bring the political complexion of the Central Committee into line with changes that had already been effected through the Secretariat's control of *nomenklatura* and appointments. The Twenty-seventh Congress elected 125 new members, about 40 percent of the full committee of 307.

174. Elizabeth Teague, "The Twenty-seventh Party Congress: Personnel Changes in the Politburo and the Secretariat," *RL* 111/86 (March 6, 1986), pp. 2, 4, 7.

175. MTS, February 25, 1986, in *FBIS*-86-38, supp. 41, pp. O1, O33–34.

176. Ibid., p. O32.

Gorbachev and the Soviet Military Establishment

Gorbachev may not have been directly involved in foreign and defense policy before becoming general secretary, but that did not mean that he was ignorant of the military or of military officers, and the same can be said of Shevardnadze. As first secretary of the Stavropol' region Gorbachev sat on the Military Council of the North Caucasus Military District, and from 1971 he was a member of the Central Committee where the periodic plenums would have kept him abreast of the major issues in defense and foreign policy. After November 1979 he was privy to Politburo deliberations and, following Andropov's election as general secretary, he could not have escaped the major internal debates of the 1983–84 period on détente, arms control, the imminence of war, the allocation of resources to defense, and the immediate needs of the military.

As one of the most powerful members of the Politburo he must have been directly involved in the process of deciding who would succeed the ailing Ustinov as minister of defense in December 1984, and what should be done about the increasingly outspoken chief of the General Staff, Marshal Ogarkov (the timing of whose reassignment to command the Western TVD suggests Gorbachev's direct responsibility for the transfer). There is evidence that Gorbachev and Ogarkov disagreed on what turned out to be the fundamental question of whether "achieving a durable peace was a fully realistic task." Ogarkov argued that it was not realistic at the present time.[177]

Sergey F. Akhromeev, sixty-one years old and first deputy chief of the General Staff, replaced Ogarkov. He had joined the General Staff in 1974 as chief of Main Operations and deputy chief of the General Staff; he became Ogarkov's first deputy in 1979, and during Andropov's brief tenure was promoted to marshal of the Soviet Union and full member of the Central Committee in 1983. During 1983 Andropov had assembled the loose coalition that took over power in 1985, and he may have identified Akhromeev as a potential member of that group. In any case, in September 1984 it would have been politically impossible to have passed over Akhromeev in favor of a younger man, even if Gorbachev had wanted to. And although Akhromeev and Ogarkov shared the same

177. Chapter 5, note 113.

ideas about contemporary operational requirements and the imminent "revolution in military affairs," they differed on the more distant future. Ogarkov had fairly revolutionary ideas about the nature and need for technological change, while Akhromeev belonged to a more evolutionary school of thought. He was also less arrogant than Ogarkov.[178]

Ustinov was succeeded by seventy-three-year-old Sergey L. Sokolov, one of the first deputy ministers of defense, an army general since 1969 with responsibility for general matters. Sokolov had a respectable operational record, with combat experience going back to 1938 on the Manchurian border, but his strength lay in defense management. While junior in military rank to Akhromeev, he outranked him within the ministerial hierarchy and was twelve years older.[179]

Sokolov's appointment would have satisfied the various sectional interests, if not the ambitions of such as Ogarkov and Politburo member Grigoriy V. Romanov, the Central Committee secretary responsible for defense industries. Sokolov was closer in age, experience, and attitudes to the old guard than to the new. His appointment reassured the military and the broader defense establishment that Soviet security concerns were being properly attended to. And the fact that he was a career officer meant that he could be excluded from full membership in the Politburo on grounds of a rarely broken precedent.[180]

There seems little doubt that in principle the military would have welcomed the concept of economic perestroika, at least in the form it was conceived during Andropov's tenure, when the emphasis was on improving the performance of the economic machinery, tightening labor discipline, and speeding the introduction of new technology. A more efficient domestic economy would relieve the continual pressure to shift resources from defense and improve the quality of those products the military drew from the civilian sector.

In practice there would have been increasing doubts as Gorbachev began to move away from those simple prescriptions and as the perestroika process acquired its own momentum and began to impinge directly

178. Rose E. Gottemoeller, *Conflict and Consensus in the Soviet Armed Forces*, R-3759-AE (Santa Monica, Calif.: Rand Corp., October 1989), pp. 17–21; Dale R. Herspring, *The Soviet High Command 1967–89: Personalities and Politics* (Princeton University Press, 1990), pp. 218–22.

179. Herspring, *Soviet High Command*, pp. 223–24, 306.

180. Marshal Grechko was a full member for less than three years, in 1973–76, and Marshal Zhukov for only three months, in 1957. The military ranks of other defense ministers who were also full members of the Politburo were largely honorific.

on the military establishment. There would have been growing doubt as to whether perestroika would serve the military's short-term interests as well as whether perestroika could in fact succeed. By the end of 1986 the military was anything but of one mind about the way things were going.

The Defense Burden

The fact that the mass of Russians have always placed the security of their homeland above their personal comfort does not imply that guns have usually had precedence over butter; the relative priority has depended on the likelihood of war. Certainly the new Soviet leadership saw the high level of investment in defense as one of the main obstacles to renewed economic growth and modernizing the Soviet industrial base. Abel Aganbegyan, who was appointed chairman of the Commission for the Study of Productive Forces a few months after Gorbachev took office, had long pointed to overspending on defense as one of the two basic sources of Soviet economic malaise.[181] According to one Soviet source, 40 percent of the output of the machine-building industry and 75 percent of spending on science was going to the military.[182]

The need to reduce the burden of defense as much as the need to reduce the danger of war explains the urgency of Gorbachev's call for arms reductions and his outspoken frustration with the slow progress in arms control negotiations. But the problem was further complicated by the revolution in military affairs that was being brought about by microprocessors, remote-sensing devices, and the application of new physical principles to conventional war. Military concern about these developments had surfaced publicly by 1981.[183]

For some time the Soviets had been facing a triangle of conflicting demands. National security (as traditionally defined) required the Soviet military to be able to fight and "not lose" a world war, should it be unavoidable. In order not to lose, it was essential that the Soviets remain abreast of the revolution in military affairs. For that to be possible it would be necessary to restructure the Soviet economy and bring it up to

181. The other was administrative-command management. Sidney I. Ploss, "A New Soviet Era?" *Foreign Policy,* no. 62 (Spring 1986), p. 53.
182. Vladimir N. Chernega, vice-rector of the MFA Diplomatic Academy, interviewed by Bill Keller, *New York Times,* November 30, 1989, p. A20.
183. N. Ogarkov, "Guarding Peaceful Labor," *Kommunist,* no. 10 (July 1981), pp. 80–91.

world standards. But the resources that had to be directed to ensuring national security imposed a burden that prevented economic restructuring.

Clearly, if this triangle of requirements were to come together, one of the corners would have to be redefined. The Soviets, however, had no control over the onrush of U.S. technological developments that was driving the revolution in military affairs. And economic perestroika was essential if the Soviet Union was not to be relegated to the ash heap of history. This meant that national security was the sole candidate for redefinition.

There were precedents for redefining national security requirements in less demanding terms, notably in the mid-1950s. A major reassessment following Stalin's death had led to the downgrading of the threat of a capitalist invasion by land and by sea, and this had enabled a large reduction in the defense burden. And the doctrinal shift in the late 1960s had obviated the need for superiority in strategic weapons. In that case, however, the need for strategic parity had remained, enmeshing the Soviets in a qualitative and quantitative nuclear arms race, while the 1970s strategy had significantly increased the requirement for conventional forces.

Given the nature of the debate underlying the 1983–84 reappraisal of Soviet defense and foreign policy, and the fact that the second Reagan administration was only marginally less hostile than the first, in 1985 it was not easy to downgrade or redefine Soviet national security requirements. While it could be argued, as did Gorbachev, that security in the nuclear age should rely more on political than military means, to the extent that was true (and it still had to be demonstrated), it only applied to averting war and it certainly did not reduce the level of forces needed to be reasonably sure of "not losing" a world war, should it be unavoidable. Indeed, the 1984 decision to lower tension in Europe (and hence the danger of war) by adopting a defensive posture facing NATO actually increased the requirement for conventional forces (at least in theory), since Soviet ground forces would lack the advantage of operational surprise if they were required to launch their offensive.

A more direct way of addressing the defense burden was to negotiate mutual reductions in armed forces, an objective the Soviets had long pursued but one that was easier specified than achieved. After fifteen years of negotiating arms control agreements, both sides' force levels and overall capability were significantly higher than they had been in 1970.

A third approach was to require the military to make more efficient use of existing resources, and an injunction to that effect had been an important aspect of Brezhnev's speech to a gathering of several hundred military command personnel shortly before he died in November 1982.[184] An extension of this approach was to challenge the military's assessment of what was needed to achieve its objective, and to seek evidence that the military was overinsuring, that it had more than was absolutely necessary.

Gorbachev adopted all these approaches in his efforts to reduce the defense burden. Within a month of taking office, he had sought to improve the chances of reducing the number of nuclear weapons by making a unilateral concession and he continued that policy during the run-up to the Geneva summit. In his report on the summit, he introduced the concept of "sufficiency" in strategic nuclear weapons at greatly reduced levels, and in his report to the party congress in February 1986 spoke of a "reasonable sufficiency."[185] The idea of sufficiency was also implicit in the statement that the armed forces would be kept at a level that would make it impossible for the enemy to have strategic superiority, which was included in the 1986 party program.[186]

But apart from the choice of words, none of this was new, because "sufficiency" in strategic weapons meant parity with the United States. That concept had already been accepted in 1969, had been publicly affirmed in Brezhnev's speech at Tula in January 1977, and had underlain the Soviet Union's approach to the SALT negotiations throughout the 1970s. What is more, the logic of the 1970s strategy required parity at as low a level as could be negotiated. In practice, however, the level depended on the United States, where deterrence theory had provided

184. *Pravda,* October 28, 1982.
185. *Pravda,* November 28, 1985, p. 1, in *FBIS*-85-232, p. R18; MTS, February 25, 1986, in *FBIS*-86-38, supp. 41, p. O34.
186. The formulation that the armed forces were maintained "at the level that excludes strategic superiority by the forces of imperialism" was used by Defense Minister Sokolov in his speech to the party congress and by others on subsequent occasions (Glickham, "New Directions," p. 15). That particular requirement had not been specified in the 1961 party program, when the target had been strategic superiority. The program had, however, required the armed forces to be able "to ensure the decisive and complete defeat" of the enemy, whereas the 1986 program only required them to be ready "to rout any aggressor." Jan F. Triska, *Soviet Communism: Programs and Rules* (San Francisco: Chandler Publishing Co., 1962), p. 105; *Pravda,* March 7, 1986, in *FBIS*-86-46, supp. 51, p. O12.

a rationale for the existing arsenal of warheads whose numbers were still growing. Similarly, the definition of what was "reasonable" was hostage to Western theories of crisis stability based on sophisticated models of a nuclear missile exchange.[187]

Conventional Force Reductions

In any case, the really large savings were to be found in general-purpose rather than strategic forces, and when Gorbachev addressed a group of senior military officers at Minsk in July 1985, he warned them that they would have to do more with less.[188] But Gorbachev must have known that exhortations of that kind were only nibbling at the edges of the problem, which stemmed from the long-standing requirement to cover the worst-case contingency of world war. The objective of "not losing a world war" had become steadily more onerous as the years went by, and the impending revolution in military affairs would make it even more demanding. And despite the vast investment of resources in meeting this requirement, in the event of war the chances of achieving that objective were at best even.

It would have become increasingly apparent that until the Soviet armed forces were relieved of that steadily growing requirement, it would be impossible to effect major reductions in Soviet military capabilities and hence relieve the burden of defense. The trouble was that as long as Soviet doctrine decreed that world war was possible, the military were bound to cover that contingency, and relief would only come if they could plan on the assumption that world war could and would be averted by political means.

In 1983–84 Gorbachev had been one of those who argued that, despite the policies of the first Reagan administration, "preconditions and circumstances" were *already* creating the conditions that would eliminate the danger of world war. In 1985, within a few weeks of taking

187. However, at some stage the Soviets must have decided not to go ahead with the production of the follow-on to the SS-20 intermediate-range ballistic missile, which was being flight-tested in April 1985, and the follow-on to the SS-18 intercontinental missile (the SS-26) which was nearing flight testing in mid-1985 (MccGwire, *Military Objectives*, p. 256, note 29, p. 498, note 43). Their nonappearance indicates that they were deleted from the Twelfth Five-Year Plan approved in March 1986.

188. Dale R. Herspring, "The Soviet High Command Looks at Gorbachev," *The Changing Strategic Landscape—Part I*, Adelphi Paper 235 (London: International Institute for Strategic Studies, 1989), p. 50; "Gorbachev: What Makes Him Run?" *Newsweek*, November 18, 1985, p. 50.

office, he obtained the agreement of the other Warsaw Pact members that "achieving a durable peace [was] a fully realistic task." He then set out to accomplish that task, in part through his campaign for new political thinking about international relations. And the 1986 party program declared in bold print that "there is no fatal inevitability of world war. It is possible to avert war and to safeguard mankind from catastrophe." While many of these same words had appeared in earlier formulas, looking to the future, the 1986 statement was firmly anchored in the present.[189]

Meanwhile Gorbachev did what he could with the doctrinal changes that had emerged from the 1983–84 reappraisal. The objective of averting world war had been given new priority at the military-technical level of doctrine, and therefore in the event of conflict in Europe, the Soviets would initially remain on the defensive. If, however, a halt to hostilities had not been negotiated within twenty to thirty days, the Soviets would revert to the 1970s strategy of mounting a blitzkrieg offensive to defeat NATO in Europe and evict U.S. forces from the Continent. The structural implications of this decision would have been worked out by mid-1986, allowing Gorbachev to plan for what he hoped would be a significant initiative on reductions of conventional arms in Europe when the Political Consultative Committee of the Warsaw Pact met in June. By adopting a defensive posture facing NATO, the Soviets would forgo the possibility of launching a surprise attack, should war seem inevitable. A surprise attack was NATO's greatest fear. If the Soviets specifically renounced that capability, they might be able to induce the West to negotiate symmetrical force reductions.

But Gorbachev took the logic one step further. By early 1986 it was clear that the Stockholm Conference on Disarmament in Europe (CDE) would fail unless the Soviet Union changed its position on intrusive verification.[190] On-site and aerial verification of ground and air forces in

189. "1986 CPSU Program," *Pravda*, March 7, 1986, in *FBIS*-86-046, supp. 051, p. O8; Jan F. Trisica, ed., *Soviet Communism: Programs and Rules* (San Francisco: Chandler Publishing, 1963), pp. 64–65; Institut Marksism-Leninizma, *Kommunisticheskaya partiya Sovietskogo Soyuzi: v rezolyutsiyakh i resheniyakh c'ezdov, konferentsiy i plenumov TsK (The Communist Party of the Soviet Union: Resolutions and Decisions of the Congresses, Conferences and Plenums of the Central Committee)*, vol. 4, 1954–60 (Moscow: Politizdat, 1960), p. 9.

190. The Conference on Confidence and Security-Building and Disarmament in Europe had been mandated in 1983 by the thirty-five-nation Conference on Security and Cooperation in Europe (CSCE), which had produced the Helsinki Agreement in August 1975 and had reconvened in 1977–78 and 1980–83 to review progress in implementation of the agreement. The first stage of the CDE (which began in January 1984 and would end in September 1986)

the European theater was, however, hard for the Soviet military to swallow, for institutional as well as operational reasons. Nevertheless, the principle of on-site inspection and "other additional verification measures" had already been accepted in respect to strategic arms reductions,[191] and the changes in military doctrine that emerged in 1984 could be used to justify acceptance of such verification at the theater level. First, once the Soviets adopted a defensive posture and forwent the possibility of strategic surprise, secrecy lost much of its importance. Second, at the military-technical level the objective of "averting war" now had priority over the objective of "not losing"; inspection, surveillance, and monitoring would reduce the likelihood of misperceptions in crises. And third, effective verification would increase NATO's willingness to negotiate mutual force reductions, which would serve to lower tension and make war less likely.

Gorbachev took these two developments, the adoption of a so-called defensive doctrine at the military-technical level and Soviet acceptance of the need for effective verification in the European theater, and linked them to a 25 percent reduction in forces in the area stretching from the Atlantic to the Urals, the latter being something that Brezhnev had already conceded in 1981.[192] Gorbachev's proposal that both sides reduce their forces in that area by 100,000–150,000 within two years, and bring the total up to 500,000 in the early 1990s, was publicized at the end of the Warsaw Pact meeting in the Budapest Appeal.[193] The reduction in arms, effective verification, and other confidence-building measures were intended to reduce the danger of surprise attack and increase strategic stability, while at the same time reducing defense expenditures.[194]

---

was to seek agreement on confidence-building measures. Only if this first stage was successful would the CSCE mandate a second stage, which might consider actual disarmament measures.

191. See Gorbachev's proposal, *Pravda,* January 15, 1986, p. 1.

192. The idea of Europe from "the Atlantic to the Urals" had first been raised by French President Charles de Gaulle, and at the 1980–83 CSCE review conference this was proposed by the French as the scope of the CDE. In his report to the 1981 party congress Brezhnev proposed that existing confidence-building measures should be strengthened and extended to cover "the entire European part of the USSR, on the condition that the Western states make a corresponding extension of the area." The Warsaw Pact statement did not repeat this caveat, but it did not withdraw it.

193. A preview of these proposals had already been shown to selected Westerners during the first half of April, and the general approach was included in Gorbachev's speech to the Eleventh Congress of the Socialist Unity Party (SED) of East Germany (TASS, April 18, 1986, in *FBIS*-86-75, pp. F1–9).

194. "Warsaw Pact Appeal to [NATO Concerning] Conventional Arms Reductions in Europe," *Pravda,* June 12, 1986, p. 1.

It seems that Gorbachev hoped that concessions on verification and surprise attack, coupled with claims of having adopted a defensive doctrine, would persuade NATO to negotiate symmetrical force reductions. However, NATO was not interested in enshrining the existing imbalance of forces in a formal agreement, even at a much lower level. And while the Soviets' intention to adopt a defensive posture at the military-technical level was an important development, its significance was lost on the West, long inured to claims that Soviet doctrine was inherently defensive. That, indeed, had been true at the political-military level, but it was hard for the West to savor these doctrinal niceties when faced by the Pact's preponderance in conventional forces.

Once more, the need to cover the contingency of world war was the obstacle to progress. In order to achieve their objective of "not losing" such a war, the Soviets would need to deny the United States a bridgehead in Europe, implying the defeat of NATO in the central region and the eviction of U.S. forces from the Continent. To achieve that objective, the Soviets required a measure of superiority over NATO. And as long as that superiority existed, the West would remain unwilling to negotiate symmetrical reductions of forces.

Establishing Political Dominance

While acknowledging the importance of military strength for the defense of the homeland and asserting that the new leadership would "never sacrifice security interests" in favor of the civilian sector of the economy, Gorbachev was explicit that in the nuclear age national security must be ensured primarily by political rather than military means.[195] Although this order of priorities was made official in the resolutions of the Twenty-seventh Party Congress, it ran counter to the established wisdom, which was based on the harsh experience of the 1930s and 1940s. This was reinforced by a perception that the capitalist urge to roll back communism in the 1950s had been deterred by the Soviet conventional capability in Europe and that it was rough strategic parity that had forced the United States to accept détente and to negotiate on limiting strategic nuclear weapons.

Four unrelated developments helped Gorbachev establish political

195. Gorbachev's interview with the chief editor of *Rude Pravo*, reported in *Ivestiya*, September 9, 1986.

dominance over the Soviet military establishment by the end of 1986: the nuclear explosion in a reactor at Chernobyl; corruption and inefficiency within the Soviet armed forces; the military's failure to implement Politburo policy on at least two occasions; and some apparently sensible decisions at the military-technical level that had extremely adverse consequences at the political-military level, resulting in a diminution of overall security.

COUNTERPRODUCTIVE STRATEGIC INITIATIVES. The 1971–72 decision to produce the SS-20 intermediate-range ballistic missile (IRBM) from components procured for the canceled SS-16 intercontinental ballistic missile (ICBM) program made excellent strategic sense, and the military rationale was still compelling in 1976–77 when the SS-20 was ready for initial deployment. Because of its vulnerability, the obsolescent SS-4 and SS-5 missile force was more a hindrance than a help to the 1970s strategy, and there were strong operational reasons for replacing it with a more responsive, accurate, and survivable system.

However, the SS-20 deployment turned out to be a political disaster, with very high military costs. It served as the catalyst for Western concerns ranging from the Soviet conventional buildup in Europe to Soviet "adventurism" in the third world and prompted NATO's agreement to the deployment of Pershing II IRBMs and ground-launched cruise missiles (GLCMs), both of which could reach targets in Russia. The acerbic negotiations on intermediate-range nuclear forces (INF) in 1981–83 contributed to the sharp rise in East-West tension and increased the danger of world war, while the final outcome was widely perceived as a defeat for the Soviet Union. To make matters worse the subsequent deployment of Pershing IIs and GLCMs seriously threatened the Soviet Union's capability to implement its operational plans in the event of war.

These costs had all been incurred before Gorbachev took office, although as a member of the Politburo he would have been aware of what was happening. There was, however, another very live issue that had even more long-term implications—namely, the ballistic-missile early-warning radar that was being built near Krasnoyarsk. The fact that the location of this radar breached the letter of the ABM Treaty was an important feature of the Reagan administration's argument that arms control agreements were against the U.S. interest because the Soviets could not be trusted.[196] More serious, the Soviet breach could be and

---

196. The treaty required radars to be located on the periphery of national territory and

was used as justification for the United States doing likewise to develop a space-based ballistic-missile defense system. As such, the Krasnoyarsk radar was a permanent embarrassment to Gorbachev as he launched his campaign to prevent the arms race from spreading into space.

Here again the location of the radar made excellent military sense. The 1970s strategy assumed a two-phase war, and a worst-case contingency for the long-drawn-out second phase envisioned the United States somehow arranging to mount a land offensive through Xinjian, outflanking Siberia. This raised the need for a secondary defense perimeter to the east of the Yenisey River securing the industrially important West Siberian Plain, and military prudence required that all major facilities should be located to the west of this line. In the case of early warning radars this could be seen as a matter of strategic necessity rather than choice.

The radar at Krasnoyarsk was intended to cover the new threat from Trident-class ballistic-missile submarines patrolling in the North Pacific, a requirement that would have emerged in the first half of the 1970s but probably after the signing of the ABM Treaty. The Soviets are unlikely to have foreseen this conflict at the time they signed the treaty, but as détente began to crumble and the danger of war increased at the end of the 1970s, and as the United States drew closer to the People's Republic of China, the military arguments for locating this radar to the west of China and Siberia became increasingly compelling.[197]

It seems likely that the Soviet military went ahead with the construction of the Krasnoyarsk radar on the basis of decisions made in the early 1970s, and that they either avoided or saw no reason for reopening the issue to political scrutiny.[198] In any case, U.S. satellites detected the

---

look outward. The Krasnoyarsk radar is located 470 miles from the southern periphery and looks northeast across 4,000 miles of Soviet territory.

197. There were savings to be made from the chosen location, but the strategic arguments are likely to have been critical. It would probably have taken two radars located on the Soviet eastern periphery (one in the permafrost zone) to provide the same coverage, but they could be outflanked by ground operations in the second phase of a world war. That was the time when the Soviet Union would be at the greatest risk of a U.S. nuclear attack, and military prudence required that early warning systems be located within the Soviet inner defense perimeter. MccGwire, *Military Objectives,* pp. 243–44.

198. At the time the final decision on location was taken (probably in 1975, in preparation for the Eleventh Five-Year Plan, due to start in 1976), the Soviets may have assumed that the SALT process would continue unchecked and that it would be possible to negotiate this technical breach through the Standing Consultative Commission in Geneva.

new construction at an early stage and the cry of "cheating" was not long in coming.

The rational military decisions made in this and the SS-20 case that were designed to enhance the security of the Soviet Union had had just the opposite effect. These examples could be generalized to argue that the adoption of the 1970s strategy, with its unexceptionable objective of increasing the chances of "not losing" a world war while avoiding the nuclear devastation of Russia, had resulted in very heavy economic, political, and military costs and had actually made war more likely.

The Soviets had always recognized that waging war was too serious a matter to be left to the generals. It was now clear that even planning for war should not be left in their hands.

MILITARY INSUBORDINATION. The military could also be charged with failing to carry out the party's instructions, as in the political decision to accept intrusive verification in the European theater. By the end of January 1986 Gorbachev had decided that conventional arms reductions depended on a successful conclusion to the negotiations at the CDE. He had learned from Oleg A. Grinevsky, leader of the Soviet delegation at Stockholm, that Soviet resistance to on-site inspections was an absolute obstacle to progress, and around the end of March the Politburo had accepted the principle of intrusive verification.[199] In April Gorbachev publicly acknowledged the need for "dependable verification at every stage" of the conventional arms reduction process, including international forms and on-site inspection.[200] Yet despite this reversal of policy, negotiations on the details of an agreement made little progress. In May Valentin Falin, the new head of Novosti, acknowledged that in spite of Politburo policy, there was continuing inflexibility on the part of the military negotiators at Stockholm; the matter was not resolved until the end of August when Marshal Akhromeev, chief of the General Staff, was sent to Stockholm with instructions to break the logjam and ensure agreement.[201]

A more serious case of military insubordination involved Afghanistan.

199. Information supplied to me by a member of the U.S. delegation at CDE.

200. Speech to SED party congress, TASS, April 18, 1986, in *FBIS*-86-75, p. F8.

201. Falin, formerly ambassador to West Germany, made his comment at a press conference in Bonn (cited by *Arms Control Reporter* [1986], p. 402-B-109). The fact that Akhromeev had been "ordered" to Stockholm was common knowledge at the CDE. Herspring notes that Akhromeev was on record as being opposed to intrusive verification and was concerned lest "monitoring . . . turn into intelligence activity" ("Soviet High Command," p. 50).

Speaking at Vladivostok at the end of July 1986, Gorbachev had announced a Politburo decision to withdraw six regiments (one tank, two motorized rifle, and three antiaircraft) by the end of the year. It appears that some time in the fall the Soviets did withdraw two antiaircraft regiments. However, two extra motorized rifle regiments were inserted and then withdrawn, and one tank unit was first reinforced from the Soviet Union, before being withdrawn as a nominal regiment.

Whether a result of misunderstanding or deliberate intent, these shenanigans must have angered Gorbachev and his colleagues. By placing in question the veracity of formal Politburo pronouncements, the phony withdrawal undermined the whole thrust of the new approach to foreign policy, with its emphasis on cooperation and political understanding that must rely in part on mutual trust.

OTHER CONTRIBUTING FACTORS. The military were spared the rigors of glasnost through the end of 1986. Nevertheless, the new openness in the rest of Soviet society and the greater publicity given to operations in Afghanistan must have had some effect on the opacity of the Soviet military establishment. Gorbachev and his colleagues must have become increasingly aware of the many glaring defects that were later exposed to public gaze, ranging from incompetence and inefficiency to blatant corruption. And it is almost certain that when Gorbachev visited the Far East in July 1986 he met Army General Dmitriy T. Yazov, who had been commander of the Far Eastern Military District since 1984 and was destined to relieve Sokolov as minister of defense in May 1987.

Through a series of articles published in 1981–85 Yazov had established a reputation as someone with strong concern about personnel matters, officer effectiveness, and troop morale. A few weeks before Gorbachev's visit, Yazov's outspoken criticism of leadership and management styles in his command received national press coverage. His emphasis on the importance of the individual soldier was comparable to Gorbachev's emphasis on the need to encourage individual initiative and personal responsibility in members of the bureaucracy and the productive work force.[202] In January 1987 Yazov was brought back to Moscow to become deputy minister of defense in charge of personnel, which makes it likely that he had spent enough time with Gorbachev or his senior advisers the previous July for them to gain some insight into the military's internal problems and the dire need for military perestroika.

---

202. Herspring, *Soviet High Command,* pp. 224–25, citing *KZ,* July 10, 1986.

A completely unrelated but nonetheless influential event was the reactor explosion at Chernobyl at the end of April 1986. It riveted attention on the catastrophic effects that any kind of war would have in heavily industrialized Europe, with its numerous nuclear power stations and chemical plants producing toxic substances. The damage that conventional military operations would cause, whether intentional or accidental, would inevitably result in the contamination of large parts of Europe by radioactive fallout and lethal gases, killing millions of noncombatants and rendering vast areas uninhabitable.

At the Geneva summit in November 1985 it had been agreed that nuclear war could not be won and must not be fought. To that dictum the stricture should now be added that war of any kind must not be fought in Europe.[203] From here it was a relatively small intellectual step to the planning assumption that a world war would not be fought but would be prevented by political means.

AKHROMEEV JOINS THE TEAM. As chief of the General Staff, Akhromeev was the senior spokesman for the military's operational interests, and his visit to Stockholm at the end of August 1986 may have marked the turning point in Gorbachev's relationship with the senior military leadership.[204] At Stockholm, Akhromeev was clearly doing the politicians' bidding, and it seems likely that by the end of the Reykjavik summit six weeks later he had been mainly co-opted by the Gorbachev leadership. He was probably not a whole-hearted supporter but thought he could best ensure the nation's security interests as a member of the team rather than the opposition.[205]

203. In the restricted journal *VM* the lead editorial in June 1986 gave as the foremost task the "prevention of war," rather than just "nuclear war" (cited by Raymond Garthoff, "New Thinking in Soviet Military Doctrine," *Washington Quarterly*, vol. 11 [Summer 1988], pp. 134–35).

204. Omission by *KZ* (August 30, 1986, p. 5) of several sentences from Akhromeev's statement at Stockholm to a Western audience was not significant; he had said that the Soviets needed to underline the concessions they were making by not insisting on the inclusion of independent air and naval exercises and by accepting the exclusion of North America. The Soviet leadership did not, however, need to draw the attention of *KZ*'s military readership to these unequal concessions.

205. Herspring concludes from Akhromeev's writings that Akhromeev decided to throw his weight behind the Gorbachev team sometime between the middle of 1986 and the end of the year ("Soviet High Command," p. 52). Others argue that the shift in alignment did not happen until 1987, citing a change in tone between Akhromeev articles published in February and December. This claim ignores the different audiences being addressed and the maturation of policy. The February article, written for Armed Forces Day, was addressed to a Soviet audience, one message being that the armed forces were about to undergo their own perestroika. The article also mentioned that military doctrine was in the process of major revision. (S. Akhromeev, "The Glory and Pride of the Soviet People," *Sovetskaya Rossiya*,

The role Akhromeev played at Reykjavik was unprecedented. While Gorbachev was clearly in charge, the chief of the General Staff led the team that conducted detailed negotiations on strategic arms reductions. He showed considerable flexibility and had significant authority to make concessions within established guidelines. This was the first time the military had been given such a central role and Akhromeev ranked alongside Shevardnadze in the overall proceedings.[206]

Continuity and Change

The most striking feature of Soviet defense and foreign policy between 1984 and the end of 1986 is the extent to which the new leadership hewed to the general line that had emerged from the 1983–84 reappraisal. Nor was that 1984 line itself entirely new. It had reaffirmed various aspects of the policy established by the 1981 party congress, notably the overriding importance of superpower agreement to limit nuclear weapons, the turn toward China, and the more pragmatic approach to countries of the third world.

The most significant change to emerge from the 1983–84 reappraisal had been the conclusion that, while peaceful coexistence was a sine qua non, it was unrealistic to count on a sustained détente relationship with the United States, certainly as long as Reagan was in office, and most probably as a general rule. A by-product of that assessment was the decision that the Soviet Union would have to adopt a more assertive policy in defense of socialist gains in the third world; otherwise the United States would assume that it had an unbridled right to intervene with military force whenever it disapproved of a country's behavior.

A quite separate decision sought to reduce the danger of world war by adopting a defensive posture facing NATO. To justify this new defensive doctrine, the Soviets had to give priority at the military-

---

February 21, 1987, in *FBIS*-87-89, pp. V3–4.) The December article was addressed to the World Marxist Movement (including readers in the Soviet Union and Eastern Europe) and was publicizing the new military doctrine that had by then been worked out and formally agreed (Marshal S. Akhromeev, "Doctrine of Averting War, Defending Peace and Socialism," *World Marxist Review*, vol. 30 [December 1987], pp. 37–47).

206. Although the proposals put forward by the Soviets at Reykjavik had been cleared by the Politburo, Akhromeev's participation allowed further concessions to be made during the course of negotiations. It also meant that Akhromeev would gain first-hand knowledge of the Reagan leadership and its factions and hence a clearer understanding of the problems facing the Gorbachev leadership.

technical level to the objective of "averting world war" at the expense
of "not losing" such a war, although the latter objective continued to
determine the size and structure of Soviet forces.

All these elements of Soviet policy remained in place through 1986.
While Soviet spokesmen affirmed the desirability of "normal" relations
with the United States, they did not spare their criticism of U.S.
imperialism and militaristic behavior or hide their conviction that the
stalemate in negotiating reductions in the size of nuclear arsenals
reflected the baleful influence of "aggressive circles" in America.
Criticism by the Gorbachev leadership of Soviet policy in the Brezhnev
period focused predominantly on the domestic arena. To the extent
that past foreign policy was criticized it concerned style rather than
substance, except in relation to arms control, where Gorbachev required
a whole new approach to negotiations. But the objectives remained
unchanged. Averting world war was still the dominant concern, while
the United States continued to be the central problem in international
relations.

In general, Gorbachev had accelerated and broadened existing policies, notably in respect to arms control and to China and the Asian-
Pacific region, and he had continued to diversify Soviet political and
economic involvement in the third world. The 1984 decision to be more
assertive in defending the gains of socialism in the third world was
a partial exception. The interposition of Soviet forces would flout
Gorbachev's prohibition against the confrontation between capitalism
and socialism taking a military form, a principle that was formally
reaffirmed at the 1986 party congress. This implied that Soviet policy on
direct military intervention had reverted to its earlier more cautious
mode.

The first twenty months of the new leadership yielded mixed results
in the field of national security. On the one hand, international tension
had been relaxed and, for the time being, the danger of war had receded.
The international image of the Soviet Union had improved sharply, from
that of a doctrinaire, intransigent, militarized state led by an ossified
gerontocracy to that of a more conciliatory and cooperative member of
the world community, led by a new and younger team that sought to
mesh Soviet national security with the broader concept of international
security.

On the other hand, very little had changed in practice. There had been no progress in arms control and the arms race continued unchecked, with the United States still determined to extend it into space. The successive concessions offered by Gorbachev had been seen by Washington as a reason to ask for more, while offering nothing in return. The United States flatly refused to halt nuclear testing and had been unimpressed by the Soviet announcement of a defensive doctrine. As recently as May 1986 Reagan had declared that U.S. military spending must be increased because the Soviets sought a communist world revolution and were outbuilding NATO.[207] The Geneva summit had done little to abate the assertive hostility of the Reagan administration which had, if anything, increased in the wake of Reykjavik. Reykjavik had also confirmed the political strength of U.S. "aggressive circles" and the pervasive influence of the military-industrial complex.

Another element of continuity with the pre-Gorbachev era was the need for Soviet policy to accommodate an unusually large number of internal contradictions. These long-existing contradictions, which had their roots in the requirements of Soviet military doctrine and Marxist ideology, had become increasingly acute since the late 1970s. The more important of them involved the need

- to avert world war; and to prepare to wage and not lose such a war, should it prove unavoidable.
- to maintain the capability to wage world war; and to negotiate the elimination of U.S. strategic nuclear systems that were designed to deter such a war.
- to retain conventional superiority in Europe; and to negotiate the elimination of NATO theater nuclear forces that were designed to balance the Soviet conventional superiority.
- to negotiate mutual reductions in conventional forces so as to reduce the defense burden; and to retain sufficient conventional superiority to be able to defeat NATO in Europe in the event of world war.
- to shift resources out of the defense sector; to remain abreast of the impending revolution in military affairs; and to provide for Soviet national security, as currently defined.

In addition to these long-standing contradictions, the new political thinking about international relations introduced several new ones.

207. *New York Times,* May 22, 1986, p. A1.

These included

- the essential role of Eastern Europe as an offensive springboard or a defensive glacis in the event of world war; and the principle of nonintervention in the internal affairs of other states.
- the zero-sum view of international relations implicit in the concept of an ideological struggle between the two social systems; and the expanding-sum approach required by the increasing interdependence of the world and the need for global solutions to global problems.
- the Marxist doctrine that Soviet foreign policy should be guided by class analysis; and the admission that other nations had legitimate interests and that their viewpoint had to be respected.

Six of these eight contradictions involved the political-military requirement to cover the contingency of world war, a war the Soviets absolutely wanted to avoid but could not afford to lose. The requirement had first emerged in 1947–48, when the contingency was seen as largely a replay with different participants of the war the Soviets had just fought and won. However, by the mid-1980s the likely scope of a world war had grown immeasurably, as had the military capability that was needed in order "not to lose."

In the Euro-Atlantic region the Soviets would have to defeat NATO on land, evict U.S. forces from the Continent, and establish a defense perimeter running from the Norwegian Sea to the Cape Verde Islands and then east across the northern part of Africa. In the Asian-Pacific region China would have to be deterred from taking advantage of Soviet involvement in Europe, Japan would have to be neutralized, the United States would have to be held at bay, and Soviet forces would have to be ready to seize Manchuria once victory was assured in Europe. In the Indo-Arabian region the Soviets would have to establish themselves securely in the Bab-al-Mandab–Horn region, and be ready to seize Chah Bahar at the head of the Arabian Sea and perhaps to drive south from Azerbaijan to Tabriz in Iran.[208]

The list of these requirements gives a sense of their scale, and the history of World War II argues that they were not overstated. The Soviets also had to match the U.S. nuclear capability and, if wartime

---

208. For justification of the requirements, see MccGwire, *Military Objectives,* chaps. 4–9.

deterrence failed, be ready to wage global nuclear war. This was contingency planning on the grand scale. The resources, human and material, that the Soviets had invested in meeting this requirement were massive, but even so they were barely sufficient, given the forces arrayed against them.

It was not only the Soviet economy that was skewed and damaged by this onerous requirement. So was Soviet foreign policy, particularly in respect to China and the nations of Western Europe, all of whom felt threatened by the large Soviet forces on their borders. Meanwhile, the strategic requirement for a sufficient margin of conventional superiority over NATO was a permanent obstacle to negotiating arms reductions, whether nuclear or conventional, strategic or theater.

Most of the contradictions that had hamstrung Gorbachev's policy initiatives stemmed from the doctrinal assumption that world war was possible, and therefore had to be prepared for. Gorbachev had, however, gotten the other Warsaw Pact nations to agree that "achieving a durable peace was a fully realistic task," and during his first twenty months he had argued consistently that national security in the nuclear age had to be ensured by political rather than military means. In the wake of Reykjavik he therefore had to decide whether to take his line of argument to its logical conclusion.

Could he afford to carry on as hitherto, making virtually no progress toward his stated goals? If he could not, the obvious way for Gorbachev to resolve the contradictions underlying Soviet policy was by means of a simple but audacious change in military doctrine. The political leadership would have to instruct the military to plan on the assumption that world war could and would be averted by political means.

CHAPTER 7

Gorbachev Assumes Command, 1987–88

UNTIL the all-important plenum at the end of January 1987, the new Soviet leadership was largely implementing ideas and policies that had been generated in the Andropov period. There was a rough consensus on the general direction to be followed and, while Gorbachev had steadily increased his power and authority, he was still nominally primus inter pares.

The first six months of 1987 were a watershed in Soviet domestic and foreign policy. As Gorbachev observed, after the January plenum, "events went in a completely different direction."[1] The period between the Central Committee's adoption of the new policy of political democratization in January and the plenum in June was a watershed, when the focus of perestroika shifted from a primary concern for the economy to a broader concern for Soviet society as a whole.

It was in this period that political opposition to this broadening process crystallized and gathered strength and that disagreement over Gorbachev's policies "changed and intensified."[2] In this period Gorbachev diagnosed past neglect as the cause of "pre-crisis conditions"[3] and

1. "Strengthening the Restructuring with Practical Actions," *Pravda,* July 15, 1987, in *FBIS*-87-136, p. R1 (see Abbreviations of Frequently Cited Sources).
2. Ibid.
3. Gorbachev, *Pravda,* June 26, 1987, in *FBIS*-87-123, p. R2.

explicitly described the task facing Soviet society as "a real revolution."[4]
And in this period the "Basic Theses" that were meant to provide the
framework for comprehensive economic reform were hammered out,
for adoption at the plenum in June.[5]

During the first six months of 1987 the lines of battle were drawn.
Subsequent events—the party conference in July 1988, the surprise
plenum which produced wholesale leadership changes at the end of
September, the various phases of the new electoral process that were
set in motion in late 1988—can be seen as successive engagements in
this ongoing political struggle, as attempts to outflank the enemy or to
bring reinforcements to the battle.

The decision that economic perestroika would fail unless the energies
of the Soviet people were directly engaged through a process of democratization had momentous domestic consequences. But the implications for
foreign policy and military doctrine were no less far reaching, because
the decision served as the catalyst that brought about a truly symbiotic
relationship between domestic perestroika and Soviet foreign policy.

Gorbachev publicized the need for democratization in an unscheduled
speech at Krasnodar in September 1986 on his way back from his summer
vacation in Stavropol'. In the following months he not only had to enlist
party support for democratization, but he had also to initiate measures
to mitigate its destabilizing effects. And to have some chance of success
he needed a peaceful international environment and external assistance
in restructuring the Soviet economy. A series of initiatives designed to
achieve these and other results can be dated to this period, of which
the most important were the decisions to reassess the superpower
relationship yet again and to adopt the planning assumption that world
war could and would be averted by political means.

In the last three months of 1986 the perestroika process acquired its
own dynamic, forcing decisions on momentous issues. The decision to
democratize set the ship of state on a new course, one that would soon

---

4. "Strengthening the Restructuring," p. R5. The term was not new, for Gorbachev in a
February 1986 interview described the demands of perestroika as a "revolutionary task"
(*Pravda,* February 8, 1986, p. 1), and in July in a speech at Khabarovsk he specifically equated
the term *perestroika* with the word *revolution* (*Pravda,* August 2, 1986, p. 1). In Mikhail
Gorbachev, *Perestroika* (Harper and Row, 1987), pp. 49–55, he refers to perestroika as a new
revolution, an extension and development of the 1917 October Revolution.

5. Ed A. Hewett, *Reforming the Soviet Economy: Equality versus Efficiency* (Brookings,
1988), pp. 348–50.

leave familiar waters for the uncharted seas that Gorbachev is now trying to navigate.

The Genesis of Perestroika

In essence, the process of economic perestroika—literally rebuilding or restructuring—was initiated by Andropov in 1983,[6] and during Gorbachev's first two years as general secretary he largely followed the path that had been mapped out in 1983–84.[7] Leadership dissatisfaction with the performance of the Soviet economy was not without precedent, including that of Nikita Khrushchev. Although the Soviet Union's growth rates in the 1950s and 1960s were high compared to those of Western European countries and the United States, the glaring inefficiencies of the system engendered repeated attempts to improve the workings of its economic machinery.

Khrushchev's efforts at reorganization in 1957, motivated as much by political as by economic considerations, introduced new inefficiencies that outweighed the marginal gains. The Brezhnev-Kosygin reforms of 1965 were carefully thought out and much more substantial than Khrushchev's and initially created the impression of having improved matters, but by the early 1970s it was clear to the Soviet leadership that more was needed. The 1973 industrial reorganization and the 1979 decree on improving planning and the functioning of the existing machinery (which was never really implemented) continued the thrust of the 1965 reforms, seeking to improve the central decisionmaking apparatus and the responsiveness of the production enterprises, but it was all to no avail.[8]

By the end of the 1970s the Soviets had identified another fundamental problem. Observing that the economic growth rate had declined steadily since the second half of the 1950s, they had concluded that an underlying

6. M. S. Gorbachev, "On Convening the 27th CPSU Congress and the Tasks Related to Its Preparation and Conduct," *Kommunist,* no. 7 (May 1985), in *JPRS*-85-013, p. 5. At the June 1983 plenum Andropov had noted that Soviet social development had reached the kind of "historic frontier where deeply qualitative changes in productive forces and a corresponding perfection of production relations have . . . become inevitable" (*Kommunist,* no. 9 [June 1983], p. 6).

7. Elizabeth Teague, "Gorbachev Answers His Critics," *RL* 280/87 (July 15, 1987), p. 7.

8. Hewett, *Reforming the Soviet Economy,* pp. 221–26. Hewett argues that the 1965 reforms did not get at the root of the problem and even if they had been properly implemented, they would not have solved the problem.

cause of the slowdown in the economy was their failure to shift from extensive to intensive development. Extensive development, which achieves growth through an increasing volume of the inputs to production (raw material, labor, capital), had been successful during the first two decades after the war but was no longer effective because the volume of inputs, labor in particular, was reaching its limits. Meanwhile, the Soviets had been unable to switch to intensive development, which relies for growth on increasing the productivity rather than the volume of the various factors of production. Far too much had been spent on trying to expand the economic base and far too little on continuously modernizing it.[9]

Measures to Improve Efficiency

When Andropov succeeded Brezhnev as general secretary in November 1982, he turned to the economy almost immediately. His prescription reflected the widespread belief that a large part of the problem lay in past failures to implement effectively the reforms that had been introduced since 1965. The basic requirement was to accelerate the process of economic development, of moving from extensive to intensive development. Andropov was brutally frank in his description of the economic system's inadequacies and of the poor performance by its leaders, planners, managers, and work force, which he exposed in the national press.[10] He stressed the need for greatly improved discipline throughout the system, in the party, in the government, and in the workplace, discipline that implied a tight link between performance and rewards to enterprises and to individuals. The administrative thrust of Andropov's reform was similar to Kosygin's in 1965, but he also encouraged discussion and debate about the economy, what was wrong with it, and why past reforms had failed. That debate broadened after his death.[11]

Besides initiating the perestroika process and opening up the economic debate, Andropov began to put together the coalition that took

9. Ibid., pp. 69–72. The influential Soviet economist Abel Aganbegian considers that intensive factors should account for two-thirds of all growth, whereas the reverse has generally been the case (ibid., p. 71). Gorbachev pinpoints the failure to shift emphasis in his report to the 27th Party Congress, MTS, February 25, 1986, in *FBIS*-86-38, supp. 41, p. O10.

10. Vera Tolz, "A Chronological Overview of Gorbachev's Campaign for 'Glasnost,' " *RL* 66/87 (February 23, 1987), p. 1.

11. Hewett, *Reforming the Soviet Economy*, pp. 257–73.

over the reins of power in March 1985.[12] Gorbachev, a full member of the Politburo since 1980 and responsible for the economy and party cadres under Andropov, was its most prominent member, and it was this coalition that continued to develop the concept of perestroika during the Chernenko interregnum from February 1984 to March 1985,[13] when Gorbachev was tenuously the number-two man in the party.

Konstantin Chernenko allowed the economic debate to continue, and Andropov's experimental introduction of a new set of economic plan indicators and incentives went ahead as scheduled in 1984 and was duly modified and extended in 1985.[14] But while Chernenko did not reverse perestroika, he allowed the drive for discipline to slacken.[15] That, and the elevation of a relative nonentity to be leader of the country, the third successive general secretary to be old and ailing, increased the sense of social crisis that had been growing steadily since the inertia of Brezhnev's final years.

Gorbachev was elected general secretary by the Central Committee on March 11, 1985, after a split vote in the Politburo and an unscripted but wholehearted speech by Andrey Gromyko supporting his candidature.[16] Gorbachev subsequently admitted that he then had still not fully grasped the scope, depth, and pervasiveness of the difficulties afflicting the Soviet political economy.[17] In his report to the Central Committee plenum on April 23, 1985, while he stressed the "newness and scale" of the problem facing Soviet society, neither his diagnosis nor his remedies differed significantly in their broad outline from what had gone before.

The main reason Gorbachev gave for the economy lagging so badly was the failure of previous leaders to spell out in detail and then implement properly the earlier reform programs. He claimed that a sharp acceleration (*uskorenie*) of economic development could be achieved if priority was given to industrial modernization, involving the application of the latest scientific and technological developments to all sectors of

12. Michel Tatu, "Seventy Years after the Revolution: What Next?" *RL* 426/87 (October 26, 1987), p. 4, note 2; Archie Brown, "The Soviet Leadership and the Struggle for Political Reform," in Paul Lerner, ed., *The Soviet Union—1988: Essays from the Harriman Institute Forum* (Crane Russak, 1989), p. 52.

13. Gorbachev, *Perestroika*, pp. 24, 27.

14. Hewett, *Reforming the Soviet Economy*, pp. 273–74.

15. Gorbachev, Report at Plenum, *Kommunist*, no. 7 (May 1985), in *JPRS*-85-13, p. 13.

16. Archie Brown, "Gorbachev: New Man in the Kremlin," *Problems of Communism*, vol. 34 (May–June 1985), pp. 7–9.

17. Gorbachev, *Perestroika*, pp. 62–63.

the national economy, machine building being the most important; if the economic machinery (planning, management, finance) was restructured to make it more effective and more responsive; and if there was a sharp improvement in the attitude to work and in the quality of organization and discipline at all levels.

A highly publicized measure aimed at this last problem, the "human factor," was the anti-alcohol program launched in May 1985,[18] while a major purpose of glasnost was to expose incompetence in bureaucracy and management. In response to the first problem, investment in machine building and metal working planned for 1986–90 was increased 80 percent over actual investment in 1981–85. And there were a series of decrees rearranging the machinery of economic administration during 1985–86.[19]

A primary means of implementing the first stage of this modernization program would be the Twelfth Five-Year Plan, which Gorbachev presented to the Twenty-seventh Party Congress for approval at the end of February 1986.[20] The thrust of his economic report to the congress was largely similar to what he had said at the plenum in April 1985. Although he pulled no punches in this later analysis of the state of the Soviet economy, Gorbachev gave the impression of being reasonably confident that progress was being made and that things were moving in the right direction, although perhaps not as fast as he would have liked.[21]

Still outstanding (although not mentioned by Gorbachev) was the formulation and acceptance of the grand design for a restructured economy that would provide the blueprint for the comprehensive and radical reforms that were needed. This would take another twelve months at least, but the need for radical reform was generally accepted. As Egor Ligachev (then seen as number two in the hierarchy) put it, there was an "urgent need for a sharp change of direction in the country's development." But his prescription was for more discipline, a strengthening of "the leadership of the party, state, economic, and social

18. This seemingly sensible measure backfired badly. It caused a serious shortage of sugar (used in illicit stills) and deprived the state of much-needed revenue from taxes on alcohol.

19. Hewett, *Reforming the Soviet Economy,* pp. 316, 322.

20. From the time of the Five-Year Plan's inception under Andropov, Gorbachev would have had primary responsibility for overseeing its development and establishing its targets. Ibid., pp. 306, 310.

21. His report to the June 1986 plenum evinced a much higher level of dissatisfaction with progress. *Pravda,* June 17, 1986, pp. 1–4.

organizations,'' and a struggle against alcoholism and "the acquisition of unearned income.''[22]

The Need to Democratize

At some time during the summer of 1986, Gorbachev seems to have realized that things were not progressing as well as predicted and to have concluded that drastic action was needed if the perestroika process was not to go the way of the previous attempts at reform. Part of the problem lay in the bureaucratic inertia of the ministries, but that had been foreseen. What had not been foreseen was the failure to engage the mass of the people in the perestroika process, the failure to overcome the average citizen's skepticism and distrust of the state and party apparatus. Unlike Ligachev, he realized that engaging the "human factor" was not a matter of improved discipline but of basic motivation.

Gorbachev concluded that unless the "human factor" could be activated, perestroika was bound to fail. He identified the problem in these words: "a house can be put in order only by a person who feels that he owns this house.''[23] The remedy lay in "democratization," an established term to which Gorbachev gave new meaning.

Gorbachev had raised the issue of democratization obliquely in his address to the Khaborovsk Party *aktiv* at the end of July. He was critical of deficiencies in the region and he stressed that party cadres must encourage active involvement by the people. He reached back to Lenin to draw the conclusion that the Soviet Union now had "an educated people which strives to participate in the political process, to play a real part in managing the affairs of society and the state.''[24]

Firm evidence of Gorbachev's far-reaching conclusion surfaced in the unscheduled speech he gave in Krasnodar on September 18.[25] He said that it had been agreed he would visit the region on the way back from vacation and that he had not planned a speech, but when he realized

22. Y. L. Ligachev, "Teaching to Think and Act in a New Way," *Pravda,* October 2, 1986, in *FBIS*-86-203, pp. R1–2. This speech could have been a response to Gorbachev's Krasnodar address, which was given wide coverage. Addressing the Academy of Sciences, Ligachev called for "a radical turning point in the way [Soviet science] operates, of fundamental changes in all spheres of its activity" (*Pravda,* October 17, 1986, in *FBIS*-86-206, p. R7).

23. Gorbachev, "On Reorganization and the Party's Personnel Policy," TASS, January 27, 1987, in *FBIS*-87-018, p. R17.

24. MDS, July 31, 1986, in *FBIS*-86-149, p. R13.

25. *Pravda,* September 20, 1986, p. 1.

how bitter the people were, he decided to address the local party *aktiv*.[26] The second part of his published address began with a strong attack on the failings of ministerial bureaucracies but then moved on to the need for democratization in all spheres of Soviet life, as the means of involving the people in the process of perestroika. Indeed, "the essence of perestroika . . . is for people to feel they are the country's master."[27]

The Krasnodar speech marked an important turning point for Gorbachev.[28] For the party and for perestroika, the turning point was the plenum in January 1987, when the scope of democratization was spelled out in Gorbachev's report "On Perestroika and the Party's Personnel Policy."[29]

Gorbachev had great difficulty in getting Politburo agreement to that controversial report. The plenum was deferred three times,[30] and disagreement over Gorbachev's policies sharpened and intensified in its wake—with good reason. Whereas previously Gorbachev had been engaged in restructuring the Soviet economy, he had now embarked on restructuring the Soviet political system. He argued that it was the only way of engaging the support of the Soviet people, of mobilizing the "human factor."

26. Gorbachev, *Perestroika*, p. 73. Among the signs that the speech had not been scheduled (although that does not mean it was unpremeditated) was the absence of the local statistics that are usually a feature of such addresses. The discussion with the Krasnodar party *aktiv* was euphemistically described as "businesslike" (*KZ*, September 19, 1986, in *FBIS*-86-189, p. R9). At the January 1987 plenum the Krasnodar territory was one of six areas singled out for mention by Gorbachev where "negative processes . . . manifested themselves in extremely ugly forms." The unfortunate first secretary of the Krasnodar *kraykom* incongruously headed the list of fairly eminent speakers in the subsequent debate.

27. *Pravda*, September 20, 1986, in *FBIS*-86-186, p. R10. Gorbachev repeated this formulation in his impromptu speech in Stavropol (*KZ*, September 19, 1986, in *FBIS*-86-189, p. R11).

28. This can be inferred from the way he refers to the occasion in *Perestroika*, p. 73. Raymond L. Garthoff, of Brookings, told me that shortly after the speech, a Soviet official alerted him to its significance. In the report of a conference at the Main Political Administration (MPA) of the Army and Navy, the chief of the MPA referred to the Central Committee decree dated September 25, 1986, "Concerning the Results of Comrade M. S. Gorbachev's trip in Krasnodar and Stavropol' Regions" (*KZ*, November 15, 1986, p. 2).

29. TASS, January 27, 1987, in *FBIS*-87-018, pp. R2–48.

30. Referring to the January plenum Gorbachev noted that "to prepare it proved a difficult matter. Suffice to say that we postponed [it] three times, for we could not hold it without having a clear idea of the main issues" ("Address to the 18th AUCCTU Congress," MTS, February 25, 1987, in *FBIS*-87-39, p. R4). An echo of the Politburo debate can be heard in Ligachev's speech on the sixty-ninth anniversary of the October Revolution, when he noted that "the process of restructuring . . . has a revolutionary character. . . . Of course, this does not mean changing the essence of our social system" (MTS, November 6, 1986, in *FBIS*-86-216, p. O4). The *Pravda* reprint of this speech (November 7, 1986) inserted additional material on steps to increase democratic participation (*FBIS*-86-218, p. O11).

January 1987 was crucial because it gave official sanction to the thesis that the acceleration of economic development, the process of perestroika, was just not possible without engaging the "decisive force" of the people, and that to engage that force required the democratization of society.[31]

Gorbachev's far-reaching proposals at the January plenum mark a sharp change in direction from what he had said about democratization eleven months earlier in his report to the Twenty-seventh Party Congress. The difference between the resolutions adopted by the two meetings is telling. The brief references to democratization in the congress resolutions implied no change in the existing situation.[32] In contrast, of the two substantive sections of resolutions passed by the January plenum, one was devoted entirely to different aspects of democratization. The resolutions ranged from changes in the electoral system, through worker participation in the management of farms and factories, to provision for democratic control of the bureaucracy from below.

The key difference was in the spirit of the resolutions. The party congress saw democracy as an indirect process, mainly involving organizations and appointed bodies. Attention to democracy meant attention to correct procedures and improved efficiency. The plenum resolutions saw democracy as a participatory process, where the talents and energy of individuals were enlisted in support of perestroika, not primarily as a means of outflanking the bureaucracy, but as a vital and essential force in its own right.

Nor were those resolutions the final answer. As Gorbachev said in July 1987: "We are now . . . going through the school of democracy afresh. We are learning."[33] He subsequently noted that "if the democratic process had developed normally" in the Soviet Union, many of the country's difficulties could have been avoided. He claimed that this lesson has been thoroughly learned and that the line has been established that "only through the consistent development of the democratic form inherent in socialism and through the expansion of self-government can [the Soviet Union] make progress. . . . Perestroika . . . can only come through democracy."[34]

31. Gorbachev later described democratization as "the engine that will ensure restructuring" ("Czechoslovak-Soviet Friendship Rally," *Pravda,* April 11, 1987, in *FBIS*-87-071, p. F8).

32. *Kommunist,* no. 4 (March 1986), in *JPRS*-86-011, pp. 101–02.

33. "Strengthening the Restructuring," p. R3.

34. Gorbachev, *Perestroika,* p. 32.

"It [was] either democracy or social inertia and conservation. There [was] no third way."[35] But by itself, democracy was not sufficient to ensure the success of perestroika and, among other prerequisites, there would need to be a major shift of resources from defense to the civilian sector of the economy. Withdrawal from Afghanistan would be some help. But a really major shift of resources would require the military to cease preparing for the contingency of world war. The January plenum appears to have been the occasion for legitimating and promulgating the classified decision that the military should develop plans based on the doctrinal assumption that world war could and would be averted by political means.

The remaining prerequisites in the field of foreign policy and defense would be harder to achieve. One required the reversal of existing policy toward the United States—a policy that had only been decided in 1983–84, when the losers of the debate in 1967–71 had been able to claim that events had proven them right. The other required a reinterpretation of Marxist-Leninist doctrine on central concepts like the correlation of forces, peaceful coexistence, and the international class struggle. Both issues were ideologically very sensitive and a lot of political blood had been spilled over the first. New policy would therefore have to be introduced gradually and without fanfare, allowing events rather than dictates to bring about change.

The Implications of Democratization

In the two years following the January 1987 plenum there were many radical changes in Soviet foreign and defense policy. These included the withdrawal from Afghanistan, the acceptance of a separate treaty on intermediate-range nuclear forces (INF), a reversal of policy toward the United States, the adoption of a new kind of military doctrine, and the announcement of very large unilateral cuts in Soviet forces. The changes in ideology included the reinterpretation of peaceful coexistence and the promotion of national interests above class interests.

The coherence in this series of initiatives in terms of timing, substance,

---

35. Gorbachev, "Address to the 18th AUCCTU Congress," p. R6.

and interdependence implies that they all stem from a single underlying concept. The evidence suggests that the process of formulating new concepts began soon after the Reykjavik summit and that a draft plan of action had been decided by the end of November 1986.

Rerigging the Ship of State

The decision to democratize the Soviet political process meant political destabilization. In essence Gorbachev—who had spoken in terms of the ship of state—was proposing to rerig the ship on the high seas, to restep its masts in midocean. This was a perilous undertaking and success required a calm maritime environment, a compliant crew, and a measure of external assistance.

The calm international environment and the availability of external assistance depended directly on good relations with the United States. The United States' capacity to prevent such assistance was matched only by its capacity to heighten international tension and increase the danger of war. But good relations could not be achieved just by asking, since American anticommunism was widespread, deep-rooted, and enduring. The Soviets had faced up to this fact during the 1983–84 reappraisal, the dominant view having been that the Soviet Union had been wrong in the late 1960s to base its foreign policy on the assumption that a long-term cooperative relationship with the United States was possible. History should have told the Brezhnev leadership otherwise, and the point appeared to have been proven when the U.S. effectively renounced détente in the second half of the 1970s.

In the spring of 1984 the Soviets had begun to plan on the assumption of an inherently hostile United States, a country with whom good relations would be a means to an end, rather than an end in themselves, since détente would not endure and could not be counted on. The United States could not be ignored, but it was a problem to be circumvented whenever possible. While it was counterproductive to try to exclude the United States, attempts at sustained cooperation were bound to fail, at Soviet expense.

However, some time in the fall of 1986 Gorbachev decided that if he was going to open the Pandora's box of democratization, good relations were an absolute practical necessity rather than a theoretical option to be adopted or rejected.[36] Good relations with the United States were, however, more easily specified than achieved. After all, in 1945 Stalin had hoped to carry the wartime collaborative relationship into the postwar era, and it was the United States and Great Britain who by the spring of 1946 had decided that Soviet behavior made normal relations impossible. And in the late 1970s it was Brezhnev who persisted in claiming that détente was still alive, long after it had become a dirty word in U.S. political circles.

The problem was that each side's interest in good relations had always been asymmetrical. The Soviet Union had little to offer that the United States could not obtain elsewhere, and there were many U.S. interest groups—ethnic, religious, ideological, and military-industrial—that for their different reasons favored or at least benefited from a hostile relationship.

Diagnosing the Problem

It may have been the bizarre experience at Reykjavik that brought these issues into focus for the Soviets. The mini summit and its aftermath demonstrated that the influence of the American military-industrial complex and the "aggressive circles" who sought the downfall of the Soviet state was too strong for the emergence of a grand compromise on strategic weapons, despite the cornucopia of concessions offered by the Soviets. Following the rhetorical success of the Geneva summit, Moscow seems to have thought that it could outflank these militaristic elements by having Gorbachev deal directly with Reagan. Reykjavik demonstrated that assessment to be wrong. Something more imaginative and far reaching would be required if the Soviet leadership was to empower that body of U.S. opinion that acknowledged that in the nuclear age there was no such thing "as national security, only international security" and recognized that guaranteeing security must rely "above all on political and not military means."

This challenge allowed a proper hearing for adherents of the less ideological, more cooperative tendency in Soviet views of the U.S. policy process and its underlying power structure, and the Soviet policies

36. The central importance of establishing good relations with the United States becomes clear when one contemplates what would have happened if the events that actually took place in 1989 had occurred in 1982–83, when the Reagan administration was at its most bellicose and confrontational.

that began to emerge in 1987 suggest that a sophisticated variant of those views prevailed. It appears to have been acknowledged that forty years before, at the very start of the cold war, the Soviet Union would have done better not to have responded in kind to the Truman Doctrine of military containment and to the buildup of U.S. strategic nuclear forces. By allowing the United States to define the competition in military terms and by responding in kind, the Soviet Union had provided the external threat that was the lifeblood of the U.S. military-industrial complex and had allowed itself to be drawn into a ruinous arms race.[37] This had played into the hands of "aggressive circles" in the United States and those who sought the downfall of the Soviet state by economic means.[38]

The critical diagnosis of past policy toward the United States blended with Gorbachev's new political thinking about international relations to yield clear-cut policy prescriptions:

- Get out of the arms race, preserving security but sacrificing national pride and what is "fair" to more important interests.
- Take active steps to de-demonize the Soviet Union, thereby denying the West its "threat."
- Plan on the assumption that world war can and will be averted by political means.

The three prescriptions were interdependent, but the most crucial was the assumption of "no world war." It was a prerequisite for de-demonizing the Soviet Union and for extricating it from the arms race; it would allow a radical reduction in the defense burden; and it would make world war less likely. The experience of the 1970s and early 1980s had shown that the age-old adage *si vis pacem para bellum* did not hold

37. Gorbachev referred to this obliquely in his speech on the seventieth anniversary of the October Revolution when he noted that the Soviet Union was "unable to make use of the enormous moral prestige with which [it] emerged from the war to consolidate peaceloving, democratic forces and to stop the organizers of the Cold War. Our reaction to the provocative actions of imperialism was not always adequate." MTS, November 2, 1987, in *FBIS*-87-212, p. 54.

38. Gorbachev referred to this in his "Address to the 18th AUCCTU Congress," p. R14, saying "Let us not repeat—automatically, without thinking—what imperialism is seeking to impose on us in the arms race." The policy of forcing the Soviet Union to invest scarce resources in the defense sector was explicitly advocated in the U.S. Defense Guidance for 1984–88 that was leaked to the press in 1982 (Richard Halloran, "Pentagon Draws Up First Strategy for Fighting a Long Nuclear War," *New York Times,* May 30, 1982, p. A1). It was implicit in an article by Defense Secretary Caspar Weinberger ("U.S. Defense Strategy," *Foreign Affairs,* vol. 64 [Spring 1986], pp. 695–96) and in a statement by Senator Sam Nunn supporting the B-2 bomber (Malcolm Brown, "Will the Stealth Bomber Work?" *New York Times Magazine,* p. 26).

good in the nuclear age. In preparing for world war the Soviets had jeopardized peace and made such a war more likely. To act on the assumption that world war would be averted by political means would of itself reduce the danger of such a war.[39]

The opposite assumption, that world war was possible and therefore must be prepared for, underlay six of the eight contradictions that bedeviled Soviet foreign policy.[40] Over the forty years that military requirements had been shaped by the contingency of world war—a war the Soviets absolutely wanted to avoid but could not afford to lose—the likely nature of such a war had progressively changed. Repeatedly Soviet forces had had to be restructured, but an enduring feature had been the offensive westward. The 1970s strategy that had so alarmed the West required the Soviets to deny the United States a bridgehead in the event of war; to defeat NATO in Europe and evict U.S. forces from the Continent required superiority in conventional forces over NATO.

This superiority lay at the root of the Soviet problem.[41] It loomed large in Western threat perceptions. It stymied negotiations on conventional force reductions, where massive cuts were needed to alleviate the Soviet defense burden. And Soviet superiority in conventional arms was the nominal reason why Washington would not negotiate seriously on preventing an arms race in space, halting it on earth, and ultimately eliminating nuclear weapons altogether—despite the fact that the U.S. president and secretary of state had each signed a formal joint statement to that effect with their Soviet counterparts.

Conventional superiority was, however, essential if the Soviets were not to lose a world war. The only way to obviate the requirement for superiority was to cease planning for the worst-case contingency of world war and to give the military a less demanding objective. Ensuring the territorial integrity and internal cohesion of the Soviet bloc, or perhaps even just the Soviet Union, would not require superiority

39. In commenting on past mistakes in Soviet military and foreign policy, V. Zagladin noted a "conceptual inconsistency. While rejecting nuclear war and waging a struggle to avert it, we nonetheless proceeded from the possibility of winning it. . . . When we brought our concept into line with reality and logic, our whole policy started to be organized differently." "Press conference at the 19th Party Conference," MTS, June 25, 1988, in *FBIS*-88-123, p. 2.

40. See final section of chapter 6.

41. Gorbachev in his speech to the French General Assembly in October 1985, referring to troop reductions in Central Europe, said, "We are prepared to reduce more troops than the Americans." He again expressed a willingness to eliminate any Soviet "surplus" during the French president's visit to Moscow in July 1986, but such asymmetrical reductions would apply to both sides. *Pravda,* October 4, 1985, in *FBIS*-85-193, p. G5; TASS, July 7, 1986, in *FBIS*-86-130, p. G5.

or surprise. And a westward offensive, which had been a strategic imperative, would be excluded because it would precipitate world war. The Soviets would therefore be able to make the major unilateral cuts needed to prime the pump of mutual reductions in forces, which would allow significant resources to be moved out of defense into the civilian sector.

Evidence of the new policies emerged in the wake of the plenum in January 1987. On February 28 Gorbachev announced that the Soviet Union was willing to sign "without delay" a separate agreement on INF.[42] The final agreement brought the inventory of intermediate- and short-range missiles on both sides to zero and required the Soviets to scrap 1,836 missiles carrying 3,136 warheads, whereas the United States had to scrap only 859 missiles carrying 859 warheads.

Gorbachev's new political thinking had already done something to de-demonize the Soviet Union, but at the end of March 1987 there was a marked shift in the tenor of Soviet diplomatic relations with the United States. Later that year Georgiy Arbatov referred obliquely to depriving the United States of its threat,[43] but in a subsequent and widely reported comment he taunted his Western interlocutor with the explicit claim that Moscow was achieving what the Western political-military establishment feared most—dissolution of the Soviet threat.[44]

The assumption of "no world war" required a completely new kind of military doctrine, and Marshal Sergey Akhromeev made reference to it in his Armed Forces Day article on February 21.[45] The assumption was implicit in Gorbachev's speech to the Trade Unions Congress on February 25, when he remarked that the "dramatic change in the very atmosphere of international relations . . . in the attitude of both ordinary people and many statesmen on . . . the question of war and peace . . . is becoming . . . more pronounced."[46] And he made it explicit in his speech to the United Nations in December 1988 when he noted that "forces already have formed in the world which one way or another are inducing the *start of a period of peace*."[47]

42. *Pravda*, March 1, 1987, p. 1.

43. "The Darkness before Dawn?" *Pravda*, September 10, 1987, p. 4, final paragraphs.

44. Soviet commentators subsequently referred to this idea often enough for it to be seen as a policy objective.

45. *Sovetskaya Rossiya*, February 21, 1987, in *FBIS*-87-39, pp. V3–4. Interestingly, when describing the source of Soviet policy, Akhromeev linked Gorbachev's February 16, 1987, speech to the International Forum with the decisions of the party congress in 1986.

46. "Address to the 18th AUCCTU Congress," p. R13.

47. *Pravda*, December 8, 1988, p. 1.

Timing

This radical redirection of Soviet defense and foreign policy was probably carried out by Gorbachev's closest advisers, rather than by the Central Committee secretariat. Although the plan of action is likely to have been mapped out by the end of November 1986,[48] Gorbachev appears to have avoided confronting his colleagues with the full analysis at this stage.[49] The conceptual analysis underlying the plan was politically sensitive and Gorbachev was already having difficulty gaining Politburo acceptance of democratization. Instead, he seems to have presented them with those elements that could be justified in their own terms and did not involve questions of Marxist-Leninist ideology or doctrine.

However, he did have a timetable in mind that was dictated by the existing plans for economic perestroika. Gorbachev's original economic strategy had two main stages: a preparatory one that would run through the end of the decade; and an implementation stage, starting with the Thirteenth Five-Year Plan in 1991, which would provide for dramatic improvements in quality and a national income growth rate of about 5 percent a year, ensuring the desired acceleration of economic development.[50]

If the economy was to be up and running by 1991, the various reforms would have to be in place and the main restructuring of the economic system completed at least a year earlier. Gorbachev indicated as much in his speech marking the seventieth anniversary of the October Revolution on November 2, 1987, twice referring to the critical importance of "the next two or perhaps three years." This period would see "the transfer from an excessively centralized command-based management system to a democratic one, based predominantly on economic methods and an optimum combination of centralism and self-management." It would be necessary "to implement deep structural improvements in the economy, to reach a turning point in the acceleration of scientific and technical progress, and in the main to restructure the economic

48. It is possible that the Delhi Declaration (November 27, 1986) stemmed from the same plan of action, but its origins are probably earlier.

49. This approach had precedents. Stephen M. Meyer notes that "Khrushchev set the agenda, along with his staff devised policy options, and then announced decisions. Often, only a handful of Politburo members knew what to expect" ("The Sources and Prospects of Gorbachev's New Political Thinking on Security," *International Security*, vol. 13 [Fall 1988], p. 130, note 13).

50. Hewett, *Reforming the Soviet Economy*, pp. 309–10.

mechanism, thus taking the decisive step in switching the economy onto the tracks of intensification."[51]

The law giving new economic authority to state enterprises, which lay at the heart of perestroika, would come into force at the beginning of 1988. At that date, enterprises producing 60 percent of industrial output would be working under the new conditions, which would apply across the board in 1989. Similarly, the new planning prices would have to be introduced by the end of 1988 to allow work to proceed on the next five-year plan.[52] Introduction of the new prices was, in the event, deferred, but despite all the problems the 1989 economic plan did depart sharply from long-established precedent by setting higher growth targets for consumer goods and social expenditures than for increasing the means of production. Meanwhile defense spending flattened out.[53]

It is clear that an important benchmark was the Nineteenth All-Union Party Conference held at the end of June 1988. Gorbachev had proposed that this conference should be held in his report to the January 1987 plenum, but it was not agreed to by the Central Committee until the June plenum. Such conferences had been convened frequently through the mid-1920s, but then ceased until 1941 when the eighteenth conference was held a few months before the German invasion. Gorbachev did not achieve all he hoped for at the conference, but the proceedings offer clear evidence of the timetable he had in mind at the end of 1986.

This time frame helps to define how the various developments in foreign policy and the extensive changes in the military aspects of national security policy fit into the overall scheme of things.

Measures to Mitigate Destabilization

One way of reducing the destabilizing effects of democratization was to get rid of the disaffected. New emigration regulations, which had been approved in August 1986, were announced by Eduard Shevardnadze at the start of the Conference on Security and Cooperation in Europe early in November, to take effect January 1, 1987.[54] More important than the

---

51. MTS, November 2, 1987, in *FBIS*-87-212, pp. 50–53.

52. Ibid. See also Hewett, *Reforming the Soviet Economy*, pp. 332–33.

53. John Tedstrom, "The Soviet Economy: Planning for the 1990s," in *Report on the USSR*, vol. 1 (December 22, 1989), p. 2. Military expenditure was frozen in 1987 and 1988 (D. T. Yazov [interview], *Izvestiya*, September 17, 1989, in *FBIS*-89-179, p. 1).

54. Philip Taubman, *New York Times*, November 6, 1986, p. A18.

announcement was the number of permits issued—40,000 in 1987 and 108,000 in 1988, compared to a mere 6,000 in 1986; the numbers of Jews, Germans, and Armenians allowed to leave in 1987 was almost fourteen times the 1,959 who emigrated in 1986.[55]

Another approach was to enlist the support of the intelligentsia. On December 19, 1986, Gorbachev personally gave Academician Andrey Sakharov permission to return to Moscow from Gor'ky, where he had been exiled since 1979 because of his outspoken opposition to the invasion of Afghanistan. On his return, Sakharov in television interviews criticized the government and reiterated his call for Soviet withdrawal from Afghanistan. But by February 1987 he had thrown his qualified support behind Gorbachev, announcing that something had definitely changed.[56]

A third initiative involved setting a deadline for the withdrawal of Soviet forces from the increasingly unpopular war in Afghanistan.[57] In his speech at Vladivostok in July 1986 Gorbachev had spoken in favor of a coalition government of national reconciliation, but at the time of his visit to India at the end of November, he went even further. Speaking to Indian journalists, Gorbachev declared that the Soviet Union was in favor of a nonaligned and independent Afghanistan, even a neutral Afghanistan. On December 7, Abdul Sattar, the first deputy foreign minister of Pakistan, made an unexpected visit to Moscow marking the resumption of bilateral negotiations. Moscow had meanwhile sent a high-level delegation to Kabul and on December 11–14 the Afghan leaders visited Moscow. These were the first such high-level visits in six years, and the Soviet media emphasized that there was "a genuine and real opportunity" for solving the problem of Afghanistan. After his return to Kabul, President Najibullah told a party meeting that Gorbachev intended to withdraw Soviet troops within eighteen months. And on January 1 Najibullah offered a general amnesty and announced a six-month ceasefire starting on January 15.[58]

---

55. The gross figures are from Dmitry Yakushkin, "A Policy of Humanism," *Sovietskaya Kultura,* June 10, 1989, in *FBIS*-89-117, pp. 8–9; figures for Jews, Germans, and Armenians were provided by the U.S. State Department.

56. Philip Taubman, *New York Times,* February 12, 1987, p. A1.

57. The United States began supplying Stinger hand-held heat-seeking antiaircraft missiles to the Mujihadeen in the summer and fall of 1986. This is unlikely to have been a major factor in the decision to set a deadline.

58. Bohdan Nahaylo, "Gorbachev-Najib Meeting Deepens Hopes For Early Settlement in Afghanistan," *RL* 470/86 (December 15, 1986), "Towards a Settlement of the Afghanistan Conflict," *RL* 16/87 (January 11, 1987), and "Gorbachev Reiterates Kremlin's Position on

This rapid sequence of events, including Sakharov's televized criticism of Soviet involvement in Afghanistan when he was released from exile, suggests the execution of a plan of action that had probably been decided by the end of November.[59] It was foreseen that the actual military withdrawal would take twelve months, and it appears that Gorbachev had the Politburo's agreement to initiate the diplomatic and political process at the beginning of January, although the timing remained a matter of dispute.[60]

Gorbachev seems to have been arguing that Soviet forces should be out of Afghanistan by July 1988, certainly no later than January 1989. His opponents were more concerned with the terms of an agreement under which a withdrawal would be acceptable and considered that an arbitrary deadline would undermine the Soviet negotiating position—as indeed turned out to be the case.[61] On March 2, 1987, Foreign Minister Shevardnadze stated that Moscow was close to setting a timetable for the withdrawal, which might take twenty-two months—that would have been January 1989. In the event, the last troops were withdrawn by February 21, 1989.[62]

The timetable had still not been agreed at the time of the June 1987 plenum, but the balance in the Politburo changed then in Gorbachev's favor. In the middle of July the deadline of January 1989 appears to have been finally accepted, with Gorbachev being given the authority to initiate the withdrawal before January 1988, if progress in the negotiations between Afghanistan and Pakistan would allow it.[63] It did not.

Afghanistan," *RL* 195/87 (May 21, 1987); Robert A. Manning, "Moscow's Pacific Future: Gorbachev Rediscovers Asia," *World Policy Journal,* vol. 5 (Winter 1987–88), p. 72; Don Oberdorfer, *Washington Post,* April 17, 1988, p. A31.

59. Gorbachev subsequently noted that "possibilities for achieving [a practical solution] emerged following the appearance of genuinely national forces headed by Najibullah on the political stage in Afghanistan in late 1986." *Kommunist,* no 4 (March 1988), in *JPRS-88-009,* p. 18.

60. By early January 1987, the U.S. State Department had concluded that the Soviets had taken the general decision to withdraw, but had yet to agree to a final timetable (Oberdorfer, *Washington Post,* April 17, 1988, p. A31). The decision was not without significant risk. Karen Dawisha noted that in March 1986 the general line in Moscow was that a Soviet withdrawal would result in a "bloodbath" unless guarantees could be provided for the People's Democratic Party of Afghanistan (PDPA).

61. According to a well-placed Afghan defector, in December 1986 Gorbachev had told Najibullah that in June 1987 he and Pakistani President Zia would agree on a twelve-month timetable for withdrawing Soviet forces. When Najibullah was summoned to Moscow in July 1987, he was again told by Gorbachev that Soviet troops would be withdrawn within twelve months (ibid).

62. Shevardnadze was speaking in Bangkok (*Agence France-Presse,* Hong Kong, March 2, 1987, in *FBIS*-87-041, p. E2).

63. In an interview with the Indonesian paper *MERDEKA,* Gorbachev noted that the withdrawal of Soviet troops from Afghanistan had already been decided in principle. He went

Najibullah was a reluctant partner in Gorbachev's plan for national reconciliation in Afghanistan and the withdrawal of Soviet troops. Following his summons to Moscow in December 1986, Najibullah did offer a general amnesty, an end to persecution for previous political activity, and respect for the nation's historical, national, and cultural traditions and for Islam. But he also made it clear that he would not compromise on his party's program for action or its ties with the Soviet Union. This unconstructive stance prompted a hurried visit by Shevardnadze and Anatoliy Dobrynin, following which Najibullah announced a plan for sharing power with the opposition.[64] He was, however, aware of the disagreement in the Politburo—in negotiations with Pakistan on the contentious issue of the time needed for a Soviet withdrawal, the Afghans seem to have used the January 1989 deadline as their final sticking point and to have refused to hasten the process.[65]

At the Washington summit in December 1987, Gorbachev offered a twelve-month timetable for withdrawing from Afghanistan. President Reagan then put obstacles in the way by disowning his administration's agreement (reached in 1985) on halting the supply of arms. It was a measure of Gorbachev's priorities that, despite this setback, he announced on February 8 that if the accord were signed by March 15, withdrawal would begin May 15 and be completed within ten months.[66] Although the accords were not finally signed until April 14, Moscow insisted that the Soviet withdrawal begin on May 15 and agreed to complete the process within nine months.[67]

While a Soviet withdrawal from Afghanistan would remove a cause of domestic disaffection and somewhat reduce the defense burden, it would also bring significant benefits in the field of foreign affairs. The presence of Soviet forces in Afghanistan was one of the "three obstacles"

---

on to say that he would have liked the withdrawal period to have been compressed [*my za to chtoby sroki vyvoda byli szhatymi*] (*Pravda,* July 23, 1987, p. 2).

64. Dobrynin was the Central Committee secretary in charge of the International Department. Najibullah made his announcement on January 1 and Shevardnadze and Dobrynin made a surprise visit on January 5. Nahaylo, "Towards a Settlement"; Oberdorfer, *Washington Post,* April 17, 1988, p. A31.

65. Pakistan was willing to accept a seven-month withdrawal. In 1986 Afghanistan had proposed forty-eight months. However, in March 1987 it proposed twenty-two (although it ultimately conceded eighteen); in early September it agreed to sixteen, and in December 1987, to twelve.

66. This public commitment was a clear signal that there would be no re-entry of Soviet troops in the event of the collapse of the PDPA.

67. Rosanne Klass, "Afghanistan: The Accords," *Foreign Affairs,* vol. 66 (Summer 1988), pp. 932–36; Selig S. Harrison, "Inside the Afghan Talks," *Foreign Policy,* no. 72 (Fall 1988), pp. 54–56.

to improved relations with China, and since the Soviet Union was already moving to reduce its forces on the Chinese border, this left the Vietnamese presence in Cambodia as the one remaining obstacle. A withdrawal from Afghanistan would improve the Soviet Union's standing with countries in the third world, especially the thirty-eight Muslim states that had been particularly outraged by the Soviet action in 1979. And it would remove a major source of dissension with the United States.

Calming the International Environment

In promoting his belief in the need for new political thinking about international relations Gorbachev had relied initially on expounding his ideas to the leaders of foreign governments or their parliamentary bodies. However, the Reykjavik summit made it clear that this was insufficient, and that if he was to outflank Western "aggressive circles" and the powerful military-industrial complex, he would have to bypass governments. The decision to mount a major campaign to bring the new political thinking to the attention of the world's opinion-forming elites appears to have been taken by the end of November, since the early invitations to attend a large international forum "For a Nuclear Free World, For the Survival of Mankind" had reached their Western addressees by December 12.

Some 300–400 people attended the three-day forum in mid-February. Gorbachev described it as "a true embodiment of world opinion," comprising as it did "politicians and journalists, businessmen and scholars, doctors and people of culture and the arts, writers and representatives of various churches."[68] In what was at that date the most fully formed exposition of "the new realities of the nuclear age," Gorbachev's address focused on the danger inherent in the nuclear arms race, which was reaching a qualitatively new stage, and on the trend in international relations toward enforced interdependence.

For many participants this was their first exposure to the new political thinking about international relations, which had been given scant coverage by the Western press.

68. MTS, February 16, 1987, in *FBIS*-87-31, p. AA16. See William F. Brazier and Joel S. Hellman, "Gorbachev's New World View," *Social Policy*, vol. 18 (Summer 1987), pp. 4–12.

The Shift in Policy toward the United States

Once Gorbachev had decided to introduce democracy, the central importance of good relations with the United States would have been self-evident. But a decision to reverse policy toward the United States differed in important ways from the decisions to withdraw from Afghanistan and to revise political-military doctrine about the likelihood of world war. The two latter policies would take a long time to put into effect, and the sooner the processes started the better. There was, however, no hurry over good relations with the United States, which would in any case depend in large part on the success of the other two initiatives. Both of the other new initiatives could be represented as adjustments to established policy. The withdrawal from Afghanistan had been approved in principle by the April 1985 plenum and the party congress in February 1986. Similarly, the new military doctrine could be seen as taking to their logical conclusion the 1984 doctrinal decision on the priority of averting war and the Twenty-seventh Party Congress's resolution that ensuring security was increasingly a political, rather than a military, task.

In contrast, the new policy toward the United States would require the reversal of decisions over which much political blood had been spilled during the previous twenty years. Soviet-American relations were central to the struggle between the two social systems and hence highly ideological. There had been significant opposition to Brezhnev's move to détente in the second half of the 1960s and to the "peace program" that was adopted at the 1971 party congress. And when détente ran into the sand ten years later, there were many, both ideologues and pragmatists, who could claim to have been proven right. They would have felt vindicated by the outcome of the 1983–84 policy reappraisal and would not look kindly on a suggestion to give détente one more try. Indeed, it would have been another reason for opposing Gorbachev on democratization.

In any case, the fall of 1986 was not a propitious time for such a proposal. As if to compensate for having been forced to exchange Gennady Zakharov for Nicholas Daniloff, both alleged to have been spying, Washington had ordered the *New Jersey* battle group to steam through the Sea of Okhotsk in September.[69] The diplomatic barging

69. *Bulletin of Atomic Scientists,* vol. 44 (September 1988), p. 63. This was the first time a U.S. battle group had operated in this semienclosed sea, an area where the Soviets were known to deploy their ballistic-missile submarines. The *New Jersey* carried nuclear-armed Tomahawk land-attack missiles. Two years before, two U.S. carrier battle groups operating

match had reached its denouement in October, when five U.S. embassy officials were ordered out of the USSR and fifty-five Soviet diplomats were told to leave the United States by November 1. It is quite likely that Gorbachev was being criticized by some of his colleagues for the concessions he had been willing to offer at Reykjavik (which the Americans had promptly pocketed), while all factions in Moscow were angered by the U.S. administration's misrepresentation of what had taken place in Reykjavik and what had been agreed.

In two hard-hitting speeches at the end of October, Secretary of State George Shultz had added insult to injury when he ruled out any arms control agreement until there was substantial Soviet progress in the area of human rights; ten days later the Reagan administration had reaffirmed its intention to breach the SALT II limits by the year's end.[70] And then to rub salt into the wound, when the arms control talks did reassemble in Geneva in November, the Soviets discovered that the negotiations had been set back rather than advanced by the Reykjavik summit.

For all these reasons it seems likely that Gorbachev and Shevardnadze decided to avoid controversy within the Politburo about the bases of Soviet policy toward the United States and chose instead to rely on a change in style that of itself would lead to improved relations, after which ideological arguments would be easier to dispose of. By February 1987 the outlook had improved somewhat. The Republicans had not done well in the mid-term congressional elections the previous November, and this supported the argument that Reagan was an aberration in the long-term trend toward a better relationship between the two social systems. Meanwhile, his administration had been weakened politically by the Iran-Contra scandal that had broken surface in the first half of November 1986, leading to a major turnover in White House staff, including the replacement of the president's national security adviser (on November 25) and chief of staff (on February 18). This stream of resignations was augmented in the new year by the departure of those who had always planned to leave at the start of the administration's final two years.[71]

in the Sea of Japan had come to within fifty miles of Vladivostok and much closer than that to the Soviet coastline (Hedrick Smith, *New York Times,* December 19, 1984, p. A1).

70. Bernard Gwertzman, *New York Times,* November 1, 1989, p. A1, and Michael R. Gordon, ibid., November 11, 1989, p. A1. The Soviets probably realized that Shultz's combative statements were aimed at the U.S. electorate; nevertheless they had to be taken at face value. The breach of SALT II involved converting the 131st bomber to carry cruise missiles.

71. Richard Perle, assistant secretary of defense for international security policy and a primary obstacle to arms control agreements, submitted his "long anticipated" resignation on March 13.

At the end of February 1987 Gorbachev took action on the new precept of getting out of the arms race at whatever cost in pride or fairness, as long as Soviet security was not thereby jeopardized. He announced that the Soviet Union was willing to negotiate a separate agreement on intermediate-range nuclear forces (INF).[72] This opened the door for Shultz to visit Moscow in mid-April, and as preparations started for the visit, U.S. embassy officials became aware of a dramatic change in the tenor of Soviet-American relations.[73] Gorbachev chose the occasion of his meeting with Shultz to announce the Soviets' readiness to scrap all their missiles in the 300–1,000-mile bracket, as well as all of their intermediate-range missiles (1,000–3,000 miles).

The visit marked a turnaround in Soviet policy toward the United States that became increasingly apparent in the following months, as the Soviets moved from the hard-nosed and accusatory stance of Gorbachev's first two years to one marked by compromise and conciliation. While the concessions on INF are certain to have been agreed by the Politburo, it seems most likely that the underlying shift in policy was treated in its early stage as a tactical adjustment in style rather than a strategic redirection. Such a redirection could not be justified in terms of existing Marxist-Leninist theory of international relations, and new theory would have to be developed before the new direction could be publicly admitted.

The Need for New Theory

A distinguishing feature of Soviet foreign policy was that it was nominally guided by the Marxist-Leninist theory of international relations. All Soviet political leaders claimed that their decisions were based on such theory, and theory and practice were considered interdependent. For example, theory was meant to allow practice to see the direction of movement in the correlation of forces, both currently and in the near future. Theory had to, however, remain abreast of practice and new theory had to be developed to take account of changes in social reality.[74]

---

72. The Soviets had begun working on the problem of how to eliminate such weapons in 1986, "and began its practical implementation in 1987" (Akhromeev television interview, MTS, October 9, 1989, in *FBIS*-89-197, p. 102).

73. The visit, announced in Washington on March 7, took place April 13–15.

74. Margot Light, *The Soviet Theory of International Relations* (St. Martin's Press, 1988), pp. 3–4.

It is clear that Gorbachev and his followers recognized the inherent conflict between the Marxist-Leninist concept of antagonistic social systems and the new political thinking about international relations with its image of an interdependent world and the need for cooperative endeavors. For example, in May 1986 Dobrynin had called for "even more profound works on international and military-political problems," citing Gorbachev on the need to bridge the gap between theoretical concepts and the new realities. He had also stressed the need to develop a new theory that reflected the realities of the nuclear age and that could provide a scientific basis for the new political thinking about international relations.[75]

Within a few weeks of taking office, Gorbachev had started to develop a new definition of peaceful coexistence, which is an inherently spongy concept, but he avoided challenging key ideological tenets directly. However, in the summer of 1986, when he came to see that without democracy perestroika must surely fail, he also realized that he could not wait for the theorists to catch up with reality. He therefore arranged for the key concepts of class analysis and the correlation of forces to be challenged directly, starting in the fall of 1986.

PEACEFUL COEXISTENCE. While peaceful coexistence excluded military confrontation, it remained a manifestation of the class struggle and therefore assumed continuing economic and ideological conflict. The official line was that "irreconcilability in the ideological struggle is an objective demand, not a subjective wish," and Marxist-Leninists had to rebuff the idea that peaceful coexistence between capitalist and socialist ideologies was possible.[76] This, of course, was the antithesis of Gorbachev's new political thinking.

The counterargument that the ideological struggle should not be allowed to dictate the nature of interstate relations had been made by

75. A. Dobrynin, "For a Nuclear-free World, As We Approach the XXI Century," *Kommunist*, no. 9 (June 1986). This article was based on his address in May to a major gathering of "scientists" (in the sense of learned people from all disciplines). The third section of the article (particularly pp. 26, 28, 30) focuses on the role of scientists in turning the new way of thinking into reality. Dobrynin quotes Goethe to the effect that "our wishes already contain the anticipation of our ability to achieve them." He goes on to note that "a social science or a policy that refuses to take into consideration this major dimension of social reality, becomes not a science but dead scientism, and not a policy but blind empiricism."

76. A. S. Milovidov and V. G. Kozlov, eds., *Philosophical Heritage of V. I. Lenin and Problems of Contemporary War* (Moscow: Voenizdat, 1972), U.S. Air Force translation (U.S. Government Printing Office, 1977), p. 217. See also Light, *Soviet Theory*, pp. 44–72.

Yuri Andropov in 1983.[77] Gorbachev followed that precept during his visit to London in December 1984, when he stressed that the most important problems facing mankind could only be solved by joint efforts. In March, four months later, a few weeks after being elected general secretary, Gorbachev described peaceful coexistence as a policy where "each system attempts to prove that it is better by force of example and not by force of arms," and he repeated this formula in his speech to the French Assembly in October and at the press conference following the November summit in Geneva.[78] To the French parliamentarians he also described peaceful coexistence as "the difficult art of taking account of each other's interests" and he added the injunction that in the present situation it was "especially important not to emulate mediaeval fanatics and not to spread ideological differences to interstate relations."[79]

In January 1986, in an authoritative article discussing Gorbachev's major proposals on strategic arms control, Evgeniy M. Primakov also touched on the meaning of peaceful coexistence. He noted that it was Lenin who had decided on the necessity of peaceful coexistence, which included an important element of constructive cooperation in various spheres. It was also Lenin who spoke of the priority of the interests of social development. In the nuclear era, when the survival of mankind and the further progress of civilization depended on the joint efforts of states with different social systems, "the Leninist theory of peaceful coexistence acquires very great significance." The new way of thinking must therefore "recognize the existence of different countries' objective interests, to seek areas where these interests coincide, and then to act with the aim of bringing them closer together."[80]

In his report to the Twenty-seventh Party Congress at the end of

77. *Pravda,* September 29, 1983. The context implied he was referring to the United States, but the choice of words made it applicable to both parties.

78. "M. S. Gorbachev Interview with the Editor of the Newspaper *Pravda,*" *Kommunist,* no. 6 (April 1985), in *JPRS*-85-012, p. 29; *Pravda,* October 4, 1985, in *FBIS*-85-93, pp. G4–5; MTS, November 21, 1985, in *FBIS*-85-225, supp. 013, p. 3.

79. *Pravda,* October 4, 1985, in *FBIS*-85-193, pp. G5, G10.

80. "Way to the Future," *Pravda,* January 22, 1986, in *FBIS*-86-016, p. AA9. Primakov had taken over as head of the Institute of the World Economy and International Relations (IMEiMO) when Alexandr Yakovlev joined the Central Committee secretariat in June 1985. In April 1989 Primakov was elected a candidate of the Politburo. He was one of the 100 noncontested party candidates for the Congress of People's Deputies, which elected him to the Supreme Soviet, where he was "chosen" to be chairman of the Council of the Union in June 1989. In March 1990 he was selected by Gorbachev to be a member of his presidential council.

February Gorbachev did not challenge directly the doctrine that the ideological struggle must persist, but he did claim that his report was guided by Marxism-Leninism, a theory that derived its vitality from its constant capacity for development. Any attempt to turn the theory into "an assortment of ossified schemes and prescriptions" was "most definitely contrary to the essence and spirit of Marxism-Leninism." He asserted that "peaceful coexistence rather than confrontation . . . should be the rule in interstate relations." While noting that "the two worlds are divided by very many things, and deeply divided, too," he considered that the "realistic dialectics of contemporary development [was] the combination of competition and confrontation between the two systems and in a growing tendency toward interdependence of the countries of the world community." He emphasized "the intrinsic complexity and contradictoriness of the paths of social progress" and noted that Lenin had stressed that "the interests of social development rank above all else."[81]

Meanwhile the congress approved the new edition of the party program describing peaceful coexistence as "the kind of international order whereby not military force, but good neighborliness and cooperation would predominate." The party was said to consider the "spread of the ideological contradictions between the two systems to the sphere of [international relations] to be inadmissible."[82]

Clearly Gorbachev's statement about the "real dialectic of modern-day world development" was seen as important.[83] But its doctrinal significance did not become clear until fifteen months later when Primakov explained that Gorbachev's statement had "rectified the distortion whereby the examination of the confrontation between . . . the socialist and the capitalist systems ignored their interdependence." He warned that "interstate relations in general cannot be the sphere in which the outcome of the confrontation between world socialism and world capitalism is settled."[84]

Primakov also noted how, until quite recently, peaceful coexistence had been seen as a breathing space before a renewed assault by capitalism

81. MTS, February 26, 1986, in *FBIS*-86-36, supp. O41, pp. O5, O2, O9.

82. *Pravda,* March 7, 1986, in *FBIS*-86-046, supp. O51, pt. 1, p. O7, pt. 3, p. O4.

83. It was repeated verbatim in the resolutions of the party congress (*Pravda,* March 6, 1986, in *FBIS*-86-044, p. O2). Aleksandr Bovin replayed the statement in "New Thinking—The Requirement of the Nuclear Age," *Kommunist,* no. 10 (July 1986), in *JPRS*-86-017, p. 129.

84. Ye. Primakov, "The New Philosophy of Foreign Policy," *Pravda,* July 9, 1987, in *FBIS*-87-134, pp. CC6, CC7, CC5.

on the Soviet Union, the first country of victorious socialism. Today, however, "we are dealing with a fundamentally new situation" and "such assessments . . . are clearly inadequate." Primakov went on to hint that, because "peaceful coexistence [had become] a vital necessity for mankind's survival," foreign policy must be based on the assumption that it was now the permanently operating condition, rather than just a breathing space. He was explicit that this would have major implications for military requirements, foreign policy methods, and the philosophy underlying the Soviet approach to international problems.[85]

Gorbachev removed any remaining doubts on this issue in his important speech to the assembled bodies of the Central Committee and the supreme soviets of the USSR and the Russian Republic gathered in the Kremlin to celebrate the seventieth anniversary of the October Revolution. He noted that "Lenin's conception of peaceful coexistence has of course undergone changes." Whereas in the beginning "it was justified primarily by the need to create the minimum external conditions for the construction of a new society," peaceful coexistence had gone on, "especially in the nuclear age, to become transformed into a condition for the survival of all mankind."[86]

CLASS INTERESTS VERSUS NATIONAL INTERESTS. Toward the end of October 1986, in a little-noticed conversation with a group of world cultural figures, Gorbachev asserted that Lenin had said that "the interests of social development and pan-human values take priority over the interests of any particular class."[87] This dubious claim on Lenin's behalf had already been floated by Evgeniy Ambartsumov in a roundtable discussion in September,[88] and Gorbachev's assertion was quoted in at least one subsequent article.[89] The remark is noteworthy because, as recently

---

85. Ibid.
86. MTS, November 2, 1987, in *FBIS*-87-212, p. 54.
87. Transcript of M. S. Gorbachev's conversation with participants in the "Issyk-kul Forum: The Times Demand New Thinking," *Literaturnaya gazeta,* November 5, 1986, in *FBIS*-86-216, p. CC23.
88. "*Izvestiya* Round Table—Demand of the Nuclear Age," *Izvestiya,* September 6, 1986, in *FBIS*-86-178, p. CC7. Ambartsumov, a section head at the Institute for the Study of the World Socialist Economy, was talking with Vitaliy V. Zhurkin, deputy director of the Institute of U.S.A. and Canada. In May 1988, Zhurkin was appointed director of the newly formed European Studies Institute.
89. E. G. Plimak, "Novoe myshlenie i perspektivy sotsialnogo obnovleniya mira" ("New Thinking and Prospects for the Social Renewal of the World") *Voprosy filosofii (Questions of Philosophy),* no. 6 (1987), p. 88. I noticed this inadvertently; no search was made. The general argument had been advanced by G. Kh. Shakhnazarov in "Logika politicheskogo myshleniya v yadernuyu eru" ("The Logic of Political Thinking in the Nuclear Era"), ibid., no. 5 (1984), p. 72.

as June that year, Dobrynin had found it necessary to reiterate that "the new political thinking does not mean in the least any abandonment of the class-oriented analysis of the problems of war and peace."[90]

The argument was advanced another stage by Aleksandr Bovin in a major three-part article that appeared in *Izvestiya* in January 1987. Drawing on the experience of World War II, he noted that national interests had proved stronger than class interests, resulting in a "combat alliance between a socialist state and one group of capitalist states, directed against another such group."[91] This was a direct challenge to established doctrine. By December 1987 the debate about the analytical priority of national interests versus class interests must have been resolved because senior Soviet visitors to the West publicized the fact that the contemporary new political thinking saw national interests as being more important than class interests.[92]

The issue nevertheless remained a matter of contention in 1988. For example, speaking in Gor'kiy in early August, Ligachev raised a question of "vital importance"—the correlation between general human values and proletarian class interests. He stressed that they were not in opposition and that there was a "primordial and deep interlinking between the general human approach and the class approach in foreign policy." He argued that "the struggle for peace and the survival of mankind is indeed also the struggle for the root interests of the working class" and concluded: "We proceed . . . from the fact that international relations are particularly class in character. . . . Any other way of putting this question introduces confusion into the consciousness of our people and our friends abroad."[93]

Earlier, Vadim V. Zagladin had tried to fudge the issue by claiming "priority for the values and interests common to all mankind, [which include] the working people's class interests."[94] In October, however, Vadim A. Medvedev, the Central Committee secretary responsible for ideology, acknowledged that "a more accurate explanation of the correlation between universal and class priorities in mutual relations

90. Dobrynin, "For a Nuclear-free World," p. 31.

91. A. Bovin, "The Soviet Disarmament Program: One Year On," *Izvestiya,* January 10, 1987, in *FBIS*-87-007, p. AA4.

92. The point was made on separate occasions by Primakov and Zhurkin.

93. "Vremya," MTS, August 5, 1988, in *FBIS*-88-152, p. 42. The *Pravda* report (August 6) only gave the last quotation, and even that was omitted from *Sovetskaya Rossiya* (*FBIS*-88-152, p. 39).

94. *Pravda,* June 13, 1988, in *FBIS*-88-116, p. 43.

between the two [social] systems" was required.[95] But this was ideological housekeeping. In July, speaking in his capacity as head of state, Andrey Gromyko had acknowledged "the priority of general human values above all else."[96] And in September Shevardnadze declared officially that "the balance of interests [was] the basis on which interstate relations should be built in the modern world." He linked the authority of the Twenty-seventh Party Congress and the Nineteenth All-Union Party Conference to the priority given to national interests, which was "inspired by Lenin's idea that 'from the viewpoint of the basic ideas of Marxism, the interests of social development rank above the interests of the proletariat.'"[97]

THE NATURE OF CAPITALISM. Subsuming the interests of the proletariat in the broader concept of universal values was one way of outflanking class analysis. Another way was to raise the possibility that capitalism was capable of learning and evolving and no longer lay within the bounds of traditional Marxist definition. This idea, advanced by Evgeniy S. Varga in the second half of the 1940s, was based on changes introduced during World War II, particularly in Great Britain where central planning had been adopted and whole industries nationalized in the wake of war.

This view continued to have a limited number of adherents, although they got little exposure in the professional literature. In 1986 Bovin developed a different kind of argument leading to the same general conclusion. Asking rhetorically whether it was possible for the U.S. leadership to recognize the realities of the nuclear age, he listed all the doctrinal reasons why not. However, he then went on to provide evidence that imperialism did in fact respond to changes in world circumstances. Furthermore, the class instinct of self-preservation, which led capitalism to attempt to destroy socialism, had been overridden by the human instinct to avoid a global catastrophe. In other words, capitalist imperialism had changed and was likely to continue to do so.[98]

Recognition that "present-day capitalism differs in many respects from what it was at the beginning and even in the middle of the 20th century" was included in the new edition of the party program, although

95. Medvedev was speaking at an international learned conference on "The Contemporary Concept of Socialism, International Scientific Conference," *Pravda,* October 5, 1988, in *FBIS-88-194,* p. 6.

96. *Pravda,* July 7, 1988, p. 4. Gromyko was welcoming the president of India.

97. Shevardnadze was addressing a Danish audience of government and business leaders in Copenhagen (*Pravda,* September 22, 1988, in *FBIS-88-185,* p. 34).

98. Bovin, "New Thinking," pp. 136–37.

firmly embedded in statements about its deepening general crisis.[99] Bovin, returning to his earlier argument, claimed in January 1987 that world developments, when seen in their broad socio-historical context, cannot have failed to influence the nature of capitalism. As he put it, "the 'nature' itself does not change. But the machinery and means of its realization change."[100] It was this change that made peaceful coexistence possible, and of course it meant that class analysis was no longer fully reliable.

In September Primakov, discussing "Capitalism in an Interconnected World," described a series of changes in the capitalist system brought about by the emergence and influence of world socialism. The picture he drew of this modern version of capitalism is surprisingly favorable, with many of the unattractive features mitigated either by socialistic developments or by the emergence of new forms of competition, both domestic and international. Among other things he concluded that the "aggravation of interimperialist contradictions does not inevitably lead to world wars," that "militarism is not a mandatory companion of even the accelerated growth of productive forces under capitalism," that intensified competition within the monopoly sector enhanced its capacity to absorb the results of scientific and technical progress, and that the prediction of "an automatic advance towards a line which would mark the collapse of capitalism [had] proved to be false." He also questioned whether the current trend in the change in the correlation of forces did in fact favor socialism.[101]

Finally, at the beginning of November 1987, Gorbachev devoted a significant part of his speech on the anniversary of the October Revolution to answering a series of rhetorical questions about the nature of capitalism and imperialism in the contemporary period. In his lengthy disquisition pointing out that it was necessary and realistic to aim for "an all-embracing system of international security in conditions of disarmament," he showed clearly that capitalism had evolved in ways very different from those foreseen by Marx and Lenin. He also noted new forms of social contradiction in the capitalist world such as the peace and environmental movements and other efforts to mitigate the adverse effects of capitalism. In other words, the human factor was

---

99. *Pravda,* March 7, 1986, in *FBIS*-86-046, supp. O51, pt. 1, p. O4.
100. Bovin, "Soviet Disarmament Program," p. AA4.
101. *Kommunist,* no. 13 (September 1987), in *JPRS*-87-020, pp. 63–69.

beginning to achieve political influence, providing grounds for his "optimistic view of the future and the prospects for creation of an all-embracing international security system."[102]

The new precedence given to national over class interests was important also in altering the concept that capitalism had an inherent tendency to give rise to war. Shifting the focus from class to national interests would bolster the argument that world war could be prevented by political means; so would the redefinition of capitalism.

THE CORRELATION OF FORCES. The precedence of national interests also altered the traditional analysis of the correlation of forces. A correct assessment of class forces had been held to be central to the analysis, which meant that a change in the alignment of class forces could lead to a change in the entire strategy of the world communist movement.[103] That would not be so in the future.

The correlation of forces is essentially a zero-sum concept where one side's gain is the other's loss. Evgeniy Ambartsumov had challenged this idea at the September 1986 roundtable, noting that because of the absolute opposition between the interests of the Western military-industrial complex and those of the Soviet Union, there was a tendency to assume an absolute opposition between U.S. and Soviet interests.[104] He went on to challenge the common assumption that whatever was bad for the United States was good for the Soviet Union, and vice versa. "After all," he said, "the advantages and long term prospects of the new thinking indeed lie in understanding the contemporary world as interdependent, as indivisible in many respects. This conclusion by the Twenty-seventh CPSU Congress is worth thinking about."[105]

His argument was given semiofficial recognition in July 1987 in what was clearly an authoritative article by Primakov entitled "The New

102. MTS, November 2, 1987, in *FBIS*-87-212, pp. 55, 59.

103. Light, *Soviet Theory*, p. 274, citing the book edited by Vadim V. Zagladin (1973).

104. Karen Dawisha notes that Ambartsumov's reemergence was itself significant, because he had been censured for his early 1980s views that the Polish crisis had occurred because of contradictions intrinsic to socialism and not because of imperialist subversion. By 1986 that argument had been resolved in favor of Ambartsumov's point of view and many other persons had lost their posts, including Richard Kozolapov, editor of *Kommunist*. Karen Dawisha and Jonathan Valdez, "Socialist Internationalism in Eastern Europe," *Problems of Communism,* vol. 36 (March–April 1987), pp. 11–12.

105. "*Izvestiya* Round Table," p. CC6. Arguments to the effect that international relations did not represent a strict zero-sum game had begun to appear in the professional literature in the second half of the 1960s (Allen Lynch, *The Soviet Study of International Relations* [Cambridge University Press, 1987], p. 39). Ambartsumov, however, was speaking from a semiofficial platform, and his statement was given tacit approval by publication in *Izvestiya*.

Philosophy of Foreign Policy." Primakov noted that the philosophy took into account "the need to recognize the objective character of different countries' national interests and not to counterpose them but to painstakingly seek areas where these interests can be combined."[106] When Primakov visited the United States in December that year, he used the term "expanding sum" to explain the thrust of Soviet policy in the Middle East and argued that the two sides must move away from the zero-sum approach that had underlain their policies in the past.

In June 1988, discussing the theses that the Central Committee would be presenting to the Nineteenth All-Union Party Conference, Zagladin noted that when formulating foreign policy in the nuclear age it was wise not to focus solely on the very real differences and disagreements that undoubtedly existed between states but to seek "common, mutually acceptable, and mutually advantageous aspects." He described Soviet policy as "striving to make the transition from confrontation to nonconfrontational cooperation" and noted that "the orientation toward a balance of power in international relations [was] gradually being replaced by the search for a balance of interests."[107] Or as the theses put it, there were grounds for hoping that national security would "increasingly move out of the sphere of the correlation of military potentials into the sphere of politics, the primacy of law, and common human morality in the fulfillment of international commitments."[108]

NEW THEORY IN PLACE. By the second half of 1988 the ideological debate was largely over and the key elements of the new theory were in place. A central concept was that the world community must unify against the threat of nuclear annihilation. At the *Izvestiya* roundtable in September 1986 Ambartsumov had posed that question rhetorically, pointing out that the anti-Hitler coalition during World War II included states with different social systems, and asking, "How about now?" A year later at the United Nations, Shevardnadze had advocated peaceful coexistence as a universal principle for relations among states, with "peace as a supreme existential value," and he asserted that one of perestroika's objectives was "to do away with . . . the split of the world into hostile alliances."[109]

106. *Pravda,* July 9, 1987, in *FBIS*-87-134, p. CC8.

107. *Pravda,* June 13, 1988, in *FBIS*-88-116, pp. 44–45. At this date Zagladin was deputy head of the International Department of the Central Committee and later became one of Gorbachev's "advisers" (*pomoshchnik*).

108. *Pravda,* May 27, 1988, in *FBIS*-88-103, p. 49.

109. TASS, September 23, 1987, in *FBIS*-87-185, p. 7.

This was part of the progressive reorienting of the key ideological concepts, but Shevardnadze made it official in his speech to the high-level three-day conference that convened at the Ministry of Foreign Affairs in late July 1988. Shevardnadze also established that "the struggle between the two opposing systems is no longer a determining tendency of the contemporary era." Rather "the ability to build up material wealth at an accelerated rate on the basis of front-ranking science and high level techniques and technology and to distribute it fairly, and through joint efforts to restore and protect the resources necessary for mankind's survival acquires decisive importance" at the modern stage.[110]

Central Committee Secretary Medvedev reaffirmed the new line at an international conference on "The Contemporary Concept of Socialism" on October 4. He called for a "return to the sources of Lenin's perception of peaceful coexistence, cleansing it of the deformations and accretions of the subsequent period." He noted that "the idea that socialism and capitalism can develop somehow in parallel is also obsolete." It was inevitable that the paths of their development would cross and, while there could be no talk of convergence, "both systems inevitably interact within the framework of one and the same human civilization." And today "when universal values are embodied with the utmost specificity, primarily in ensuring mankind's survival," the correlation between universal and class priorities "comes to the foreground of international relations, and constitutes the nucleus of the new political thinking."[111]

This three-day conference, convened to thrash out what "socialism" meant within the framework of perestroika and the new political thinking, and the earlier conference at the Ministry of Foreign Affairs, convened to work out the implications for the conduct of Soviet foreign policy, marked the realignment of Marxist-Leninist theory with the realities of the nuclear age. There was still room for argument, but the major contradictions between traditional theory and the new thinking had been resolved in the latter's favor.

---

110. *Pravda,* July 26, 1988, p. 4. About 900 people attended this important conference, which was nominally reviewing the implications of the Nineteenth All-Union Party Conference held at the end of June. Following the plenary speeches, it broke up into eight sections, each headed by a deputy foreign minister. Some 300 people contributed to the discussions. Participants, drawn from a wide range of organizations, ministries, institutes, and political and party organs, included the chief of the General Staff, the deputy chairman of the KGB, two senior Central Committee secretaries, and the president of the Academy of Sciences.

111. *Pravda,* October 5, 1988, in *FBIS*-88-194, p. 6.

Collateral Policy Initiatives

Besides the shift in policy toward the United States and the initial steps to redefine the Soviet theory on international relations, 1987 saw a new effort to achieve reconciliation between the parties to regional conflict.

There were objective reasons why regional conflicts were liable to work against a calm international environment. Other countries could become involved and, if the superpowers were drawn in, there was the danger of military confrontation and escalation to major conflict or even world war.

But there were also subjective reasons. Washington tended to use the extent of Soviet involvement in regional conflicts as a measure of unacceptable behavior. The precipitate deterioration in Soviet-American relations in the second half of the 1970s was an example of this correlation, and it was accompanied by a steady rise in international tension, culminating in the first Reagan administration.

The correlation reflected a U.S. view that all Soviet activity beyond Soviet borders was inherently illegitimate, while the United States had the worldwide role of defending freedom against the encroachments of Marxist socialism. Despite this double standard, Gorbachev urged the settlement of regional conflicts in his speech to the International Forum in February 1987, listing the Arab-Israeli conflict, "the Iran-Iraq war, the Central American crisis, the Afghan problem, the situation in the south of Africa and in Indochina."[112] And during the next two years the Soviets were active in helping to find solutions to the underlying issues.

Soviet policy toward Afghanistan had for some time favored a negotiated settlement based on reconciliation between the warring factions,[113] but in January 1987 Najibullah had been forced to make serious overtures to the Mujihadeen, and this policy of active reconciliation persisted during the negotiations on the Soviet troop withdrawal and beyond. In November 1987 the reconciliation program had included the proclamation of Islam as the country's official religion; permission for the formation of non-Marxist parties; an invitation to the former king of Afghanistan to head a transitional government; and the inclusion of representatives of the opposition in a government.[114]

---

112. MTS, February 17, 1987, in *FBIS-87-31*, p. AA22.
113. See for example, Gorbachev's Vladivostok speech, *Pravda,* July 28, 1986, p. 1.
114. Viktor Yasmann, "The New Soviet Thinking in Regional Conflicts: Ideology and Politics," *RL* 493/87 (December 3, 1987), p. 4.

Referring to the Middle East in a speech honoring the Syrian leader Hafez al-Asad at the end of April 1987, Gorbachev was explicit that the emphasis on military power as a way of settling the conflict "had become completely discredited."[115] Earlier that month, Soviet diplomatic activity had been partly responsible for the outcome of the meeting of the Palestine National Council, which saw a reconciliation of Yasir Arafat with many radical critics.[116] Meanwhile Soviet policy shifted from discouraging to encouraging PLO involvement in U.S.-mediated negotiations with Israel, and this was important to the initiation of direct talks between U.S. representatives and the PLO toward the end of 1988. Soviet pressure is generally considered to have been behind the conciliatory statement authored by Yasir Arafat's press secretary at the Arab summit in June that year.[117]

In Angola, the ruling Popular Front for the Liberation of Angola (MPLA) was already committed to launching a major offensive that had been in preparation for two years and had involved the Soviet rearmament of the Angolan armed forces (the FPLA) in early 1987. Angola was something of a special case because of the direct involvement by South African forces and because internal unrest in the South African Republic in 1984–86 had raised hopes that the apartheid regime in Pretoria might be faltering. However, the offensive in July 1987 failed, and although the military situation was subsequently stabilized and then reversed in the MPLA's favor (following major Cuban reinforcements), Angola joined the other regional conflicts as a suitable case for conciliation.

In August 1987 the MPLA resurrected the prospects of a political settlement based on linking the withdrawal of Cuban forces from Angola with the withdrawal of South Africa from Namibia (and hence southern Angola) in compliance with UN Resolution 435. After many vicissitudes this led to the agreements signed on December 22, 1988, which could be seen as a vindication of the policy of reconciliation. Whereas the Soviet-supported Cuban involvement in Angola in the mid-1970s had justified a rapid buildup of South African armed forces and a forward military policy that was not limited to Angola, negotiations had resulted in the

---

115. *Pravda,* April 25, 1987, p. 2.
116. Fred Halliday, "Gorbachev and the 'Arab Syndrome': Soviet Policy in the Middle East," *World Policy Journal,* vol. 4 (Summer 1987), p. 416.
117. Helena Cobban, *Beyond Crisis Management: The Superpowers and the Syrian-Israeli Military Theater* (Washington, D.C.: Center for Strategic and International Studies, forthcoming).

first withdrawal of white imperial power in Southern Africa since the negotiations on Southern Rhodesia–Zimbabwe in 1980.[118]

However, the protagonists of reconciliation could not ignore that the successful defense of Cuito Cuanavale air base in southern Angola, the buildup of Cuban forces in early 1988, and their move into southwestern Angola were important factors in persuading South Africa to negotiate and in the shape of the final agreement.[119]

In the Horn of Africa, having normalized its relations with Somalia in October 1986, Moscow was pressing in 1987 for a rapprochement between Ethiopia and Somalia.[120] But in terms of Primakov's injunction that it was "particularly important to stop examining regional conflicts from the angle of Soviet-U.S. rivalry," the most striking development was the pressure brought on Nicaragua.[121] On his return from Moscow at the beginning of November 1987 Daniel Ortega, head of the Sandinista government, announced that Nicaragua would carry out in full the agreement for a peaceful settlement in Central America that had been concluded that August by the presidents of the five Central American states. Ortega also announced a number of measures to increase pluralism, including relaxing restrictions on the political opposition and the independent press and allowing members of the opposition to become part of the country's administration.[122]

A natural corollary to this deliberate shift away from seeking to gain unilateral advantage in regional conflicts to a policy of conflict resolution and conciliation was a greater emphasis on the role of the United Nations. The Soviets were already on record as favoring an enhanced role for "the United Nations and other international organizations [in] preserving peace, ending the arms race and achieving disarmament."[123] However, in September 1987 *Pravda* published a major article by Gorbachev written to coincide with the opening of the forty-second session of the

118. S. Neil MacFarlane, "The Soviet Union and Southern African Security," *Problems of Communism,* vol. 38 (March–June 1989), pp. 81, 84–87.

119. The continuing importance of the armed struggle in the third world was stressed in a 1987 article that supported the "new thinking." The article noted that in recent decades the armed struggle had "in many respects determined the success of the anti-imperialist movement of the oppressed peoples." Plimak, "New Thinking," p. 79. See also Viktor Yasmann, "The New Political Thinking and the 'Civilized' Class Struggle," *RL* 292/87 (July 29, 1987).

120. David E. Albright, "The USSR and the Third World in the 1980s," *Problems of Communism,* vol. 38 (March–June 1988), p. 66.

121. Primakov, "The New Philosophy," p. CC9.

122. Yasmann, "New Soviet Thinking," p. 5.

123. "Communique of the Conference of the Warsaw Pact Political Consultative Committee," *Pravda,* June 12, 1986, in *FBIS*-86-114, p. BB7.

General Assembly, which focused on how to establish "a comprehensive system of international security" and invited the UN member countries and the world public to discuss the problem. Shevardnadze's address to the General Assembly later that month elaborated on Gorbachev's ideas. And during the fall the Soviet Union paid off all the peacekeeping and other charges that it had refused to accept in the past.[124]

Necessary but Not Sufficient

The controversial conclusion that economic perestroika would fail unless the energies of the people were directly engaged through democratization had carried the day in the closing months of 1986, despite significant opposition in the Politburo and Central Committee. Democratization implied political destabilization. Whereas a nonconflictual external environment had previously been seen as important to the success of perestroika, it was now absolutely essential. Good relations with the United States were no longer a matter of choice, but a vital necessity. The United States had a unique capacity to disturb the peace of the world and to prevent the provision of economic assistance by other Western nations, while itself being potentially the most important source of high-technology aid and business know-how.

Good relations with the United States could not be had for the asking but would need to be bought through a sea change in Soviet policy that avoided confrontation and sought conciliation, regardless of the merits of the various cases. This required the redefinition of the concept of peaceful coexistence and, indeed, most of the key tenets of Marxist-Leninist international relations theory. Gorbachev and his supporters were anyway in favor of such changes, which were essential if the new political thinking about international relations was to be adopted as Soviet foreign policy.

Relations with the United States were set on a new track at the end of March 1987, which saw a new tone in Soviet diplomatic discourse. Meanwhile Gorbachev's supporters were already embarked on the ideologically sensitive process of redefining key elements of Marxist-Leninist theory and justifying the shift from a zero-sum to an expanding-sum conception of international relations. The new concepts and defini-

124. Carlotta Gall, "The Burden of Empire," *RL* 512/87 (December 16, 1987), p. 3.

tions were legitimized and promulgated at the large Ministry of Foreign Affairs conference and the international conference on the contemporary concept of socialism held in late July and early October 1988. These meetings were tied to the All-Union Party Conference held at the end of June 1988 that had approved Gorbachev's new political thinking and reaffirmed that only a political approach to resolving the world's conflicts and other problems was practical.[125]

While necessary, these developments were not, however, sufficient. The West, though ready to cite Marx or Lenin to prove hostile intent, had little understanding of the role of theory in Soviet policy or the significance of the changes which were, after all, "only words." Similarly, the new tone in Soviet diplomatic discourse could be dismissed as a tactical shift, the move to conciliation a sign of economic duress, and the withdrawal from Afghanistan a replay of Vietnam. None of these developments could be taken as proof of a Soviet change of heart, least of all the proposal to scrap all nuclear weapons, which could only be a propaganda ploy designed to embarrass the West.

Meanwhile, Soviet forces continued to be deployed in Eastern Europe, superior in numbers to the NATO forces ranged against them, and clearly configured for a blitzkrieg offensive. Until that offensive overhang was removed, Western political-military establishments would remain unconvinced that the Soviet threat, which for forty years was perceived to dominate the international landscape, had changed in any substantive way.

---

125. Editorial on All-Union Party Conference Resolution, *Pravda*, July 6, 1988, in *FBIS-88-130*, p. 43.

CHAPTER 8

Rethinking War, 1987–88

THE NEED to prepare for the contingency of world war determined the size, structure, and posture of the Soviet armed forces from 1948 through 1986. It defined Soviet geostrategic requirements and was an important factor in shaping Soviet foreign policy.

For the first eight years of that period, military requirements had been based on the doctrinal assumption that world war was inevitable. This assumption was relaxed in 1956 to be replaced by the doctrine that, given the necessary sociopolitical conditions, it was theoretically possible to avert world war; meanwhile world war remained a possibility that had to be covered. The Soviet assessment of the likelihood of world war has fluctuated over the years, mainly reflecting the level of East-West tension. For example, the danger was seen to be low in the early 1970s, even during the Arab-Israeli war. There is, however, good evidence that in 1983 the Soviets saw a significant possibility of war with the United States.[1]

In the first half of 1984 the Soviets decided to adopt a defensive posture facing NATO; this was intended to lower international tension and strengthen the hand of the European peace movements, and thereby to reduce the danger of world war. The question also arose whether it was realistic to think in terms of obviating the danger of world war while capitalist imperialism was so evidently assertive. Marshal Nikolay Ogarkov clearly thought it was not. Mikhail Gorbachev thought it was, and shortly after taking office he got the leaders of the other Warsaw Pact countries to agree that "achieving a durable peace was a thoroughly realistic task."

---

1. Annual Edinburgh Forum, 1987. See also chap. 10, notes 13–24.

In the numerous speeches that Gorbachev made during his first two of years in office, two reasons for his belief in the central importance of achieving a durable peace stand out. One was the strong conviction that mankind could not continue to teeter on the brink of the nuclear abyss without falling in.[2] The other was the hardheaded appreciation that restructuring the Soviet economy required a massive shift of resources from defense to the civilian sector. Gorbachev was also convinced that the age-old adage "if you want peace, prepare for war" did not hold up in the nuclear age and that preparing for world war actually made such a war more likely. Hence the numerous assertions that security in the nuclear age must depend primarily on political rather than military means.

If preparing for world war made war more likely, the logical course of action was to cease preparing for such a war. The Soviets had ducked this issue in 1983–84, which was understandable in the prevailing circumstances. But in 1986 there were compelling economic reasons for ceasing to invest scarce resources in preparing to fight a war that "could not be won and must not be fought," as the joint statement from the Geneva summit implied. Furthermore, the requirement to be able to wage world war was an absolute obstacle to cutting the levels of conventional forces, to eliminating strategic and theater nuclear weapons, and to modifying Soviet policy toward Eastern Europe.

However, existing military requirements were based on the long-standing assumption that world war was possible, and to change those requirements would require a change in military doctrine. If the Soviet military establishment was to cease preparing for world war, it must be told to assume that such a war could and would be averted by political means. This required a change in the planning assumption about the likelihood of war.

Problems of Understanding

To instruct the General Staff to develop plans based on the assumption that world war could and would be prevented by political means was, in

2. As Gorbachev said when addressing the Soviet people in the wake of Reykjavik, "We are firmly convinced that the protracted, feverish state of international relations harbours the threat of a sudden and disastrous crisis. Practical steps are needed away from the nuclear abyss." "Vremya," MTS, October 14, 1986, in *FBIS*-86-199, p. DD1 (see Abbreviations of Frequently Cited Sources).

essence, the same as telling it to plan on the assumption that there would be no world war.

Although there is a Western precedent for precisely this kind of planning assumption, there is an instinctive resistance to the idea among Western analysts of Soviet policy.[3] A major reason is that some kind of worldwide conflict remains conceivable. This is, not, however, a valid objection, because it ignores the distinction between a statement of fact and an assumption adopted for the purpose of formulating plans and requirements.

It is somewhat like the building trade in most parts of the United States, which uses engineering criteria that assume that earthquakes are impossible despite the fact that in many areas they are conceivable. But the analogy is only partial because the Soviet assumption is not only that world war can be avoided but that it can be averted by political means. To cease preparing for world war is itself a political initiative that contributes to the process of neutralizing the danger of such a war.

The analogy also misses the distinction between the kind of full-blooded conflict between the specially structured forces that have been facing each other for some forty years and the inherently limited conflict that is all that would be possible once both sides ceased structuring their forces for world war.

This relates to another invalid objection—that whatever its political instructions, the Soviet military would continue to hedge against the possibility of worldwide conflict with the West. Of course it would. It is the General Staff's responsibility to plan a response to all conceivable contingencies, using whatever means are available to the Soviet armed forces. But that is just the point. Under the new assumption, the resources allocated to the military would not be sufficient to wage world war in a coherent fashion. Yes, the military would continue to have contingency plans to cover the worst case, but those plans would bear no relation to the 1970s strategy, or to world war as it had been envisaged for the previous thirty-five years. And while plans for world war of some

3. In 1919 the British adopted a "ten-year rule," whereby the three services were instructed to plan on the assumption that they would not be engaged in a major conflict during the next ten years; this planning assumption was reaffirmed every year until the early 1930s. For Soviet precedents when, for planning purposes, they ruled out various kinds of war, see Jacob Kipp, "Soviet Military Strategy and Doctrine in the Inter-war Period: Between Ideology and Macht Politika," *Papers on the Military and the Origins of the Second World War* (U.S. Army Center for Military History).

kind would exist, Soviet forces would no longer be structured or postured for that contingency.

Some Westerners, who are uncomfortable with the planning assumption of "no world war," argue that the Soviets continue to assume that world war is possible but have reduced their preparations for such a war in order to make it less likely. This argument ignores the evidence that the Soviet Union is in the process of dismantling the forces it needs to wage world war, as that contingency had been traditionally envisaged. But the argument also fails in terms of policy.

For the last thirty years the Soviets have faced a choice of two evils. They could develop and deploy forces that, in the event of world war being inescapable, would have a reasonable chance of not losing the war and (since the mid-1970s) of avoiding the nuclear devastation of the Soviet Union—this meant arms racing and increasing tension. Or they could focus all their efforts on averting world war, including ceasing to prepare for such a contingency, which would allow them to withdraw from the arms race and concentrate on mutual force reductions. To choose a middle road would be to achieve the worst of both worlds—a significant possibility of world war and certain defeat should it occur.

Other analysts argue that the change in Soviet doctrine stems from the assessment that victory in Europe could no longer be achieved. This argument reflects the ingrained belief that the Soviet Union had an urge to seize Western Europe, a prize that would be gained through victory in war. This belief was enshrined in NATO deterrence doctrine, which viewed the world through the lens of Munich and assumed that war would be precipitated by Soviet aggression. It largely ignored the experience of Sarajevo and World War I, and played down Soviet concern about a world war that grew out of a chain of unintended consequences.

This view includes a silent assumption that the Soviet Union, like Germany in the late 1930s, saw war as being beneficial, the obverse of the Soviet view that war is an unmitigated disaster, something to be avoided at almost all costs. This Western viewpoint implies that, for forty years, the Soviet Union engaged in a ruinous arms race with NATO in the hope that at some instant it could successfully invade Western Europe. It must also assume that the Soviets think only in terms of benefits (in this case, the possession of a war-devastated Western Europe) and ignore costs (which might include the nuclear devastation of the Soviet Union). Only such implausible assumptions make it possible to argue that the Soviet Union had chosen to reverse the military posture it sustained at such cost for forty years and to withdraw from Eastern Europe because it concluded that victory in Europe was no longer possible.

In other words, neither of these arguments provides a satisfactory explanation for the momentous change in Soviet policy in Europe, including the Soviets' ready agreement to reductions in Soviet ground forces that are ten to twenty times larger than those accepted by NATO.[4] Meanwhile, the argument that the Soviets have adopted the planning assumption of "no world war" does explain all the evidence.[5] However, to understand the full implications, the assumptions must be expressed as a statement of probability—namely, that world war is ruled to be not possible.

Planning assumptions are probability statements. They locate contingencies on a continuum of possibilities that lie between the categorical extremes of inevitable and impossible. In analytical terms, this continuum divides into three logically distinct parts, comprising the two terminals (or end zones) and the broad middle zone that stretches between inevitable at one end and not possible at the other. When an assumption moves in or out of an end zone, it may require consequential (and sometimes fundamental) changes in dependent aspects of military doctrine, such as objectives, strategy, and the structuring of forces.

Unlike the Marxist-Leninist theory of international relations, where divergent concepts such as class interests and national interests coexist and compete for priority, doctrinal assumptions about the likelihood and nature of a world war are mutually exclusive. World war is either possible or it is not possible; it cannot be both. Similarly the nuclear devastation of the Soviet Union in such a war is either inevitable or it is not; it cannot be both.

This is not just an exercise in symbolic logic. As tables 2-1 and 2-2 make clear, the doctrinal decision, in late 1966, that it was no longer inevitable that a world war would be nuclear had immense consequences. This seemingly subtle adjustment in assumptions required the reformulation of wartime objectives, which led to fundamental changes in strategy

---

4. See chap. 10, notes 63–65.

5. It was also able to predict the unilateral force cuts and the Soviet withdrawal from Eastern Europe. This prediction took the form of asserting that there were no longer any war-related (as opposed to political) reasons for deploying Soviet forces in Eastern Europe or for maintaining conventional superiority over NATO. See Michael MccGwire, "A Mutual Security Regime for Europe?" *International Affairs* (London), vol. 64 (Summer 1988), pp. 361–79.

and operational concepts and the consequential restructuring of Soviet forces to support the new 1970s strategy. Eight years later, the West was beginning to recognize these changes in the structure of Soviet forces and their patterns of operational behavior, but the far-reaching implications in terms of wartime objectives and strategy only became apparent after the underlying change in assumptions had been identified in the 1980s.[6]

Similarly, the evidence of change in Soviet military behavior had been steadily accumulating since 1987, but this mass of information only fell into an intelligible pattern once it was appreciated that Soviet military requirements were no longer driven by the objective of "not losing" a world war. Doctrinal assumptions about the likelihood of world war must therefore have changed; the military must have been told to plan on the assumption that there would be no world war and to develop plans for some lesser contingency.[7]

The new military doctrine, publicized in mid-1987, gave overriding priority to averting war, rather than waging it, as had been the case hitherto. But the new doctrine was not sufficient on its own to explain the far-reaching changes in Soviet military policy and behavior. Only when Gorbachev's dictum that preparing for world war made such a war more likely was added did the doctrine become sufficient; to achieve the objective of averting world war, the Soviets must cease preparing to wage it.

In terms of military planning, which includes weapons procurement and force development, ceasing to prepare for world war had to be "legitimized" by a doctrinal assumption that there would be no world war. Assumptions of this kind are not peculiar to the Soviets, and on both sides planning assumptions have played a central role in military policy. The West, however, has rarely been explicit about the doctrinal assumptions that underlie its approach to military requirements, mainly to preserve alliance cohesion. And the Soviets have not employed explicit terminology to discuss the changes they were setting in train. Nevertheless, carefully formulated assumptions are the basis of good military planning.

---

6. See Michael MccGwire, *Military Objectives in Soviet Foreign Policy* (Brookings, 1987), chaps. 3–9.

7. See Michael MccGwire, "Rethinking War: The Soviets and European Security," *Brookings Review*, Spring 1988, pp. 1–9.

Planning Assumptions

Assumptions about future contingencies—explicit or implicit—are a prerequisite for all kinds of forward planning. Farmers make assumptions about the weather and future markets; developers make assumptions about interest rates, the cost of labor and materials, and population trends; shipbuilders make assumptions about trade flows and the supply and demand of commodities; transportation authorities make assumptions about the future movement of goods and people. And in the sphere of national security, political leaders make assumptions about the likelihood and nature of future conflict.

Military establishments formulate their requirements for men, weapons, and equipment on the basis of the assumptions that are (or should be) made at the highest political level. In the 1960s the U.S. Department of Defense planned on the assumption that the United States might be involved simultaneously in two and one-half wars—a major conflict in Europe, a war like that in Korea or Vietnam (including Chinese participation), and a lesser conflict that might break out in the Middle East or somewhere else. With the adoption of the Nixon doctrine, announced in mid-1969, the planning assumption was changed to one and one-half wars. The China contingency was dropped, while war between NATO and the Warsaw Pact remained on the books.

This approach to planning made sense for the United States, which enjoyed overwhelming preponderance in its hemisphere and was separated from its serious enemies by thousands of miles of ocean. Through the 1950s, when it also enjoyed global economic preponderance, the United States could well think in terms of finding its forces engaged in two different parts of the world outside Europe, with the possibility that the Soviet Union would take advantage of that involvement to launch an assault on NATO. However, by the end of the 1960s, the United States had discovered that its economy could not sustain a large war without some form of national mobilization and that its citizens would not support a large war outside the NATO area. President Nixon therefore dropped the requirement to wage such a war and undertook the gradual withdrawal of U.S. forces from Vietnam. In doing so, he implicitly renounced the objective that had justified military intervention in the first place—namely, preventing the spread of communist regimes in Asia.

Thus the objectives and planning assumptions that had guided the U.S. military for some twenty years were arbitrarily changed by political fiat. Military planners had worked on the assumption that American involvement in a major war against an enemy other than the USSR was possible. After 1970, planning proceeded on the assumption that there would be no such war and steps were taken to mend fences with China. It was not developments in the international arena but domestic factors that brought about the change, including the new president's world view.

It was, of course, still accepted that armed conflict between NATO and the Warsaw Pact was possible, and it was assumed that, if such conflict were not halted at a very early stage, it would most likely develop into a world war. American forces were shaped to prevail in such a war, with particular emphasis being placed on the strategic nuclear element.

The Soviets made planning assumptions comparable to those of the United States. They did not have the option of ignoring lesser contingencies, since their potential enemies were arrayed on their borders. World war was seen as inevitable from 1948 to 1956, and from 1956 through 1986 it was seen as still being possible. For most of the 1960s, a conventional war with China fell outside the scope of Soviet plans for world war, but the adoption of the 1970s strategy brought plans for the separate contingencies into line. Thereafter, in preparing for world war, the Soviets would also acquire the military capability needed for lesser contingencies on the Soviet periphery.

Semantic Imprecision

Although the United States and the Soviet Union invested vast resources in covering the contingency of world war, and trained and exercised their forces to carry out their plans for such a war, neither side used that specific terminology. The Americans explained the structure and employment of their forces in terms of deterrence. The Soviets spoke in equally general terms of rebuffing imperialist aggression. Both of these objectives were formulated in the 1948–53 period, at which time they adequately reflected the situation as perceived by the opposing sides. But these objectives continued to underpin the two sides' rhetoric even though they soon lost their utility as determinants of military requirements.

The actual danger facing the Soviet Union was the possibility of a world war that would be precipitated in some way by the imperialists. If the Soviets failed to deny the United States a bridgehead in Europe, the capitalist West would be able to build up its forces and launch a land and air offensive against the USSR and bring down the Soviet government. The minimum objective, therefore, was "not to lose" a world war; as evidenced by the structuring of the Soviet armed forces from the end of the 1940s, that overarching objective determined Soviet military requirements for almost forty years.

The Soviets' imprecision in expressing their objective was primarily a result of progressive change. It was not critical since the equally imprecise concept of "victory" that permeated the military-technical level of Soviet doctrine encompassed the more precise formulation of "not losing." This imprecision persisted into 1990, in part because the traditional objective of rebuffing aggression had become significantly closer to the actual mission of the Soviet armed forces under the new military doctrine. The result of the imprecision was that while it could be inferred with considerable confidence that the Soviet General Staff had, *in effect,* been told to plan on the assumption of "no world war" or some equivalent assumption, there had yet to be an explicit (as opposed to implicit) reference in the open literature to such an assumption.

There were two good reasons for this reticence. One was the ease with which the assumption could be discredited. It would seem that initially Gorbachev did intend to adopt the assumption openly—he went to some lengths to get Warsaw Pact agreement that "achieving a durable peace was a thoroughly realistic task," and at the April 1985 plenum and at Geneva in November he insisted that world war could be prevented.[8] Following the Geneva summit he interpreted the joint statement as saying that he and Reagan considered nuclear war to be impossible (*nevozmozhnyy*).[9]

Gorbachev was, however, adept at identifying future obstructions to political progress and, as he demonstrated when redefining the Marxist-Leninist theory of international relations, skillful in devising ways to outflank them. His indirect approach can be seen at work in the case of the new military doctrine, with its implicit planning assumption of no world war.

In May 1986, at a large conference at the Ministry of Foreign Affairs, Gorbachev did not address the issue directly but chose instead to attack existing planning assumptions by ridiculing the long-held idea that the Soviet Union should be as strong as any possible coalition of states opposing it. He said that the Soviets could not permit themselves "the

8. See chap. 6.
9. MTS, November 21, 1985, in *FBIS*-85-225, supp. 13, p. 7.

luxury of imitating the United States, NATO, and Japan in all their military-technical novelties."[10] But that and the strength to match the opposing coalition was exactly the capability the Soviet Union would need if it were not to lose a world war! No nation deliberately plans to lose a war, least of all the Soviet Union, and Gorbachev's statement indicated that at that stage he was already positioning himself to be able to require the General Staff to plan on the assumption that world war would be prevented by political means.

The other reason was perhaps even more important. To declare that world war was (in effect) impossible was to flout a primary tenet of Marxist-Leninist theory. Theory held that until socialism became the predominant system, the danger of world war would remain. Gorbachev had no desire to forge an alliance between the ideologues and the military on this crucial issue, and obfuscation was the obvious answer.

The debate about military requirements that surfaced in the spring of 1987 and the different statements about the new approach to ensuring security were therefore couched in imprecise terms such as averting war, reasonable sufficiency, and a defensive doctrine. The attraction of those terms was that they had already been legitimized by the decisions that had emerged from the 1983–84 reappraisal. Now, however, they were to be used to advance concepts that were fundamentally different from those they had applied to in the 1984–86 period.

The Assumption of "No World War"

It is quite likely that many, perhaps most, of the participants in the open debate that surfaced in 1987 about military requirements remained unaware of the fundamental change in objectives and underlying doctrine, believing that it was just a matter of shifting from an offensive to a defensive strategy and ensuring that no more than "enough" was invested in defense. This would explain the extremely diffuse nature of the argument, and why the professional debate on these issues failed completely as a predictor of the political decisions that were taken on unilateral cuts in forces in 1988 and the proposals advanced at the Vienna talks on conventional force reductions in 1989.[11]

10. Quoted by Eduard Shevardnadze in speech to the Foreign Ministry conference in July 1988. *Pravda,* July 26, 1988, in *FBIS*-88-143, p. 30.

11. See, for example, Stephen M. Meyer, "The Sources and Prospects of Gorbachev's New Political Thinking on Security," *International Security,* vol. 13 (Fall 1988), pp. 124–63.

But despite the semantic confusion, there can be little doubt that Gorbachev and his associates were definitely thinking in terms of "no world war." Their statements clearly indicated that they had accepted the logic of the political-military situation, and their practical initiatives, proposals, and concrete actions during the next three years provide evidence that the concept was central to their thinking. The coherent series of events could not have been driven by the woolly concepts of a defensive doctrine and reasonable sufficiency.

Soviet policymakers brought up in the Marxist-Leninist tradition would have found the assumption that world war could be averted by political means easier to stomach than would their Western counterparts. Since war was a function of class antagonisms, basic Marxist theory assumed that once capitalism had faded from the face of the earth, so would war. In 1956 it was decreed that war between the two social systems (world war) was no longer fatalistically inevitable, and doctrine was gradually modified to say that social forces were emerging that would make it possible actively to avert world war, even before the final demise of capitalism. In 1984, the doctrinal disagreement between Gorbachev and Marshal Ogarkov was over whether those forces were already sufficiently developed to allow planning on the assumption that Soviet political measures would be sufficient to neutralize the danger of world war or, as Gorbachev put it, to achieve a durable peace.

In other words, the military's instructions to develop plans based on the assumption that world war would be prevented by political means was no more than the final step in a process of doctrinal evolution that had been under way for some thirty years. Furthermore, this final step could be seen as an inescapable corollary to changes in the theory of international relations being introduced by Gorbachev. Traditional theory saw world war as a by-product of the two social systems. But, as Shevardnadze said at the Ministry of Foreign Affairs' July 1988 conference, "the struggle between the two opposing systems is no longer a determining tendency of the contemporary era." Peaceful coexistence was being redefined to remove the element of ideological struggle, and it was being argued that capitalism had not followed the predicted hostile trajectory. Meanwhile the class struggle was no longer a determinant of Soviet foreign policy and the pursuit of national interests meant that both sides were now equally eager to avert world war.

In such circumstances, it was not a great leap of faith to adopt the assumption that world war could be averted by political means.

Nevertheless, it was an audacious decision, and in November 1987 Gorbachev may have been defending that audacity in his Kremlin address on the seventieth anniversary of the October Revolution. Early on, he noted that it was the revolutionary dialectics of Marxism that had "helped to accomplish, literally on the border between the possible and the impossible, the political and moral feat of the Brest Peace Treaty that saved thousands and thousands of lives and the very existence of the Socialist fatherland."[12] For Gorbachev, Brest-Litovsk was a prime example of clear thinking, the result of Lenin having accepted the realities of March 1918 and being courageous enough to act accordingly, even though his decision was in most ways counterintuitive. Similarly, Gorbachev had recognized and accepted the realities of the nuclear age and was acting in accordance with those realities.

The implications of the decision to base Soviet military requirements on the assumption that world war would be averted by political means were as far-reaching and widespread in their effects as the decision to democratize. However, unlike the decision to democratize or the realignment of Marxist-Leninist theory of international relations and the reversal of policy toward the United States, the need to redefine military doctrine probably raised no significant disagreement within the new political leadership. Everyone was convinced of the need for economic reform, and there was general agreement that the success of perestroika would depend in large part on being able to transfer scarce resources from the defense sector to the civilian economy.

In 1984 the debate on doctrine had been set aside rather than resolved, but by the end of 1986 the new leadership had reestablished political dominance over military policymaking. Full realization of the Soviet Union's dire economic straits meant that a change in military doctrine was unavoidable, however distasteful that might be to the armed forces.

Military resistance to the change in doctrine, to the redefinition of objectives, to the reformulation of military requirements, to the restructuring of Soviet forces overlapped and mingled with resistance to the perestroika process, once that began to be applied to the armed forces. Again, the political leadership almost universally supported the concept of perestroika as tighter discipline, improved cost effectiveness, and more individual initiative and personal responsibility. And they

12. MTS, November 2, 1987, in *FBIS*-87-212, p. 40.

regarded these values as relevant to the military, where greater efficiency would enhance national security while reducing the burden of defense.

This kind of perestroika (and its adjunct glasnost) began to be applied to the armed forces in the wake of the January 1987 plenum. The resulting overlap of evidence has led to the confusion in Western analyses of two quite different kinds of restructuring (or perestroika) affecting the Soviet military establishment. The one of interest to this study involved the higher levels of doctrine and strategy and had its origins in the new political thinking about international relations. The other kind of restructuring was part of domestic perestroika and involved the effectiveness and efficiency of the armed forces.

Perestroika and the Military

For most of Gorbachev's first two years in office, the armed forces considered themselves to be largely excused from the perestroika process, which they saw as being directed at the civilian economy and the party political apparatus. Improving efficiency and preparedness had always been a military requirement and, to the extent that perestroika had any relevance for the armed forces, it was seen to be the responsibility of the party organs. During these two years the military was also spared the rigors of glasnost, and in the main it carried on in the same old ways. The number of articles and letters about perestroika in the military press increased after the 1986 party congress, suggesting that the requirement was being taken somewhat more seriously, but by the end of 1986 support within the armed forces was still only lukewarm.[13]

The situation changed abruptly after the January 1987 plenum, on which occasion Gorbachev made it clear that the armed services, along with the foreign and state security (KGB) services, were no longer to be considered sacrosanct.[14] In the plenum's wake, the military began to come under criticism regarding discipline, morale, performance on training exercises, and misuse of resources. The military leadership got the message, and there was a surge of articles in military publications

13. This summary is based on Dale R. Herspring, *The Soviet High Command 1967–1989: Personalities and Politics* (Princeton University Press, 1990), chap. 7. See also the generally critical remarks of Army General Aleksey Lizichev in November 1986, when summing up a conference at the Main Political Administration of the Army and Navy, of which he was chief ("Evaluate More Sharply, Act Decisively," *KZ*, November 15, 1986, p. 2).

14. TASS, January 27, 1987, in *FBIS*-87-018, pp. R45–46.

on the importance of perestroika. In their Armed Forces Day articles on February 21, 1987, the minister of defense, Army General Sergey Sokolov, and the chief of the General Staff, Marshal Sergey Akhromeev, both stressed at length the importance of perestroika. The previous year Sokolov had barely mentioned the subject, and Akhromeev not at all.

Their statements were mainly lip service. On May 28, 1987, however, the military was delivered into Gorbachev's hands when a young West German piloted a light aircraft through seven hundred kilometers of Soviet airspace and landed it on Red Square in front of the Kremlin. Within two days the minister of defense had been summarily retired, as was Marshal Aleksandr Koldunov, commander-in-chief of the air defense forces, while other officers down the chain of command were retired, demoted, or reprimanded.[15] At the plenum one month later, Gorbachev used this "unprecedented incident" as an example of the "indiscipline, slipshod work, negligence, and irresponsibility [in] our society, even the army." He went on to declare in the name of the Politburo and the Defense Council "that there must be no doubt, either in the party or among the people, of the USSR Armed Forces' ability to defend the country."[16]

Sokolov's forced retirement allowed Gorbachev to replace him with Army General Dmitriy T. Yazov, whom he had already brought back from the Far East in January to be the deputy minister responsible for personnel. Shortly after becoming minister of defense, Yazov particularized Gorbachev's general indictment, berating the officer corps, including generals and admirals, for having failed to grasp the essence of perestroika, especially the fact that the process must start with themselves.[17]

The Civilianization of Military Planning

One outcome of the painful process of glasnost and perestroika within the military was the appointment of forty-nine-year-old Colonel General Mikhail A. Moiseev, then commander of the Far Eastern Military District, to succeed Marshal Akhromeev. Akhromeev retired as chief of

15. Timothy Colton, "Gorbachev and the Soviet Military," in Susan L. Clark, ed., *Gorbachev's Agenda: Changes in Soviet Domestic and Foreign Policy* (Westview Press, 1989), p. 181.

16. *Pravda,* June 26, 1987, in *FBIS*-87-123, p. R11.

17. D. T. Yazov, "Perestroika in the Work of Military Cadres," *VIZ,* no. 7 (1987), p. 6; cited by Colton, "Gorbachev and the Soviet Military," pp. 181–82.

the General Staff in early December 1988, shortly before Gorbachev announced a unilateral reduction in Soviet military strength by 500,000 troops.[18] Moiseev had been chief of staff to Yazov in the Far East and had taken his place when Yazov was appointed deputy minister of defense in January 1987.

From Gorbachev's point of view, there were obvious attractions to Moiseev's appointment. The senior professional job in the military went to a man who shared Yazov's ideas about the importance of effective leadership and management, was junior in rank to Yazov (unlike Akhromeev), and was also eight years younger than Gorbachev. Like the forty-five-year-old Rear Admiral Sergey G. Gorshkov whom Nikita Khrushchev had appointed commander-in-chief of the Soviet navy in 1956, Moiseev was appointed over the heads of many more senior officers. Gorshkov's job had been to restructure the fleet, a task that required wholesale cuts in naval programs, including a 60 percent cut in planned production-tonnage.

The significant fact in Moiseev's case was the replacement of a senior marshal who had fought in the Second World War and whose expertise lay in the higher realms of strategic planning by a young colonel general. Moiseev had no experience of war (not even in Afghanistan) and he had never served on the General Staff.[19] The unexpected appointment reflected the political conclusion that it was essential to bridge the gap between the sociopolitical and military-technical levels of doctrine, a decision that Gorbachev had reached by the end of 1986, if not much earlier. As Andrey Kokoshin put it later, there had to be a "complete correspondence between the political and the military-technical components of the state's military doctrine."[20]

Under Leonid Brezhnev, military-technical doctrine had increasingly become the preserve of the General Staff and various military institutions. It had, however, become very clear by the mid-1980s that seem-

18. Akhromeev's retirement is unlikely to have been a resignation in protest against the force reductions. That was not the Soviet way, and to have been effective it would have to have taken place six to twelve months earlier. Once Akhromeev had led the military across the critical hurdle of unilateral force cuts, he could retire, voluntarily or involuntarily. An informed Soviet observer suggested that leaking news of the retirement just before Gorbachev's speech to the United Nations may have been a ploy by Akhromeev to ensure that he would be kept on as a military adviser to Gorbachev.

19. Moiseev only graduated from the General Staff Academy in 1982.

20. "Aleksandr Svechin: On War and Politics," *International Affairs* (Moscow), no. 11 (November 1988), p. 121. Kokoshin, a deputy director of the Institute for the Study of the United States and Canada, was one of the more influential participants in the debate on military requirements.

ingly sensible and well-thought-out military decisions intended to enhance the security of the Soviet Union had had the opposite effect. They had made war more likely, while incurring heavy political, economic, and even military costs. The General Staff were not, therefore, in a position to resist when the political leadership insisted that the upper reaches of military-technical doctrine should henceforth come within the purview of the broader political-military establishment, including the Ministry of Foreign Affairs and the international department of the Central Committee Secretariat. Akhromeev's replacement by Moiseev in December 1988 was a clear indication that the higher levels of strategic planning and the formulation of military requirements were now within the purview of the civilian establishment, while the military's primary responsibility was for the care, maintenance, and efficient performance of the armed forces.

By April 1987 Gorbachev had ensured that discussion of military-technical issues would be more wide-ranging by expanding the *nomenklatura* that had been established in the first half of 1984 to address the problems introduced by the U.S. strategic defense initiative and to bring scientific methods to bear on the wider problems of strategic nuclear arms control. The extended *nomenklatura* would now include members of the various policy institutes.[21] The 1984 *nomenklatura* would now cover the whole military field, with particular attention being paid initially to the requirement for conventional forces in the defense of the Soviet Union. The end result was "a new community of those who dealt with [the problems of international security] on a regular basis [comprising] physicists, mathematicians, experts on large technical systems [and] political scientists."[22]

Redefining National Security Requirements

It was one thing to assert that in the nuclear age there was no such thing as national security, only international security. It was something

21. In May 1987 the issues underlying the concept of "sufficiency," which became so prominent in the following eighteen months, had hardly been addressed by the political-military analytical community. Robert Legvold, *The New Political Thinking and Gorbachev's Foreign Policy,* Occasional Paper 3 (Tokyo: Research Institute for Peace and Security, May 1987), p. 25.

22. Andrey Kokoshin, "Systems Research and Issues of International Security," paper prepared for Conference of the International Institute of Applied Systems Analysis (IIASA), June 1988.

else to reshape Soviet military thinking and the structure of Warsaw Pact forces so that the expanding-sum concept of mutual security could become a reality. The attempt was particularly problematic when the new thinking about international relations was dismissed in the West as utopian, propagandistic, or both, and the United States showed no inclination to view the competition in other than zero-sum terms or to renounce its efforts to preserve its military superiority.

The New Military Doctrine

Akhromeev's Armed Forces Day article in February 1987 contained embryonic references to the new military doctrine, which he related to the "new political thinking, [the] new approaches" to foreign and defense policy. These were based on the premise that "safeguarding of security . . . can and must be resolved primarily by political means, by lowering the level of military confrontation, limiting and reducing arms, and strengthening trust and international cooperation."[23]

The first clear indication of what the new doctrine implied appeared in the statement issued by the Warsaw Pact's Political Consultative Committee at the end of its annual meeting on May 28–29, 1987, in Berlin. This proposed reducing forces in the European theater to a level where "neither side, in ensuring its own defense, would have means for a sudden attack on the other side, or for carrying out offensive operations in general."[24] At first glance, this Berlin statement appeared to be a relatively minor elaboration on the comparable statement made the previous year at Budapest. But there was a crucial difference between the 1986 notion of being willing to renounce the capability for surprise attack and the 1987 intention to forgo the capability for offensive operations in general; the difference lay in the ability to carry out existing war plans.

It was true that the loss of operational surprise would have made it harder to defeat NATO in Europe and evict U.S. forces from the Continent, but the task would have still been manageable. If, however, the Soviets forwent the capability for offensive operations in general,

23. "The Glory and Pride of the Soviet People," *Sovetskaya Rossiya,* February 21, 1987, in *FBIS*-87-39, pp. V2–4. Interestingly, when describing the source of Soviet policy, he linked Gorbachev's speech to the International Forum the previous week with the decisions of the party congress in 1986.
24. *Pravda,* May 31, 1987, in *FBIS*-87-104, p. BB21.

then the task would become impossible. But if the Soviets were "not to lose" a world war, the successful discharge of that task was an imperative. No General Staff deliberately plans to lose a war. It had therefore to be assumed that in stating their willingness to forgo the capability for offensive operations in general, the Soviets were revealing their intention to cease covering the contingency of world war. This implied that the Soviet General Staff had been told to develop plans based on the assumption that there would be "no world war," to assume that world war could and would be prevented by political means.

The two Warsaw Pact statements also differed in how they addressed the question of a defensive doctrine. In the words of the 1986 Budapest Appeal, "the military concepts and doctrines of the military alliances must be based on defensive principles." The 1987 Berlin statement declared that "the military doctrine of the Warsaw Treaty member states is strictly a defensive one." The latter is a categorical statement describing a present condition, whereas the 1986 version was an appeal, looking to a future condition.

That this distinction was not accidental can be seen in Yazov's book, published a few months after he became minister of defense. He asserted that "Soviet military doctrine regards defense as the main type of military operation for repelling aggression."[25] This was something distinct from the adoption of a defensive posture facing NATO as decided in 1984; no such change in the relative priority of offense and defense appears to have occurred between 1984 and 1986.[26] The different wording in the successive Warsaw Pact statements, it later turned out, reflected two very different doctrinal concepts, and the Soviets tended to use the qualifier "defensive" for both.

25. D. T. Yazov, *Na strazhe sotsializma i mira (On Guard over Socialism and Peace)* (Moscow: Voenizdat, 1987), p. 32. The book was sent for typesetting on August 28 and released to the press on October 9, 1987.
26. The 1986 edition of *VES*, which included amended entries introducing the military-technical requirement to avert war and the 1984 concept of "military stability," did not question the long-standing priority accorded the offensive. Nor could such a change in the relative priority of offense and defense be discerned from a comparison of two books entitled *Istoriya voennogo isskustva* published by Voenizdat. One, published in 1984, was a textbook for military academies; the authors' collective was led by B. V. Panon; the book was released to the press on October 28, 1983. The other, published in 1986, carried the Officers Library insignia; it was edited by Lieutenant General P. A. Zhilin, the authors' collective being led by M. M. Kiryan; it was sent for typesetting on March 29, 1984, and released to the press on January 23, 1985. Because of the new emphasis on defense that became evident in 1984, I sought evidence of a change in doctrinal priority during 1984–86, but without success.

The preamble to the Berlin statement in May 1987 asserted that "the military doctrine of the Warsaw Treaty . . . is subordinated to the task of preventing war." Yazov, referring to that statement, noted that it was "the first time in the existence of various military-political alliances [that] a military doctrine was openly proclaimed which *is subordinated to the mission of preventing war, both nuclear and conventional.*"[27] If this was the first time (certainly the Budapest Appeal had made no such assertion), then this had to be a *new* doctrine. Akhromeev had implied as much in his Armed Forces Day article when he said that doctrine was being *created and developed.* He had also signaled the nature of the change, defining the doctrine as "a system of fundamental views on the essence and *prevention of war.*"[28]

Some of the implications of this new doctrine were fleshed out by Akhromeev in December 1987 in an authoritative article discussing the Warsaw Pact statement.[29] One of three particularly significant points was a redefinition of what military doctrine was now about. For the best part of seventy years, doctrine had concerned "the essence, objectives and nature of a possible future war . . . and the preparation of the country and armed forces to wage it."[30] In the future it would concern "*the prevention of war . . . and the preparation of their countries and the armed forces to ward off aggression.*" Akhromeev explained that this "modern definition" reflected "the new assumptions [*ustanovka*]" of Warsaw Pact military doctrine. Like Yazov, he stressed that this was "*the first time* that the proposition of averting war has been included in such a straightforward and sharp formulation" in the definition of what doctrine was about. Doctrine was now "aimed against war . . . instead of preparation for war."[31]

He went on to explain that the revised doctrine reflected the realities of the nuclear-space age and was designed to solve "two cardinal problems: first of all *to prevent and avert* both a nuclear and a

27. Yazov, *On Guard,* p. 27.
28. "Glory and Pride," pp. V2–4; emphasis added.
29. Sergey Akhromeev, "Doctrine of Averting War and Defending Peace and Socialism," *Problemy mira i sotsializma* (*Problems of Peace and Socialism*), December 1987, pp. 23–28. *Problems* is published in 40 languages and circulates in 145 countries; the English-language version is entitled *World Marxist Review,* vol. 30 (December 1987), pp. 37–47.
30. *VES* (1986), p. 240; M. A. Gareev, *M. V. Frunze: Voenyy teoretik* (*M. V. Frunze: Military Theorist*) (Moscow: Voenizdat, 1985), p. 418.
31. "Doctrine," p. 41. The new doctrine was implied in the 1987 Warsaw Pact statement, but not specified.

conventional war; and second to provide socialism with a reliable defense."[32] The ordering of the two problems was itself significant, not only because it was new[33] but because it required the military, in providing for the defense of socialism, not to decrease the sense of security of others. The revised doctrine implicitly favored nonoffensive means of defense.

The second significant point concerned the three key propositions (*polozheniya*) that were said to reflect the defensive orientation of the revised doctrine. The first two cannot be demonstrated short of conflict—namely, that the Warsaw Pact countries (1) have no aggressive designs and (2) will never, under any circumstances, be the first to initiate military operations (unless themselves the object of attack) and will never be the first to use nuclear weapons. The third proposition requires that the development of the armed forces be based on the principle of maintaining the military-strategic balance at the lowest possible level required for defense.[34]

The third significant point concerned the primacy of the political aspects of military doctrine and the assumption that "there is no fatal inevitability of world war, and that it can be averted, however great the threat to peace now being posed by the policy of the aggressive circles of imperialism."[35] This disposed authoritatively of the argument advanced by Marshal Nikolay Ogarkov in 1983–84 (which no doubt persisted in some quarters) that the possibility of neutralizing the danger of world war must not be confused with the reality of doing so, and that meanwhile the danger of war could actually increase.

All but explicit in the new definition of military doctrine was the requirement to refrain from preparing for world war. The experience of 1975–85 had shown that in preparing for world war the Soviets had made such war more likely. Military doctrine was now about averting war. The Soviets must therefore cease preparing for world war. That logical conclusion was reinforced by the political assessment that forgoing the capability to fight such a war would, of itself, make such a war less likely. The military would therefore be required to plan on the assumption that world war could and would be averted by political means.

Akhromeev made the assumption explicit in a television interview in

32. Ibid., pp. 40–41.
33. Previously, the two problems had had equal ranking; *VES* (1986), p. 240.
34. "Doctrine," pp. 41–42.
35. Ibid.

October 1989 when he interrupted to assert, "No, I think that in present conditions not only nuclear war but also a so-called war using conventional systems in Europe is impossible." Because there are two hundred fifty-six nuclear power stations in Europe, plus thousands of factories with dangerous chemical facilities "such a war is impossible . . . and I even believe that no one wants it." But he then added the military man's caveat, "But that does not mean that the possibility of it coming about is totally excluded."[36]

The New Overarching Strategic Objective

When the Soviet General Staff was told to develop new plans based on the assumption of "no world war," they would also have been given (or have had approved) the objective those plans would be designed to achieve. Such an objective (like the one it replaced) would be expressed in very broad terms. Its general thrust is evident in key statements, in the domestic and political-military situation that prevailed in the first half of 1987, and in subsequent developments.

In February 1987 Gorbachev asserted, "We have been and will keep doing everything necessary to absolutely guarantee our security and the security of our friends and allies, so that no one is tempted to test our borders."[37] Akhromeev described the new definition of military doctrine that was formulated in the first half of 1987 as "a system of fundamental views . . . on the prevention of war, on military [structuring,] on the preparation of the [Warsaw Pact countries and their] armed forces to ward off aggression, and on the modes of conducting armed struggle in defense of socialism."[38] And there is the May 29, 1987, statement on the Warsaw Pact's military doctrine.

This suggests that *at that stage* the General Staff would have been given an objective like "ensure the territorial integrity and political cohesion of the Soviet bloc." For the first time, Soviet military doctrine would be truly defensive. By mid-1988, however, the long-term objective

36. MTS, October 9, 1989, in *FBIS*-89-197, p. 101. Akhromeev was exaggerating. For a listing of nuclear power stations and other potentially dangerous facilities in the European theater, see Alexei A. Vasiliev, "Nuclear Weapons and the Reduction of Nuclear Weapons," in Robert D. Blackwill and F. Stephen Larrabee, eds., *Conventional Arms Control and East-West Security* (Duke University Press, 1989), tables 1, 2.

37. Speech to the 18th Congress of the All-Union Council of Communist Trade Unions (AUCCTU), MTS, February 25, 1987, in *FBIS*-87-39, p. R14.

38. "Doctrine," p. 41.

must have been reformulated. This new and more limited objective would have been expressed in terms of "ensuring the territorial integrity of the Soviet Union." The military was meanwhile left with the problem of devising a graceful way of withdrawing, while still keeping up its guard.

The Process of Restructuring

In his February 1987 Armed Forces Day article, Akhromeev noted that "Soviet military doctrine . . . *is being* created and developed in accordance with CPSU policy and the principle of the new political thinking."[39] Subsequent statements make it clear that this was a completely new doctrine. It is therefore very likely that besides the decision on democratization, the January plenum was also the occasion for legitimating the decision on the need for a fundamental change in military doctrine.

Until the most recent changes in the structure of Soviet rule, plenums provided the ideal opportunity for promulgating high-level secret decisions of this nature. The Central Committee included the key leaders of the armed forces, the defense industry, and the foreign policy, party, and state apparatus, who constituted a de facto subcommittee for considering matters concerning national security.[40]

Because Soviet political discourse is wordy and often oblique, and also for the reasons described earlier, it is likely that in putting the need for new military doctrine before the plenum, Gorbachev or his representative would have used widely accepted terms and concepts rather than come out openly about the revised assumption or the new strategic objective. The central importance of averting world war, the primary role of political means in reducing the threat and ensuring national security, the futility of attempting to match the military capability of all potential enemies, the economic necessity of providing no more for defense than would be sufficient to rebuff aggression, the inherently defensive nature of Soviet military doctrine, all would have been woven together to invoke the need for a major revision of Soviet military doctrine. These terms and concepts were duly used by all sides in the

39. "Glory and Pride," pp. V2–4; emphasis added.
40. I inferred this practice initially from the coincidence of the December 1966 plenum with the shift in doctrine on the nature of a world war that led to the 1970s strategy. MccGwire, *Military Objectives,* pp. 392–404.

subsequent debate about what was needed to ensure the security of the Soviet Union—about "how much was enough."

By mid-March 1987 the Warsaw Pact had been informed that the Soviet Union had adopted the concept of "sufficiency" as the criterion for determining its military requirements.[41] The crucial question, of course, was "sufficient for what?" and it gradually became clear that sufficiency was introduced as a verbal surrogate for the new, more limited, overarching strategic objective. May 1987 saw the first article in the professional literature on "reasonable sufficiency," signaling the beginning of an open debate on how to define sufficiency and what was implied by a defensive doctrine.[42]

At the end of May, following the annual meeting of the Warsaw Pact's Political Consultative Committee (PCC), both the conference communiqué and the statement on military doctrine emphasized the defensive doctrine and the concept of sufficiency. And the proposal to renounce the capability for offensive operations in general implied that the Soviets were intending to cease preparing to wage world war.[43] In other words, by mid-1987 the new direction had been established and the main thrust of the new doctrine had already been described in a book authored by the newly appointed minister of defense.[44]

The May PCC meeting discussed the emerging agreement on eliminating intermediate-range nuclear forces (INF) in Europe and authorized the establishment of a special commission on questions of disarmament and a "multi-lateral group for current reciprocal information" as permanent organs of the Pact. The communiqué also expressed "a readiness to rectify in the course of reductions the inequality that had emerged in some elements [of the armed forces] by way of corresponding cuts on the side that is ahead." The communiqué issued after the foreign ministers' meeting in October reaffirmed the readiness to "eradicate

41. Don Oberdorfer, *Washington Post,* April 26, 1987, p. D1. Oberdorfer told me that the senior Eastern European official who provided this information in mid-March implied that this was a quite recent event. The information could have been passed at the Warsaw Pact working group of experts on conventional arms reductions in Europe, which met in Sophia on March 11 (TASS, March 12, 1987).

42. R. Hyland Phillips and Jeffrey I. Sands, *Reasonable Sufficiency and Soviet Conventional Defense: Evidence of a Civil-Military Divergence on Conventional Force Posture?* prepared for the Soviet Security Studies Working Group (SSSWG) (Center for International Studies, MIT, May 1988).

43. *Pravda,* May 30 and 31, 1987, in *FBIS*-87-104, pp. BB10–21.

44. Yazov, *On Guard,* p. 27. Andrey Kokoshin identified the Warsaw Pact statement as the public change in military doctrine ("Restructure Forces, Enhance Security," *Bulletin of Atomic Scientists,* vol. 44 [September 1988], p. 37).

imbalances through corresponding reductions." It also advocated "the elimination of bases on foreign territory [and] the return home of all troops stationed abroad," although this was not specifically in the European context.[45]

Work on the new doctrine presumably continued throughout the summer and fall of 1987, and the ramifications would have been discussed at the late November meeting of the Pact defense ministers, which coincided with the publication of Akhromeev's article giving the first full explanation of the doctrine. The doctrine also provided the military rationale for treating INF as a separate issue and for the gross asymmetry in the number of missiles to be destroyed under the treaty that would be signed at the Washington summit on December 8.

In an interview preceding the summit, Gorbachev expressed Soviet willingness to address without delay the question of conventional asymmetries in Europe, and at the end of December he asserted that the Soviet Union strongly favored the elimination of existing imbalances and asymmetries.[46] At the summit, Gorbachev made proposals concerning the conventional force talks in Vienna, which were not, however, reflected in the summit joint statement.[47] But in his speech following the signing ceremony Gorbachev referred to the prospect of reaching agreement on a considerable reduction of conventional forces at the next summit in Moscow.[48]

Having disposed of the INF question, the Soviets refocused attention on the problem of conventional force reductions. During November and December 1987 it was rumored that a special interagency commission headed by Colonel General Vladimir N. Lobov had been formed to establish the parameters of what was practical in terms of unilateral reductions (Lobov, at that time head of the main operational directorate

45. *Pravda,* May 31, 1987, in *FBIS*-87-104, pp. BB14, 18; *Pravda,* October 20, 1987, in *FBIS*-87-210, pp. 9, 11. The May communiqué only referred to the arms control commission; the October communiqué described both that and the group on reciprocal information as permanent organs. The question of imbalances had first been raised in the communiqué following the March 19, 1987, meeting of foreign ministers. It was not referred to following the meeting in October 1986.

46. Interview with U.S. NBC television, TASS, December 1, 1987, in *FBIS*-87-230, p. 16; meeting with Franz-Josef Strauss, chairman of the West German Christian Social Union, TASS, December 29, 1987, in *FBIS*-87-250, p. 35.

47. In his press conference following the Moscow summit in 1988 Gorbachev noted that at the meeting between Shultz and Shevardnadze that had preceded the Washington summit in December 1987, Shevardnadze had offered a formula to resolve the issue of the mandate for the conventional force talks in Vienna. Gorbachev proposed this same formula at the Washington summit. *Pravda,* June 2, 1988, in *FBIS*-88-107, p. 13.

48. *Pravda,* December 9, 1987, in *FBIS*-87-236, p. 17.

of the General Staff, was subsequently appointed chief of staff to the commander-in-chief of the Warsaw Pact). By mid-1988, Akhromeev wrote a year later, "the political and military leaders of [the Soviet] government had jointly reached the conclusion that unilateral force cuts were possible."[49] It was rumored that the Lobov commission had concluded that a cut of half a million troops was practical, while a group headed by Academician Evgeniy Velikov had proposed a cut of one million.[50] If true, the second group would probably have been a stalking horse to make Lobov's proposal more acceptable.

This general conclusion would have been communicated to the leaders of the other Warsaw Pact countries at the PCC meeting in Warsaw on July 15 and 16, 1988.[51] Ten days before that meeting Gorbachev had asserted that there were "no questions pertaining to the reduction of armed forces and arms on which [the Soviets] would refuse to hold talks with the NATO States."[52] He is rumored to have warned the other leaders at the PCC meeting to prepare themselves for the withdrawal of Soviet forces from Eastern Europe in the not too distant future. Already he had "agreed in principle" to a complete withdrawal from Hungary.[53] And ten days after the meeting Shevardnadze told an important in-house conference at the MFA that "the restriction of the military activities of all states to the territories within their national borders is in both the general interest and our own interest."[54]

49. Marshal S. Akhromeev, "Open Letter to the Chief Editor of the Journal," *Ogonek*, no. 50 (December 1989), p. 6. The "joint" nature of the conclusions is probably exaggerated.

50. The Velikhov commission was an assemblage of scientists and analysts who were members of the new *nomenklatura* established in the first half of 1984 to help shape the Soviet response to the U.S. strategic defense initiative. By the end of 1987 the commission had started work on alternative conventional arms control regimes. Robert Legvold, "Gorbachev's New Approach to Conventional Arms Control," *Harriman Institute Forum*, vol. 1 (January 1988); also in Paul Lerner, ed., *The Soviet Union 1988* (Crane Russak, 1989), pp. 10–11.

51. The question of unilateral troop withdrawals was certainly discussed. Poland and Hungary were strongly in favor, while East Germany and Czechoslovakia expressed doubts. Kay Withers, *Baltimore Sun*, July 17, 1988, p. A4.

52. *Pravda*, July 6, 1988, in *FBIS*-88-129, p. 43. Speech at luncheon for Hungarian leader.

53. Karoly Grosz, who visited Moscow at the beginning of July 1988 after taking over the leadership of Hungary from Janos Kadar, subsequently claimed that Gorbachev had "agreed in principle" to his request that Soviet troops be withdrawn (Jim Hoagland, *Washington Post*, January 23, 1990, p. A21). During the preceding twelve months there had been persistent rumors of unilateral troop withdrawals from Eastern Europe. In early July 1988, the U.S. government leaked information that there were "increasing indications" that the Soviets might withdraw troops from Hungary (John M. Goshko, *Washington Post*, July 9, 1988, p. A15; Michael R. Gordon, *New York Times*, July 9, 1988, p. 1).

54. Shevardnadze's speech to the practical-learned conference at the MFA, *Vestnik ministerstva inostrannykh del USSR (Herald of the Ministry of Foreign Affairs)*, no. 15 (August 1988), in *FBIS*-88-184 (annex), p. 37.

The principle of unilateral cuts in Warsaw Pact forces was reflected in the statement on conventional arms reductions in Europe issued at the end of the PCC meeting. It proposed a three-stage process, the first of which would concentrate on removing asymmetries in the two sides' troop strength and holdings of various types of weapons.[55] This was not the first time a three-stage process had been suggested. It had been advanced during the Moscow summit (May 29–June 2, 1988), although the United States had not responded to what Gorbachev called a "bold and totally realistic plan."[56] It had been spelled out in some detail by Shevardnadze at the United Nations ten days later[57] and again by Gorbachev when speaking to the Polish Sejm on July 11.[58]

The practical aspects of these reductions in Soviet and other Pact forces were worked out during the next few months, with a detailed analysis carried out "by the leadership of the Ministry of Defense, of the [separate] services of the armed forces and of their [respective] branches, and by the scientific research institutes and military academies."[59] On December 7, in his speech to the United Nations, Gorbachev announced that the Soviet Union would make a unilateral cut of 500,000 in the strength of its forces by the end of 1989.[60] And in February 1989 the commander-in-chief of the Warsaw Pact and his chief of staff, both of whom had been in post since the mid-1970s, were replaced by men who could be seen as Gorbachev appointees.[61]

---

55. *Pravda,* July 17, 1988, pt. 1, p. 1. The need for a three-stage process was inherent in the 1987 Warsaw Pact statement and in the concept of a mutual security regime that was embedded in the new political thinking. It would involve (1) unilateral cuts, (2) mutual reductions, and (3) defensive restructuring of the remaining forces. See MccGwire, "A Mutual Security Regime for Europe?" pp. 361–79, and Michael MccGwire, "The New Challenge of Europe," testimony before the Panel on Defense Burdensharing of the House Committee on Armed Services, May 17, 1988, both written well before the Soviets made their proposal.

56. Press statement, MTS, June 1, 1988, in *FBIS*-88-106, pp. 27, 30.

57. *Pravda,* June 9, 1988, in *FBIS*-88-111, p. 6.

58. *Pravda,* July 12, 1988, pp. 4–5.

59. Akhromeev, "Open Letter," p. 6.

60. *Pravda,* December 8, 1988, p. 2.

61. Army General Petr G. Lushev who took over as commander-in-chief had commanded the Soviet Group of Forces in Germany from July 1985 until being brought back to Moscow as a first deputy minister of defense in July 1986. Colonel General Vladimir M. Lobov, his chief of staff, had been first deputy chief of the General Staff and head of the Main Operations Directorate. Lobov was sixteen years younger than Army General Anatoliy I. Gribkov, whom he replaced. Three years earlier Lobov had been moved to the General Staff from commanding the Central Asian military district; he had replaced Yazov there in 1984 and would have continued to interact with him. Before going to Germany in 1985, Lushev had commanded the politically sensitive Moscow military district since December 1980. There he would have gotten to know Gorbachev, who had become a full member of the Politburo in October 1980.

Akhromeev claimed in his December 1989 letter in *Ogonek* that the figure of 500,000 had only been presented to the political leadership for approval after a military analysis carried out in the second half of 1988. But his assertion in an interview in March 1989, that the General Staff had planned the cuts in the spring and summer of 1988, just before his visit to the United States in July,[62] is more likely to reflect the actual course of events.[63] A detailed military analysis would have been needed to determine how the agreed reductions were to be apportioned among existing forces to maximize the remaining military capability, and it would have been carried out in the second half of 1988, as Akhromeev's letter states. But it must have been preceded by a much broader analysis that would have come up with a round figure of 500,000, which was then given to the military to work with. Such an analysis would have involved many elements of the state and party apparatus, including the Ministry of Foreign Affairs and probably those who would be responsible for absorbing that number of people into the work force. That fits well with the rumors about Lobov's commission, and with information that by the end of 1987 Viktor Karpov's arms control department in the MFA had begun to address the problem of alternative conventional arms regimes.[64] It fits not at all with Akhromeev's claims.[65]

The force reductions were designed not only to reduce the asymmetry in ground forces facing NATO, but also to remove one of the three "obstacles" to good relations to China, by reducing the concentration

---

The recall of Lushev to Moscow as the third first deputy minister of defense in July 1986 after only one year in Germany may have been designed to threaten Akhromeev's tenure and bring him into line behind Gorbachev policies. In any event, that was the end result. See chap. 6, note 205.

62. Ken Adelman, *Washington Times,* March 27, 1989, p. D3.

63. In his "Open Letter" to *Ogonek,* Akhromeev was trying to demonstrate that the 500,000 reduction was justified by the "improvement in the international situation, reduction in military tension and the threat of war," but that thereafter all cuts would have to be reciprocal. He was trying to show that Soviet force requirements were based on objective military criteria and calculations and that further unilateral cuts could not be justified without change in the external factors.

64. Legvold, "Gorbachev's New Approach," p. 11.

65. In a television interview in October 1989, in which Akhromeev expostulated against attacks on the military in *Ogonek,* he said that after it was decided that unilateral cuts were possible, the military leadership received instructions "to work this through" (which sounds more like the sequence described here). Although Akhromeev claimed that the military worked on how much could be done and when, he also noted that the military made many reports to the Defense Council, which made many suggestions until the military finally came up with the "precise figure" of 500,000. This gives the strong impression of the military being forced to come up with the answers that conformed to predetermined aggregate numbers and timetable. MTS, October 9, 1989, in *FBIS*-89-197, pp. 97–98.

of Soviet troops on that border.[66] Subsequent statements indicated that 200,000 of the 500,000 would come from the Far East, 60,000 from the southern region (where the Soviet forces would already have been withdrawn from Afghanistan), and the remaining 240,000 from the European theater. Of the latter, 50,000 would come from Eastern Europe, including six tank divisions. If cuts by the allies were included, this meant a reduction of Warsaw Pact forces in Eastern Europe by 106,000 men and more than 7,000 tanks.

The size and details of the Soviet force cuts appear to have been tailored to break the logjam in conventional force reductions in Europe. The overall size of Soviet unilateral force reductions was 20 percent more than NATO's highest demand at the negotiations on mutual and balanced force reductions. The number of Soviet tanks to be withdrawn was exactly equal to the number of tanks added to the Warsaw Pact inventory in Central Europe between 1967 and 1987. And the number was exactly equal to the number specified by U.S. Senator Samuel Nunn in his March 1987 proposal.[67]

The course of events in 1987–88 followed the general timetable in which 1991, and the start of the Thirteenth Five-Year Plan, was the crucial target date. It is most unlikely that Gorbachev expected to be able to turn around the military behemoth in less than two years, especially since the INF treaty would require that the military, during the first twelve months, stomach scrapping more than twice as many missiles as the United States. The beginning of 1989 therefore would have been planned as the date for initiating unilateral cuts in conventional forces. As with the withdrawal from Afghanistan, with the redefinition of the Marxist-Leninist theory of international relations, and with the restructuring of the domestic political system, June 1988 was a critical deadline—in this case for deciding on the overall size of the unilateral reductions.

The cuts of 500,000 men would represent a reduction in strength of 12 percent and would be completed by the end of 1990. During the same period the military budget would be reduced by 14.2 percent and the production of arms and equipment by 19.5 percent, resulting in a saving

66. This was possible because it would no longer be necessary to deter or prevent China from exploiting Soviet involvement in Europe in the event of world war.

67. Phillip A. Karber, "Soviet Implementation of the Gorbachev Unilateral Military Reductions," in *Impact of Gorbachev's Reform Movement on the Soviet Military,* Hearings before the House Armed Services Committee, 100 Cong. 2 sess. (GPO, 1988), p. 57.

of 30 billion rubles on what had been allowed in the 1986–90 plan.[68] Thus, by the beginning of the five-year plan in 1991 Gorbachev would have set in motion the process of moving "from an economy of armament to an economy of disarmament," which he advocated in his speech to the United Nations in December 1988. Reductions in strength were planned to continue during the 1990s, but on a bilateral basis as both sides' forces were first drawn down and then repostured and restructured so as to be unambiguously defensive.

Defensive or Reasonable Sufficiency?

In his speech to the Congress of the All Union Council of Communist Trade Unions in February 1987, Gorbachev asserted that the Soviet armed forces would "not make a single step in excess of the demands and requirements of sensible sufficient defense." He went on to refer to the U.S. policy of trying to force the Soviet Union to invest scarce resources in the defense sector, saying, "Let us not repeat—automatically without thinking—what imperialism is seeking to impose on us in the arms race."[69] The national security *nomenklatura* was further expanded in early 1987 to include members of the policy-oriented social science institutes such as the Institute of World Economy and International Relations (IMEiMO) and the Institute for the Study of the United States and Canada (ISKAN), and its terms of reference were extended to include military-technical aspects of theater warfare. This was clearly intended to challenge the military's monopoly of expertise and hence professional advice in this area, and to generate elite support for the unilateral force reductions that lay ahead.

The public debate that occupied the pages of professional journals and other types of media was therefore mainly designed to air the underlying issues, to undermine long-standing military assumptions, and to develop a range of options that had previously been excluded from consideration. In this it can be seen to have been successful. As a debate about what was needed to ensure Soviet national security it was, however, singularly deficient.

There was little indication that the participants understood the larger

68. Gorbachev speaking to representatives of the Trilateral Commission in Moscow, TASS, January 18, 1989, in *FBIS*-89-012, p. 10; Akhromeev, "Open Letter," p. 6; D. T. Yazov (interview), *Izvestiya,* September 17, 1989, in *FBIS*-89-179, p. 2.

69. MTS, February 25, 1987, in *FBIS*-87-39, p. R14.

rationale underlying the existing size, structure, and posture of Soviet forces or were aware of why that rationale need no longer apply. Perhaps this was not surprising, since Soviet strategic plans for the worst-case contingency of world war would have been closely held, and only a few within the political-military establishment would have been privy to the overarching concept for waging world war. Furthermore, few of the civilian institute members (*institutniki*) who now joined the fray had any understanding of what was involved in planning for war. Indeed, most of them held the military establishment and its leadership in ill-disguised contempt, and they saw their primary purpose as demonstrating that the Soviet armed forces were much larger than necessary, rather than trying to understand the genesis of Soviet military requirements. Some of the younger members combined the intellectual arrogance of the academic "whiz kids" whom Robert McNamara took with him to the Pentagon in 1961 with the excessive national self-denigration that was prevalent among American intellectuals in the wake of Vietnam. Everything was the Soviet Union's fault and much of it could be blamed on military obtuseness and the belief that more was better.

The *institutniki* attacked along two main lines. One seems to have been intended to increase the acceptability of a defensive doctrine and to give the concept military respectability by providing historical examples of its use at the military-technical level. Given the primacy that had been accorded to offensive operations for almost seventy years—a primacy that had seemingly been validated by war—it was not easy to argue for the priority of the strategic defensive in contemporary circumstances. However, skillful use was made of historical examples to present that case—the German defeat at Kursk in 1943, for instance, was analyzed to demonstrate the effectiveness of a carefully thought out and prepared defensive strategy that consciously rejected the option of an offensive.[70] The defensive phase of the battle of Kursk was, of course, followed by a highly successful counteroffensive, which the military view as one of the decisive victories of the Second World War.[71]

70. This followed in the wake of Akhromeev's 1984 article on the battle of Kursk in *VIZh* (see chap. 5, note 34).

71. A. Kokoshin and V. Larionov, "The Battle of Kursk in the Light of Contemporary Defensive Doctrine," *MEiMO*, no. 8 (August 1987), pp. 32–40. See also Kokoshin, "Aleksandr Svechin." Kokoshin and Major General Larionov, a doctor of historical science and professor at the General Staff Academy, are two of the most thoughtful and professional critics of traditional military thinking.

The other approach was to use the criterion of "sufficiency" to challenge the existing structure and strength of Soviet forces, while the military used the same criterion to defend it. There was little real substance to this debate and its lineaments were not hard to predict. Opinion would spread along a continuum running from those who considered that the country could never have enough military strength to those who believed that the territorial integrity and political cohesion of the Soviet bloc could be ensured mainly by political means. The continuum could be expected to divide into two main divisions, reflecting different judgments and attitudes on matters such as the nature of capitalism and the political-military threat, the role of military force in national security, the relative importance of offense and defense, and the possibility of distinguishing between offensive and defensive weapons.

The civilian analyst could be predicted as likely to have a more sanguine set of attitudes and beliefs that favored "reasonable" sufficiency, and the military would be likely to be less sanguine, favoring a more concrete concept of "defensive" sufficiency. While this was the rough pattern, in neither case were the concepts clearly defined, nor was the use of "reasonable" or "defensive" in distinguishing between the two concepts always consistent.[72]

As a contribution to decisionmaking the debate was deficient because the participants never clarified their assumptions or addressed the central question, "sufficient for what?" Instead, they based their analyses on unargued attitudes and beliefs, with results that were largely predictable. But until that central question had been addressed and the adoption of a new overarching objective justified, there were really no grounds for claiming that in the past the military had been provided with more than was needed. Even in the European theater, where there was a clear preponderance of Soviet ground forces, the chances of achieving the wartime objective of defeating NATO and evicting U.S. forces from Europe were certainly no better than even, and probably less.

The leadership may have had several reasons for choosing not to specify the new and more limited objective before launching the debate. The assumption underlying the new objective was vulnerable to highly persuasive (albeit invalid) public objection. Furthermore, the process of redefining key tenets of Soviet international relations theory would not

---

72. Phillips and Sands, *Reasonable Sufficiency*.

be far enough advanced until the second half of 1988 to fully justify adoption of the new assumption. Meanwhile, wartime objectives were known to very few persons, and there were sound military arguments for not disclosing the projected change. It was not accidental that the analysis of how to apportion the 500,000 troop reduction was carried out by the *rukovodstvo,* the leadership of the Ministry of Defense, of the individual services, and of their separate branches.[73]

But the debate was never intended to determine how much was enough, because that could not be decided until the nature of the future threat environment became clear. By committing the Soviet Union to unilateral force cuts, the leadership hoped to break the logjam in conventional force negotiations and set in motion a process of mutual force reductions whose final outcome could not be forecast. Meanwhile the role of the civilivan analyst was to take at face value and then dismantle military assertions about the nature of the political-military threat that were used to justify requirements, and to challenge the long-standing primacy of the offensive, with its need for military superiority.[74]

The Warsaw Pact goals of forgoing the capacity for surprise attack and even the capability for offensive operations in general, combined with public adoption of a defensive doctrine (even though it meant different things to different people), were sufficient to bound the scope of the debate and to exclude from discussion the long-standing requirement to seize NATO Europe in the event of war, even though this was never made explicit. Within these parameters, a central question was the type of counteroffensive capability that would be needed to ensure a secure defense.

This aspect of the debate can best be understood by visualizing a fourfold division overlying the twofold division between ''reasonable'' and ''defensive'' sufficiency. At one extreme there would be a full counteroffensive capability, analogous to what the Soviets had at Kursk; although it would be defensively postured, the resource allocation would not be significantly different from the existing capability for offensive operations in Europe. At the other extreme would be an absence of any

73. Akhromeev, ''Open Letter,'' p. 6. The term *rukovodstvo* suggests that the problem was not just given to the various staffs but handled at a higher and more restricted level.

74. Personal communication from Dale Herspring, who in discussion with well-placed Soviet officials learned that the intended role of the civilian analyst was to force the military to address all these issues.

offensive capability and complete reliance on nonoffensive means of defense that would ensure the aggressor's frustrated withdrawal.[75]

Neither extreme would have been a serious candidate for adoption by the leadership. A Kursk-type capability would involve minimal change and save few resources. And while Gorbachev was personally interested in nonoffensive means of physical defense,[76] in 1987–88 the idea was still too novel and imprecise and the nature of the future threat too unclear for it to have been salable. This left the two middle categories: a limited counteroffensive capability, able to clear friendly territory and restore the status quo ante, and a significant counteroffensive capability, capable of repulsing the aggressor and then defeating him on his own territory.

Judged by their stated opinions, the military would have advocated a more extensive counteroffensive capability, while the political leadership would have favored the more limited counteroffensive capability, verging on nonoffensive means of defense. The final capability would reflect a political decision that would depend on the emerging political-military situation on the Soviet periphery, and on progress in the negotiations to establish a mutual security regime in Europe. Meanwhile, the exclusion from consideration of anything larger than a relatively modest counteroffensive capability was sufficient at this time for the leadership's purposes.

The Implications for Military Requirements

The long-term implications of assuming "no world war" could be worked out in theory, but there remained the short-term realities and

75. This fourfold division differs in parameter and purpose from four variants described by A. Kokoshin and V. Larionov in June 1988, which were intended as analytical models for evaluation in terms of strategic stability and conflict termination. In the first, the defender moves over to the offense almost immediately, leading to a series of meeting engagements (a strategic offensive operation). The second was a replay of Kursk (operational-strategic), the third a limited counteroffensive (tactical-operational), and the fourth a nonoffensive defense relying on counterattacks (tactical). Variant one is unstable; only variant four is seen to be stable. Variant one described the strategy that emerged from the 1984 adoption of a so-called defensive doctrine, but it would not meet the new criteria in the 1987 Warsaw Pact statement. Unless it served as a straw man, its inclusion is evidence of the disjunction between the professional debate and the actual redirection of policy. "Opposing General Purpose Forces in the Context of Providing Strategic Stability," *MEiMO*, no. 6 (1988), pp. 23–31.

76. Letter from M. Gorbachev, dated November 16, 1987, to Messrs. von Muller, von Hippel, Bozrup, and Nil.

the problem of how to get from here to there. Before a mutual security regime emerged in Europe and before Gorbachev's "period of peace" was realized in practice,[77] the Soviet military would face a world that, in major respects, had not changed since Brezhnev died in 1982. Although compared to the first half of the decade, East-West tension had been sharply reduced by 1987, the armed confrontation in Europe continued in place and NATO was resolutely set on weapons modernization. The dangers of dissension within the Warsaw Pact and the likelihood of internal unrest in the member nations must inevitably increase. Meanwhile the Reagan administration remained prone to confrontational sallies and had yet to renounce its attempt to restore U.S. military superiority, which would upset the strategic balance.[78]

In the process of moving from the existing situation to some international security system that would depend on Western cooperation for its success, the Soviet military would have to meet complex and conflicting requirements. Convinced or not, they would have to assume that the Gorbachev leadership would take whatever political measures were necessary to prevent any conflict on the periphery of the Soviet bloc (including the inter-German border) from escalating to world war. It was true that a political veto on Soviet forces initiating offensive operations would work to limit such conflicts. On the other hand, the opposing forces in place around the periphery of the Soviet bloc were capable of major and sustained warfare. Furthermore, the U.S. declaratory doctrine of horizontal escalation, if acted on, would undermine political attempts to contain any conflict that did erupt.

In 1987–88 the Soviet armed forces were preoccupied with very real concerns as they set about planning to withdraw from Afghanistan, developing and adopting a radically new military doctrine, opening up their forces to on-site inspection, preparing to scrap two whole categories of nuclear missiles, and planning major unilateral cuts in their ground forces. The future did not look reassuring. Meanwhile, the military as an institution was being exposed to the rigors of perestroika and glasnost

77. Gorbachev's speech to the United Nations, *Pravda,* December 8, 1988.
78. While the annual increase in U.S. defense authorization had flattened out in fiscal 1986, the annual total was still about twice that for fiscal 1980, and in June 1987 Defense Secretary Caspar Weinberger, speaking in London on the fortieth anniversary of the Marshall Plan, called for further strengthening of NATO. In February 1988 two U.S. warships (claiming innocent passage) deliberately entered Soviet territorial waters off the Crimea, where they were deliberately bumped by Soviet warships.

and its intellectual primacy in the field of military thought was being challenged and often belittled by the *institutniki*.

Besides challenging professional military opinion, the *institutniki* also had an unwitting role in de-demonizing the Soviet Union and thus denying the Western military-industrial complex a Soviet threat. It did not matter, therefore, that they were holding forth on Soviet military requirements without any real understanding of the strategic logic underlying existing force size and structure, and without being aware of the critical assumption of no world war or its far-reaching implications. From Gorbachev's point of view they were fulfilling their intended purpose, but by the same token they were *not* a primary source of advice on future military requirements.[79] And because the military's arguments were usually concerned with institutional as well as strategic factors, and because they and the civilian analysts had different time frames in mind, it is not surprising that the public debate was not a good predictor of emerging Soviet policy.

The best way of understanding the implications of the assumption of "no world war" is to start from the assumption that drove Soviet military planning from 1948 to 1986. A comparison of the military requirements that flow from these opposing assumptions will make the implications clear.

Geostrategic Considerations

The new assumption meant that goestrategic requirements that had been generated by both the 1970s and the 1960s strategies for world war would lapse.

WESTERN EUROPE. There was no longer the requirement, specified in the 1970s strategy, to defeat NATO in Europe, evict U.S. forces from the Continent, and deny the West a bridgehead. Nor would Europe need to serve as an alternative socioeconomic base from which to rebuild the shattered socialist economies in the event of intercontinental escalation, as called for by the 1960s strategy. Therefore there would no longer be conflict between the military-technical objective of persuading the United States to withdraw its forces from Europe in peacetime and the

---

79. According to Herspring, in a personal communication, the *institutniki*'s own assessment of their influence in early 1990 accords with this conclusion.

political-military objective of ensuring that the United States remain in Europe to prevent or contain a resurgence of German power.

EASTERN EUROPE. Fearing aggression by a capitalist coalition led by the United States and Great Britain, in 1947–48 the Soviets had set out to turn Eastern Europe into a defensive glacis, both in an ideological and in a territorial sense. The area subsequently evolved into a cross between an ideological empire and a military alliance; meanwhile the economic links between Moscow and its satellites became steadily more significant, initially for the Soviets and subsequently also for the Eastern Europeans.

The importance of Eastern Europe as a military glacis increased over the years, but while the defensive role continued to be significant, the area gained a new importance as the springboard for offensive operations against Western Europe in the event of war. The salience of this role increased sharply with the 1970s strategy, and almost all members of the Warsaw Pact had a part to play. These parts became even more important following the Soviets' 1983–84 reappraisal and the decision to remain on the defensive for the first twenty to thirty days of a major conflict.

The assumption of "no world war" dramatically affected Soviet strategic interests in the Eastern European satellites, changing the plot and writing out their parts. These countries would not even be needed as a physical buffer against invasion, because that would imply world war. And as a political buffer, their effectiveness would be hindered rather than helped by the presence of Soviet troops, a lesson that had been driven home in Afghanistan.

In other words, the presence of Soviet forces in Eastern Europe was no longer a strategic imperative. However, Soviet military involvement had acquired political significance as an instrument of alliance solidarity. The military integration achieved through Warsaw Pact channels was important in promoting the political cohesion of the Soviet bloc and enhancing the authority of the Communist parties in the different countries, at least as long as they remained in power.

CHINA. Under the 1960s strategy, Manchuria was to serve as an alternative socioeconomic base from which to rebuild a devastated socialist system. Under the 1970s strategy Manchuria would be taken over at the end of the first phase of a world war in order to weaken China, to deny the United States access to the Yellow Sea, and to strengthen the Soviet military-industrial base for the long-drawn-out struggle with an undamaged United States and other remnants of the capitalist system in the second phase. The requirement for the capability to seize Manchuria would now lapse.

THE THIRD WORLD. An important reason for Soviet military involvement in the third world had been to establish the political, physical, and operational infrastructure needed to support Soviet strategy in the event of world war. Thus in the 1960s the Soviets had sought access to naval support facilities in Egypt, leading to deeper involvement in Egyptian affairs than otherwise might have been warranted. The adoption of the 1970s strategy prompted a shift in strategic emphasis away from the Mediterranean to the Horn of Africa. Similarly, geostrategic considerations had a role in shaping the pattern of Soviet arms supply to third world countries.

The concept of an extended defense perimeter and the prospect of a protracted second phase of a world war, whose course and duration were hard to predict, meant that a strategic rationale could easily be found for military involvement in peacetime. But the assumption of "no world war" meant that in future Soviet policy toward the third world could avoid the distortions induced by geostrategic considerations. A weak case could be made for retaining the forward base in Vietnam to cover the possibility of conflict with China[80] or the slim possibility of some deal on the U.S. base at Subic Bay in the Philippines. But as a general rule (and excluding the Soviet national security zone), the idea of "strategic imperatives" could be ruled out of policy considerations in respect to the third world.

The Military-Industrial Base

Adopting the limited objective of ensuring the territorial integrity and internal cohesion of the Soviet bloc would allow a significant reduction in the size of the Soviet armed forces and hence the transfer of resources to the civilian sector. That was evident. Less obvious were the implications of forgoing the capability to wage world war in terms of the military-industrial base.

The 1970s strategy had envisaged an intense and sustained arms race during the second phase of a world war, since both sides' military-industrial bases would be undamaged. The U.S. system had demon-

80. MccGwire, *Military Objectives*, p. 209.

strated its ability to build up its industrial capacity rapidly when challenged. For the Soviets to compete in such a race, they needed to have most of the industrial facilities already in place.[81] In other words, the defense burden went beyond the military-industrial capacity to sustain the existing force structure (including reserves) to include a large mobilization base that would only be brought on line in the event of world war but would otherwise remain underutilized or unused.

The Implications for Arms Control

The assumption of "no world war" affected all elements of the arms control process, but in the case of conventional forces in Europe it allowed the Soviets to completely change their approach to negotiations.

CONVENTIONAL FORCES IN EUROPE. Because there was no longer a requirement to be able to launch a conventional blitzkrieg, the Soviets no longer needed ground forces superior to those of NATO. They could therefore make the unilateral cuts needed to bring the two sides' forces in balance, and that would allow the process of mutual force reductions to move ahead. But the new objective also had broader implications.

While both NATO and the Warsaw Pact sought to avert world war in their different ways, both sides had the minimum objective of "not losing" a war, should it prove inescapable. For the Soviets, this meant denying the United States a bridgehead, and that implied the defeat of NATO in Europe. For NATO not to lose the war, it had to deny the Soviets victory in Europe, but it did not itself need victory. The asymmetry in requirements caused an action-reaction process that fueled an arms race and prevented the emergence of a stable military balance. It also meant that arms control negotiations were inherently zero sum—one side's gain was the other's loss. The process therefore exacerbated East-West hostility, rather than ameliorating it.

The new objective meant that the two sides' requirements would now be symmetrical. This implied that negotiations to achieve mutual force reductions could be expanding sum—both sides would gain even when asymmetrical cuts were involved—while the development of nonoffensive means of defense would become a practical proposition. As negotiations progressed, the inherent conflict between NATO's dual objectives of "averting" and "not losing" a world war would be resolved in favor

81. Ibid., pp. 44, 58–59.

of "averting" war; the direction of the action-reaction process would be reversed and, in combination with economic factors, would provide a downward pressure on force levels.

THEATER NUCLEAR FORCES. The 1970s strategy sought to avoid resort to nuclear weapons in the European theater, lest it precipitate intercontinental escalation; by 1974 it had been decreed that Soviet forces would not be the first to use nuclear weapons. The Soviets had also concluded that a nuclear environment would hinder rather than help their blitzkrieg, and the military preference was for a denuclearized Europe. In the absence of that situation, it was necessary to have nuclear weapons in the Soviet theater inventory, partly to discourage NATO from going nuclear and partly to avoid being at a military disadvantage if NATO did escalate.

The military objection to the so-called zero option proposed by the Reagan administration in 1981 was that it eliminated medium-range missile systems, where the Soviets held an advantage, but left nuclear delivery aircraft, where NATO had a sizable advantage. The Soviets were prepared to pay a certain price to prevent the deployment of Pershing II missiles, but not as high as that. At Reykjavik they had been willing to accept that price, but only as part of a package deal that would include a U.S. pledge to abide by the terms of the 1972 Antiballistic Missile (ABM) Treaty, as those terms had originally been understood.

The new objective removed the military objections to the zero option. There would be no Soviet blitzkrieg, and it was implicit in the planning assumption of "no world war" that there would be no premeditated aggression by NATO. In such circumstances Gorbachev's objective of a nuclear-free world argued for eliminating whatever categories of nuclear weapon the United States would agree to, even if it meant having to destroy a larger number of weapons than the Americans.

As a separate but important consideration, an agreement on intermediate-range nuclear forces would resuscitate the arms control process. If there were no INF agreement, the record would show six years of arms control ending in 1975, after which the process had effectively run into the sand.[82] If there were an agreement, arms control would have a twenty-year track record, achieved largely by Republican presidents. It would be difficult, if not impossible, for a future American leadership to

---

82. Although SALT II was signed in 1979, there was little significant progress between the follow-up to the Vladivostok summit in November 1974 and the Vienna summit in June 1979. The treaty was never submitted for ratification.

put the arms control process into reverse, as elements within the first Reagan administration had tried to do.

The military had every reason to support the objective of eliminating nuclear weapons in the European theater, even though the focus on missiles (to the neglect of aircraft) in the on-going negotiations meant that, initially, the Soviets would have to destroy many more weapons than the West. This asymmetry was acceptable because it removed the new strategic threat that had emerged with the deployment of Euromissiles in late 1983, because it was the only way to get the process under way, and because those weapons were only a part of the overall military balance in Europe and Asia.

STRATEGIC NUCLEAR FORCES. Under the 1970s strategy and the old objective, strategic nuclear forces had two distinct roles, one immediate and the other latent. The immediate role was to deter the United States from striking at the Soviet Union as U.S. forces went down to defeat in Europe. The land-based force provided the primary deterrent, while sea-based systems served as insurance against U.S. technological ingenuity devising some way of rendering the land-based deterrent impotent. The latent role became operational if this wartime deterrence failed, at which time these same weapons were needed to balance the U.S. capability to fight a nuclear war.

It was this latent war-fighting role—the 1960s strategy—that determined the mix of the intercontinental-ballistic-missile (ICBM) force; the heavy missiles, equipped with multiple independently targeted reentry vehicles (MIRVs) covered a pre-planned target set of fixed facilities, while the single-warhead mobile light missiles provided the strategic reserve for use in the post-exchange phase. Under the 1970s strategy, Soviet interests were best served by parity at as low a level as could be negotiated.

The assumption of "no world war" meant the demise of both of these wartime roles, while war-fighting considerations would no longer need to determine the force mix. Since the peacetime deterrence of nuclear attack could be ensured by a relatively small number of missiles, this would seem to suggest that a large unilateral cut in strategic forces should be possible. In practice, the size of the force would have to be determined by political considerations, the most weighty being the United States' unwillingness to negotiate limitations or reductions of any category of weapon in which it held a significant advantage.

Both the new political thinking and the new military doctrine reinforced the 1970s objective of strategic nuclear parity at as low a level as could be negotiated and provided new reasons for arguing that if less was better, then none was best. The Soviet military probably had doubts about that extension of the logic, because of the third-country problem and the difficulties and dangers of taking the final steps. The military's primary concern was to avoid any developments that would disrupt the strategic equilibrium that had been achieved at such cost through the strategic arms limitation talks (SALT), and it was of "special importance" to ensure that this strategic equilibrium was maintained as forces were reduced by the two sides.[83]

Furthermore, there was an important and widely based constituency within the Soviet Union that would resist any move to relinquish that parity voluntarily. In any case, unilateral cuts in Soviet strategic forces would not help rid the world of nuclear weapons, because the United States would happily pocket the concessions and offer nothing in return. There was therefore no reason to reverse the long-standing political assessment that rough strategic parity was a milestone in Soviet-American relations. This need for parity was reinforced by the United States' persistent and frequently reiterated belief in "negotiating from a position of strength," its tendency to see crises as a way of forcing political concessions, and its past (and self-approving) resort to brinkmanship, including explicit and implied threats to use nuclear weapons.[84]

The U.S. strategic arsenal (in which the Soviets counted sea-launched cruise missiles) would have to be bargained down and Soviet strategic nuclear delivery vehicles (SNDVs) would become most important as bargaining counters. They would be used to persuade the United States to follow through on the proposals to reduce the inventories of both sides to the 1,600 SNDVs and 6,000 warheads that had been agreed in principle at Reykjavik, and also to help persuade the United States to refrain from extending the arms race into space.

When these reductions in strategic weapons would come about was another matter. Even the fleeting agreement at Reykjavik had foreseen that it would take at least ten years to implement the reductions, and

---

83. Yazov, "Doctrine," pp. 42–43.
84. See MccGwire, *Military Objectives,* pp. 217–18, discussing Anatoliy Gromyko's article, "The Caribbean Crisis," in V. V. Zhurkin and Ye. M. Primakov, eds., *Mezhdunarodnye konflikty (International Conflicts)* (Moscow: Izdatel'stvo Mezhdunarodnye Otnosheniya, 1972). Zhurkin is head of the European Studies Institute and Primakov subsequently became head of IMEiMO, and in 1989 a member of the Central Committee and chairman of the Council of the Union.

the previous fifteen years' experience provided no certainty that the negotiations could be successful or that the United States would continue to honor existing agreements.

DEFENSE AGAINST ANTIBALLISTIC MISSILES. The new objective did not affect the Soviet Union's adamant opposition to the deployment of strike weapons in space. By deploying such systems the United States would place in question the assumption of "no world war" and threaten the viability of the new objective of ensuring the territorial integrity of the Soviet bloc.

The new objective did, however, affect the Soviet position on territorial ABM systems, as that position had been reflected in the provisions of the 1972 ABM Treaty. The 1966 doctrinal shift and the consequential formulation of the 1970s strategy had led the Soviet Union to reverse its earlier belief in ABM defenses. The change from strategic preemption to a policy of launch-on-warning and to the objective of avoiding the nuclear devastation of the USSR gave new importance to the credibility of wartime deterrence. Credibility required the certainty that Soviet missiles, once launched, would strike home on North America. It was because an effective territorial defense system could undermine such certainty that in 1969 the Soviets had pressed for an ABM Treaty that would prohibit the deployment of such a system.

The assumption of "no world war" removed the need for wartime deterrence and hence this concern about credibility. Meanwhile the seemingly inexorable spread of nuclear weapons and of the means of delivering them had introduced new arguments in favor of ABM defenses that would be capable of warding off attacks from third parties. Although such a capability would most probably require a more extensive territorial deployment than that allowed by the existing ABM Treaty, the issue remained open.

General-Purpose Forces

The assumption that world war could and would be prevented by political means had the most immediate impact on Soviet ground forces and their supporting aviation. The traditional mission of defending the homeland would, of course, remain, but even that would have different implications if the possibility of world war was ruled out.

GROUND FORCES AND SUPPORTING AVIATION. In the European theater, the 1970s strategy required the Soviets to defeat NATO in Europe, evict

U.S. forces from the Continent, and establish an extended defense perimeter. This required a significant measure of superiority over NATO and the capability for deep air attacks and a blitzkrieg ground offensive. It also required the capability to ensure sustained political and military control of the nonallied countries encompassed by the defense perimeter.[85] The new objective would not require superiority over NATO and a blitzkrieg would be prohibited. The ground forces' offensive capability would be limited to that required to restore the situation in the event of enemy aggression.

In the Asian-Pacific theater the 1970s strategy required the Soviets to deter, and if necessary defend against, an attempt by China to profit from the Soviet involvement in the European theater. It also required the Soviets to have the capability to take over Manchuria, once they had achieved their main objectives in Europe.[86] Both of these requirements lapsed under the new objective. Force requirements on the Chinese border would now be determined by the nature of Sino-Soviet relations, the type of regime in Beijing, the strength and disposition of Chinese forces, and the likelihood that China would provoke conflict with the Soviet Union.

In the Indo-Arabian theater, the 1970s strategy required the Soviets to establish control over the Horn of Africa and to be prepared for a range of military activity in the Persian Gulf area. The Horn was the southeastern fulcrum of the extended defense perimeter, and if the trans-Siberian railroad were blocked, the Soviets would need to ship supplies either via the Suez Canal or from the head of the Arabian Sea.[87] The importance of the Horn would lapse under the new objective, as would the need to ship military supplies to the Far East via Iran and the Persian Gulf or via Afghanistan and Chah Bahar. The shipment of military supplies might still be needed in the event of war with China, but the Soviets should be able to use the Suez Canal.

Renouncing the 1970s strategy and adopting the new objective would allow major unilateral reductions in ground forces in the European and Asian-Pacific theaters. In the Indo-Arabian theater it would remove whatever geostrategic justification there might have been for remaining in Afghanistan. It would not, however, affect requirements in the Transcaucasian military district, because of the continuing possibility of

85. MccGwire, *Military Objectives,* pp. 77–89, 128–60.
86. Ibid., pp. 161–70.
87. Ibid., pp. 183–210.

U.S. military intervention in the Gulf area outside the circumstances of world war.

NATIONAL AIR AND SPACE DEFENSE. The new objective did not remove existing requirements to defend the Soviet bloc against attack from the air, but the likely scale of attack and hence the density of the defenses could be reevaluated. However, the Korean airliner incident in September 1983 and the landing of a plane in Red Square in May 1987 illustrated the need to be able to control Soviet air space and prevent hit-and-run intruders. In the event of conflict on the Soviet periphery, the national air defense system would also need to be able to seal off the combat zone from the Soviet hinterland.

The new objective would not reduce the requirement for early warning of an attack by ballistic missiles or some other type of SNDV, if only to identify the source of the attack. To the extent that they were effective, existing ABM systems should remain in place for the time being as insurance against the possibility of attack on Moscow by a third party.

AIR STRIKE FORCES. Under the old objective, medium-range strike aircraft such as the Badger and the Backfire were intended for delivering conventional or nuclear ordnance against distant targets such as carrier battle groups, amphibious assault groups, and various facilities deep in NATO's rear. The Blackjack long-range bomber was seen in the West as a strategic nuclear delivery platform and came under the counting rules of SALT and the strategic arms reductions talks (START); it is, however, likely that its primary mission was selected conventional strikes during the first phase of a world war and operations in support of the extended defense perimeter during the second phase.

Under the new objective, phase-two missions disappeared, as did the need for strikes deep in NATO's rear. However, U.S. carrier battle groups would have an autonomous capability to intervene in conflicts that might erupt on the Soviet periphery, and the requirement to counter them would persist.

NAVAL FORCES. The navy's claim for additional resources to implement the 1970s strategy had already been largely reversed during the 1976–77 policy review, when the concept of closing off the Arctic by establishing command of the Norwegian Sea had been scrapped as too costly to achieve and sustain. Nevertheless, the assumption of "no world war" would have dealt a final blow to the naval missions in phase two of a world war that Admiral Gorshkov had promoted so strongly in the first half of the 1970s.

Similarly, missions related solely to phase one would no longer be relevant. These included helping to seize the Baltic and Black Sea exits, providing flank support to the armies advancing in the Western and Southwestern theaters of military action (TVDs) and into arctic Norway, and using cruise-missile-armed submarines to outflank NATO air defenses and deliver conventional strikes on theater nuclear weapons based in Great Britain. The navy had also had to be prepared to attack NATO's sea lines of communication (SLOCs) if ground operations in the Western TVD bogged down.

Because some of these missions would have been carried out seriatum by the same units, the actual saving in naval forces would be less than might be expected. In any case, the new objective of ensuring the territorial integrity of the Soviet bloc encompassed the traditional naval mission of securing the USSR's maritime frontiers, to which had now been added the requirement to ensure the security of the Soviet nuclear-powered ballistic-missile submarine (SSBN) force.

The Soviets' stated objective was to negotiate very large cuts in strategic nuclear delivery vehicles (including sea-launched cruise missiles); if they had their preference, they would most likely choose to dispense first with the sea-based element of their nuclear force. The SSBNs lacked the inherent protection that being on sovereign territory provides the ICBM force and they introduced additional problems of command and control. Mobile land-based systems embody many of the advantages while avoiding the disadvantages of the SSBNs—including the high cost of the naval forces required to protect them. Such an arrangement would, however, be difficult to negotiate, since the United States had always seen the Soviet ICBM force as the greatest threat and its own ICBMs as relatively vulnerable.

As long as the Soviet Union was stuck with sea-based systems, the SSBN force would require protection against intruding submarines.[88] Even if it were agreed at START to cut sea-based SNDVs by 50 percent, this would have less than a proportionate effect on the requirement for

---

88. It could be argued that, in the absence of world war, there was no requirement to defend the SSBN force against Western attempts to draw down its strength. However, the protection of SSBNs in peacetime comes under the objective of ensuring the physical integrity of the Soviet Union.

supporting forces, which would be needed for area defense as much as for direct protection. Carriers would continue to be needed to provide sea-based air support, including denying the use of the air to U.S. antisubmarine aircraft.

Naval forces would also have to contribute to national air defense, one of the three overarching tasks of the armed forces.[89] They could provide early warning of attack by aircraft or cruise missile from the maritime axes, and warships could be used as off-shore missile batteries to shoot down low-flying intruders or force them to fly high enough to be detected by land-based radar.

There remained the more specifically naval problem of the U.S. carrier battle groups. The mission of countering these forces went back to the 1950s and, despite the assumption of "no world war," they still posed a threat, because of their nuclear capability. If negotiations on ridding Europe of nuclear weapons were successful, the carriers would provide the United States with the unilateral capability to influence a limited conflict on the Soviet periphery with the threat or use of tactical nuclear weapons.

Removing nuclear weapons from U.S. carriers would therefore be the primary focus of naval arms control. Nor was that an unrealistic objective. With world war a diminishing possibility, the U.S. navy's primary mission would be the projection of military force in the third world, where the use of nuclear weapons was politically unthinkable. Given that constraint, a properly regulated nonnuclear maritime environment was very much in the U.S. navy's interests. It would sharply improve the U.S. navy's capability with regard to Soviet naval forces (including land-based maritime air) and obviate the future threat of a nuclear maverick in the third world.

While the Soviets might talk of unilateral reductions in U.S. carriers to offset unilateral reductions in Soviet ground forces, the number of carriers (as opposed to their nuclear capability) was not an important issue. Indeed, it could be argued that continuation of the United States' self-appointed role as "world gendarme" (as the Soviets call it) could only damage the U.S. international standing while highlighting the Soviet Union's noninterventionist stance.

89. N. P. V'yunenko and others, *Voenno-morskoy flot: rol', perspektivy razvitiya, ispol'zovanie* (*The Navy: Its Role, Prospects for Development, and Employment*) (Moscow: Voenizdat, 1988), p. 35.

The Obstacle Removed

By the end of 1988 Soviet military doctrine, strategy, and requirements had been set on a completely new track, while the military establishment was itself being subjected to radical change. In addition to the domestic disruptions of glasnost and administrative perestroika, military units in Europe were exposed to the challenge of inspection by NATO officials in 1987, and this intrusive verification was extended to facilities throughout the USSR in 1988, as the process of destroying the INF missiles got under way. By the end of 1988 the Soviet armed forces had been committed to a reduction of 500,000 troops, with no compensation of any kind from the West. Meanwhile, there had been a wholesale turnover in the upper echelons of the military leadership, with retirements, demotions, and replacements, and the military-technical levels of doctrine and planning were being subjected to public scrutiny by civilian analysts.

But these changes affecting the military establishment were insignificant compared to the changes in Soviet defense and foreign policy that were made possible by the assumption of "no world war."

Soviet military behavior served for forty years in the West as a metaphor for the objectives of the world communist movement and as irrefutable evidence of the Soviet Union's efforts to dominate the world by military means.[90] However, by the end of 1988 there had been a sea change in that behavior. The Soviet acceptance of intrusive verification of theater as well as strategic forces, the readiness to destroy twice as many missiles as its opponents under the INF Treaty, the withdrawal from Afghanistan, the exchange of visits by the ministers of defense and heads of the joint staffs, and then the announcement of massive unilateral force cuts, these and other developments made it impossible for U.S. "aggressive circles" and their allies in the Western military-industrial complex to continue using the Soviet military threat to justify anti-Soviet policies.

By assuming "no world war," the Soviets resolved six of the eight main contradictions underlying their defense and foreign policy. This

---

90. See statements by Secretary of Defense Caspar Weinberger in "Face the Nation," CBS television, March 13, 1983; *USA Today,* August 11, 1983; Fred Hiatt, *Washington Post,* April 11, 1984. Internal repression was the other half of the metaphor, justifying the view of the Soviet Union as an "evil empire," set on destroying the "free world."

allowed a completely new approach to conventional arms control and to relations with other nations on the Eurasian landmass, and a potentially massive shift of resources from defense to the civilian economy. While it had been essential to redefine the Marxist-Leninist theory of international relations in order to allow the reversal of policy toward the United States, on its own that would not have been enough. The West would have dismissed the new theory as propaganda and the reversal of policy as a tactical ploy. Concrete evidence of a sea change in Soviet military behavior was needed to persuade an understandably skeptical Western political-military establishment that a new era in East-West relations was beginning.

And such a change in Soviet military behavior could only be justified if it were first assumed that world war could and would be averted by political means.

CHAPTER 9

Running with the Storm, 1989–90

BY THE END OF 1988 Mikhail Gorbachev had succeeded in initiating the "real revolution" that he believed was needed if the Soviet Union was to escape the economic stagnation and social anomie that afflicted the country and its people.

Gorbachev had set in motion a process that would shift the locus of political and administrative decisionmaking from the party apparatus to state organs responsible at all levels to democratically elected bodies. Marxist-Leninist theory had been reworked to yield an expanding-sum view of international relations, where the emphasis was on cooperation and conciliation rather than conflict and confrontation. Policy toward the United States had been set on a new track. And a new perception of national security had allowed the very substance of military doctrine to be redefined, leading to a radical change in the scale and nature of Soviet force requirements.

Gorbachev and his supporters were successful in initiating revolutionary change everywhere except in the Soviet economy, where perestroika was running two to three years behind plan. Elsewhere the seeds of change had taken root and the revolutionary process was under way. By the end of 1989 the Communist party apparatus would be challenged by a democratically elected body whose powers would flower steadily. Union republics would be agitating for independence. In foreign policy, the new emphasis on self-determination and the unacceptability of foreign intervention would introduce new factors into relations with the countries of Eastern Europe. And in the sphere of national security, involvement of the *institutniki* in the debate on Soviet defense requirements and the armed forces' exposure to the rigors of glasnost would result in the steady erosion of the military leadership's authority.

The January 1987 plenum had initiated the process of political democratization and had legitimated the doctrinal assumption that world war would be prevented by political means. These two initiatives put in train a series of developments that generated a veritable storm of change. In 1989 Gorbachev set course to run with that storm, rather than butt into those dangerous seas. He may not have foreseen the full scope of all the consequential developments or the speed with which they would come about. However, by running with the storm rather than resisting change, Gorbachev was able to make the continual course corrections needed to preserve the integrity of the ship of state. Spars might be lost or damaged, but good seamanship should be able to avoid swamping in the raging seas and preserve the hull intact.

Restructuring the Political System

At the January 1987 plenum, Gorbachev had proposed that an all-Union party conference be convened in June 1988. This was the first step in a process designed simultaneously to wrest power from the party bureaucracy, provide for democratic participation at all levels, and increase his capacity to propel events in the desired direction.

It was the ossified bureaucracy that Gorbachev saw as the problem, not the concept of a party of dedicated activists who could energize the political economy. Democratization was a way of clearing out the deadwood and ensuring that the party's influence reflected the competence of its members and not the positions they held. Rather than diminishing the party's leading role, he intended "to intensify the party's influence on social processes . . . by concentrating efforts" on elaborating theory and analyzing social processes, and then "influencing public opinion."[1]

It would be the first such conference to be held since 1941, and Gorbachev's immediate purpose was to use it as a means of rejuvenating the composition of the Central Committee, and to alter various party statutes. Otherwise both would remain unchanged until the next party

1. This was the formulation used by V. A. Medvedev in his speech to the international learned conference on the Contemporary Concept of Socialism, *Pravda,* October 5, 1988, in *FBIS*-88-194, p. 6 (see Abbreviations of Frequently Cited Sources).

congress that was scheduled for 1991. The June 1987 plenum finally agreed to holding the conference but not that it should have the authority Gorbachev sought. It nevertheless would serve his wider purpose of extending the political field of battle, giving him more room for maneuver and, since the proceedings would be televised, informing the Soviet people of the issues at stake.

In the months immediately preceding the conference the political struggle intensified over the selection of delegates and the substance of the theses that the Central Committee would submit to the conference. There was a conservative attack on perestroika in March 1988, but this served to strengthen Gorbachev's position and the theses adopted by the plenum in May 1988 were more radical than would have been possible twelve months earlier. In many respects the conference resolutions went further than the theses, despite the fact that 90 percent of the delegates were regular party apparatchiks.[2]

The main purpose of both the theses and the conference resolutions was to initiate the process of shifting power from the party to state organs. This was to be achieved by "fully restor[ing] the role and power of the councils of people's deputies as sovereign organs of popular representation," by restoring "the councils' real governing powers, and to refer for their examination and solution all concrete questions of state, economic and sociocultural life, without exception," and by establishing "the real supremacy of the councils over executive organs." This presupposed "a cardinal enhancement of the country's supreme organ of power," the Supreme Soviet.[3] Meanwhile the power of the party apparatus was to be weakened by diluting the *nomenklatura* system, by requiring multicandidate elections with limited terms in office, and by prohibiting concurrent appointments to party and state positions.[4]

After the conference had clarified the distribution of political support and authorized movement in a general direction, Gorbachev moved to consolidate the potential gains, calling a surprise plenum followed by a special session of the Supreme Soviet at the end of September. This saw Andrei Gromyko's replacement by Gorbachev as chairman of the

2. Michel Tatu, "19th Party Conference," *Problems of Communism*, vol. 37 (May–August 1988), pp. 5–6; "Resolutions of the 19th All-Union CPSU Conference: On Political Reform," *Kommunist*, no. 10 (July 1988), in *JPRS*-88-016, pp. 37, 42–46.

3. "Central Committee Theses for the 19th All-Union Party Conference," *Pravda*, May 27, 1988, in *FBIS*-88-103, p. 45.

4. Ibid., pp. 43–44.

Presidium (the titular head of state) and changes in the membership and responsibilities of the Politburo.

The tactic of taking decisive action shortly after a gathering or election had clarified the distribution of forces became a standard political maneuver. In terms of strengthening Gorbachev's position in relation to the party, the most important change approved by the September 1988 plenum was grouping the departments of the Central Committee Secretariat and placing them under the purview of six commissions comprising members of the Central Committee plus some nonmembers. This prepared the way for transferring executive authority from the Secretariat to the commissions at the November 28 plenum that preceded the meeting of the Supreme Soviet. This move significantly weakened the power of the permanent officials of the central party apparatus and nominally transferred that power to the elected Central Committee. However, the commissions were convened rarely. Day-to-day control therefore lay with their chairmen, and those heading the three most politically sensitive commissions were strong supporters of Gorbachev.[5]

The special session of the Supreme Soviet at the end of November 1988 passed laws amending the Constitution and arranging multicandidate elections for a Congress of People's Deputies. The elections were held on March 26, and by the time of the next plenum, a month later, Gorbachev had extracted the resignation of 110 "dead souls" from the Central Committee and Auditing Commission who no longer held the appointments that had justified their "election" at the party congress in 1986. These forced resignations and the promotion of 24 loyalists from the ranks of candidate members finally gave Gorbachev control of the Central Committee. His position within the upper echelons of the Communist party was further strengthened at the plenum in September 1989 when two of the leading conservatives were dropped from the Politburo.[6]

In May 1989, less than a year after the Nineteenth Party Conference, the new Congress of People's Deputies convened for its first session. Almost 2,900 candidates had competed for the 1,500 territorial and

---

5. Dawn Mann, "Gorbachev's Position Consolidated," *RL* 436/88 (October 4, 1988); Alexander Rahr, "Gorbachev Changes Party Structure," *RL* 519/88 (November 30. 1988).

6. Elizabeth Teague, "Gorbachev Outfoxes the Opposition," and "Gorbachev and the KGB Profit from Politbureau Reshuffle," *Report on the USSR,* vol. 1 (May 12, 1989), pp. 1–3, and (September 29, 1989), pp. 4–6.

national-territorial seats; the other 750 members were elected by various all-Union organizations, including the Communist party. The congress elected a newly configured Supreme Soviet and a bicameral legislature comprising the Council of the Union and the Council of Nations (each with 271 members), which elected Gorbachev as its chairman. By the end of its second session in late November 1989 the Supreme Soviet had adopted twenty-nine decisions, resolutions, and laws, rejected a number of nominations for ministerial appointments, rejected a proposed ban on strikes, and generally shown itself a body to be reckoned with.[7]

On February 27, 1990, the Supreme Soviet approved Gorbachev's proposal that the Soviet Union should move to an executive presidency, which would strengthen the executive branch of government while weakening the powers of the legislature. On March 15, exactly five years after Gorbachev was elected general secretary, an extraordinary session of the Congress of People's Deputies elected Gorbachev to be the first president for a four-year term. It also abolished the constitutional priority of the Communist party, opening the way to a multiparty system. The constitutional revision also required the president to appoint a ten-member advisory body or Presidential Council, whose membership was announced on March 24. Only five were members of the Politburo, and three were non-Slavic.

Meanwhile, preparations were under way for the Twenty-eighth Party Congress, scheduled for July 1990, eight months earlier than normal. At the March plenum Gorbachev presented a draft party platform and a set of rules to be approved by the congress, which were designed to dispel the party's image as "a bureaucratic, official apparatus." He also argued that it should not be a parliamentary party but "the vanguard political force in society"; Communists would be too busy "solving the country's urgent problems" to have time for "trivial parliamentary games."[8]

Under the new party rules, the Politburo, headed by the general secretary, would be replaced by a presidium, headed by the chairman of the party and his two deputies who, together with the leaders of the Union republics' Communist parties, would be ex officio members.

7. Dawn Mann, "Legislative Reform," *Report on the USSR,* vol. 1 (December 29, 1989), pp. 1–3.

8. *RFE/RL* (U.S. Radio Free Europe/Radio Liberty) *Daily Report,* no. 52 (March 14, 1990), p. 4.

Other members would be elected by the Central Committee and ratified by the congress. Party officials would be limited to two terms in office, local party organizations would control the selection and election of delegates to party congresses, and senior members of the party would have to submit themselves for reelection. However, Gorbachev's proposal that top leaders should be elected by the party congress rather than the Central Committee was not accepted, and the principle of "democratic centralism" was reinstated.[9]

Although Gorbachev did not achieve everything he had hoped for at the March plenum, the new rules represented further weakening of the party by diffusing its powers and making it significantly more democratic. The Twenty-eighth Party Congress in July would provide an even more important opportunity for reshaping the party. Meanwhile, the creation of an executive presidency with its advisory council would sharply reduce the Politburo's influence on government policy, freeing Gorbachev from the need to seek consensus there and in the Central Committee.

Undoubtedly, the political struggle would continue. However, within forty months of the January 1987 plenum, Gorbachev had completely recast the country's structure of governance, shifted political power from the party apparatus to democratically elected state organs, and in a truly remarkable way consolidated and augmented his own power and authority.[10]

The Nationalities Question

The Soviet Union has always claimed that it was a union of more than one hundred nationalities. However, most of the nationalities are very small, and the twenty-two largest make up almost 98 percent of the total population. In practical terms, just over half the population is Russian, another 20 percent are also Slavs (Ukranian and Byelorussian), another 20 percent are traditional Islamic people, 3 percent are Christian Caucasians (Armenians and Georgians), and 3 percent are Balts.[11] The fifteen

9. *RFE/RL Daily Report,* no. 62 (March 28, 1990), pp. 5–6; "Draft CPSU Statutes," *Pravda,* March 28, 1990, p. 2.

10. Elizabeth Teague and Dawn Mann, "Gorbachev's Dual Role," *Problems of Communism,* vol. 39 (January–February 1990), pp. 1–14, describe the state of policy in early 1990.

11. Paul A. Goble, *Washington Post,* March 25, 1990, pp. C1–2.

Union republics range in size from Estonia with a population of 1.6 million to the Russian Soviet Federated Socialist Republic (RSFSR), which stretches from the Baltic to the Pacific and has a population of 147 million. All but one are dominated by a single ethnic group,[12] and each republic includes "autonomous" republics, regions, and districts with concentrations of other ethnic groups.

The new leadership appears to have been unprepared for the nationalistic response evoked by the anticorruption drive, glasnost, and democratization. Nor was it ready for the violence that broke out against ethnic enclaves—notably against the largely Armenian group in the autonomous region of Nagorno-Karabakh, located within the Union Republic of Azerbaijan. However, although a major and enduring problem for Moscow, this violence had less serious long-term consequences than the surge of nationalism in the Union republics, particularly the three Baltic republics.[13]

Publication of the draft laws to implement the proposals of the Nineteenth Party Conference on restructuring government evoked strong protests in October 1988 from Georgia and the Baltic republics and led to the formation of independent nationalist bodies. The republics argued that the new structure would result in more rather than less centralization (as had been proposed by the conference) and that it reduced the relative representation of the non-Russian republics in the Council of Nationalities. After correcting some sloppy drafting that had caused disagreement and making various concessions, the Supreme Soviet passed new laws amending the Constitution and providing for the election of deputies on December 1, 1988. However, the roots of the problem were deep, and there was a basic disjunction of interests between the central government in Moscow and the governments of the Baltic republics.

Starting with demands for increased republican "sovereignty," linguistic separatism, and various forms of economic autonomy, nationalist forces steadily extended their influence and the scope of other demands, until these coalesced into a call for full political independence. The election in March 1989 for the USSR Congress of People's Deputies demonstrated the level of popular support. In Lithuania, candidates

---

12. The population of Kazakhstan is 36 percent Kazakh and 41 percent Russian; the Russians, who began colonizing the area in the late eighteenth century, are concentrated in the northern half.

13. Ibid.

nominated by the Reconstruction Movement, Sajudis, won thirty-six of the thirty-nine districts where they ran, while senior state and party officials were roundly beaten. Similarly, the Popular Fronts in both Latvia and Estonia, although public organizations rather than political parties, made a strong showing, with three quarters of the Latvian deputies being affiliated with the Front.[14]

Official defiance of Moscow reflected the differing levels of demographic primacy within the three republics. In Latvia, with a population of 2.7 million, 50 percent Latvian and 36 percent Russian (the Latvians being concentrated in rural areas and upper-age groups), the Popular Front's influence increased steadily at the expense of Soviet authority. But the Communist party still maintained a monopoly on power at the end of 1989. However, in 1990 the party showed signs of splitting, with an ethnic Latvian wing advocating independence from Moscow.[15]

Estonia, 68 percent of whose 1.6 million people were Estonian and 28 percent Russian, had in 1988 formally asserted the right to reject Soviet laws that infringed local autonomy. In 1989 the Estonian Supreme Soviet passed a law requiring two years' residence to vote in local elections, but this had to be withdrawn. In February 1990, however, elections were held for an independent Congress of Estonia, an unofficial alternative legislature chosen from citizens of the interwar republic and their descendants. At the end of March the newly elected Supreme Soviet declared its intention of cooperating with the congress. It also declared the Soviet annexation in 1940 to have been invalid, reaffirmed prewar Estonia's de jure existence, and made clear its intention to resume that independent status in due course. Meanwhile, the Estonian Communist party split, with one group pledged to break away from Moscow.[16]

Lithuania, with a 3.7 million population that was 80 percent Lithuanian and 9 percent Russian, moved more precipitately, perhaps emboldened by Moscow's acquiescence to the replacement of communist governments throughout Eastern Europe, and thinking that if the opportunity were not seized it would be lost. In September 1989, the Lithuanian Supreme Soviet declared the 1940 annexation by the Soviet Union to

14. Saulius Girnius, "Lithuania," Riina Kionka, "Estonia," and Dzintra Bungs, "Latvia," *Report on the USSR,* vol. 1 (December 29, 1989), pp. 23–30.

15. See Juris Dreifelds, "Latvian National Rebirth," *Problems of Communism,* vol. 38 (July–August 1989), p. 77–94.

16. See also Rein Taagepera, "Estonia's Road to Independence," *Problems of Communism,* vol. 38 (November–December 1989), pp. 11–26.

have been invalid. In December, following a republican decree abolishing the Communist party's official primacy, the party voted to break with Moscow and described its goal to be "an independent, democratic Lithuania." The declaration that the 1940 annexation was invalid was reaffirmed by the republic's newly elected Supreme Soviet in February 1990, which elected the non-Communist leader of the Sajudis as president. On March 11 the Supreme Soviet declared Lithuania to be a sovereign state, legally free of the Soviet Union.[17] This declaration was, however, resolved to be illegal by an overwhelming majority of the USSR Congress of People's Deputies, and it was rejected by Gorbachev, leading to direct confrontation.

These developments posed a dilemma for Moscow. In legal terms the Baltic republics could be seen as a special case. They had existed as sovereign states for twenty-two years between the wars, and it could be shown that their legal accession to the Soviet Union had involved military coercion and rigged referendums. Their annexation was therefore of dubious legality in a way that did not apply to the other spoils of World War II or to earlier wars. Given the ongoing process of rectifying the distortions of Stalin's policy, a strong case could be made for admitting the special circumstances of 1940 and acknowledging that the Baltic republics had an inherent right to independence.

There were also practical reasons for doing so. By virtue of their location, ethnic makeup, and existing infrastructure the Baltic republics were ideally situated to serve as the major economic interface between Western Europe and the Soviet Union. They became a self-financing region at the beginning of 1990 and there had been talk of turning them into free-trade zones, but to reap the full benefits of the interface-entrepot role the Baltic republics would need the spur of independence.

Meanwhile, the strategic imperatives that had justified their annexation in 1940 and their retention after the war had ceased to apply once it was ruled that world war would be averted by political means. In the past, their territory had provided defense in depth to Leningrad and their coastline and bases were essential to naval command of the Baltic. The requirement for early warning of air attack remained, but ways could be found to arrange for that. In the future, therefore, it would be more appropriate to view the Baltic republics in terms of the Soviet-Finnish relationship. That had proven to be a satisfactory way of achieving

17. See V. Stanley Vardys, "Lithuanian National Policies," *Problems of Communism,* vol. 38 (July–August 1989), pp. 53–76.

physical security, while opening the Soviet Union to Western technology and trade.

Gorbachev was not, however, operating in a political vacuum. For a start, the Baltic republics' push for independence came as the Supreme Soviet in Moscow was reworking the law on the federal relationship that linked the fifteen republics in a single union and delimited the powers of the USSR and the republics. It was also preparing a law, which hitherto had not existed, on the mechanics of secession. This required that two-thirds of the voters opt for secession and that there be a five-year transition period during which the political, military, and economic terms would be negotiated.[18] However, this constitutional obstacle could perhaps have been circumvented by a grandfather clause that recognized the Baltic republics as a special case. This would have met a central objective of the perestroika process—namely, a civil society ruled by law and not by political fiat.

The more intractable obstacle to a flexible approach was the possibility that the secession of the Baltic republics would start the disintegration of the Soviet Union, the unravelling of the tsarist empire. The events in Eastern Europe in 1989, particularly the move toward a unified Germany, had already exposed Gorbachev to the charge that his policies were endangering the security of the Soviet Union. And while it could be argued that the security advantage of a defensive glacis did not justify the political and economic costs of maintaining the Warsaw Pact, that did not read across to the Baltic states. World war or not, why give up territory that had inherent strategic importance and that had first come into Russia's possession in the eighteenth century?

It was true that many within government and academic circles saw the breakup of the Soviet Union as inevitable. Some believed that only Byelorussia could be counted on to remain linked with the RFSFR, while others included the eastern (non-Catholic) part of the Ukraine and the northern (non-Muslim) part of Kazakhstan, and there were also other variants.[19] Some intellectuals saw this process of disintegration and

18. *RFE/RL Daily Report*, no. 67 (April 4, 1990), pp. 4–5. The two-thirds requirement followed sound constitutional practice, but Estonia might not be able to meet it. This explains Estonia's insistence that as a sovereign state it was not subject to the Soviet constitution.

19. Phillip A. Petersen, "The Emerging Soviet Vision of European Security," paper presented at a Seminar on Soviet Decision-Making at NATO Headquarters, Brussels, March 19, 1990, updated to April 17, 1990, pp. 21–25; John B. Dunlop, "Ethnic Russians on Possible Breakup of the USSR," *Report on the USSR*, vol. 2 (March 2, 1990), pp. 16–17.

reconsolidation as not only inevitable but ultimately beneficial to all concerned, but popular feeling was more difficult to gauge.

Among the Russians, who made up 50 percent of the Soviet population, there were certainly those who were strongly in favor of preserving the imperial borders of the USSR. These would include many, if not most of those serving in all-Union organizations, ranging from the military and internal security organizations to the party bureaucracies, state institutions and industries, and professional and trade unions. But other Russians saw "Russia" as a nation rather than an empire, and while its essential character and boundaries differed between groups of protagonists, such a nation would even gain from relinquishing the non-Russian areas.[20]

These different possibilities could flourish under glasnost, but they were not ideas that Gorbachev could entertain publicly in 1990. Despite the new structure of governance, he was still vulnerable to the charge that he was destroying the fabric of the country that so many had died for in the Great Fatherland War, a charge that linked many different interests inside and outside the party.

Furthermore, he had his own agenda. Now that the appropriate political structure was in place, he hoped that perestroika would transform the Soviet Union into an entity that others would wish to join rather than leave. That would, however, take time. Meanwhile he must resist developments that would lead to premature defections.

The Problem of Eastern Europe

In June 1986, addressing the Polish party congress, Gorbachev had described the Soviet bloc as "an international reality, an alliance of states linked by political, economic, cultural and defense interests." He had gone on to say that "to tear one country or another from the socialist community" would represent an encroachment "on the entire postwar order, and, in the final analysis, on peace."[21]

However, in November or December 1986 Gorbachev informed a meeting of Eastern European party chiefs that in the future they could

20. Roman Szporluk, "Dilemmas of Russian Nationalism," *Problems of Communism,* vol. 38 (July–August 1989), pp. 15–35.
21. MTS, June 30, 1986, in *FBIS*-86-126, p. F3.

not expect Soviet military intervention to keep them in power.[22] And in January 1987 Gorbachev embarked on a path that placed in question the postwar order in Europe. Gorbachev considered it essential that the energies of the people be engaged directly through democratization; otherwise perestroika would surely fail. However, once proclaimed in the Soviet Union, democracy could not be denied to the nations of Eastern Europe, where it would combine with nationalism to create an explosive mix.

A necessary corollary of the decision to democratize was the adoption of a new military doctrine and the development of plans based on the assumption that world war could and would be averted by political means. Without such a reshaping of plans, it would not be possible to achieve major reductions in general-purpose forces, or to put pressure on the United States to negotiate seriously on reducing strategic nuclear forces. The very fact of forgoing the capability to wage world war was reason for reshaping plans since war would be less likely and peace thereby strengthened. But the new military doctrine would place in question the postwar order in Europe, which had been seen as the basis for stability and peace.

It is likely that Gorbachev's ideas about Eastern Europe would have reflected those of his mentor Yuri Andropov, whose career had started in the Karelo-Finnish region where he was a protégé of the Finnish-born member of the Politburo, Otto Kuusinen. It was Kuusinen who assembled the group of young consultants that Andropov inherited when he joined the Secretariat in 1962 and who turned out to be the bellwethers of Gorbachev's revolution.[23] It seems that Andropov saw Soviet relations with Finland as the proper model for relations between the Soviet Union and the countries of the Warsaw Pact, and since this was all part of the new political thinking about international relations that Gorbachev inherited, he is likely to have shared the same general view.[24]

22. Raymond L. Garthoff (personal communication) was told this in July 1990 by a deputy director of the Institute for the Study of the World Socialist Economy.
23. Petersen, "Emerging Soviet Vision," p. 2. Petersen lists Fedor Burlatsky, Georgi Arbatov, Aleksandr Bovin, and Oleg Bogomolov as members of "the Andropov circle."
24. Ibid., p. 5. In 1989 a member of Bogomolov's institute specifically proposed "Finlandization" as the appropriate relationship with the countries of Eastern Europe (Andranik Migranyan, "For Discussion: Epitaph for the Brezhnev Doctrine: The USSR and Other Socialist Countries in the Context of East-West Relations," *Moscow News,* no. 34 [August 27, 1989], p. 6).

Gorbachev would also have been influenced by the ideas emanating from the Institute for the Study of the World Socialist Economy. Its director, Oleg Bogomolov, had been one of Kusinen's young consultants. In an article on the need for political and economic reform he noted that "a collective search was underway for a new socialist society." He highlighted the main trends: moving away from command-administrative and mobilization-ordering forms of management, with accompanying changes in the laws of ownership and the restoration of commodity-money relations through markets; restructuring the political mechanisms, involving the introduction of democratic procedures and increased public control, while recognizing the complexity of social interrelationships and the impossibility of unanimity; questioning the relationship between the party and the state and society at large; and increasing the involvement of socialist countries in the international community.[25]

The institute's foreign affairs department was headed by Vyacheslav Dashichev, a diplomatic historian who had fought in World War II and had worked with the General Staff until he was recruited by Bogomolov in 1967. By his account, in 1977 his section had warned of the impending crisis in Poland and in confidential memorandums to the Central Committee he had criticized the invasion of Afghanistan in 1980 and in 1981 had recommended accepting the Reagan administration's proposal for eliminating all intermediate-range nuclear forces.[26] These ideas would have been congenial to Gorbachev, who would have been familiar with the confidential papers produced by Bogomolov's institute since he was responsible for relations with the bloc countries before his election as general secretary in 1985.

Dashichev started from the proposition that in Eastern Europe the status quo had proven to be "exceptionally burdensome politically, economically, militarily, and psychologically," and that its continuation, besides being quite unnecessary, was "undermining the vital

25. Oleg Bogomolov, "The World of Socialism on the Road of Restructuring," *Kommunist*, no. 16 (November 1987), in *JPRS*-88-003, pp. 61–68. For a pointed criticism of the Soviet political economy see the interview with Bogomolov in *Izvestiya*, May 14, 1987, in *FBIS*-87-101, p. S1.

26. Jonathan Haslem, "Soviet Policy toward Western Europe since World War II," in G. Breslauer and P. Tetlock, *Learning in U.S. and Soviet Foreign Policy* (Washington, D.C.: National Research Council, National Academy of Sciences, forthcoming). The protest about Afghanistan was in a letter dated January 20, 1980, signed by Bogomolov and other members of the institute; it was published in *Literaturnaya gazeta*, no. 11 (March 16, 1988).

foundations of the Soviet Union."[27] He argued that by the late 1950s the Stalinist administrative-command system had begun to reveal its ineffectiveness, but neither Khrushchev nor Brezhnev recognized that the Soviet Union had moved from being seen as the liberator from fascism to being the oppressor and opponent of change. This led to the profound crisis that affected most Eastern European countries in the 1980s, by when the Soviet Union had effectively been deprived of its social, political, and economic levers.

Meanwhile, use of the military instrument "would have catastrophic consequences, not only for [the Eastern European] countries and the entire system of East-West relations, but also for the policy of perestroika in the USSR." As a consequence, Eastern Europe had gradually changed "from being a security zone into a zone of danger and instability." Besides being dangerous in its own right, "the forcible establishment of Soviet dominance over Eastern Europe [was] one of the main reasons for unleashing of the Cold War by the West . . . and the fierce confrontation in Europe."[28]

Dashichev faced up to what the withdrawal of Soviet dominance would imply for German reunification and argued that unification was in fact essential to the building of a common European house or home. He saw reunification as something that would come about "when the East-West confrontation in Europe [began] to give way to all-European cooperation."[29] He recognized that West German involvement in the economic integration of Western Europe was irreversible, but he saw this as being beneficial. It would prevent the use of "the economic might of the Common Market for political purposes that [ran] counter to the interests of the Soviet Union," and would avoid the conversion of "the Common Market into a closed grouping," or "zone to which the access of commodities from Eastern Europe [would] be limited."[30]

When these background factors are joined with the course of events

27. Vyacheslav Dashichev, "The Concept of an All-European House and the German Question" (unpublished paper). This paper was in most respects identical to a speech delivered by Dashichev in Berlin on April 18, 1989, before Gorbachev's visit to Bonn in June, which was published in *Der Spiegel,* no. 6 (1990), pp. 142–58. In March 1990, Dashichev told Phillip A. Petersen that the speech/paper was virtually the same as the one he had presented to the Ministry of Foreign Affairs in the fall of 1987.

28. Dashichev, "Concept"; he made the same point, and again blamed Brezhnev for the situation, in "East-West: The Search for New Relations," *Literaturnaya gazeta,* no. 20 (May 18, 1988), p. 14.

29. Dashichev, "Concept."

30. Dashichev, speech in Berlin, cited by Petersen, "Emerging Soviet Vision," pp. 8–9.

in 1987–89, a pattern begins to emerge. In March 1987, in the communiqué following their regular meeting, the Warsaw Pact foreign ministers mentioned imbalances; that marked the beginning of a nine-month series of Warsaw Pact and Soviet statements that referred to asymmetrical reductions with increasing specificity. The May 1987 meeting of the Warsaw Pact Political Consultative Committee (PCC) set in train a process that led to the question of unilateral force cuts by all members of the Pact being a key item on the agenda of the Pact's next regular meeting in July 1988.

May 1987 can be seen as the watershed in Warsaw Pact developments. The PCC set up a special commission on questions of disarmament and a multilateral group for current reciprocal information, the latter perhaps being concerned with the destabilizing effects of perestroika and glasnost. The PCC also established a commission to consider the implications of a Soviet military withdrawal from Eastern Europe by the year 2000.[31] The Soviets admitted that in this period there was debate (and dissension) among the leadership about the future of the two Germanies.[32]

In mid-1988 a special commission on Soviet national security issued a report that concluded that cuts of 500,000 troops were feasible and that Soviet forces could be withdrawn completely from Czechoslovakia and Hungary.[33] During the same period Gorbachev informed the other members of the Warsaw Pact of the Soviet intention to make unilateral force reductions. These were welcomed by Poland and Hungary, while Czechoslovakia and East Germany had reservations.

Also in mid-1988, the Nineteenth Party Conference in Moscow initiated a process that would lead to a more democratic form of Soviet government. Multicandidate elections were scheduled for the spring of 1989 and a new kind of Supreme Soviet with real powers would be

31. Petersen gleaned this during an interview for the "Emerging Soviet Vision" and follow-up interviews in March 1990.

32. See Michael J. Sodaro, *Moscow, Germany and the West, from Khrushchev to Gorbachev* (Cornell University Press, 1990), chap. 10, notes 135–58. In September 1987 a senior official of the West German foreign ministry mentioned a report, which had originated with East German officials, that the Soviets had established a commission to study a possible German confederation (Gary Lee, *Washington Post,* October 12, 1987, p. A30). The Soviets denied the report, but it lends credence to the rumors that in mid-1987 Bogomolov's institute was ordered to study the political implications of a Soviet withdrawal from Eastern Europe, with particular reference to the two Germanies.

33. See chap. 8; on Hungary and Czechoslovakia, see Haslem, "Soviet Policy." The commission, which drew on the work of Bogomolov's institute, may have been the one headed by Lobov, though his group might have been a military wing of some larger commission.

chosen by the newly elected Congress of People's Deputies by the middle of that year. Meanwhile, early in October 1988 the Academy of Social Sciences of the party's Central Committee convened a conference of more than one hundred senior social scientists from the socialist countries on "The Contemporary Concept of Socialism."

In his introductory speech at the conference, Vadim A. Medvedev, the Politburo member with oversight of ideology, stressed that removing the distortions did not imply a simple return to Leninism, but rather a reinterpretation of Leninism in light of contemporary conditions. In essence, he called for a root-and-branch rethinking of socialism, in order to achieve the kind of society that Gorbachev had described in his report to the party conference. He dismissed many cherished doctrinal tenets, stressed the need for diversity, and emphasized the central importance of a democratic approach. He noted that the Soviet Union was attempting to create a new system of power and management that would rely on the idea of a socialist rule-of-law state and a ramified network of organizations and institutions to express the multitude of social interests. The party would still have a leading role, but its structure, functions, and methods needed to be profoundly democratized.[34] The conference conclusions noted that "the level of development of the social sciences in the socialist countries [did] not measure up to present-day demands."[35]

The pattern of events in 1987–88 argues strongly that the Gorbachev leadership deliberately set in motion the process that would lead to the collapse of communist rule throughout Eastern Europe by the end of 1989.[36] The desanctification of Marxist-Leninist dogma, the push to rethink the meaning and substance of socialism, the emphasis on democratizing both the state and the party, and the plans for unilateral force reductions and the withdrawal of Soviet forces, each on its own was a radical development. In combination their implications were revolutionary.[37]

Meanwhile, the Soviet Union had declared the "impermissibility of interference in [another country's] internal affairs under any pretext

34. *Pravda,* October 5, 1988, in *FBIS*-88-194, pp. 4–6.
35. TASS, October 6, 1988, in *FBIS*-88-196, p. 8; *FBIS*-88-195, pp. 5–7.
36. Karen Dawisha provides evidence of this in *Eastern Europe, Gorbachev and Reform: The Great Challenge,* 2d ed. (Cambridge University Press, 1988), chap. 7. See also Vladimir V. Kushin, "Gorbachev's Evolving Attitude toward Eastern Europe," *Report on the USSR,* vol. 1 (August 4, 1989), pp. 8–12.
37. Karen Dawisha told me she believes that the Soviet leadership had decided by mid-1989 to allow socialism as previously defined to collapse, both inside the Soviet Union and in Eastern Europe; in Eastern Europe "they even gave it a shove."

whatsoever," in a joint statement at the end of Gorbachev's visit to Yugoslavia in March 1988.[38] The same message was implicit in Gorbachev's report to the party conference in June that year. In February 1989, Bogomolov discussed with equanimity the possibility that changes in Hungary might result in a Western-style bourgeois democracy like Austria's or Sweden's, and that Hungary would remain a member of the Pact. He asserted that all the Eastern European countries needed to escape the Stalinist form of socialism, although some of the leaders did not understand that.[39]

It could be said that Gorbachev chose to kill communism in order that a redefined form of socialism should survive and flourish. Not the communism envisaged by Marx and Lenin, but the atrophied communism of Stalin, the stultified, self-serving communism of the party bureaucrats and the inefficient and corrupt apparatchiks. He was therefore unperturbed when the first round of elections in Poland produced a large majority for Solidarity in June 1989, ensuring that the Communist party would lose its ruling position.

Speaking to the Council of Europe early in July, Gorbachev asserted that "respect for each people's sovereign right to choose a social system as it sees fit represents a most important precondition for a normal European process." He noted that countries' social and political orders had changed in the past and might do so again in the future, but that was "exclusively the affair of the people themselves." He stressed that "any interference in internal affairs of whatever kind, any attempts to limit the sovereignty of states, both of friends and allies, no matter whose it is, is impermissible."[40]

He went on to assert that "the philosophy of . . . the all-European home excludes . . . the very possibility of the use of force or the threat of force, above all military—alliance against alliance, *within an alliance,* wherever it might be."[41] Although the words were different, these same

---

38. *Pravda,* March 19, 1988, in *FBIS*-88-054, p. 35.
39. MDS and Budapest Domestic Service, February 8, 1989, in *FBIS*-89-026, pp. 33–34. At a meeting with the Hungarian secretary general in March, Soviet leaders made it clear that Moscow would not interfere with Hungary's plans for multiparty elections (*Pravda,* March 26, 1989, p. 4). In personal correspondence and conversation Jacob Kipp told me that his informants in Hungary (analysts, military specialists, and noncommunist politicians), reported that Moscow endorsed the plans that were formulated in July 1989 to hasten the reform process by opening their frontiers with other Eastern European states and with Austria, an initiative that served as the catalyst for change in East Germany.
40. MTS, July 6, 1989, in *FBIS*-89-129, p. 29.
41. Ibid. Emphasis added.

principles were reiterated in the declaration issued by the PCC of the Warsaw Pact two days later, following its annual meeting.[42]

Shortly thereafter Egor Ligachev noted that the declaration stated that the Soviet Union "must not interfere in the internal affairs" of another member of the Pact.[43] This principle of nonintervention was reaffirmed in the joint statement at the end of Gorbachev's visit to Finland in October; it declared that "there can be no justification for any use of force; whether by one military-political alliance against another, or within such alliances."[44]

There seems little doubt that by 1989 Gorbachev was fully aware of the storm that his policies were brewing in Eastern Europe and was determined to run with that storm, accepting that it would take him into uncharted seas. If he had any doubts, they would have been removed by the Chinese response to the demonstrations in Tiananmen Square during his visit to Beijing at the beginning of June. The sharp deterioration in China's relations with the West would have buttressed his case against those who were resisting the democratization of Eastern Europe.

Thereafter, Moscow appears to have actively abetted the process whereby popular forces removed existing Communist party regimes from power in East Germany, Czechoslovakia, and Bulgaria, the German case being the most blatant.[45] This is not to say that the Soviets foresaw the rapidity with which events would move, particularly in the case of East Germany. But it is certain that Moscow had addressed the possibility of some kind of unified Germany as far back as mid-1987, and the final outcome is likely to have been less of a surprise in the Soviet Union than in the West.

For ten years after World War II, Moscow had sought a neutral unified Germany. Following West Germany's accession to NATO in 1955, Moscow accepted the division as irreversible—however, East Germany did not join the Warsaw Pact until 1964, and even then the size of its

42. This was the first time such principles were incorporated in the PCC's declaration. Furthermore, the wording was significantly more specific and imperative than the routine sentiments included in the communiqués summarizing the 1987 and 1988 proceedings.

43. Ligachev, on Hungarian television, "Panorama," July 17, 1989, cited by Kushin, "Gorbachev's Evolving Attitude," p. 12, note 17. Evgenii Ambartsumov also referred to the Warsaw Pact statement as making "it clear that events such as the invasion of Czechoslovakia and of Afghanistan can never happen again" (Kevin Devlin, "Brezhnev Doctrine Dead: No More Invasions," *Report on the USSR*, vol. 1 [September 29, 1989], p. 15, citing *la Republica* [Rome], August 13–14, 1989).

44. *Pravda*, October 27, 1989, in *FBIS-89-207*, p. 41.

45. Sodaro, *Moscow, Germany and the West*, chap. 10; Dawisha, *Eastern Europe*, chap. 7.

forces was kept proportionally low.[46] With the advent of Gorbachev's "new political thinking," of the concept of a common European home, and of the view that the division of Europe should be overcome, new ways of countering the potential threat of a resurgent and revanchist Germany became feasible. German unity and the modalities of Germany's reincorporation in a restructured European political system were once again an open question.[47]

Military Dislocation and Disruption

Like the Communist party apparatus, the Soviet military establishment was buffeted by perestroika, glasnost, and then democratization, but it was also troubled by problems stemming from the new political thinking about international relations and from the fundamental change in military doctrine that took place in 1987. By mid-1988 the decision-in-principle had been made to cut forces unilaterally; the numbers were announced by Gorbachev in December 1988, despite overt disagreement in military circles over what were seen as unwarranted concessions to the West. Meanwhile, glasnost was exposing military maladministration and some corruption in the armed forces, at the same time that those forces were being called on to provide aid to the civil power in quelling ethnic violence.

The military was, however, better off in psychological terms than the party, for its core role of defending the homeland was not under attack. Its problem was a matter of identifying the appropriate mix between military and political means of providing for the country's security and recognizing that military requirements could be cut by reducing the threat through political accommodation.

Gorbachev and his colleagues did not deny that there had been a significant threat in the past, nor did they claim that the threat had evaporated. In his report to the party conference in June 1988, Gorbachev had asked rhetorically whether the imperialist sources of aggression and wars had really vanished; his reply was emphatic: "No! We are not forgetting the threat to peace from imperialist militarism and we believe that for the moment no guarantees have been provided for the irreversibil-

46. Michael MccGwire, *Military Objectives in Soviet Foreign Policy* (Brookings, 1987), p. 129.
47. Dawisha, *Eastern Europe,* chap. 7.

ity of the positive processes that have begun."[48] Similarly, Eduard
Shevardnadze, having asserted that disarmament was the top priority of
foreign policy, broke off to note: "Here, it is essential to repeat that
in no instance does this replace the need for the greatest possible
strengthening of defense. The peace of the Soviet people should be
thoroughly protected."[49]

Nevertheless, despite this verbal support by the political leadership
and the relatively minor actual (as opposed to projected) cuts in the
allocation of resources to defense procurement, by 1989 the armed
services faced steadily increasing disruption and dislocation. While the
metaphor of a ship running before the storm could be applied to the body
politic as a whole, for the Soviet military the appropriate metaphor was
that of a protracted rearguard action—a withdrawal from well-known
and long-established positions to some new location in totally unfamiliar
territory at some unknown distance to the rear; a withdrawal carried
out in an increasingly unfriendly environment, where the formerly
deferential and supportive populace became ever more disrespectful and
obstructionist; a withdrawal from a situation where military objectives
and strategy were clearly defined, to one where nothing was clear, and
most things would not be decided until some unspecified time in the
future.

Military Requirements

The more straightforward implications for military requirements are
outlined in chapter 8. But requirements are determined by doctrine and
military science, both of which had to undergo fundamental reshaping.
They both cover much the same field, doctrine being fixed at any one
period, while science (*nauka*) is subject to debate and change.

In the Soviet Union, military science is properly understood in its
original sense of knowledge and disciplined inquiry. Among its six main
elements are military art and military structuring (*stroitel'stvo*), the latter
term meaning organizing, building, and developing the armed forces.
Military art comprises strategy, operational art, and tactics, art (*isskus-*

48. MTS, June 28, 1988, in *FBIS*-88-125S; Taku, "19th CPSU Conference," p. 13.
49. Shevardnadze was addressing the conference staged by the Ministry of Foreign Affairs
to discuss the implications of the party conference; *Vestnik ministerstva inostrannykh del
USSR* (*Herald of the Ministry of Foreign Affairs*), no. 15 (August 1988), in *FBIS*-88-184
(annex), p. 13.

tvo) being understood in its original sense of technics or applied knowledge, hence the military craft or craft of war. All this would need to be rethought. But what were the new parameters of analysis?

For forty years military doctrine and science had been primarily concerned with the worst-case contingency of world war, and the Soviet Union had structured and postured its forces to fight such a war. Henceforth the military must plan on the assumption that world war could be averted and prepare instead for lesser contingencies of limited conflict on the Soviet periphery.

In itself this was no mean task, given the length and variety of the Soviet Union's land and sea frontiers and the diversity of countries ranged against them. In the past that task had always been subsumed under the larger problem of world war. Now it was a problem in its own right. But the military had to plan on the basis of an unknowable future, whose parameters were the subject of continuing negotiation and where the nature and level of threat remained uncertain, since the threat depended on policy decisions by the Western powers in general and the United States in particular.

The main political guidelines were that the end product must be unambiguously defensive and that the forces must be no more than "sufficient" to ensure the secure defense of the Soviet Union. These guidelines were adequate when the immediate objective was to remove the offensive overhang facing NATO and Manchuria and to start the process of negotiating mutual force reductions in the European theater and the Far East. But beyond that, how could "sufficiency" be calculated if the nature of the future threat environment was not known? And assuming that a cooperative security regime for Europe would ultimately emerge from the negotiating process, how could security be ensured in the meantime?

In these fluid circumstances, most of established military art was open to challenge, but the debate had to be in terms of hypothetical future scenarios rather than concrete circumstances. History could be used to demonstrate the advantage of the defense or to develop theories about the military effectiveness of nonoffensive means of defense. But how could the need for forces with lead times of five to fifteen years be forecast when the range of possible futures was so great? In the naval field, for example, how could the requirements for maritime defense be calculated, when the scope of the mission depended on whether it would be necessary to protect nuclear-powered ballistic-missile submarines

(SSBNs) and on the nature of the threat from air- and sea-launched cruise missiles (ALCMs and SLCMs), both of which depended on the progress of the strategic arms reductions talks (START)?

It was easy enough for the Soviets to set about dismantling the vast military machine so laboriously restructured in the 1970s and the first half of the 1980s. But exactly when should the process be halted? And how did they arrange for the military machine still to be able to perform its designated function should the need arise at any stage of the dismantling process?

In principle, the final size and shape of the armed forces had been specified in numerous declarations and statements. For nuclear weapons, the stated objective was their elimination, along with chemical weapons and any other weapons of mass destruction. For general-purpose forces, the objective was a level sufficient to ensure a secure defense with greatly reduced forces, while denying the option of a surprise attack or offensive operations in general. These two objectives were to be achieved by the end of the century and preferably sooner.

In practice, both objectives raised major problems. Despite U.S. statements at presidential and secretary of state level supporting the objective of eliminating nuclear weapons, it was clear that the political-military establishment in the United States continued to set great store by large nuclear arsenals, particularly at the strategic level. As for general-purpose forces, even if a counteroffensive capability were ruled out and emphasis placed on nonoffensive means of defense, sufficiency would still depend on the military capability of possible opponents and their potential political alignment. The Soviet Union did not enjoy the U.S. luxury of overwhelming predominance in a hemisphere that was separated from other major powers by thousands of miles of water.

The final size and shape of the general-purpose forces would therefore depend on political decisions about international trends, about the balance between political and military means of ensuring security, about the nature of the threat, and about the level of defense expenditure the economy could sustain. Those political decisions could not be made for at least two or three years, and probably much longer, by when political trends in Europe and the progress in arms control negotiations would be clearer. By then it might be possible to judge whether the United States was likely to subscribe to the new political thinking about international relations; or would it strive to preserve its military superiority and continue to act as the gendarme of the world? Could the irreversibility of the "positive trends," as Gorbachev put it in June 1988, be guaranteed or not?

Professional debate and public discussion would meanwhile proceed unchecked. There would continue to be books and articles on the type of war that remained inherent in the existing inventories of weapons and equipment, which would be affected only marginally by the unilateral force cuts.[50] But there would also be debate about the emerging military order and the best way to provide for Soviet security in the unknown future, an area where the *institutniki* would often find themselves at odds with military professionals.

This future-oriented discussion would cover the full range of subjects, from strategic and operational concepts to the appropriate structure of forces. It would revert to the 1920s debate about the appropriate role of the armed forces and the best way to man them.[51] It would revive consideration of territorial militias and ask whether full-time professional military forces would be more cost effective than conscript forces led by professional officers and senior noncommissioned officers.

While illuminating the range of possible options, this debate was unlikely to be a useful predictor of the final outcome or of the way stations needed to get there. Gorbachev had been reasonably specific on the general shape of the outcome he sought, but the outcome was heavily dependent on cooperation by the West, particularly the United States. To achieve that outcome required a sustained process, and Gorbachev had been prepared to make concessions to start the process and keep it moving. But domestic political considerations as well as the requirements of national security would necessarily impose limits on asymmetrical concessions.

At some stage the Soviet leadership would have to decide whether it was fully realistic to continue pursuing its stated objective, and if not, what lesser objective was feasible and acceptable. At that stage, the

50. For a sampling of this debate see *Soviet Defense News* (Soviet Security Studies Working Group, Massachusetts Institute of Technology, 1989), vol. 1, nos. 1–6; ibid. (1990), vol. 2, no. 1.

51. M. Andrew Hulse, "Time, Technology and Conventional Arms Control: Soviet National Security Policy toward the Next Century" (1989), notes Soviet references to the 1921–25 period as being analogous to the present. In the 1920s the Soviet Union reduced its standing army from 5.5 million to 562,000, approximately 90 percent, over three years. This cadre force of 36 regular divisions remained between 562,000 and 680,000 until late 1937, when Stalin ordered full mobilization and the Soviets began filling out the 84 territorial divisions.

military could be given precise directions. Meanwhile the military had to continue conducting its withdrawal in as good order as could be managed in the difficult circumstances that it faced.[52]

Personnel Problems

Perestroika and glasnost exposed deficiencies throughout the military leadership, man management, operational readiness, and the efficient use of resources. But the process was aimed at solving rather than creating problems and, while disruptive, perestroika generally worked to improve military effectiveness and morale. However, developments in two areas worked to lower morale and to reduce effectiveness, particularly among the officer corps.

The assault on the military officer's self-respect, pride of service, and sense of purpose was especially damaging. The assault, as much implicit as explicit, came from several directions. Core beliefs, such as the threat posed by capitalist imperialism, were now said to have been false. Cherished values like the primacy of the offensive or the pursuit of victory no longer held true. Unilateral force reductions implied that existing strategies had been misconceived. Within government, the General Staff was no longer the only source of professional advice, and it was increasingly bypassed during the policy-formulation stage and only brought in to plan the detailed implementation of agreed policy.

The military was meanwhile subjected to public assault in professional publications and the popular press. This ranged from attacks by academics on the strategic justifications for existing and future requirements, to challenges by journalists on various aspects of military affairs, including the size of the defense budget. Whereas the military previously had had a clear understanding of its role and generally had been held in high regard, it was now continually criticized for old thinking and for its contribution to the country's economic problems.[53]

Public disenchantment with the military was becoming manifest in the increase in draft evasion and the desertion rate. With arms limitations

52. For a useful review of the new Soviet approach to national security and some of its practical long-term implications, see Minister of Defense Dimitriy T. Yazov, "New Model of Security and the Soviet Armed Forces," *Kommunist,* no. 18 (December 1989) in *JPRS*-90-003, pp. 43–50.

53. Criticism included complaints that the officer corps, particularly its senior members, was unduly privileged, and that the military, living in its barracks with its own economy, was divorced from society.

and reductions the number-one priority of foreign policy, the average officer began to wonder what purpose he was serving and to worry about the future of his career.

While these developments tended to undermine morale throughout the officer corps, troop reductions introduced a different kind of problem, with forced retirements at different stages of officers' careers. The initial reduction of 500,000 men—the first stage of an extended process—would affect about 100,000 officers. The main problem was facing an unknown future, after leaving a high-prestige career with good perquisites. But other difficulties included the level of pension entitlement and the arrangements for resettlement, including the question of family accommodation. Family housing posed major problems also for the military units being withdrawn from Eastern Europe but not being disbanded. By February 1990 more than 173,000 families of officers and warrant officers were without accommodation.[54]

Political Concerns

Although the Gorbachev leadership was at pains to applaud the part played by the Soviet armed forces in World War II and to blame a combination of imperialist behavior and Stalin's obsessions for the emergence of the cold war, the conclusion was inescapable: for forty years, Soviet national security had been on the wrong track. Many officers found this hard to stomach, but the military was conditioned to accept political rulings on the nature of the external threat and on the best way of ensuring the security of the Soviet Union. The problems in Eastern Europe were clear for all to see, as were the costs of trying to contain them by military intervention, an option that had effectively lapsed by the mid-1980s. The withdrawal of Soviet forces was therefore accepted as inevitable. However, the fragmentation of the Soviet Union was another matter, particularly because the rise of nationalism could be traced directly to glasnost, to the introduction of democratization, and to the party's weakened authority and loss of centripetal force.

The military leadership had a legitimate interest in the nationalities question. Although the Ministry of Internal Affairs (MVD) and the Committee on State Security (KGB) were nominally responsible for

54. Interview with Army General D. T. Yazov, "Defending the People's Security," *Pravda,* February 23, 1990, in *FBIS*-90-037.

internal security, the armed services had been called on to deal with ethnic violence in Azerbaijan, and they could well be used in the future to prevent illegal secession from the Union. In his criticism of the draft party program in early 1990, the chief of the General Staff noted the absence of any reference to the army's internal function.[55]

The military was also anxious to have the political leadership check "antimilitary propaganda" which, together with the growing sense of ethnicity and nationalism, was an increasing cause of draft evasion and desertion and contributed to the lowering of military morale. Gorbachev, despite glasnost, urged the press to be more constructive and "truthful and respectful" in its attitudes toward the military, and as the prospects of domestic turbulence increased, there were signs that the political leadership was moving to mend its fences with the military establishment.[56]

The military's political concerns were not, however, limited to the political cohesion of the Union, domestic stability, and the status of the armed forces within Soviet society. They extended to doubts as to whether Gorbachev's efforts to reduce the threat by political means were as effective as claimed. A particularly sharp criticism was advanced in February 1990 by Colonel General Boris Gromov, the well-thought-of commander of Soviet forces in Afghanistan who had been promoted and appointed to command the important Kiev military district.

Gromov claimed that despite Soviet unilateral force reductions and other concessions, the United States was "not hurrying to reduce its armed forces, to withdraw its troops from territories of other countries, to liquidate military bases spread around the USSR; [its] fundamental emphasis [was] on the modernization of its conventional weapons." Gromov concluded that the United States still sought strategic superiority over the Soviet Union.[57] This growing concern about the continuing lack of U.S. reciprocity was expressed a month or so later by Marshal Akhromeev and by other Soviet senior officers in conversations with U.S. visitors to Moscow.

55. Mikhail Moiseev, "We Share the Same Task," *KZ*, February 10, 1990, cited by Stephen Foye, "Chief of General Staff Criticizes Draft Party Platform," *Report on the USSR*, vol. 2 (March 2, 1990), p. 1.

56. Foye, "Chief of General Staff," citing *Pravda*, February 13, 1990, pp. 1–2; Alexander Rahr, "Gorbachev Moves to Placate and Forestall Disgruntled Military Establishment," *Report on the USSR*, vol. 2 (March 16, 1990), p. 6.

57. Stephen Foye, "Rumblings in the Soviet Armed Forces," *Report on the USSR*, vol. 2 (March 16, 1990), pp. 1–2, citing *Pod znamenem leninizma* (*Under the Banner of Leninism*), no. 2 (1990), pp. 32–36.

Arms Limitations and Reductions

The negotiations on arms control managed to resist being caught up in the political storm generated by Gorbachev. On taking office in January 1989, the Bush administration had embarked on a protracted interagency strategic review, while the U.S. defense bureaucracy pressed ahead with existing weapons programs and the White House called "for more proof of Gorbachev's good intentions."[58] The weapons programs included the follow-on Lance missile, a newly developed theater nuclear weapon designed to fill the "gap" caused by the elimination of intermediate-range nuclear forces (INF).[59]

Negotiations on Conventional Forces in Europe

Popular resistance to the deployment of the follow-on Lance in West Germany, combined with the approaching NATO fortieth-anniversary summit, forced the White House to short-circuit the review process and put forward constructive proposals for negotiating reductions in conventional forces in Europe (CFE). Until then, NATO's approach had been to take Soviet concessions, which were substantial, as its due entitlement. For example, if the final ceilings were 20,000 tanks, 20,000 artillery pieces, and 30,000 armored combat vehicles, the Warsaw Pact would have to get rid of roughly 39,000 tanks, 30,000 artillery pieces, and 40,000 armored combat vehicles; NATO would only have to eliminate 10,690 tanks, no artillery pieces, and about 16,900 troop carriers.[60] Meanwhile, NATO had insisted that negotiations be limited to ground force weapons, the area where the Pact forces were at an advantage, but had refused to countenance Soviet proposals to agree to negotiate on personnel numbers, or on the reduction of aircraft, an area of NATO advantage.[61]

At the anniversary summit in July, President Bush proposed that NATO should agree to include aircraft in the CFE talks and he accepted

58. Spurgeon M. Keeny, Jr., "When Bush Comes to Shove," *Arms Control Today*, vol. 19 (June–July 1989), p. 2.

59. The 70-mile Lance missile deployed in 1972 would be replaced by a 300-mile missile designed to escape the constraints of the INF Treaty. The United States had made future deployment of this missile into yet another test of alliance cohesion.

60. "Conventional Forces in Europe after CFE," Fact Sheet (Washington, D.C.: Arms Control Association, May 1990). The numbers are based on Warsaw Pact data.

61. Ted Greenwood, "CFE—Taking Aim at Aircraft," *Arms Control Today*, vol. 20 (March 1990), p. 14.

negotiations on personnel numbers. His proposed ceiling of 275,000 on troops stationed outside national borders in Europe would require the withdrawal of 30,000 U.S. troops, a cut of 10 percent, and of 325,000 Soviet troops, a cut of 50 percent.[62] Bush also proposed that agreement on CFE should be reached within six to twelve months and be implemented by 1992 or 1993. Although NATO's subsequent proposals on aircraft excluded carrier aviation and made no allowance for the Soviet Union's particular requirements for air defense,[63] the Soviets accepted the challenge to reach an agreement by the end of 1990. Negotiations began to make progress, with the Soviet Union continuing to make most of the substantive concessions.[64]

The need for unilateral concessions had been accepted by the Soviet military leadership, but its members were concerned about the absence of any indication that the United States and its allies shared the broader political perspective that was shaping Soviet policy. As Gorbachev, Shevardnadze, Akhromeev, and other leaders had made clear, the Soviet Union was moving from a primary reliance on military means of providing for national security to a reliance on political means, a central feature of which would be some form of cooperative security regime.

The immediate problem was how to move from a system of opposing military alliances and heavily armed forces structured for war to a quite different kind of military posture focused on strategic stability, defensive sufficiency, and nonoffensive means of defense. To make rapid progress in this direction required both sides to adopt a cooperative, expanding-sum approach, aimed at realizing mutual benefits rather than at preserving whatever relative advantage was possible. The expanding-sum approach underlay the Soviet Union's unilateral force cuts, the initiative that had gotten the process moving. It also justified the Soviets accepting NATO's proposals for new, equal levels of major ground force weapons, even though the reductions would be twenty to thirty times larger for the Warsaw Pact than for the West.[65]

62. The Soviets were willing to accept a ceiling of 300,000, but only if U.S. allies were included in the ceiling. The British and French together had about 120,000 troops in this category, but they were unwilling to cut their troops. Stanley Resor, "Malta Meeting Charts a New Course for Arms Control," *Arms Control Today,* vol. 19 (December 1989–January 1990), p. 8.

63. Greenwood, "CFE," pp. 15–18.

64. Stanley Resor, "Arms Control in Jackson Hole: Baker/Shevardnadze and Beyond," *Arms Control Today,* vol. 19 (October 1989), p. 12.

65. Jonathan Dean, "Negotiated Force Cuts in Europe: Overtaken by Events?" *Arms Control Today,* vol. 19 (December 1989–January 1990), p. 12.

Developments in the Soviet Union and Eastern Europe since 1987 had been studiously ignored by NATO, which persisted with a zero-sum approach, seeking to put the Soviets at a further disadvantage rather than reach an equitable agreement. The CFE talks were seen as an opportunity to nail down the unexpected concessions offered by the Soviets, not as the precursor to a wide-ranging political-military settlement in Europe. There was, in fact, no agreement among the members of NATO as to what their negotiating objectives were, and the emphasis was on maintaining the status quo ("if it ain't broke, don't fix it") and on the stability of the balance between the alliances, rather than on developing a new form of political structure.[66]

Developments in Eastern Europe during the second half of 1989, culminating in November with the breaching of the Berlin Wall, made this negative approach politically untenable. The surprise mini summit at Malta in December marked a new stage in U.S.-Soviet relations; Bush expressed his support for Gorbachev and perestroika and agreed to accelerate the arms control process, decisions that won broad approval in the United States. Both leaders committed themselves to push their bureaucracies to reach agreement on a CFE treaty, which should be ready in time for a multilateral (twenty-three-nation) summit before the end of 1990.[67]

The impending reunification of Germany was another catalyst for change within NATO and many of the European members of the wartime Grand Alliance had serious reservations about the implications of reunification. The Bush administration, aligning its actions with German aspirations, gained new maneuvering room within the alliance and began to press for a review of NATO strategy. This led to a proposal in early July 1990 that the NATO doctrine of "flexible response," with its reliance on first use of nuclear weapons, be modified. Meanwhile, at the Washington summit in May, Bush had acceded to Gorbachev's urging that the Conference on Security and Cooperation in Europe (CSCE) be used at least as one forum for deliberations on European security.

Strategic Arms Reductions

The long-drawn-out negotiations on reducing strategic arms had come to a halt in 1989 when the Bush administration embarked on the strategic

66. Barry Blechman, "Breaking with Convention: The Start of New European Force Talks," *Arms Control Today,* vol. 19 (April 1989), p. 4.
67. Resor, "Malta Meeting," pp. 6–8.

review that led to a proposal for additional verification measures—a further block to progress.[68] There were strong forces within the U.S. administration that, for a variety of reasons, opposed proceeding with START. There was also a broadly based sentiment that unless the Soviets were prepared to make significant concessions beyond those the Reagan administration had pocketed following Reykjavik, the existing stalemate was in the United States' interest.

As with CFE, the two sides had different negotiating objectives. The Soviet Union sought to reduce the size of the nuclear arsenals, achieving parity at as low a level as possible. The United States sought to retain its effective strategic superiority, the absolute size of the inventories being unimportant. It was symptomatic that during the START negotiations (1982–90) the number of U.S. warheads rose from 11,000 to 13,000.[69] The Soviet priority was on reducing numbers across the board; the U.S. emphasis was on reducing numbers in those areas where the Soviets held an advantage (as in heavy intercontinental ballistic missiles) but allowing maximum numbers in areas where the United States had the edge.[70]

This unproductive process was, however, prised from the hands of the bureaucracy when Secretary of State James A. Baker III met with Foreign Minister Shevardnadze for two days in September 1989 at Jackson Hole, Wyoming. The two leaders of the superpowers furthered that progress when they decided at the Malta summit that all issues of principle should be resolved by the summit scheduled for June, with the final drafting of a treaty to take a few months longer.[71]

Again it was the Soviet Union that made the concessions needed to achieve agreement.[72] At U.S. insistence, SLCMs would be exempt from

68. Paul Warnke, President Carter's chief arms control negotiator, noted that "in arms control, verification is the last resort of scoundrels, who if they can't think of any other reason not to have an agreement, will claim the unverifiability of that agreement" (*Arms Control Today,* vol. 19 [August 1989], p. 7).

69. Similarly, between 1970 and 1975, the height of the SALT negotiations, the number of U.S. strategic warheads rose from about 1,900 to 6,850. In 1970–75 the Soviet inventory rose from about 1,700 to 2,700 and in 1982–90 from 8,794 to just under 11,000.

70. In discussing the disagreement on how to count ALCMs, Richard Burt, the U.S. chief negotiator on START, explained that the Soviets wanted a system that would limit numbers while the United States wanted one that would allow large numbers. "Ambassador Richard Burt on the State of START," *Arms Control Today,* vol. 20 (February 1990), p. 4.

71. "Arms Control in Jackson Hole," p. 9.

72. Paul C. Warnke caught the flavor in his comment that "[Soviet] insistence that a Start treaty be mutually negotiated rather than designed to suit U.S. preferences, should not be construed as intransigence" ("Soviet Intransigence on Arms Control? No, Just Sensible Negotiating," *New York Times,* April 13, 1990, p. A31). In an article justifying the emerging

the long-agreed ceiling of 1,600 strategic nuclear delivery vehicles (SNDVs) and 6,000 warheads, and different counting rules would apply to U.S. and Soviet ALCMs.[73] The projected outcome would require the United States to reduce its arsenal from about 13,000 to 11,000 warheads (to roughly their level in 1982 at the beginning of the START process), leaving it with a potential advantage of about 3,000 warheads.[74]

Enduring Objectives

The Soviets' readiness to make concessions in order to reach agreement on arms limitations and reductions did not imply that they were willing to compromise their long-range policy objectives. Those objectives had been clearly articulated and repeatedly reaffirmed:

- to reduce and ultimately eliminate nuclear weapons;
- to prevent the deployment of strike weapons in space;
- to reduce and restructure conventional forces in Europe so that they would be sufficient only for defense.

The long-range prospect of a cooperative security regime in Europe justified Soviet concessions to set the CFE process in motion. Although the emerging political situation remained unclear, a follow-up conference on conventional forces in Europe would provide the opportunity for negotiating key issues. By that time, Western electoral pressure for compromise by NATO would be stronger. Air defense remained a central concern, and in that context the U.S. refusal to discuss limitations of naval forces was particularly worrisome. In all circumstances, but particularly if the objective of a denuclearized Europe was achieved, U.S. carrier aircraft could have a major influence on a conflict in Europe. The Soviets registered their concern about this issue, but it was something that could be left to a later stage.

---

agreement, Richard Burt highlighted the asymmetrical advantages the United States would enjoy ("START's Misguided Critics," *Washington Post,* June 10, 1990, p. C7).

73. In justifying their proposals, U.S. negotiators made ingenious use of concepts like stability, verifiability, and even fairness. Large numbers of ALCMs were said to be stabilizing; SLCMs could not be verified and must therefore be excluded from the ceiling of 1,600 SNDVs; it was not fair that ALCMs should count as much as a ballistic-missile warhead.

74. R. Jeffrey Smith, *Washington Post,* May 14, 1990, p. A15. The "concessions" involved the withdrawal of a U.S. demand that the Soviets raise the lower range for ALCMs from the 600 kilometers agreed at SALT II to 800 kilometers. In exchange, a new nonnuclear ALCM, intended for use against Soviet air defense, would be exempt from the limits. On this same occasion the United States proposed a new ceiling on mobile land-based missiles that would only affect the Soviet Union.

The Soviets changed their tactics on preventing the arms race from being extended into space, but not their objective. In September 1989 Shevardnadze announced that the Soviet Union would no longer insist that the agreement on START depended on Soviet concern regarding the strategic defense initiative being met. He noted instead the Soviet Union's right to withdraw from the START obligation if the United States failed to comply with the Antiballistic Missile Treaty. Moscow had recognized that its adamant opposition to the SDI and to the reinterpretation of the 1972 ABM Treaty had been counterproductive.

Although the Bush administration persisted with that new interpretation, the chances of an SDI system ever being deployed were steadily diminishing. The effects of a vanishing Soviet threat and pressure to reduce U.S. expenditure on defense were reinforced by a growing consensus that antimissile defenses were not in the U.S. interest. It was increasingly likely that in the next few years the United States would be willing to reaffirm the principles underlying the 1972 treaty in a new version that would establish precisely what kinds of military activity were permissible in space.

The Soviets also adjusted their timetable and intermediate goals regarding the elimination of nuclear weapons. It was recognized that the Western belief in the virtues of nuclear deterrence was too widespread and deeply implanted for the elimination of nuclear weapons to be acceptable in the near future, and minimum deterrence was therefore defined as the intermediate objective. The adoption of this Western concept did not, however, imply that the Soviet leadership had reversed its position that nuclear deterrence was a dangerous concept that could not provide the basis for cooperative security. Rather, minimum deterrence was an interim goal that was capable of attracting widespread Western political support in the radically changed threat environment, support that would persuade the U.S. administration to negotiate the kind of sweeping cuts in strategic nuclear weapons that Gorbachev had been advocating since 1985.

This stepped approach and the persistence of the long-range objective were clearly articulated in December 1989 by the Soviet defense minister, Army General Dmitriy Yazov. Noting that "the creation of a new model of security is not a day's task," he explained the need for "a number of intermediate stages" and spoke of "gradual movement from super-armament to sufficiency, to a democratic, nuclear-free, non-violent world." Yazov acknowledged the past role of strategic parity in preventing war, a war that capitalism would have initiated if it had been left with a nuclear monopoly, but he noted that parity was "like balancing on an edge between war and peace. The higher the level of parity, the more dangerous."[75]

He went on to aver that "reliance on military strength or the threat of its use" led to confrontation, to increased tension and arms racing, and "thus, to the gradual self-elimination of the restraining effect of military strategic parity." Noting "an accelerating slide toward global catastrophe," Yazov asserted that "the threat of destruction which hangs over mankind has made the elimination of weapons of mass destruction . . . not only an urgent task, but also an indispensable condition for survival." He also declared "the literally vital necessity of reducing the parties' military strategic balance to the lowest possible level, completely excluding nuclear and other types of mass annihilation weapons from this balance."[76]

Clearly, the official line was still that nuclear weapons made nuclear war possible; hence they should be eliminated. Minimum deterrence was just an interim objective on the way to achieving that larger goal.

Prospects for the Future

In the five years following Gorbachev's accession to power in March 1985, truly remarkable developments had taken place in the Soviet Union and Eastern Europe. Gorbachev, besides proving to be a consummate politician, had shown himself to be a man of vision and strong beliefs. There were three main strands of his coherent worldview. He showed a genuine and deep-seated concern for mankind, whose survival was most immediately endangered by the possibility of nuclear war. But mankind was also threatened in the longer term by a range of global problems that would require global solutions that would depend on international cooperation.

He had an equally strong concern for the future well-being and status of the Soviet Union, both as the embodiment of historic Russia and as the manifestation of socialism's potential. He also firmly believed that Marx and Lenin had, in their time, provided crucial insights to the nature

75. D. M. Yazov, "New Model of Security," pp. 44–45.
76. Ibid.

of social systems. While their prognosis of capitalist development had turned out to be wrong, and their expectations of the working class were too idealistic, the underlying values that constituted the socialist vision of national and world society remained essential to the welfare of mankind.

Besides vision and belief, Gorbachev had also shown that he was willing to take policy decisions to their logical conclusion, and that in the long term he would not tolerate internal contradictions in those policies. Thus, once he concluded that the energies of the Soviet people would need to be directly engaged if economic perestroika was not to fail, he accepted that the existing command-administrative system would have to go, that full democratization was essential, and that half measures would produce the worst of all worlds.

Similarly, having castigated the United States for its readiness to intervene in the affairs of other states, especially those in its own hemisphere, Gorbachev moved to apply the same principle to the Soviet national security zone, notably Eastern Europe. In doing so, he brought Soviet policy toward Eastern Europe into line with the domestic drive for democratization and with the emphasis in the new political thinking on the supreme virtue of human life and the need for personal development.

Having recognized the increasing interconnectedness of world developments and the need for cooperative solutions, he moved to change Marxist-Leninist theory, which still defined international relations in terms of the class struggle. In the field of national security, having acknowledged that the Soviets in covering the contingency of world war in the 1970s had made the worst-case outcome more likely, Gorbachev took the analysis to its logical conclusion and required the military to cease preparing for world war. And on the basis that it was nuclear weapons that made the catastrophe of nuclear war possible, he pressed for their elimination through negotiations.

In five short years, Gorbachev and his colleagues had brought about a fundamental change in the political structure of the Soviet Union, had introduced a completely new approach to Soviet national security, and had offered a new perception of international relations to the world community. These were remarkable achievements. However, the Soviet economy remained intractable.

The new leadership had been unsuccessful in tapping the unused reserves of productive capacity; instead output had steadily declined. Rather than having a restructured economy up and running by 1990, the

Soviet Union still had to implement major reforms and the central problem of retail prices had to be addressed. It was even in question whether the policies adopted by Gorbachev could possibly succeed in moving from a command-administrative economy to some kind of market socialism.

Meanwhile, democratization and the idea of self-determination, combined with the relaxation of central party control, had brought problems on the periphery of the Soviet-Russian empire, ranging from ethnic violence in Azerbaijan and the Turkic republics lying east of the Caspian Sea to a serious drive for secession in the Baltic republics and in Georgia.

Five years to the day after Gorbachev was elected general secretary of the Soviet Communist party on March 15, 1985, he was elected to the newly created post of president of the Soviet Union. Responsibility for success or failure lay squarely on Gorbachev's shoulders as he embarked on the second five years of leading the country. He had shown amazing political dexterity and continued to hold the middle ground, but it was hard to tell what lay ahead for the Soviet Union.

The unknown factors were to what extent Gorbachev had succeeded in manning the key positions at all levels of the political economy with competent people; whether grass-root ideas and attitudes toward risk and individual enterprise had changed; and whether the political economy was ripe and the leadership ready for the kind of painful measures that would be needed to bring the Soviet Union around to the new tack of market socialism.

Had the window of opportunity been missed? Would output continue to decline and the economy become increasingly fragmented and disorderly, leading to increasing pressure for regional autonomy? Would conditions deteriorate to the extent that the reformers in Moscow would be totally discredited and replaced by a repressive conservative regime that would restore discipline, reassert centralized control, and steadily stifle the democratic process?

CHAPTER 10

Beyond the Cold War

THE CHANGES that have taken place in the Soviet bloc since 1985 caught the world by surprise, and the establishments of the West (political, military, intellectual) have been understandably reluctant to relinquish the certitudes of the cold war. The cold war set the agenda, identified friend and foe, justified military intervention, and generally defined right thinking. However, it also narrowed the West's perspective and foreshortened its policy horizons, to the neglect of broader trends in world developments. Willy-nilly, the West must now shed those restrictive lenses, expand its horizons, and view the mounting problems of the world in their proper context.

To apprehend the future it is necessary to understand the past. One purpose of this book is to clarify the reasons underlying Soviet foreign policy behavior since World War II, particularly in respect to the military element that has loomed so large in Western perceptions and analysis. Another is to describe the course of events and the reasons underlying the fundamental change in Soviet defense and foreign policy that first became evident in 1987.

Past Western behavior also needs to be examined. As the world moves beyond the cold war and looks toward the possibility of a more cooperative world order, two kinds of questions about past Western policies need to be addressed. The relationship between Western policies and change in the Soviet Union needs to be reviewed, and the nature of Western policies themselves and the validity of the assumptions underlying them must be questioned. Those assumptions must be evaluated in their own terms with the benefits of hindsight and without the bias of cold war loyalties.

The findings in this book are of obvious relevance to such a reevaluation. Here, however, the analysis is limited to examining the claim that the tough policies of the first Reagan administration brought about the change in Moscow. This chapter also considers what lies ahead for the Soviet Union, how various possible outcomes could affect the outside world, and the extent to which the favorable changes in Soviet military requirements are reversible.

Did Confrontation Pay Off?

Mikhail Gorbachev came to power in the wake of Ronald Reagan's first administration. Because of this coincidence there is a tendency to impute a causal relationship between Reagan's confrontational policies and the sharp rise in U.S. defense budgets, on the one hand, and the changes in Soviet defense and foreign policy since 1987, on the other.[1] The facts do not support such a relationship. What they do show is a link between the policies of the first Reagan administration and the Soviets' defense and foreign policy reevaluation in 1983–84. But the findings of that reappraisal of policy set the Soviet Union on a course that would have been extremely detrimental to U.S. interests, if Gorbachev had not changed policies in 1987.

The assumption that it was the confrontational policies of the Reagan administration that led to the Gorbachev revolution is not only wrong, it is dangerous. It obscures the fact that Soviet perception of the likelihood of war increased sharply in 1981–84. In itself that was an undesirable state of affairs, but for a variety of reasons, this perception reached a dangerous peak in November 1983, when the Soviets evidently misinterpreted a NATO command-post exercise as indicating that the West was actually preparing for nuclear war.

Meanwhile, the assumption that a confrontational stance is productive panders to a bullying strain in U.S. foreign policy that works against the nation's long-term interests. The implication is that if toughness worked when dealing with the Soviet Union during the first Reagan administration, then it is a recipe for action in the future. If it worked with the Soviets, then it will work with other major powers.

1. This view is not limited to the political right. For a variant, see John Lewis Gaddis, "Hanging Tough Paid Off," *Bulletin of Atomic Scientists,* vol. 45 (January–February 1989), pp. 11–14.

The Reagan Years

The decision to reorient Soviet policy stemmed from a combination of three factors: the bankruptcy of established policies; autonomous new thinking; and concern about the danger of war. To a large extent the failure of established policies, domestic and foreign, can be attributed to deficiencies in the Soviet system and not to Western initiatives. A central problem was the economy's inability to move from extensive to intensive development, which resulted in increasing stagnation. This, combined with the ossification of the party apparatus, corruption in high places, and a general sense of drift, led to growing sociopolitical anomie and a breakdown of work discipline. To be sure, Western containment was a background condition and the arms race imposed a heavy burden, but Soviet economic problems were fundamentally structural. They could not have been solved by rearranging the allocation of resources between defense and the civil economy.

It so happened that during Ronald Reagan's presidency two obstacles to change in the Soviet Union were removed. One was the generation of Soviet citizens who had experienced the fateful events of 1920–60. Its removal by death and disability in 1982–85 resulted in a generational change of leadership. The other obstacle stemmed from the long-standing and perfectly reasonable political-military assumption that world war was inherently possible; the obstacle was the military requirement to cover that contingency. The audacious decision in January 1987 that the Soviet military should develop plans based on the assumption that world war would be prevented by political means signaled the demolition of that obstacle.

That obstacle might have been demolished earlier if the Soviets had not concluded that the danger of world war had increased sharply with the advent of the Reagan administration. The United States showed an explicit disdain for the nuclear arms control process and simultaneously increased its weapons procurement, culminating in the strategic defense initiative announced in March 1983. Furthermore, the first Reagan administration adopted a highly ideological and sharply confrontational policy with its crusade against communism and casual talk of the inevitability of war with the Soviet Union.[2]

It was these U.S. developments that justified the 1983–84 reappraisal of Soviet defense and foreign policy, yielding a series of decisions that

2. See chap. 4.

were unfavorable to Western interests. In other words, the policies of the first Reagan administration did provoke a Soviet reaction, but it was the opposite of what American advocates of a confrontational policy claim it to be. It did prompt a shift in Soviet policy, but the shift was toward greater intransigence, not in the favorable direction that emerged three years later under Gorbachev.

The Soviet Response

In terms of the four images of the United States that competed for dominance in Soviet policymaking circles, the outcome of the 1983–84 reappraisal was a further shift toward the Stalinist image of an unchanging and unchangeable capitalist system. And it represented another setback for those advocating Varga's image of the United States as a more malleable opponent, with whom compromise and cooperation would be feasible (see figure 5-1).

There was a sharp increase in the allocation of resources to defense. Cuts in weapons production in the 1981–85 five-year plan were reversed, and the plan for 1986–90 provided for a rise of about 40 percent in military expenditure, even though national income was projected to increase by only 22 percent.[3] Production of tanks, which had been cut back to 2,000 in 1981 from the annual rate of about 3,000 in 1976–80, was brought back to the higher rate by 1983. Similarly, the annual production of self-propelled field artillery had been increased by 10 percent by the end of the 1981–85 five-year plan. A further increase in tank production was called for in the 1986–90 five-year plan.[4] Meanwhile, the decision to go ahead with the deferred flight-testing of the fifth-generation intermediate-

3. M. Gorbachev's report to the Central Committee Plenum, *Pravda*, December 10, 1989, in *FBIS*-89-236, p. 55. Even after Gorbachev had taken office, military expenditures were planned to increase in 1987–88 by 10 billion rubles (Dmitry T. Yazov, "New Model of Security and the Armed Forces," *Kommunist*, no. 18 [December 1989], in *JPRS*-90-003, p. 47 [see Abbreviations of Frequently Cited Sources]).

4. A graph in *Allocation of Resources in the Soviet Union and China,* Hearings before the Subcommittee on National Security Economics and the Subcommittee on Technology and National Security of the Joint Economic Committee, 101 Cong. 1 sess. (U.S. Government Printing Office, 1990) pt. 14, p. 19, shows the drop and rise in tank production. The actual increase in the annual rate would have been significantly greater in 1986 than the average shown for 1986–90 because military outlays were frozen in 1987–88 and subsequently cut (Yazov, "New Model of Security," p. 47). The increase in tank production above the 1981–85 plan was achieved at the expense of armored combat vehicles, the combined total of tank and ACV production holding steady at about 7,000 a year during the period (against 9,000–9,500 in 1976–80). See U.S. Department of Defense, *Soviet Military Power* (GPO, 1983), p. 80; ibid. (1985), pp. 98, 75; ibid. (1986), p. 113.

range and intercontinental ballistic missiles (IRBMs and ICBMs) appears to have been taken in late 1982 or early 1983.[5] Similarly, anti-surface warship programs that had been curtailed following the 1976–77 decisions were reinstated at this period.[6]

In 1982 the Soviets achieved the capability for continuous photographic surveillance by satellite and in 1983 the capability for continuous detection of ICBM launches. By the end of 1982 there had been a significant increase in the production of military transport aircraft at the expense of civilian production. By the end of 1983 the Chelyabinsk tractor plant was producing tank chassis for the first time since the 1940s, and a second factory had been converted from tractor to tank production. Also by the end of 1983 a new facility for storing nuclear weapons was under construction in the Far East, the first to be built in a decade.[7]

While significant in themselves, these increases represented only the most visible tip of defense investment. In 1984 the U.S. Central Intelligence Agency saw these and other Soviet responses as being driven by U.S. developments—"a building defense budget, new initiatives in continental defense, improvements in force readiness and a potentially massive space defense program."[8] The full scope of the Soviet response to Reagan's policies cannot be known because many of the decisions taken in the first half of the 1980s would have been reversed following the reorientation of defense policy in 1987. One can, however, be certain that the response was substantial.

In terms of foreign policy, Andrei Gromyko summed up the Soviet response in his speech at the United Nations in September 1984 when he noted that the period of détente was something in the past and launched a root-and-branch attack on U.S. policy.[9] The United States remained the most important actor in the international arena, but good

5. Michael MccGwire, *Military Objectives in Soviet Foreign Policy* (Brookings, 1987), p. 499.

6. These renewed naval building programs can be seen as a direct response to the increased threat of carrier air strikes that was implicit in the sharp rise in U.S. appropriations for naval new construction and in the reversal of the mid-1970s decision to reduce carrier battle groups from fifteen to twelve. The threat was made explicit in statements by Reagan's secretary of the navy and by the assertive forward deployment of U.S. attack carriers.

7. An intelligence report itemizing evidence that the Soviets saw an increasing danger of war was leaked to the *Washington Times* in July 1984 and subsequently became more generally available. See Jay Mallin, Sr., *Washington Times,* July 26, 1984, p. A1, and July 27, 1984, p. A1.

8. Ibid., July 27, 1984, p. A17.

9. See A. A. Gromyko speech at the 39th session of the UN General Assembly, TASS, September 27, 1984, in *FBIS*-84-190, pp. CC1–14.

relations with the United States had to be seen as a means to an end (such as arms control) rather than an end in itself. It would not be allowed to constrain Soviet policy in the third world, where the United States was increasingly intolerant of Marxist regimes and ready to use coercive force to get its way. To defend the gains of socialism, the Soviet Union would need to adopt a more assertive policy in the third world and accept the increased chance of Soviet-U.S. military confrontation.

Meanwhile, the sharp rise in tension engineered by the Reagan administration effectively prevented the Soviet leadership from drawing the correct conclusion from the adverse developments in Europe from 1978 to 1983. In the 1970s, the Soviets had restructured their forces to increase the possibility of avoiding the nuclear devastation of the Soviet Union in the event of world war—a war the Soviets absolutely wanted to avoid but could not afford to lose. This restructuring had alarmed the West, raised tension, and contributed to the election of Reagan and his supporters.

If the overriding objective was to avoid world war, and if preparing to fight such a war made it more likely, the obvious response was to cease preparing for that war. Despite being correct in logic—and, as Gorbachev subsequently demonstrated, in terms of practical policy—that conclusion could not even be considered in the threatening political climate of 1983–84, a climate deliberately engendered by the Reagan administration. Instead, the Soviets adopted the palliative of shifting from their politically provocative offensive posture to a more reassuring defensive posture facing NATO, but they continued to prepare for the worst case of world war.

The Soviet reaction to the policies of the first Reagan administration could have been foreseen, for it was the kind of reaction to be expected from any proud and powerful nation. Rather than knuckle under, the Soviets responded in kind. They did not abandon the idea of arms control, but they did go ahead with the flight-testing and deployment of fifth-generation ICBMs and they subsequently reinstated their plan for deployment of the SS-20 IRBM. In the third world they became more assertive in providing military support to protégés and clients, and they probably embarked on developing the capability for naval interposition. Meanwhile they continued to plan for the possibility of world war and added the contingency of major conflict with the United States in the region north of the Persian Gulf.

None of these developments were in the interest of the United States, the West, or the world at large. Yet they were decided by a leadership headed by Yuri Andropov, mentor of the group of enlightened foreign policy specialists who would come to prominence under Gorbachev. If this damaging response to Reagan's policies emerged when Andropov was general secretary, it is not hard to visualize what the Soviet reaction might be to similar policies in less favorable circumstances.

Confrontation Was Counterproductive

Rather than prompting the conciliatory style of Soviet foreign policy that emerged in 1987, the crusading rhetoric and confrontational policies of the first Reagan administration made it impossible for that favorable trend to emerge earlier and could easily have prevented it from emerging at all.

In 1981–82 the Soviet succession was not preordained and there was no certainty that Leonid Brezhnev would be followed by Andropov, or that the latter would survive just long enough to move his followers into key positions. Andropov's nonideological approach to foreign policy was not widely supported in the Politburo, and another general secretary would have brought in people with very different views. But even with Andropov as general secretary it was never certain that Gorbachev would succeed Konstantin Chernenko. And it does seem as if Gorbachev was essential to the emergence at this time of democracy in the Soviet Union and of the new political thinking about international relations.

Reagan is said to have been a lucky president, and never more so than in dealing with the Soviet Union. Gorbachev, who was chosen as general secretary because of his competence as a party apparatchik and economic manager, turned out to be a radical in the field of defense and foreign policy. His ideas about national security, dismissed as propaganda or utopian by the Western political-military establishment, allowed him to break the action-reaction cycle and to spurn the U.S. challenge to a new round in the arms race.

But this was despite the assertive policies of the Reagan administration, not because of them. Gorbachev had made it clear that before he could embark on major arms control initiatives, it was essential for him to meet Reagan, to find out whether the president really believed in his administration's rhetoric and bellicose posturing and whether there was any common ground between the two sides. At the November 1985 summit Gorbachev had found a narrow strip of ground that the two leaders posted with their statement that nuclear war could not be won and must never be fought.

In this particular respect, personal credit must go to Reagan.[10] His sincere revulsion against nuclear weapons prompted him to engage in serious negotiations about limiting them, first at Reykjavik in 1986 and subsequently over the Treaty on Intermediate-Range Nuclear Forces (INF) in 1987. He signed the latter despite public objections by the supreme allied commander Europe (a U.S. general), objections that confirmed the claim by Alexander Haig that the "zero option" proposed in 1981 had been designed to be nonnegotiable.

In the circumstances of 1981–83 the zero option was indeed nonnegotiable, despite the Soviet military being in favor of a nonnuclear European theater. But in 1987, Soviet assumptions about world war had changed and so had the Soviet military requirement for INF. A successful arms control agreement and the elimination of a complete category of nuclear weapons were now the priority objectives. It was these changes that enabled agreement on the INF Treaty, with its asymmetrical numbers, and not the intransigence of the first Reagan administration.

In fact, the effects of American intransigence appear to have been quite different from what was imagined or intended. Members of the administration and their right-wing supporters evoked classic Marxist-Leninist images of capitalism in such caricature that in the new reformist atmosphere of the Soviet Union they could be discounted. Their very extremism reinforced the argument that they were not representative of the United States as a whole. This probably helped engender, and certainly lent plausibility to, the inspired idea of outflanking the most intensely committed anti-Soviet zealots in the United States by denying them their lifeblood—the Soviet military threat.

Confrontation Was Dangerous

Within a few months of the Reagan administration's taking office in January 1981, concern about the imminent danger of world war began to rise in Moscow. It had been hoped that Ronald Reagan, like Richard

10. According to a close adviser, it was Reagan who personally insisted that his speech announcing the strategic defense initiative should promise the elimination of all nuclear weapons (Janne E. Nolan, *Guardians of the Arsenal: The Politics of Nuclear Strategy* [New York: Basic Books, 1989], p. 16).

Nixon, would moderate his rhetoric and his policies once in office, but that did not happen. The active hostility toward the Soviet Union displayed by the first Reagan administration, its call for a crusade against communism, and the persistent emphasis on "relentless Soviet expansionism" that would have to be checked by military force, if necessary, were matched by the sharp increase in U.S. defense spending and the more assertive employment of U.S. forces, particularly the navy.[11]

This behavior was worrying because it represented an acceleration of the anti-Soviet trend that had emerged in 1978 and increased sharply in early 1980, following the invasion of Afghanistan. The election of President Reagan had in large part been a backlash to the post-Vietnam syndrome. It had brought "anti-Soviet elements" and representatives of "U.S. aggressive circles" to positions of influence in Washington, and a president who could speak quite calmly about waging nuclear war in Europe.[12]

President Reagan's remark was particularly disturbing. It fitted the Soviets' belief that the Reagan administration was prepared to incur the political costs of deploying the Euromissiles (and resisted negotiating on intermediate-range nuclear forces) because the Pershing II missiles would allow the United States to engage the Soviets with military force in Europe, without risking the devastation of North America.

While the idea of a deliberate nuclear attack was inherently improbable, U.S. behavior generated enough uncertainty about the intentions of the Reagan administration to justify establishing special measures to provide strategic early warning of plans to attack the Soviet Union. A list of indicators was drawn up, which ranged from long-range preparations like building up emergency blood banks, increasing Western civil defense preparedness, and stockpiling food, to short-range indicators such as troop movements or unusual political and diplomatic activity in the capitals of NATO. At the end of November 1981 this list was sent for action to military and KGB intelligence representatives in the capitals of all NATO members and certain other countries.[13]

11. See last part of chap. 4, particularly notes 78–86.
12. Bernard Gwertzman, *New York Times,* October 18, 1981, p. A1; Richard Halloran, ibid., October 21, 1981, p. A1; Bernard Gwertzman, ibid., October 22, 1981, p. A1.
13. According to Oleg Gordievskiy, a KGB colonel, who began passing information to the British in 1973, the operation was known as RYaN, the Russian acronym for nuclear-missile attack. Gordon Brook-Shepherd, *The Storm Birds: Soviet Postwar Defectors* (Weidenfeld and Nicholson, 1989), pp. 329–31.

American behavior in 1982 was no more reassuring. The substance of the highly classified Defense Guidance that was leaked to the press in May could be seen as supporting the assessment that the United States was preparing for war, if not in the near future, then certainly in the longer term. That conclusion could also be inferred from U.S. strategic weapons programs. In March 1983, Reagan made his "evil empire" speech and two weeks later announced the strategic defense initiative which, among other things, was touted as being able to render the Soviet ICBM force impotent. Earlier that month there had been a press report of a presidential directive declaring that a change in Soviet internal policy was a primary U.S. goal, a report that appeared to be confirmed by the secretary of state's testimony to Congress in June.[14]

March and April also saw a major U.S. exercise in the northwest Pacific. The largest deployment of naval forces in the area since World War II, the three-week exercise involved three carrier battle groups as well as B-52 bombers and other shore-based aircraft. It was explicitly designed to highlight the vulnerability of Soviet military facilities on the exposed Kamchatka Peninsula. Evading Soviet surveillance, one of the carrier battle groups steamed toward the heavily defended Kuriles chain and U.S. navy aircraft flew over one of the islands.[15]

The tension generated by these naval operations would have been a factor in the Soviet decisions that led to the shooting down in September of what turned out to be a Korean airliner that had flown over Kamchatka and Sakhalin and appeared to be heading straight for Vladivostok. Given the circumstances, the Soviets saw the Reagan administration's response to this tragic accident as exaggerated and possibly planned. The incident and its aftermath provided the backdrop to Andropov's "declaration" on September 28th, a statement that had an "electrifying and sobering effect" on the Soviet populace, among at least some of whom it was understood to imply a significant possibility of war with the United States.[16]

Tension continued to rise as the deadline for the deployment of

14. See chap. 4, notes 79–82. See also Seymour M. Hersch, *"The Target Is Destroyed": What Really Happened to Flight 007 and What America Knew About It* (Random House, 1986), p. 16.

15. Hersh, *Target*, pp. 17–18, citing congressional testimony.

16. See chap. 5, notes 5–11. For a discussion of the evidence of sharply increasing Soviet concern about the danger of war, see MccGwire, *Military Objectives*, pp. 294–306.

Euromissiles drew near, with no sign of compromise in the U.S. position. On October 24 the Soviets announced plans to emplace SS-23 missiles with a 500-kilometer range in East Germany and Czechoslovakia if the United States went ahead with the deployment. On October 25 the United States invaded Grenada, roughing up the Soviet ambassador in the process. Meanwhile General Secretary Yuri Andropov was gravely ill with kidney failure, agreement had still to be reached on his successor as general secretary, and the lines of authority in Moscow were blurred.[17]

The deployment of Euromissiles was scheduled for November 23. By coincidence, the Autumn Forge series of annual NATO exercises began on October 31. This included the command-post exercise Able Archer (November 2–11), which was designed to practice NATO procedures for releasing nuclear weapons in the central region.

In response to the improved Soviet capability for a "standing start" offensive, NATO had introduced ways of speeding up the transition to a wartime posture. This included greater autonomy for military commanders to order precautionary measures, and the concern to shorten reaction time had resulted in a wide diffusion of the authority to alert and mobilize forces. Also, NATO had developed the means for carrying out a "rapid, deep and potentially devastating" strike against Soviet forces at the onset of war, to disrupt a Warsaw Pact offensive.[18]

Perhaps because the format of NATO's messages had changed, Soviet intelligence began to have doubts about the true purpose of the Able Archer exercise and to question whether the series were designed to conceal preparations for a premeditated attack, perhaps tied to the deployment of Euromissiles. Details of the Soviet response are not public, but it is known that Moscow called for immediate reports of war indicators from their intelligence agents in foreign capitals, and the Soviet military is said to have responded particularly vigorously on November 8–9 (though in what ways remains unspecified).[19]

Given that the NATO exercise ran its full course, ending on November 11, it seems likely that Western command authorities were not aware of the Soviet reaction at the time. The full implications only became clear

---

17. This draws on the chronology compiled by Robert Windren, NBC Nightly News. Although the attack on barracks in Beirut in which 242 U.S. marines were killed is not directly relevant, it occurred on October 23. See also Dusko Doder, "Soviets Charge U.S. Plane Wounded a Russian at Embassy in Grenada," *Washington Post,* October 29, 1983, p. A13.

18. Paul B. Stares, *Command Performance: The Neglected Dimension of European Security* (Brookings, forthcoming), chap. 1.

19. Brook-Shepherd, *Storm Birds,* p. 330.

as the result of subsequent analysis.[20] If this was an intelligence failure, it was probably a fortunate one. Discussing the change in NATO's nuclear release procedures, Paul Stares concluded that with such "an inflammable mixture, the possibility of inadvertent escalation leading to spontaneous combustion was inherent."[21] There is no knowing what escalatory process might have been triggered if NATO authorities had understood the implications of the Soviet response at the time.[22]

It may have been this incident that caused the Soviets to moderate their internal propaganda about the imminent danger of war.[23] Nevertheless, that propaganda continued to contain the message that the state of U.S.-Soviet relations was comparable to those between Nazi Germany and the USSR in 1941, and that the Soviet Union would not be surprised again.

In the wake of Able Archer and the deployment of Euromissiles that began two weeks later, the Soviets took a series of measures designed to improve their readiness for war. For example, a directive terminating military support for the harvest (primarily transport) was issued in March 1984. In East Germany a major ammunition plant went on three shifts, more than doubling its output. Troops were held back from rotation, strengthening the forces already deployed in the central region. The number of "special forces" in Eastern Europe was increased. Inside the Soviet Union civil defense had a high salience in the media and there was an unprecedented civil defense exercise, when some eight hundred people walked fifty kilometers. On the basis of this and other evidence, the Central Intelligence Agency concluded that the Soviets considered that the danger of war was greater than it had been before the deployment of Pershing II missiles and that the Soviets were probably taking national readiness measures at a deliberate pace.[24]

The Reagan administration was, however, reluctant to accept that the Soviets were really worried about the possibility of war. Nor was it

20. Bruce G. Blair's analysis suggests that the Soviets instituted nuclear alert measures and he suspects that the decision to do so was made by the General Staff (*The Logic of Accidental Nuclear War* [Brookings, forthcoming]).

21. Stares, *Command Performance.*

22. By subsequently adjusting their practices in such exercises, NATO authorities tacitly acknowledged that there had been grounds for misunderstanding. Brook-Shepherd, *Storm Birds,* p. 333.

23. Blair, *The Logic,* suggests that if it was the General Staff that initiated nuclear alert measures, this may have been one reason for the reassignment in September 1984 of then chief of the general staff, Marshal Nikolay Ogarkov.

24. See Jay Mallin, Sr., *Washington Times,* July 27, 1984, p. A12.

willing to concede that its confrontational policies and the resulting increase in the international tension made war more likely. Indeed, it argued that the opposite was true—that the Soviets, recognizing the international arena to be more dangerous, would respond by being more cautious. They would refrain from initiatives that the United States would have had to counter with military force, leading to conflict.[25]

Complementing this view was the contention that because the Soviets had achieved strategic parity, they would be led to embark on military initiatives that would have to be checked by force, resulting in conflict.[26] Deterrence theory, doctrinaire anti-Sovietism, and the lens of Munich led the Reagan administration to assume that war could only come about through some Soviet action that the United States failed to deter. The possibility of inadvertent war was discounted. Confrontational U.S. policies and high tension were seen as enhancing deterrence, and not as making war more likely.[27]

It has been said that the danger of war in U.S. policy lies in the conduct of policy as if there was no danger of war,[28] and this was never more true than during the first Reagan administration. Policymaking circles in Washington remained immune to the palpable concern about the possibility of inadvertent world war, evidenced by a surge in the growth of peace and antiwar movements in Europe, the United States, and elsewhere. Increasingly, this concern estranged those who had counted themselves among the United States' most passionate admirers. Noting the administration's "unworthiness of style and madness of purpose," one such admirer admitted to the "reluctant and terrible conviction that the greatest threat to the peace of humanity is the United States." By coincidence, these remarks by an internationally renowned journalist appeared in the *New York Times* two days after the NATO exercise Able Archer, when the world may have unknowingly approached the brink of inadvertent nuclear war.[29]

25. I heard this argument advanced in all seriousness in 1983 by a senior State Department official at a seminar of specialists on the Soviet Union.

26. See chap. 4, note 78.

27. Members of the Reagan administration were not finally persuaded of the Soviet concern about the imminence of war until they read a report by Oleg Gordievskiy on "Soviet Perceptions of Nuclear Warfare," written after he defected, in mid-1985. Brook-Shepherd, *Storm Birds,* pp. 333–34.

28. The aphorism is said to have originated with Professor Carl Fredreich von Weisecker, physicist, brother of the president of West Germany, and founding member of the International Institute for Strategic Studies. Quoted by Georgiy Arbatov, who was cited by Charles Kiselyak, "Round the Prickly Pear: SALT and Survival," *Orbis,* vol 22 (Winter 1979), p. 833.

29. Jan Morris, *New York Times,* November 13, 1983, p. E21.

Standing Firm

The claim that the democratization of Eastern Europe came about because the West "stood firm" is extraordinarily presumptuous. It is only true in the sense that if the West had succumbed to communism, the change might not have come about. In any other sense, the evidence belies the assertion.

In terms of "standing firm," NATO policy toward the Soviet Union and Eastern Europe did not alter appreciably after the mid-1950s. Before then, the United States talked of "roll back," a dangerous slogan that led to false expectations, notably in Hungary. Thereafter, "standing firm" had had no appreciable effect on Soviet decisions to use force or the threat of force to suppress unrest in Eastern Europe—for example, in 1956 in Hungary, 1968 in Czechoslovakia, or 1981–82 in Poland. Why, therefore, should it suddenly take effect in 1989?

By 1989 there had been a sea change in the Soviet view of Eastern Europe's role in national security. Democratization in Moscow and the policy of nonintervention abroad demanded a new relationship with the countries in the region. And the Soviets judged that the nations of Western Europe would refrain from enlisting the Eastern Europeans in an anti-Soviet bloc. That judgment would have been confirmed in mid-1989 by the evidence that the Bush administration had finally acknowledged the fundamental nature of the rethinking in Moscow and was prepared to support rather than exploit it. It would have been difficult to make such a judgment during the first Reagan administration.

It was these changes that enabled the democratization of Eastern Europe. The democratization was effected by the people in each country. Those who had "stood firm" were the dissidents who had managed to endure and survive despite attempts to eradicate them. In 1989 the West merely watched in amazement, as powerless to influence events (except in a negative way) as it had been in 1956, 1968, and 1981–82.

What Lies Ahead?

There is an array of possible outcomes to the ongoing attempt to restructure the Soviet political economy. Gorbachev may be fully successful, and it is conceivable that the Soviet Union will emerge intact as a powerful nation with a fully developed economy which, if not among the leading two or three, would be a strong competitor in the world economy. It is also conceivable that the attempt will fail utterly, resulting in political and economic disintegration which could lead to various levels of anarchy, brigandage, and perhaps even full-scale civil war.

Many other possibilities lie between these extremes, including a state of repressive stagnation, with similarities to the final century of the Ottoman Empire or to Spain once it started its imperial decline. There is the strong probability that some or all of the ethnically distinct republics that lie on the Soviet periphery and were later accretions to the Russian Empire will break away, either completely or through some constitutional rearrangement. Indeed, this is only to be expected, since the Russian Empire was a fifteenth century coeval of the Spanish, Portuguese, British, French, and Dutch empires, none of which now exist.

The British, French, and Dutch withdrew from empire in the wake of World War II because their subject races had learned from them the principles of national freedom and democracy, and the imperialists had meanwhile lost the will to empire and the readiness to suppress mass dissent with deadly force. Something comparable happened in the Soviet Union during Gorbachev's first five years. If the Soviet withdrawal from empire can be arranged gracefully, there could be benefits all around. It would allow a new and more homogeneous Russian state to emerge, one that could be economically as strong as, and politically stronger than, the sprawling Soviet Union with its eleven nonslavic ethnic republics.

Each outcome would have different implications for the citizens of the Soviet state, ranging from highly beneficial to utterly disastrous. For Western leaders, the crucial question in the 1990s is what these different outcomes would portend for international security and the well-being of their respective countries. What might the different outcomes imply in terms of a military threat to the West?

Many Western defense analysts were initially unwilling to forgo the image of a Soviet threat that had provided their predominant professional focus. Every military concession offered by the Soviet Union was therefore reinterpreted to show how it was really intended to improve the Soviet capability for offensive operations.

Initially such analysts based their arguments on the change in force-to-space ratios, which would make it harder for NATO to defend the central region. It was, however, difficult to sustain this objection once the scale of unilateral cuts and Soviet plans for repositioning forces became known. But it could be argued that there was still no evidence of cuts in Soviet weapons programs. This was true, but their argument ignored the important point that until the Soviets knew the nature of their future requirements, which must depend on the outcome of negotiations with the West, it would be imprudent to make large cuts in weapons production. Moreover, because of procurement lead times, a decision to halt production could take months to years to manifest itself in weapons deliveries, depending on the type of weapon. And Western intelligence could not identify such a change for a further year or two.

The more judicious analysts, who accepted that there would be cuts in forces and weapons production, shifted their concern to the future Soviet military establishment. Some argued that while smaller, Soviet forces would be "leaner and meaner" and inherently more capable than the juggernaut whose sheer mass had so worried NATO for forty years.[30] Others argued that the primary purpose of perestroika was to provide a breathing space. During this *peredyshka* the economy would be brought up to world standards and then the Soviet Union would rearm, using the latest technologies, while the capitalist world continued to nod.

The argument assumed that the Soviets would be able to achieve their economic goals, that they could match the West's onrushing progress in technology, and that the Soviet people would accept the defense burden in the absence of a threat to the homeland. It also presupposed Western inertia in the face of Soviet rearmament. None of those assumptions could be supported by the experience of the previous thirty years.

Strategic Deception

A resolute few among the Western analysts continued to insist that perestroika and the new conciliatory approach to international relations was a massive exercise in strategic deception.[31] And it was, of course,

30. For a rebuttal of this type of argument, see Joshua M. Epstein, *Conventional Force Reductions: A Dynamic Assessment* (Brookings, 1990), pp. 83–84.

31. A letter dated January 22, 1990, from the Security and Intelligence Foundation (Arlington, Virginia) enclosing a reprint of a declassified CIA report on "The Trust," a deception operation mounted in 1921–27, draws attention to the "uncanny resemblance it bears to the current Soviet policies"; the letter suggests "that [the possibility that current Soviet policies are fraudulent] must be considered." It does, however, make the caveat "that it would be a grave error to assume so." For a broad sampling of this kind of thinking, see Brian D. Dailey and Patrick J. Parker, *Soviet Strategic Deception* (Lexington Books for the Hoover Institution Press, 1987).

true that Gorbachev's new political thinking and the way it was propagated bore an uncomfortable resemblance to the "peace offensives" that the Soviet Union had launched over the years.

The most disturbing precedent was the International Economic Conference held at Genoa in 1922, when the Soviets (as today) needed desperately to rebuild and restructure their economy. To further its Genoa objectives of political-military stabilization and the expansion of trade, the Lenin leadership had secretly adopted a duplicitous policy designed to create the impression that it had moderated its revolutionary doctrine.[32]

But ideological fervor was at its height in 1922, whereas in 1990 large tracts of Marxist-Leninist theory have either been reformulated or discarded as outdated. In 1922 the newly formed Soviet state had just emerged from a brutal civil war and it was forced to look for aid from hostile governments that had done their best to prevent that emergence. Dissembling at Genoa was the only way to ensure the survival of the Soviet state; the revolutionary rhetoric was therefore muted, but there was no corresponding change of policy in Moscow. That is the critical distinction. By the end of the 1980s, Soviet policy and behavior were closely aligned with Soviet rhetoric.

However, Gorbachev remains a socialist.[33] He may no longer believe that "for all its unevenness, complexity, and contradictions, mankind's movement toward socialism and communism is inexorable,"[34] but he still sees socialism as "a dynamic and transnational system that is capable of reforming itself." He "wants a socialism which absorbs all the advanced experience of world development, which is based . . . on the achievement of human progress" while "renouncing everything that deformed [it] in the thirties and led it into stagnation in the seventies."[35]

Gorbachev sees socialism as "a system of genuine . . . humanism in which man is really the measure of all things . . . a system with an efficient

32. Franklyn Griffiths, *Genoa plus 51: Changing Soviet Objectives in Europe,* Wellesley Paper 4 (Toronto: Canadian Institute for International Affairs, June 1973), pp. 23–32.

33. In May 1990 Gorbachev reiterated his support of socialism in a speech to the Congress of People's Deputies of the Russian Soviet Federated Socialist Republic, before the election of Boris Yeltsin as president of that congress. He criticized Yeltsin for wanting to separate the RSFSR from socialism. MTS, May 23, 1990, in *FBIS*-90-101, p. 105.

34. The 1986 CPSU Program, as adopted at the 27th PC, *Pravda,* March 7, 1986, in *FBIS*-86-046, supp. 051, p. O8.

35. Karen Dawisha, "Eastern Europe and Perestroika under Gorbachev: Options for the West," 1988, p. 1. See also the Editors, *Mikhail S. Gorbachev: An Intimate Biography* (Time Books, 1988).

and dynamic economy based on the best achievements of scientific-technical progress . . . on various forms of public and private property . . . [where] the working people are the real masters of production and [where] earnings are directly linked with the results of one's labor . . . a system with social justice, combining social guarantees of man's vital requirements . . . with the . . . principle of distribution according to one's work . . . a highly cultured and moral system . . . a society . . . that rejects consumerism, lack of spirituality and cultural primitivism . . . a system of genuine sovereignty of the people in which all working people are guaranteed full opportunity . . . to participate in the management of social processes.''[36]

Similarly, the redefinition of Marxist-Leninist tenets regarding the struggle between the two social systems and the inevitable collapse of capitalism does not mean that the Soviet leadership has revised the unfavorable assessment of U.S. cold war policies that was explicit in its statements during Gorbachev's first two years and implicit in his key appointments. That assessment was based mainly on U.S. behavior. While the Soviets now accept their share of the blame in shaping that behavior, they also know that the larger part of American foreign policy stems from impulses in the domestic polity, and that the coalition of anti-Soviet forces retains considerable influence within U.S. political circles.

The fact that the Soviet leadership still sees the United States as potentially hostile does not, however, mean that the shift in policy in the first half of 1987 was deceitful. Rather, it reflected the judgment that it took two to quarrel and that if the Soviet Union refused to prepare for war with the United States and went out of its way to conciliate it in the third world and over details of arms reductions in Europe, the more reasonable elements would gain influence within the American body politic, thereby improving the prospects for good relations, which had become an end in themselves.

Nor is the Soviet campaign for new political thinking about international relations deceitful. Certainly it is largely propagandistic, but it is propaganda in the Western sense of public diplomacy and not the Goebbellian sense of the ''big lie.'' The Soviets are quite open in their effort to bypass political-military establishments and put their case for rethinking international relations directly to Western electorates and to

36. ''Gorbachev's report to the 19th CPSU Conference,'' MTS, June 28, 1988, in *FBIS*-88-125S, pp. 34–35.

nongovernmental elites throughout the world. Nor do they pretend that this is an exercise in international altruism. From the start Gorbachev held that a tranquil international environment was a necessary adjunct to economic perestroika. He also told the Soviet people that unless they could reverse the adverse economic and social trends that had emerged in the 1970s, the Soviet Union would be sidelined by history and the future of socialism imperiled.

In short, the duplicitous behavior of the Soviets at Genoa in 1922 is of little relevance to the Soviets' current exercise in strategic redefinition. The tumultuous events since 1988 cannot reasonably be seen as part of a long-range communist plan to overthrow capitalism. The rejection of most of the central tenets of Marxist-Leninism, the fall of communist governments throughout Europe, the readiness to forgo the leading role of the Communist party and move to a multiparty system in the Soviet Union, massive unilateral force cuts and the demoralization of the military, political unrest and physical violence in the peripheral ethnic republics, and a move to secession by the Baltic states cannot be made the products of traditional communist ideology by any twist of logic.

Is Russia Innately Expansionist?

For most of the nineteenth century the British, in a glorious example of the pot calling the kettle black, insisted that the Russians were inherently expansionist. After World War II, that accusation was recruited to the cause of inflating the Soviet threat—it was the combination of innate Russian aggressiveness with the Marxist vision of a socialist world that made the Soviet Union so dangerous. This argument gained force after the invasion of Afghanistan in 1979, when the hoary British canard of Russia's historic drive for warm-water ports was resurrected.[37] In the wake of the Korean airliner being shot down in 1983, the Reagan administration made it clear that the problem lay as much with Russia as with communism.[38]

This image of an inherently expansionist Russia, combined with the idea of communist military world domination, prompts fear that somehow the Soviet Union will manage to pose a serious threat to the West during the next decade. But is that image justified? Was Russia's international behavior during the four hundred years that preceded the

37. See chap. 4, note 28.
38. See Vice President Bush's speech in Vienna, cited in chap. 4, note 83.

First World War notably different from that of the other European powers?

The European global expansion based on trade and colonization that would come to dominate the world in the first half of the twentieth century began to gather momentum in the sixteenth century. States bordering the Atlantic expanded overseas, while Russia, hemmed in to the west and south, expanded over land to the east. Russian policy under the tsars was certainly no more expansionist in those four centuries than that of other Western (or westernized) powers, and probably less so.

Russian colonial expansion had largely run its course by 1885, when the "grab for Africa" by the Western Europeans was just getting under way. Russian involvement in China had trailed by more than forty years that of the Western maritime powers, who had engaged in two punitive wars in 1839–42 and 1858–60 in the attempt to force the failing Manchu Empire to open its hinterland to trade and investment. Russian penetration of northern China was halted and reversed in 1905 after war with Japan, while the Western (or westernized) assault on China continued in various forms until 1945.[39]

Meanwhile, Russian behavior toward the inhabitants of the areas it conquered was well within contemporary norms. There was colonization of the northern Caucasus, Bashkira, and isolated points in the Kazakh steppes and parts of Turkestan, but no attempt was made to Russify the local population.[40] Unlike the Portuguese and Spanish (and to a lesser extent the French), the Russians did not consider it their mission to spread Christianity, by force if necessary. Nor did they relocate or effectively eliminate the original inhabitants of the territories they occupied, as did the mainly British settlers in Australia and North America.[41]

In Europe, Russia's frontiers had been largely established by the end of the eighteenth century, by when it had finally pushed back the Swedish and Polish-Lithuanian empires to the west and the Ottoman Empire to the south. The period of the Napoleonic Wars added Bessarabia and the

39. A later development was the Mongols' rebellion against China in 1911–12. The Mongols sought protection from Russia, and were reluctantly provided with arms, and the new state of Outer Mongolia did become a de facto Russian protectorate. Hugh Seton-Watson, *The Russian Empire, 1801–1917* (Oxford University Press, 1967), p. 683.

40. Ibid., pp. 737, 740.

41. It is estimated that before 1600, something like one million Indians lived north of the Rio Grande. In 1783, the newly independent United States had a settler population of little more than three million. Geoffrey Barraclough, ed., *The Times Atlas of World History* (London: Times Books, 1979), pp. 220–21, 236.

Caucasian territories of the Persian Empire and detached Finland from Sweden to become an autonomous grand duchy beholden to the tsar. The war also brought Russia into Europe, with its armies campaigning in northern Italy and finally in France, and at the time of Napoleon's defeat in 1814, Russia was the most powerful continental power.[42]

It is misleading to explain Russian policy in Europe during the nineteenth century in terms of a simple urge to expand, nor does the evidence support such an explanation. In 1828, for instance, having advanced to the border of Turkey, Russia renounced all claims to the conquered lands (Romania and most of Bulgaria), except for the relatively small area between the Russian frontier and the Danube delta, which allowed it to enjoy freedom of navigation on that major waterway. Yet this was at a time when Russia still largely enjoyed the political prestige and military strength it had acquired in defeating Napoleon, and in going to war against Turkey it was fulfilling its treaty commitments to Great Britain and France.[43]

Once Russia had pushed back the borders of encroaching empires, the possession of European territory ceased being an end in itself, as long as influence and security could be achieved by other means. As a grand duchy (1809), Finland was allowed to keep its own laws and institutions, and these were respected by Russia for nearly a century.[44] Reestablishing Poland as a separate kingdom under the tsar (1815) was another, if less successful, example of an alternative to full incorporation into the Russian Empire.

Following Napoleon's defeat in 1814, Russia's interest in Europe went beyond a concern for national influence and security to embrace the idea of a new system of international order and peaceful cooperation that would be embodied in the Holy Alliance. This was the personal conception of Tsar Alexander I, who drafted the text of the compact himself, and it was motivated in part by strong religious convictions. It was also motivated by the fear of revolution, a threat to sovereign rule and a threat to peace, the French revolution being seen as the root cause of the Napoleonic Wars.[45]

42. Ibid., pp. 163, 196, 204.

43. In going to war with Turkey in 1827–28, Russia made the greatest military contribution to the liberation of Orthodox Greece. The terms of the subsequent peace also confirmed the autonomy (under Ottoman suzerainty) of Serbia and the two Romanian principalities. Seton-Watson, *Russian Empire,* pp. 297–302.

44. Ibid., p. 115.

45. Although nominally open to all nations, the Holy (or Triple) Alliance (1820) was formed

All in all, Russian policy in Europe was well within the norms of contemporary great-power behavior. Indeed, when it is compared to the punitive conditions the Germans imposed on the new Soviet state in the Treaty of Brest-Litovsk in 1918 or Great Britain's worldwide gains at the end of World War I, Russian policy in Europe during the previous century was notably nonacquisitive, if not actually benign.

Communist Military Expansionism

If Russia is not inherently expansionist, what then of communism? Marxism-Leninism was always explicit that the capitalist system was destined to fail and would be replaced by world socialism. But it spoke in terms of historical inevitability, of inexorable social forces, not of military conquest. Indeed, once the civil war was behind them, the Soviets consistently refuted the idea that war by itself caused revolution, or that revolution could be exported. Military forces were needed to defend socialist gains against capitalist attempts to reverse them. This requirement was vividly demonstrated by the intervention of counterrevolutionary capitalist forces during 1918–21 and was revalidated many times thereafter. But the idea of communist world military domination was a capitalist bogey and not a Marxist-Leninist concept.

It is true that many of the territories that took the opportunity to secede from the tsarist empire in the wake of the revolution were reincorporated by the Red Army during and after the civil war. But that reflected a mix of greater Russian nationalism and a variant of "socialism in one country"—the whole country, as it had existed for most of the revolutionaries' lives! Another large chunk of the tsarist empire was recovered in 1939 and 1940 when, in collusion with Nazi Germany, the Soviets took over the eastern part of Poland, the Baltic states, and Bessarabia (Moldavia). But war with Germany was seen to be inevitable, the Germans were clearly set on invading Poland, and if the Soviets did not help themselves, the Germans surely would. The Soviets therefore took over the territory to the east of the 1919 Curzon Line, the population of which was largely Byelorussian or Ukrainian.[46] Within twelve months

---

by the three autocratic monarchies, Russia, Prussia, and Austria. Great Britain refused to join and worked through the Quadruple Alliance (1815) or Concert of Europe. Seton-Watson, ibid., pp. 174–76; H. A. L. Fisher, *A History of Europe* (Fontana Library, 1966), vol. 2, pp. 960–62.

46. This line was established in December 1919 by the Allied Supreme Council as the provisional frontier between Russia and Poland on the basis of population distribution.

a similar process was applied to the Baltic states (which had been Russian territory before 1918)—and that extra depth made the fragile difference between failure and success in the later defense of Leningrad.

It was World War II—a war the Soviets did their best to avoid—that brought communism to the countries of Eastern Europe. Three of them, pursuing their separate interests, had been more or less willing allies of the Germans and they suffered the consequences as the Soviets drove the Axis forces to defeat. Romania had served as the southern springboard for Hitler's invasion and had provided some thirty divisions and incurred nearly half a million casualties against the Russians, as it sought to extend its frontier to the River Bugg. Hungary had joined the Axis even earlier, in November 1940, and its troops had fought against Yugoslavia as well as the Soviets, while its transportation system was essential to the supply of both the Balkan and the Russian fronts. And although Bulgaria had not declared war against the Soviet Union nor sent troops to fight there, it had allowed the German navy to use its ports.

Meanwhile, in Yugoslavia, Albania, and Greece, it was the communist partisans who dominated the indigenous resistance movements and were best placed to take over as the Germans withdrew. They did assume power in Albania and Yugoslavia, and might have done so in Greece if British forces had not been used to reinstate the prewar monarchy.[47]

Those who claim that Soviet communism has sought military domination of the world must explain away certain Soviet behavior at the end of World War II. The Soviets withdrew forces that, in the process of driving back the Germans, had advanced about 250 miles into Norway; they withdrew from Finland, Yugoslavia, Czechoslovakia, and the strategically located island of Bornholm in the Baltic; they agreed to four-power control of Berlin, a city captured by the Soviets and well behind their lines; at British request, they made Bulgaria withdraw its army from Thrace and the Aegean coast; and they refused help to the grassroots communist insurgency in Greece.

In the 1950s the Soviet Union relinquished military bases in Porkala, Finland, and in Port Arthur, China; withdrew from Austria; and failed

---

However, in the spring of 1920 Poland and its Ukrainian allies sought to profit from the civil war and seize a large part of Russia. Although the assault was repelled, by the time of the armistice in October 1920, about half of Byelorussia and a substantial part of the Ukraine were behind Polish lines.

47. Stalin had accepted that Greece came within the British sphere of influence in exchange for British recognition that Romania fell within the Soviet sphere.

to occupy Afghanistan, even when the formation of the Central Treaty Organization in 1958 linked Iran and Pakistan in an anti-Soviet alliance, an alliance that could be seen as breaching the Soviet-Iranian treaty of 1921. The failure to act against Afghanistan is particularly telling since it was at this time that the United States and Great Britain intervened militarily in Lebanon and Jordan.

If the Soviets have been seeking military domination of the world, how can the structure and deployment of their forces since World War II be explained? Such an objective would argue for deploying no more forces facing NATO than were necessary to secure the European borders of the Soviet empire. These deployments would be designed to tie down Western military resources while freeing the maximum number of Soviet forces for use elsewhere. Why did the Soviets fail to exploit the advantage of their adjacency to the Persian Gulf area—the weakest part of the U.S. girdle of containment—rather than giving the Southern TVD the lowest priority in men, arms, and equipment? Why did the Soviets not develop a worldwide capability to project force, comparable with that of the U.S. navy and marines? And, having developed a limited naval capability to operate, if not survive in distant waters by the end of the 1960s, why did the Soviets cut back these deployments in the second half of the 1970s?

If the Soviets believed in territorial expansion, why did they not take over Xinjiang in the mid-1960s, while China was embroiled in its cultural revolution? In the late 1960s, with more than half a million Americans tied down in Vietnam, the British committed to withdrawing from east of Suez, but the U.S. tilt to China and the arming of Iran yet to come, why did the Soviets not use their military preponderance to achieve gains in Iran? And if the invasion of Afghanistan in 1979 was an example of planned expansionism, why did the Soviet Union choose to mount the operation in midwinter and only use limited force?

What If Gorbachev Falls?

While Gorbachev has assumed increasing importance as a national leader and while his political adroitness may have been essential to achieving the peaceful revolution in the Soviet leadership, his achievements were only possible because he represented a significant body of influential opinion in the upper reaches of the party and state apparatus, which steadily gained adherents as the revolution took hold. Foreign affairs spokesman Gennady Gerasimov has claimed that a new kind of

Soviet society would have emerged in any case, because "the country was pregnant with [perestroika]," and that if something should happen to Gorbachev, others would take his place and continue the reforms.[48]

Gerasimov's assessment may or may not be valid. But if domestic developments do bring about the downfall of the Gorbachev leadership and its replacement by a more or less reactionary regime, would everything return to where it was in the first half of the 1980s? These are obviously matters of central importance to the citizens of the Soviet Union. But for the world at large, the insistent question is what such a change would imply for Soviet relations with the rest of the world, particularly with the United States and with the countries bordering the Soviet Union, especially China and Europe.

THE EFFECT ON MILITARY REQUIREMENTS. For the rest of the world, the crucial question is what the fall of the Gorbachev leadership would imply in terms of Soviet military policy. Would there be a return to the size, structure, and posture of Soviet forces that existed in the first half of the 1980s? This military capability was a key element of the East-West confrontation, because the West used Soviet military behavior as a metaphor for Soviet foreign policy and global aspirations.

The short answer is no. This categorical response is possible because the size, structure, and posture of Soviet forces in the first half of the 1980s was determined by the objective of "not losing" a world war, should it be inescapable. That same objective had driven requirements in the 1950s, 1960s, and 1970s. Initially the requirement was manageable, if burdensome, representing an updated version of the Soviet Union's capability in World War II. The 1960s saw the addition of nuclear weapons, which immeasurably complicated the battlefield but did not impose an incommensurate burden on the economy. The 1970s strategy was something far more demanding, requiring that theater nuclear capabilities be replicated with conventional weapons and that the military-industrial base be prepared for a long-drawn-out war against an undamaged North America. The 1980s brought emerging technologies and new means of destruction to the battlefield, requiring a defense industry quite different from the one the Soviets had so laboriously built in the postwar period.

Over forty years the scale of Soviet military requirements had increased almost unnoticeably, increment by increment, driven by new

48. Interview on Radio-Television Arts Network, February 26, 1990, in *FBIS*-90-043, p. 24.

technology, changes in threat, and adjustments to strategy, covering a contingency that became steadily less plausible. By the second half of the 1980s the burden had become intolerable. In 1987 the Gorbachev leadership decided to cease covering the contingency of world war and set in motion the process of dismantling the existing force structure and its associated industrial base. Until then, Soviet military capabilities had been justified by the worst case of world war. The new leadership ruled that such a war could and would be prevented by political means. It is inconceivable that a future leader, for *domestic political reasons,* would reverse that decision and reshoulder the burden of preparing for world war.

It is necessary to be clear about exactly what is being said. The contingency of world war had, by the second half of the 1970s, required that the Soviets be able to defeat NATO in Europe using conventional means only, evict U.S. forces from the Continent, and prevent their return. To prevent the return of U.S. forces required an extended defense perimeter and the capability to establish political control over the western half of the Eurasian landmass, the northern parts of Africa, and the Arabian Peninsula. In the eastern half of Eurasia the Soviets needed the conventional capability to deter Chinese involvement and subsequently to seize Manchuria. The Soviet navy had to be prepared for global war against a maritime coalition. And since it was unlikely that the Soviets would be able to avert NATO's resort to nuclear weapons in Europe, they had to prepare for theater nuclear war and also be prepared for the possibility that wartime deterrence would fail, leading to intercontinental escalation.

It is this burden that the Soviets will not reshoulder for domestic political reasons. Nor will they reshoulder the burden of holding down Eastern Europe so that it can serve as a defensive glacis or springboard for a westward offensive in the event of world war. It took political courage in 1987 to assume away the possibility of world war, but Gorbachev will have been proven right if events show that political negotiation can, indeed, dissolve the military threat to Russia.

If, however, negotiations bog down, or the United States persists in trying to preserve overall strategic superiority and insists on deploying strike weapons in space, then Gorbachev would be proven wrong. This would support the case of those in Moscow who argued that the possibility of world war should not be excluded from contingency planning and formulating military requirements. Similarly, if Washington were to act on the assumption that Soviet concessions in the third world were the West's due entitlement, were to refuse to accommodate what the Soviet Union sees as its legitimate interests, and were to adopt the role of world gendarme, using force to promote its interests as it saw fit, this would prove the case of those who argued that the essence of capitalist imperialism was immutable.

There is no combination of personal and domestic factors that could conceivably lead some future Soviet leadership to reshoulder the burden of world war, but certain kinds of Western behavior could do so. It would be particularly unfortunate if, in an emotional response to events inside the Soviet Union—say, the brutal suppression of internal dissent or the use of military force to prevent the secession of a Baltic republic—the United States returned to the confrontational policies of the first Reagan administration. That would surely prove the Soviet hardliners right, and clinch their argument that the United States still believed in negotiating from a position of strength and took conciliation to be a sign of weakness. Like all capitalists, it would be said, U.S. leaders only understand the language of countervailing force.

OTHER EVENTUALITIES. By the end of 1989 it could be asserted with confidence that, no matter what group or individual came to power in Moscow, there was no combination of domestic or personal circumstances that would lead the Soviet Union to reshoulder the burden of being able and ready to fight a world war—the worst-case contingency that shaped military requirements in the 1970s and 1980s. That, however, says nothing about how Moscow might react in the future to problems or opportunities *on its borders* where the use of military force might be appropriate. In such circumstances the nature and world outlook of the Soviet government would be critical. A reactionary regime would be more likely to resort to force than the present leadership, with its remarkably consistent emphasis on nonintervention and primary reliance on political instruments of policy.

However, to conclude that a conservative regime would be likely to place greater value on military power than does the Gorbachev leadership is quite different than claiming that an authoritarian regime would respond to domestic unrest by embarking on foreign adventures. The latter response cannot be shown to be part of recent tsarist or Soviet history. The more relevant example is 1801, when Alexander I made peace abroad in order to turn to reform at home.[49] If the Soviet

49. Seton-Watson, *Russian Empire,* p. 83.

political economy is to start functioning properly, some kind of reform, democratic or authoritarian, will continue to be needed, whatever kind of regime holds power in Moscow.

The notion of foreign adventures omits the crucial element of an external threat to the homeland. It was that threat (and the Nazi application of its racist ideology in the western parts of the Soviet Union) that brought the country together to defeat the Germans in World War II. And it was the external threat implicit in the U.S. strategic nuclear capability and in the rehabilitation of Germany and Japan that was used to justify switching priorities in the late 1940s from reconstruction to rearmament and that provided substance for the increasingly ritualistic mission of "rebuffing imperialist aggression" during the next forty years.

A recent development is the reemergence of Russian slavophile nationalism as a political force. There is evidence of a patriotic backlash against Gorbachev's conciliatory foreign policies and against the intellectual establishment's readiness to blame the Soviet Union for all unfavorable developments since World War II and for much that went wrong in the interwar years. This backlash would be akin to the reaction of the American right to the post-Vietnam syndrome, a backlash that brought the first Reagan administration to power, with its religious fundamentalism and Manichaean view of the world.

In the nineteenth century, a sense of Russian moral superiority and the rejection of the West's subversive culture gave rise to the alternative concept of panslavism. It was an inherently restricted concept and it was fostered by the image of Orthodox Christian coreligionists and fellow Slavs being brutally oppressed by the Muslim Turks. In the last decade of the twentieth century, panslavism would seem to have little potential as a political concept outside the boundaries of the Soviet Union.

Another danger in the short term, which will be removed in a few years, involves the presence of Soviet troops on what was East German soil. These troops did not create a problem when the communist regime fell, or during the subsequent move to reunification. However, the continued presence of Soviet troops on East German soil could become a major political issue that could be played up by the different political parties in Germany and perhaps in certain of the NATO allies.

Yet another question involves the role of the armed forces in dealing with ethnic violence, responding to guerilla war by nationalist groups in, for example, Georgia, and ensuring the continuing cohesion of the Soviet state. There are considerable dangers and difficulties in using conscript forces to provide aid to the civil power, particularly when the unrest has ethnic roots, and there are indications that the internal troops of the Ministry of Internal Affairs (MVD) are being built up for this role, in which they will be supported by KGB border troops and special forces.[50] While the Soviet armed forces may be used in these roles, by the time such internal problems were serious enough to start affecting the size and structure of military requirements, the Soviet Union would be on the brink of political disintegration.

The question of civil war involves a concept that is distinct from conflict that stems from attempts to secede from the Soviet Union, which are really wars of independence. It is true that internal disagreement on the desirability of secession could lead to a form of civil war, as for example in the Ukraine. But civil war implies conflict between different elements of the same society, and at this stage it is difficult to identify core issues (apart from secession) that would justify taking up arms. It is hard to have a war about competence or getting the economy moving. And while there are those who would like to return to the bad old days and reimpose "discipline," this would justify a political coup, but that body of opinion does not have sufficient strength to impose its will by military force, leading to civil war. It is, of course, possible that such a regime might attempt to reintroduce a centralized coercive system gradually. However, with a well-educated citizenry that had been exposed to glasnost and had tasted democracy, this would be much more difficult to achieve than was the case in the 1920s.

Overview

The major and so far mainly peaceable social, political, and economic revolution taking place in the Soviet Union is certainly not a massive exercise in strategic deception, designed to entrap the West.

There is no *historical* reason for supposing that the restructured state that finally emerges from this process of change will have innate expansionist or aggressive tendencies, and the bogey of a communist drive for *military* domination of the world will remain the myth it has always been.

50. Mark Galeotti, "Police and Paramilitaries: Public Order Forces and Resources," *Report on the USSR*, vol. 2 (June 8, 1990), pp. 6–9.

The decision to restructure and democratize the Soviet political system can be seen as a correction rather than an innovation. In terms of political participation and popular representation the Soviets are returning to the dominant trend in Western political development since the second half of the eighteenth century, a trend that communism nominally supported and never disavowed, while reversing it in actual practice.[51]

The Soviet decision to walk away from the cold war is much more momentous. This is not a return to the mainstream of Western international relations practice, which is something the Soviets had always adhered to, despite using a somewhat different frame of analysis. The "new political thinking" that justified the redirection of Soviet defense and foreign policy in 1987 stems from a divergent trend in Western theory that has long existed but began to gain new intellectual substance in the 1960s.

The mainstream of Western international relations theory has been the self-styled "realist school" which reflects the experience of the 1930s, when Germany, Italy, and Japan were set on territorial expansion. This school of thought came to dominate Western policymaking in the wake of World War II, and the divergent trend was seen, by academic and practitioner alike, as of no practical relevance to the Hobbesian world of international politics. Now, however, a superpower has applied the divergent theory in practice and claims that its security and world standing has been significantly enhanced.

The Inevitability of Change

In one sense the changes that have taken place in the Soviet Union and Eastern Europe represent a sudden reversal of policy. In a more important sense they are just the culminating stage of a series of incremental adjustments. As the number of adjustments grew, they effected a change in quality; in some cases, however, there was an abrupt shift, as when an incremental fall in temperature turns water into ice.

That kind of shift occurred in the evolution of the Soviets' doctrinal

---

51. Marx argued that "freedom consists in transforming the state from an organ dominating society into one completely subordinate to it" ("Critique of the Gotha Program," cited by Robin Fox, "Marxism's Obit Is Premature," *Nation*, May 14, 1990, p. 664).

assumption about the likelihood of world war. That doctrine moved from the categorical extreme of "inevitable" in the first half of the 1950s, through the broad middle ground of "possible" during the 1960s, 1970s, and early 1980s, into the other extreme of "not possible" in the second half of the 1980s. It was, however, the cumulative process that applied to the relentless advance of military technology, which made warfare so complex and so devastating that it verged on the impossible and ultimately the absurd.

The cumulative process also applied to the Soviet theory of international relations, where the mounting evidence that Marxism-Leninism did not work in the developing world was reinforced by the failure of the concept of competing global economic systems. In the world at large the correlation of forces turned against the Soviet Union in the first half of the 1970s, the adverse effects being exaggerated because Moscow badly misjudged the trend. Mounting economic problems provided a backdrop to all else: a stagnant domestic economy; an increasing defense burden; and the rising costs of third world commitments.

The one true reversal of doctrine concerned the dominant image of the United States. Whereas the trend had been toward the Stalinist image of an unchangeable United States, a trend that was accentuated in 1983–84, in 1987 it was reversed sharply and Varga's image of a malleable United States became dominant (see figure 5-1). Adopting that image in the wake of the Reykjavik summit required an act of faith—faith that, appearances to the contrary, the military-industrial complex and "aggressive circles" did not have a stranglehold on the U.S. political process, and faith that a conciliatory Soviet policy would not be taken for weakness but would allow the "more sober" elements to gain ascendancy in Washington.

In respect to Soviet foreign policy, these trends and changes all tended in the same direction and could be justified in socialist terms. Similarly, the emergence of a globalist view could be seen as an extension of communism's universalist ideas about mankind, and concern about world poverty and illiteracy as a variant of the focus on the working class. The catalyst for change was the decision to democratize and its corollary, the assumption of "no world war." The effect was to turn Gorbachev's new political thinking about international relations from a set of worthy aspirations into a framework for Soviet foreign policy in the nuclear age.

The Implications for Europe

For forty years the Soviet Union posed the threat of military invasion in Western Europe. The threat was one of capabilities, reflecting the requirement that Soviet forces be able to defeat NATO in Europe and evict U.S. forces from the Continent, should world war prove inescapable. However, in December 1988, Gorbachev announced unilateral force cuts of 500,000 troops, 240,000 of them in the European theater. At the subsequent negotiations on reductions of conventional forces the Soviets accepted further asymmetrical cuts which, when implemented, would have the effect of lifting the capabilities threat to Western Europe. During 1989, Moscow withdrew its support from the communist regimes of Eastern Europe; by the end of the year all of those regimes had either been replaced or been remodeled, and early in 1990 it became clear that Germany would be reunified.

The political and military disintegration of the Warsaw Pact, and the inevitable demoralization of Soviet forces stationed in Eastern Europe, meant that by mid-1990 (if not much earlier) the capabilities threat to Western Europe had, for all practical purposes, dissolved.

In the short to medium term, the process of disintegration is irreversible. Soviet forces had entered Eastern Europe in 1944–45 in the course of defeating Germany, and in many countries they were welcomed as liberators. It was their military presence that had allowed the Soviets to establish political hegemony in particularly favorable circumstances, not least because their system could be seen to have prevailed in the crucial test of war. To reimpose that hegemony in the 1990s would require the Soviet Union to go to war with the states of Eastern Europe, invading and occupying those countries whose people would now be active enemies rather than nominal allies. Although the Soviet Union will continue to possess the military wherewithall to wage such a war for some time to come, the military-political will and the domestic support for such a war will be totally lacking unless some clearly defined and major threat should emerge in Eastern Europe.

In the long term, it is most unlikely that a regime might emerge in Moscow that had autonomous territorial ambitions, given the experience of the last two hundred years. Soviet forces could, however, be drawn back into Eastern Europe in the event of internal or interstate conflict in the region. In those circumstances (and assuming the absence of unilateral Western intervention), Soviet forces might become involved in resolving the conflict, in peacekeeping, or in reestablishing political order. Or, in a revised version of the 1930s, an Eastern European state might call on Soviet support against a resurgent Germany. Or should the threat of a world war emerge, the Soviet Union might find itself on the opposite side from the United States and the Western Europeans.

Soviet perceptions of the threat of world war will continue to be directly related to U.S. behavior. Thus the threat would resurface if, for whatever reason, the United States were to deny the legitimacy of the Soviet state and to seek to undermine it; if the United States were to embark on arms racing as a way of impoverishing the Soviet Union while reinforcing U.S. military superiority; and if the United States were to seek to emplace strike weapons in space, weapons that would nominally be for defensive purposes but would, in practice, provide the key to a U.S. first-strike capability while posing a continuous threat to the Soviet Union of instantaneous political decapitation.

Those possibilities are not fanciful, since they are what the first Reagan administration sought to do. The reemergence of a U.S. policy designed to threaten the Soviet Union would prove that those who resisted Gorbachev's policies in the 1980s had been right all along. It would confirm that the United States mistook conciliation for weakness and that the security of the Soviet Union could not be entrusted primarily to political means. Whether it was a manifestation of capitalism or imperialism, the United States had not changed, world war continued to be a live possibility, and it must therefore be prepared for.

In other words, the future threat environment and the role of the Soviet Union in that environment will depend in large measure on Western policies in general and U.S. policies in particular. This is not just a question of avoiding emotional responses to unfolding world events. One of the lessons of the last forty-five years is the pernicious effect of worst-case analysis. To a significant extent, both sides generated real threats, each to its *own* security, by focusing on hypothetical worst-case contingencies and responding in kind.

Looking to the Future

The Soviet Union has learned a lesson, jettisoned worst-case analysis, and made the audacious decision to base its military requirements on the assumption that world war will be prevented by political means. But it has gone beyond that to argue that in the nuclear age there can be no such thing as national security, only international security, a mutual or cooperative regime where the security of other nations is as important to each nation as its own sense of national security.

The Soviets have extended this cooperative approach to international relations in general, where the emphasis is on interdependence and the need to move away from the concept of a balance of power toward a balance of interests. Whereas Marxist-Leninist theory had been premised on a zero-sum view of the world, where capitalism's gain would be socialism's loss, the new political thinking advocates an expanding-sum approach where both sides would gain through compromise and cooperation.

Cooperative Security in Europe

There is little evidence that the political-military establishments of the West are intellectually prepared for the major adjustment in attitudes that will be needed for them to join in such a cooperative approach. Meanwhile, it is not clear how much longer the Soviets will be able to make unilateral or asymmetrical concessions before internal opposition to this one-sided situation becomes too strong for the Gorbachev leadership to resist.[52] To some extent this imbalance applies to the negotiations over strategic nuclear weapons, but it is in the negotiations on conventional force reductions in Europe (CFE) that Western attitudes lag most obviously behind changing realities.

One of the three main reasons for this potentially dangerous lag is the belief that economic duress is driving Soviet forces cuts, so NATO has nothing to do but sit back and wait. Another is the assumption that the cold war and the military confrontation in Europe was entirely the fault of the Soviet Union, rather than the outcome of complex international and domestic circumstances in the 1944–47 period, where neither side can be entirely absolved or blamed for the outcome, and where each side inadvertently succeeded in fulfilling the other's dire prophecies.[53] Believing right to have been entirely on its side, the West considers

52. Army General Albert Makashov caught the mood of the opposition in his address to the founding congress of the Russian Communist party. He noted that "Germany is reuniting and will probably become a member of NATO, Japan is becoming the decisive force in the Pacific. Only our wise peacocks are crowing that no one is going to attack us." David Remnick, *Washington Post,* June 20, 1990, p. A31.

53. See Michael MccGwire, "The Genesis of Soviet Threat Perceptions" (Brookings, 1988).

unilateral Soviet concessions to be its due entitlement. This belief has been reinforced by the idea that NATO has in some way "won" the cold war, and that such concessions represent the fruits of victory.

The third and most damaging reason is that NATO has been unable to make the conceptual about-face required to deal with radically changed circumstances. Its approach to negotiations is still zero sum, the objective being to improve NATO's military standing relative to the Warsaw Pact, rather than the expanding-sum objective of devising a way of safely dismantling the opposing military structures and replacing them with some kind of cooperative security regime. Through mid-1989, Western commitment to arms negotiations remained half-hearted, and participation was seen more as an aspect of alliance management than a means of changing the nature of the confrontation in Europe. The tendency was to pocket Soviet concessions and then press for more while resisting Soviet proposals that NATO make comparable asymmetrical reductions or that aircraft be included in the negotiations, an area where NATO held the advantage. Meanwhile, the primary preoccupation of NATO's political-military establishments was how to compensate for the unforeseen outcome of the INF negotiations and how to ensure that NATO's force modernization plans were not set back.

By the end of 1989, events in Europe had convinced the Bush administration that fundamental change was indeed afoot in the Soviet bloc. This did not, however, change the U.S. approach to the CFE negotiations—the objective was still to extract the maximum concessions from the Soviets while holding firm to positions that benefited NATO unilaterally. Aircraft had been included in the negotiations, but that was an unintended concession, the price for West German agreement to NATO plans for nuclear modernization. Not until the summit in May 1990 did the United States show any willingness to acknowledge Soviet concerns about moving promptly on the question of developing a mutual security regime to replace the existing structure of opposing alliances. And yet it was the prospect of such a regime, reaching from the Atlantic to the Urals, that had justified the political decision by the Soviet Union to make sweeping concessions in order to enable mutual force reductions in Europe.

The West has yet to acknowledge formally that such a regime is in the interests of everyone, and not just the Soviet Union. It has yet to move the creation of such a regime to the top of its political agenda. And it has yet to recognize that the assumptions underlying a cooperative security regime are the antithesis of those underlying NATO, and that a choice has to be made.

It was understandable that the West should have hesitated before accepting the unexpected developments and accompanying Soviet statements at face value. But NATO now is like a man trying to cross a river by stepping stone—at some stage he must change his weight from his back foot to his front foot; otherwise he will fall in. Similarly in Europe, if the West wants to move to a new type of politico-legal regime, it must explicitly forgo the assumptions around which NATO and its central doctrine of deterrence are structured. It must shift its concern from enhancing NATO's deterrent capability to dismantling and reshaping the existing military structures so as to provide for cooperative security in Europe. The West cannot have it both ways. The reluctance to relinquish the security blanket of NATO for the untried benefits of a cooperative security regime is understandable, but the question "*Who is NATO now deterring from doing what*?" has yet to be addressed.

Europe has been presented with an opportunity to resolve a problem it has been trying to deal with for one hundred seventy-five years. The challenge is to devise a politico-legal structure that will allow the quarrelsome races in Europe to live peaceably together.[54] In the past, in the wake of major war, the victors imposed a new order on the vanquished. This time the mold has been broken peaceably and forums such as the Conference on Security and Cooperation in Europe are already in place. During the enforced division of Europe, states within each of the opposing blocs learned to live in peace and in several cases traditional enmities were muted and may have largely evaporated. The political maturation during that period, particularly among the states of the Soviet bloc, make resolving the problem of Europe a better possibility than it has ever been.

The Causes and Risks of War

Not only in respect to Europe but in international relations in general, "old thinking" characterizes the Western approach to security. In this broader arena, the political-military establishments of NATO do not just face the Gorbachev leadership. Rather, they are pitted against an unusual

---

54. It is important to make the distinction between Europe as a geostrategic region that extends from the Atlantic to the Urals and Europe as a geopolitical concept, which excludes the Soviet Union.

alliance between the new thinkers in Moscow and like-minded people around the world, including important Western elites and some political parties.

As Gorbachev has stressed, there is nothing particularly original about the new political thinking, which draws on a well-established body of Western thought whose principles underlie the Charter of the United Nations. What is unusual is that a great power has chosen to base its policies on those principles, demonstrating in the process that its own security and the security of others have been thereby increased.

The radical change in the climate of international relations between the first and second halves of the 1980s is obvious to all. What has still to be grasped is the extent to which Gorbachev's new political thinking diverges from the established way of thinking in the West, particularly in respect to questions of peace and war. The two sides differ fundamentally on the causes and risks of war and on the merits and dangers of deterrence doctrine and of large inventories of nuclear weapons.

These differences existed long before Gorbachev came to power, reflecting the very different historical experiences of the two superpowers and their very different geostrategic circumstances. It was, however, the new political thinking that brought this fundamental divergence into focus. Gorbachev argues that the new realities of the nuclear age demand new thinking about international relations. The U.S. establishment does not admit these new realities. Nor does it share the Soviet concern about the danger of arms racing or Gorbachev's conviction that to deliberately teeter on the brink of the nuclear abyss is an invitation to disaster.

The disagreement is as fundamental as is the disagreement about handguns in America. The pro-gun lobby argues that it is not guns that kill people, but people that kill people. The gun-control lobby argues that it is guns that kill people and that if guns were not easily available, fewer people would be killed. Along the same lines, Gorbachev argues that it is the existence of nuclear weapons that makes nuclear war possible and he urges their elimination.[55] The United States insists that

55. For a discussion of this issue that focuses on the European theater, see Alexei A. Vasiliev, "Nuclear Weapons and the Reduction of Conventional Weapons," in Robert D. Blackwill and F. Stephen Larrabee, eds., *Conventional Arms Control and East-West Security* (Duke University Press, 1989), pp. 442–60. The late Vasiliev, who wrote the chapter in 1988–89, was head of the Political-Military Department of the Institute for the Study of the United States and Canada and was subsequently appointed to the six-member Soviet delegation to the CFE talks in Vienna. For a critique of nuclear deterrence, see V. Dmitriev and Colonel V. Strebkov, "Outdated Concept" and "From the Strategy of Deterrence to Strategic Stability," *KZ*, April 10 and June 5, 1990, in *FBIS*-90-074, pp. 1–2, and *FBIS*-90-110, pp. 2–3.

nuclear weapons actually prevent nuclear war.[56] It is joined in this opinion by the political-military establishments of NATO and by most Western defense intellectuals.

Gorbachev acknowledges that it will not be easy to cast aside ways of thinking that have endured for centuries, even millennia. Nevertheless, he insists that the age-old adage "if you seek peace, prepare for war" does not hold true in the nuclear age. To avoid world war, one must cease preparing to wage it, and that implies massive cuts in nuclear inventories and the ultimate elimination of nuclear weapons. The Soviets are not claiming that this solution is a panacea or that the elimination of nuclear weapons can be accomplished easily. Rather, they see a choice between two hazardous policies, only one of which offers the possibility of a satisfactory outcome.

In the Soviets' view, deterrence policies point toward ultimate disaster. They consider that deterrence theory has been largely responsible for the nuclear arms race and explains why strategic inventories have risen steadily during twenty years of negotiations that were nominally aimed at limitations and reductions. In the European theater it is, in effect, an "obstacle to the shift from confrontation to cooperation."[57] The theory justifies other nations seeking to acquire a nuclear capability, and the process of proliferation thus steadily gathers momentum. The chance of nuclear weapons being used accidentally or deliberately increases exponentially. Nor is it clear how one or both superpowers would use their nuclear predominance to preserve peace and order in such a world.

The alternative to deterrence is to develop some kind of politico-legal regime based on the elimination of nuclear weapons and the prohibition of their production. What such a regime would involve is not clear, but the Soviets see the move toward banning chemical weapons as a pilot for the more difficult endeavor, since the same kinds of problems are

56. There having been no world war, it is claimed that it was nuclear deterrence that kept the peace for forty years. That assertion rests on the assumptions that world war could only come about through some Soviet action that the United States failed to deter; that the Soviets had an urge to territorial expansion and were set on taking over Western Europe by military force; and that given a strong Soviet urge to aggression, nothing less than the threat of devastating the Soviet Union with nuclear weapons would have deterred them from invading Western Europe. None of these assumptions stands up to analysis. See Michael MccGwire, "Deterrence: The Problem, Not the Solution," in Roman Kolkowicz, ed., *Dilemmas of Nuclear Strategy* (Frank Cass, 1987), pp. 24–32.

57. Vasiliev notes that the doctrine of deterrence "forc[es] us to cling to these weapons, to worry about their buildup and modernization" ("Nuclear Weapons," p. 446).

involved.[58] Central to any such regime would be the prior obligation of the superpowers to observe its terms. The Soviets have stressed that "the democratization of international relations" is a necessary prerequisite for universal security.[59] As Shevardnadze noted when addressing the UN General Assembly, "If the term 'great power' is to be retained at all, it is only in the sense of great responsibility to the rest of the world."[60]

Such a regime would be part of the broader comprehensive security system that the Soviet Union has been promoting through the United Nations, whose role it wishes to enhance so that it can become a "unique global center for ensuring universal and regional security and the security of each country." International law would need to be developed to underpin such a comprehensive system, and the thrust of such a program could be expressed in the motto "security, trust and cooperation through law."[61]

Realism and Idealism

These are important proposals with very wide political appeal. Yet they are dismissed as utopian by Western leaders, particularly those in the United States and Great Britain who belittle statements of principle and pride themselves on pragmatism. The tendency has been to treat the proposals as a propaganda ploy rather than a serious attempt to address the realities of the nuclear age.

Gorbachev's new political thinking is, however, firmly anchored in a well-established body of Western international relations theory. This divergent trend in theory emerged in the second half of the nineteenth century, when circumstances were not ripe for the ideas being put forward and the concepts were characterized as utopian. But as Aleksandr Bovin put it, utopia is merely history waiting to be written, and the failure of these concepts in the 1930s can be blamed on prematurity rather than impracticality.

Since World War II these "utopian" concepts have steadily taken concrete form. One expression of these concepts is the European Economic Community, which brings long-standing enemies like Great

58. Ibid., p. 457.
59. Eduard Shevardnadze in Denmark, *Pravda,* September 22, 1988, in *FBIS*-88-185, p. 37.
60. *Pravda,* November 28, 1988, in *FBIS*-88-188, p. 6.
61. Ibid., pp. 3, 5.

Britain, France, and Germany together in a supernational organization to which the member states are progressively conceding sovereign powers. Another is the continually growing family of organizations, institutions, and initiatives that come under the general umbrella of the United Nations. They have gradually gained legitimacy and influence, despite the United Nations Organization being used as an arena for the East-West struggle, with each side seeking to manipulate the UN for its own purposes and prevent the other from achieving its ends. It is not the failures that are surprising but the accumulating record of success, including successes in peacekeeping and conflict resolution.

And it was surely utopian to have expected that 172 state entities, negotiating for thirteen years, could produce a completely new legal regime covering the use of the sea and its resources. Yet such a treaty was indeed negotiated, with both the United States and the Soviet Union playing major parts in the successful outcome. In December 1982, 119 states signed the UN Convention on the Law of the Sea, and all but 15 of the remaining 53 states signed within two years.[62] The Law of the Sea negotiations were, however, routine compared to the developments in the Soviet Union and Eastern Europe since 1987, developments that would have been dismissed as wishful thinking if postulated in 1985. Not least among these developments was the reversal of Soviet policy toward the United Nations; that organization may be able to achieve its potential as it ceases to be an arena for superpower rivalry and intersystem competition.

There remains, however, a fundamental divergence of opinion on the nature of international relations that starts from a basic disagreement on the realities of the nuclear age and extends to questions concerning the risk of war, the role of military force, and the danger inherent in nuclear

62. Three major powers—the United States, Great Britain, and the Federal Republic of Germany—did not sign the treaty; the twelve other states ranged from Tonga and the Holy See to Turkey and Syria. The U.S. refusal to sign was offically related to dissatisfaction with the international regime for the management of deepsea minerals but reflected deep concern about constraints on freedom of action. It was largely ideological reasons that led the Reagan administration to repudiate the work of its four predecessors, and to persuade Great Britain and West Germany to refuse to sign the treaty. The abstention of these three industrialized nations did not, however, invalidate the treaty-making process. The convention, which enters into force twelve months after 60 states have ratified their signatures, had 43 ratifications by May 1990. (For comparison, it was eleven years before the Vienna Convention on the Law of Treaties [1969] entered into force.) Most of the provisions of the Law of the Sea treaty (320 articles and nine annexes) are being observed and tested as customary law. John King Gamble, Jr., "Status of the 1982 Convention on the Law of the Sea," *Marine Policy Reports* (University of Delaware, Center for the Study of Marine Policy), July 1988, pp. 1–5.

weapons. This disagreement goes well beyond the opposing viewpoints implied by the words "realist" and "utopian" or "idealist." To the extent those labels are used to distinguish between the established Western approach to international relations and the divergent trend that is now reflected in the new political thinking, the labels are seriously misleading.

In describing the opposing schools of thought in the late 1930s, E. H. Carr identifies realism with political practice and professionals and idealism with theory and intellectuals.[63] It is, however, the doctrine of nuclear deterrence—the concept that lies at the heart of Western thinking about security—that is the highly theoretical construct, a doctrine devised by academics and intellectuals. It is based on abstractions such as game theory and "strategic man," and scant attention was paid to the practical realities of Soviet capabilities and intentions in the 1948–53 period. It was the theoretical ramifications of deterrence doctrine that were used to rationalize the strenuous U.S. resistance to reducing the strategic nuclear arsenals to 6,000 warheads apiece in the second half of the 1980s.[64] Meanwhile, it was the "utopian" ideas about a European community and United Nations peacekeeping that were advocated and then implemented by hardheaded professionals and their political masters.

It was theory that extended the logic of the realist approach to embrace the idea of basing Western security on the threat of nuclear devastation[65] and fostered the belief that increased tension did not increase the risk of war. It was, however, empirical evidence that convinced the Soviet Union that in seeking to improve its chances of not losing a world war, it had in fact made war more likely, leading to the "utopian" reversal of Soviet military policy and the withdrawal from Eastern Europe.

63. *The Twenty Years' Crisis: 1919–1939* (London: Macmillan, 1939), pp. 11–21.

64. John D. Steinbruner has estimated that roughly 75 percent of the industrial capability and a comparable proportion of the military infrastructure in either the United States or the Soviet Union could be effectively destroyed with 2,000 nuclear warheads, and such a retaliatory strike could be guaranteed by an initial inventory of 3,000 warheads apiece ("Revolution in Foreign Policy," in Henry J. Aaron, ed., *Setting National Priorities: Policy for the Nineties* [Brookings, 1990], p. 79). In May 1990 roughly 13,000 U.S. warheads and 11,000 Soviet warheads were deployed.

65. Hans J. Morgenthau argued that international politics was about "interests defined as power" and that nations sought to maximize power as a way of protecting and promoting their interests. Since he believed that politics were governed by objective laws that have their roots in human nature, the implication of his argument was that nations *ought* to seek to maximize their power (*Politics Among Nations*, 5th ed. [Knopf, 1973], pp. 4–5). His magisterial textbook (1st ed. [Knopf, 1948]) shaped the minds of generations of scholars and practitioners in the United States.

Western thinking is still firmly grounded in the thought processes of the 1948–53 period and, having "won" the cold war, the United States shows little inclination to review the past and reevaluate its policies in broader terms. When it does (and the sooner the better), it will need to guard against the stereotyping of these outdated labels.

The difference between the idealist and the realist does not lie simply in the difference between optimism and pessimism, but in their time horizons. The realist is a short-term pessimist who plans for the worst case; but he is implicitly a long-term optimist who assumes that if today's problems can be dealt with, the future will look after itself. The idealist is a short-term optimist who thinks that today's problems are manageable; but he is also a long-term pessimist, who doubts that the future will look after itself and is convinced that worst-case assumptions will lead to the worst of all worlds.

With so-called idealism discredited by the experience of the 1930s, a distorted form of realist thinking and a zero-sum view of the world held sway for forty years in Washington and Moscow.[66] Those forty years saw an escalating arms race which brought some 30,000 nuclear warheads into each side's arsenal and built up massive inventories of tanks, artillery, armored combat vehicles, and aircraft.

Largely because neither side harbored the intentions imputed to it by the other, there was no war in Europe, the focus of the costly arms race. Cognitive dissonance did, however, ensure repeated crises and periods of high tension, while the risk of inadvertent conflict was inherent in the two sides' confrontational policies, postures, and behavior. Wars were meanwhile fought elsewhere in the world, conflicts that were exacerbated and fueled by the superpowers' ideological struggle, with dire consequences for the peoples concerned.

A Time for Choice

The Soviets have now rejected the zero-sum way of thinking and adopted an expanding-sum approach to foreign policy. It may be utopian, but the results have been startling and are widely seen to have been beneficial to the Soviet Union and to most other nations. It is not important that this change was partly brought about by economic duress; it is the effects of the change that matter, and those effects are very real.

---

66. Both sides' realist policies were distorted by ideology. Western policy was further distorted by deterrence theory.

The West now faces a choice. It can ignore the new thinking that brought about these changes and concentrate on gathering the fruits; it can assume that these favorable developments were the result of Western policies rather than fundamental changes in the Soviet Union; and it can persist with the ideas and attitudes that served the European nations well during the first four hundred years of their global expansion, but for the last hundred have proved to be increasingly dysfunctional and actively destructive. Or the West can acknowledge the new realities of the nuclear age and accept the challenge of the new political thinking on international relations.

A new agenda is already at hand and has been publicly articulated by Mikhail Gorbachev, although he is the first to disclaim authorship. It comprises well-established ideas that are firmly grounded in Western thinking on international relations. Parts of that agenda have been incorporated in statements issued jointly by the Soviet Union and Brazil, Canada, Finland, India, Italy, and West Germany.[67] And the agenda reflects the conclusions reached by the three international commissions that were set up at the instigation of the General Assembly of the United Nations on international development issues (1977), on disarmament and security issues (1980), and on environment and development (1983).[68]

It remains to be seen whether the West, and the United States in particular, will accept the challenge of this new agenda and join in moving international relations and the conduct of great-power foreign policy into a new era. It is now five hundred years since the quarrelsome nations of Europe embarked on the path that would lead to a brief period of global domination by their descendants, a period that is surely past. If the perestroika process implies the resolution of intra-European conflict, what does that portend for the larger international system and the prospects of world order?

---

67. On October 19, 1988; November 22, 1989; October 26, 1989; November 27, 1989 (the Delhi Declaration, discussed in chap. 6); November 30, 1989; and June 13, 1989, respectively.

68. The commissions were chaired, respectively, by Willy Brandt, Olaf Palme, and Gro Brutland, all former prime ministers; their reports were Willy Brandt and Anthony Sampson, eds., *North-South: A Program for Survival* (MIT Press, 1980), *Common Security: A Blueprint for Survival* (Simon and Schuster, 1984), and *Our Common Future* (Oxford University Press, 1987).

The Analytical Approach

THE METHODOLOGY used in this study is known as "objectives analysis," which features four basic characteristics.[1]

First, the focus is on the "why" of Soviet policy, rather than on the "what." Rather than simply describing Soviet behavior and associated policies, the methodology emphasizes the development of testable hypotheses that can explain the motivations shaping past and present behavior and that can predict future behavior.

Second, the hypothesized motivations are expressed formally in terms of Soviet planning assumptions, hierarchies of objectives, operational missions, and force requirements. These formulations can be tested using concrete evidence, while allowing one to grasp the far-reaching implications of seemingly subtle changes in wording or behavior.

Third, the fact of change, be it in assumptions, objectives, threat perceptions, or military technology, lies at the heart of the analysis. Emphasis is placed on identifying and dating changes in these and other factors and on investigating the consequences.

And fourth, all information is analyzed in the context of what amounts to an externally inferred frame of reference. The inferences used are derived from a wide range of information of different types and sources, using a variety of analytical techniques.

The inferences impute a logical connection between hypothesized objectives and observed behavior. The validity of the logical inferences made is judged in terms of overall consistency with the evidence rather than more narrowly in terms of direct historical documentation. The

---

1. For an early application of this methodology, see Michael MccGwire, *Military Objectives in Soviet Foreign Policy* (Brookings, 1987).

analysis thus generates implicit reasons for Soviet actions that are not necessarily formulated in the same way by Soviet decisionmakers.

The methodology underlying objectives analysis was developed incrementally between 1965 and 1986, a time when the particular characteristics of the Soviet system facilitated the techniques involved. From that analysis there emerged the central conclusion that the Soviet Union's military behavior, the structure and posture of its forces, and much of its foreign policy were shaped by the need to prepare for the worst case of world war, a contingency the Soviets saw as inherent in the antagonisms of the opposing social systems.

Since 1987 there has been a radical change in the analytical environment. Soviet policy has been in a state of flux, assumptions about peace and war have undergone fundamental revision, military doctrine is still being reworked, and glasnost has produced a mass of raw information, including a flood of statements and published material that varies greatly in value as evidence.

Despite the far-reaching nature of changes, the "objectives" approach to analyzing Soviet defense and foreign policy retains its importance and the associated techniques are still valuable, particularly at the higher levels of analysis. But the greatest contribution of the objectives approach to the analysis of current developments is the coherent and well-tested explanation it provides of Soviet military behavior in the 1948–86 period, which is a prerequisite to understanding what has happened since 1987.

The Multidimensional Hypothesis

Western explanations of Soviet defense and foreign policy are necessarily hypotheses. The analytical challenge is to develop an internally consistent hypothesis that is amenable to testing and that can accommodate all the existing evidence and explain all related developments.

The quality of such hypotheses (explanations) depends largely on their internal analytical structure. This structure must be able to order and interpret the existing mass of information, translate new information into evidence, and direct the analyst to other evidence. It must be able to accommodate change and anticipate it. And it should also provide the means for identifying the policy implications of nuanced changes in the pattern of evidence, and the means to "operationalize" relatively small adjustments in policy pronouncements or shifts in doctrinal formulations.

It takes a complex and detailed hypothesis to meet these requirements, and it was found that a hierarchy of objectives that spanned all levels of analysis provided the best analytical structure for the 1948–86 period. The concept of objectives is central to military planning in all countries, and the Soviets have applied it with systematic rigor, reflecting the centralized nature of the political system and the General Staff's top-down approach to formulating military requirements.

The analytical structure can be visualized as a skeletal ball, with the overarching national objective lying at the center. The hierarchy of objectives radiates outward in an unbroken logical sequence to the detailed missions and tasks of the separate services and of their various arms at the operational level, and beyond that to the design specifications for individual weapons. In analytical practice, pathways out from the center are developed as required to support specific analyses, and the amount of detail in any such hierarchy depends on the analytical focus. For analytical convenience, branches of the hierarchy can be broken off and treated as self-contained hierarchies, but they remain causally linked to the higher-order objectives and to other parts of the main hierarchy.

This hierarchical structure reflects an idealized model of national security planning and decisionmaking, a process driven by strategic imperatives. However, the structure also reflects the realities of the Soviet political-military apparatus, at least as it existed before 1988. The Soviet Union was a mono-organizational society in which a complex pattern of bureaucracies strove to achieve centrally formulated goals.[2] Military doctrine was an officially adopted *system* of views on basic questions about war, including the nature of a future war, the appropriate objectives in such a war, and the likely way it would be waged. Doctrine reflected the Marxist belief in law-governed regularities in all social phenomena, including war.

Decisions on political-military issues were made at Politburo level, routinely by the Defense Council, with the full Politburo ruling on the most important and controversial matters. The implementation of those decisions at the military-technical level was the responsibility of the Higher Industrial Commission (VPK), which coordinated research and

2. T. H. Rigby, "Introduction: Political Legitimacy, Weber and the Communist Mono-organizational Systems," in T. H. Rigby and Ference Feher, eds., *Political Legitimation in Communist States* (St. Martin's Press, 1982), pp. 10–11.

development and the production of weapons systems, and of the General Staff. The result was a top-down (center-out) structure that strove to enforce consistency and conformity with centrally decided policies and doctrine. This aim was helped by the ground forces' domination of the defense establishment as a whole and of the General Staff in particular.

The Soviet Union's geostrategic situation, the scale of its military requirements, and the Marxist-Leninist approach to solving problems yielded abundant information that allowed one to develop a well-supported hierarchy of objectives. Two kinds of evidence were fairly readily available. There was the concrete evidence provided by the structure, disposition, and deployment of Soviet forces, by Soviet weapons procurement programs, and by Soviet operational concepts. At the other end of the continuum there were authoritative doctrinal statements about the likely nature of a future war and the methods of waging it. These statements varied greatly in clarity and specificity, but they could be fleshed out by the professional debates in the military press.

There was a direct relationship between those two bodies of evidence. The structural link that joined them and made sense of the relationship was the hierarchy of objectives. The nature of war determined the scope of the objectives and those objectives determined missions, which determined requirements, which became manifest as weapons systems and operational behavior. The inductive analysis of the hardware evidence complemented, corrected, and verified the deductive analysis of military objectives, and the overlap of the two analyses allowed the internal consistency of the overarching hypothesis to be tested against relevant Soviet behavior.

For obvious reasons, the Soviets did not spell out their wartime objectives, but the hierarchy could be reconstructed using this combination of inductive and deductive approaches. It involved the concurrent analysis of four different elements of Soviet military policy: military doctrine and the relevant aspects of ideological theory; the hierarchy of strategic objectives implied by the doctrine; the characteristics, structure, and deployment of Soviet forces; and the procurement programs that produced these forces.

In the process of analysis, a series of testable hypotheses emerged whose proof lay in the details of weapons programs, military exercises, and policy pronouncements. There were other hypotheses that depended on war for validation, but the hierarchy of objectives provided a logical basis for postulating Soviet behavior in those opaque policy areas where direct evidence was lacking.[3] Soviet policy evolved during those four decades, as did the underlying objectives, but that was an aid to analysis. Any significant shift reverberated through the tightly planned system, precipitating a cascade of changes that resulted in observable differences in operational concepts and force structure, and anomalies in established patterns of production.

The reasons for change were numerous and included the reformulation of doctrinal assumptions, the emergence of new technology or the coming availability of new capabilities, and new or revised perceptions of threat. It was important to date the change correctly. The wrong date generated misleading explanations of the motivations underlying subsequent developments, and hence false interpretations of the new policy. Meanwhile, the fact of change had analytical significance. It was impermissible to use evidence that originated before a decision to change policy as a part of the explanations of Soviet policy subsequent to that change. On the other hand, comparison of the evidence from before and after a change threw light on both the old and the new policies.

Combining the examination of changes over time with the different analytical approaches that make up objectives analysis produced a dynamic multidimensional analytical matrix that established the logical relationship between different data and provided a concrete but evolving framework within which to evaluate published material and public pronouncements. The matrix determined the context (and hence the meaning) of ambiguous evidence, directed the search for missing evidence, and was continuously testing the evolving hypothesis for consistency. The hypothesis meanwhile generated subordinate ones that were implied by the logic of the matrix and that could be tested in their turn.

The original process of developing this complex hypothesis can be likened to reconstructing the path of a long-dead explorer by piecing

3. Soviet policy on initiating the use of nuclear weapons illustrates this claim. In 1983, having identified the doctrinal shift that occurred toward the end of 1966 and then having developed the 1970s hierarchy of strategic objectives, I drew the conclusion that the 1970s strategy would eschew first use of nuclear weapons (MccGwire, *Military Objectives*, pp. 50–51, 54–55). There was some textual evidence that supported a new policy of launch-on-warning at the strategic level, but it was widely discounted, while "common sense" argued that the Soviets would not forgo the option of nuclear preemption in the theater. My conclusion was therefore dismissed as unfounded. However, in 1988 Raymond L. Garthoff came across an authoritative reference to a secret decree issued in 1973–74 instructing the military to plan and prepare on the assumption that the Soviet Union would *not* be the first to use nuclear weapons, thus confirming my prediction (*Deterrence and the Revolution in Soviet Military Doctrine* [Brookings, 1990], p. 83).

together the work of different mapmakers and then using new carto-graphic methods to remove contradictions and fill in the gaps. However, once the path has been identified, it is analytically more useful to describe it in simplified terms. In the same way that a schematic map of a rail or road transit system makes it easier to see where one is going and to recognize when one is on the wrong line, an explanation of Soviet military policy that is expressed in terms of key decisions and changing objectives makes it easier to see what should lie ahead and to recognize when future behavior is consistently off track. The purpose is not to describe, but to explain and to predict.

The Analytical Techniques

An important feature of objectives analysis was the use of five different techniques to develop the evidence that was used to build, test, and extend the multidimensional hypothesis. Unprocessed information can seriously mislead, and a common mistake has been to take such raw information, whether some pronouncement or a new weapon system, and adduce it as evidence of Soviet motivations without first evaluating the information within the proper context.

The various analytical techniques were developed over time, with the two types of hardware analysis being the first to emerge.[4] One was concerned with the characteristics of Soviet weapons systems and the way they were disposed, deployed, and exercised. This was referred to as either requirements or mission analysis, because it identified both the requirement the weapon systems had originally been intended to meet and its actual mission in the event of war, which might be different. The other type was procurement analysis, which sought to reconstruct various weapons programs over time. Although the two techniques were conceptually distinct, there was a symbiotic relationship between them and they were used in close conjunction.

Next to emerge was the concept of decision periods, responding to the evidence from hardware analysis that continuity of weapons

---

4. The focus was initially on Soviet naval developments. Naval forces and warship building programs were particularly suitable for this type of analysis. For an early exposition of these techniques, see Michael MccGwire, "Naval Capabilities and Intentions" and "Soviet Naval Procurement," in Royal United Service Institution, *The Soviet Union in Europe and the Near East: Her Capabilities and Intentions* (London, 1970).

programs was the exception rather than the rule. Identifying the nature and timing of changes in policy was obviously crucial to the larger picture.

The analysis of doctrinal statements emerged much later. The focus was on identifying the planning assumptions that underlay Soviet policy and it moved steadily into the higher reaches of doctrine and on to Marxist-Leninist ideology and the Soviet theory of international relations. At this same period it was realized that the different kinds of evidence developed by these various techniques all formed part of a hierarchy of objectives. The idea was latent in the analysis of missions and requirements, and the hierarchy linked them directly to the overarching objectives that shaped Soviet defense and foreign policy.

Common to all these techniques was the focus on the why of Soviet behavior, rather than the what, a focus that reflected the level of analysis. At the military-technical or "colonel's" level of analysis, the contingency planner focuses on Soviet capabilities and assumes worst-case intentions. At the politico-strategic or "ministerial" level, the policy planner is interested in the most likely case and should therefore compare the Soviets' capabilities with their essential requirements and analyze their interests and their intentions.

These different focuses yield different conclusions, each appropriate to its own level of analysis. To ignore this distinction at the ministerial level is to commit the "colonel's fallacy" which, without analyzing Soviet interests or intentions, just assumes the worst.

Requirements or Mission Analysis

The technique of requirements or mission analysis lies at the heart of objectives analysis. By bringing the "why" question to bear directly on the Soviets' military behavior, on the size and structure of their forces, and on the characteristics of their weapon systems, it extracts the kind of information needed for decisionmaking at the ministerial level. In the absence of requirements or mission analysis, the policy planner has to rely on the information provided by the "what" questions being used for capabilities analysis at the colonel's level, where the focus is on how to defeat the Soviets in war, rather than how to deal with them in peace.

The Soviets stress the importance of the main or primary mission, the main axis of advance, and so on, and careful analysis of the structure, composition, characteristics, and employment of specific forces will usually disclose their primary mission. One of two pitfalls that must be avoided is thinking in terms of Western vulnerabilities, rather than Soviet requirements; they are not mirror images. The other pitfall is fastening on some secondary purpose that is also being served (or could be served by the existing capability) and promoting it to the primary place. The mistake is particularly likely when the secondary purpose mirrors Western concepts or reflects Western fears.

This happened repeatedly in the naval sphere, where the two sides' operational concepts and requirements diverged most sharply, and the West persistently imputed Mahanist ambitions to the Soviet Union. For example, the Soviet navy's shift to forward deployment in the first half of the 1960s was explained in Mahanist terms of overseas expansion, whereas those exposed forces were originally intended to counter the U.S. capability to launch nuclear strikes against the Soviet Union from distant sea areas and to deny the United States the option of withholding its naval strike forces for use at a later stage of a war.

Those vulnerable deployments of Soviet naval forces in distant sea areas dominated by Western maritime power became comprehensible once viewed in the context of the Soviet 1960s strategy for world war. Fine-grained analysis of the pattern of Soviet operations in the Mediterranean and the Indian Ocean confirmed that developing the capability to discharge the wartime mission was the primary purpose, whereas political influence-building was at best a by-product, and an uncertain one at that.

Similarly, each of the three Soviet classes of air-capable ship was successively claimed to be intended for the Western-style mission of "power projection." Those claims were successively disposed of when the ships entered service, the Moskva class being configured to carry antisubmarine helicopters, the Kiev being able to deny Western maritime patrol aircraft a free ride over the Norwegian Sea, and the Tbilisi able to provide limited air cover to Soviet naval forces operating in such areas. None had been designed for power projection, although the Tbilisi has some capability in that respect.

An example of focusing on Western vulnerabilities is provided by the Western interpretation of the Soviet submarine buildup that got under way in the early 1950s. The program was originally planned to yield a force of 1,200 diesel submarines by 1965, and it was understandable that the West should jump to the conclusion that the Soviets were preparing to attack NATO's sea lines of communication.

If, however, that had been true, then how did one explain this evidence: the concentration of submarines in the Baltic and Black Sea fleets, whose exits were in NATO hands, and the relatively small number in the Northern Fleet, which had unimpeded access to the Atlantic; the failure to build tenders that would allow Soviet submarines to operate from ports in France and Norway, as soon as those ports were seized; and the fact that only 15 percent of the planned submarine force would be optimized for distant-water operations, while the characteristics of the remaining 85 percent made them unsuitable for operating in the mid-Atlantic.

Those submarines were, however, very well suited for operations in the Black Sea, Baltic, and Sea of Japan, and in conjunction with other forces, including shore-based aircraft, were intended to provide a defense against the demonstrated Western capability to project and sustain continental-scale armies by sea. The use of submarines in this role followed established Soviet practice and would contribute to the Soviet navy's primary mission of defending the homeland against seaborne attack.[5]

These examples illustrate the need for fine-grained analysis but also demonstrate the importance of evaluating information about hardware within the broadest strategic context. This includes dating the decisions that underlie the activity or hardware being analyzed. Because of long lead times it frequently happened that by the time a weapon system was ready for deployment, the operational requirement it had originally been designed to meet had changed, perhaps because of a change in the Western threat or because of a change in Soviet strategy. This placed an important limitation on what could be inferred from the characteristics of a weapon system.

More serious, information on the capabilities of a weapon system, even though accurate, could actively mislead if it was interpreted in the wrong context. For example, if the original design characteristics of a weapon could meet redefined operational requirements equally well,

5. This is being wise after the event. It was not until 1959 that the evidence fell into place, when I learned that staff exercises at the Frunze naval academy in the 1945–48 period focused on defense against seaborne invasion. Nevertheless, besides overlooking the traditional Russian emphasis on submarines in the area defense role, Western assessments ignored that as early as 1937 (responding to the Japanese naval buildup), the newly formed Pacific Fleet had a force of 67 submarines, that the Soviet Union had 218 submarines when it was invaded in 1941, and that prewar building plans called for a force of 400 submarines, when the threat from the maritime axes of attack was relatively slight.

then the change in Soviet requirements or a fundamental shift in strategy would be obscured. This happened in the case of the fourth-generation SS-18 "heavy" intercontinental ballistic missile (ICBM) whose design characteristics would have been specified in the first half of the 1960s.

At that time Soviet strategy was predicated on getting in the first blow if war became inescapable, and this would include preemptive strikes on U.S. nuclear delivery systems. Western analysts ascribed that counterforce role to the SS-18 when its characteristics became known in the first half of the 1970s. By then, however, the new Soviet strategy was in effect, which ruled out the option of striking first.

Henceforth, Soviet ICBMs would be launched on warning of attack, if that were possible, but the Soviets had to assume that a significant part of their ICBM force would be put out of action. In such circumstances, the SS-18's accuracy and throw-weight remained as important as hitherto, since the greater the capability of those missiles that survived a U.S. first strike, the better.

This mistake might have been caught if the implications of the SS-18's characteristics had been evaluated against a reconstruction of the third-generation ICBM programs (see appendix B), while a thorough analysis of Soviet doctrinal writings in the first half of the 1970s would certainly have yielded the correct answer.[6] Instead, Western analysts compounded their error by drawing on Soviet doctrinal writings in the 1960s, which supported the mistaken conclusion that the Soviets still had an offensive, preemptive, counterforce strategy. This "evidence" did not, however, take account of the shift in military doctrine that had been decided in December 1966 and had begun to have visible effects by the end of the 1960s.[7]

The imputed role of the SS-18 and the somewhat smaller SS-19 was important to the claim that the United States faced a "window of strategic vulnerability" which, although discounted subsequently, had significant political repercussions. But the distortions introduced by the use of this

6. Starting in 1969 (with one important precursor in 1967), Soviet pronouncements indicated a shift from a policy of preemption to one of launch-on-warning. Raymond L. Garthoff, "Mutual Deterrence and Strategic Arms Limitation in Soviet Policy," *International Security,* vol. 3 (Summer 1978), pp. 129–32.

7. For the type of analysis that was influential in shaping the mistaken appreciation, see Joseph D. Douglass, Jr., and Amoretta N. Hoeber, *Soviet Strategy for Nuclear War* (Hoover Institution Press, 1979). Of the eighty-seven articles listed in the bibliography, 40 percent were published before 1967 and none were published later than 1969.

outdated evidence went far beyond the role of the SS-18. When that evidence was melded with current information on the fourth generation of Soviet ICBMs and the improvements in their theater capabilities, the case could be made that the Soviets believed victory to be possible in a nuclear war and were actively preparing to achieve such a victory should war occur.[8]

This led to the conclusion that the United States' capacity to deter Soviet aggression was less than complete, and thus to Presidential Directive 59 and the "countervailing strategy" that required the United States to develop a capability for waging protracted nuclear war.

Common to all these examples of mistaken Western assessments was a focus on the what of Soviet behavior and a neglect of the why, an emphasis on Western vulnerabilities rather than Soviet requirements. Not that requirements or mission analysis slights Soviet capabilities or ignores Western vulnerabilities. Rather, those analyses provide the basis for a process that goes on to explain, not just describe.

But requirements or mission analysis does more than just explain. It also forecasts Soviet behavior and thus can provide early warning of change. Once a well-tested explanation of past and present behavior has been developed, nonconformance with the forecast is a strong indicator of a change in underlying policy. For example, it was the evidence that emerged in the first half of 1987 that the Soviets were moving in a direction that would prevent them from meeting their long-established requirements for war in Europe that alerted me to the fundamental change in Soviet military doctrine about the likelihood of world war.

Procurement Analysis

Procurement analysis has several purposes. One is to develop models of various defense industries such as shipbuilding or missile production, which allows one to establish building rates, patterns of production, and so forth. Another is to establish the genesis of individual weapons programs and to locate them in the large picture. These, in turn, allow one to identify and date changes in underlying policy, because of the disruption caused to existing programs. And beyond that, the models

---

8. Leon Sloss and Marc Dean Millott, "U.S. Nuclear Strategy in Evolution," *Strategic Review*, vol. 12 (Winter 1984), p. 24.

developed by procurement analysis provide the internal structure for the hypotheses generated by mission or requirements analysis, somewhat in the same way that the hierarchy of objectives provides the internal structure for the comprehensive multidimensional hypothesis.

The technique originated with the analysis of postwar naval building programs, which were numerous, subject to successive changes, and constrained by a finite shipyard capacity. A close analysis of warship deliveries and the characteristics of successive classes uncovered various practices and procedures that prevailed in naval design and procurement and that determined the pattern of production in the naval sector of the shipbuilding industry. Once a crude model of the industry had been constructed, the analysis became a reiterative process as the model's "rules" were elaborated and progressively refined to achieve consistency. The model meanwhile became a hypothesis that made predictions and could be tested.

This process suggested such organizing concepts as generations of weapons platforms and systems and vintages of weapons and key components. It also yielded analytical concepts such as design decision, lead time, delivery period, pipeline inertia, notional production lines, and key limiting factors, concepts that were found to apply equally to other kinds of weapon programs.[9] It was also found possible to reconstruct the pattern of programs that had been planned but subsequently canceled.

The process of reconstructing weapons programs is analogous to the analysis used in rock mechanics. In seeking to learn the internal composition of a rock formation, the geologist extracts a series of cores, which tell him the relative location and composition of successive strata. They also tell him about faults, folds, and shifts, from which he is able to infer the history of that rock formation, reaching back millions of years.

In the case of Soviet weapons programs the "core" is extruded by the Soviet production process, with successive generations of weapons and their platforms being analogous to the rock strata. Ideally this centrally planned process would lay down successive strata in regular unbroken layers, as successive generations of weapons followed each other into service. In practice there are changes in requirements, leading

9. For an explanation of these terms, see Michael MccGwire, ed., *Soviet Naval Developments: Capability and Context* (Praeger, 1973), chap. 16.

to the cancellation or amendment of the original plan, which create faults and folds in the strata.

The geologist is able to infer what caused the faults and folds in a rock formation by analyzing the evidence within a larger geological picture such as plate tectonics. Similarly, anomalies in the pattern of weapons programs should alert the analyst to the fact of change in the larger picture, and the reason for change can then be sought.

Although strata are folded or broken, by referring to established patterns and the factors limiting production, the analyst can infer what was originally planned before the external force brought about change. In the case of canceled naval programs, further evidence was provided by the systems (weapons, sensors, propulsion) that the ships would have carried. Because they had been provided for in the five-year plan, those systems were usually applied to other platforms.[10] This allowed one to use simple arithmetic to work out the number of units that had originally been programmed.[11] Identifying the "geology" of successive programs in this way was made possible by the Soviets' practice of continuous procurement, their emphasis on series production, the five-year planning process, the way they allocated production facilities, and the fact that they were usually working within clearly defined constraints.

Procurement analysis is a powerful but neglected technique. Soviet weapons programs came within the ambit of capabilities analysis, where the focus was on what was being currently produced and when it would become operational, while the pattern of production over time was largely ignored. The idea that the pattern could yield valuable evidence of canceled decisions and plans forgone was not only foreign to most analysts, but the reconstruction process violated the canons of evidence that applied to current production.[12]

10. For example, the air-defense and antisubmarine units of the truncated Moskva program were applied to the Kresta program to produce the SAM Kotlin, while the original Kresta systems were used to convert Krupny to Kanin.

11. For example, the conversion of only 8 regular Kotlins to SAM Kotlin and the taking in hand of all 8 Krupnys for conversion to Kanin confirmed the model's prediction that both Kynda and Kresta had been programmed at 12 units. The fact that 10 Kresta IIs (fitted with Moskva antiaircraft [AA] and antisubmarine warfare [ASW] systems) were built, rather than the 8 predicted by the model, argued that the Moskva class (only two of which were delivered) had also been originally programmed at 12 units. The Moskva's AA and ASW systems were of the next generation, and the need to get them to sea to meet the new requirements that had prompted these changes in naval building programs justified extending the production of Kresta hull-propulsion platforms by two units.

12. For examples of procurement analysis see app. B; MccGwire, *Military Objectives,* apps. B, D; MccGwire, ed., *Soviet Naval Developments,* chap. 16.

Deducing Change—The Decision Period

The Soviet five-year planning cycle provided for incremental change, for systematic product improvement, and for upgrading successive generations of platform, weapons, and equipment by incorporating new design and technology. One had to distinguish between that kind of evolutionary change, on one hand, and, on the other hand, abrupt or out-of-cycle change that required a change in established plans, even if the decision to change happened to coincide with the planning cycle. Such out-of-cycle change was almost certain to produce anomalies in the established pattern of production.

The process of reaching a decision on the need for out-of-cycle change can be pictured as a wave form. The rear slope of the wave represents the period when perceptions of the need for change build up to a crest of a top-level agreement in principle. The front slope of the wave represents the series of implementing decisions that stem from this acceptance of the need for change and constitutes what I have labeled the "decision period." Both slopes and the crest of the decisionmaking wave have to be analyzed to establish the exact nature of the change, why it was decided on, and what the implications were or are.

The initial evidence of change varied. In rare cases it could be inferred from a public pronouncement. But it often happened that a change of policy first became manifest several years later as anomalies in weapons programs or new patterns of deployment and operation. In such cases it was essential to date the underlying decision period correctly, and this required that proper allowance be made for lead time (which was usually underestimated), while the tendency to link changes in deployment patterns of weapons programs with the nearest significant event had to be resisted.

Misdating the decision period generated misleading explanations of the motivations underlying specific developments. A classic example is the still widely held belief that the Soviet Union's discomfiture during the Cuban missile crisis in October 1962 led to the Soviet navy's shift to forward deployment in 1963–64 and the buildup of Soviet ICBMs that began in 1965. Both of those developments and the renewed emphasis in that period on ground forces and frontal aviation can be tied to the defense initiatives adopted by the Kennedy administration in the early months of 1961.[13]

13. The change in the ground forces' fortune is usually tied to Nikita Khrushchev's

This earlier date yields a very different explanation, which is supported by detailed analysis of the three developments. The prospective surge in the U.S. sea-based nuclear capability prompted the Soviet navy's move forward in strategic defense. The mass production of Minuteman ICBMs that would be emplaced in silos in the American Midwest required that Soviet ICBM programs be restructured. And the military debate that was prompted by the Kennedy initiatives led to a partial withdrawal from Khrushchev's overconcentration on nuclear missile warfare and the return to traditional verities announced at the Twenty-second Party Congress in October 1961. What the Cuban crisis did do was to confirm the validity of these earlier Soviet decisions taken in 1961–62.[14]

Unless there is unambiguous evidence of a decision-in-principle, such as a public pronouncement, identifying the crest of the decisionmaking wave is an iterative four-stage process. First comes the alert that something has changed. Next one establishes the decision period from which the observed changes emanated; each change must be analyzed separately and the clustering of these dates locates the front slope of the decisionmaking wave in time. One then crosses to the back slope to identify the circumstances that prompted the need for change. Fourth, one postulates a decision-in-principle that would fit this evidence. One then repeats the process.[15]

In focusing on how to identify a single decision-in-principle or decision period, one must be sensitive to the fact that at any one time the information being analyzed will represent the overlapping outputs of several separate decisions made at different times in the past. Sometimes the effects will be confusing, like the wave pattern in a pool into which stones are being tossed at intervals, and the evidence will seem contradictory.[16] At other times the effects will be mutually reinforcing,

---

replacement by Leonid Brezhnev in 1964. However, John McDonnell's analysis of the Soviet debate during the first six months of 1961 indicates that the decision-in-principle was reached in July–September 1961 ("Khrushchev and the Soviet Military Industrial Complex: Soviet Defense Policy, 1959–61" [Halifax, Nova Scotia: Dalhousie University, Center for Foreign Policy Studies, 1979], pp. 73–82).

14. It also prompted adjustments to Soviet ICBM targeting policy, to the role of large-type torpedo-armed diesel submarines, and to Soviet policy on naval arms supply.

15. For a demonstration, see MccGwire, *Military Objectives,* app. A, which identifies the doctrinal shift in December 1966.

16. Nuclear submarine deliveries in the 1968–82 period provide an example; see ibid., app. C.

and here one must avoid assuming that just one of several successive decisions can explain the full range of evidence over time.[17]

The problem is analogous to that faced by the scientist who needs to analyze a fluctuating phenomenon such as sound. He uses a Fourier transform to convert it into a spectrum, which describes the sound as a series of volumes at distinct pitches.[18] A closer analogy might be the problem faced by an astronomer who is trying to describe and explain the evolving universe. The signals he receives today were generated by different events that are millions of years apart in time. Besides building up a composite picture from a large number of different frequencies, the astronomer has to sort out which signals belong to which event.

The Role of Doctrine

Until mid-1987, Soviet military doctrine concerned "the essence, objectives and nature of a possible future war . . . and the preparation of the country and forces to wage it." Since doctrine was an officially adopted system of views authorized at the highest political level, it would seem that all the analyst needed to do was to acquire a thorough understanding of Soviet doctrinal writings and everything would fall into place. In practice it was less simple.

For a start, Soviet writing did not separate out doctrine from military science, a term that is best understood in its original sense of knowledge and disciplined inquiry.[19] Military science talks about much the same thing as doctrine but its findings are fluid and subject to continual debate, whereas doctrine is fixed at any given period. It is often not easy to tell science and doctrine apart, besides which the analyst must decide which elements of doctrine are grist to his mill.

Doctrine covers a continuum that runs from the general to the specific. In formal terms, doctrine divides between theory, programmatic analysis (which determines the nature of the operating environment), and strategy and tactics, a division that applies to both international relations and

17. For example, the increasing emphasis on conventional weapons and ground forces in the European theater reflected a series of reinforcing decisions. The process started in 1961–62 and continued throughout the 1970s. See ibid., pp. 24–28, 55–56.

18. The Fourier transform is a mathematical technique that decomposes such phenomena into a set of sinusoidal components. Ronald N. Bracewell, "The Fourier Transform," *Scientific American*, vol. 260 (June 1989), p. 86.

19. Similarly, *isskustvo,* usually translated as *art,* should be understood in its original sense of technics or applied knowledge, which is a subset of science or knowledge. The term is best translated as *military craft* or *the craft of war.*

military conflict. In the case of military doctrine it is analytically convenient to divide this continuum into theory, assumption, and prescriptions.

Theory describes, analyzes, and categorizes the essential structure of the social environment, the forces at work in it, and social phenomena such as conflict and war, and at the highest level it merges with the theory of international relations and Marxist ideology. However, those kinds of questions are only sometimes important to Soviet military analysis. At the other end of the continuum, the prescriptions establish priorities, rules, and procedures for the conduct of war, and these are mainly important to those analysts who address the question of how the Soviets would actually fight a war.

The primary concern of objectives analysis is to explain Soviet military behavior short of war, and the rationale underlying the structure and deployment of Soviet forces in peacetime. Planning assumptions are therefore of paramount importance. Since World War II, two sets of assumptions have determined Soviet military policy. One concerned the possibility of world war; the other concerned the likely nature of such a war.

Assumptions about the possibility of world war merged with ideological theory, and until 1956 such a war was seen as being inevitable. A reformulation of ideology in 1956 made it possible to rule that world war was no longer inevitable, but this did not affect the substance of Soviet military requirements. Whether world war was inevitable or merely possible, Soviet forces had to be structured to cover the worst-case contingency. Estimates of the likelihood or imminence of war would affect decisions on the allocation of resources to flesh out the force structure, but they did not affect the disposition of forces, the logistical infrastructure, or the size of the military-industrial base.

As long as world war was possible, military requirements would be determined by Soviet assumptions about the likely nature of such a war. The crucial assumption was whether or not it was inevitable that a world war would be nuclear and involve massive strikes on the Soviet Union. It was that assumption that dictated the choice of the two primary wartime objectives that would best promote the long-term well-being of the Soviet state, while not losing the war. From those two objectives all others have stemmed (see table 2-2).

Soviet assumptions about the likely nature of a world war were reflected in contemporary Soviet writings. The material was inherently ambiguous, but one could infer whether or not, at any particular period, the Soviets assumed that a world war would inevitably be nuclear. In late 1966 the Soviets changed their assumption from inevitable to not inevitable; since the decision had far-reaching consequences, the Soviets took pains to conceal the shift. Secrecy increased the chance of achieving strategic surprise in the event of war, while concealing from the West the Soviet Union's vulnerability as it embarked on the process of restructuring its forces to implement the new strategy required by the new hierarchy of objectives.[20]

The doctrinal shift in 1966 highlighted the usefulness of the continuum of possibilities as an analytical tool. As discussed in the early part of chapter 8, planning assumptions are probability statements. They locate contingencies on a continuum of inevitable and impossible. In analytical terms, this continuum divides into three logically distinct parts, comprising the two terminals (or end zones) and the broad middle zone that stretches between inevitable at one end and not possible at the other.

The great bulk of doctrinal assumptions is located in the ambiguous middle zone and, beyond indicating that the Soviets are sensitive to the unpredictability of war and seek to prepare for all eventualities, those assumptions do not tell one much. When, however, an assumption moves from that middle zone into an end zone, or vice versa, one needs to pay attention. The adjacent assumptions are mutually exclusive (in the sense that an event cannot be both inevitable and not inevitable, or possible and not possible), and the new assumption may require a major change in existing policies, as was the case in 1966 and 1987.

A final point about doctrine as an analytical tool is the distinction to be made between the practical concerns of the General Staff and the content of theoretical writings. Doctrinal writings, including staff handbooks and what was taught at the higher military schools, covered the full span of possibilities, with world war as just one among a range of contingencies. The General Staff, however, was mainly preoccupied with preparing for the contingency of world war, the worst case that dominated Soviet military concerns from 1948 onward.

This was particularly true in the 1970s, when the General Staff was fully involved in the wholesale restructuring of Soviet strategy, operational concepts, force structure, and weapons specifications, in

---

20. For the doctrinal shift see MccGwire, *Military Objectives,* pp. 30, 387–400. This shift was not referred to explicitly until 1985 (M. A. Gareev, *M. V. Frunze: veonnyy teoretik* [*M. V. Frunze: Military Theorist*] [Moscow: Voenizdat, 1985], pp. 239–40).

order to support the new hierarchy of objectives required by the doctrinal reformulation that was agreed at the end of 1966. This preoccupation was reinforced by objective circumstances since the end of the 1950s, which made the possibility of major conflict with the United States outside Europe extremely remote.

Despite discussion of such a contingency in doctrinal writings, for all practical purposes the General Staff would have planned on the assumption that major conflict with the United States implied war in Europe, and hence world war. That would require the immediate launch of an offensive against NATO. However, that assumption was undermined by the possibility of major conflict with the United States in the area north of the Persian Gulf that emerged in 1979–82, which raised the new possibility of having to hold in the west, while fighting to the south.

No matter that the possibility of limited war with the United States had been discussed in doctrinal writings. As discussed in chapter 2, the practical consequences of this concrete possibility and its effects on military thinking would have been of quite a different order.

Figuring Out Soviet Objectives

Choosing the optimal objective is the key to success in war, and the process takes careful thought and consideration. Similarly, deducing Soviet objectives is a painstaking process, and the precise way one chooses to word the various objectives is a matter of considerable importance.

For example, the traditional Soviet mission of "defending the home-land" worked well for the navy, the national air defense troops, and, if one accepted Western deterrence theory, the strategic rocket forces. It could not, however, account for the posture of Soviet ground and air forces facing NATO. Nor could it explain the radical change in Soviet missile programs, in targeting philosophy, and in the structure of Soviet forces in Eastern Europe and on the Chinese border in the 1970s.

The only explanation that would cover all five services over time was that they had been structured and postured for the worst-case contingency of world war. In such a war the Soviets had good reason to believe that the U.S. objective would be to overthrow the Soviet state, and they could clearly not afford to lose such a war. That must be the minimum objective. It was significantly different from the oversimplified concept of defending the homeland and, while it encompassed the same general idea, it was more demanding.[21]

Throughout the 1948–86 period the size, structure, disposition, and posture of the Soviet armed forces clearly expressed the objective of "not losing a world war."[22] It is hard to exaggerate the analytical importance of formulating this overarching objective in such specific terms. It provides a fully satisfactory justification for the changing size and structure of Soviet forces in the postwar period. It highlights the extent to which Soviet foreign policy behavior was shaped by the need to prepare for the worst case of world war. And by relinquishing that objective (while continuing "to defend the homeland"), Mikhail Gorbachev was able to adopt a completely new approach to Soviet defense and foreign policy, and to justify major unilateral cuts in Soviet military strength.

The process of developing a hierarchy of objectives is demonstrated in chapter 3 of *Military Objectives,* which shows how the 1960s hierarchy had to be completely restructured as a result of the doctrinal shift in December 1966. (The results are summarized in tables 2-1 and 2-2 of this book.) The decision that it was no longer inevitable that world war would involve massive strikes on the Soviet Union meant that it was possible (and hence necessary, in order to "promote the well-being of the Soviet state") to adopt the wartime objective of "avoiding the nuclear devastation of the USSR." This replaced "preserving the socialist system" as one of the two primary wartime objectives, and at the same time made inoperative the other primary objective of "destroying the capitalist system." That could only be achieved with a nuclear strike, which would ensure U.S. retaliation and the devastation of the USSR.

Once again, the precise wording was important. To avoid any kind of nuclear attack on the Soviet Union would obviously be preferable but, given the role of nuclear weapons in U.S. strategy, that objective was unlikely to be achieved. If that happened, military logic would require the Soviets to revert to the 1960s strategy, with its certainty of mutual

21. The Soviets did refer to the mission of the armed forces as "securing the defense of the Soviet fatherland." Although this objective was too general for analytical purposes, it is implied by the more specific one used in objectives analysis. Should the Soviet armed forces lose a world war, the Soviet state would be overthrown and the armed forces would therefore have failed in their mission of securing the defense of the fatherland. "Defense of the homeland" was little more specific than the U.S. objective of "deterrence," a catchall concept that was used to justify all types of weapons programs and most kinds of military deployment.

22. Choice of the formulation "not losing," rather than "winning" or "victory" is explained in chap. 2.

devastation. By specifying nuclear devastation as the thing to be *avoided,* the 1970s objective allowed for limited U.S. strikes on the USSR, without predetermining how the Soviets would react. Their response would be able to reflect the circumstances at the time, balancing the objective of avoiding the nuclear devastation of the USSR against the higher-order objective of not losing the war.

Textual Analysis

Information derived from Soviet pronouncements and writings contributed to the evolving multidimensional hypothesis and in the process it was realized that objectives analysis had a potentially important role in analyzing textual material, which was inherently ambiguous. This ambiguity stemmed from the difficulty of knowing why a particular statement was made or piece written, who the primary audiences were, and whether the information should be taken at face value. The problem of validity is indicated by the terms used at various times by Western analysts to categorize this type of material: propagandistic, genuflection to party line, Aesopian, surrogate, concrete expression of doctrine, authoritative, and even factual.

The difficulties posed by this inherent ambiguity were compounded by the sheer volume of the material, and the result was that it could be used to prove almost anything. Yet most Western analyses of Soviet policy were largely based on information derived from public pronouncements and writings, and this information was also used to add an extra dimension to analyses of Soviet capabilities, which focused mainly on hardware. On what basis, then, did the analyst select information from this mass and apply it as evidence to support his conclusions? Equally important, how did the policymaker choose between opposing arguments based on the same material?

The latter problem was well illustrated in the second half of the 1970s when Raymond L. Garthoff and Richard Pipes, drawing on the same textual material, reached diametrically opposed conclusions on Soviet strategic nuclear doctrine.[23] This was no mere academic dispute. The Pipes viewpoint was congenial to the political mood of the 1970s and had

23. "A Garthoff-Pipes Debate on Soviet Strategic Doctrine," *Strategic Review,* vol. 10 (Fall 1982), pp. 36–63.

an important influence on his "Team B" report in 1976.[24] And yet, if one relied solely on the contents of the textual material, there was no way of choosing between the two arguments.[25] Clearly, an externally derived frame of reference was needed to select and interpret information from textual material, and it was found that the complex hypothesis that lay at the heart of objectives analysis could meet that requirement.

For textual material that was more than a few years old, the analytical matrix provided a concrete framework derived from the hard evidence of policy outputs in the shape of Soviet behavior, and the published information verified and fleshed out that framework and was itself reinterpreted through the analytical lens of the comprehensive explanation. For relatively current statements and writing, the matrix provided a robust and well-developed hypothesis that allowed the information to be evaluated in its proper context, and perhaps to signal a change in Soviet policy.

The matrix provides a ready means of deciding who was right in the Garthoff-Pipes debate. Pipes relied heavily on writings from the 1960s, which reflected the outdated doctrine that underlay the 1960s strategy, a doctrine that was reformulated at the end of 1966. Garthoff's more systematic analysis of Soviet writings identified a shift of focus in the 1967–74 period from a policy of nuclear preemption to one of launch-on-warning. This reflected the changed doctrine that underlay the 1970s strategy, a change that Pipes remained unaware of.[26]

Given the analytical backgrounds of the two debaters, it is not surprising that Garthoff should have been proved right.[27] But also

24. Professor Pipes, a specialist in nineteenth-century Russian intellectual history, achieved prominence in the field of Soviet military analysis when the Ford administration staged a competitive assessment of the Soviet threat in the second half of 1976. Analysts from the Central Intelligence Agency (Team A) were pitted against an outside group chaired by Pipes (Team B), given access to the same classified data, and required to come up with independent estimates. Pipes's thesis was originally publicized in "Why the Soviet Union Thinks It Could Fight and Win a Nuclear War," *Commentary,* July 1977. He linked that article to Team B in his book, *U.S.-Soviet Relations in the Era of Détente* (Westview Press, 1981), pp. xvi–xvii.

25. Cori Dauber, "Validity Standards and the Debate over Nuclear Strategic Doctrine," *Defense Analysis,* vol. 5 (Summer 1989), pp. 115–28.

26. See Garthoff, "Mutual Deterrence"; Douglass and Hoeber, *Soviet Strategy.*

27. Garthoff (a colleague of mine) had been reading Soviet material for some forty years. His service with the State Department meant that he had been closely involved with Soviet affairs for most of that period and also had had a fair amount of contact with Soviet officials and others at a time when such contacts were rare. He continued to have access to a very wide range of publications, read a vast body of material, had excellent Russian, numerous contacts in the Soviet Union, voluminous files, and a prodigious memory, and the selection process was now largely intuitive.

Garthoff had developed a comprehensive explanation of Soviet behavior that had a well-developed, if largely implicit, internal analytical structure which he had tested and tuned over the years. And although that structure was internally rather than externally generated, Garthoff's particular experience allowed him to avoid the pitfall of circularity. Few analysts had his advantages, and most analysts, lacking an externally derived frame of reference, face a very real problem of how to avoid circularity in the selection and interpretation of evidence.

Besides establishing the context in which textual material should be analyzed, and the proper background to that analysis, the multidimensional hypothesis also suggested what questions to "ask" the material. Only sometimes did textual material "volunteer" information, and the choice of question would determine what the answer would be about. The material might contain information that was more interesting or important, but if one were unaware of the right question, that information would remain undiscovered.

Similarly, the hypothesis was important in identifying the central issues underlying Soviet discussions of higher-order policy questions. For example, it was not until subsequent analysis had uncovered the doctrinal shift in late 1966, leading to a restructuring of Soviet wartime objectives and the adoption of the 1970s strategy, that one could grasp that in 1972–73 the commander-in-chief of the Soviet navy had been arguing about the role of the navy in a two-phase world war that did not escalate to a nuclear exchange.[28] In 1973, this possibility did not even cross our minds.

The problem of identifying the correct context, the importance of asking the material the right questions, the difficulty of uncovering the subject of debate, all underlined the inherent ambiguity of textual material, particularly at the higher levels of analysis. It was much less ambiguous at the lower levels, at the operational and tactical levels of doctrine. As the targeted audience got larger and less aware of underlying assumptions, and as the purpose became that of informing, educating, and prescribing, ambiguity became counterproductive from the Soviet point of view. The information at this level was therefore much more specific, and systematic analysis would usually yield concrete results.

28. The argument was contained in eleven articles totaling some 54,000 words published in 1972–73 in the navy's house journal *Morskoy sbornik* (*Naval Journal*), under the name of Admiral Sergey S. Gorshkov. This material was analyzed intensively in 1973–78, but Western analysts did not identify the core of the argument, which would have allowed everything else to fall into place. See MccGwire, *Military Objectives,* app. C.

This did not, however, imply that one could count on this type of information at the higher levels of analysis. Nor could its absence be taken as negative evidence. Neither the open literature nor restricted-circulation material like *Voennaya mysl'* (*Military Thought*) would have been a primary means of communication about higher-order questions of national policy, military doctrine, and strategy. In a closed society like the Soviet Union, there must obviously have existed a comprehensive system of classified communication, and what emerged in the open literature was an attenuated echo, with key elements missing.

This points to the root problem with textual analysis. Unless the analyst has an externally derived frame of reference that can order the information, establish the context, and indicate the questions that need asking, he or she will have to rely on preconceptions to make those choices. Those preconceptions, whether personal or institutional, will shape the final answer, and to a large extent the analyst will get out what he or she puts in.

Despite glasnost, the requirement for an external frame of reference remains, and not only because elements of classified communication will necessarily persist. In conditions of fast-moving change, final outcomes will depend on political decisions made at some future date when the relevant circumstances have clarified. While indicating the range of options, the current debate does not predict outcomes. Meanwhile, the volume of material to be considered has greatly increased and glasnost has compounded the difficulties of deciding on the authoritativeness of opinions and pronouncements. Moreover, much of the debate is ill informed, both about the past and about current considerations.

Objectives analysis allows one to get a handle on this mass of material. First, one hypothesizes the main issues that the Soviet military need to address if they are to meet the requirements implied by the new objective that stemmed from the planning assumption of "no world war." Once those issues have been postulated, one can foresee the range of opinion that is likely to exist on the various questions and hence predict the scope and nature of each debate.

The debates can then be monitored to see how they conform to the predicted pattern, and to watch for evidence that contradicts the central hypothesis or its subsidiaries. In addition, one can postulate an outcome to each debate that would be compatible with the body of ideas on international relations, national security, and the needs of the Soviet economy that have been developed by the Gorbachev leadership. The different debates can then be continually evaluated against those benchmarks.

Overview

In describing the different techniques that contribute to objectives analysis, I have drawn parallels with cartography, rock mechanics, and astronomy, but perhaps the best analogy for the overall approach is paleontology. The analyst is trying to infer the full skeletal structure of the hypothesis from partial evidence and, like the paleontologist, uses a range of analytical approaches to compensate for the dislocations of time and space.

Objectives analysis builds on traditional methods and does not replace them.[29] The multidimensional hypothesis can accommodate all the information presented by traditional analyses, although it often interprets that information in a different way. Unavoidably, the hypothesis is also the frame of reference that transmutes information into evidence, but the problem of circularity is minimized by combining different types of information and a variety of analytical techniques. In practical terms, for any one type of information the frame is externally generated.

In satisfying the analytical demands of different types of information and inferential approaches, alternative explanations are progressively excluded. By allowing "why" questions to lead the analysis, objectives analysis opens up avenues of inquiry that are as fruitful as they are unforeseen. This focus on the reasons underlying old and new policies generates a stream of implied consequences, many of which can be verified, and the central hypothesis is continually being tested.

For those predictions that cannot be verified, it is analytically more rigorous to infer the missing pieces of a well-evidenced logical structure than to base conclusions on Western vulnerabilities or practice, combined with fragmentary and outdated textual material that lends itself to

29. The techniques of bureaucratic, institutional, and interest-group analysis that are so essential to understanding the "why" of U.S. defense policy were, however, only sometimes of help in explaining Soviet military behavior. It was the *outcome* of internal debates that was important at this level of analysis, and only occasionally were the details of the debate significant. Naval policy was a frequent exception to that generalization, as was Soviet policy in the third world. Meanwhile, unless they were grounded in the central hypothesis, conclusions drawn from these kinds of analysis could be seriously misleading.

multiple interpretations. The principle at work is the one that allows physicists to predict the existence of a still unknown subatomic particle. They may never find it, but if the mathematics of the theory (the logic of the analysis) are sound, the theory will be adopted until falsified, or superseded by a better one.

Objectives analysis fosters good analytical practices. It develops robust hypotheses that predict future outcomes; it generates a stream of if-then propositions and encourages one to devise new ways of getting at the underlying evidence; it exposes silent assumptions and sensitizes one to the dangers of circularity; it highlights anomalies and prompts one to ask why; it focuses attention on the possibility of change and drives one to reevaluate existing analyses; it imposes order on the mass of data, allowing one to operationalize information on current developments; and it forces one to look at the situation through Soviet rather than Western eyes.

Only by viewing the world through Soviet eyes can one get at the question of motivation. The central importance of this question is highlighted by the analogy of a man walking about a city. While there might be no disagreement about the path the man had already taken, his future path would depend on the purpose of his walk. Was he going to visit a friend, exploring a strange city, exercising the dog and expected back for supper, or trying to evade his followers? Each explanation yields a different forecast and it will also affect the description of the path already taken.

A successful explanation of Soviet military policy must, therefore, combine the analysis of both the why and the what. Unfortunately, the great majority of Western analysts have been preoccupied with what questions. This was particularly true of those involved in capabilities analysis, which focused on policy outputs, such as the characteristics of weapons and the details of their deployments. But many explanations of the underlying policies were also mainly descriptive, the analytical focus being on the substance of the policies rather than why they were chosen. Needless to say, this did not prevent silent assumptions about Soviet motivations from coloring those descriptions of Soviet policy.

This is not just a matter of analytical niceties. For the last forty years, Western explanations of what motivated Soviet military developments played directly to questions of peace and war. Soviet military behavior dominated Western analyses and perceptions of Soviet intentions, and the West failed to see that a reasonable concern for the possibility of world war shaped and distorted Soviet foreign policy in ways that often ran counter to the Soviet Union's broader interests. Both sides were guilty of the colonel's fallacy and relied on worst-case assessments at the ministerial level of analysis which led to a nuclear arms race that endangered the fate of mankind.

Reconstructing Soviet Missile Programs

APPENDIX D OF *Military Objectives in Soviet Foreign Policy* described the development of Soviet strategic rocket forces during the period 1955–85, the analysis being based on a reconstruction of the different missiles programs and their successive adaptation to changing military requirements.

While introducing no new information, this appendix lays out the evidence in greater detail and expounds at greater length the analysis that underlay the reconstruction of actual and projected missile programs. The approach is an extension of the methodology developed for analyzing Soviet naval building programs that has been described elsewhere[1] and is made possible by the Soviets' structured approach to weapons procurement before 1987.

The methodology required simple arithmetic, patience, and persistence. A number of missile programs have to be combined to create a plausible production schedule, and the aim is to devise one that will accommodate all the available information. The latter includes the annual cumulative total of all intercontinental ballistic missiles (ICBMs) deployed, plus the designer of each missile system, the year that system entered service (initial deployment), and the number of missiles that

---

1. See Michael MccGwire, "Soviet Naval Procurement," in Royal United Service Institution, *The Soviet Union in Europe and the Near East: Her Capabilities and Intentions* (London: 1970), and Michael MccGwire, ed., *Soviet Naval Developments: Capability and Context* (Praeger, 1973), pp. 176–210. For an exposition of the methodology see Michael MccGwire, *Military Objectives in Soviet Foreign Policy* (Brookings, 1987), app. B.

Table B-1. *Deployment Schedules for Intercontinental Ballistic Missiles, 1961–73*

Year	Postulated deployment						Cumulative deployment	
	SS-6	SS-7	SS-8	SS-9	SS-11	SS-13	Postulated	Observed
1961	4	6	...	...	...	...	10	...
1962	...	48	...	...	...	...	58	...
1963	...	48	12	...	...	...	118	80
1964	...	48	11	...	...	...	177	180
1965	...	36	...	12ª	...	...	225	225
1966	...	...	...	48	144	...	417	340
1967	...	...	...	48	240	...	705	720
1968	...	...	...	48	144	...	897	900
1969	...	...	...	48	48	48	1,041	1,060
1970	−4	...	...	48	240	12	1,337	1,350
1971	...	...	...	36	144	...	1,517	1,520
1972	...	...	...	...	36	...	1,553	1,550
1973	...	...	...	...	34	...	1,587	1,587
Total	0	186	23	288	1,030	60	1,587	1,587

Sources: For initial year of postulated deployment, U.S. Defense Department, *Soviet Military Power, 1985* (U.S. Government Printing Office, 1985), p. 41; for following years, see text. For observed deployment, Albert Wohlstetter, "Is There a Strategic Arms Race?" *Foreign Policy*, no. 15 (Summer 1974), p. 13, fig. 1; U.S. Defense Department, *Statement of Secretary of Defense Robert S. McNamara before the House Armed Services Committee on the FY 1968–72 Defense Program and 1968 Defense Budget*, 91 Cong. 1 sess. (GPO, 1967), p. 41; *Department of Defense Annual Report, Fiscal Year 1969*, p. 54; *Fiscal Year 1970*, p. 42; *Fiscal Year 1971*, p. 102; *Fiscal Year 1972*, p. 165; *Fiscal Year 1973*, p. 40; *Fiscal Year 1975*, p. 50.

a. Initial deployment of SS-9 derives from arithmetic of table. See text and note 29.

were deployed. The dates and figures for the period 1961–73 are shown in table B-1.[2]

The totals at the bottom of table B-1 are hard numbers that have been accepted as the basis of arms control agreements. The observed cumulative totals in the right hand column are less exact, although they combine the information from declassified reports by the U.S. Department of Defense with data extrapolated from the figures in Albert Wohlstetter's authoritative 1974 article.[3] This is so partly because these figures, particularly for the early years, represent relatively raw intelligence which had yet to be refined by time, and also because of the difficulty of knowing when individual missiles became operational and hence part of the Soviet inventory. That difficulty applies equally to establishing the date when a new type of missile first entered service or "deployed."

2. See also Robert P. Berman and John C. Baker, *Soviet Strategic Forces: Requirements and Responses* (Brookings, 1982), a mine of relevant information.

3. "Is there a Strategic Arms Race?" *Foreign Policy*, no. 15 (Summer 1974), p. 13. It can be safely assumed that Wohlstetter drew on classified data.

Launcher deployment can be used as a surrogate for missile production, bearing in mind that no allowance is made for the additional production needed to meet the requirement for spares, testing, reloads, and so forth. Linking the two allows one to combine the evidence of force levels with the dynamics and constraints of the planning-production process, with its five-year plans and predetermined annual production rates. The postulated deployment programs in table B-1 are idealized in the sense of reflecting planned rather than actual rates for any one year, but the analysis of Soviet naval building programs has shown that the differences average out. The planned rate is the key indicator that allows one to reconstruct programs that are canceled or curtailed.

The SS-9 ICBM Program

In the case of intercontinental-range ballistic missiles the reconstruction process starts with the SS-9 third-generation "heavy" missile; 288 were deployed between 1965 and 1972 (table B-1). By the end of 1969, 282 silos had been completed or were under construction, and in the first half of 1970 work was started on another 24; however, only 6 of these were completed, the other 18 being abandoned.[4]

If work began on 24 silos in the first half of 1970, the annual construction rate must have been either 24 or 48. Only the latter could achieve a deployment of 288 missiles in seven to eight years, which implies a production rate of 48 a year. The program had been halted after only six years' production (288 = 6 × 48), although the abandoned silos imply that at least a seventh year's production had been planned. Subsequent developments provided persuasive evidence that the program had, indeed, been planned to run for ten years, as normal practice would lead one to expect.

By abandoning the construction of 18 silos in 1970, the Soviets signaled that they were curtailing the deployment of SS-9 to 288 missiles, rather than some higher figure that had been planned. This did not satisfy the United States, whose negotiators continued to press the Soviets to cut back the SS-9 heavy-missile force to the arbitrary number of 250 launchers. In 1971 the Soviets responded by constructing an additional

---

4. Personal recollection of Raymond L. Garthoff as a member of the U.S. negotiating team at the strategic arms limitation talks.

4 silos at 5 of the 48 missile sites, increasing the number of missiles at those sites from 6 to 10.[5] The implicit threat was that if the United States was not satisfied with the concessions the Soviet Union had already made, the latter would go ahead as originally planned and deploy 10 missiles at all 48 sites, for a total of 480.

This evidence argues that a ten-year production run of SS-9 had been programmed, to deploy at a rate of 48 missiles a year. How do these numbers fit in with the information on the other programs and the overall pattern of deployment?

The Original ICBM Production Plan

First, it must be recognized that missile deployments during the 1960s stem from the 1961 decision period, which effected major changes in the original production and deployment plan that had been decided in 1957–58. As explained in appendix D of *Military Objectives,* the evidence of missile flight-testing, test of nuclear warheads, and actual deployments indicates that in 1957–58 the Soviets adopted their standard three-stage approach to the requirement for ICBMs, and the second, third, and fourth generations of ICBM represented the initial, interim, and final application of this new capability.

The first generation of ICBMs, the SS-6 designed by S. P. Korolev's bureau, was unsuccessful and is not relevant to this analysis. The evidence indicates that it was originally planned to start deploying the second generation, the 5-megaton SS-7 and SS-8, designed by the M. K. Yangel and the Korolev bureaus, respectively, in 1961. These missiles would have been followed in 1966 by the 20-megaton SS-9 and SS-10 from the same two design bureaus, and in the third five-year period (1971–75) the "superheavies" would have been deployed.[6]

What production rate was originally planned in 1957–58 for the second- and third-generation missiles? The arithmetic of the SS-7 deployment requires an annual rate of about 50, arguing that the production rate of this second-generation missile designed by Yangel was the same as the

5. These 20 silos were completed and occupied in due course by fourth-generation SS-18s, bringing the total of heavy missiles to 308. The 288 SS-9 silos were later converted to house SS-18.

6. See MccGwire, *Military Objectives,* pp. 481–82, for firm evidence of these superheavy missiles and the strategic concept of "area devastation."

rate for the SS-9, its third-generation successor—that is, 48 a year, giving an overall rate of 96 a year.[7]

This would have yielded a force of 480 5-megaton and 480 20-megaton ICBMs by the end of 1970. It would have been capable of achieving the "area devastation" of North America in the event of war, although this requirement would not be met fully until the "final" stage, when the fourth-generation systems, including superheavies, would replace the relatively primitive 5-megaton second-generation systems.

The evidence of missile flight-tests and actual deployments indicates that in the second five-year period (1966–70) the Soviets planned to augment the two-track program of heavy ICBMs (SS-8, SS-10) with a third type, the SS-13 light missile. This 600-kiloton solid-fuel mobile missile from V. N. Nadiradize's design bureau was intended as the strategic reserve and would be followed by an improved version in the third five-year period. In the event, the Soviets were not successful in developing solid-fuel propulsion. Deployment of the SS-13 was delayed by three years and when it did take place, the missiles were emplaced in silos.

Meanwhile, as a result of adopting the 1960s strategy at the end of 1959, the original plan had to be amended because that strategy was predicated on being able to launch a preemptive nuclear strike in the event that world war was seen to be unavoidable. Korolev had chosen to develop rocket motors using nonstorable liquid fuel; hence neither the second-generation SS-8 nor the third-generation SS-10 would be able to meet the new operational requirement. The Soviets would therefore have to rely on the SS-7 and its successor, the SS-9.[8]

This suggests that the planned production rate of SS-7 and SS-9 ICBMs would have been doubled, using the facilities that had been earmarked for the missiles from Korolev's design bureau. However, before that could take effect, the defense initiatives adopted early in 1961 by the incoming U.S. administration completely changed the

7. In 1962 the U.S. estimate of future ICBM deployment was 65 to 120 a year (see Wohlstetter, "Is There a Strategic Arms Race?" pp. 12–13).

8. Twenty-three SS-8s were in fact deployed. These would have been missiles whose manufacture was far enough advanced in 1959–60 for the principle of "pipeline inertia" to have justified their completion. The decision to actually deploy these missiles in 1963–64 was probably tied to the Soviet failure to emplace some 40 medium-range ballistic missiles in Cuba in the fall of 1962. That unsuccessful initiative had been prompted by the U.S. deployment of the silo-based Minuteman ICBM, which technologically outflanked existing Soviet strategy and plans (see below).

strategic picture. Among other things, there emerged a new requirement to cover the Minuteman ICBM, which would be emplaced in silos in the U.S. Midwest and would escape the effects of the area devastation strategy.

The SS-11 Program

The Soviets met this new requirement by adapting the design of a variable-range ballistic missile that was being developed by V. N. Chelomey's bureau for use against U.S. carrier strike forces when they approached to launch nuclear attacks on the Soviet Union. This adaptation, the SS-11 ICBM, would carry a 1-megaton warhead that could be targeted against individual silos, the poor accuracy of the system being less important than the fact that the whole Minuteman force would be put directly at risk. It made sense as an interim response, while a more effective hard-target counterforce weapon was being developed.[9]

The Planned Deployment Rate

What production rate for SS-11 did the Soviets decide on in 1961? Clearly, it was a high-volume program, since 960 SS-11s were deployed in 1966–71. Furthermore, the observed cumulative total of all types of ICBM jumped by 380 in 1967, of which only 48 could be accounted for by SS-9s, and in the two years 1967–68 it increased by almost 500, of which only 96 could have been SS-9s. On the other hand, the cumulative total rose by only 160 missiles in 1968, of which as many as 96 could have been SS-9s and SS-13s. In other words, the high production rate of SS-11s did not remain constant during the eight years the system was being deployed.

By trial and error, an SS-11 deployment rate of 240 (5 × 48) a year was found to fit the arithmetic of the observed cumulative totals in table B-1, allowing that there was a hiatus in 1968–69, equivalent to about

---

9. The original decision to develop the SS-11 was in line with the established policy of posing some kind of counter to any threat to the Soviet homeland and of addressing a new problem with a series of concurrent responses (initial, interim, final) rather than waiting until the final solution became available.

one year's production. This hiatus could be explained in part by the completion of the Minuteman deployment in 1967, since it was that program that had generated the original requirement for SS-11s.

In late 1960 the Soviets had warned the incoming Kennedy administration that they would respond in kind to a U.S. buildup of ICBMs.[10] Congress had authorized Minuteman production at 360 a year, and launchers were brought into service at a rate of 20–25 a month (240–300 a year) between December 1962 and June 1965.[11] There had, however, been talk of doubling the production rate to 720 a year, and the final size of the Minuteman force was not decided until 1964.[12]

Production Facilities

There was no provision in existing plans for the high-volume production of SS-11, a program that would run at five times the rate that had been planned for the SS-9 and SS-10 systems ($240 = 5 \times 48$). Therefore, SS-11 production would have to usurp facilities that been earmarked for other programs that had originally had been scheduled for deployment in the second half of the 1960s.

An obvious candidate was the set of facilities that would have been allocated to producing the missile from which the SS-11 was derived.[13] Another candidate was the set of facilities that had originally been scheduled to produce Korolev's SS-8 and its successor the SS-10 but was then reallocated to the SS-7 and SS-9 programs when nonstorable rocket fuel was ruled to be operationally unacceptable. Assuming that those two sets of production facilities could each sustain a deployment of 48 missiles a year, the remaining 144 missiles could have been produced by the facilities that in 1961 were already engaged in producing the SS-5.

10. Arthur M. Schlesinger, Jr., *A Thousand Days: John F. Kennedy in the White House* (Houghton Mifflin, 1965), p. 301.

11. Desmond Ball, *Politics and Force Levels: The Strategic Missile Program of the Kennedy Administration* (University of California Press, 1980), pp. 46–53.

12. Joseph Alsop, "Shortening the Missile Gap," *New York Herald Tribune*, February 7, 1961. The U.S. Joint Chiefs of Staff favored a force of 1,600 missiles, while the Strategic Air Command was lobbying for "thousands," and from 1961 to 1963 the "approved" number fluctuated between 800 and 1,300 (John Prados, *The Soviet Estimate* [Dial Press, 1982], pp. 114–15).

13. For the SS-11 to have deployed in 1966, as it did, deployment of the original system must have been far enough advanced to meet the same schedule. Given Nikita Khrushchev's personal interest in Chelomey's design bureau and in that particular missile system, one can assume that facilities had been allocated for its production.

Deployment of the SS-5, a 2,200-mile intermediate range ballistic missile (IRBM) had begun in 1961 but was curtailed after little more than 100 launchers had entered service.[14] The number is too small to extrapolate an annual rate, but the underlying missile production capacity can be inferred by reference to the SS-4 program. That 1,000-mile system entered service in 1959 and more than 600 SS-4 launchers were deployed at a rate of about 75 a year. The SS-5 was, in essence, a parallel program and, if one assumes a comparable pattern of deployment had been planned, this would require a missile production rate of 144 a year, since each SS-5 launcher was provided with a reload.

The silo-based Minuteman largely undermined the cost-effective Soviet strategy of area devastation and generated a new requirement for counterforce point-targeting. Because it would take at least ten years to develop missile systems that could meet that requirement, the SS-11 was programmed for ten rather than five years' production. So was the SS-9, to compensate for the loss of the SS-10 production facilities. Meanwhile, various strategic requirements that had been identified in 1957–58 and reaffirmed in 1959 would have to be deferred or left unmet—namely, half of the ICBMs intended for the area devastation of North America; 80 percent or more of the IRBMs intended for fixed targets in Eurasia; and all of the variable-range ballistic missiles (VRBMs) intended for mobile targets on the Eurasian periphery such as carrier strike forces and army groupings.

The 1967 Policy Review

In any circumstances, therefore, the future of the SS-11 program would have come under review when it became certain in 1966–67 that the U.S. Minuteman force would be limited to 1,000 missiles, even though the first year's production of Soviet SS-11s was only then entering service.[15] But December 1966 also saw the reformulation of Soviet military doctrine to the effect that it was no longer inevitable that world war would be nuclear, and even if it were, it would not necessarily involve the nuclear devastation of the Soviet Union.

14. Reasons for concluding that the program was curtailed are given in MccGwire, *Military Objectives*, p. 503.

15. At the prevailing rate of deployment, the 1,000th SS-11 would enter service in 1970 and the full program would yield a force of 2,400 ICBMs by 1975–76.

As discussed in chapter 2, the new doctrine had far-reaching implications. Besides necessitating the restructuring of wartime objectives and the introduction of the fundamentally new 1970s strategy that eschewed nuclear preemption, the new doctrine removed the long-standing requirement for strategic nuclear superiority, which hitherto had dictated the size of Soviet strategic missile programs.

The hiatus in the deployment of SS-11s in 1968–69 can be explained in large part by the fundamental review of wartime strategy, operational concepts, and consequential force requirements that took place in 1967, the conclusions being evidenced by naval, ground force, and frontal aviation weapons programs that entered service in the 1970s and early 1980s. In the case of the SS-11, the decision was to continue producing 48 SS-11 ICBMs a year but to adapt the remaining 80 percent of the SS-11 production capacity to manufacturing variable-range missiles. These SS-11 VRBMs would be for use against fixed and mobile targets on the Eurasian continent and its periphery, remedying the shortfall in regional coverage that had resulted from the 1961 reallocation of missile production facilities.

In making this decision, an additional consideration would have been the earlier conclusion, reached in about 1962–63, that the more effective way of countering the Minuteman force would be to use the heavy SS-9 to disable the Minuteman launch control centers (there was 1 for every 10 missiles) rather than target each Minuteman silo with an SS-11.[16]

Following the sharp drop in SS-11 deployments in 1968–69, the programmed rate of 240 a year was regained in 1970. Assuming that the year's hiatus in production caused by the policy review would not have been subsequently made up, this reconfiguration of the SS-11 program would have resulted in a force of 960 ICBMs and 1,200 VRBMs by 1975–76. By then the fourth generation of "light" missiles (Yangel's SS-17 and Chelomey's SS-19) would be ready for deployment.

The Effects of SALT

This was not, however, to be. The strategic arms limitations talks (SALT) got under way toward the end of 1969, and in the first half of 1970 the Soviets decided to halt the manufacture of third-generation

16. See Berman and Baker, *Soviet Strategic Forces*, pp. 117–18 and table C-6.

strategic systems once those missiles already in the production pipeline had been completed. Missile silos whose construction had only recently begun were therefore abandoned. Besides the 18 SS-9 silos mentioned earlier, in the first half of 1970 the Soviets abandoned 10 SS-11 silos, 20 SS-13 silos, and another 30 silos about which it was too early to say whether they were SS-11s or SS-13s.[17]

The result of this decision to curtail the production of strategic missiles was that the SS-13 completed deployment at 60 ICBMs in 1970 and the SS-9 completed at 288 in 1971. The SS-11 did not, however, complete until 1973 because another 60 silos were constructed in a former SS-4–SS-5 field in southwest Russia.[18] This brought the total of SS-11s to 1,030, of which 670 were ICBMs targeted on North America and 360 were VRBMs targeted on the Eurasian continent and its periphery.[19]

The Production of Fourth-Generation Systems

Fourth-generation systems were scheduled to start deploying in 1975–76 and production would therefore begin during the 1971–75 five-year plan, whose details would have been finalized in 1970. The abandonment of newly started silos in the first half of that year and the subsequent curtailment of third-generation programs is evidence that the Soviets had by then decided on a ceiling of 1,587 on the number of missiles to be counted as ICBMs in SALT I.[20] That number was subsequently increased to 1,607 by the 20 heavy launchers whose silos were started in 1971, and that number was formalized in the SALT accords signed in 1972.

17. Personal recollection by Raymond L. Garthoff.

18. These were occupied initially by SS-11 VRBMs, which were subsequently replaced by fourth-generation SS-19 VRBMs, likewise designed by Chelomey.

19. For the analysis underlying the identification of VRBMs, see MccGwire, *Military Objectives,* pp. 505–15.

20. This conclusion is not undermined by work having started in 1971 on the construction of 60 light silos for SS-11 and SS-19 missiles. The different lead times involved allow that the initiation of this new construction and the abandonment of 60 newly started light silos in the first half of 1970 both stemmed from the same decision, which would have reflected two considerations. Given the curtailment of the SS-11 program, it would have been necessary to decide on the final mix of VRBMs and ICBMs at this time. Meanwhile, once it became clear that launchers would be the unit of account at SALT I, there was no purpose in building silos that would be unable to house fourth-generation systems, except in the case of the 6 SS-9 silos, where the centrality of heavy missiles in the SALT negotiations could not brook such delay.

Of that total, 209 were second-generation SS-7s and SS-8s, scheduled to be replaced by additions to the inventory of submarine-launched ballistic missiles. This would leave a force of 1,398 third-generation land-based missiles, of which 1,038 were ICBMs targeted on North America and 360 were VRBMs covering regional targets.[21] It was these 1,398 (say 1,400) missiles that would need to be replaced by fourth-generation systems, and those would in due course have to be replaced by fifth-generation systems. The latter would be specifically designed to meet the new requirements generated by the 1970s strategy, but they would not be ready for deployment before the mid-1980s.[22]

Beginning in about 1973, the conversion of existing missile silos to house fourth-generation systems proceeded at about 150 a year, and by the first half of 1979 about 920 had either been finished or were in hand. However, following the signing of SALT II, the conversion of about 100 of the SS-11 silos to launch SS-17s and SS-19s (about 50 of each) was aborted, and the final total of fourth-generation systems was 818. This conformed to the SALT II ceiling of 820 for any missiles that had been tested with multiple independently targeted reentry vehicles (MIRVs).[23]

As finally deployed, the fourth-generation missiles comprised 308 SS-18s from Yangel's design bureau, which replaced (and added to) the heavy missiles in the SS-9 force, plus 150 SS-17s (Yangel) and 360 SS-19s (Chelomey), which replaced about 60 percent of the SS-11 force. There is only limited information on the detailed pattern of deployment of these three systems, but the following explanation accommodates what evidence is available and conforms to the practices adopted by the Soviets in respect to their second- and third-generation systems.[24]

Production of fourth-generation systems was planned to run for ten years at a rate that would sustain an annual deployment of 144 missiles. These would be manufactured in three sets of facilities, each able to produce at the established rate of 48 missiles a year. One set of facilities was allocated to the production of Chelomey's SS-19 while the other

21. The Soviet ICBM force was therefore comparable in numbers to the U.S. force (1,000 Minutemen and 54 Titans) but lagged badly in quality.

22. The original design specifications for the fourth-generation systems dated back to the first half of the 1960s, before the 1966 shift in military doctrine.

23. Raymond L. Garthoff, *Perspectives on the Strategic Balance* (Brookings, 1983), p. 15, and *Détente and Confrontation: American-Soviet Relations from Nixon to Reagan* (Brookings, 1985), p. 793, note 114.

24. For fragmentary information on deployments, see *The Military Balance* (London: International Institute for Strategic Studies), annual issues, 1974–82.

two sets were allocated to the production of Yangel's SS-17 and SS-18, although not divided equally between them. For the first four years, Yangel's facilities were apportioned as 72 for the SS-18 and 24 for the SS-17. The SALT ceiling of 308 heavy SS-18s would be reached during the fifth year of the program and it was planned that the SS-18 facilities would then become available to the SS-17, giving a production rate of 96 SS-17s a year.

This unbalanced allocation was necessitated by the terms of SALT II, whose lineaments began to emerge in 1973 and whose general parameters were clear by the end of 1974. If production facilities had been divided equally, only 274 heavy SS-18s would have been deployed before the ceiling on MIRVed ICBMs was breached. Hence the decision to deploy the permitted maximum of 308 SS-18s, before turning to build up the SS-17 force.

It so happened that Chelomey's SS-19 proved to be more successful than Yangel's SS-17. In the wake of SALT II, production of the SS-17 was therefore halted, less than halfway through the planned deployment, by when less than a quarter of the projected force had entered service. The production of SS-19 meanwhile continued, until 360 missiles had been deployed, which was three-quarters of the planned program.

The SS-16 ICBM and the SS-20 IRBM

The design specifications for fourth-generation ICBMs would originally have been formulated in 1963–64 and were driven by three requirements, two of them long-standing, one new. The established requirements were area devastation, the SS-9's designed role, which would be assumed by the SS-18; and survivable strategic reserve, the SS-13's intended role, which would be assumed by the SS-16. The new requirement was to destroy hard targets, which would be met by the newly designed (and competing) SS-17 and SS-19 systems.

Apart from some adjustments to the mission of area devastation, and despite the 1967–68 restructuring of wartime objectives, these three requirements remained valid throughout the 1970s and continued to provide an operational justification for all four fourth-generation systems. There was, however, an important qualification. In 1963–64, the Soviets were seeking strategic superiority and the deployment of ICBMs had been programmed at 336 a year. In 1970 the aim was strategic parity and the Soviets decided that only 1,400 fourth-generation missiles would be deployed, at a rate of no more than 144 a year.

Canceling the SS-16 Program

Although the SS-16 began flight testing roughly on schedule in 1972, the Soviets decided not to proceed to series production and deployment, leaving the field to the other three systems. Several reasons can be found for this decision. One was the impending availability of nuclear-powered ballistic-missile submarines (SSBNs) to fill the role of a strategic reserve, since the new SSBNs would carry missiles capable of striking at North America from Soviet home waters.

Another reason was the need to deploy a modern IRBM to replace the first- and second-generation SS-4s and SS-5s. The third-generation replacements had been unsuccessful, and the plan to replace the obsolescent SS-4s and SS-5s with VRBMs had been stymied by the SALT counting rules. This gap in regional coverage could be filled by making use of SS-16 design and development, its long-lead procurement, and the production facilities that had been earmarked for the SS-16 program to produce a fourth-generation IRBM, the SS-20.

A third reason was the gross imbalance in warheads that was emerging, threatening the Soviet goal of parity. The United States was already embarked on deploying 550 MIRVed Minuteman IIIs and it was in the cards that the remaining 450 single-warhead Minutemen would also be replaced. The submarine-launched Polaris missile was likewise being replaced by the MIRVed Poseidon. From the viewpoint of 1970–71 it made military sense for the Soviets to devote the full production of 144 missiles a year to MIRVed systems rather than allocate part to producing the 600-kiloton single-warhead SS-16.

Nor would it have made sense to reverse this decision in 1973–74, when the parameters of SALT II began to emerge, and not only because the necessary production facilities were by then committed to the SS-20 program. The requirement for a survivable strategic reserve would be met by the Delta classes of SSBN (albeit suboptimally), and the operational shortfall that would result from SALT II lay in VRBMs and MIRVed ICBMs. Meanwhile, it was by no means certain that a treaty would ever be signed, which is why the Soviet military pressed ahead with converting silos to launch fourth-generation missiles, even after the agreed limit of 820 had been passed.

Lastly, it is possible that the Soviets had yet to solve all the problems they had had with solid-fuel propulsion. Many Western analysts believed this to have been the case, but this may have been a post facto rationalization of the failure to deploy the system. It is to some extent belied by the successful deployment of the SS-20, which used two of the SS-16's three propulsion stages. Meanwhile, it is certain that the cancellation of the SS-16 program was not in response to U.S. pressure to forgo the deployment of mobile systems, which was something the Soviets absolutely could not accept. The 1970s strategy had increased the importance of ICBM survivability, and this was to be achieved by making two of the three fifth-generation systems mobile.

The SS-20 Program

As discussed in chapter 3, the SS-20 deployment was curtailed in 1979 as part of the Soviets' unsuccessful attempt to head off a NATO decision to deploy the Pershing II. Nevertheless there is sufficient information to infer the underlying pattern of production.

The construction of SS-20 missile bases began in 1975, and in both 1978 and 1979 work started on nine new bases, each with nine launcher emplacements. However, in 1980 new starts fell off and tapered to a halt in 1982. Correspondingly, the deployment of SS-20 missiles got under way in 1977, built up to a brief plateau in 1980 and 1981, and then fell away over the next three years, yielding a force of 378 missiles emplaced in 42 bases.[25] This pattern is typical of a program that has been brought to a halt in midcourse. The tailing off is evidence of pipeline inertia, and the timing implies a decision taken in mid-1979.

Having failed to prevent the deployment of Pershing II, the Soviets resumed the construction of missile bases in June 1984. By April 1985, 414 SS-20 launchers had been deployed in 46 missile bases and work was

---

25. Raymond L. Garthoff, "The Soviet SS-20 Decision," *Survival,* vol. 25 (May–June 1983), pp. 118–19, notes 7, 18; John Cartwright and Julian Critchley, *Nuclear Weapons in Europe* (Brussels: North Atlantic Assembly, 1984), p. 18.

proceeding on another 8 sites.[26] Those 56 bases would hold a total of 486 launchers, the equivalent of six missile armies of three divisions each.[27]

New starts on missile bases in 1978 and 1979 indicate an underlying production rate of 81 missile launchers a year, a rate that should have allowed the force of 486 launchers to be deployed in six years. The SS-20 program did not, however, get into its full stride until 1980, and even if it had been allowed to run to plan, it would probably have been 1984–85 before the force was fully deployed.

Meanwhile, established practice makes it likely that missile (as opposed to mobile launcher) production was programmed for 72 a year, requiring a seven-year program. When account is taken of the requirement for each launcher to have a reload, the notional production rate rises to 144. That is a familiar number and it is also the rate that was postulated above for the SS-5 IRBM program, as it would originally have been planned.

It seems likely that the production schedules for the SS-20 missile and its launcher were different. The launcher may have needed a somewhat longer lead time, and initial deployment of the system may have depended on its availability.

The Analytical Process

The presentation in this appendix started with the SS-9 program because the details of silos being abandoned in 1970 and additional silos being started in 1971 provide reasonable concrete evidence of a ten-year program with an annual deployment of 48.

I was, however, unaware of that information when I embarked on this reconstruction process in 1985. At that stage I only knew the totals of different missile systems and the year of their initial deployment, and the observed cumulative annual totals. From that data alone, however, one could infer an annual deployment rate of about 50 a year for the SS-7 and SS-9, and 250 a year for the SS-11, allowing a hiatus in about 1968–69. It was only when I discussed my findings with Raymond

26. "New Soviet Missile Sites Reported," *New York Times,* April 23, 1985.
27. This figure is compatible with the information available to U.S. officials in 1976 that the Soviets were planning to produce "about 1,200" SS-20s (William Beecher, *International Herald Tribune,* September 10, 1976). A reload for each launcher plus 25 percent for maintenance replacement, proof testing, and so forth, would require a total of 1,215 missiles.

Garthoff that I learned about the abandoned silos, which yielded the hard number of 48 for the SS-9 deployment rate and concrete evidence of a ten-year program. This allowed me to refine my earlier analysis, while validating my hypothesis.

Similarly, I was ignorant of the actual rate at which the fourth-generation missiles had been deployed when I concluded that the inventory of third-generation missiles implied a fourth-generation force of some 1,400 missiles that would deploy at about 140 a year. On the basis of the Soviets' practice with their third-generation systems I hypothesized an annual rate of 144, and only subsequently did I come across information that the deployment rate had been about 150 a year.

In other words, one does not need a great deal of information before one is able to start factoring the numbers. This allows one progressively to build up patterns of deployment and deduce planned production rates and runs, imposing order on what at first seems an unmanageable set of figures. Soviet weapons programs have always been constrained, and once one has identified those constraints the patterns begin to emerge. For third-generation systems the constraint was production facilities. For fourth-generation systems the primary constraint was the SALT ceilings, with production facilities being secondary.

Missile deployments are used as a surrogate for production, and the actual production process remains unknown. Nor is it known how the facilities that built third-generation missiles relate to those that built fourth-generation systems, but there is likely to have been some underlying consistency. In the case of naval building programs this consistency was captured by the concept of a "notional production line," which allowed one to project future output as shipyards moved successively from building gun cruisers to assembling nuclear submarines (and so on) during the 1950–70 period. In a similar way, the notion of a set of production facilities that could support the deployment of 48 missiles a year appears to have had continuing analytical utility in the 1960–85 period.

The factor 48 was used consistently to construct table B-1, and the resultant fit between the "postulated" and "observed" cumulative annual totals is better than the fit in table D-1 in *Military Objectives*.[28]

---

28. The one major disparity is 1966, when there was a shortfall of 77 on a postulated deployment of 192 missiles. That was the year of the SS-11's initial deployment and a shortfall

In that table I used 60 as a factor for SS-11 and SS-13, on the grounds that the missiles were emplaced in fields of 60. However, the results were less satisfactory, since the pattern of missile emplacement is not directly related to the annual rate of deployment.

In another change, I have allowed Yangel's SS-7 and SS-9 programs in table B-1 to abut directly, yielding a combined deployment of 48 missiles in 1965. In the earlier analysis I assumed a shortfall, to cover the disruption of rejigging production facilities, but the cumulative fit was less satisfactory. Lastly, the 1965 date for the initial deployment of the SS-9 derives from the arithmetic of the table, rather than official sources, while conforming to the logic of advancing the planned deployment of SS-9 in response to the 1961 Kennedy initiatives.[29]

---

of some kind is not surprising, given the convoluted genesis of the system and the fact it was being produced in such large numbers. But U.S. intelligence may also have had difficulty in deciding how many of these newly deployed missiles were operational. In any case, the observed total jumped by 380 in 1967, which was far above the annual production capacity; hence the observed total for 1966 must be suspect as an indicator of planned deployment.

29. Berman and Baker, *Soviet Strategic Forces,* p. 82, gives 1966; U.S. Department of Defense, *Soviet Military Power,* 4th ed. (1985), p. 41, gives 1964. The construction of the first SS-9 silo would have been well under way, if not nearly complete, by the end of 1964. It may have been premature for U.S. intelligence to claim that this worrisome new system was operational.

Index